Acronyms, Initialisms & Abbreviations Dictionary

Supplement

ISSN 0270-4404

Acronyms, Initialisms & Abbreviations Dictionary

Supplement

Volume 2 of
Acronyms, Initialisms & Abbreviations Dictionary
Twenty-Eighth Edition

*A Guide to Acronyms, Abbreviations,
Contractions, Alphabetic Symbols, and Similar Condensed Appellations*

Covering: Aerospace, Associations, Banking, Biochemistry, Business, Data Processing, Domestic and International Affairs, Economics, Education, Electronics, Genetics, Government, Information Technology, Internet, Investment, Labor, Language, Law, Medicine, Military Affairs, Periodicals, Pharmacy, Physiology, Politics, Religion, Science, Societies, Sports, Technical Drawings and Specifications, Telecommunications, Trade, Transportation, and Other Fields

Mary Rose Bonk,
Editor

GALE GROUP

Detroit
New York
San Francisco
London
Boston
Woodbridge, CT

Editor:	Mary Rose Bonk
Associate Editor:	Pamela Dear
Assistant Editor:	Phyllis Spinelli
Data Capture Manager:	Ronald D. Montgomery
Project Administrator:	Gwendolyn S. Tucker
Data Capture Specialist:	Constance Wells
Data Capture Assistants:	Katrina Coach, Elizabeth Pilette
Manufacturing Manager:	Dorothy Maki
Buyer:	NeKita McKee
Product Design Manager:	Kenn Zorn
Graphic Artist:	Mike Logusz
Manager, Technical Support Services:	Theresa A. Rocklin
Senior Programmer:	Charles Beaumont
Programmer/Analyst:	Magdalena Cureton-Streicher

Library of Congress Catalog Number 84-643188
ISBN 0-7876-3385-2
ISSN 0270-4404

Printed in the United States of America

Contents

Gale's publications in the acronyms and abbreviations field include:

***Acronyms, Initialisms & Abbreviations Dictionary* series:**

Acronyms, Initialisms & Abbreviations Dictionary (Volume 1). A guide to acronyms, initialisms, abbreviations, and similar contractions, arranged alphabetically by abbreviation.

Acronyms, Initialisms & Abbreviations Supplement (Volume 2). An interedition supplement in which terms are arranged alphabetically both by abbreviation and by meaning.

Reverse Acronyms, Initialisms & Abbreviations Dictionary (Volume 3). A companion to Volume 1 in which terms are arranged alphabetically by meaning of the acronym, initialism, or abbreviation.

***Acronyms, Initialisms & Abbreviations Dictionary* Subject Guide series:**

Computer & Telecommunications Acronyms (Volume 1). A guide to acronyms, initialisms, abbreviations, and similar contractions used in the field of computers and telecommunications in which terms are arranged alphabetically both by abbreviation and by meaning.

Business Acronyms (Volume 2). A guide to business-oriented acronyms, initialisms, abbreviations, and similar contractions in which terms are arranged alphabetically both by abbreviation and by meaning.

***International Acronyms, Initialisms & Abbreviations Dictionary* series:**

International Acronyms, Initialisms & Abbreviations Dictionary (Volume 1). A guide to foreign and international acronyms, initialisms, abbreviations, and similar contractions, arranged alphabetically by abbreviation.

Reverse International Acronyms, Initialisms & Abbreviations Dictionary (Volume 2). A companion to Volume 1, in which terms are arranged alphabetically by meaning of the acronym, initialism, or abbreviation.

***Periodical Title Abbreviations* series:**

Periodical Title Abbreviations: By Abbreviation (Volume 1). A guide to abbreviations commonly used for periodical titles, arranged alphabetically by abbreviation.

Periodical Title Abbreviations: By Title (Volume 2). A guide to abbreviations commonly used for periodical titles, arranged alphabetically by title.

A Word about
Acronyms, Initialisms & Abbreviations
Dictionary Supplement

> Contains nearly 10,000 newly coined or newly found terms

As acronyms continue to simplify and accelerate modern communication, the need for timely access remains essential. Publication of this supplement to the twenty-eighth edition of *Acronyms, Initialisms & Abbreviations Dictionary (AIAD)* makes terms available while their currency is at a peak, keeping you informed and up to date in a constantly expanding field.

Timely Coverage

The more dynamic fields of endeavor tend to generate the largest number of acronyms. *Acronyms, Initialisms & Abbreviations Dictionary Supplement (AIAD-S)* reflects this trend by providing increased coverage in:

- Artificial Intelligence

- Business

- Internet

- Psychology

- Travel

Current events and new technology often produce abbreviated designations intended as time and space savers. Colorful examples in this supplement include:

- BTDT...Been There Done That

- FROG..Finished Room over Garage

- Po5...Party of Five

- RIP..Rodent Impact Program

Major Sources Cited

AIAD-S, like *AIAD*, contains entries from a wide variety of sources. Although many terms are from published sources, the majority of entries are sent by outside contributors, are uncovered through independent research by the editorial staff, or are located in miscellaneous broadcast or print media references. Therefore, it is impossible to cite a source on every entry in *AIAD-S*. It was felt, however, that the citation of selected sources would assist the user in his or her research.

A code for the source of the entry (represented in small capital letters within parentheses) is given only for those print sources that provided at least 50 items. Complete bibliographical information about the publications cited can be found in the List of Selected Sources following the User's Guide. The editor will provide further information upon request.

Acknowledgments

In addition to the in-house staff, other people have contributed significantly to the compilation of this supplement. The editor wishes to thank Hoyt Hammer, Monica Langley, James U. Rose, Janet I. Rose, and Tracey Head Turbett for their contributions.

Available in Electronic Format

AIAD and *AIAD-S* are available for licensing on magnetic tape or diskette in a fielded format. The database is available for internal data processing and nonpublishing purposes only. For more information, call 800-877-GALE.

Comments and Suggestions Are Welcome

Users can make unique and important contributions to future supplements and new editions by notifying the editor of subject fields that are not adequately covered, by suggesting sources for covering such fields, and even by sending individual terms they feel should be included.

User's Guide

Acronyms, Initialisms & Abbreviations Dictionary Supplement comprises two sections, providing numeric and alphabetic access to entries either by acronym or by meaning.

By Acronym Section

Acronyms are arranged alphabetically in letter-by-letter sequence, regardless of spacing, punctuation, or capitalization. If the same abbreviation has more than one meaning, the various meanings are then subarranged alphabetically in word-by-word sequence. Entries may contain some of the elements noted in the example below:

Abbreviation or acronym ——————
Location ——————
English Translation——————
Sponsoring Organization ——————

AP...............Absolute Pardon
A/P...............Account-Purchase Phrase
A & P ....Agricultural and Pastoral
ap...............Antiperiplanar [*Chemistry*]
AP...............Appendectomy
APA ....Automobile Protection Association [*Canada*]
APB ....All Points Bulletin
APC ....Anno post Christum Natum [*Latin*]
APC ....Archives Publiques du Canada [*Public Archives of Canada*]
APC ....Area Planning Council [*Department of Education*]
APCA............Aft Power Controller Assembly (MCD)

—— Meaning or Phrase
—— Subject area
—— Language
—— Source code (Decoded in the List of Selected Sources)

By Meaning Section

Terms are arranged in word-by-word sequence according to the explanation of the acronym. Minor parts of speech (articles, conjunctions, prepositions) are generally not considered in the alphabetizing. If a particular explanation of the acronym has more than one initialism representing it, the various choices are then subarranged alphabetically, letter-by-letter, as they are in the *By Acronym* section.

Meaning or Phrase ——————

Second Audio Program...SAP
Second Audio Program...SAPRO
Second Audio Program...SECAP
Second Base [*Baseball*]..2B
Secondary School Admission Test Board [*Princeton, NJ*]..SSATB
Secretariat for Catholic-Jewish Relations ....CJR
Secretariat Europeen des Fabricants d'Emballages Metalliques Legers [*European Secretariat of Manufacturers of Light Metal Packages*]..........SEFEL
Secretariat for Hispanic Affairs [*National Conference of Catholic Bishops*].......................SHA
Secundum [*Latin*]..SEC
Secure Acoustic Data Relay.................................SADR

—— Abbreviation or Acronym

List of Selected Sources

Each of the print sources included in the following list contributed at least 50 terms. It would be impossible to cite a source for every entry because the majority of terms are sent by outside contributors, are uncovered through independent research by the editorial staff, or are located in miscellaneous broadcast or print media references.

Unless further described in an annotation, the publications listed here contain no additional information about the acronym, initialism, or abbreviation. The editor will provide further information about these sources upon request.

(ABAC) "Abbreviations, Acronyms, and Initialisms." <http://www.pnl.gov/ag/usage/acroel.html> (27 January 2000)

(ADWA) *Abbreviations Dictionary; A Practical Compilation of Today's Acronyms and Abbreviations.* By Robert S. Wachal. Boston: Houghton Mifflin Co., 1999.

(AEBE) *Acronyms in Electronics Business and Engineering.* By Ken Westover. Boulder, CO: Cliff Canyon Publishing Co., 1998.

(ALHF) "Alaska Housing Finance Corporation Glossary." <http://www.ahfc.state.ak.us/index.htm> (18 October 1999)

(ARMP) "Global Change Acronyms and Abbreviations." <http://www.arm.gov/docs/index/html> (8 February 2000)

(AUEG) "Acronyms Used by Environmental Groups and Agencies." <http://www.etd.ameslab.gov/etd/library/acronyms/acronym.html> (2000)

(AVGL) "Aircraft Owners and Pilots Association Aviation Glossary." <http://www.aopa.ch/xgloss.htm> (20 October 1999)

(CARB) "Carbon Dioxide Information Analysis Center--Acronyms and Abbreviations." <http://www.cdiac.esd.oorni.gov/cdiac/pns/acronyms.html> (18 July 1996)

(CCCA) *ABC Pocket Guide for the Field on C3 Acronyms; An Anthology of Command, Control, and Communications Acronyms and Abbreviations.* 2d ed. Edited by Charles R. Wolfson. Geneva, IL: ABC TeleTraining, Inc. 1986.

(CGWS) *The Comprehensive Guide to Wireless Resources; Definitions and Acronyms, and National Trade Shows, Association and Publication Listings.* By Lawrence Harte and Steven Kellogg. Fuquay-Varina, NC: APDG Publishing, 1998.

(COBU) "Common Business and Professional Abbreviations and Acronyms." <http://www.instantaccess.co.uk/infozone/abbraviations.html> (27 January 2000)

(CTAS) "CTAS Acronym Dictionary." <http://www.ctas.arc.nase.gov/acronyms> (10 October 2000)

(CWA) "Civil War Acronyms." <http://www.antiqueresources.com/articles/cwacronms.html> (1998)

(DAVI)   *Medical Abbreviations; 14,000 Conveniences at the Expense of Communications and Safety*. 9th ed. By Neil M. Davis. Huntingdon Valley, PA: Neil M. Davis Associates, 1999.

(DEMM)   "Department of Emergency Management Master List of Acronyms." <http://bcem.co.bay.fl.us/dem/htm> (27 January 2000)

(DIPS)   *The Dictionary of Psychology*. By Raymond J. Corsini. Philadelphia: Taylor and Francis, 1999.

(FUCW)   "Frequently Used Contractions in National Weather Service Products." <http://www.awc-kc.noaa.gov/info/domestic_contractions.html> (16 November 1999)

(GRST)   "Glossary of Remote Sensing Terms." <http://ceo1409.ceo.sai.jrc.it:8080.2/tutorials/glossary> (5 October 1999)

(HEAS)   "Acronyms and Abbreviations Used in Health and Safety Executive Information Services." <http://www.healthandsafety.co.uk/acronyms.html> (26 September 2000)

(HLLA)   "Honeywell Abbreviation and Acronym Dictionary." <http://www.cas.honeywell.com/ats/acronym.html> (27 January 2000)

(IAS)   "International Arctic Science Committee." <http://www.iasc.no/acronyms.htm> (20 October 1999)

(IDAI)   *The International Dictionary of Artificial Intelligence*. By William Raynor. Chicago: Glenlake Publishing Co., Ltd., 1999.

(IOWA)   "Iowa Department of Natural Resources Quick Facts." <http://www.state.ia.us/government/dnr/part1.htm> (19 October 1999)

(ITCA)   *Internet Terms and Computer Acronyms, A Useful Guide*. By Mary Brookhart. Charlotte, NC: Southeast Consulting, Inc., 1998.

(MARI)   "Glossary of Marine Abbreviations." <http://www.royalsunalliance.ca/rsa.arine/glossabbrevdisp.html> (26 September 2000)

(MELL)   *Melloni's Illustrated Dictionary of Medical Abbreviations*. By John Melloni and Ida G. Dox. Pearl River, NY: Parthenon Publishing Group, Inc., 1998.

(MGMA)   "Medical Group Management Association's Book of Acronyms for Medical Practice Executives." <http://www.mgma.com/library/acronyms.html> (19 October 1999)

(MLOA)   "Marconi--List of Acronyms." <http://www.fore.com/atm-edu/acronyms.html> (1999)

(NAU)   "The Nautical Institute; Acronyms and Abbreviations." <http://www.nautinist.org/acronyms.htm> (20 October 1999)

(NAV)   "Navoceano Acronym List." <http://www.navo.hpc.mil> (12 November 1993)

(NDBD)   *The New Dickson Baseball Dictionary*. By Paul Dickson. San Diego, CA: Harcourt, Brace, and Co., 1999.

(NTIO)   *NTC's Dictionary of Acronyms and Abbreviations*. Compiled by Steven R. Kleinedler. Edited by Richard A. Spears. Lincolnwood, IL: NTC Publishing Group, 1996.

(NUJO)   "Initials, Credentials, Abbreviations Found on Medical Resumes."
           <http://www.nursesearch.net/initials.html> (1 February 2000)

(PIAV)   "Pilot's Magazine's A to Z Aviation Jargon." Compiled by James Allan and Mike Jerran.
           <http://web1.hiway.co.uk/avaition/pterms.html> (10 October 2000)

(PIPO)   *Pilot's Pocket Handbook*. 4th ed. N.p.: Flight Time Publishing, 1999.

(RIMS)   "Rimship AS Forkortelser." <http://www.rimship.no/sider/liste.html> (26 September 2000)

(ROAS)   "Acronym and Abbreviation Server Results." <http://www.ucc.ie/cgi-bin/acronym> (20
           September 1999)

(SARE)   "Safety and Related Acronyms." <http://www.labsafety.org/acro.htm> (1999)

(SG)   *Standard & Poor's Stock Guide*. New York, NY: Standard & Poor's, 2000.

(SPST)   "Space Station Acronyms." <http://www.spacefllight.nasa.gov/cgi-bi> (1999)

(TRID)   "Travel Industry Dictionary." <http://www.hometravelagency.com/dictionary/itra/html> (15
           August 2000)

(USCA)   "U.S. Census Bureau Abbreviations and Acronyms." <http://www.census.gov/cgi-
           bin/main/alacro.pl> (20 October 2000)

Numerics
By Acronym

2DC.............. Two-Dimensional Cloud (ARMP)

3DNEPH....... Three-Dimensional Nephanalysis (ARMP)

3G................ Third Generation

5-FU............. 5-Fluorouracil [*Medicine*]

5HT.............. Five-Hydroxytrptamine [*Chemical name of serotonin*] (DIPS)

5HTP............ Five-Hydroxytryptophan [*Chemical precursor to serotonin*] (DIPS)

6-MP........... 6-Mercaptopurine [*Medicine*]

6-TG............. 6-Thioguanine [*Medicine*]

16PF .... Sixteen Personality Factor Questionnaire [*R. B. Cattell*] (DIPS)

90210 .... Beverly Hills 90210 [*Television program title*]

1

A

By Acronym

a	Absent (ADWA)
a	Acceleration (NTIO)
A	Across (ADWA)
A	Airport Area (PIPO)
a	Alto
a	Amplitude (DIPS)
A	Asked Price (SG)
A	Response Amplitude (DIPS)
A2D	Analog-to-Digital (AEBE)
AA	Administering Agency (SARE)
aa	After Arrival (MARI)
A/A	Air to Air (PIPO)
AA	All-Around [Rodeo term]
AA	Anaplastic Anaemia [Medicine]
AA	Anticipatory Account (ABAC)
aa	Arteries (ADWA)
AA	Associate Advisor
aa	Author's Alteration (ADWA)
AAAA	Alaskan AIDS Assistance Association
AAAA	Always Afloat Always Accessible (RIMS)
AAAPP	American Association of Applied and Preventive Psychology (DIPS)
AABP	American Association of Bovine Practitioners
AAC	Ableauctions.comInc. [AMEX symbol]
AAC	American Association for Counseling (DIPS)
AACE	Association for the Advancement of Computing in Education
AACF	Asian-American Christian Fellowship
AACN	American Association of Critical-Care Nurses
AACP	American Association of Clinical Psychologists (DIPS)
AAD	Attitude Anomaly Detector (ADWA)
AADP	Asian-American Donor Program (NUJO)
aae	Above Aerodrome Elevation [Aviation] (PIAV)
AAFC	Agriculture and Agri-Food Canada
AAG	American Association of Geographers (CARB)
AAHCC	American Accreditation Health Care Commission (HOAS)
AAI	Administrative Authority Identifier [Computer science]
AAIA	American Association of Independent Architects
AAIAG	Adventure Activities Industry Advisory Committee (HEAS)
AAL	Asynchronous Transfer Mode Adaptation Layer (ITCA)
AAMOF	As a Matter of Fact (ADWA)
A&A	Astronomy and Astrophysics
A&C	Activation and Checkout [NASA] (SPST)
A&E	Arts and Entertainment (ADWA)
a&h	Accident and Health (ADWA)
A&P	Great Atlantic and Pacific Tea Company (NTIO)
A and R	Artists and Repertory (ADWA)
AAO	Adjacent Arctic Ocean (ARMP)
A-A-O	Awake-Alert-Oriented (ADWA)
AAP	Association of Applied Psychologists (DIPS)
AAR	Acceptor of Action Results (DIPS)
AARA	Amsterdam-Antwerpen-Rotterdam Area (RIMS)
AARC	Alternative Agricultural Research and Commercialization Center
A-ARCS	Arctic Atmospheric Radiation and Cloud Station (ARMP)
AARS	Automated Aircraft Reporting System (ADWA)
AAS	Annual Activities Summary (ABAC)
AAS	Ascending Activating System (DIPS)
AAS	Audio Automatic Switch (CCCA)
AAT	Animal-Assisted-Therapy (ADWA)
AATM	At All Times (PIPO)
AATS	Ames Airborne Tracking Sunphotometer (ARMP)
AATSR	Advanced Along Track Scanning Radiometer
AAU	Amateur Athletic Union (NTIO)
AAWF	Auxiliary Aviation Weather Facility (PIPO)
ab	Abbreviation (ADWA)
ABA	Adrenergic Blocking Agent (DIPS)
aba	Adrenergic Blocking Agent (DIPS)
AB&R	Adventures of Batman and Robin
Abb	Abbess (ADWA)
abbr	Abbreviate (ADWA)
abbrev	Abbreviate (ADWA)
ABC	Acting Bureau Chief (DEMM)
ABC	Advanced Booking Charters [Travel industry] (TRID)
ABC	Advanced Breast Cancer [Medicine]
ABC	Alliance of Business Consultants (COBU)
ABCCC	Airborne Command and Control Center (ROAS)
ABC Islands	Aruba, Bonaire, and Curacao Islands (NTIO)
ABCL	Automatic Barrier Crossing, Locally Monitored (HEAS)
ABCT	Airborne Battalion Combat Team [Army]
abd	Abdicated (ADWA)
ABDR	Aircraft Battle Damage Repair (ADWA)
ABEND	Abnormal End of Task (ADWA)
ABF	Australian Boxing Federation
ABHI	Association of British Healthcare Industries (COBU)
ABI	Acquired Brain Injury (ADWA)
abl absol	Ablative Absolute (ADWA)
ABLE	Argonne Boundary Layer Experiment (ARMP)
ABMT	Autologous Bone Marrow Transplantation (ADWA)
ABMTR	Autologous Blood and Marrow Transplant Registry (ADWA)
ABN	Abnormal (ADWA)
abn	Airborne (ADWA)
ABO	Annular Beam Oscillator (ADWA)
Aborg	Aboriginal (ADWA)
ABP	Archbishop (ADWA)
ABPCO	Association of British Professional Conference Organisers (COBU)
ABR	Aeroballistic Rocket (ADWA)
ABR	Automatic Bit Rate
ABREMA	Activity Based Risk Evaluation Model of Auditing
ABRFC	Arkansas Basin Red River Forecast Center (ARMP)
ABRP	Auto Body Repair and Painting
abs	Abdominal Muscles (ADWA)
abs	Absent (ADWA)
abs	Absolute (ABAC)
ABS	Alternative Billing Service
ABS	Association of Business Schools (COBU)
ABS	Assumption Based System [Logic system] (IDAI)
ABSA	Association of Building Services Agencies (COBU)
ABSBH	Average Busy Season Busy Hour
absol	Absolute (ADWA)
abstr	Abstract (ADWA)
abv	Above (ADWA)
a/c	Account Current (ADWA)
ac	Air-Cool (ADWA)
AC	Area Coordinator (DEMM)
AC	Authentication Center (CGWS)
AC/A	Accommodative Convergence/Accommodation (ADWA)
ACA	Advanced Computer Applications (CARB)
acad	Academic (ADWA)
AC&S	Attitude, Control, and Stabilization [NASA] (SPST)
ACARS	Aircraft Communication and Recording System (CARB)
ACAVC	Advisory Committee on Agricultural and Veterinary Chemicals (AUEG)
acc	According (ADWA)
ACC	Audio Communications Controller (ROAS)
ACCA	Chartered Association of Certified Accountants (COBU)
ACCBD	Advisory Committee on Conservation of Biological Diversity (AUEG)
ACCE	American College of Childbirth Educators (NUJO)
ACCEL	American College of Cardiology Extended Learning (ADWA)
ACCELS	American Council for Collaboration in Education and Language Studies
ACCENT	Association of Centres of Excellence in Foreign Language Training (COBU)
Access	Accessory
ACCESS	Architectural and Transportation Barriers Compliance Board (ADWA)
ACCH	Associated Control Channel (CGWS)
ACCINTNET	Air Combat Command Intelligence Network (ADWA)
ACCL	Accelerated Networks [NASDAQ symbol]
ACCL	American Canadian Caribbean Line (TRID)
ACCM	Atmospheric General Circulation Model (CARB)
ACCMP	Army Command Control Master Plan (CCCA)
ACCOLC	Access Overload Class (CGWS)
accomp	Accompaniment (ADWA)
accrd	Accrued (ADWA)
ACCRI	Wright's Anaesthesia and Critical Care Resources on the Internet (ADWA)
ACCS	Army Communications and Control System (ROAS)
ACCS	Automated Calling Card Service (ROAS)
ACCSH	Advisory Committee on Construction Safety and Health (SARE)
ACCSQ	Airborne Command Control Squadron (CCCA)
acct	Accountant (ADWA)
accum	Accumulate (ADWA)
accus	Accusative (NTIO)
ACD	Advanced Conceptual Design (ABAC)
AC/DC	Alternating Current/Direct Current (NTIO)

3

ACE............ Achieving the Competitive Edge (ABAC)
ACE............ Association of Conference Executives (COBU)
ACE............ Automatic Calibration and Equalization
ACECCIS...... Allied Command Europe Command Control Information System (CCCA)
AceNET........ Appalachian Cooperative Economics Network
ACENVO....... Association of Chief Executives of National Voluntary Organisations (COBU)
ACER.......... Advisory Committee on Environmental Resources (AUEG)
ACES.......... Adaptation Controlled Environment System (ADWA)
ACES.......... Applied Computational Electromagnetics Society
acet .... Acetone (ADWA)
ACF/NCP...... Advanced Communications Function/Network Control Program (ITCA)
acft .... Aircraft (ADWA)
ACF/TCAM ... Advanced Communications Function for the Telecommunications Access Method (ITCA)
ACF/VTAME... Advanced Communications Function for the Virtual Telecommunications Access Method Entry (ITCA)
Ach .... Acetylchlorine (DIPS)
ACH .... Acetylcholine
achiev........ Achievement (ADWA)
AC/HR........ Aircraft per Hour (CTAS)
ACIO .... Assistant Chief Inspecting Officer (HEAS)
ACIPR........ Adjacent Carrier Interference Protection Ratio (CGWS)
ACIS.......... Altitude Compensation Induction System
ack........... Acknowledge (ADWA)
acl .... Alto Clarinet
ACL........... Approved Carriage List (HEAS)
ACL........... Atmospheric Convergence Line
ACLA.......... Aclara BioSciences [NASDAQ symbol] (SG)
ACLS.......... Adult and Community Learning Services
ACLs.......... Alternate Concentration Limits (ADWA)
ACM........... Access Control Machine
ACM........... Asbestos Containing Material
ACM........... Asian Christian Male (ADWA)
ACM........... Attitude Calibration Module [NASA] (SPST)
ACM........... Automatic Communications Monitor (CCCA)
ACMD .... Advisory Council on the Misuse of Drugs (HEAS)
ACMSU .... Atmospheric Chemistry Modelling Support Unit
acn........... Accordion
ACNP.......... Acute Care Nurse Practitioner
ACOA .... Adult Children of Alcoholics (DIPS)
ACOC .... Area Control Operation Center (CCCA)
ACON .... Air Conditioned (TRID)
ACP-ASIM.... American College of Physicians-American Society of Internal Medicine
ACPC .... Association of Coffee Producing Countries
ACPV .... American College of Poultry Veterinarians
ac-q .... Accelerator Globulin (ADWA)
acq........... Acquire (ADWA)
ACQIP .... Ambulatory Care Quality Improvement Program (ADWA)
ACR .... Available Cell Rate (MLOA)
ACRB .... Acquisition Career Record Brief [Army]
ACRD .... Acquisition Career Record Briefs [Army]
ACRFG .... Assembly Contingency Radio Frequency Group (SPST)
ACROS........ Airborne Cloud-Radiation Observing System (ARMP)
ACRP .... Adjusted Community Rate Proposal
ACRV .... Astronaut Crew Rescue Vehicle [NASA]
ACS........... American Car Buying Service
ACS........... Association of Consulting Scientists (COBU)
ACSA .... American Center for Social Awareness (ADWA)
ACSB .... American Society for Cell Biology
ACSN .... Aspartame Consumer Safety Network (ADWA)
ACSOE .... Atmospheric Chemistry Studies in the Oceanic Environment
A/cs rec...... Accounts Receivable (ADWA)
acst........... Acoustic (ADWA)
ACST.......... Association of Consulting Science and Technology (COBU)
ACSW .... Association of Certified Social Workers
ACT............ Acceptance and Commitment Therapy [Developed by Steven Hayes] (DIPS)
ACT............ Advanced Cell Technology
ACT............ American College Test (NTIO)
actg .... Acting (ADWA)
ACTI.......... Activ Card SA ADS [NASDAQ symbol] (SG)
ACTIVE........ Advanced Controls Technology for Integrated Vehicles (ADWA)
ACTM.......... Atmospheric Chemical Transport Model (CARB)
ACTP.......... American College Testing Program (DIPS)
ACT-UP........ AIDS Coalition to Unleash Power [An association] (NTIO)
ACU .... Attitude Control Unit (ADWA)
ACUFOS....... Australian Centre for UFO Studies
acv........... Actual Cash Value (ADWA)
ACVD .... Arteriosclerotic Cardiovascular Disease (ADWA)
ACW.......... Antarctic Circumpolar Wave
ACZ .... Aerodrome Control Zone [Aviation] (PIAV)
ad .... Adapter (ADWA)
A/D............ Aerodrome (PIAV)
AD............ Agent's Discount (TRID)
A/D............ Analog to Digital (CGWS)
AD............ Antimatter Decelerator
AD............ Area Director (HEAS)
A/D............ Arrival/Departure (CTAS)
AD............ Art Deco
AD............ Attachment Disorder
ADA .... Aerodrome Advisory Area (PIPO)

ADA .... Anomalous Diffraction Approximation (ARMP)
ADACS .... Attitude Determination and Control Subsystem (ADWA)
ADAD.......... Alzheimer Disease and Associated Disorders (ADWA)
ADALT .... Advanced Radar Altimeter (CARB)
adapt.......... Adaptation (ADWA)
Adapt.......... American Disabled for Attendant Programs Today (ADWA)
ADARG......... Adolescent Argumentativeness Scale [Roberto and Finucane, 1997]
adb .... Accidental Death Benefit (ADWA)
ADB .... Advise if Duplicate Booking [Travel industry] (TRID)
ADB .... Air Discount Bulletin [Travel industry] (TRID)
adbom .... Abdominal (ADWA)
ADC .... Advanced Developing Country (ADWA)
ADC .... Affiliated Data Center (CARB)
ADCOM .... Address Commission (RIMS)
ADCOM .... Aerospace Defense Command (CCCA)
add .... Addition (ADWA)
ADD .... Architecture Description Document (SPST)
add/col .... Additional Collection [Travel industry] (TRID)
ADDH .... Attention-Deficit Disorder with Hyperactivity (DIPS)
addn .... Addition (ADWA)
ADDNET........ Acid Deposition Data Network [Environmental Protection Agency] (CARB)
addnl .... Additional (ADWA)
ADDS .... Advanced Data Dictionary System (ITCA)
ADE .... Array Drive Electronics (ADWA)
ADFRF .... Ames-Dryden Flight Research Facility [NASA]
ADHF .... American Digestive Health Foundation
ADI .... Attitude Director Indicator (PIPO)
ADIL .... Annual Digest and Reports of Public International Law Cases [A publication]
adj .... Adjectival (ADWA)
ADJ .... Adjusting Schedule of Reinforcement (DIPS)
ADJ IBL .... Adjusted Interest-Bearing Liabilities
ADL .... Activities for Daily Living
ADL .... Advanced Development Laboratory (CCCA)
adm .... Administration (NTIO)
ADM........... Air Data Module (HLLA)
ADM........... Angular Dependence Model (ARMP)
admin .... Administrator (ADWA)
ADMP .... Air Defense Master Plan (CCCA)
ADN .... Any Day Now (ADWA)
ADNO .... Advise if Not Okay [Travel industry] (TRID)
ADO .... Adecco SA ADS [NYSE symbol] (SG)
ADOA .... Advise on Arrival [Travel industry] (TRID)
ADOL .... Adolescence Directory Online (ADWA)
ADON .... Assistant Director of Nursing (NUJO)
ADP .... Adult Diploma Program
ADP .... Astrophysical Data Program [NASA]
ADPE .... Automated Data Processing Equipment (CTAS)
AD-PEO........ Autosomal Dominant-Progressive External Ophthalmoplegia
ADR .... Adverse Drug Reaction (DIPS)
ADR .... Air Data Reference (HLLA)
ADR .... American Depository Receipts
ADR .... Depositary Receipts
ADS .... Acid Deposition System [EPA] (AUEG)
ADS .... Approved Dosimetry Service (HEAS)
ADS .... Astrophysics Data System [NASA]
ADSET .... Association for Database Services (COBU)
ADSS .... Alcohol and Drug Services Study (ADWA)
ADT........... Abstract Data Type (AUEG)
ADT........... Air Data Tester (HLLA)
ADT........... Automatic Data Transition (CCCA)
ADTE .... Aviation Development Tactics and Evaluation Department [Military]
ADTK .... Advise if Ticketed [Travel industry] (TRID)
adv........... Advance (ADWA)
Adv........... Advent (ADWA)
Adv........... Adventure
ADVA .... Adolescent Verbal Aggressiveness Scale [Roberto and Finucane, 1997]
advb........... Adverbial (ADWA)
ADVLAM ...... Advanced Laminate Analysis Code (SPST)
ADVN .... Advise as to Names [Travel industry] (TRID)
ADVR .... Advise as to Rate [Travel industry] (TRID)
advs........... Adverbs (ADWA)
ADWAS........ Abused Deaf Women's Advocacy Services (ADWA)
AE .... Adverse Event
AE .... American English (ADWA)
AE .... Area Executive (HEAS)
AEA .... Adult Education Act
AEA .... Alpha Energy Analysis (ABAC)
AEBR .... Aerosol Extinction-to-Backscatter Ratios (ARMP)
AEC .... Administrative, Executive, and Clerical (HEAS)
AEC........... Atomic Energy Commission (AUEG)
AECP.......... Army Experimentation Campaign Plan
AED .... Automated External Defibrillator
AEDE .... Annual Effective Dose Equivalent (ABAC)
AEE .... Association for Environmental Education (AUEG)
aef .... Aerodromes Environmental Federation (PIAV)
AEF .... Average Emission Factor (CARB)
AEGIS .... AIDS Education Global Information System (ADWA)
AEK .... All Electrical Kitchen (ADWA)
AELDS .... Advanced Earth Location Data System (ADWA)
AEOS .... Advanced Electro-Optical System (ADWA)
AEPA.......... Alberta Environmental Protection and Enhancement Act [Canada]
AER........... Atmospheric Environmental Research, Inc. (ARMP)

AERI	Atmospheric Emitted Radiance Interferometer	(ARMP)
aero	Aeronautical	(ADWA)
AERO	Aeronautics Maintenance	
aerodyn	Aerodynamics	(ADWA)
acron	Aeronautics	(ADWA)
Aeron	Aeronautics	
aeronaut	Aeronautics	(ADWA)
AERP	Aquatic Effects Research Program	(AUEG)
AERT	Average Evoked Response Technique	(DIPS)
AES	Adlai E. Stevenson	(ADWA)
AES	Airborne Emission Spectrometer	(ARMP)
AESOP	Association for Energy Systems, Operations, and Programming (ABAC)	
AETP	Acquisition Education and Training Program [Army]	
AEX	Amsterdam Exchanges N.V. [Netherlands]	
AF	Acre-Feet	(ADWA)
AF	Action Figure	
af	Affix	(ADWA)
Af	Afghan	(ADWA)
AF	A-Frame	
af	Audio Frequency	(ABAC)
AFAICR	As Far as I Can Recall	(ADWA)
AFAICS	As Far As I Can See [Online dialog]	
AFAICT	As Far as I Can Tell	(ADWA)
AFAIKT	As Far As I Know Today [Online dialog]	
AFAIR	As Far As I Know [Online dialog]	
AFAIR	As Far As I Recall	(ADWA)
AFAM	Adaptive Fuzzy Associative Memory	(IDAI)
AFBPS	Associate Fellow of the British Psychological Society	
AFC	Automatic Flow Controller	
AFCD	Automatic Flue Closing Device	(HEAS)
A/FD	Airport Facilities Directory	(PIPO)
AFDB	Agri-Food Development Branch [Canada]	
AFEN	Atlantic Frontier Environmental Network	
AFEWES	Air Force Electronic Warfare Effectiveness Simulator	(ADWA)
aff	Affairs	(ADWA)
AFF	Associate Administrator for Airway Facilities	(CTAS)
affd	Affirmed	(ADWA)
affg	Affirming	(ADWA)
afft	Affidavit	(ADWA)
Afg	Afghanistan	(ADWA)
AFGIHS	Air Force Geographic Information Handling System	(ADWA)
AFH	Above Field Height	(PIPO)
A-Fib	Atrial Fibrillation	(ADWA)
AFIN	Air Force Intelligence	(CCCA)
AFIO	Air Force Intelligence Officer	(CCCA)
AFIS	Airborne Flight Information Service	(HLLA)
Afk	Afrikaans	(ADWA)
afl	Alto Flute	
AFLC	Antiferroelectric	
AFOB	Archaeological Fieldwork Opportunities Bulletin [A publication]	
AFP	Alphafotoprotein Test	
Afr	African	(NTIO)
AFRC	Air Force Reserve Command	
Afrik	Afrikaans	(ADWA)
AFRL	Air Force Research Laboratory	
AFS	Available for Sale	
AFSAT	Air Force Satellite	(CCCA)
AFSCF	Air Force Satellite Communications System	(CCCA)
AFSFC	Air Force Space Forecasting Center	(ADWA)
AFSPS	Arrival First Sea Pilot Station	(RIMS)
AFT	Actual Flying Time [Travel industry]	(TRID)
AFY	Acre-Feet per Year	(ADWA)
ag	Agricultural	(ADWA)
A/G	Air-to-Ground	(PIAV)
Ag	August	(ADWA)
AGA	Angle of Attack [Aviation]	(PIPO)
AGIT	Antenna Group Interface Tube	(SPST)
agl	Above Ground Level	(PIAV)
AGN	Active Galactic Nuclei	
AgNIC	Agriculture Network Information Center	
agr	Agricultural	(ADWA)
agr	Agriculture	(NTIO)
AGR	Alphaglucosylrutin [Antioxidant]	
AGRA	American Genetic Resources Alliance	
AGRAS	Air-Ground Radiotelephone Automated Service	(CGWS)
AGRASCCN	Air-Ground Radiotelephone Automated Service Credit Card Number (CGWS)	
A/G ratio	Albumin-Globulin Ratio	(ADWA)
agri	Agricultural	(ADWA)
agric	Agricultural	(ADWA)
Agric	Agriculture	
agron	Agronomy	(ADWA)
agst	Against	(ADWA)
AGW	All Going Well	(RIMS)
AGWP	Absolute Global Warning Potential	(CARB)
AH	Air Heater	(CARB)
A-h	Ampere-Hour	(ADWA)
ah	Ampere-Hour	(NTIO)
A/H	Anchor Handling	(RIMS)
AHA	American Hyperloxia Association	
AHC	Alternating Hemiplegia of Childhood	
AHCA	Agency for Health Care Administration	(DEMM)
AHD	Attention-Deficit Hyperactivity Disorder	(DIPS)
AHDL	Analog Hardware Description Language	(AEBE)
AHDL	Analog Hardware Descriptive Language	(ADWA)
AHF	American Hull Form	(MARI)
AHIP	Academy of Health Information Professionals	(NUJO)
AHMA	American Hotel and Motel Association	(TRID)
AHP	American Home Products	
AHP	Association Health Plan	
AHRIS	Automated Health Research Information System	(ADWA)
AHRQ	Agency for Healthcare Research and Quality	
AHS	American Horticultural Society	
AI	Accident Investigator	(SARE)
AI	Adapter Interface	(ADWA)
ai	Airborne Intercept	(ADWA)
AI	Allegheny International	
A/I	Anti-Ice	(PIPO)
AIA	Advance Informed Agreement	
AIAA	Area of Intense Aerial Activity [Aviation]	(PIAV)
AIAC	Agriculture Industry Advisory Committee	(HEAS)
AIAC	Artificial Intelligence Advisory Committee	(AUEG)
AIB	Asbestos Insulation Board	(HEAS)
AIBS	All-Important Box Score [Baseball term]	(NDBD)
AIC	Active Instability Control	(HEAS)
AIC	Australian Institute of Cartographers	
AICC	Automatic Intercept Communications Controller	(ROAS)
AID	Aircraft Identifier	(CTAS)
AID	Aircraft Identification	(CTAS)
AID	Automated Interaction Detector	(AUEG)
AIES	Advanced Imagery Exploitation System	(CCCA)
AIF	Audio Interchange Format	
AIFF	Audio Interface Format	
AiGaN	Aluminum Gallium Nitride	
AIH	American Institute of Hypnotherapy	
AIHCE	American Industrial Hygiene Conference and Exposition	(ADWA)
AILC	Adult Independent Living Center	(ADWA)
AILC	All-Important Loss Column [Baseball term]	(NDBD)
AIM	Atlantic Isopycnic Model	
AIME	Amount of Invested Mental Effort	
AIMS	Advanced Inventory Management System	
AIO	Advances in Osteoporosis	(ADWA)
AIOSH	Associate of the Institute of Occupational Safety and Health	(HEAS)
AIP	Aryl Hydrocarbon Receptor-Interacting Protein	
AIPAC	American-Israeli Political Action Committee	
AIR	Alternative Internet Resource	
AIRD	Assembly Implementation Requirements Document [NASA]	(SPST)
AIREP	Aircraft Weather Report	(CARB)
AIRS	Airline Inventory Redistribution System	
AIRST	Advanced Infrared Search and Track	(ADWA)
AIS	Action Item System	
AIS	Active Isolated Stretching	
AIS	Address Information System	(AUEG)
AIS	Automated Information Security	(ADWA)
AISSP	Automated Information Systems Security Program	
AIT	Assembly, Integration, and Test	(ADWA)
AIT	Auditory Integrated Training	
AIT	Auditory Integration Training	
AITP	Arctic Ice Thickness Project	(CARB)
AIV	Assembly-Integration-Verification	(ADWA)
AIZ	Aerodrome Information Zone [Aviation]	(PIAV)
AJ	Administration of Justice	
AJ	Astronomical Journal [A publication]	
AJCL	American Journal of Comparative Law [A publication]	
AJRA	American Junior Rodeo Association	
AKC	Access Pharmaceuticals [AMEX symbol]	(SG)
AKDC	Automatic Key Distribution Center	(CCCA)
AL	Active List	(NDRD)
al	Alcohol	(ADWA)
Al	Aluminum	(ABAC)
Ala	Alabama	(ADWA)
ALA	Association of London Authorities	(HEAS)
ALAA	Associate of the Library Association of Australia	
ALARA	As Late as Reasonably Achievable	(ADWA)
Alas	Alaska	(NTIO)
ALASAT	Air Launched Anti-Satellite	(CCCA)
ALATE	As Low as Technically and Economically Praticable	(ABAC)
Alb	Albanian	(ADWA)
alb	Albumen	(ADWA)
Alba	Alberta	(ADWA)
alc	Alcohol	(ADWA)
Alcan	Alaska-Canada	(ADWA)
Ald	Alderwoman	(ADWA)
ALD	Anoxic Limestone Drains	
ALE	Application Launching and Embedding [Computer science]	
ALEC	Alternative Local Exchange Carrier	(CGWS)
ALEP	Adaptive Learning Environments Program	
ALEXIS	Array of Low Energy X-Ray Imaging Sensors	(ADWA)
alg	Algebra	(ADWA)
Alg	Algerian	(ADWA)
ALGOL	Algorithmic-Oriented Language	(ADWA)
ALH	Advanced Liquid Hydrogen	(ADWA)
ALI	Adult Literacy Initiative	
ALI	Allowable Limit of Intake	(ABAC)
ALIAS	Aircraft Laser Infrared Absorption Spectrometer	(CARB)
alk	Alkali	(ADWA)
alky	Alkalinity	(ADWA)
alle	Alloisoleucine	(ADWA)
All ER	All England Law Reports [A publication]	

allus .... Allusion (ADWA)
alm .... Alarm (ADWA)
ALMA.......... Atacama Large Millimeter Array
ALO............. Analytical Laboratory Operations (ABAC)
ALOS .... Advanced Land Observation Satellite (ARMP)
ALOS .... Advanced Land Observing Satellite [*Sponsored by Japan Space Agency*]
alp .... Alpine (ADWA)
ALPA........... Air Line Pilots Association
ALPD .... Automated Large Panel Display (CCCA)
alphanumeric... Alphabetical and Numerical (ADWA)
ALPI............ Asbestos Licensing Principal Inspector (HEAS)
ALRI............ Adult Literacy Resource Institute
ALS............. Approach Lighting System [*Aviation*] (PIPO)
alt .... Alteration (ADWA)
ALT .... Alternative Schedule of Reinforcement (DIPS)
alter............ Alteration (ADWA)
ALTH........... Allos Therapeutics [*NASDAQ symbol*] (SG)
altm .... Altimeter (ADWA)
ALTV........... Association of Local Television Stations, Inc.
ALU............. Allou Health & Beauty Care
ALU............. Asbestos Licensing Unit (HEAS)
alum .... Alumna (NTIO)
alum .... Alumnae (ADWA)
alw.............. Allowance (ADWA)
AM .... Administration Manager (HEAS)
am .... Ammeter (ADWA)
AM .... Amplitude Modulated (PIPO)
Am .... Amsterdam Stock Exchange (SG)
AMAG .... Agricultural Machinery Advisory Group (HEAS)
AMAP........... Arctic Monitoring and Assessment Program (ARMP)
AMB............ Acquisition Management Branch [*Army*]
amb .... Ambassador (ADWA)
AMC............ All My Children [*Television program title*]
AMC............ Antecedent Moisture Condition (ADWA)
AMD............ Advisory Map Display (HLLA)
amd .... Amended (ADWA)
AMD............ Associated Manufacturing and Design [*Alexandria, Virginia*] (ABAC)
Ame .... America (ADWA)
AMED........... Allied and Alternative Medicine (ADWA)
AMEDDC&S... Army Medical Department Center and School
AMEI............ Association of Medical Expenses Insurers (COBU)
AMEL........... Airplane Multi-Engine Land (PIPO)
AmerF.......... American French (ADWA)
AmerInd....... American Indian (ADWA)
AmerSp........ American Spanish (ADWA)
AMES........... Airplane Multi-Engine Sea (PIPO)
AMES........... Ames Laboratory
Ameslan....... American Sign Language (NTIO)
AmEx .... American Express (NTIO)
AMF .... Assistant Manager of Facility Transition (ABAC)
AMI .... Airline Modifiable Information (HLLA)
ammo .... Ammunition (ADWA)
Amn .... Airman (ADWA)
AMNH .... American Museum of Natural History (AUEG)
AMO............ Aircraft Maintenance Officer
Amoco .... American Oil Company (NTIO)
amort.......... Amortization (ADWA)
AMOSS .... Airline Maintenance and Operation Support System (HLLA)
AMP .... Augmented Materials Production (ABAC)
AMPE.......... Automatic Message Processing Equipment (CCCA)
AMPL-FT..... Access Michigan Periodical List-Full Text
AMPS........... Advanced Mobile Phone System
AMRS .... Advanced Microwave Scanning Radiometer (ARMP)
AMS............. Automated Meteorological Station (AUEG)
amsl............ Above Mean Sea Level (PIAV)
AMST........... American Studies
AMT .... Automotive Technology
AMTEX........ American Textile Industry (ABAC)
Amtrak........ American Track (NTIO)
AMTS........... Advanced Moisture and Temperature Sounder (CARB)
amu .... Atomic Mass Unit (ABAC)
AMV............ AmeriVest Properties [*AMEX symbol*] (SG)
AMVETS....... American Veterans (ADWA)
an .... Above Named (ADWA)
AN............... Added Name [*Travel industry*] (TRID)
ANAA .... Advanced Nucleic Acid Analyzer
ANADA......... Abbreviated New Animal Drug Application [*Food and Drug Administration*]
anal .... Analogous (ADWA)
Anal .... Analysis
analyt .... Analytical (ADWA)
ANAP .... Anionic Neutrophil Activating Peptide (ADWA)
ANARE........ Australian National Antarctic Research Establishment (CARB)
anat............ Anatomical (ADWA)
ANBS .... Asian Network of Biological Sciences (CARB)
ANC .... Aerojet Nuclear Company (ABAC)
ANCS........... Automated Nautical Charting System (ADWA)
and .... Andante (ADWA)
And .... Andorran (ADWA)
ANED .... Alive No Evidence of Disease [*Medicine*]
anes............ Anesthesia (ADWA)
ANF............. Advanced Nuclear Fuels Corp. (ABAC)
ang .... Angiogram (ADWA)
Ang .... Angola (ADWA)

Angl............ Anglican (ADWA)
Anglo-Ind.... Anglo-Indian (ADWA)
Anglo-Ir ...... Anglo-Irish (ADWA)
angst .... Angstrom (ADWA)
anhyd.......... Anhydrous (ADWA)
ANLP .... Association for Neuro-Linguistic Programming (COBU)
ANM............ Assistant Nurse Manager (NUJO)
ann .... Annals (ADWA)
ANN .... Artificial Neural Network (IDAI)
Anniv .... Anniversary
anniv .... Anniversary (ADWA)
annot........... Annotated (ADWA)
ANP .... Actual Navigation Performance (HLLA)
ANPN .... Adult Numeracy Practitioners Network
ANSIR.......... Advanced Navigation System Inertial Reference (HLLA)
Ant .... Antarctica (ADWA)
ant .... Antiquity (ADWA)
ANTH .... Anthropology
ANTHAM ..... Antwerp-Hamburg Range (RIMS)
anthol .... Anthology (ADWA)
anthro .... Anthropology (ADWA)
anthrop .... Anthropological (ADWA)
anthropol .... Anthropological (ADWA)
antilog......... Antilogarithm
antiq........... Antiquarian (ADWA)
ANTS .... Antenna Subsystem (ADWA)
ANWD .... Alpha/Numeric Wall Display (CCCA)
Anzac.......... Australia and New Zealand Army Corps (ADWA)
AO............... Aorta (ADWA)
AO............... Arctic Oscillation
AO............... Atmosphere-Ocean (CARB)
AOA .... Airport Operators' Association (PIAV)
aoa .... Any One Accident (MARI)
AOAC .... American Organization of Analytical Chemists (ABAC)
AOB .... Air Operating Base (CCCA)
aob .... Any One Bottom (MARI)
AOC .... Airline Operations Center (CTAS)
AOC .... All Other Contents (MARI)
AOCL .... Automatic Open Crossing Locally Monitored (HEAS)
AOCMS........ Attitude and Orbit Control Measurement System (ADWA)
AOCR........... Automatic Open Crossing, Remotely Monitored (HEAS)
AODC .... Acridine Orange Direct Count (CARB)
AoE .... Airport of Entry (PIAV)
aoe .... Any One Event (MARI)
AOE .... Area of Emphasis (SPST)
AOG .... Aircraft on Ground (PIAV)
AOHA .... Administrators in Oncology/Hematology Assembly (ADWA)
aol .... Any One Loss (MARI)
AOL .... Arrow of Light [*Boy Scouts of America*]
AOM............ Award of Merit [*Boy Scouts of America*]
aoo .... Any One Occurrence (MARI)
aor .... Aorist (ADWA)
AOS .... Academic Operating System
AOS .... Aerosol Observing System (ARMP)
AOSS .... Auxilliary Operator Service System
AOT .... Astronomical Observation Template (ADWA)
AOTC .... Associated Offices Technical Committee (HEAS)
aov .... Any One Vessel (MARI)
aovov .... Any One Voyage (MARI)
A/P.............. Account Paid (ADWA)
A/P.............. Airport (PIAV)
AP............... Annual Premium (MARI)
AP............... Aorticopulmonary (ADWA)
Ap............... Apostle (ADWA)
ap............... Apothecary (ADWA)
AP............... Assistant Principal
APA............. Aerodromes Protection Agency [*British*] (PIAV)
APA............. Also Printed As (ADWA)
APACHE .... Acute Physiology and Chronic Health Evaluation (IDAI)
A-part .... Alpha Particle (ADWA)
APAS........... Androgynous Peripheral Attachment System [*NASA*] (SPST)
APAU........... Accident Prevention Advisory Unit (HEAS)
APBL........... Automatic Power Boom Lowering (HEAS)
APC............. Accident Prevention Council (ABAC)
APC............. Adaptive Predictive Correction (CGWS)
A-P-C .... Adenoidal-Pharyngeal-Conjunctival (ADWA)
apc............. Automatic Phase Control
APD .... Auditory Processing Disorder
APD .... Avalanche Photon Device (CCCA)
APE............. Adaptive Physical Education
APE............. Aerosol Photoemission (HEAS)
APEC........... Asia-Pacific Economic Cooperation (ARMP)
APELL.......... Awareness and Preparedness for Emergencies at Local Level (HEAS)
aper .... Aperture (ADWA)
APEX........... AntiProton Experiments
APF............. Asian Professional Female (ADWA)
APF............. Assigned Protection Factor (SARE)
APG .... Administration Planning Group (HEAS)
APG .... Ambulatory Patient Group (ADWA)
aphet .... Aphetized (ADWA)
API.............. Aerial Photo Interpretation (AUEG)
API.............. American Petroleum Institute (HEAS)
API.............. Asian and Pacific Islander (ADWA)
APID .... Application Identification (ADWA)

APIH	Association of Professional Hygienists (SARE)
APIL	Association of Personal Injury Lawyers
ApJ	Astrophysical Journal [*A publication*]
APL	Adult Performance Level
Apl	April (ADWA)
apl	As per List (MARI)
APL	Atlas Pipeline Ptnrs. LP [*AMEX symbol*] (SG)
APLS	Advanced Pediatric Life Support (NUJO)
APLS	Antiphospholipid Syndrome (ADWA)
APM	Amplitude and Phase Modulation (CCCA)
APM	Antenna Pointing Mechanism (ADWA)
APM	Associate Program Manager (CTAS)
APM	Astronaut Positioning Mechanism [*NASA*] (SPST)
APMC	Associate Program Manager for Contracting (CTAS)
APME	Attitude Pointing Mechanism Electronics (ADWA)
APMGC	Associate Program Manager for General Counsel (CTAS)
APML	Associate Program Manager for Logistics (CTAS)
APMO	Associate Program Manager for Operations (CTAS)
APMP	Associate Program Manager for Procedures (CTAS)
APMQ	Associate Program Manager for Quality (CTAS)
APMR	Associate Program Manager for Requirements (CTAS)
APMSE	Associate Program Manager for System Engineering (CTAS)
APMT	Associate Program Manager for Test (CTAS)
APN	Advanced Practice Nurse (NUJO)
APN	Asia-Pacific Network (ARMP)
apo	Apoenzyme (ADWA)
apo-E	Apolipoprotein-E (ADWA)
APP	Adjustable Premium Policy (MARI)
app	Apparently (ADWA)
APP	Approved (CTAS)
APPA	American Public Power Association (HEAS)
APPA	Association of Physical Plant Administrators (SARE)
appar	Apparent (ADWA)
Appd	Approved (MARI)
appl	Appliances (ADWA)
appmt	Appointment (ADWA)
appr	Approximate (ADWA)
approx	Approximate (ADWA)
appt	Appoint (ADWA)
APR	Apple Print Recognizer [*Handwriting recognition system*] (IDAI)
Apr	April (ADWA)
APS	Arrival Pilot Station (RIMS)
APS	CollegeLink.com, Inc. [*AMEX symbol*] (SG)
APT	Advanced Personnel Testing (ADWA)
APT	Advanced Processing Technology (ABAC)
APT	Airline Passenger Tariff [*Travel industry*] (TRID)
APTI	Advanced Processing Technology Institute (ABAC)
apu	Auxiliary Power Unit (ADWA)
apx	Appendix (ADWA)
AQC	Analog Quantum Computers
AQR	Aquarius (ADWA)
AQRP	Association of Qualitative Research Practitioners (COBU)
AQUA	Analytical Quality Assurance (HEAS)
A/R	Accounts Receivable (NTIO)
AR	Analytical Reagent (ABAC)
Ar	Aramaic (ADWA)
ar	Arrival (ADWA)
AR	Authors' Registry
Arab	Arabian (ADWA)
Arab	Arabic (NTIO)
ARAG	Amsterdam-Rotterdam-Antwerp-Gent Range (RIMS)
Aram	Aramaic (ADWA)
ARAM	Automated Remediation Assessment Methodology (ABAC)
ARARs	Applicable, Revelant, or Appropriate Requirements (ADWA)
ARB	Airworthiness Review Board (PIAV)
ARB	Alternate Reconstitution Base (CCCA)
arb	Arbitrageur (ADWA)
ARB	Arthritis and Rheumatism Branch
ARBA	Army Review Boards Agency
ARC	Airlines Reporting Corporation (TRID)
Arc	Arcade (ADWA)
ARC	Automatic Radial Centering [*Aviation*] (PIPO)
ARCA	Areas Requiring Corrective Action [*Department of Emergency Management*] (DEMM)
ARCA	Attached Resupply Carrier [*NASA*] (SPST)
ARCAL	Aircraft Radio Control of Aerodrome Lighting (PIAV)
ARCC	Acquisition Reform Communications Center
arc csc	Arc Cosecant (ADWA)
arch	Archaism (ADWA)
archit	Architecture (ADWA)
ARCS	Atmosphere Radiation and Cloud Station (ARMP)
arc sec	Arc Secant (ADWA)
arc sin	Arc Sine (ADWA)
ARCSYM	Arctic Regional Climate System Model (ARMP)
arc tan	Arc Tangent (ADWA)
ARET	Association for Rational Emotive Therapists (COBU)
ARF	Aerosol Radiative Forcing (ARMP)
ARFCN	Absolute Radio Frequency Channel Number (CGWS)
arg	Argent (ADWA)
Arg	Argentinean (ADWA)
ARGOS	Advanced Research and Global Observation Satellite (ADWA)
ARH	Atmospheric Radiative Heating (ARMP)
ARI	Aries (NTIO)
ARI	Autism Research Institute
arid ID	Arid Integrated Demonstration (ABAC)

ARIES	Antarctic Reception Imagery for Environmental Studies
ARISE	Advanced Radio Interferometry Between Space and Earth
ARISS	Amateur Radio on the International Space Station
aristo	Aristocrat (ADWA)
arith	Arithmetic (NTIO)
Ariz	Arizona (ADWA)
Ark	Arkansas (ADWA)
ARL	Australian Radiation Laboratory (CARB)
ARM	Argonne Remote Manipulator
Arm	Armenian (ADWA)
ARMSAT	Atmospheric Radiation Measurement Satellite (CARB)
ARNet	Acquistion Reform Network
ARP	Accrued Rights Premium (MARI)
ARP	Advisory Review Panel
ARP	Aerodrome Reference Point [*Aviation*] (PIAV)
ARPANet	Advanced Research Projects Agency Network
ARPERSCOM	Army Reserve Personnel Command
ARPT	Arrow Point Communications [*NASDAQ symbol*] (SG)
ARq	Authentication Request (ADWA)
arr	Arranged (ADWA)
Arr TL	Arranged Total Loss (MARI)
ARs	Authentication Response (ADWA)
ART	Advanced Reasoning Tool (IDAI)
art	Article (NTIO)
art	Artillery (ADWA)
ART	Automated Regression Tester [*Computer science*] (ITCA)
ARTEMIS	Advanced Relay Technology Mission
ARTEMIS	Advanced Research Testbed for Medical Informatics (ADWA)
ARTPR	Approved Regulations for Transportable Pressure Receptacles (HEAS)
ARTS	Advanced Radio Technology Subcommittee (CGWS)
arty	Artillery (ADWA)
ARVN	Army of the Republic of North Vietnam (NTIO)
AS	Added Segment (TRID)
AS	Advanced Schottky (AEBE)
AS	Agricultural Safety (HEAS)
A/S	Air-Speed (PIPO)
AS	American Stock Exchange (SG)
AS	Anglo-Saxon (NTIO)
AS	Anvil Stratus (ARMP)
AS	Asbestos Shingles
As	Asian (ADWA)
AS	Asperger's Syndrome
AS	Atmospheric Science
A/S	At Sight (ADWA)
AS	Autistic Spectrum
As	Oakland Athletics [*Baseball team*] (NTIO)
ASA	Accredited Safety Auditor [*International Loss Control Institute*] (SARE)
ASA	Astronomical Society of the Atlantic
ASA	Atlantic Southeast Airlines
ASA	Atmosphere Spectroscopy Applications (CARB)
ASA	Aviation Supplies & Academics
ASAALT	Assistant Secretary of the Army for Acquisition, Logistics and Technology
ASAC	Asian Standards Advisory Committee (HEAS)
ASARS	Airborne Synthetic Aperture Radar System (CCCA)
ASAS	Advanced Solid State Array Sensor (CARB)
ASC	Advising Schedule Change [*Travel industry*] (TRID)
ASC	Arctic Stratus Cloud (ARMP)
asc	Ascending (ADWA)
A-SCAT	Advanced Scatterometer (CARB)
ASCATT	Advanced Scatterometer (CARB)
ASCII	American Standard Language for Information Interchange
ASCII	American Standards Committee for Information Interchange (ARMP)
ASCM	Advanced Spaceborne Computer Module
ASD	Aircraft Situational Display (CTAS)
ASD	Analytical Spectral Devices (ARMP)
ASD	Autistic Spectrum Disorder
ASDAR	Aircraft-to-Satellite Data Relay System (ADWA)
ASE	Adult Secondary Education
ASE	Airline-Selected Equipment (HLLA)
ASE	Available Solar Energy (ADWA)
ASEL	Altitude Select [*Aviation*] (PIPO)
ASEMA	Asbestos Safety Equipment Manufacturer's Association (HEAS)
ASES	Airplane Single-Engine Sea (PIPO)
ASF	Atmospheric Stabilization Framework (AUEG)
asg	Assigned (ADWA)
ASGPA	Assembly of Surgical Group Practice Administrators (ADWA)
ASH	Edwin Ashdown [*Publisher*]
ASHPRF	American Society of Hospital Pharmacists Research and Education Foundation
ASIA	Asia Info Holdings [*NASDAQ symbol*] (SG)
ASIG	American Special Interest Group (ADWA)
ASLA	Australia School Library Association
ASLH	American Speech-Language-Hearing Foundation
ASLI	Automatic Safe Load Indicator (HEAS)
ASLIC	Asbestos Licensing Regulations (HEAS)
asm	Assembly (ADWA)
ASM	Assistant Scoutmaster [*Boy Scouts of America*]
ASN	Abstract Syntax Notation (MLOA)
ASO	Assistant Scientific Officer (HEAS)
ASOS	Automated Surface Observation System [*Aviation*] (PIPO)
ASOS	Automatic Surface Observing System (ARMP)
asp	Abnormal Spindle

ASP............	Advanced Strip Processor
ASP............	Application Service Provider
ASP............	Area Settlement Plan (TRID)
ASP............	Arrival Sequencing Program (CTAS)
ASP............	Association of Sales Professionals
ASPG.........	Automatic Data Processing Standards Policy Group (CCCA)
ASPI..........	Advanced Small Computer Systems Interface (ADWA)
ASPIIRE.......	Associations of Service Providers Implementing IDEA Reforms in Education
ASPIS.........	Abandoned Site Program Information System (SARE)
ASPM.........	Aspect Medical Systems [*NASDAQ symbol*] (SG)
ASPW.........	Any Safe Port in the World (RIMS)
ASR	Aerosol Scattering Ratio (ARMP)
ASR	Applied Space Resources
ASR	Available Solar Radiation (ADWA)
assem........	Assembly (ADWA)
assim.........	Assimilated (ADWA)
assoc........	Association (NTIO)
asstd.........	Assisted (ADWA)
assy..........	Assembly (ADWA)
Assyr	Assyrian (ADWA)
AST...........	American Segment Trainer [*NASA*] (SPST)
AST...........	Aspartate Transaminase
ASTC.........	Application-Specific-Integrated Chip (ADWA)
ASTI..........	Absolute Solar Transmittance Interferometer (ARMP)
astrol........	Astrological (ADWA)
astrol........	Astrology (NTIO)
astron	Astronomer (ADWA)
astronaut	Astronautics (ADWA)
ASV...........	Absorptive Stripping Voltametry (ABAC)
ASVD........	Analog Simultaneous Voice/Data Technology (ITCA)
asx...........	Alto Saxophone
asym.........	Asymmetric (ADWA)
At.............	Ampere-Turn (ADWA)
AT.............	Assistive Technology
AT.............	Atlantic Time (ADWA)
at.............	Atmosphere (ADWA)
aT.............	Attotesla (ADWA)
AT.............	Automatic Transmission (NTIO)
ata	Atmosphere Absolute (ADWA)
ATA...........	Aviation Training Association (COBU)
ATA-2.........	Advanced Technology Attachment Interface with Extensions [*Computer science*] (ITCA)
ATAGS	Advanced Technology Anti-G Suit (ADWA)
ATB...........	Agricultural Training Board (COBU)
ATB...........	Antenna Test Bed (SPST)
ATCCS	Army Tactical Command and Control System (ROAS)
atch..........	Attach (ADWA)
ATCM........	Air Toxics Control Measure (SARE)
ATD...........	Alpha Track Detector (ABAC)
ATDNSHINC...	Any Time Day/Night Sundays and Holidays Included (RIMS)
ATDPS	Attitude Toward Disabled Persons Scale (DIPS)
ATDRS	Advanced Tracking and Data Relay Satellite (ADWA)
ATF...........	Aerodrome Traffic Frequency (PIPO)
ATF...........	Atmospheric Transmission Factor (CARB)
ATFDS	Automated Ticket and Fare Determination System [*Travel industry*] (TRID)
ATG...........	Automatic Test Generation
ath	Athletic (ADWA)
athl	Athlete (ADWA)
ATI	Air Transport Indicator (HLLA)
ATIES........	Association of Temporary and Interim Executive Services (COBU)
ATIRCM	Advanced Threat Infrared Countermeasures (ADWA)
ATL...........	Americans for Technology Leadership
ATLAS........	Airborne Turnable Laser Absorption Spectrometer (CARB)
ATM...........	Advanced Trauma Management [*Army*]
ATM...........	Amateur Telescope Maker
ATM...........	Analog-to-Time Module
ATM...........	Asynchronous Transmission Mode (AEBE)
atm	Atmosphere (ADWA)
ATM...........	Automatic Teller Machine (NTIO)
atmos	Atmospheric (ADWA)
Atmos	Atmospheric
ATMOS	Atmospheric Trace Spectroscopy (ARMP)
ATMS	Automated Transportation Management System (ABAC)
ATNAVICS....	Air Traffic Navigation, Integration and Coordination System [*Army*]
ATO...........	Airport Ticket Office (TRID)
ATO...........	Air Traffic Operations (CTAS)
ATOC.........	Army Tactical Operations Center (CCCA)
ATR...........	Acceptance Test Review (CTAS)

ATR...........	Air Traffic Plans and Requirements Service (CTAS)
ATR...........	Air Traffic Requirements (CTAS)
ATR...........	Approved Tank Requirements (HEAS)
ATRA	Assistive Technology Resource Alliance (ADWA)
atRY..........	All-Trans-Retinylester
ATS...........	Active Thermal System (SPST)
ATS...........	Air Transport Systems (HLLA)
ATS...........	Automatic Tracking System (ABAC)
ATSL..........	Along the Same Line (ADWA)
att.............	Attachment (ADWA)
attr...........	Attractive (ADWA)
attrib.........	Attributively (ADWA)
ATUTC........	Actually Time Used to Count (RIMS)
ATW..........	Around the World (TRID)
AU.............	Austerity
Au.............	Australian Stock Exchange (SG)
AuC...........	Authentication Center (CGWS)
aud	Audience (ADWA)
aud	Auditor (ADWA)
aug	Augmentative (ADWA)
Aug	August (ADWA)
augm.........	Augmentative (ADWA)
AUK..........	Authorized User Key [*Computer science*] (ITCA)
AURIO........	Auroral Imaging Observatory (CARB)
Aus	Australia (ADWA)
AUSPECC.....	Australian Pacific Economic Cooperation Committee
Aust	Australia (ADWA)
Austl	Australia (ADWA)
Austral	Australia (NTIO)
AutCom.......	Autism National Committee
auth	Authority (ADWA)
Auth Ver	Authorized Version (ADWA)
auto	Automobile (ADWA)
AUTOB........	Automatic Observing Station (PIPO)
AUX	Auxiliary Verb (ADWA)
Aux	Fitted with Auxiliary Engine (MARI)
A/V............	Ad Valorem [*According to Value*] [*Latin*] (NTIO)
A-V............	Arteriovenous (ADWA)
av	Average (ADWA)
Av	Average (MARI)
AVA	Antiovarian Antibody (ADWA)
AVAS	Additivity and Variance Stabilization (IDAI)
AVD	Acoustic Variable Density (CARB)
avdp..........	Avoirdupois (NTIO)
Avest	Avestan (ADWA)
avg............	Average (ABAC)
avgas.........	Aviation Gasoline (ADWA)
AVIA..........	American Vocational Information Association
AVL...........	Available (ADWA)
avlbl	Available (ADWA)
AVN	Avanir Pharmaceuticals 'A' [*AMEX symbol*] (SG)
avn...........	Aviation (ADWA)
AVN	Russian Military News Agency
AVP...........	Approximate Vertical Profile (CTAS)
AVR...........	Avitar, Inc. [*AMEX symbol*] (SG)
AVS...........	Availability Status Messages [*Travel industry*] (TRID)
AVSC.........	Access to Voluntary and Safe Contraception (ADWA)
A-V Shunt....	Arteriovenous Shunt (ADWA)
AVSSCS.......	Audio-Visual Service Specific Convergence Sublayer
avtur..........	Aviation Turbine Fuel (PIAV)
AW............	Another World [*Television program title*]
AWE..........	AT&T Corp-Wireless Grp. [*NYSE symbol*] (SG)
awk...........	Awkward (ADWA)
AWO	Animal Welfare Officer (SARE)
AWP...........	Any Willing Provider
AWP...........	Any Will Provider (ADWA)
AWRS	Automatic Weather Reporting Station (PIPO)
AWS...........	Aural Warning System [*Aviation*] (PIPO)
AWS...........	Automated Weather Station (ARMP)
AWST.........	Aviation Week & Space Technology (CCCA)
AWT...........	Advanced Wastewater Treatment (ADWA)
AWUNW.......	Associated Western Universities-Northwest (ABAC)
AWW	Alert Severe Weather Watch (PIPO)
Awy...........	Airway (PIAV)
ax	Axiom (ADWA)
Ax	Axis (DIPS)
AY.............	Any (ADWA)
AYG	Anything (ADWA)
az..............	Azure (ADWA)
AZA............	Azimuth Angle (ARMP)
AZE............	Azerbaijan (ADWA)

B
By Acronym

b	Bar (ABAC)
B	Beacon Available [*Aviation*] (PIPO)
B	Bid Price (SG)
B	Boston Stock Exchange (SG)
b	Breadth (ADWA)
B	Bunt [*Baseball term*] (NDBD)
B2B	Business-to-Business
B/A	Bank Angle [*Aviation*] (PIPO)
ba	Bathroom (ADWA)
BAA	Broad Agency Announcement
BABA	Biomass and Biofuels Association (COBU)
bact	Bacterial (ADWA)
bacteriol	Bacteriology (ADWA)
BAIC	Barring of All Incoming Calls (CGWS)
bal	Balcony (NTIO)
balc	Balcony (ADWA)
BALFRAM	Balanced Force Requirements Analysis Model (CCCA)
Balt	Baltic (ADWA)
BAM	Business Administration Manager (ABAC)
BAMS	Bulletin of the American Meteorological Society [*A publication*] (ARMP)
Banana	Build Absolutely Nothing Anywhere Near Anybody (ADWA)
B&B	Bed and Breakfast (TRID)
B&B	Bold and the Beautiful [*Television program title*]
B and E	Breaking and Entering (ADWA)
B and L	Building and Loan (ADWA)
B&O	Baltimore and Ohio (ADWA)
B&R	Batman and Robin
B&R	Budgeting and Reporting (ABAC)
B and S	Bourbon and Soda (ADWA)
B&U	Buildings and Utilities (ABAC)
B&W	Babcock & Wilcox Co. (ABAC)
BAOC	Barring of All Outgoing Calls (CGWS)
Bap	Baptist (NTIO)
BAPC	British Association of Print and Copyshops (COBU)
BAPE	Benign Asbestos Pleural Effusion (HEAS)
BAPS	Baseline Air Pollution Station (AUEG)
bapt	Baptized (ADWA)
BAPT	British Association of Psychological Types (COBU)
bar	Barometer (NTIO)
BAR	Broad Area Review
BARM	Block Acceptance Reporting Mechanism (ADWA)
BARRITT	Barrier Injected Transit Time (CCCA)
barsx	Baritone Saxophone
bas	Basal (ADWA)
BAS	Basic Inspection (HEAS)
BAS	Batman, the Animated Series
BAS	Behavioral Activation System
BAS	Behavioral Approach System (DIPS)
BAS	Block Acquisition Sequence (ADWA)
BAS	Brigade Aid Station [*Military*]
BASELT	British Association of State English Language Teaching
bast	Basket
BAT	Baseball Assistance Team (NDBD)
bat	Battalion (ADWA)
BAT	Biological Tolerance Value (HEAS)
BATGE	Biosphere-Atmosphere Trace Gas Exchange (CARB)
batt	Battalion (ADWA)
BB	Bareback Riding [*Rodeo term*]
Bb	Bareboat (RIMS)
BB	Baseball (NDBD)
BB	Batboy (NDBD)
BB	Biomass Burned (CARB)
bb	Books (ADWA)
BB	Buffet Breakfast [*Travel industry*] (TRID)
BB4N	Bye Bye for Now [*Internet dialog*]
BBB	Before Breaking Bulk (RIMS)
BBB	Blood-Brain Barrier (DIPS)
BBFN	Bye-Bye for Now (ADWA)
BBHIR	Broadband Hemispherical in Flux Radiometer (CARB)
BBHSR	Broadband Hemispherical Solar Radiometer (CARB)
BBP	Baseband Processor
BBP	Bloodborne Pathogen (SARE)
BBR	Bank Buying Rate (TRID)
BBROYGBVGW	Black, Brown, Red, Orange, Yellow, Green, Blue, Violet, Grey, White [*Electronic component color codes*] (ROAS)

BBS	Be Back Soon [*Online dialog*]
BBS	Behavior Based Safety (SARE)
BBSS	Balloon-Borne Sounding System (ARMP)
BC	Black Carbon (CARB)
bc	Blind Copy (NTIO)
BC	Bureau Chief (DEMM)
BCA	Boeing Commercial Airplanes (HLLA)
BCAR	British Civil Air Requirements (PIAV)
bcc	Body Centered Cubic (ABAC)
BCC	British Company Law Cases [*A publication*]
BCD	Base Catalyzed Destruction (ABAC)
BCE	Book Club Edition (ADWA)
B cell	Bone-Marrow-Derived Cell (ADWA)
BCF	Backup Computational Facility (CCCA)
bcf	Billion Cubic Feet (ADWA)
BCF	Black Christian Female (ADWA)
BCG	Boston Consulting Group
BCH	Broadcast Channel (CGWS)
bchd	Bunched
BCHFT	Beachfront [*Travel industry*] (TRID)
BCI	Board of Chief Inspectors (HEAS)
bcl	Bass Clarinet
BCL	Batch Command Language [*Computer science*]
BCLC	Butterworths Company Law Cases [*A publication*]
BCM	Black Christian Male (ADWA)
bcn	Beacon (ADWA)
BCP	Base Communications Processor (CCCA)
BCP	Bioconcentration Potential (ADWA)
BCP	Blue Cone Pigment
BCP	Break Cloud Procedure [*Aviation*] (PIAV)
BCPL	Basic Commercial Pilot's License (PIAV)
BCPS	Bureau of Compliance Planning and Support [*Department of Emergency Management*] (DEMM)
BCR	Baseline Change Request (ARMP)
BCRU	British Committee on Radiological Units (HEAS)
BCSR	Boeing Computer Services Richland, Inc. (ABAC)
BCTDC	British Columbia Trade Development Corporation (ABAC)
BCY	Breast-Conserving Therapy (ADWA)
bd	Baud (ABAC)
B/D	Bills Discounted (ADWA)
BD	Biological Defense
BD	Bouffees Delirantes [*An acute delusional disorder*] (DIPS)
BDA	Bandwidth Demand Assignment (CCCA)
BDC	Battelle Development Corporation (ABAC)
BDCPEC	Brunei Darussalam National Committee for Pacific Economic Cooperation
bde	Brigade (ADWA)
bd ft	Board Foot (ABAC)
bdg	Binding (ADWA)
BDG	Brigade
BDIL	British Digest of International Law [*A publication*]
bdl	Bundle (ADWA)
bdle	Bundle (ADWA)
BDM	Block Data Message (CTAS)
BDPP	Barrier Development Program Plan (ABAC)
BDR	Battery Discharge Regulator (ADWA)
bdry	Boundary (ADWA)
Bds	Barbados (ADWA)
BDS	Bomb Disposal Squad (ADWA)
BDW	Block Descriptive Word [*Computer science*] (ITCA)
Bdx	Bordeaux (ADWA)
bdy	Boundary (ADWA)
Bdy	Burgundy (ADWA)
BE	Battelle Europe (ABAC)
Be	Beaume Scale (ADWA)
BE	Both Ends (RIMS)
BE	Bulk Encryption (CCCA)
BE	Business Education
BEA	Basic Education Act [*1977*]
BEAST	Breacher's Explosive Access Selectable Tool
bec	Because (ADWA)
BEC	Bose-Einstein Condensate
BEC	Buccal Epithelial Cells
BEEM	Ballistic Electron Emission Microscopy
BEEM	Bond-Equivalent Effective Margin
Beep	Borough President (ADWA)

beg	Begin (ADWA)
BEH............	Behaviorally/Emotionally Handicapped
Belg	Belgian (ADWA)
BELS	Biological Exposure Limits (HEAS)
BENCHMARC...	Biodegradation of Environmental Chemicals Modeled with Aquatic, Relative-Rate Coefficients (AUEG)
Beng	Bengal (ADWA)
BENL	Basic English in the Native Language
BER............	Bit Error Rate (CGWS)
BERSA	British Elastic Rope Sports Association (HEAS)
BERT..........	Bit Error Rate Test
BESA	British Association of Educational Supplies (COBU)
BESP..........	Building Energy Standards Program (ABAC)
BEST..........	Basic English Skills Test
BetaII........	Revised Beta Examination, Second Edition [*C. E. Kellogg, N. W. Morton*] (DIPS)
betw...........	Between (ADWA)
BEU............	Business Efficiency Unit (HEAS)
BEV............	Billion Electron Volts (AEBE)
BEZS	Bandwidth Efficient Zero Suppression (ADWA)
BF	BASF AG ADS [*NYSE symbol*]
BF	Batman Forever
BF	Boundary Facility (ARMP)
BF	Breast Feeding
B/F	Brought Forward (ADWA)
BF	Bullfighting [*Rodeo term*]
BFB............	Bromoflurobenzene (ABAC)
BFE............	Base Flood Elevation (DEMM)
BFI.............	Brigade Force Initiative [*Army*]
BFN............	Bye for Now (ADWA)
bfo.............	Beat Frequency Oscillator (AEBE)
BFSK..........	Binary Frequency Shift Keying (CCCA)
BFSN	Beam Forming & Switching Network (CCCA)
BGI.............	Basic Ground Instructor [*Aviation*] (PIPO)
bgt	Bought (ADWA)
bgtr............	Bass Guitar
BH..............	Behaviorally Handicapped
BH..............	Black Hole
B/H.............	Bordeaux/Hamburg Limits (MARI)
BHC	Backhaul Check (TRID)
bhd	Bulkhead (ADWA)
BHI.............	Bechtel Hanford Incorporated (ABAC)
BHL............	Berkshire Hills Bancorp [*AMEX symbol*]
bHLH	Basic Helix-Loop-Helix
BHM...........	Basic Health Management
BHPA	British Hang-Gliding and Paragliding Association (PIAV)
BHSS	British Health and Safety Society (HEAS)
BI..............	Bell Industries [*AMEX symbol*] (SG)
Bi..............	Bisexual (ADWA)
BI..............	Both Inclusive (RIMS)
B/I.............	Broadcast Interrupt (CCCA)
BI..............	Built-In (ADWA)
BIA.............	Bioelectric Impedance Analysis (DIPS)
BIA.............	Bioluminescence Immunoassay
BIAF...........	Bisexual Asian Female (ADWA)
BIAM..........	Bisexual Asian Male (ADWA)
Bib.............	Bible (NTIO)
bib.............	Biblical (ADWA)
BIBF...........	Bisexual Black Female (ADWA)
bibl............	Biblical (ADWA)
bibliog........	Bibliographer (ADWA)
bibliogr........	Bibliography (ADWA)
BIBM..........	Bisexual Black Male (ADWA)
BIC.............	Bayesian Information Criteria (IDAI)
BIF.............	Binary Information File [*Computer science*]
BIFET.........	Bipolar Field Effect Transistor (ADWA)
BIFM..........	British Institute of Facilities Management (COBU)
BIHF...........	Bisexual Hispanic Female (ADWA)
BIHM..........	Bisexual Hispanic Male (ADWA)
BIIC...........	British Insurers' International Committee (MARI)
BIJF	Bisexual Jewish Female (ADWA)
BIJM	Bisexual Jewish Male (ADWA)
bil..............	Bilateral (ADWA)
BIMAS	BioInformatics Molecular Analysis Section
BIND	Berkeley Internet Name Domain [*Computer science*] (ITCA)
bio.............	Biology (NTIO)
BIOFAM	Binary Input-Output Fuzzy Adaptive Memory (IDAI)
BIOH	British Institute of Occupational Hygiene (HEAS)
biol	Biologist (ADWA)
Biosci.........	Bioscience
BIOSYNOP ...	Biological Synoptic Ocean Prediction (CARB)
biotech	Biotechnology (ADWA)
BIP.............	Band Interleaved by Pixel (ADWA)
BIP.............	Behavior Intervention Plan
BIP.............	Buffering in Progress
BIRG	Basking in Reflected Glory (DIPS)
BIS.............	Behavioral Inhibition System
BIS.............	Border Intermediate System
Bish	Bishop (NTIO)
BitBlt	Bit-Block Transfer (ADWA)
BITC...........	Burned in Time Codes
BITS...........	Baseline Information Tracking System (ABAC)
BJC............	Bubble Jet Color
BJ Crim	British Journal of Criminology [*A publication*]
BJIB & FL....	Butterworths Journal of International Banking & Financial Law [*A publication*]
BJIR............	British Journal of Industrial Relations [*A publication*]
BJLS	British Journal of Law & Society [*A publication*]
bjo	Banjo
BK..............	Because (ADWA)
bk	Black (ADWA)
BK..............	Burger King
bkbndr	Bookbinder (ADWA)
bkg.............	Bookkeeping (ADWA)
bkgd...........	Background (ADWA)
BKHM.........	Bookham Technology plc ADS [*NASDAQ symbol*] (SG)
bklr............	Black Letter (ADWA)
bkpg...........	Bookkeeping (ADWA)
bkpr...........	Bookkeeper (ADWA)
bks	Barracks (ADWA)
bkt	Basket
bl	Bale (ADWA)
BLA............	Biologic License Application
BLACA	British Literary and Artistic Copyright Association
BLAST.........	Bates Large Acceptance Spectrometer Toroid
BLAST.........	Bell Labs Layered Space-Time
Blast	Blocked Asynchronous Transmission [*Computer science*] (ITCA)
BLC	Belfort Laser Ceilometer (ARMP)
BLCY..........	Balcony [*Travel industry*] (TRID)
Bld.............	Baled
bld.............	Boldface (ADWA)
blk.............	Black (ADWA)
B-LLI..........	Broadband-Low Layer Information [*Telecommunications*] (MLOA)
BLLRS	Blood Lead Laboratory Reference System (ADWA)
BLM...........	Buccolingual Masticatory Syndrome (DIPS)
BLND	Blind Passenger [*Travel industry*] (TRID)
Blnd...........	Blond (ADWA)
BLOSA	Beam Line Operations and Safety Awareness (SARE)
BLPRT	Blueprint Reading
BLR............	Blue Light Radiation (HEAS)
BLR............	Business Law Review [*A publication*]
Bls	Bales (MARI)
BLT	Bilateral Lung Transplantation (ADWA)
B/L Ton	Bill of Lading Ton (MARI)
Blu.............	Blue (ADWA)
BLX	Boundary Layer Experiment (ARMP)
BLZE	Blaze Software [*NASDAQ symbol*] (SG)
bm	Beam (ADWA)
BM.............	Blood Monitoring [*Medicine*]
BMA...........	Bolt Motor Actuator (SPST)
BMDSC........	Ballistic Missile Defense Systems Command (CCCA)
BMES	Bone Marrow Edema Syndrome [*Medicine*]
BMHB	British Materials Handling Board (HEAS)
BMLR..........	Butterworths Medico-Legal Reports [*A publication*]
BMM...........	British Marine Mutual (RIMS)
BMP...........	Batch Message Processing Program [*Computer science*] (ITCA)
BMP...........	Behavior Management Plan
BMP...........	Bit-Mapped File
BMR...........	Basal Metabolism Rate (NTIO)
BMT	Ballistic Missile Technology
BMT	Beam Management Terminal
BMT	Behavior Management Plan
BMUA	British Marine Underwriters Associations (MARI)
bn	Bassoon
BN..............	Bayesian Network [*Graphical Model*] (IDAI)
B/N.............	Booking Note (RIMS)
BNCC	Base Network Control Center
bnd	Bound (ADWA)
BNFL..........	British Nuclear Fuels
BNIF...........	Bayesian Network Interchange Format (IDAI)
BNLI...........	British National Lymphoma Investigation
BNNRC........	Behavioral Neurogenetics and Neuroimaging Research Center (ADWA)
BNO	Binary Non-Consecutive Ones (CCCA)
BNS	Billed Number Screening
B/O.............	Best Offer (ADWA)
BO..............	Boomerang
BO..............	Building Operation (HEAS)
BOA...........	Basic Ordering Agreement (ADWA)
BOB	Bunker on Board (RIMS)
BOBW	Best of Both Worlds (ADWA)
BOD	Basic Oxygen Demand (SARE)
Bol.............	Bolivian (ADWA)
bol.............	Bolus (ADWA)
BOL............	Burst Out Laughing [*Internet dialog*]
BOMC	Book-of-the-Month Club (ADWA)
BOO	Collegiate Pacific [*AMEX symbol*]
BOOTP	Boot Parameters Protocol [*Computer science*] (ITCA)
BOR	Board of Regents (DEMM)
Bor.............	Borough (ADWA)
BORCAL	Broadband Outdoor Radiometer Calibration (ARMP)
BOREXINO	Boron Experiment
BOS	Bank of Scotland
BOSS	Build-to-Order Software Selector
bot	Botanical (ADWA)
BOU	Alain Boublil Music Limited [*Publisher*]
Boul	Boulevard (NTIO)
BOUT	About.com
BOVESPA	Bolsa de Valores do Sao Paulo [*Sao Paulo Stock Exchange*] [*Brazil*]

bp	Birthplace (ADWA)
bp	Blood Pressure (NTIO)
BP	Blood Pressure
BP	Borough President (ADWA)
BP	Breakfast Plan [*Travel Industry*] (TRID)
BPA	Business Professionals of America
BPC	Biomass Production Chamber (ADWA)
bpd	Barrels per Day (ADWA)
BPF	Black Professional Female (ADWA)
BPHC	Bureau of Primary Health Care
bpl	Birthplace (ADWA)
BPM	Black Professional Male (ADWA)
BPMD	Batelle Project Management Division (ABAC)
BPO	Bargain Purchase Option (ADWA)
BPO	Battelle Portland Operations (ABAC)
BPR	Bilateral Program Review (SPST)
BPR	Boarding Pass Reserve [*Travel industry*] (TRID)
BPR	Bureau of Preparedness and Response [*Department of Emergency Management*] (DEMM)
BPR	Business Process Reengineering
Bps	Bytes per Second (AEBE)
bps	Bytes per Second (ADWA)
BPVC	Boiler and Pressure Vessel Code (ABAC)
BPW	Business and Professional Women (ADWA)
bq	Becquerel (ABAC)
BQMI	Bohmian Quantum Mechanics I [*Physics*]
BR	Batman Returns
br	Bedroom (ADWA)
B/R	Bills Receivable (ADWA)
BR	Bottoms Recycle (ABAC)
br	Brass
Br	Breadth (RIMS)
br	Bridge (NTIO)
Br	British (ADWA)
Br	Brother (NTIO)
Br	Brown (ADWA)
BR	Bull Riding [*Rodeo term*]
BRA	Basic Rate Access
bra	Brassiere (ADWA)
brat	Bratwurst (ADWA)
Braz	Brazilian (ADWA)
BrazPg	Brazilian Portuguese (ADWA)
BRC	Business Reply Card
BRCS	Business Residence Custom Service
BRD	Biological Resource Division
brd	Board (ADWA)
Bret	Breton (ADWA)
brev	Brevet (ADWA)
brg	Bearing (ADWA)
BRGC	Binary Reflected Gray Code
BRHR	Basic Research and Human Resources (ADWA)
BRI	Brain Response Interface
brig	Brigade (ADWA)
Britcom	British Sitcom (ADWA)
BritRail	British Railway (TRID)
brkfst	Breakfast (ADWA)
brl	Barrel (ADWA)
Brld	Break Load (RIMS)
brlp	Burlap (ADWA)
BRM	Basic Reference Model
BRM	Bureau of Recovery and Mitigation [*Department of Emergency Management*] (DEMM)
Brn	Brown (ADWA)
BRO	Ben R. Oppenheimer [*California Institute of Technology*]
Bro	Brother (ADWA)
BRO	Bull Riders Only [*An association*]
BROB	Bunkers Remaining on Board (RIMS)
bros	Brothers (ADWA)
BRPSU	British Rail Privatisation Safety Unit (HEAS)
BRS	Basic Rate Service
Brshd	Brushed
brt	Bright (ADWA)
Brt	Gross Tonnage (RIMS)
BRU	Battery Reconditioning Unit (ADWA)
brwnstn	Brownstone (ADWA)
b/s	Bill of Sale (ADWA)
BS	Blown Save [*Baseball term*] (NDBD)
BS	Broadcast Station (PIPO)
BS	Business Sensitive (ABAC)
BSB	Business Services Branch (HEAS)
BSC	Biological Sciences Center
BSCS	Bachelor of Science Degree in Computer Science
BSCs	Business Service Centers (ADWA)
BSD	Business Services Division (HEAS)
BSDL	Boundary Scan Descriptor Language [*Computer science*]
BSEC	Binary Symmetric Erasure Channel (CCCA)
bsh	Bushel (ADWA)

BSI	Basic Sine In (TRID)
bsk	Basket (ADWA)
Bs/L	Bills of Lading (ADWA)
BSN	Block Sequence Number (CCCA)
BSO	Basic Sine Out (TRID)
BSP	Blatant Self-Promotion (ADWA)
BSP	Building Systems Program (ABAC)
BSRC	Battelle Seattle Research Center (ABAC)
BSRD	Behavioural Sciences Research Division (HEAS)
BSS	Basic Safety Standards Directive (HEAS)
BSSDF	Bidirectional Surface-Scattering Distribution Function [*Computer graphics*]
bsst	Brick or Stone Built, Slated or Tiled (MARI)
BST	Basic Services Terminal
BST	Brief-Stimuli Technique (DIPS)
BSTF	Battle Staff Training Facility [*Marine Corps*]
BSTJ	Bell Systems Technical Journal [*A publication*] (CCCA)
BSX	Bermuda Stock Exchange Ltd.
BT	Back Trajectory (ARMP)
BT	Bandwidth Time (CCCA)
BT	Bit Test (ROAS)
bt	Boat (ADWA)
BT	Brightness Temperature (ARMP)
BTAB	Barrier Technical Advisory Board (ABAC)
BTAS	Batman, the Animated Series
btbn	Bass Trombone
BTC	Bit Test and Complement (ROAS)
BTC	Booktech.com, Inc. [*AMEX symbol*] (SG)
BTD	Brightness Temperature Difference (ARMP)
BTD	Business Travel Department (TRID)
BTDT	Been There, Done That [*Internet dialog*]
BTH	Bold-Type Headings
bthn	Basset Horn
BTI	Boyce Thompson Institute [*Cornell University*]
BTL	Backplane Transceiver Logic (AEBE)
btl	Bottle (ADWA)
btn	Button (ADWA)
BTO	Bachman Turner Overdrive (ROAS)
BTP	British Transport Police (HEAS)
BTPON	Business Telephony on Passive Optical Network [*Telecommunications*] (ROAS)
btr	Better
BTR	Bit Test and Reset [*Telecommunications*] (ROAS)
BTR	British Tax Review [*A publication*]
BTS	Bit Test and Set (ROAS)
BTS	Board Tracking System (ROAS)
btty	Battery (ADWA)
btu	British Thermal Unit (NTIO)
BTX	Beacon Transmitter (ADWA)
BU	Bungalow
bu	Bureau (ADWA)
bu	Bushel
BU	Business Unit (ROAS)
Bud	Budweiser (ADWA)
BUFR	Binary Universal Form for Representation (ADWA)
bul	Bulletin (ADWA)
Bulg	Bulgarian (ADWA)
bur	Buried (ADWA)
Bur	Burma (ADWA)
Burm	Burmese (ADWA)
Bus Law	Business Lawyer [*A publication*]
BUTE	Bent Up Trailing Edge [*Aviation*] (PIPO)
BUWC	Baptist Union of Western Canada (ROAS)
BV	Bay Window Villa
BV	Bed Volume (ABAC)
BV	Bulk Volume (ROAS)
BVC	Billing Validation Center (ROAS)
BVP	Blood Volume Pulse (ADWA)
bw	Birthweight (NTIO)
BW	Bulk Water (CARB)
BW	Business Wire (ROAS)
BWAD	Brackish Water Arrival Draft (RIMS)
Bway	Broadway (NTIO)
BWC	Bandwidth Compression (ROAS)
BWHC	Babcock & Wilcox Hanford Co. (ABAC)
BWI	British West Indies (TRID)
BWID	Buried Waste Integrated Demonstration (ABAC)
BWIP	Basalt Waste Isolation Project (ABAC)
BWL	Bursting with Laughter [*Internet dialog*]
BWM	Broadcast Warning Message (ROAS)
BWO	Battelle Washington Office (ABAC)
BWTS	Bandwidth Test Set (ROAS)
Bx	Biopsy [*Medicine*]
bxd	Boxed (ADWA)
BYBL	British Yearbook of International Law [*A publication*]
byp	Bypass (ADWA)
Bz	Benzene (ABAC)

C

By Acronym

C .... Charm (ADWA)
c .... Circumference (ADWA)
C .... Coefficient of Contingency (DIPS)
C .... Coefficient of Mean Square Contingency (DIPS)
C .... Color Response [*Used in Rorschach tests*] (DIPS)
C .... Contingency Coefficient (DIPS)
c .... Copyright (ADWA)
c .... Cubic (NTIO)
C2C .... Consumer-to-Consumer
C4ISR .... Command, Control, Communications, Computers, Intelligence, Surveillance, and Reconnaissance [*Military*]
C7 .... Common Channel Signaling System No. 7 (CGWS)
ca .... Carcinoma (ADWA)
Ca .... Cathode (DIPS)
CA .... Caudality (DIPS)
CA .... Certificate Authority
CA .... Child Abuse (DIPS)
CA .... Clean Air
CA .... Coefficient Association (DIPS)
CA .... Communication Apprehension
CA .... Communication Arts
CA .... Conservation Authority [*Canada*]
CA .... Control Architecture (SPST)
CA .... Corrugated Asbestos
CAA .... Central Arid Asia (CARB)
CAA .... Civil Aviation Authorities (CTAS)
CAA .... Critically Alarm Annunciators (ABAC)
CAAFU .... Civil Aviation Authority Flying Unit (PIAV)
CAASD .... Center for Advanced Aviation System Development (CTAS)
CAB .... Cabletelevision Advertising Bureau, Inc.
CABG .... Coronary Artery Bypass Grafting [*Medicine*]
CAC .... Community Assistance Consultant (DEMM)
CAD-CAM ...... Computer-Aided Design and Computer-Aided Manufacture (NTIO)
CADIZ .... Canadian Air Defense Zone (PIPO)
CADRE .... Computer-Aided Data Retrieval and Evaluation Software (AUEG)
CADS .... Clinical Administrative Data Service (ADWA)
CAEHR .... Center for the Advancement of Electronic Health Records (ADWA)
CAEN .... Computer-Aided Engineering Network (ADWA)
CAF .... Cathodic Anodic Filaments
CAF .... Cellular Anti-Fraud (CGWS)
CAF .... Clean Air Facility (CARB)
CAF .... Cleared As Filed [*Aviation*] (PIPO)
CAF .... Corporate Asset Funding Unit
CAFCO .... Commercial Asset Funding Company
CAGE .... Contractor and Government Entity Code
CAH .... Care at Home
CAKE .... Case Tool for Knowledge Engineering (IDAI)
cal .... Caliber (ADWA)
cal .... Calibration (ADWA)
Cal .... California (NTIO)
Cal .... Calorie (NTIO)
calc .... Calculate (ADWA)
calc .... Calculus (NTIO)
CALD .... Caldera Systems [*NASDAQ symbol*] (SG)
Cal LR .... California Law Review [*A publication*]
Cal-OSHA ..... California Division of Occupational Safety and Health (SARE)
CalTrans ...... California Department of Transportation (SARE)
Cam .... Cambridge (ADWA)
cam .... Camouflage (ADWA)
CAM .... Computer-Aided Manufacture (NTIO)
CAMEO .... Creating a More Efficient Office (HEAS)
CaMKII .... Calcium-Calmodulin-Dependent Protein Kinase II
CAMP .... Capital Asset Management Process (ABAC)
campanol .... Campanology (ADWA)
CAMZ .... Caminus Corp. [*NASDAQ symbol*] (SG)
Can .... Canal (NTIO)
can .... Cancellation (ADWA)
CAN .... Cooperative Agreement Notice
CANA .... Convulsant Antidote for Nerve Agent
Canad .... Canadian
Can BJ .... Canadian Bar Journal [*A publication*]
canc .... Canceled (NTIO)
CanCom .... Women's Cancer Information Project (ADWA)
CANCPEC ..... Canadian National Committee for Pacific Economic Cooperation
CANDA .... Computer Assisted New Drug Application [*Food and Drug Administration*]

C&MS .... Chemistry and Materials Science
C&PCC .... Core and Payload Control Centers [*NASA*] (SPST)
CANP .... Civil Aviation Notification Procedure (PIAV)
CANT .... Citizens Against Nuclear Trash [*An association*]
CANUTEC ..... Canadian Transport Emergency Center (HEAS)
Cap .... Capitation
CAP .... Capricorn (NTIO)
CAP .... Collaborative Arrival Planning (CTAS)
CAP .... Communications Access Processor (CCCA)
CAP .... Condition Assessment Programme (RIMS)
CAPD .... Central Auditory Processing Disorder
CAPD .... Central Auditory Processing Disorder
caplet .... Capsule/Tablet (NTIO)
CAPP .... Committee for the Advancement of Professional Practice (DIPS)
Caps .... Capsule (NTIO)
CAPS .... Computer Aided Planning System (HEAS)
CARA .... Chemical Assessments and Related Activities (AUEG)
carbo .... Carbohydrate (ADWA)
CARDS .... Comprehensive Aerological Reference Data Set (ARMP)
Caricom ...... Caribbean Community (ADWA)
CARL .... Colorado Association of Research Libraries (AUEG)
CARLA .... Center for Advanced Research on Language Research
CARN .... Certified Addictions Registered Nurse (NUJO)
CARP .... Carpentry
carp .... Carpentry (ADWA)
carr .... Carrier (ADWA)
CARS .... Climate Applications Referral System (CARB)
CARS .... Corrective Action Reporting System (AUEG)
CAS .... Calibrated Ancillary System [*NASA*] (SPST)
cas .... Cassette (ADWA)
cas .... Castle (ADWA)
CAs .... Catecholamines (DIPS)
CASA .... Centre on Addiction and Substance Abuse [*Columbia University*]
CASTNet ...... Clean Air Status and Trends Network
CaT .... Cambridge Antibody Technology
cat .... Catapult (ADWA)
cat .... Cataract (ADWA)
CAT .... College Admission Test (DIPS)
Catal .... Catalan (ADWA)
Cath .... Cathedral (NTIO)
cath .... Catheter (ADWA)
cath .... Cathode (ADWA)
CATI .... Computer-Aided Testing and Implementation (ITCA)
CATIAC .... Cotton and Allied Textiles Industry Advisory Committee (HEAS)
CATsat .... Cooperative Astrophysics and Technology Satellite [*Sponsored by the University of New Hampshire*]
CAU .... Cryptograph Ancillary Unit (CCCA)
cauc .... Caucasian (NTIO)
caus .... Causative (ADWA)
cav .... Caveat (ADWA)
CAV .... Community Assistance Visit (DEMM)
CAV .... Constant Air Volume (SARE)
CAVOK .... Ceiling and Visibility [*Aviation*] (PIAV)
CAW .... Current Acid Waste (ABAC)
CAWP .... Cost Accounting Work Plan (ABAC)
CAWR .... Control of Asbestos at Work Regulations (HEAS)
CAWS .... Common Aviation Weather Sub-System (PIPO)
c/b .... Carry Back (ADWA)
cb .... Centibar (ADWA)
CB .... Control Bus (SPST)
CBA .... Cell-Based Array (AEBE)
CBA .... Cost Benefit Analysis (ROAS)
CBBG .... Cabin Baggage [*Travel industry*] (TRID)
CBBS .... Computer Bulletin Board System
CBC .... Carolina Bird Club (ROAS)
CBCH .... Cell Broadcast Channel (CGWS)
cbcl .... Contrabass Clarinet
CBDS .... Constraint Based Diagnostic System (ROAS)
CBDT .... Consultative Board for Diver Training (HEAS)
CBE .... Certified Breastfeeding Educator (NUJO)
CBE .... Charting by Exception
CBEST .... California Basic Education Skills Test (ROAS)
CBFT .... Cubic Feet (RIMS)
CBGA .... Ceramic Ball Grid Array
CBH .... Catalyst Bed Heater (ADWA)
CBH .... Cloud Base Height (ARMP)

CBHP	Community Breast Health Project (ADWA)
CBI	China, Burma, India (ADWA)
CBIS	Cincinnati Bell Information Systems (ROAS)
CBLA	Carolina Brown Lung Association (ROAS)
CBM	Certified Ballasts Manufacturers [An association]
CBM	Current Bibliographies in Medicine [A publication] (ADWA)
CBMT	Clinical Bulletin of Myofascial Therapy [A publication] (ADWA)
CBMTS	Chemical and Biological Medical Treatment Symposia (ADWA)
CBN	Cancer Biotherapeutics Newsletter [A publication] (ADWA)
cbn	Carbine (ADWA)
cbn	Contrabassoon
CBOE	Chicago Board of Options Exchange (ROAS)
CBP	Coded Block Pattern (ROAS)
CBPS	Chemical, Biological, Protected Shelter
CBR	Content-Based Retrieval
CBRIDS	Chemical, Biological and Radiological Integrated Reconnaissance System [Army]
CBZ	Coastal Building Zone (DEMM)
CC	Call Control (CGWS)
CC	Cape Cod
CC	Combined Cycle (CARB)
CC	Command & Control (CCCA)
CC	Complexant Concentrate (ABAC)
CC	Crime Control
CCA	Compliance Cost Assessments (HEAS)
CCAA	California Clean Air Act (SARE)
CCAM	Collision and Contamination Avoidance Maneuver (ADWA)
CCAP	Coastal Change Analysis Program (ROAS)
CCAR	Compact Car (TRID)
CCAS	Contribution-Based Compensation and Appraisal System [Army]
CCATS	Commodity Classification Automated Tracking System
CCBE	Central Canada Broadcast Engineers (ROAS)
CCBS	Conventional Core-Barrel Sampling (ABAC)
CCC	Ceramic Chip Carrier
CCC	Coastal Coordination Council [Texas]
CCC	Command Control & Communications (CCCA)
CCC	Compromised Container Caps [Jerry Mason, 1995] (SARE)
CCC	Computer Control Center (ROAS)
CCC	Creators' Copyright Coalition
CCC	Customer Care Consultant (ROAS)
CCCL	Coastal Construction Control Line (DEMM)
CCCSP	Comprehensive Capitol Complex Security Plan (DEMM)
CCCT	Clomiphene Citrate Challenge Test (ADWA)
CCD	Charged Coupled Device
CCD	Configuration Coordinate Diagram
CCDM	Control of Communicable Diseases in Man (ADWA)
CCEMHC	California Coalition for Ethical Mental Health Care
CCF	Canadian Cystic Fibrosis Foundation
CCF	Consolidated Communications Facilities [NASA] (SPST)
CCFY	Contractor's Current Fiscal Year (ROAS)
CCH	Common Control Channel (CGWS)
CCHARR	Co-Ordinating Committee on Health Aspects of Radiation Research (HEAS)
cckw	Counterclockwise (NTIO)
CCLEx	Close Combat Leadership Exercise [Military]
CCLI	California Clearinghouse for Library Instruction
CCM	Call Control Module (CCCA)
CCM	Central Customer Manager
CCM	Certified Case Manager (NUJO)
CCM	Cold Crucible Melter (ABAC)
CCMP	Cabot Microelectronics [NASDAQ symbol] (SG)
CCMP	Communications Control and Management Processor
CCMS	Centre for Coastal & Marine Sciences
CCN	Chris-Craft Industries
CCN	Critical Care Nurse (NUJO)
CCO	Close Combat Optics
CCOM	Control Center Operations Manager (ADWA)
CCOU	Construction Central Operations Unit (HEAS)
CCP	Campus Custom Publishing (ADWA)
CCP	Certified Computer Programmer (ROAS)
CCP	Conference Control Protocol (CCCA)
CCP	Cooperative Compliance Program (SARE)
CCR	Cloud Cover Radiometer (ADWA)
CCR	Covenants, Conditions, and Restrictions (ROAS)
CCRG	Children's Cancer Research Group [England]
CCRN	Certified Critical Care Registered Nurse (NUJO)
CCRN7	Credit Card Return Notice (TRID)
CCS7	Common Channel Signaling System Number 7 (CGWS)
CCSM	Control Center Systems Manager (ADWA)
CCT	Central Control Terminal (ROAS)
CCT	Clomiphene Challenge Test (ADWA)
CCTA	Central Computer and Telecommunications Authority (COBU)
CCTR	Cochrane Controlled Trials Register (ADWA)
CCU	Conference Control Unit (CCCA)
CCV	Calling Card Validation (ROAS)
CCW	Command and Control Warfare (ADWA)
CD	Central Detector
CD	Certified Deposit (ROAS)
CD	Chemistry Division (CARB)
CD	Clearance Delivery [Aviation] (PIPO)
CD	Coasting Drive
CD	Color Display (ROAS)
CD	Communication Deviance (DIPS)
CD	Conceptual Design (ABAC)
CD	Conduct Disorder (DIPS)
CD	Conference Director (CCCA)
CD	Consultation Distance (HEAS)
CD	Consultative Document (HEAS)
CD	Contract Direction (SPST)
C/D	Country Damage (MARI)
CD	Culminating Demonstration
CD	Cycle Day (ADWA)
CDAC	Certified Drug and Alcohol Counselor (NUJO)
CDCF	Cumulative Discounted Cash Flow
CDCR	Conceptual Design and Cost Review (CARB)
CDDIS	Crustal Dynamics Data Information System (ARMP)
CDDN	Certified Developmental Disabilities Nurse (NUJO)
CDEP	Cimate Dynamics and Experimental Prediction (ARMP)
CDG	Code Division Multiple Access Development Group (CGWS)
cdg	Commanding (ADWA)
CDG Rail	Carriage of Dangerous Goods by Rail Regulations (HEAS)
CDGS	Carbohydrate Deficient Glycoprotein Syndrome
CDHF	Central Data Handling Facility (ADWA)
CDI	Capacitive Deionization (ADWA)
CD-I	Compact Disc Interactive (AEBE)
CDIM	Clerkship Directors in Internal Medicine (ADWA)
CDL	Cloud Detection Lidar (ARMP)
CDLS	Contractor Depot Logistics Support (CTAS)
CDM	Construction Design and Management (HEAS)
CDMHP	County Designated Mental Health Professional (ROAS)
CDMP	Cartilage-Derived Morphogenic Proteins [Medicine]
CDMRP	Congressionally Directed Medical Research Programs
CDMS	Certified Disability Management Specialist (NUJO)
CDNC	Cloud Drop Number Concentration (CARB)
CDOA	Career Development and Outplacement Association (COBU)
CDOS	Concurrent Disk Operating System (ROAS)
CDP	Central Data Processor (CCCA)
CDP	Chemical Demilitarization Program [Army]
CDP	Conceptual Design Plan (ABAC)
CDP	Custom Defense Package
CDR	Communicable Disease Report (HEAS)
CDR	Conceptual Design Report (ABAC)
CDR	Conceptual Design Review (ABAC)
CD-RDx	Compact Disk-Read Only Memory Data Exchange Standard (ROAS)
CDRG	Catastrophic Disaster Response Group (DEMM)
CD-RW	Compact Disk-Read or Write
CDS	Canadian Defense System (CCCA)
CDS	Cockpit Display System
CDS	Common Display System (HLLA)
CDT	Call Data Transmitter (ROAS)
CDTA	Compass Diagnostic Test of Arithmetic (DIPS)
CDU	Cesium Demonstration Unit (ABAC)
CD-XA	Compact Disk-Extended Architecture (ROAS)
CE	Combustion Efficiency (CARB)
CE	Community Education
CEA	Cause-and-Effect Analysis (CARB)
CEA	County Education Authority
CEAP	Certified Employee Assistance Professional
CEAS	Comprehensive Emergency Assistance System
CEC	California Energy Commission (ABAC)
CEC	Common Equipment Card [Telecommunications] (MLOA)
CEC	Cooperative Engagement Capability [Military]
CECA	Connecticut Educators Computer Association
CEDA	Canadian Electrical Distributors Association
CEDR	Comprehensive Epidemiologic Data Resource (ADWA)
CEEB	College Entry Examination Board (ADWA)
CEEL	Community Emergency Exposure Level (SARE)
CEELT	Cambridge Examination in English for Language Teachers
CEEMAC	Certification of Electrical Equipment for Mining Advisory Council (HEAS)
CEERT	Coalition for Energy Efficiency and Renewable Technologies
CEFFA	Committee for Electrical Equipment for Use in Flammable Atmospheres (HEAS)
CEHN	Children's Environmental Health Network (ADWA)
CEI	Conducted Electromagnetic Interference
cel	Celesta
cel	Celluloid (ADWA)
CEL	Chemical Engineering Laboratory (ABAC)
celcrts	Cell Crates
celeb	Celebrity (ADWA)
cell	Cellular (ADWA)
CELSS	Controlled Ecological Life Support System
CELTA	Certificate in English Language Teaching for Adults
CEM	Cloud Ensemble Model (ARMP)
CEMA	Colorado Educational Media Association
CEMA	Connecticut Educational Media Association
CEMP	Comprehensive Emergency Management Plan (DEMM)
Cen	Cenozoic (NTIO)
Cent	Centerfold
cent	Central (NTIO)
CENT	Computer, Electronics, and Networking Technology
CENTRALL	Center for Research and Lessons Learned [Army]
CEO	Catalyzed Electrochemical Oxidation (ABAC)
CEO	Configuration Engineering Office (SPST)
CEOC	County Emergency Operations Center (DEMM)
CEOS	Centre for Earth Observation Science
CEOS	Child Exploitation and Obscenity Section
CEPAC	Central Eastern Pacific Routes (PIPO)
CEPE	Centre for Electrical Power Engineering [Glasgow]
CEPS	Center for Earth and Planetary Studies

CEPS........... Cluster Environmental Protection Specialist (SARE)
CER............. Character Error Rate (CCCA)
CERA .... Catcher's Earned Run Average [*Baseball term*] (NDBD)
CERC .... Coal Energy Research Committee
CERD .... Committee for the Elimination of Racial Discrimination
CERES .... California Environmental Resources Evaluation System (AUEG)
CERF .... California Education and Research Federation
CERFNET .... California Education and Research Federation Network
CERIAC .... Ceramics Industry Advisory Committee (HEAS)
CERN .... Chinese Ecological Research Network (CARB)
CERP .... Capitol Emergency Response Plan (DEMM)
cert .... Certainly (ADWA)
cert .... Certificate (ADWA)
certif .... Certificated (ADWA)
CES .... Consumer Electronics Show
CESD .... Communications Electronics Security Department (HEAS)
CET .... Cerebral Electrotherapy (DIPS)
ce Ta .... Center Tank (RIMS)
CETN .... Certified Enterostomal Therapy Nurse (NUJO)
CETTR......... Crew and Equipment Translation Techniques and Routing [*NASA*] (SPST)
CEVI............ Common Equipment Voltage Indicator
cf .... Calfskin (ADWA)
CF .... Carbon Fraction (CARB)
cf .... Center Field [*Baseball term*] (NDBD)
CF .... Central Facility (ARMP)
CF .... Construction Forces (ABAC)
C/F .... Custom Finished
CFA .... Center for Astrophysics [*Harvard-Smithsonian*]
CfA .... Center for Astrophysics
CFAGB .... Carbon Fraction of Above Ground Biomass (CARB)
CFB .... Call Forward Busy
CFC .... Currency Forwards Contract
CF/CV .... Counter Force/Counter Value (CCCA)
cfd .... Cubic Feet per Day (ADWA)
CFDS .... Centralized Fault Display System (HLLA)
CFE .... Customer Furnished Equipment
CFF .... Calories from Fat
cff .... Critical Flicker Frequency (DIPS)
CFFZ .... Call-for-Fire-Zone [*Army*]
CFI .... Common Flash-Memory Interface
CFIT .... Culture-Fair Intelligence Test (DIPS)
CFIT .... Culture-Free Intelligence Test (DIPS)
CFLE .... Certified Family Life Educator
cfm .... Cubic Feet per Minute (ABAC)
CFMD.......... Confirmed (TRID)
CFMT .... Concentrator and Feed Make-Up-Tank (ABAC)
CFO .... Cancel Former Order
CFOC .... Chief Financial Officers Council
cfsm .... Cubic Feet per Second per Square Mile (ADWA)
CFSS........... Certified Fragrance Sales Specialist (ADWA)
CFV .... Canyon Forest Village
CFV .... Cell for Voting (ADWA)
CFWTL......... Chronic Freshwater Toxicity Level (ABAC)
cg .... Centigram (NTIO)
CG .... Coordinating Group
CGA .... Column Grid Array
cga.............. Conga
CGAM .... Centre for Global Atmospheric Modelling
CGBA .... Commercial Generic Bioprocessing Apparatus (SPST)
CGC .... Charles G. Chandler
CGCP .... Canadian Global Change Program (CARB)
CGES .... Center for Global Environmental Studies (CARB)
CGL............. Center for Group Learning
CGMS .... Coordination Group for Meteorological Satellites (ADWA)
CGN .... Concentrator Group Number
CGRN .... Certified Gastroenterological Registered Nurse (NUJO)
CGW .... Color Graphics Workstation
CGW .... Computer Graphics World
Ch .... Channel (NTIO)
CH............... Chester Music [*Publisher*]
CH............... Course Heading [*Aviation*] (PIPO)
CHA .... Canadian Hyperlexia Association
CHA .... Corporate Hospitality Association (COBU)
CHAIN .... Chained Schedule of Reinforcement (DIPS)
Chal............ Chaldean (ADWA)
Chald .... Chaldean (ADWA)
Champ......... Champion (ADWA)
CHAMP .... Change Management Programme (HEAS)
CHAMP .... Churn Analysis, Modeling, and Prediction (IDAI)
Chan .... Channel (ADWA)
CHAN .... Chemical Hazard Alert Notices (HEAS)
Chanc.......... Chancellor (NTIO)
CHAOS......... Canadian High Acceptance Orbit Spectrometer
Chap............ Chaplain (ADWA)
CHAP .... Community Health Accreditation Program (ADWA)
char .... Characteristic (ADWA)
chard .... Chardonnay (ADWA)
CHART......... Continuous Hyperfractionated Accelerated Radiotherapy (ADWA)
CHASE .... Complete Health and Safety Evaluation Scheme (HEAS)
CHCK .... Channel Check
CHCS .... Chemical Hazards Communications Society (HEAS)
CHD .... Congenital Hip Dysplasia
CHE .... Co-Ordinator of Health Education (HEAS)
CHEA .... Council for Higher Education Accreditation

chem .... Chemistry (NTIO)
CHEMAG ...... Chemicals in Agriculture Advisory Group (HEAS)
Chem-FET .... Chemical Field Emission Transistor (ABAC)
chemo .... Chemotherapy (NTIO)
CHEMSAFE... Chemical Industry Scheme for Assistance in Freight (HEAS)
CHEMWARN... Chemical Warning
CHES .... Certified Health Education Specialist (ADWA)
C-HFET .... Complementary Heterostructure Field Effect Transistor (ADWA)
chg............. Change (ADWA)
chgd............ Charged (ADWA)
Chgo .... Chicago (NTIO)
CHGRP......... Change Group
CHHA .... Coastal High Hazard Area (DEMM)
Chi .... Chicago (ADWA)
CHI............. Consumer Health Information (ADWA)
CHILPEC ...... Chilean National Committee for Pacific Economic Cooperation
CHIN........... Community Health Information Network
CHIP .... Community Health Information Partnerships (ADWA)
CHIPS .... Cosmic Hot Interstellar Plasma Spectrometer [*Developed to study a gas cloud surrounding the solar system*]
CHITA .... Community Health Information Technology Alliance (ADWA)
chl .... Chloroform (ADWA)
CHL .... Crown-Heel Length (ADWA)
chm .... Checkmate (ADWA)
chm .... Chimes
CHMIS......... Community Health Management Information Systems (ADWA)
CHMOD........ Change Mode
CHN .... Community Health Nurse (NUJO)
CHNT .... Change Name To [*Travel industry*] (TRID)
CHO .... Chemical Hygiene Officer (SARE)
CHO .... Chinese Hamster Ovary
chol .... Cholesterol (ADWA)
CHOPT......... Charterers' Option (RIMS)
chor .... Choreographed By (ADWA)
CHOWN........ Change Owner
CHP .... Certified Health Physicist (SARE)
CHP .... Certified Health Professional (SARE)
CHPN .... Certified Hospice and Palliative Care Nurse (NUJO)
chpn............ Chairperson (ADWA)
chron .... Chronological (ADWA)
chronol .... Chronological (ADWA)
CHS .... Chlorinated Hydrocarbon Solvents
CHSG .... Construction Health and Safety Group (HEAS)
CHT .... Certified Hemodialysis Technician (NUJO)
CHTR .... Charter [*Travel industry*] (TRID)
CHU .... China Unicom ADS [*NYSE symbol*]
CHW .... Cladding Hull Waste (ABAC)
ci .... Class Interval (DIPS)
CI .... Control Interval [*Computer science*] (ITCA)
CIAg............ Chief Inspector of Agriculture (HFAS)
CIAO .... Critical Infrastructure Assurance Office
CIB .... Combat Infantry Badge [*Army*]
CIC .... Campus Improvement Council
CIC .... Consumer Information Catalog (AUEG)
CID .... Critical Incident Detection (HEAS)
CIDEM .... Center for Inherited Disorders of Energy Metabolism (ADWA)
CIDGAP........ Critical Incident Debriefing for General Aviation Pilots
CIDI .... Central Index of Dose Information (HFAS)
CIDS .... Comfortable Interpersonal Distance Scale (DIPS)
CIE .... Center for International Economics (AUEG)
CIE .... Chinese Institute of Electronics (CARB)
CIE .... Commercial Internet Exchange
CIESCO........ Commercial Industrial Trade Receivables
CIESIN .... Center for International Earth Sciences Information Network (ARMP)
CIF.............. Central Issuing Facility [*Army*]
CIF.............. Chief Inspector of Factories (HEAS)
CIHI .... Center for International Health Information (ADWA)
CIHR .... Canadian Institutes of Health Research
CIIT .... Chemical Industry Institute of Technology (SARE)
CIL .... Coal India Limited (CARB)
CILT .... Center for Innovative Learning Technologies
CIM .... Chief Inspector's Memo (HEAS)
CIMAH .... Control of Industrial Major Accident Hazards Regulations (HEAS)
CIMB........... Central Institute for Molecular Biology [*East Berlin*]
cimb .... Cimbalom
CIMM........... Chief Inspector's Management Meeting (HEAS)
CIN .... Convective Inhibition (ARMP)
CINCAD....... Commander-in-Chief Aerospace Defense Command (CCCA)
CINCC .... Coal Industry National Consultative Council (HEAS)
CINCH......... Competitive Impulse, Non-Carcinogenic Hypergol
CINCLANT.... Commander-in-Chief, Atlantic Command (DEMM)
cinemat .... Cinematography (ADWA)
CIP .... Communications Improvement Plan (CCCA)
CIP .... Critical Infrastructure Protection (DEMM)
CIPP .... Comprehensive Integrated Planning Process (ABAC)
CIPR .... Center for Imaging and Pharmaceutical Research (ADWA)
CIPRIS .... Coordinated Interagency Partnership Regulating International Students
cir .... Circuit (NTIO)
CIR............. Commonwealth of Independent Republics
circ .... Circuit (ADWA)
circ .... Circulation (NTIO)
circ .... Circumcised (ADWA)
CIRCE .... Cornell Institute for Research in Chemical Ecology
circum .... Circumference (NTIO)

CIRR	Commercial Interest Reference Rate (RIMS)
CIRRIS	Cryogenic Infrared Radiance Instrument for Shuttle [*NASA*]
CIRS	Certified Insurance Rehabilitation Specialist (NUJO)
CIRT	Cirrus Test (CARB)
CIS	Colliery Information System (HEAS)
CISL	Center for the Improvement of Student Learning
CISMM	Chief Inspector's Specialist Management Meeting (HEAS)
CISS	Community Integrated Service Systems (ADWA)
CIT	Circumstellar Imaging Telescope
cit	Citizen (NTIO)
CIT	Continuous Improvement Team
CIT	Current Injection Test (CCCA)
CITT	Canadian International Trade Tribunal
CIU	Crypto Interface Unit (CCCA)
civ	Civilian (NTIO)
CIVL	Concept Integration and Verification Laboratory [*NASA*] (SPST)
C-JAM	Combination Job Analysis Method (DIPS)
CJQ	Civil Justice Quarterly [*A publication*]
CJR	CORUS Entertainment 'B' [*NYSE symbol*]
ckb	Cookbook
CKCM	Click Commerce [*NASDAQ symbol*]
CKE	Cumulus Kinetic Energy (CARB)
CK-MB	Creatine Kinase Myocardial Band
CKML	Conceptual Knowledge Markup Language (IDAI)
ckt	Circuit (ADWA)
ckw	Clockwise (ADWA)
cl	Centiliter (ADWA)
C/L	Centre-Line [*Aviation*] (PIAV)
CL	Chlorine
Cl	Chlorine (ABAC)
cl	Clarinet
Cl	Class (SG)
Cl	Clause (MARI)
CL	Colonial
CL	Comparison Level (DIPS)
CL	Convective Precipitation Over Land (ARMP)
CL	Current Law [*A publication*]
CL	Runaway Centerline Lights [*Aviation*] (PIPO)
CLA	Children's Liver Alliance (ADWA)
CLAlt	Comparison Level for Alternatives (DIPS)
CLARCS	Copyright Licensing Agency Rapid Clearance Service
CLASS	Committee for Library Advocacy and Student Success
CLB	Configurable Logic Block (AEBE)
CLBRR	Centre for Land and Biological Resource Research [*Canada*]
CLC	Clean Lakes Clearinghouse (AUEG)
CLC	Consequential Loss Committee [*Insurance*] (MARI)
CLCB	Charged Liquid Cluster Beam (ROAS)
CLCP	Certified Life Care Planner (NUJO)
CLCW	Command Link Control Word (ADWA)
CLD	Chronic Lyme Disease
cld	Cooled (ADWA)
CLDC	Competitive Long Distance Coalition
CLDN	Calling Line Directory Number
cldy	Cloudy (ADWA)
CLEF	Certified Licensed Evaluation Facility
CLEK	Collaborative Longitudinal Evaluation of Keratoconus (ADWA)
CLEX	Cloud Layer Experiment (ARMP)
clg	Ceiling (ADWA)
CLI	Critical Line Item (CCCA)
CLI	Current Legal Information [*A publication*]
CLIBCON	Chiropractic Library Consortium (ADWA)
Clim	Climatic
clin	Clinical (ADWA)
CLIP	Crew Loads Instrumental Panel [*NASA*] (SPST)
CLIST	Command List [*Computer science*] (ITCA)
CLIVAR	Climate Variability and Predictability (ARMP)
CLJ	Cambridge Law Journal [*A publication*]
clkg	Caulking (ADWA)
CLL	Celltech Group ADS [*NYSE symbol*] (SG)
CLM	Career-Limiting Maneuver (ADWA)
CLMI	Comprehensive Loss Management, Inc., of Minneapolis (SARE)
CLN	Celsion Corp. [*AMEX symbol*]
cln	Clean (ADWA)
CLNC	Certified Legal Nurse Consultant (NUJO)
CLNCDEL	Clearance Delivery (PIPO)
CLP	Current Legal Problems [*A publication*]
Clpk	Cell Pack
CLQ	Cell-Loc, Inc. [*Alberta Stock Exchange*]
CLR	Commonwealth Law Reports [*A publication*]
clrb	Coloring Book
CLS	Canadian Light Source
CLS	Combat Lifesaver [*Army*]
CLS	Constant Level Signalling (CCCA)
CLSR	Computer Law & Security Report [*A publication*]
CLSS	College-Level and State Services
CLST	Closet (ADWA)
CLTL	Comple Tel Europe NV [*NASDAQ symbol*] (SG)
CLW	ClearWorks.net, Inc. [*AMEX symbol*]
CLYB	Current Law Year Book [*A publication*]
cm	Circular Mail (NTIO)
CM	Circular Minute (HEAS)
CM	Common Market (ADWA)
CM	Controlled Manual (ABAC)
cm	Cumulative (SG)
CMA	Cement Manufacturers' Association (CARB)

CMAA	Central Missouri Astronomical Association
CMAC	Centralized Maintenance and Administration Center
CMAP	Climate Modeling, Analysis, and Prediction Program (ARMP)
CMAWS	Common Missile Approach Warning System (ADWA)
CMB	Configuration Management Board
CMC	Carlanita Music [*Publisher*]
cmc	Critical Micelle Concentration (ADWA)
CMCC	Canadian Memorial Chiropractic College
CMD	Centralized Message Distribution [*Computer science*]
CMD	Classification of Mental Disorders (DIPS)
cmd	Command (ADWA)
CMDF	Combined Main Distributing Frame
cmdg	Commanding (ADWA)
CMDS	Computer Management and Development Services
CMEIS	Continuing Medical Education Information Services (ADWA)
CMEO	Crying My Eyes Out [*Online dialog*]
CMF	Configuration Management Facility (CTAS)
CMI	Compatibility Modification Inference (IDAI)
CMIB	Cellular Message Information Block
CMIIW	Correct Me If I'm Wrong (ADWA)
cmil	Circular Mil
CMIS	Configuration Management Information System
CML	Certified Master Locksmith
CML	Current Model Logic
CMLS	Contractor Maintenance and Logistics Support (CTAS)
CMO	Configuration Management Organization (CTAS)
CMP	Captioned Media Program
CMP	Certified Meeting Professional (TRID)
CMPE	Certified Medical Practice Executive (ADWA)
CMPH	Clinical Microbiology Procedures Handbook [*A publication*] (ADWA)
CMPL	Commercial Materials Processing Laboratory (SPST)
cmpt	Compute (ADWA)
CMR	Commercial Mail Relay
CMRO	Comarco
CMRS	Clinical Magnetic Resonance Society (ADWA)
CMS	Cable Management Software
CMS	Chemical Management System (ABAC)
CMS	Children's Memory Scale [*M. Cohen*] (DIPS)
CMS	Clinical Micro Sensors
CMS	Compact Muon Solenoid
CMSE	Command Management Systems Engineer (ADWA)
CMT	Communications Maintenance Terminal
CMTS	Cable Modem Termination System
CMV	Circuit Mode Voice
CMWS	Common Missile Warning System (ADWA)
CN	Cemetery Net (CCCA)
C/N	Credit Note (ADWA)
CN	Cyanide (ABAC)
CNC	Clinical Nurse Consultant (NUJO)
CNCB	Clinical Nutrition Certification Board (ADWA)
CNCPEC	China National Committee for Pacific Economic Cooperation
CNCS	Cryptographic Net Control Station (CCCA)
CND	Commission on Narcotic Drugs (ADWA)
CNE	Continuing Nursing Education (ADWA)
CNF	Conjunctive Normal Form (IDAI)
CNFN	Cable News Financial Network (ADWA)
CNMMN	Commission on New Minerals and Mineral Names [*Mineralogical Association*]
CNN	Certified Nephrology Nurse (NUJO)
CNNFn	CNN Financial News
CNPC	China National Petroleum Corp.
CNR	Center for Naval Research (CCCA)
CNR	Complex Node Representation
CNRI	Council for National Research Initiatives
CNRS	Cornerstone Internet Solutions
cns	Central Nervous System (DIPS)
CNS	Certified Niche Specialist (TRID)
CNSD	Certified Nutrition Support Dietitian (NUJO)
CNSR	Comet Nucleus Sample Return
CNSZ	Central Nevada Seismic Zone
CNT	Contract
cnt	Cornet
CNTF	Commander Naval Task Force (CCCA)
cntrs	Containers
CNVRT	Convertible (ADWA)
CNVRTBL	Convertible (ADWA)
cnvt	Convert (ADWA)
Cnx	Calnexin
c/o	Care Of (NTIO)
c/o	Carry Over (ADWA)
C/O	Certificate of Origin (ADWA)
co	Company (NTIO)
Co	Comparison Stimulus (DIPS)
CO	Conventional
Co	County (ADWA)
COA	Certificate of Authenticity (ADWA)
COA	Certified Ophthalmic Assistant (NUJO)
COAA	Course of Action Analysis [*Military*]
COACP	Contract of Affreightment Charter Party (RIMS)
COAPEC	Coupled Ocean-Atmosphere Processes and their Effect on Climate
coax	Coaxial Cable (ADWA)
COB	Consolidated Operating Base (CCCA)
COBLDN	Closing of Business London (RIMS)
cobot	Cooperative Robot (ADWA)
COBS	Care of the Body Surface (DIPS)

COBS	Central on Board Softwear (ADWA)
COC	Country of Commencement [*Travel industry*] (TRID)
COCO	Corinthian Colleges [*NASDAQ symbol*] (SG)
COCS	Common Occupational Classification System (ABAC)
COD	Crown Office Digest [*A publication*]
CoDE...........	Coherent Digital Exciter (ADWA)
COE.............	Commission on Ecology (AUEG)
coef	Coefficient (ADWA)
coeff	Coefficient (ADWA)
COESA	Canada-Ontario Environmental Sustainability Agreement
C of A	Certificate of Airworthiness [*Aviation*] (PIAV)
C of E	Certificate of Experience [*Aviation*] (PIAV)
c of g	Centre of Gravity [*Aviation*] (PIAV)
C of P	Centre of Pressure [*Aviation*] (PIAV)
CoFR...........	Certification of Flight Readiness [*NASA*] (SPST)
cog..............	Cognate (ADWA)
COH	Court of Honor [*Boy Scouts of America*]
COHN..........	Certified Occupational Health Nurse (NUJO)
COHN-S	Certified Occupational Health Nurse Specialist (NUJO)
COI..............	Cone of Influence (ADWA)
COI..............	Critical Oxygen Index (HEAS)
coin-op........	Coin-Operated (ADWA)
COINS.........	Community Oriented Intelligence Network System (CCCA)
Col..............	Colombia (NTIO)
Col..............	Colonial (ADWA)
col	Colony (NTIO)
col	Coloratura
Col..............	Colossal
cola	Cost-of-Living Adjustment (NTIO)
collat	Collateral (ADWA)
Coll Ed........	Collector's Edition
colloq..........	Colloquial (NTIO)
Col LR	Columbia Law Review [*A publication*]
colog	Cologarithm (ADWA)
COLPECC	Colombia National Committee for Pacific Economic Cooperation
com	Combustion (ADWA)
COM............	Comedy Central (ADWA)
com	Commercial
Com	Common (SG)
Com	Commonwealth (ADWA)
com	Communication (NTIO)
com	Communist (NTIO)
CoM.............	Consequence Management (DEMM)
COMAH........	Control of Major Accident Hazards (HEAS)
comb	Combined (NTIO)
comb	Combining (ADWA)
comb	Commander (ADWA)
COMC	Commander Carrier (CCCA)
Comdex	Communications and Data Processing Exhibition (ADWA)
comm	Commerce (NTIO)
comm	Commercial (ADWA)
COMM	Communications (PIPO)
Comm..........	Community (ADWA)
ComMet........	Commercialization Model for Environmental Technologies (ABAC)
commo	Commodore (ADWA)
ComNavAirLant...	Commander Naval Air, Atlantic
comp	Comparative (ADWA)
comp	Compensation (NTIO)
comp	Complete (NTIO)
comp	Composition (ADWA)
compander...	Compressor-Expander (ADWA)
compar........	Comparative (ADWA)
compl	Complement (ADWA)
compo	Composition Material (ADWA)
compt	Compartment (ADWA)
Comr............	Commissioner (ADWA)
COMSOC......	Communications Society (CCCA)
COMSS	Council of Musculoskeletal Specialty Societies (ADWA)
COMSTAT ...	Communications Satellite Corporation (ITCA)
COMT	Certified Ophthalmic Medical Technologist (NUJO)
con..............	Concerto (ADWA)
con..............	Conclusion (NTIO)
con..............	Confidence (NTIO)
con..............	Confidence Game (ADWA)
Con	Congo (NTIO)
conc............	Concerning (ADWA)
Conc	Concerto
CONC	Concurrent Schedule of Reinforcement (DIPS)
concl...........	Conclusion (ADWA)
concn..........	Concentration (ADWA)
cond............	Condenser (ADWA)
Cond	Conductor (NTIO)
CONDAM......	Construction Design and Management Regulations (HEAS)
Conelrad......	Control of Electromagnetic Radiation (NTIO)
conf	Confidential (ADWA)
confab	Confabulation (ADWA)
Confed........	Confederate (NTIO)
confed.........	Confederation (ADWA)
config	Configuration (ADWA)
cong............	Congregation
cong............	Congregational (NTIO)
con game	Confidence Game (ADWA)
CONIAC........	Construction Industry Advisory Committee (HEAS)
conj	Conjunctive (ADWA)
CONJ	Conjunctive Schedule of Reinforcement (DIPS)

con man	Confidence Man (ADWA)
conn............	Connotation (ADWA)
CONQUEST...	Computerized Needs-Oriented Quality Measurement Evaluation System (ADWA)
Cons	Conservative (ADWA)
cons............	Consigned (ADWA)
cons............	Consonant (NTIO)
Cons	Constable (NTIO)
cons............	Constitution (NTIO)
cons............	Constructed (NTIO)
consec.........	Consecutive (ADWA)
const	Constable (ADWA)
Const	Constitution (ADWA)
cont	Continent (ADWA)
contemp	Contemporary (NTIO)
contempt	Contemptuous (ADWA)
contg	Containing (ADWA)
contn	Continuation (ADWA)
CONTOUR	Comet Nucleus Tour [*NASA's study of photochemical processes in comet comas*]
contr	Contract (ADWA)
Contr	Controller (ADWA)
contrail........	Condensation Trail (ADWA)
contrib.........	Contributing (NTIO)
CONUSA	Continental United States Army (DEMM)
conv............	Convention (NTIO)
Conv	Conventual (ADWA)
Conv	Conveyancer, Conveyancer & Property Lawyer [*A publication*]
conv............	Convocation (ADWA)
CONVINCE ..	Consortium of North American Veterinary Interactive New Concept Education (ADWA)
COO	Conduct of Operations (SARE)
COO	Continuity of Operations (CCCA)
COOL	Cost of Ownership Luminator
Co-op..........	Cooperative (NTIO)
co-op	Cooperative (ADWA)
coord	Coordinate (ADWA)
COP	Certification of Proposal
COP	Change Over Point [*Aviation*] (PIPO)
COP	Communications Output Processor (CCCA)
COP	Community Outreach Program (DIPS)
Cop.............	Coptic (ADWA)
cop.............	Copy (ADWA)
COPA	Child Online Protection Act
COPP	Cyclophosphamide, Vincristine, Procarbazine, and Prednisone [*Medicine*]
COPPA	Children's Online Privacy Protection Act
COPS	Continuously Operating per Fluorocarbon Sniffer (CARB)
COR	Center for Orthopaedic Research (ADWA)
COR	Communications Operating Requirement (CCCA)
COR	Communications Outage Recorder [*NASA*] (SPST)
cor	Cornet (ADWA)
CORD..........	Council of Emergency Medicine Residency Directors (ADWA)
Corn............	Cornwall (ADWA)
corol	Corollary (ADWA)
coroll	Corollary (NTIO)
Corp............	Corporal (ADWA)
corp	Corporation (NTIO)
Corpl...........	Corporal (ADWA)
corprcrat......	Corporate Bureaucrat (ADWA)
CORR..........	Clinical Orthopaedics and Related Research (ADWA)
corr.............	Corrugated (ADWA)
correl..........	Correlative (ADWA)
corresp........	Correspondence (ADWA)
corrupt.........	Corruption (ADWA)
CORU..........	Cabinet Office Deregulation Unit (HEAS)
COS	Canadian Oncology Society
cos..............	Consul (ADWA)
cos..............	Cosine (ABAC)
cosec..........	Cosecant (ADWA)
Co-SITREP ...	County Situation Report [*Department of Emergency Management*] (DEMM)
CoSLA	Convention of Scottish Local Authorities
COSMIC	Chajnantor Observatory Sub-Millimeter International Collaboration
COSNA........	Composite Observing System for the North Atlantic (ADWA)
COSTED	Committee on Science and Technology in Developing Countries (ADWA)
COSTEP	Comprehensive Supra Thermal and Energetic Particle (ADWA)
COSTR	Collaborative Solar-Terrestrial Research (ADWA)
COT.............	Certified Ophthalmic Technician (NUJO)
cot	Cotangent (NTIO)
cot	Cottage [*Travel industry*] (TRID)
COTT...........	Committee of Ten Thousand (ADWA)
coun............	Counsel (ADWA)
COVE	Council on Vocational Education
COW	Cellsite on Wheels (ADWA)
COW	Conference Order Wire (CCCA)
COX-2	Cyclooxygenase-2
CP..............	Capability Performance
CP..............	Cellular Provider (CGWS)
cP..............	Centipoise (ABAC)
cp	Coupon (ADWA)
CP..............	Cultural Practices (ADWA)
C/P.............	Custom Painted
CPA.............	Centrally Planned Asia (CARB)

CPA.............. Claims Payable Abroad [*Insurance*] (MARI)
CPA.............. Combined Paging and Access (CGWS)
CPA.............. Community Program Administrator (DEMM)
CPAC .... Civilian Personnel Advisory Center [*Army*]
cp and nc .... Can't Play and No Chance [*Baseball term*] (NDBD)
CPC.............. Certificate of Public Convenience (CGWS)
CPC.............. Cheap Personal Computer (ADWA)
cpd............... Compound (ADWA)
CPD .... Concurrent Product Development
CPD .... ConSeal Private Desktop
CPDB .... Clinical Pathway Database (ADWA)
CPDF .... Cumulative Probability Density Function (CCCA)
CPE.............. Cellular Provider Equipment (CGWS)
CPF.............. Cleft Palate Foundation (ADWA)
CPFR .... Collaboration Planning Forecasting Replenishment
CPFS........... Computer Program Functional Specification (CTAS)
CPFT........... Certified Pulmonary Function Technician (NUJO)
CPHQ .... Certified Professional in Healthcare Quality (NUJO)
CPHU .... County Public Health Unit (DEMM)
CPIT............ California Psychological Inventory Test (DIPS)
cpl .... Complete (ADWA)
CPLD .... Complex Programmable Logic Device (AEBE)
cpm .... Counts per Minute (ABAC)
CPMF........... Command Post Modern Processor (CCCA)
CPMS........... Civilian Personnel Management Services
CPMSM....... Colonial Police Meritorious Service Medal [*British*]
CPO .... Chief Privacy Officer
CPON .... Certified Pediatric Oncology Nurse (NUJO)
CPP.............. Calling Party Pays (CGWS)
CPP.............. Certified Pain Practitioner (NUJO)
CPP.............. Cloud Photopolarimeter (CARB)
CPPD .... Calcium Pyrophosphate Deposition Disease (ADWA)
CPRA .... Canadian Professional Rodeo Association
CPRS .... Cloud Profiling Radar System (ARMP)
CPS.............. Chips per Second (CCCA)
CPS.............. Collective Protection Shelter [*Army*]
CPST........... Capstone Turbine [*NASDAQ symbol*]
CPsychol...... Chartered Psychologist
Cpt............... Captain (NTIO)
CPT.............. Cognitive Processing Therapy (DIPS)
CPT.............. Cone Penetrometer (ABAC)
cpt .... Counterpoint (ADWA)
cptd .... Carpeted (ADWA)
CPWR .... Center to Protect Workers' Rights (SARE)
CQM............. Channel Quality Measurement (CGWS)
CQMA .... Cost/Quality Management Assessment (ABAC)
CQSA .... Chartered Quantity Surveying Association (COBU)
CQT............. Channel Queue Table (CCCA)
CR............... Calf Roping [*Rodeo term*]
CR............... Cancellation Ratio (CCCA)
CR............... Change Record (TRID)
CR............... Commissioned Research
C/R.............. Counter Rotating [*Aviation*] (PIPO)
Cr................ Crane (RIMS)
cr .... Credit (NTIO)
Cr................ Creek (NTIO)
cr .... Creek (ADWA)
CR............... Crossing Restrictions (CTAS)
C ration .... Canned Ration (ADWA)
CRBOH........ Canadian Registration Board of Occupational Hygienists (SARE)
CRC .... Climate Research Committee (CARB)
CRCIA .... Columbia River Comprehensive Impact Assessment (ABAC)
CRDB........... Crew Requirements Data Base [*NASA*] (SPST)
CREAM .... Comprehensive Risk Evaluation and Management (ABAC)
CREP .... Conservation Reserve Enhancement Program [*Michigan*]
crep .... Crepitation (ADWA)
CRF.............. Cell Relay Function (MLOA)
CRF.............. Continuous Schedule of Reinforcement (DIPS)
CRFA .... Cancer Research Foundation of America (ADWA)
CRFH .... Cray Fish Co. ADS [*NASDAQ symbol*] (SG)
CRI.............. Cancer Research Institute
CRI.............. Climate Research Institute [*Oklahoma State University*] (CARB)
CRI.............. Collective Routing Indicator (CCCA)
CRI.............. Compositional Rule of Inference (IDAI)
crim............. Criminal (ADWA)
criminol........ Criminologist (ADWA)
Crim LQ .... Criminal Law Quarterly [*A publication*]
Crim LR .... Criminal Law Review [*A publication*]
CRIR .... Caitlin Raymond International Registry (ADWA)
CRISP .... Consortium Research on Indicators of System Performance (ADWA)
crit .... Critic (NTIO)
crit.............. Criticism (NTIO)
crit.............. Criticized (ADWA)
CRL.............. Carbon Released from Living Biomass (CARB)
CRL.............. Certified Reporting Limit (ABAC)
CRL.............. Charles River Labs. [*NYSE symbol*]
cr/lf........... Carriage Return/Line Feed (ADWA)
CrM.............. Crisis Management (DEMM)
CRM............. Customer Relationship Management
CRN .... Cash Refund Notice (TRID)
cRNA........... Complementary Ribonucleic Acid (ADWA)
CRNFA .... Certified Registered Nurse First Assistant (NUJO)
CRNH........... Certified Registered Nurse Hospice (NUJO)
CRNO........... Certified Registered Nurse in Ophthalmology (NUJO)
CRO .... Cancelling of Policy Returns Only [*Insurance*] (MARI)

Croat........... Croatian (ADWA)
CROB .... Cargo Remaining on Board (RIMS)
croc .... Crocodile (ADWA)
CROS .... Contract-Research Organisations
CRP .... Community Research Project
CRP .... Crop Reserve Program (ADWA)
crpt............. Carport (ADWA)
CRQ .... Chronic Respiratory Questionnaire (ADWA)
CRR .... Carbo Ceramics [*NYSE symbol*]
CRS .... Can't Remember Stuff (ADWA)
CRS .... Cavity-Ringdown Spectrometer (CARB)
Crt.............. Calreticulin
crt .... Court (ADWA)
crt .... Crate
CRUFAD...... Clinical Research Unit for Anxiety Disorders (ADWA)
CRW .... Cladding Removal Waste (ABAC)
crypto .... Cryptography (ADWA)
cryst........... Cyrstallography (ADWA)
CRYT .... Cryogen Tank (SPST)
c/s.............. Call Sign (PIAV)
CS.............. Carbon Stored (CARB)
cs................ Cesarean Section (ADWA)
CS.............. Cloudscope (ARMP)
Cs................ Conscious (DIPS)
CS.............. Constant-Speed [*Propeller*] (PIAV)
CSA.............. Certified Surgical Assistant (NUJO)
CSA.............. Charge Sensitive Amplifier
CSA.............. Chinese Society of Astronautics (CARB)
CSA.............. Continental Stratus Archive (ARMP)
CSAB........... Center for the Study of American Business
CSACC .... Customer Service Administration Control Center (ROAS)
CSAE........... Canadian Society for Engineering in Agriculture, Food, and Biological Systems
CSB............. Chemical Safety and Hazard Investigation Board
CSC............. Combat Stress Control [*Army*]
csc.............. Cosecant (NTIO)
CSCA .... Cardiovascular/Thoracic Surgery and Cardiology Assembly (ADWA)
CSCA .... Central States Communication Association
CSE............. Center for Social Epidemiology (ADWA)
CSE............. Committee on Special Education
CSE............. Control and Switching Element (CCCA)
C section ..... Caesarean Section (NTIO)
C-section ..... Cesarean Section (ADWA)
CSEEE .... Center for the Study of Environmental Endocrine Effects (ADWA)
CSEPP .... Chemical Stockpile Emergency Preparedness Program (ABAC)
CSEQ .... College Student Experinces Questionnaire
CSETI .... Center for the Study of Extraterrestrial Intelligence
CSFM........... California State Fire Marshall (SARE)
CSFM........... Commercial Spent Fuel Management (ABAC)
csg.............. Casting (ADWA)
CSHEMA ..... Campus Safety, Health, and Environmental Management Association (SARE)
CSHS .... Cancer and Steroid Hormonal Study (ADWA)
CSI.............. Center for the Study of Intelligence
CSI.............. Consumer Safety Inspector [*Food and Drug Administration*]
csk.............. Countersink (ADWA)
CSL............. Central Science Laboratory
CSL............. Climate Simulation Laboratory (ARMP)
CSL............. Command Selection List [*Army*]
CSL............. Commission on Student Learning
CSLA .... California School Library Association
CSML .... Child's Meal [*Travel industry*] (TRID)
CSMS .... Colorado Springs Mineralogical Society
CSN .... Children's Safety Network (ADWA)
CSO .... Computer Security Officials (ADWA)
CSO .... Consumer Safety Officer [*Food and Drug Administration*]
CSOC .... Consolidated Satellite Operations Center (CCCA)
CSP............. Combined Sensor Program (ARMP)
CSP............. Communications Signal Processor (CCCA)
CSPAAD ...... Coarse Sun Pointing Attitude Anomaly Detection (ADWA)
CSPED .... Concurrent Semiconductor Production and Equipment Development
CSPI............ Certified Specialist in Poison Information
C-spine .... Cervical Spine (ADWA)
CSQ .... Coping Strategies Questionnaire (DIPS)
CSR .... Center for Scientific Review [*National Institutes of Health*]
CSR .... Comprehensive Spending Review
CSR .... Customer Support Room (SPST)
CSRM .... Clouds, Storms, and Regional Meteorology
CSS............. Cellular Subscriber Station (CGWS)
CSS............. Combined Sewer System (ADWA)
CSS............. Communications Selector Switch (CCCA)
CSS............. Contaminated Surface Soil (ABAC)
CSS1........... Cascading Style Sheets Level 1
CSSM.......... Center for Subatomic Structure of Matter [*Australia*]
CST............. Central Standard Time (AUEG)
CST............. Commercial Satellite Terminal (CCCA)
CSTC........... Consolidated Satellite Test Center (ADWA)
CSTC........... Consolidated Space Test Center
CSU/DSU ..... Customer Service Unit/Data Service Unit [*Computer science*] (ITCA)
CSW............. Caustic Slurry Waste (ABAC)
CSW............. Certificate in Social Work (ADWA)
CSWMP .... County Solid Waste Management Plan [*California*] (SARE)
CSWP .... Committee on the Status of Women in the Profession
Ct................ Carat (NTIO)
ct .... Certificate (ADWA)

CT	Chlamydia Trachomatis [*Medicine*]
CT	Circle Trip [*Travel industry*] (TRID)
CT	Conduction Time (DIPS)
CT	Cottage
Ct	Count (NTIO)
Ct	Countertenor
CT1	Cordless Telephone-1st Generation (CGWS)
CT2	Cellular Telephone-2nd Generation (CGWS)
CTA	Combined Transcortical Aphasia (DIPS)
CTA	Condominium Travel Associates (TRID)
CTBL	Cloud-Topped Boundary Layer (ARMP)
CTBT	Comprehensive Test Ban Treaty (AUEG)
CTC	Common Toxicity Criteria [*Medicine*]
CTCB	Contact's Business Phone (TRID)
CTCH	Contact's Home Phone (TRID)
CTCI	CT Communications [*NASDAQ symbol*] (SG)
CTD	Cheapest to Deliver (ADWA)
CTD	Corporate Travel Department (TRID)
CTEFLA	Certificate in the Teaching of English as a Foreign Language to Adults
CTF	Capture the Flag (ADWA)
ctf	Certificate (NTIO)
Ctf	Certificates (SG)
ctf	Certified (ADWA)
ctg	Cartridge (ADWA)
ctge	Cartage (ADWA)
CTIA	Capacitive Feedback Transimpedance Amplifier (ADWA)
CTICU	Cardiac Thoracic Intensive Care Unit
CTIP	Coalition for Travel Industry Parity (TRID)
CTL	Certificate Trust Lists
CTL	Communications Technology Laboratory (CCCA)
CTLM	Centillium Communic. [*NASDAQ symbol*]
CTM	Chemical Transport Model
CTM	Circle Trip Minimum [*Travel industry*] (TRID)
ctmo	Centimo (ADWA)
CTN	Certified Transplant Nurse (NUJO)
ctn	Cotangent (ADWA)
CTO	Central Technical Operations (HLLA)
CTO	City Ticket Office [*Travel industry*] (TRID)
CTO	Clinical Trials Office [*Medicine*]
cto	Concerto (ADWA)
CTOF	Charge Time-of-Flight (ADWA)
CTP	Cytidine 5c-Triphosphate (ADWA)
CTPECC	Chinese Taipei Pacific Economic Cooperation Committee
CTRC	Canadian Television and Radio Commission (CGWS)
ctrl	Control (ADWA)
CTS	Clinical Trials Supplies
CTSA	Channel Tunnel Safety Authority (HEAS)
CTTS	Consolidated Theater Target Services [*Military*]
CTU	Channel Terminating Unit (CCCA)
CTVC	Closed Loop Television Camera (SPST)
ctvo	Centavo (ADWA)
Ctx	Contractions (ADWA)
Cty	County (ADWA)
CU	Cryptographic Unit (CCCA)
Cu	Cumulus (ADWA)
CUAP	College and University Affiliations Program
cube	Cubicle (ADWA)
CUFON	Computer UFO Network
CUFORN	Canadian UFO Research Network
CUITN	Common User Installation Transport Network
CUL	Catch You Later (ADWA)
cul	Culinary (ADWA)
cult	Culturo (ADWA)
cum	Cumulative (ADWA)
Cumb	Cumbria (ADWA)

cUMP	Cyclic Uridine 3c, 5c-Monophosphate (ADWA)
cur	Currency (NTIO)
CUR	J. Curwen & Sons [*Publisher*]
curr	Currency (ADWA)
curric	Curriculum (ADWA)
cust	Custodian (ADWA)
CV	Central Valley Trucks
CV	Check Visit (HEAS)
CV	Code Violations (ADWA)
cv	Column Volume (ABAC)
CV	Container Vessel (TRID)
cv	Convertible (ADWA)
CV	Counter Value (CCCA)
CVB	Convention and Visitors Bureau (TRID)
CVCC	Controlled Vortex Combustion Chamber (ROAS)
CVFP	Charted Visual Flight Procedure (PIPO)
CVIC	Center for Violence and Injury Control (ADWA)
CVICU	Cardiovascular Intensive Care Unit (NUJO)
CVO	Credentials Verification Organization (ADWA)
CVP	Content Vectoring Protocol
cvr	Cover (ADWA)
CVS	Chorionic Villus Sampling (ADWA)
CVS	Composite Variability Study (ABAC)
cvt	Convertible (ADWA)
CVVH	Continuous Veno-Venous Hemofiltration (NUJO)
CVVHD	Continuous Veno-Veno Hemodialysis (NUJO)
CW	Chemical Wavelength (CCCA)
c/w	Consistent With (ADWA)
C/W	Continue With [*Medicine*]
CW	Convective Precipitation Over Water (ARMP)
C/W	Country Western (ADWA)
CWA	Chemical Warfare Agent (ABAC)
CWA	County Warning Area [*Department of Emergency Management*] (DEMM)
CWCN	Certified Wound Care Nurse (NUJO)
CWCS	Control of Work in Confined Spaces (HEAS)
CWHC	Community Wholistic Health Center (ADWA)
CWIS	Campus-Wide Information Server
CWL	Chemical Wavelength Laser (CCCA)
CWMS	Commercial Waste Management Statement (ABAC)
CWOC	Catholic Women of the Chapel
CWS	College World Series [*Baseball*] (NDBD)
CWSF	Customer Waste Solidification Facility (ABAC)
CWT	Code Walk-Through (CTAS)
CWTA	Canadian Wireless Telecommunications Association (CGWS)
CWV	Columnar Water Vapor (ARMP)
CWW	Clinic Without Walls (ADWA)
cx	Cervix (ADWA)
CXBR	Cosmic X-Ray Background Radiation
Cy	County (ADWA)
Cy	Cyanide (ADWA)
cy	Cycle (ADWA)
Cy	Cylinders (RIMS)
CYBA	Charter Yacht Brokers Association (TRID)
cyber	Cybernetic (ADWA)
cyc	Cyclopedia (ADWA)
cycl	Cyclopedia (ADWA)
CYL	See You Later (ADWA)
CYM	Cyan-Yellow-Magenta (AEBE)
cym	Cymbals
Cym	Cymric (ADWA)
CYR	Cyber Sentry, Inc. [*AMEX symbol*]
CYTD	Calendar Year to Date (ABAC)
cytol	Cytological (ADWA)
CZ	Consultation Zone (HEAS)
Czech	Czechoslovakia (NTIO)

D
By Acronym

d	Deuteron	(ADWA)
d	Deviation	(DIPS)
D	Down	(ADWA)
d	Drachma	(ADWA)
d	Drive Stimuli	(DIPS)
D	Drive Strength	(DIPS)
D	Selection Index [*H. J. Eysenck*]	(DIPS)
D2A	Digital-to-Analog	(AEBE)
Da	Danish	(ADWA)
DA	Dining Area	(ADWA)
D/A	Disbursement Account	(RIMS)
DAA	Data Availability Acknowledgment	(ADWA)
DAAC	Data Active Archive Center	(CARB)
DAAIS	Danger Area Activity Information Service	(PIAV)
DABM	Defense Against Ballistic Missiles	(CCCA)
DAC	Design Analysis Cycle	(SPST)
DAC	Digital-to-Analog Conversion	
DAC	Disaster Application Center [*Department of Emergency Management*]	(DEMM)
DACC	Directory Assistance Call Completion	(CGWS)
DACS	Danger Area Crossing Service	(PIAV)
DACS	Data Acquisition and Control Subsystems	(ADWA)
DACS	Department of Agriculture and Consumer Services	(DEMM)
DACS	Designers and Artists Copyright Society	
DACS	Digital Aeronautical Chart Supplement	(CTAS)
DAD	Device for Automated Desensitization	(DIPS)
dAdo	Deoxyadenosine	(ADWA)
DAEDALUS	Documenting Aerosol Electromagnetics, Defining Aerosol Lifetimes and Understanding Sources [*Research station*]	(CARB)
DAF	Divorced Asian Female	(ADWA)
DAFNE	Double Annular Factory for Nice Experiments	
DAG	Data Acquisition Glove	
dag	Decagram	(ADWA)
dag	Dekagram	(NTIO)
DAI	Direct Aqueous Injection	(ABAC)
DAI/GC	Direct Aqueous Injection/Gas Chromatography	(ABAC)
DAM	Divorced Asian Male	(ADWA)
D-AMPS	Dual-Mode Advanced Mobile Phone System	(CGWS)
Dan	Danish	(ADWA)
D&D	Decontamination and Decommissioning	(ABAC)
D & D	Distress and Diversion Cells at Air Traffic Control Centres [*British*]	(PIAV)
D&D	Drug and Disease Free	(ADWA)
D&E	Dilation and Extraction	(ADWA)
D&S	Domination and Submission	(ADWA)
D&X	Dilation and Extraction	(ADWA)
DAP	Days All Purposes	(RIMS)
DAP	Diagnostic Accreditation Program	(ADWA)
DAP	Disaster Assistance Programs	(DEMM)
DAP	Dispatch Applications Processor	(CGWS)
DAPO	Do All Possible [*Travel industry*]	(TRID)
DAS	Data-Assimilation System	(CARB)
DAS	Defensive Aid System	
DAS	Deputy Assistant Secretary	(ABAC)
DAS	Developmental Apraxia of Speech	
DAS	Differential Ability Scales [*C. D. Elliott*]	(DIPS)
DAS	Direct Access System	(CARB)
DAS	Dreaded Abbreviation Syndrome	
DAS	Dual Address Space [*Computer science*]	(ITCA)
DASH	Dietary Approaches to Stop Hypertension	
dat	Dative	(ADWA)
DAU	Decryption Authentication Unit	(ADWA)
DAVB	Digital Audio Video Broadcasting	
DAWS	Defense Automated Warning System	(ADWA)
DB	Damp Basement	(ADWA)
Db	Decibel	(DIPS)
DB	Direct Broadcast	(CARB)
db	Doublebass	
DBA	Design Business Association	(COBU)
d/b/a	Doing Business As	(NTIO)
DBEHO	Deputy Borough Environmental Health Officer	(HEAS)
DBF	Department of Banking and Finance	(DEMM)
dBI	Decibels Referenced to Isotropic Gain	(ADWA)
DBIR	Directory of Biotechnology Resources	(ADWA)
DBLB	Double Room with Bath	(TRID)
dble	Double	(ADWA)

DBLN	Double Room without Shower or Bath	(TRID)
DBLS	Double Room with Shower	(TRID)
DBL SKIN	Double Skinned	(RIMS)
dBm	Decibels Above or Below 1 Milliwatt	(AEBE)
dBm	Decibels per Milliwatt	(ADWA)
DBME	Database Management Environment	
DBPR	Department of Business and Professional Regulation	(DEMM)
dBW	Decibels Referenced to One Watt	(ADWA)
DC	Dawson's Creek [*Television program title*]	
DC	Delta Clipper	
DC	Direct Chill	(HEAS)
DC	Direct Cost	
DC	Direct Costs	(MARI)
d/c	Discharge	(ADWA)
DC	Discharge Capacity	(RIMS)
dc	Discontinue	(ADWA)
DC	Docking Compartment [*NASA*]	(SPST)
DC	Dry Chemical	(PIPO)
DCA	Department of Community Affairs	(DEMM)
DCA	Directory Client Agent	
DCB	Disk Control Block	(ROAS)
DCC	Dependent Care Connection	(ADWA)
DCC	Digital Communications Corp.	(CCCA)
DCCPS	Division of Cancer Control and Population Sciences	(ADWA)
DCE	Defense Coordinating Executive [*Department of Defense*]	(DEMM)
DCEG	Division of Cancer Epidemiology and Genetics	(ADWA)
DCEHO	Deputy Chief Environmental Health Officer	(HEAS)
DCEI	Dobson Communic. 'A' [*NASDAQ symbol*]	(SG)
DCF	Data Capture Facility	
DCF	Department of Children and Families	(DEMM)
DCGN	Distributed Communications Grid Network	(CCCA)
DCI	Decided Cases Index	(HEAS)
DCI	Deputy Chief Inspector	(HEAS)
DCI	Desktop Color Imaging	
DCIF	Deputy Chief Inspector of Factories	(HEAS)
DCIO	Deputy Chief Inspecting Officer	(HEAS)
DCIS	Ductal Carcinoma in Situ [*Medicine*]	(ADWA)
DCMDE	Defense Contract Management District East	
DCMDI	Defense Contract Management District International	
dCMP	Deoxycytidylic Acid	(ADWA)
DCMS	Distributed Call Measurement System	
DCO	Defense Coordinating Officer [*Department of Defense*]	(DEMM)
DCP	Directorate Controlled Project	
DCP	Division of Cancer Prevention	(ADWA)
DCP	Division of Capital Police	(DEMM)
DCPBX	Digitally Connected Private Branch Exchange [*Telecommunications*]	(ROAS)
DCS	Direct Credits Society	(ADWA)
DCS-1800	Digital Communications System on 1800 MHz Band	(CGWS)
DCT	Digital Cordless Telephone	(CGWS)
DCT-1800	Digital Cellular Communications-1800	(CGWS)
DCU	Digital Conference Unit	(CCCA)
DCX	Delta Clipper Experimental	
DD	Definitive Design	(ABAC)
Dd	Delivered	(MARI)
DD	Development Disorder	
DD	Differential Detection	(CCCA)
DDA	Data Delivery Acknowledgment	(ADWA)
DDB	Deductive Database	(IDAI)
D/DBP	Disinfectant and Disinfection Byproduct	(ADWA)
DDC	Defense Distribution Center	
DDDP	Detailed Design Data Package	(ABAC)
DDF	Data Distribution Facility	(ADWA)
D/DF	Drug and Disease Free	(ADWA)
DDI	Dideoxyinosine	(ADWA)
DDIC	DDi Corp. [*NASDAQ symbol*]	(SG)
DDL	Domain Dynamics Ltd.	
DDN	Data Delivery Notice	(ADWA)
DDPH	Deputy Director of Public Health	(HEAS)
DDRMI	Digital Distance Radio Magnetic Indicator	(HLLA)
DDRSDRAM	Double-Data-Rate Synchronous Dynamic Random Access Memory	(AEBE)
DDSO	Developmentally Disabled Service Office	
DDT	Dual-Double Tandem Axle	(PIPO)
DDTE	Design, Development, Test, and Evaluation	(ADWA)
DDW	Digestive Disease Week	(ADWA)

DE.............. District Executive [*Boy Scouts of America*]
DE.............. Donor Eggs (ADWA)
DEAF........... Deaf Passenger [*Travel industry*] (TRID)
deb............. Debutante (ADWA)
DEBRA........ Dystrophic Epidermolysis Bullosa Research Association (ADWA)
dec............. Declaration (ADWA)
dec............. Decoration (ADWA)
decaf......... Decaffeinated Coffee (ADWA)
decd.......... Deceased (ADWA)
decl........... Declension (NTIO)
decn.......... Decision (ADWA)
decon......... Decontamination
DED........... Darkness Emitting Diode (AEBE)
DED........... Death-Effector Domain
ded............ Deduct (ADWA)
DEECS .... Digital Electronic Engine Control System (ADWA)
DEF........... Deaf
def............. Definite (ADWA)
def............. Definitely (ADWA)
deg........... Degree (NTIO)
DEH........... Director of Environmental Health (HEAS)
DEHO........ District Environmental Health Officer (HEAS)
DEHS.......... Director of Environmental Health Services (HEAS)
DEL........... Data Evaluation Laboratory (ADWA)
del............. Delegation (ADWA)
Del............ Delete (NTIO)
deli........... Delicatessen (ADWA)
delic......... Delicious
DELTA........ Diploma in English Language Teaching for Adults
delts .... Deltoid Muscles (ADWA)
DEM........... Democratic (ADWA)
Dem.......... Democratic (NTIO)
dem.......... Demodulator (ADWA)
dem.......... Demonstrative (NTIO)
dem.......... Demurrage (ADWA)
DEM........... Division of Emergency Management (DEMM)
demo......... Demonstration (ADWA)
demob........ Demobilize (ADWA)
demon........ Demonstrative (ADWA)
demonstr ..... Demonstrative (ADWA)
den........... Denotation (ADWA)
DENIS......... Deep Near-Infrared Survey
denom........ Denomination (NTIO)
dent.......... Dental (NTIO)
dent........... Dentistry (ADWA)
DEP........... Department of Environmental Protection (AUEG)
dep........... Departure (NTIO)
dep........... Deposed (ADWA)
Dep............ Depositary Receipts (SG)
depr.......... Depreciation (ADWA)
dept.......... Deputy (ADWA)
DEQ........... Delivered Ex Quay (RIMS)
der............ Derivative (ADWA)
deriv.......... Derivation (ADWA)
derm.......... Dermatology (ADWA)
derog......... Derogatory (ADWA)
DERWeb....... Dental Education Resources on the Web (ADWA)
DES........... Delivered Ex Ship (RIMS)
Des........... Desert (NTIO)
des........... Designation (ADWA)
DES........... Destination End System [*Telecommunications*] (MLOA)
DESC.......... Defense Energy Support Center
desc.......... Descending (ADWA)
DEST.......... Domestic Emergency Support Team [*Federal Bureau of Investigation*] (DEMM)
destn .... Destination (ADWA)
det............ Detachment (ADWA)
DETLA........ Double Extended Three-Letter Abbreviation (ADWA)
detn.......... Determination (ADWA)
DEU........... Dead-End User (ADWA)
DEV........... Duck Embryo Origin Vaccine (ADWA)
Develop....... Development
DEWS.......... Distant Early Warning System (CCCA)
DF.............. Decal Film
DF.............. Direction-Finding (PIAV)
DF.............. Distribution From (CCCA)
DFAR .... Defense Federal Acquisition Regulations
DFCD.......... Data Format Control Documents (ADWA)
DFCO.......... Deputy Federal Coordinating Officer (DEMM)
DFE........... Decision Feedback Equalization (AEBE)
DFGC.......... Digital Flight Guidance Computer (HLLA)
DFM........... Dust, Fume and Mist (HEAS)
DFR........... Department of Fisheries Research (HEAS)
Dfs............. Distributed File System [*Computer science*]
dft............. Defendant (ADWA)
DG............. Data Group (SPST)
D/G........... Directional Gyro (PIPO)
DG............. Directorate General (HEAS)
dgl............ Dangling Construction (ADWA)
dGMP........ Deoxyguanylic Acid (ADWA)
dgt............ Digit (ADWA)
DH.............. Darling Husband (ADWA)
DH.............. Dear Husband
DH.............. Decoherent Histories
DH.............. Developmentally Handicapped

DH.............. Doubleheader [*Baseball term*] (NDBD)
D/H........... Drug History
DHA........... Duck Head Apparel [*AMEX symbol*]
DHC........... Direct Hydrophilic Conjugation
DHCN.......... Daily Historical Climate Network (CARB)
DHDATSBE... Despatch Half Demurrage on All Time Saved Both Ends (RIMS)
DHDWTSBE.. Despatch Half Demurrage on Working Time Saved Both Ends (RIMS)
DHEA .... Dihydroeplandrosterone (ADWA)
DHEAS........ Dihydroeplandrosterone (ADWA)
DHF........... Dihydrofolic Acid (ADWA)
DHJ........... Doing His Job (ADWA)
DHM........... Divorced Hispanic Male (ADWA)
DHMM........ Director of Hazardous Materials Management (SARE)
DHP........... Direct High Power (ADWA)
DHSMV....... Department of Highway Safety & Motor Vehicles (DEMM)
Di.............. Didymium (ADWA)
DIA........... Dow Jones Industrial Average
diab .... Diabetic (ADWA)
diag .... Diagonally (ADWA)
diag .... Diagram (NTIO)
dial........... Dialectal (ADWA)
DIARAD....... Dual Irradiance Absolute Radiometer (ADWA)
DIBOL........ Digital Interactive Business Oriented Language [*Computer science*] (ITCA)
DICE.......... Data Integration and Collection Environment (ADWA)
DICE.......... Dynamic Integrated Climate Economy (CARB)
dict........... Dictation (ADWA)
diet .... Dietary (ADWA)
Diet........... Dietitian (ADWA)
dif............ Difference (NTIO)
diff............ Difference (ADWA)
DiG........... DiGeorge Syndrome
digiverse .... Digital Universe (ADWA)
dil............. Dilute (ADWA)
DIMCH........ Diesel Mechanics
din............ Dining Room (ADWA)
dioc .... Diocesan (ADWA)
DIP........... Difference in Perils (MARI)
dip............ Diploma (ADWA)
diph .... Diphtheria (ADWA)
dipl............ Diploma (ADWA)
DIPT.......... Direct Intraperitoneal Insemination [*Medicine*] (ADWA)
dir............ Direction (ADWA)
DIRB.......... Dissimilar Iron Reducing Bacteria (ABAC)
DIRCM........ Directed Infrared Countermeasures (ADWA)
Dir Cut....... Director's Cut
DIS........... Defense Intelligence Service (CCCA)
dis .... Discontinued (TRID)
dis .... Disintegration (ABAC)
DIS........... Disney Channel (ADWA)
dis .... Distant (ADWA)
disab .... Disability (ADWA)
disc........... Discovered (ADWA)
disch .... Discharge (ADWA)
disco......... Discotheque (ADWA)
DISIDA........ Diisopropyl Iminodiacetic Acid (ADWA)
dis/min....... Disintegration per Minute (ABAC)
DISORT...... Discrete Ordinate Radiative Transfer (ARMP)
disp .... Dispensary (ADWA)
displ.......... Displacement (ADWA)
diss........... Dissertation (ADWA)
dis/sec....... Disintegrations per Second (ABAC)
distn .... Distillation (ADWA)
distr .... Distributor (ADWA)
distrib......... Distributive (ADWA)
DIT............ Development Integration Test (SPST)
DIT............ Discrete Trial Training
DITC.......... Ditech Communications
DIVA .... Determination, Integrity, Vitality, and Aspiration [*Self-esteem plan devised by fitness instructor Terri Walsh*]
DIW .... Deionized Water (ABAC)
dk............. Dock (ADWA)
dkg........... Dekagram (ADWA)
dkl............ Dekaliter (ADWA)
dkm.......... Dekameter (ADWA)
dkt............ Docket (ADWA)
DL............. Den Leader [*Boy Scouts of America*]
DL............. Distance Learning (HEAS)
DL............. Driver's License (SARE)
DLC........... Decision Level Concentration (ABAC)
DLC/LLC ..... Data Link Control/Logical Link Control (ADWA)
DLD........... Direct Link for the Disabled, Inc. (ADWA)
DLES.......... Department of Labor and Employment Security (DEMM)
DLG-E........ Digital Line Graph-Enhanced (CARB)
DLIS.......... Defense Logistics Information Service
DLO........... Document-Like Objects
DLOSP........ Dropping Last Outwards Sea Pilot (RIMS)
Dlove......... Deficiency Love [*A. Maslow*] (DIPS)
DLS............ Date Last Seen [*Medicine*]
DLS............ Disaster Legal Services (DEMM)
DLT........... Dose Limiting Toxicity [*Medicine*]
dlvy............ Delivery (ADWA)
DLX........... Deluxe Room [*Travel industry*] (TRID)
DM............. Data Manager (CTAS)

Dm	Data Mobile Channel (CGWS)
dm	Decimeter (ABAC)
DM	Deep Monitoring (CARB)
dm	Drum
DM	Dust and Mist (SARE)
DMA	Department of Military Affairs (DEMM)
DMA	Digraph Matrix Analysis (SPST)
DMA	Direct Memory Access
DMAT	Disaster Medical Assistance Team (ADWA)
DMC	Directional Minimum Check [*Travel industry*] (TRID)
DMF	Decayed, Missing, and Filled Teeth (ADWA)
DMG	Dimethylglyoxide (ABAC)
DMH	Data Message Handler (CGWS)
dmkit	Drum Kit
DML	Direct Memory Load (ADWA)
DMM	Digital Multimeter (AEBE)
DMNH	Denver Museum of Natural History
DMO	Destination Marketing Organization (TRID)
DMORT	Disaster Mortuary Response Team (DEMM)
DMQL	Data Mining Query Language (IDAI)
DMR	Detailed Mission Requirements (ADWA)
DMS	Department of Management Services (DEMM)
DMS	Dynamic Mechanical Spectroscopy
DMSO	Division Medical Supply Office [*Army*]
DMT	Data Management Team (ARMP)
DNase	Deoxyribonuclease (ADWA)
Dneeds	Deficiency Needs [*A. Maslow*] (DIPS)
DNF	Disjunctive Normal Form (IDAI)
DNRC	Department of Natural Resources and Conservation (AUEG)
DNSC	Defense Nuclear Facilities Safety Board
DNSI	Direct-Normal Solar Irradiance (ARMP)
DO	Dangerous Occurrence (HEAS)
DOAS	Differential Optical Absorption Spectroscopy (SARE)
DOB	Duplication of Benefits (DEMM)
dobe	Doberman Pinscher (ADWA)
DOC	Department of Corrections (DEMM)
Doc	Doctor (NTIO)
DoD	Dissolved Oxygen Demand
DoDIIS	Department of Defense Intelligence Information System (ADWA)
DOEA	Department of Elder Affairs (DEMM)
DOF	Division of Forestry (DEMM)
DOHS	Department of Health Services (SARE)
DOI	Department of Insurance (DEMM)
DOL	Dock Owner's Liability [*Insurance*] (MARI)
DOM	Data Quality Message (ADWA)
DOM	Dissolved Organic Macromolecules (CARB)
dom	Domestic (TRID)
dom	Dominant (ADWA)
Dom	Dominican (NTIO)
dom	Dominion (NTIO)
DOMS	Director of Military Support [*Army*] (DEMM)
Don	Donegal (ADWA)
DONUT	Direct Observation of the Nu Tau
DOP	Dropping Outward Pilot (RIMS)
dopa	Dihydroxyphenylalanine (ADWA)
DOPG	Duty Officers Procedure Guide [*Department of Emergency Management*] (DEMM)
DOR	Department of Revenue (DEMM)
Dor	Doric (ADWA)
DOS	Day Optical Scope
DOS	Degree of Sensitization (ABAC)
DOS	Denial of Service (ADWA)
DOS	Director of Studies
DOST	Direct Oocyte-Sperm Transfer [*Medicine*] (ADWA)
DoT	Department of Transport (PIAV)
DOTES	Doctrine, Organization, Training, Equipment, and Supporting Facilities [*Military*]
DOTMPL	Doctrine, Organization, Training, Materiel, Personnel and Leader Development [*Army*]
doublexing	Double-Crossing (ADWA)
DP	Demolition Proceeding (ADWA)
DP	Designated Player [*Baseball term*] (NDBD)
DP	Diagnostic Processor (CCCA)
dp	Differential Pressure (ABAC)
dp	Dot Pitch (ADWA)
DP	Dynamic Planner (CTAS)
dpa	Displacements per Atom (ABAC)
DPAG	Dangerous Pathogen Advisory Group (HEAS)
DPC	Data Product Code (ADWA)
DPD	Drug Product Database (ADWA)
DPE	Data Processing Engineer (ADWA)
DPF	Divorced Professional Female (ADWA)
dph	Diamond-Pyramid Hardness (ABAC)
DPIG	Disaster Preparedness Improvement Grant (DEMM)
DPL	Denied Persons List
DPLX	Duplex (TRID)
DPM	Demand Planning Module
DPM	Divorced Professional Male (ADWA)
DPMO	Defense Prisoner of War/Missing Personnel Office
DPN	Dynamic Probabilistic Network (IDAI)
DPO	Days Post-Ovulation [*Medicine*] (ADWA)
DPP	Default Protection Plan [*Travel industry*] (TRID)
DPR	Department of Pesticide Regulation [*California*] (SARE)
DPRS	Directors' & Producers' Rights Society
DPS	Detroit Public Schools [*Michigan*]
dps	Disintegrations per Second (ABAC)
DPS	Distributed Problem Solving (IDAI)
dpt	Department (NTIO)
dpt	Deponent (ADWA)
dptr	Departure (TRID)
DQ	Disqualify (ADWA)
DQA	Data Quality Assessment (ABAC)
DQPSK	Differential Quadrature Phase-Shift Keying (AEBE)
DQPSK	Differential Quadri-Phase Shift Keying (CCCA)
DQT	Design Qualification Test (CTAS)
dr	Debtor (ADWA)
dr	Dining Room (NTIO)
D/R	Distance to Cell Radius Ratio (CGWS)
DRA	Deficit Reduction Act (ADWA)
DRA	Design Requirements Agreement (SPST)
DRAM	Dataram
dram	Dramatic (NTIO)
dram	Dramatist (ADWA)
DRAS	Descending Reticular Activating System (DIPS)
DRC	Damage Received in Collision [*Insurance*] (MARI)
DRC	Disaster Recovery Center (DEMM)
DRE	Display Remoting Enhancement (CCCA)
DREAM	Data Requirements, Evaluation, and Management (ABAC)
drec	Descant Recorder
DRFM	Digital Radio Frequency Memory (ADWA)
drh	Differential Reinforcement of High Rate [*B.F. Skinner*] (DIPS)
drl	Differential Reinforcement of Low Rate [*B.F. Skinner*] (DIPS)
DRM	Digital Rights Management
DRM	Disaster Recovery Manager (DEMM)
DRM	Distribution Requirements Module
DRO	Disaster Recovery Operations (DEMM)
DRP	Data Record/Playback (CTAS)
drq	Discomfort-Relief Quotient (DIPS)
DRS	Dexterous Robotics System [*NASA*] (SPST)
DRS	Digital Radio System (CCCA)
DRS	Direct Receiving Station (ADWA)
DRS	Direct Reference System (TRID)
drsg	Dressing (ADWA)
DRTS	Data Relay Test Satellite [*Sponsored by Japan Space Agency*]
DRU	Data Recovery Unit (ADWA)
DSA	Directory Server Agent
DSC	Digital Source Collector
DSC	Directed Scattering Coefficients (ARMP)
DSC	Discovery Channel (ADWA)
DSCO	Deputy State Coordinating Officer [*Department of Emergency Management*] (DEMM)
DSD	Direct Stream Digital (ADWA)
DSD	Documentary Sight Draft (MARI)
DSD	Drop Size Distribution (ARMP)
DSDM	Dynamic Systems Development Method [*Computer science*] (ITCA)
DSDS	Data Storage and Distribution System (ADWA)
DSE	Display Screen Equipment (HEAS)
DSECT	Dummy Section [*Computer science*] (ITCA)
DSHS	Department of Social and Health Services
DSI	Daily Sum Insured [*Insurance*] (MARI)
DSI	Deputy Superintending Inspector (HEAS)
DSITMS	Direct Sampling Ion Trap Mass Spectrometry (ABAC)
DSL	Document Style Language (ADWA)
DSLAM	Digital Subscriber Line Access Multiplexer (MLOA)
DSM	Diagnostic Statistical Manual
DSP	Device Support Processor [*Computer science*] (ITCA)
DSP	Digital Signal Processing
DSR	Damage Survey Report [*Department of Emergency Management*] (DEMM)
DSR	Direct Solar Radiation (ARMP)
DSRC	Dedicated Short Range Communications
DSRS	Drug Services Research Survey (ADWA)
DSS	Data Support Section (ARMP)
DSS	Defense Security Service
DSS	Department of Special Services
DSS	Double-Shell Slurry (ABAC)
DSS	Double-Simultaneous Stimulation (DIPS)
DSSF	Double-Shell Slurry Feed (ABAC)
DSSG	Defense & Space Systems Group (CCCA)
DST	Directorate of Science and Technology (HEAS)
DSTR	DualStar Technologies
DSTS	Defensive System Technology Study (CCCA)
DSU	Data Servicing Unit (CTAS)
DSUM	Data Summary (ADWA)
DSVT	Digital Secure Voice Terminal (CCCA)
DSX	Digital Service Cross-Connect (MLOA)
dT	Diphtheria (ADWA)
DTA	Disk Transfer Address (ADWA)
DT&E	Design, Testing, and Evaluation (ABAC)
DTaP	Diphtheria, Tetanus, and Acellular Pertussis (ADWA)
DTAS	Digitas, Inc. [*NASDAQ symbol*] (SG)
DTBA	Date to Be Advised (MARI)
DTE	Data Terminal Equipment
DTEFLA	Diploma in the Teaching of English as a Foreign Language to Adults
DTF	Dental Treatment Facility
DTHK	Digital Think, Inc. [*NASDAQ symbol*] (SG)
DTIA	Dive Travel Industry Association (TRID)
DTL	Designated Transit List (MLOA)
DTL	Detailed Time Line (SPST)
DTL IE	Designated Transit List Information Ethernet (MLOA)

DTM............	Data Transfer Module (ADWA)
DTM............	Device Test Module
DTM............	Digital Transportation Marketplace
DTMF..........	Dial Tone Multiple Frequency [*Telecommunications*] (MLOA)
DTPS	Diffuse Thalamic Projection System (DIPS)
DTR	Dietetic Technician Registered (NUJO)
DTRA	Defense Threat Reduction Agency
DTS............	Data Transmission Subsystem (CCCA)
dts	Delirium Tremens (DIPS)
DTVE...........	Digital Television Element (CCCA)
DU	Deregulation Unit (HEAS)
DU	Distribution Uniformity (ADWA)
Du..............	Duchy (NTIO)
Du..............	Dutch (ADWA)
DUAT	Direct User Access Terminal System (PIPO)
Dub............	Dublin (ADWA)
Dubl............	Dublin (ADWA)
DUMBO........	Down Under the Manhattan Bridge Overpass [*New York*]
DUR	Driving under Revocation (SARE)
Dur.............	Durham (ADWA)
DUS	Driving under Suspension (SARE)
D/V..............	Dual Valuation [*Insurance*] (MARI)
DVD	Developmental Verbal Dyspraxia
DVDM	Data Voice Digital Multiplexer (CCCA)
DVD-R	Digital Versatile Disk-Recordable (ADWA)
DVD-RAM	Digital Versatile Disk-Random Access Memory (ADWA)
DVD-ROM	Digital Versatile Disk-Read Only Memory (ADWA)
DVD-RW	Digital Versatile Disk-Read-Write (ADWA)
DVG	Dunvagen [*Publisher*]
DVO	Diffuse Viewing Only (SARE)
DVSA	Diversa Corp. [*NASDAQ symbol*] (SG)
DW..............	Darling Wife (ADWA)
D/w.............	Deadweight (MARI)
D/W	Discussed With [*Medicine*]
D/W	Dying with Dignity (ADWA)
dwnstrs........	Downstairs (ADWA)
DWR	Doppler Weather Radar (ADWA)
DWR	Dual Wavelength Ratio (ARMP)
DWSF	Dry Well Storage Facility (ABAC)
DWSN	Dandy-Walker Syndrome Network (ADWA)
DWT...........	Deadweight Tonnage (ADWA)
dx	Diagnosis (ADWA)
DX.............	Diagnosis
DX.............	Distant Radio Reception (AEBE)
DXF............	Drawing Interchange File (ADWA)
DXF............	Drawing Interchange Format
dy	Dyne (NTIO)
DYNPOS	Dynamic Positioning (RIMS)
DYOH..........	Do Your Own Homework (ADWA)
DYSIM	Dynamic Simulator (CTAS)
DYUU..........	Delta Luminance Color Difference
dz................	Dozen
DZ..............	Dropping Zone (PIAV)

E
By Acronym

e	Electric
e	Engineer (ADWA)
e	Error (ADWA)
E	Excitatory Tendency (DIPS)
E	Experimental Group (DIPS)
E	Extra (ADWA)
E	Index of Forecasting Efficiency (DIPS)
E	Potential (DIPS)
E2PROM	Electrically Erasable Programmable Read Only Memory (AEBE)
E2PROM	Electrically Eraseable Programmable Read Only Memory (CGWS)
E3	Electronic Entertainment Expo (ADWA)
E4E	Enterprise for the Environment
ea	Each (NTIO)
EA	Electron Affinity (ABAC)
EA	Electronic Arts, Inc.
EA	Environment Agency (HEAS)
EA	Evolutionary Algorithm (IDAI)
EA	Export Administration
EA75	Explosives Act 1875 (HEAS)
EAA	Earth Attitude Angle (ADWA)
EAA	Environment of Evolutionary Adaptedness
EADB	Emergency Authorities Database [Department of Defense] (DEMM)
EAEO	Equal Access End Office (CCCA)
EAF	Experimenter's Analysis Facility (ADWA)
EAG	Eagle Wireless Intl. [AMEX symbol] (SG)
EAHCA	Education for All Handicapped Children [1975] (DIPS)
EAHCA	Education of All Handicapped Children Act
EAM	Encapsidated Adenovirus Minichromosome
e&ea	Each and Every Accident (MARI)
e&el	Each and Every Loss (MARI)
e&eo	Each and Every Occurrence (MARI)
E&I	Engineering and Installation (CCCA)
E&M	Earth & Magnet (MLOA)
EAP	Elvis Aaron Presley (ADWA)
EAP	Emergency Action Plan (SARE)
EAP	English for Academic Purposes
EAR	Emergency Action Room (CCCA)
EAR	Engineering All Risks (MARI)
EARA	Environmental Auditors Registration Association (COBU)
EAS	Extended Address Set (CCCA)
EASA	Electrical Apparatus Service Association, Inc.
EASe	Electronic Auditory Stimulation Effect
EASE	Estimation and Assessment of Substance Exposure (HEAS)
EASOE	European Arctic Stratospheric Ozone Experiment (CARB)
EAT	Earnings after Taxes (ADWA)
EAT	Estimated Approach Time [Aviation] (PIAV)
EAT	Expected Approach Time (PIPO)
EAWEP	East Asia and Western Pacific (CARB)
EAZO	Energy Active Zones of the Ocean (CARB)
eb	Electric Bass
EB	English Breakfast (TRID)
EBAA	European Business Aircraft Association (PIAV)
EBBR	Energy-Balance Bowen Ratio (CARB)
EBD	Emotional/Behavioral Disorder
EBHT	Electron Beam High Throughput Lithography
EBITDA	Earnings Before Interest, Taxes, Depreciation, and Amortization
EBL	External Blood Loss (ADWA)
EBM	Evidence-Based Medicine
EB/NO	Energy per Bit to Noise (CCCA)
EBOZ	Ebola Virus, Zaire Strain (ADWA)
EBPP	Electronic Bill Presentment and Payment
EBRT	External-Beam Radiation Therapy (ADWA)
EBS	Electrical Brain Stimulation (DIPS)
e-business	Electronic Business (ADWA)
EC	Earth Coverage (CCCA)
Ec	Ecuador (ADWA)
EC	Elemental Carbon (CARB)
EC	Emergency Contraceptive
ec	Emerging Company (ADWA)
EC	Environment Canada
EC	Exercise Countermeasure (SPST)
EC	Experiment Center (ARMP)
ECAD	Engineering Computer-Aided Design
ECAL	Electronic Calibration (ADWA)
ECAO	Environmental Criteria and Assessment Office (AUEG)
ECAR	Economy Car (TRID)

E-cash	Electronic Cash (ITCA)
e-cash	Electronic Cash (ADWA)
ECB	Enhanced Cordless Base (CGWS)
ECCI	Eastern Canada Cat Institute (ROAS)
eccl	Ecclesiastical (NTIO)
Eccl Gk	Ecclesiastical Greek (ADWA)
ECC RAM	Error Checking and Correcting Random-Access Memory
ECCS	Emergency Command and Control System (DEMM)
ECDC	Early Childhood Direction Center
ECDL	External Cavity Diode Laser (ARMP)
ECEAP	Early Childhood Education Assistance Program
EC-GC	Electron Capture-Gas Chromatograph (ADWA)
E-Check	Electronic Check (ITCA)
ECI	Employment Consultants Institute (COBU)
ECL	Effluent Charge Law [1976]
ECM	Electric Counter Measure (CCCA)
ECM	External Chemical Messenger (DIPS)
ECM	External Configuration Model (MLOA)
ECN	Environmental Change Network
ECO	Emergency Coordinating Officer [Department of Emergency Management] (DEMM)
ECO	Extra-Contractual Obligations (MARI)
ECoG	Electrocorticogram (DIPS)
ECOGAS	European Council of General Aviation Support (PIAV)
ecol	Ecology (ADWA)
E-com	Electronic Commerce (ITCA)
e-commerce	Electronic Commerce (ADWA)
econ	Economics (ADWA)
econ	Economist (ADWA)
ECONET	Environmental Communications Network
ECORC	Eastern Cereal and Oilseed Research Centre [Ottawa, Canada]
ECOS	Education and Career Opportunities System
ECPECC	Ecuadorian Committee of the Pacific Economic Cooperation Council
ECR	Effective Cleaning Radius (ABAC)
eCRM	e-Customer Relationship Management
ECSE	Early Childhood Special Education
ECSL	European Centre for Space Law (CARB)
ECSU	Electrical Certification Support Unit (HEAS)
ECT	Explosive Cutting Tape
ECU	Emergency Care Unit (ADWA)
ecu	European Currency Unit (NTIO)
Ecua	Ecuador (ADWA)
ECWS	Element Control Workstation [NASA] (SPST)
ecx	Electronic Catalogs
ed	Education (ADWA)
ED	Electrical Damage (ADWA)
ED	Employment Department (HEAS)
ED	Energy Division (CARB)
EDA	Elevation Difference Accuracy (CARB)
EDACS	Enhanced Digital Access Communications System (CGWS)
EDCT	Expected Departure Clearance Time (PIPO)
EDFG	Edge Device Functional Group
EDG	Employment Department Group (HEAS)
EDGE	Enhanced Data Rate for Global Evolution
EDGE	Enhanced Data Rates for Global Evolution
EDI	Equivalent-Damage Index (CARB)
edit	Editor (ADWA)
EDL	Ethernet Data Link (ADWA)
EDP	Emergency Department Physician (NUJO)
EDP	Ethylene Diamine Pyrocatechol
EDP	External Diploma Program
EDR	Electrodialysis Reversal (ADWA)
EDR	Electronic Dictionary Research (IDAI)
E-dress	Electronic Address (ADWA)
EDS	Early Deployment System (ABAC)
EDS	Enter Day Stop Order (ADWA)
EDSA	Eating Disorders Shared Awareness (ADWA)
EDU	Error Detection Unit (CCCA)
educ	Educational (ADWA)
EE	Environmental Education
EE	Export Enforcement
EEATCS	Early External Active Thermal Control System [NASA] (SPST)
EEAW	Environmental Education Association of Washington
EECMB	Electrical Equipment Certification Management Board (HEAS)
EEEE	eMachines, Inc. [NASDAQ symbol] (SG)
EEES	End-Effector Exchange System (ABAC)

EEG	Electroencephalograph	(DIPS)
EEG	Electroencephalographic	(DIPS)
EEMS	Enhanced Expanded Memory System	(ADWA)
EES	End to End System	
EF	Efficiency	(ADWA)
EFA	Examining for Aphasia [*J. Eisenson*]	(DIPS)
EFAT	Essential Field Artillery Task [*Army*]	
EFATO	Engine Failure At or After Take-Off [*Aviation*]	(PIAV)
EFCI	Explicit Forward Congestion Indication [*Telecommunications*]	(MLOA)
EFCN	Explicit Forward Congestion Notification [*Telecommunications*] (MLOA)	
EFDS	eFunds Corp. [*NASDAQ symbol*]	
eff	Effective	(TRID)
eff	Efficiency	(ADWA)
effic	Efficiency	(ADWA)
EFFNCY	Efficiency	(ADWA)
EFM	Electronic Fetal Monitor	(ADWA)
EFris	East Frisian	(ADWA)
EFS	Encrypting File System [*Computer science*]	
EFS	Event Free Survival [*Medicine*]	
EFST	Essential Fire Support Task [*Army*]	
Eg	Egypt	(NTIO)
Eg	Egyptian	(ADWA)
EGA	Enhanced Graphics Adapter	(AEBE)
EGA	Enhanced Graphics Array	(ADWA)
EGmc	East Germanic	(ADWA)
EGME	Ethylene Glycol Methyl Ether	(PIPO)
E-GSM	Extended Global System for Mobile Communication	(CGWS)
EGTA	Ethyleneglycotetraacetic Acid	(ADWA)
egtr	Electric Guitar	
Egypt	Egyptian	(ADWA)
egyptol	Egyptology	(ADWA)
EHAC	Enroute High Altitude Chart [*Aviation*]	(PIPO)
EHC	Emergency Housing Consortium	
eHEAL	Electronic Health Economics Analysis Letters	(ADWA)
eHEL	Electronic Health Economics Letters	(ADWA)
EHHE	Environmental Hazards and Health Effects	(ADWA)
EHIS	Environmental Health Information Services	(ADWA)
EHPC	Extended High Priority Command	(ADWA)
EHR	Environmental Health Review	(ADWA)
EHz	Exahertz	(ADWA)
EI	Electron Impact	(ABAC)
EI	Explosives Inspectorate	(HEAS)
EID	Emergency Isolation Device	(HEAS)
EID	Equipment Interface Development	
EIL	Environmental Impairment Liability Insurance	(SARE)
EIM	Electronic Image Management	(ITCA)
e-ink	Electronic Ink	(ADWA)
EIP	Equipment Improvement Project	
EIS	Electronic Information Standards	(ADWA)
EIS	Engineering Integrity Society	(COBU)
EIU	Even If Used	(RIMS)
EJASA	Electronic Journal of the Astronomical Society of the Atlantic [*A publication*]	
el	Elevated	(NTIO)
el	Elevated Railroad	(ADWA)
el	Elevation	(ADWA)
ELAC	Enroute Low Altitude Chart [*Aviation*]	(PIPO)
ELCI	Employers' Liability Compulsory Insurance	(HEAS)
ELCTEX	Enforcement Liaison Certification for Transport of Explosives	(HEAS)
ELD	Electronic Liquor Dispenser	(TRID)
elec	Electricity	(NTIO)
elect	Electronic	(ADWA)
electr	Electricity	(ADWA)
elem	Elementary	(NTIO)
elev	Elevation	(ADWA)
ELI	Elite Pharmaceuticals [*AMEX symbol*]	(SG)
elig	Eligible	(ADWA)
elipt	Eliptically	(ADWA)
Eliz	Elizabethan	(ADWA)
ELLPAT	Environmental Lead Laboratory Proficiency Analytical Testing	(SARE)
ELM	Elaboration-Likelihood Model [*R.E Petty & J. T. Cacioppo*]	(DIPS)
ELM	Electronics Module	(ADWA)
ELMC	Electrical Load Management Center	(ADWA)
ELMF	European Large Magnetic Field Facility	
ELN	Environmental Librarian's Network	(ADWA)
ELOA	Educational Leave of Absence	(ABAC)
ELOQ	Eloquent, Inc. [*NASDAQ symbol*]	(SG)
ELOY	eLoyalty Corp. [*NASDAQ symbol*]	(SG)
ELPAT	Environmental Lead Proficiency Analytical Testing Program	
ELSI	Electronic Licensing & Security Initiative	(ITCA)
ELSS	Extravehicular Life Support System	(ADWA)
EM	Electromigration	
EM	Energy Module	(SPST)
EMA	eMagin Corp. [*AMEX symbol*]	(SG)
EMA	Emergency Medicine Assembly	(ADWA)
EMA	Employment Medical Adviser	(HEAS)
EMA	Extra Mileage Allowance [*Travel industry*]	(TRID)
EMAC	Exercise-Associated Muscle Cramping	
E-Mail	Electronic Mail	(AUEG)
EMAN	Economy Car with Manual Transmission	(TRID)
EMAnj	Educational Media Association of New Jersey	
EMBBS	Emergency Medicine Bulletin Board System	(ADWA)
EMCG	Emcor Group	
EMD	Employment Medical Division	(HEAS)

emer	Emergency	(ADWA)
EMER	Emergency Travel	(TRID)
EMFP	Ethnic/Racial Minority Fellowship Programs	(ADWA)
EMG	Electromyograph	(DIPS)
EMG	Electromyographic	
EMGY	Emergency	(ADWA)
EMI	Educable Mentally Impaired	(ADWA)
EMI	EMI Music Publishing	
EML	Estimated Maximum Loss	(MARI)
EMMP	Environmental Monitoring and Mitigation Plan	(ABAC)
e-money	Electronic Money	(ADWA)
emp	Empire	(ADWA)
emp	Empress	(ADWA)
EMPATF	Emergency Management Preparedness and Assistance Trust Fund (DEMM)	
EMPL	Estimated Maximum Probable Loss	(MARI)
EMPRS	Enroute Mission Planning and Rehearsal System [*Army*]	
EMRA	Emergency Medical Response Agency	(ADWA)
EMRG	eMerge Interactive 'A' [*NASDAQ symbol*]	(SG)
EMRS	Electronic Medical Record System	(ADWA)
EMS	Early Mortality Syndrome	
EMS	Excess Mileage Surcharge [*Travel industry*]	(TRID)
E-MSAW	Enroute Minimum Safe Altitude Warning [*Aviation*]	(PIPO)
EMSC	Emergency Medical Services for Children	(ADWA)
EMSL	Environmental Monitoring Systems Laboratory [*Environmental Protection Agency*]	(CARB)
EMSU	Epidemiology and Medical Statistics Unit	(HEAS)
EMTC	Emergency Management Training Center	(DEMM)
emu	Electromagnetic Unit	(ADWA)
emu	Electromagnetic Units	(ABAC)
EMUO	Early Morning Urine Osmolality [*Medicine*]	
EMV	Electron Multiplier Voltage	(ABAC)
EN	Endocardium	(ADWA)
EN	European Norms	(SARE)
ENA	Employment Nursing Adviser	(HEAS)
ENB	Explosives Notified Body	(HEAS)
ENC	Eisenhower National Clearinghouse	
ENC	Emergency News Center	(DEMM)
ENC	Encore	(ADWA)
ency	Encyclopedia	(ADWA)
encyc	Encyclopedia	(NTIO)
endec	Encoder-Decoder	(AEBE)
endo	Endocrine	(ADWA)
ENDO	Endometriosis	(ADWA)
eng	Engineer	(NTIO)
Eng	English	(ADWA)
engg	Engineering	(ADWA)
engin	Engineering	(NTIO)
engr	Engineer	(ADWA)
ENIAC	Electronic Numerical Integrater and Computer	(AEBE)
enl	Enlisted	(ADWA)
ENO	Emerging Healthcare Organization	(ADWA)
ENO	Enoch & Cie [*Publisher*]	
ENP	EntrePort Corp. [*AMEX symbol*]	
ENR	Energizer Holdings [*NYSE symbol*]	(SG)
ENRICH	European Network for Research on Global Change	(CARB)
Ens	Ensign	(NTIO)
ENS	Epidermal Nevus Syndrome	
ENT	Event Number Translator	
entom	Entomology	(ADWA)
environ	Environment	(ADWA)
Env LM	Environmental Law Monthly [*A publication*]	
Env LR	Environmental Law Reports [*A publication*]	
EO	Electronics Lock Overhead [*NASA*]	(SPST)
EO	Emergency Operation	(ADWA)
EO	Erasable Optical Disk	(ITCA)
EO-1	Earth Observing One [*NASA*]	
EOA	End of Activity	(ADWA)
EOC	Earth Observation Center	(CARB)
EOG	Electrooculograph	(DIPS)
EOG	Electro-Oculography	(ADWA)
EOG	Executive Office of the Governor	(DEMM)
eohp	Except as Otherwise Herein Provided	(MARI)
EOI	Earth Observation Initiative	
EOI	End of Irradiation	(ABAC)
EOM	Extraocular Motion	(ADWA)
EOMF	Extraocular Motion Full	(ADWA)
EONC	eOn Communications [*NASDAQ symbol*]	(SG)
EOPM	Electro-Optic Phase Modulation	(CARB)
EOR	Equal Opportunities Review [*A publication*]	
EOR Dig	Equal Opportunities Review Discrimination Law Case Digest [*A publication*]	
EOS	European Optical Society	
EOS-Chem	Earth Observing Satellite-Chemistry [*NASA*]	
EOSI	Earth Observation Science Initiative	
EOSP	Earth Observing Scanning Polarimeter	(CARB)
EOT	End of Thread	(ADWA)
EOTA	Eastern Ontario Trails Alliance [*Canada*]	
EP	Evolutionary Programming	(IDAI)
EP	Explorer Platform [*NASA*]	
EP	Extra Player [*Baseball term*]	(NDBD)
EPAC	Eastern Pacific	(CCCA)
EPAct	Energy Policy Act	(ADWA)
EPAD	Electrically Powered Actuation Device	(ADWA)
EPAT	Early Psychosis Assessment Team	(ADWA)

EPC............	European Policy Committee (HEAS)
EPC............	Evidence-Based Practice Centers (ADWA)
EPCE..........	Electrical Power Consuming Equipment (SPST)
ePCS..........	Electronic Publishing Clearing Services
EPDM.........	Ethylene-Propylene Terpolymer (SARE)
EPHDP.......	Electronic Public Health Development Project (ADWA)
EPHIN........	Electron Proton Helium Instrument (ADWA)
EPI............	Extrapyramidal Involvement (DIPS)
Epis...........	Epistle (ADWA)
Episc.........	Episcopal (NTIO)
Episc.........	Episcopalian (ADWA)
Epist.........	Epistle (ADWA)
EPLO..........	Emergency Preparedness Liaison Officer (DEMM)
EPO...........	European Patent Organisation (HEAS)
EPPA..........	Emissions Prediction and Policy Analysis
EPPP..........	Examination for Professional Psychology Programs (DIPS)
EPRCA........	Enhanced Proportional Rate Control Algorithm
E-print.......	Electronic Print (ADWA)
EPRS	Eprise Corp. [NASDAQ symbol] (SG)
EPRT..........	Engine Pressure Ratio Transmitter (HLLA)
EPSS..........	Electrical Power Subsystem (ADWA)
EPTox........	Extraction Procedure Toxicity
EP TOX	Extraction Procedure Toxicity Test (SARE)
e-publishing...	Electronic Publishing (ADWA)
e-purse.......	Electronic Purse (ADWA)
EPV...........	Extended Precision Vector (ADWA)
EQ.............	Emotional Quotient (ADWA)
eq.............	Equation (ABAC)
eq.............	Equations (ADWA)
eq.............	equivalent (ABAC)
EQC...........	European Question Committee (HEAS)
EQL...........	Equilization (MLOA)
EQL...........	Estimated Quantitation Limit (ABAC)
equiv	Equivalence (ADWA)
equiv	Equivalent (NTIO)
E/R............	Early Run
Er.............	Erbium (ABAC)
ER.............	Explicit Rate (MLOA)
ER.............	Exploratory Research (ABAC)
ER.............	External Ratio (ABAC)
ERA...........	Ecological Risk Assessment (ABAC)
ERA...........	Educational Recording Agency
ERA...........	Environmental Risk Assessment (SARE)
ERA...........	Executive Recruitment Association (COBU)
ERA...........	Expedited Response Action (ABAC)
ERASER.......	Enhanced Recognition and Sensing Radar (ADWA)
ERBES	Earth Radiation Budget Explorer Satellite (CARB)
ERC...........	Endometriosis Research Center (ADWA)
ERDAS........	Earth Resource Data Analysis
ERF...........	Engineering Research Facility (ADWA)
ERI............	Earthquake Research Institute
ERIC..........	Emergency Response Intervention Card (HEAS)
ERM...........	Electronic Records Management
EROOS........	Entity-Relationship Object-Oriented Specifications (ITCA)
EROPS........	Extended Range Operations (PIAV)
EROS	European River Ocean System (CARB)
ERP...........	Emergency Response Plan (SARE)
ERQ...........	Endorsement Request (TRID)
erron.........	Erroneously (ADWA)
ERSP	Electronic Reservations Service Provider [Travel industry] (TRID)
ert............	Earth Relative Time (ADWA)
ERT...........	Enhanced Readiness Test (ABAC)
ERT...........	Execution Reference Time (CCCA)
Erx...........	Empty Spiracles-Related Retinal-Homeobox
ESA...........	Equatorial South America (CARB)
ESATCOM ...	Emergency Satellite Communications System (DEMM)
ESB...........	Electrostimulation of the Brain (DIPS)
ESB...........	Executive Support Branch (HEAS)
Esc...........	Escape (NTIO)
ESCBA........	Escape Self-Contained Breathing Apparatus (SARE)
ESCM.........	Extended Services Communications Manager [IBM Corp.]
ESD...........	Electrostatic Dissipative (SARE)
ESD...........	Emergency Shutdown Device (HEAS)
ESD...........	Emission Standards Division (AUEG)
ESDIS	Earth Science Data and Information System (CARB)
Esdr..........	Esdras (ADWA)
ESF...........	Emergency Support Function [Department of Emergency Management] (DEMM)
ESF...........	European Social Fund (HEAS)
ESFJ..........	Extroversion Sensing Feeling Judging (ADWA)
ESFP.........	Extroversion Sensing Feeling Perception (ADWA)
ESH...........	Electric Surface Heating (HEAS)
ESI............	Environmental Sustainability Initiative
e-site........	Electronic Site (ADWA)
Esk...........	Eskimo (ADWA)
ESLOA........	English as a Second Language Oral Assessment
ESM...........	Engineering Scab Melter (ABAC)
ESM...........	Equipment Support Module (ADWA)
ESMR.........	Enhanced Specialized Mobile Radio (CGWS)
ESNet........	Food Safety Network
ESPAW	Elementary School Principals' Association of Washington
ESSB.........	Electrical Self-Stimulation of the Brain (DIPS)
ESSC.........	Environmental Systems Science Centre
EST...........	Eastern Standard Time (TRID)
EST...........	Electroconvulsive Shock Therapy (DIPS)

EST............	Electro-Sleep Therapy (DIPS)
EST............	Emergency Support Team [National Guard] (DEMM)
est............	Estate (ADWA)
Est............	Estonia (NTIO)
Est............	Estonian (ADWA)
EST............	Exercise Stress Testing
estab.........	Established (ADWA)
e-stamp......	Electronic Stamp (ADWA)
ESTC..........	Explosives Safety Transport Committee (HEAS)
ESTEC.........	European Space Research and Technology Centre (CARB)
ESTEC.........	European Space Research Technology Center (CCCA)
ESTJ	Extroversion Sensing Thinking Judging (ADWA)
e-store........	Electronic Store (ADWA)
ESTP..........	Extroversion Sensing Thinking Perception (ADWA)
ESW..........	Enhanced Sludge Washing (ABAC)
ESWL.........	Electrohydraulic Shock Wave Lithotripsy (ADWA)
ET.............	Endotrachial (ADWA)
ET.............	Extended Technology (ITCA)
ET.............	External Training (HEAS)
ETA...........	Embryo Toxicity Assay (ADWA)
e-tailing......	Electronic Retailing (ADWA)
ETAW.........	Evapotranspiration of Applied Water (ADWA)
ETB...........	Environmental Technology Building (ABAC)
ETC...........	Expected Time of Completion (RIMS)
ETD...........	Expected Time of Departure (RIMS)
E-TDMA.......	Enhanced Time Division Multiple Access (CGWS)
ETDN	Electronic Ticket Delivery Network [Travel industry] (TRID)
ETEC..........	Enteroinvasive Escherichia Coli (ADWA)
ETF...........	Earth Terminal Facility (CCCA)
ETF...........	Embryo Toxic Factor (ADWA)
ETFS..........	Exchange-Traded Funds
ETG...........	Enhanced Target Generator (CTAS)
Eth...........	Ethiopian (ADWA)
Eth...........	Ethylene (RIMS)
ethnol........	Ethnologist (ADWA)
E ticket.......	Electronic Ticket [Travel industry] (TRID)
ETP...........	Early Termination of Pregnancy (ADWA)
ETPS..........	Educational Theorem Proving System (IDAI)
ETR...........	Equal Transit Rate (ADWA)
Etr...........	Etruria (ADWA)
e-trader	Electronic Trader (ADWA)
ETS	Electrical Transcranial Stimulation (DIPS)
ETS	European Telephone Service (CCCA)
ETS	Expected Time of Sailing (RIMS)
ETSR..........	Extraterrestrial Solar Spectral Irradiance (ADWA)
ETS-VIII	Engineering Test Satellite-VIII [Developed to study geostationary satellite bus technologies]
etym..........	Etymology (NTIO)
eu.............	Entropy Unit (ABAC)
EUP...........	Early Upper Paleolithic
euph	Euphonium
euphem	Euphemistic (ADWA)
EUS...........	Esophageal Ultrasonography (ADWA)
EUT...........	End User Terminal
eV.............	Electron Volt (ABAC)
ev.............	Evening (ADWA)
evac..........	Evacuation
eval	Evaluation (ADWA)
evan..........	Evangelist (ADWA)
evang.........	Evangelical (ADWA)
evap..........	Evaporate (ADWA)
eve...........	Evening (ADWA)
EVE...........	Exemplary Voluntary Effort (ABAC)
EVL...........	Electronic Visualization Laboratory
EVM...........	Evaluation Module (AEBE)
EVMS.........	Earned Value Management System [Army]
evn...........	Electric Violin
EVOL..........	Evolving Systems [NASDAQ symbol] (SG)
EW.............	Edwards Lifesciences [NYSE symbol] (SG)
EW.............	Egg White
EW.............	Electronic Welfare (CCCA)
e-wallet......	Electronic Wallet (ADWA)
EWGA.........	Executive Women's Golf Association (ADWA)
EWM..........	Weintraub Music [Publisher]
EWMP........	Efficient Water Management Practice (ADWA)
ex.............	Examination (ADWA)
ex.............	Executive (NTIO)
ex.............	Expenses (NTIO)
ex.............	Expiration (NTIO)
ex.............	Expires (NTIO)
ex.............	Express (NTIO)
ex.............	Extra
exam	Examination (ADWA)
exc...........	Excellent (NTIO)
exc...........	Except (ADWA)
exch..........	Exchange (NTIO)
excl..........	Excluding (ADWA)
exclaim......	Exclamation (ADWA)
EXEC..........	Execution Statement (ITCA)
EXEL..........	Exelixis, Inc. [NASDAQ symbol] (SG)
exfcy.........	Extra Fancy
EXFO..........	EXFO Electro-Optical Engineer [NASDAQ symbol]
exjbo	Extra Jumbo
exlge	Extra Large
EXLITE	Extended Life Tire (ADWA)

EXLOC .... Expanded Localizer (PIPO)
exlong .... Extra Long
exor .... Executor (ADWA)
EXP .... Expanded Polystyrene (HEAS)
Exp. .... Experience Balance [*Used in Rorschach tests*] (DIPS)
exp .... Experiment (ADWA)
exp .... Exponent (ADWA)
expat .... Expatriate (ADWA)
expd .... Experienced (ADWA)
expr .... Expressing (ADWA)
expt .... Experiment (ADWA)

expt .... Export
exptl .... Experimental (ADWA)
expwy .... Expressway (ADWA)
expy .... Expressway (NTIO)
exrx .... Executrix (ADWA)
EXST .... Extra Seat [*Travel industry*] (TRID)
ext .... Executor (ADWA)
ext .... Extended (NTIO)
ext .... Extinction (DIPS)
ext .... Extremity (ADWA)
EXTN .... Extensity, Inc. [*NASDAQ symbol*] (SG)
Ezk .... Ezekiel (ADWA)

F

By Acronym

F .... Fail (ADWA)
f .... Farthing (ADWA)
f .... Feminine (ADWA)
f .... Fluency (DIPS)
F .... Fly [*Baseball term*] (NDBD)
F .... Flyout [*Baseball term*] (NDBD)
f .... Focal Distance (NTIO)
F .... Form Response [*Used in Rorschach test scoring*] (DIPS)
F .... Foul Fly [*Baseball term*] (NDBD)
F .... F ratio (DIPS)
f .... Luminous Flux (DIPS)
F .... Variance Ratio (DIPS)
F/A .... Fire and Accident [*Insurance*] (MARI)
FA61 .... Factories Act 1961 (HEAS)
FAA .... Fluid Applied Asphalt (ABAC)
FAACTS .... Free Aids Advice Counseling Treatment Support (ADWA)
FAAGL .... Foundation of the American Association of Gynecologic Laparoscopists (ADWA)
FAALC .... Federal Aviation Administration Logistics Center (ADWA)
fab .... Fabulous (ADWA)
FAB .... Fraction Actually Burned (CARB)
FABF .... Fraction of Agri-Residue Burned in Fields (CARB)
fac .... Facilities (ADWA)
fac .... Facsimile (NTIO)
FAC .... Federal Advisory Committee
FAC .... Florida Administrative Code (DEMM)
FAC .... Forward Air Controller [*Military*]
FAC .... Freestanding Ambulatory (ADWA)
FACES .... Fund for African and African-American Cultural and Educational Solidarity, Inc.
FACM .... Functional Analytic Causal Model (DIPS)
FACMPE .... Fellow of the American College of Medical Practice Executives (ADWA)
FACNP .... Fellow of the American College of Nuclear Physicians (ADWA)
Fac/Oblig ..... Facultative/Obligatory (MARI)
FAD .... Fraction Actually Degrades (CARB)
FADD .... Feline Attention Deficit Disorder
FADEC .... Full Authority Digital Electronic Control
FAF .... Food and Agriculture Forum
FAFNAR .... Financial Aid Form Need Analysis Report
FAGR .... Fractional Antedating Goal Response (DIPS)
Fah .... Fahrenheit (ADWA)
FAHCT .... Foundation for the Accreditation of Hematopoietic Cell Therapy (ADWA)
Fahr .... Fahrenheit (NTIO)
FAID .... Factory and Agricultural Inspectorate Division (HEAS)
FAIM .... Fair Market, Inc. [*NASDAQ symbol*] (SG)
FAIM .... Foundation for the Advancement of Innovative Medicine (ADWA)
FALIA .... Fellow of the Australian Library and Information Association
fam .... Familiar (NTIO)
FAM .... Family Channel (ADWA)
FAM .... Fuzzy Associative Memory (IDAI)
FAMC .... Federal Agricultural Mortgage Corporation (ADWA)
Fam LQ .... Family Law Quarterly [*A publication*]
FAMR .... Family Resources
FAN .... Fetal Alcohol Network (ADWA)
f and a .... Fore and Aft (ADWA)
F&AP .... Fire and Allied Perils [*Insurance*] (MARI)
F&Ex .... Fire and Explosion (HEAS)
F&GPC .... Finance and General Purposes Committee (HEAS)
F&O .... Facilties and Operations (ABAC)
F&R .... Functions and Requirements (ABAC)
fanzine .... Fan Magazine (ADWA)
FAP .... Familial Adenomatous Polyposis
FAP .... Familial Polyposis Coli Gene [*Medicine*]
FAP .... Final Approach Point (PIPO)
Far .... Faraday (ADWA)
FAR .... Fetus at Risk [*Medicine*] (DIPS)
FAR .... Field Action Request (CTAS)
FAR .... Free of Accident Reported (MARI)
FARA .... Formula Air Racing Association (PIAV)
fas .... Fascicle (ADWA)
FAS .... Final Approach Segment (PIPO)
FAS .... For a Second [*Internet dialog*]
FAS .... Free Alongside Steamer (MARI)
FASCODE ..... Fast Atmospheric Signature Code (ARMP)

FASS........... Federation of Animal Science Societies
FAST........... Fast Auroral Snapshot Explorer
FasT........... Federal Assessment Team [*Department of Emergency Management*] (DEMM)
FAST........... Folding Articulated Square Truss (SPST)
FAST........... Food Allergy Survivors Together (ADWA)
FAST........... Fourier Amplitude-Sensitivity Test (CARB)
fath............ Fathom (ADWA)
FB............. Fraction Burned Annually (CARB)
FBA............. Functional Behavioral Assessment
FBB............. Federal Bulletin Board (ADWA)
FBCR.......... Filter Bank Combiner Radiometer (CCCA)
FBF............. FleetBoston Financial
FBFM.......... Flood Boundary Floodway Map (ADWA)
FBN............. Fly-by-Night (HLLA)
FBO............. Fixed Base Operation (PIPO)
FBOC.......... Figural Bottle Opener Collectors (ADWA)
FBX............. First City Bank [*AMEX symbol*] (SG)
FC............. Figures and Captions
FC............. Fire Control (ADWA)
fc............. Foot-Candle (NTIO)
FC............. Foster Care
FCA............. Free Carrier (RIMS)
fcap............ Foolscap (ADWA)
fcc............. Face-Centered Cubic (ABAC)
FCC............. Fleet Command Control (CCCA)
FCC............. Fractional Cloud Cover (ARMP)
FCCA.......... Florida-Caribbean Cruise Association (TRID)
FCCI............ Fuel-Cladding Chemical Interaction (ABAC)
FCG............. Field Consultant Group (HEAS)
fch............. Franchise (MARI)
FCI............. Family Care International (ADWA)
FCIM........... Federated Council for Internal Medicine (ADWA)
FCL............. Foldback Current Limiter (ADWA)
FCL............. Fuel-Cell Energy
FCLB........... Federation of Chiropractic Licensing Boards (ADWA)
FCN............. Facilities Change Notice (ABAC)
FCO............. Facility Control Office (CCCA)
FCOD.......... Fire, Collision, Overturning, and Derailment [*Insurance*] (MARI)
FCP............. Final Control Point (PIPO)
fcp............. Foolscap (ADWA)
FCP............. Fracture Control Plan (SPST)
FCPWG........ Federal Credit Policy Working Group
FCR............. Family Court Reporter [*A publication*]
FCR............. Forwarding Agents' Certificate of Receipt [*Insurance*] (MARI)
FCS............. Fiber Channel Standard [*Computer science*] (ITCA)
FCS............. Future Combat System [*Army*]
FCSSRCC..... Free of Capture, Seizure, Strikes, Riots, and Civil Commotions [*Insurance*] (MARI)
fcst............. Forecast (PIAV)
FCT............. Forwarding Agents' Certificate of Transport [*Insurance*] (MARI)
FCV............. Free-Column Volume (ABAC)
FCV............. Full Contract Value [*Insurance*] (MARI)
FCVC.......... Flow Controlled Virtual Circuit (MLOA)
fcy............. Fancy (ADWA)
FD............. Fire Break Door (MARI)
FD............. Foundation Damage (ADWA)
FD............. Frame Discard (MLOA)
FD............. Functional Directory (HEAS)
FD&C.......... Food, Drugs, and Cosmetics (NTIO)
FDD........... Freight, Demurrage, and Defence [*Insurance*] (MARI)
FDD........... Freight Demurrage Deadfreight (RIMS)
FDE........... Failure Detection Electronics (ADWA)
FDIS........... Free Discharge (RIMS)
FDISK......... Fixed Disk (ADWA)
FDLE.......... Florida Department of Law Enforcement (DEMM)
FDMU .... Flight Data Management Unit (HLLA)
FDNB .... Fluoro-2, 4-Dinitrobenzene (ADWA)
FDO........... For Declaration Purposes Only (MARI)
FDOR.......... Four-Door Car (TRID)
FDP............. Fatigue Decreased Proficiency [*NASA*] (SPST)
FDR............. Formal Dining Room (ADWA)
FDROTFL..... Falling Down Rolling on the Floor Laughing (ADWA)
FDX............. Full Duplex
FE .... Field Evaluation (CTAS)
FEA............. Far East (CARB)

FEA	Fire Extinguishing Appliances (MARI)
FEC	Forward Error Control (CCCA)
FEC	Full Economic Cost
FECA	Florida Electrical Cooperative Association (DEMM)
fed	Federal (NTIO)
fed	Federated (ADWA)
FED	Field Emission Device (ADWA)
FEDIX	Federal Information Exchange, Inc.
FEDMAP	Federal Geologic Mapping Project (CARB)
fedn	Federation (ADWA)
FEHEM	Front-End Hardward Emulator (ADWA)
FEIL	Florida Emergency Information Line (DEMM)
FEL	Felicity [Television program title]
FeLV	Feline Leukemia Virus (ADWA)
fem	Female (NTIO)
FEMA	Finite Element Model of Material Transport through Aquifers (CARB)
FEMIS	Federal Emergency Management Information System (ABAC)
Fem LS	Feminist Legal Studies [A publication]
FEMP	Facility Effluent Monitoring Plan (ABAC)
FEN	Fenfluramine [Medicine] (DIPS)
FEOM	Full Extraocular Movement (ADWA)
FEPD	Finance Efficiency and Planning Division (HEAS)
FER	Fundamental Expenditure Review (HEAS)
FERT	Federal Emergency Response Team (DEMM)
FET	Field-Emission Transistor (ABAC)
FETC	Federal Energy Technology Center
FETLA	Further Extended Three-Letter Acronym (ADWA)
FEU	Functionally Equivalent Unit (SPST)
feud	Feudalism (ADWA)
FEV	Forced Expectorant Volume [Medicine]
ff	Folios (ADWA)
ff	Fortissimo (ADWA)
FF	Free Format (CARB)
FFB	Foundation Fighting Blindness (ADWA)
FFDE	Fit for Duty Evaluation (DIPS)
fff	Fortississimo (ADWA)
FFI	Flexible Film Isolator (HEAS)
FFMC	Federal Financial Managers Council
FFR	For Future Reference [Internet dialog]
FG	Fidelity Guarantee [Insurance] (MARI)
FG	Fine Grain (ADWA)
FG	Functional Group
FGCS	Future Ground Combat Systems [Army]
FGF-2	Fibroblast Growth Factor-2
FGTS	Flammable Gas Tank Safety (ABAC)
FGU	From the Ground Up (MARI)
FH	Food for the Hungry (ADWA)
FHBC	Federation of Historical Bottle Clubs (ADWA)
FHBM	Floodway Hazard Boundary Map (ADWA)
FHCQ	Foundation for Health Care Quality (ADWA)
FHFA	Florida Housing Finance Agency (DEMM)
FHI	Food for the Hungry International (ADWA)
FHINC	Friday Holidays Included (RIMS)
FHMO	Federal Hazard Mitigation Officer (DEMM)
FHP	Florida Highway Patrol (DEMM)
fhp	Friction Horsepower (ADWA)
FHR	Fetal Heart Rhythm [Medicine] (ADWA)
FHST	Fixed Head Star Tracker
FHST	Fixed Head Star Trackers
FHTL	First-Class Hotel (TRID)
FIA	Facility Inventory Assessment (ABAC)
FIA	Feline Infectious Anemia (ADWA)
FIA	Fire Island Association
FIAC	Foundries Industry Advisory Committee (HEAS)
FIAS	Flow-Injection Analysis System (ABAC)
FIC	Factory Inspectorate Circular (HEAS)
fict	Fiction (NTIO)
fict	Fictitious (ADWA)
fid	Fidelity (ADWA)
FiFI	Fire Fighting (RIMS)
fig	Figuratively (ADWA)
FIGS	Fully Integrated Groups (ADWA)
FIL	Father-in-Law (ADWA)
FIM	Factory Inspectorate Minute (HEAS)
FIM	Flight Interruption Manifest [Travel industry] (TRID)
FIN	Factory Inspectorate Note (HEAS)
fin	Finish (ADWA)
Fin	Finland (NTIO)
Fin	Finnish (ADWA)
FIN	Fish Information Network (CARB)
fin indep	Financially Independent (ADWA)
Finn	Finnish (ADWA)
FINS	Fire Island National Seashore
fin sec	Financially Secure (ADWA)
FINU	Finance Unit (HEAS)
FIOST	Free In and Out Stowed and Trimmed (RIMS)
FIRA	Furniture Industry Research Association (HEAS)
FIRE	Fire Pond, Inc. [NASDAQ symbol] (SG)
fireplc	Fireplace (ADWA)
FIRST	Far Infrared and Submillimeter Telescope
FIRSTCHA	First Access Channel (CGWS)
FIRSTCHP	First Paging Channel (CGWS)
FIS	Fennoscandian Ice Sheet
FIS	Flood Insurance Study (ADWA)
FISM	Factory Inspectorate Specialist Minute (HEAS)

FIT	Free in Trimmed (RIMS)
FITL	Flight Increment Training Load [NASA] (SPST)
FK	Fish Kill (AUEG)
FL	Flexileave (HEAS)
fl	Floor (NTIO)
fl	Flute
FLAGU	Flammables and Gas Policy Unit (HEAS)
FLAS	Foreign Language and Area Studies
FLASH	Fast Low-Angle Shots
FLC	Federal Laboratory Consortium (ABAC)
FLC	Ferroelectric
FLD	L.A.T. Sportswear [AMEX symbol] (SG)
FLDOT	Florida Department of Transportation (DEMM)
fl dr	Fluid Dram (NTIO)
flg	Flugelhorn
FLIM	Fluoresence Lifetime Imaging Microscopy
FLIP	Family Limited Partnership
flmb	Film Bagged
flmw	Film Wrapped
flmwrpd	Film Wrapped
FLNG	Florida National Guard (DEMM)
fl oz	Fluid Ounce (NTIO)
FLP	Flameproof (HEAS)
FLR	Family Law Reports [A publication]
FLSASP	Florida State Agency for Surplus Property (DEMM)
flt	Flat
flt	Flight (TRID)
FLTF	Field Lysimeter Testing Facility (ABAC)
FLTOPS	Fleet Operations (CCCA)
FLUTD	Feline Lower Urinary Tract Disorder
FM	Friends of Mineralogy
fm	From (NTIO)
FMA	Fibromyalgia Syndrome
FMAP	Flood Mitigation Assistance Program (DEMM)
FMAS	Financial Management Accounting System (HEAS)
FMCDU	Flight Management Control and Display Unit (HLLA)
FMD	Financial Markets Development
FMD	Fluorescent Multilayer Disc
FMD-ROM	Fluorescent Multilayer Disk
FMGEC	Flight Management Guidance Envelope Computer (HLLA)
FMGP	Fungal Mitochondrial Genome Project
FMI	Fermilab Main Injector
FMP	Florida Marine Patrol (DEMM)
fMRI	Functional Magnetic-Resonance-Imaging (DIPS)
FMS	Fathoms (RIMS)
FMS	Fibromyalgia Syndrome
FMU	Field Management Unit (HEAS)
F/N	Fixing Note (RIMS)
FNAR	Financial Need Analysis Report
FNARS	Federal National Radio System (DEMM)
FNATS	Federal National Teletype System (DEMM)
FNAVS	Federal National Voice System (DEMM)
FNCS	Food, Nutrition, and Consumer Service
FNS	Fuzzy Neuron Syndrome
FNT	Frontline Communications [AMEX symbol] (SG)
FNT Pr	Frontline Commun. Cv'B' Pfd. [AMEX symbol] (SG)
FOA	Full Operational Assessment (CTAS)
FOB	Fiberoptic Bronchoscope
FOB	Fuel-Oil Blend (ABAC)
FOC	Fleet Operational Center (CCCA)
FOC	Free of Claims [Insurance] (MARI)
FOCC	Forward Analog Control Channel (CGWS)
FOCUS	Field Operations Computer System (HEAS)
FOD	Field Operations Directorate (HEAS)
FODabs	Free of Damage Absolutely [Insurance] (MARI)
FOG	Forecast Generator [Canadian natural language generation system] (IDAI)
FOG	For Our Guidance (RIMS)
fol	Folio (NTIO)
FOM	Flag, Ownership, or Management (MARI)
FOM	Formula One Management
FOM	Fortnightly Operational Minute (HEAS)
FOMMS	Flight Operations Maintenance Management System [NASA] (SPST)
FOP	Form of Payment (TRID)
for	Foreign (NTIO)
FORS	ForSoft Ltd.
FP	Fielding Percentage [Baseball term] (NDBD)
FP	Field Portable
FP	Final Payment (TRID)
FP	First Paragraph
fp	Freezing Point (NTIO)
FPA	Food and Environmental Protection Act (HEAS)
FPA	Free of Particular Average Unless Caused By (MARI)
FPA71	Fire Precautions Act 1971 (HEAS)
FPA Abs	Free of Particular Average Absolutely (MARI)
FPCM	Floor Plate-Conditioned Culture Medium
FPLD	Field Programmable Logic Device (AEBE)
fpm	Feet per Minute (PIAV)
FPR	Flight Planned Route (PIPO)
FPTPEC	France Pacific Territories National Committee for Pacific Economic Cooperation
FPU	Finance and Planning Unit (HEAS)
FPX	Kodak Flashpix Image Format
FQTV	Frequent Traveler (TRID)
fr	Fair

Fr	Father (NTIO)
FR	Fixed-Ratio Schedule of Reinforcement (DIPS)
FR	Flame Resistant (SARE)
FRA	Fuzzy Rule Approximation (IDAI)
FRAGO	Fragmentation Order [Army]
FRAV	First Available (TRID)
FRC	Financial Reconstruction Commission
FRC	Free of Reported Casualty [Insurance] (MARI)
FRC	Full Route Clearance [Aviation] (PIPO)
FRCMO	Floating Rate Collateralized Mortgage Obligation
Free Ex Ins	Free of any Extra Insurance (RIMS)
FRF	Field Record Form (ABAC)
FRGO	Fargo Electronics [NASDAQ symbol] (SG)
FRN	Friendly Ice Cream [AMEX symbol]
FRO	Fire Risk Only [Insurance] (MARI)
frof	Fire Risk on Freight [Insurance] (MARI)
FROG	Finished Room over Garage
FRP	Federal Response Plan (DEMM)
FRP	Fiber-Reinforced Polymer
FRS	Fleet Replacement Squadron [Military]
Fr wa	Fresh Water (RIMS)
FS	Fast-Spiking
fs	Femtosecond (ABAC)
FS	First Scan
FS	Flying Surgeon (NUJO)
FS	For Sale
FS	Free Sale (TRID)
FSA	Farm Service Agency
FSA	Farm Services Agency (DEMM)
FSA	Fluidic Self-Assembly [Allied Technology]
FSAC	Food Safety Advisory Centre (HEAS)
FSC	Forward Support Company [Military]
FSC	Fuel System Controller (HLLA)
FSCSS	Flexible Satellite Communications Systems Simulator (CCCA)
FSD	Flight Situation Display
FSD	Fluid System Design [NASA] (SPST)
FSDM	First Stage Digital Multiplexer (CCCA)
FSFC	Florida State Fire College (DEMM)
FSHN	Food Science and Human Nutrition
FSI	Fuzzy Singleton Inference (IDAI)
fsk	Frequency-Shift Keying
FSO	Fire Safety Officer (HEAS)
FSP	Family Support Plan
FSR	Fleet Street Reports [A publication]
FSR&CC	Free of Strikes, Riots, and Civil Commotion [Insurance] (MARI)
FSRC	Frontier Science Research Conferences
FSS II	Fear Survey Schedule II [Psychology] (DIPS)
FSST	Fastnet Corp. [NASDAQ symbol] (SG)
FSSU	Field Scientific Support Unit (HEAS)

FST	Field Sobriety Test (SARE)
FST	Finger Skin Temperature (HEAS)
FST	Frit Slurry Transport (ABAC)
FSV	Free Steered Vehicle (HEAS)
FSW	Forward-Swept Wing
FT	Fashion Technology
FT	For Trade
FT	Free Troposphere (CARB)
FTA	Feed Test Algorithm (ABAC)
ft-c	Foot-Candle (ABAC)
FTDMA	Fixed Time Division Multiple Access (CCCA)
FTF	Fisheries Task Force
fth	Fathom (NTIO)
FTH	Feedback Threshold (CCCA)
FTHL	Flag Telecom Hldgs. [NASDAQ symbol] (SG)
ftl	Faster Than Light (NTIO)
ft-L	Foot-Lambert (ABAC)
ftl	Foot-Lambert (DIPS)
ft-lb	Foot-Pound (NTIO)
FTO	Flying Training Organisation (PIAV)
FTP	Field Task Proposal (ABAC)
FTS	Federal Technology Service
ft/s	Feet per Second (ABAC)
FTS	Full Turbulence Simulation (CARB)
FTTA	Federal Technology Transfer Act (AUEG)
FUDS	Fluids Utility Distribution System [NASA] (SPST)
FUFOR	Fund for UFO Research, Inc.
fur	Furlong (NTIO)
furn	Furnished (NTIO)
FV	Flight Visibility (PIPO)
FVC	Forward Analog Voice Channel (CGWS)
FVS	Fetal Valproate Syndrome
F/W	Fly Wheels
FWAD	Fresh Water Arrival Draft (RIMS)
fwd	Forward (NTIO)
fwd	Fresh Water Damage [Insurance] (MARI)
FWDD	Fresh Water Departure Draft (RIMS)
FWF	Firewall Forward (PIPO)
FWIS	First World Communic 'B' [NASDAQ symbol] (SG)
FWP	Field-Work Proposal (ABAC)
FWPCA	Federal Water Pollution Control Act [1972] (CARB)
FWR	Functional Work Recording (HEAS)
FWWTA	Fraction of Waste Water Treated Anaerobically (CARB)
FYG	For Your Guidance (RIMS)
FYMOP	Five Year Master Objectives Program (CCCA)
FYP	Five Year Program (CCCA)
FYTD	Fiscal Year to Date (ABAC)
FYWP	Fiscal Year Work Plan (ABAC)
FZL	Freezing Level (ARMP)

G
By Acronym

G .... Acceleration of Gravity Force (PIPO)
g .... Gauss (ABAC)
G .... General Ability (DIPS)
G .... General Admission (NTIO)
GA .... Global Advisor
GA .... Gradient Angle (PIPO)
GA .... Green Arrow
G/A .... Ground to Air (PIPO)
GAAC .... General Aviation Awareness Campaign (PIAV)
GAAP .... Generally Accepted Accounting Principles
GAD .... General Average Deposit (MARI)
GADV .... Gross Arrived Damaged Value (MARI)
GAFOR .... General Aviation Visual Flight Forecast (PIAV)
GAI .... Guided Affected Imagery (DIPS)
GAL .... General Average Loss (MARI)
gal/d .... Gallons per Day (ABAC)
GALEX .... Galaxy Evolution Explorer
gal/min .... Gallons per Minute (ABAC)
gal/s .... Gallons per Second (ABAC)
GAM .... Generalized Additive Model (IDAI)
Gam .... Republic of The Gambia (NTIO)
GAMA .... General Aviation Manufacturers Association (PIAV)
G&C .... G & C Music Corporation
GAR .... Gate Acceptance Rate (CTAS)
GASBEND ... Good and Safe Port Both Ends (RIMS)
GASIL .... General Aviation Safety Information Leaflet (PIAV)
GASMAP ..... Gas Analysis System for Metabolic Analysis of Physiology [NASA] (SPST)
GASP .... Gas Accumulation Over Spreading Pools (HEAS)
GASV .... Gross Arrived Sound Value (MARI)
GATM .... Global Air Traffic Management (HLLA)
GB .... Barrel Racing [Rodeo term]
GBC .... GBI Capital Management [AMEX symbol] (SG)
gbo .... Goods in Bad Order (MARI)
GBS .... Global Broadcast Services
GBST .... Ground-Based Software Tool (HLLA)
GBT .... Green Bank Telescope (ROAS)
GBYSO .... Greater Boston Youth Symphony Orchestras (ROAS)
GC .... Gas Chromatography
GCCD .... Global Climate Change Digest [A publication]
gcd .... Greatest Common Divisor (NTIO)
GCD .... Ground Controlled Descent (ROAS)
gcf .... Greatest Common Factor (NTIO)
GCI .... General Circuit Interface
GCMD .... Global Change Master Directory [NASA]
GCP .... Glareshield Control Panel (HLLA)
GCRA .... Generic Cell Rate Algorithm (MLOA)
GCRIO......... Global Change Research Information Office
gcs............. Glasgow Coma Scale [Medicine]
GCSD .... Government Communications Systems Department (SPST)
GDA .... Gimbaled Dish Antenna (CCCA)
GDF .... Geophysical Data Facility
GDG .... Generation Data Group [Computer science] (ITCA)
GDN .... Group Dispatch Number (CGWS)
GDPO .... General Development Procedure Order (HEAS)
GEAE.......... GE Aircraft Engines
GED .... General Education Degree (DIPS)
GEDEX .... Greenhouse Effect Detection Experiment (CARB)
GEFD .... Geophysical and Environmental Fluid Dynamics
GEM .... Galileo Extended Mission
GEM .... Gemini (NTIO)
GEM .... Genetically Engineered Machine (ABAC)
GEM .... Geospace Environment Modeling (CARB)
gen .... Gender (NTIO)
Gen .... Genesis (NTIO)
GENESIS ..... Global Environmental and Ecological Simulation of Interactive System (CARB)
GenSAA ...... Generic Spacecraft Analyst Assistant (IDAI)
GENU .... Genuity, Inc. 'A' [NASDAQ symbol]
GEO .... Geostationary Earth Observation (CARB)
GEODS........ Ground Electro-Optical Deep Space Surveillance System (CCCA)
Geog........... Geographic
geog .... Geography (NTIO)
geol .... Geology (NTIO)
geom .... Geometry (NTIO)
GEOROT....... Geographical Rotation (RIMS)

Geosat......... Geodesy Satellite (CARB)
ger .... Gerund (NTIO)
GER .... Global Environmental Research
GERB .... Global Earth Radiation Budget
Germ .... German (NTIO)
GERT .... General Employee Radiation Training (SARE)
GEWEX .... Global Energy and Water Experiment (ARMP)
GF............... Grapple Fixture (SPST)
GFA............. Geophysical Focus Area (ARMP)
GFR .... Gromerular Filtration Rate
GFT .... General Flying Test (PIAV)
GG rate....... Guaranteed Group Rate [Travel industry] (TRID)
GH .... Gas Heater (CARB)
GHGB.......... Good Health is Good Business (HEAS)
GI............... Gender Identity (DIPS)
gi .... Gill (NTIO)
GI............... Global Indicator (TRID)
GI............... Guest Investigator
GICS .... Generic Intelligence Control System (ABAC)
GIF .... Graphics Interchange File [Computer science] (ITCA)
GIFTS.......... Geostationary Imaging Fourier Transform Spectrometer [NASA's proposed launch date is 2003]
GIGM .... Giga Media Ltd. [NASDAQ symbol] (SG)
GIILS .... Guide to Integrated Information Literacy Skills [A publication]
GIIR .... Grazing Incidence Infrared (ABAC)
GIPSA .... Grain Inspection, Packers, and Stockyards Administration
GIS .... Geographical Information System (ARMP)
GIT.............. Goods in Transit (MARI)
GIT.............. Group Inclusive Tour [Travel industry] (TRID)
GITS............ Government Information Technology Services
GL............... Green Lantern
GL............... Guiding Light [Television program title]
GLB TRG...... Global Trigger
GLD .... Generalized Logic Diagram (IDAI)
GLESS .... Gearless (RIMS)
GLFT........... Great Lakes Fishery Trust
gliss............ glissando (NTIO)
GLL............. Laidlaw Global [AMEX symbol]
glock........... Glockenspiel
GLSEN .... Gay, Lesbian, and Straight Education Network
GLW............ Gross Laden Weight (HEAS)
GLZ............. Window Glazing
GM .... Guidance Memoranda (HEAS)
GM .... GunMar Music [Publisher]
Gmb............ Good Merchantable Brand (MARI)
GMCC .... Ground Mobile Command Capability (CCCA)
GMP............ Genetically Modified Plant (CARB)
Gmq............ Good Merchantable Quality (MARI)
GMTC.......... Gland Manufacturers' Technical Committee (HEAS)
gmv............ Gram Molecular Volume (ABAC)
GN .... Georgian
GN .... Guidance Note (HEAS)
GNS .... German North Sea (RIMS)
GNS .... Global Navigation System (HLLA)
GNSSU........ Global Navigation Satellite Sensor Unit (HLLA)
GNT .... Genstar Therapeutics [AMEX symbol] (SG)
GO .... Goal Orientation (DIPS)
GO .... Guest Observer
GOAM .... GoAmerica, Inc. [NASDAQ symbol] (SG)
GOB .... General, Organic, and Biochemistry
GOCE .... Gravity Field and Steady State Ocean Circulation Explorer
GOCL-II........ Gordon Occupational Check List II [A checklist of 240 descriptions of activities related to occupations that do not require a college degree, developed by L.V. Gordon] (DIPS)
GOES .... Geostationary Observatory Earth Satellite (CCCA)
GOES .... Geostationary Orbiting Environmental Satellite
GOES-M....... Geostationary Operational Environmental Satellite M [NASA]
GOES-N....... Geostationary Operational Environmental Satellite N [NASA]
GOES-O........ Geostationary Operational Environmental Satellite O [NASA launch date proposed for April 2004]
GOF .... Global Ocean Flux (CARB)
GOI .... Government of India (CARB)
GOIN .... Global Observation Information Network (CARB)
GOLIP .... Ground Operations and Logistics Integration Panel [NASA] (SPST)
GOMI .... Global Ozone Monitoring Instrument (CARB)
GoS............. Grade of Service (CGWS)

GP..............	Gas Producer
GPARS........	Generic Phased Array Radar Simulator (CCCA)
GPB	Gravity Probe B
GPC	Graphics Performance Characterization (AEBE)
GPCI	Graphics Processor Command Interface
GPE............	Gas Phase Etching
GPF............	General Purpose Facilities (ABAC)
gph	Gallons per Hour (PIAV)
GPI.............	Ground Point of Interception (PIPO)
GPIRS	Global Positioning/Inertial Reference System (HLLA)
gpm	Gallons per Minute (ABAC)
GPR	Good Partial Remission [*Medicine*]
GPRS	General Packet Radio Service
GPRS	General Packet Radio System
gps............	Gallons per Second (ABAC)
GPS	General Problem Solving (IDAI)
GPS	Good Practices Standard (ABAC)
GPSP	General Purpose Simulation Program [*Computer science*] (ITCA)
GPSS	General Purpose Satellite System (CCCA)
GPSSU........	Global Positioning System Sensor Unit (HLLA)
GPST	Group Seat Request [*Travel industry*] (TRID)
GPU	Group Personnel Unit (HEAS)
GR	Gender Role (DIPS)
gr...............	Great (NTIO)
Gr	Greek (NTIO)
grad............	Graduated (NTIO)
GRAPE........	Gravity Pipe [*A specialized computer*]
GRAS	Generally Regarded as Safe (NTIO)
GRB	Gamma-Ray Bursters
GRC	Gordon Research Conferences
Grd.............	Grade
GRE	Gas Release Event (ABAC)
GRE	General Research Equipment (ABAC)
GRE	Government Research Establishment
GRID...........	Gay-Related Immune Deficiency (DIPS)
grid OD........	Grid Organizational Development (DIPS)
GRIF	Graduate Research, Internship, and Fellowshhip
GRIT	Graduated and Reciprocated Initiatives in Tension Reduction [*C. Osgood*] (DIPS)
GRL	Government Research Laboratories
GRNN..........	General Regression Neural Network (IDAI)
GRP	Grant Prideco [*NYSE symbol*] (SG)
GS..............	Grand Slam [*Baseball term*] (NDBD)
G/S.............	Groundspeed [*Aviation*] (PIAV)
GS..............	G. Schirmer, Inc. [*Publisher*]
GSA	Geographical Service Area (CGWS)
GSBR..........	Geosynchronous Space Based Radar (CCCA)
GSC	Golay Sequential Coding (CGWS)
GSC	Guide Star Catalog
GSCH..........	Gesell Developmental Schedules [*Clinical method for the study of sensorimotor growth of preschool children*] (DIPS)
GSFP	Group Soviet Forces Germany (CCCA)
GSL.............	Gulf Stream Locale (CARB)
GSN	Gifted with Special Needs
GSN	Global Seismic Network (CARB)
GSOL	Global Sources [*NASDAQ symbol*] (SG)
GSPDC........	Geostationary Satellite Precipitation Data Centre (CARB)
GSRN..........	Global Surface Radiation Network (CARB)
GSSC	General Support Services Contractor (ABAC)
GSSP	Generally Accepted System Security Principles [*Computer science*] (ITCA)
GST............	Greenwich Standard Time (NTIO)
G/T..............	Gain to System Noise Temperature (CCCA)
GT..............	Gun to Target
GTE.............	General Telephone & Electric Company (CCCA)
GTF.............	Generalized Trace Facility [*Computer science*] (ITCA)
GTIA............	Golf and Travel Industry Association (TRID)
GTL.............	Gunning Transceiver Logic (AEBE)
GTP.............	General Third Party [*Insurance*] (MARI)
GTSB	Glyphosate-Tolerant Soya Beans
GTSB	Glyphosate-Tolerant Soybeans
GTTLB.........	GT Group Telecom 'B' [*NASDAQ symbol*] (SG)
Guad...........	Guadelupe (NTIO)
guar............	Guarantee (NTIO)
guar............	Guaranteed (NTIO)
GUARNG......	Guam Army National Guard
GW..............	Glaxo Wellcome
GWDU.........	Ground Window Display Utility [*NASA*] (SPST)
GWP............	Gross Written Premiums [*Insurance*] (MARI)
GWRAC.......	General World Radio Administrative Conference (CCCA)
GWRBI........	Game-Winning Run Batted In [*Baseball term*] (NDBD)
GWS	Groundwater Surveillance (ABAC)
GWTSA	Gamma-Weighted Two-Stream Approximation (ARMP)
gyn..............	Gynecology (NTIO)

H
By Acronym

H	Hazards (PIPO)
H	Hold [*Baseball term*] (NDBD)
h	Hour (NTIO)
H	Human Figure (DIPS)
h	Hybrid
h	Precision of Process (DIPS)
HA	Hatch (RIMS)
Ha	Hawaii (NTIO)
HAA	Heterocyclic Aromatic Amines
HAAP	High-Altitude Aerial Photograph (CARB)
HACD	Home Area Customer Dialing (ROAS)
HACMP	High Availability Cluster Multi-Processing [*IBM Corp.*]
HAI	Helicopter Association International (TRID)
HALSS	High-Altitude Lidar Sensing Station (CARB)
HAM	Hand Held Monitor (HEAS)
HAMOCC	Hamburg Ocean Carbon Cycle
HANA	Hanaro Telecom ADS [*NASDAQ symbol*] (SG)
HAND	Handspring, Inc. [*NASDAQ symbol*]
H&K	Heckler & Koch
HARB	Homestead Air Reserve Base (DEMM)
HARM	Harwell Acid Rain Model
HaRP	Harrier Review Panel [*Military*]
HARRTF	Hurricane Andrew Recovery and Reconstruction Trust Fund (DEMM)
HASAC	Health and Safety Advice Centre (HEAS)
HASCOG	Health and Safety Co-Ordinating Group (HEAS)
HASP	Houston Automatic Spooling Program [*Computer science*] (ITCA)
HAVi	Home Audio Video Interoperability
HAWNA	Hawaiian Studies
HazCom	Hazard Communication (SARE)
HAZMIT	Hazard Mitigation (DEMM)
HB	Hyperion Bay [*Television program title*]
HBF	Harmless Bulk Fertilizer (RIMS)
HBFG	Host Behavior Functional Group
HBIG	Hepatitis B Immunoglobulin (HEAS)
HBP	Hit by Pitch [*Baseball term*] (NDBD)
HBSA	Harvard Business School Association (COBU)
HC	Health Circular (HEAS)
HC	Heptachlor (ABAC)
HC	Hydraulic Conductivity (ABAC)
HC	Hypothetical Construct (DIPS)
hca	Harmonica
HCA	Heterocyclicamine
HCB	Hexachlorobutadeine (ABAC)
HCCD	Historical Canadian Climate Database (CARB)
HCCI	Health Care Coordination Initiative [*Federal Government of Canada, Veterans Affairs*]
HCE	Heptachlor Epoxide (ABAC)
HCE	Human Capital Exchange
HCl	Hydrogen Chloride (ABAC)
HCL	Hardware Compatibility [*Computer science*]
HCQIP	Health Care Quality Improvement Program
HCS	Host Computer System (CTAS)
HD	Hard Disk (AEBE)
HDD	High-Density Disk [*Computer science*] (ITCA)
Hdg	Heading (PIAV)
HDL	High-Level Design Language (AEBE)
HDLCM	High Density Line Conditioning Module
HDLTSBENDS	Half Despatch Lay Time Saved Both Ends (RIMS)
hdqrs	Headquarters (NTIO)
HDR	HPSC, Inc. [*AMEX symbol*]
HDRL	High-Dose Reference Laboratory (CARB)
HDSL	High Density Subscriber Loop (CGWS)
HDU	Heat-Dissipation Unit (ABAC)
HDWTS	Half Demurrage Weather Timed Saved (RIMS)
HEAD	Higher Education Affairs Directorate
HEAL	Health Education and Adult Literacy
HEAS	Health Effects Assessment (AUEG)
HEC	Header Error Check (MLOA)
HEC	High Energy Corona (ABAC)
HECB	Higher Education Coordinating Board
heck	Heckelphone
HEDNA	Hotel Electronic Distribution Network Association (TRID)
HEDSET	Harmonised Electronic Data Set (HEAS)
HEL	Hazard Evaluation Laboratory Limited [*Herts, England*]
HELDK	Helicopter Deck (RIMS)
HELLO	Helping Educators Link Learners Online
HEMF	High-Efficiency Metal Fiber (ABAC)
HERA	Hadron-Electron Ring Accelerator
HeRA	Hermes Robotic Arm
HES	Home Electronic Systems (HEAS)
HESSI	High Energy Solar Spectroscopic Imager [*NASA*]
HEW	Half Energy Width
HEX	Helsinki Exchanges Group Ltd Oy
hex	Hexadecimal (AEBE)
hex	Hexagon (NTIO)
HFC	Hybrid Fiber Coaxial
HFDL	High Frequency Data Link (HLLA)
HFL	Highly Flammable Liquid (HEAS)
HFSM	High Fidelity Simulation Model (SPST)
hgt	Height (NTIO)
HH	Her Highness (NTIO)
HH&E	Human Health and the Environment (SARE)
HHE	Health Hazard Evaluation (HEAS)
HI	Hazard Installation (HEAS)
HI	High-Intensity Lights (PIPO)
HIAL	High Intensity Approach Lighting [*Aviation*] (PIAV)
HIG	Hazardous Installation Group (HEAS)
HII	Healthcare Integrated Svcs. [*AMEX symbol*] (SG)
HILJ	Harvard International Law Journal [*A publication*]
HIMSS	High-Resolution Microwave Spectrometer Sounder (CARB)
Hind	Hindi (NTIO)
HIP	Higher Intermediate Point (TRID)
HIPAA	Health Insurance Portability & Accountability Act
HIPU	Hazardous Installation Policy Unit (HEAS)
HIRDLS	High Resolution Dynamics Limb Sounder
HIRL	High Intensity Runway Edge Lights (PIPO)
HIRLAM	High-Resolution Limited Area Model (ARMP)
HIRS	Health Information Resources Service
HISL	High Intensity Strobe Light [*Aviation*] (PIAV)
hist	Historical (NTIO)
HITRAN	High-Resolution Transmission (ARMP)
HITRAN	High Resolution Transmission Molecular Absorption Database (CARB)
HKCPEC	Hong Kong Committee for Pacific Economic Cooperation
HL	High Latitude (ARMP)
HL	Holds List [*Travel industry*] (TRID)
HLC	Heavy Lift Capability
HLDW	High-Level Defense Waste (ABAC)
HLOS	High Level Languages Operations per Second (CCCA)
HLR	Housing Law Reports [*A publication*]
HLS	Hyperbaric Lighting Set [*NASA*] (SPST)
HLWS	High-Level Waste Solidification (ABAC)
hm	Hectometer (ABAC)
HM	Her Majesty (NTIO)
HMAC	Hot Mix Asphaltic Concrete (ABAC)
HMAI	Her Majesty's Agricultural Inspectorate (HEAS)
HMBP	Hazardous Materials Business Plans (SARE)
HMD	HLM Design [*AMEX symbol*] (SG)
HME	Hierarchical Mixtures of Experts (IDAI)
HMEI	Her Majesty's Explosives Inspectorate (HEAS)
HMEP	Hazardous Materials Emergency Preparedness (DEMM)
HMGP	Hazard Mitigation Grant Program (DEMM)
HMIG	Hazardous Materials Indentification Guide (SARE)
HMIM	Her Majesty's Inspectorate of Mines (HEAS)
HMIPIS	Her Majesty's Industrial Pollution Inspectorate for Scotland (HEAS)
hmn	Harmonium
HMNII	Her Majesty's Nuclear Installations Inspectorate (HEAS)
HMO	Hazard Mitigation Officer [*Department of Emergency Management*] (DEMM)
HMS	Heavy Metal Scraps (RIMS)
hMSC	Human Mesenchymal Stem Cells
HMSU	High-Resolution Microwave Sounding Unit (CARB)
HN	Health Notice (HEAS)
HNC	Holistic Nurse Certified (NUJO)
HNMC	Honda New Model Center
HO	Homestead
HOD	Host-on-Demand [*Computer science*] (ITCA)
HOMG	Home Grocer.com, Inc. [*NASDAQ symbol*] (SG)
Hon	Honduras (NTIO)
Horg	Hammond Organ
hort	Horticultural (NTIO)
HOST	Healthcare Open Systems and Trials

HOT	High-Occupancy Toll Lane
HOUND	Humble, Old, Unattractive, Nonverbal, and Dumb (DIPS)
hp	Harp
HP	Highway Patrol (SARE)
HP	Hit by Pitch [*Baseball term*] (NDBD)
HPBID	Host Processor/Bus Interface Dedicated (SPST)
HPC	High Performance Computer
HPD	Health Policy Division (HEAS)
HPI	High-Pressure Isolation
HPLC	High-Precision Liquid Chromatography (CARB)
HPLMN	Home Public Lands Mobile Network (CGWS)
HPNA	Home Phoneline Networking Alliance
HPS	Hops per Second (CCCA)
HPT	Health Physics Technician (ABAC)
HPT	Home Pregnancy Test
HPU	Hand Portable Unit (CGWS)
HR	Heating Rate (ARMP)
HR	High Rise
HRA	Highlands Restricted Area (PIAV)
HRC	High Resolution Camera
HREE	Heavy Rare-Earth Elements
HRFIMS	High-Resolution Field-Ionization Mass Spectrometry (ABAC)
HRH	Her Royal Highness (NTIO)
HRLJ	Human Rights Law Journal [*A publication*]
HRNTB	Halstead-Reitan Neuropsychological Test Battery [*Intended to measure brain functioning*] (DIPS)
HROI	High-Resolution Optical Instrument (CARB)
HRPAO	Human Resources Professionals Association of Ontario [*Canada*]
HRR	Hardy-Rand-Rittler [*Test for color blindness*] (DIPS)
HRR	Health Risk Review (HEAS)
HRSS	High Resolution Surveillance System (CCCA)
HRTF	Head-Related Transfer Functions
HRU	Human Resources Unit (HEAS)
HRU	Hydrostatic Release Unit (TRID)
HS	Hazardous Substance (SARE)
HS	Hierarchical Sequential Organization [*Computer science*] (ITCA)
Hse	House
HSI	Hot Section Inspection [*Aviation*] (PIPO)
HSM	Hierarchical Storage Management [*Computer science*]
HSM	Hierarchic Sequential Access Method [*Computer science*] (ITCA)
HSO	Health & Safety Officer (SARE)
HSP	Highly Sensitive Person
HSP	High Speed Photometer
HSP	Hispanic Broadcasting 'A' [*NYSE symbol*]
HSPI	Health and Safety Policy Liaison (HEAS)
HSSPLAN	Health Service Support Plan [*Army*]
HT	Herald Tribune [*A publication*]
HT	Hilly Terrain (CGWS)
HTCE	Historical Tank Content Estimate (ABAC)
HTE	High Temperature Elongation
HTF	Hard to Find
HTHL	Horizontal Takeoff Horizontal Landing
HTLV	Human T-Cell Leukemia Virus (NTIO)
HTM	Held to Maturity
HTM	High Tempature Melter (ABAC)
HTP	House-Tree-Person (DIPS)
HTS	High-Temperature Superconducting
http	Hypertext Transport Protocol (CARB)
HTVL	Horizontal Takeoff Vertical Landing
HVCB	Hawaii Visitors and Convention Bureau (ROAS)
HVFL	Heavy Fuel (RIMS)
HVI	Hypervelocity Impact (SPST)
HVPM	High Vapor Pressure Metals (ABAC)
H/W	Heavy Weathering
HWAD	Hawthorne Army Depot [*Umatilla, Oregon*]
HWCL	Hazardous Waste Control Law [*California*] (SARE)
HWI	Hazardous Waste Inspectorate (HEAS)
HWIS	Hazardous Waste Information System (SARE)
HWMU	Hazardous Waste Management Units (SARE)
hwy	Highway (NTIO)
HX	Have Cancelled [*Travel industry*] (TRID)
HXD	Hard X-Ray Detector
H/Y	Heavy Tarnish
hyp	Hypotenuse (NTIO)
hypoth	Hypothesis (NTIO)
HYREX	Hydrological Radar Experiment
HZO	MarineMax
HzSC	Hazardous Substances Consent (HEAS)

I

By Acronym

I	Electric Flow in Amperes (NTIO)
I	Imaginary Number (NTIO)
I	Index Number (DIPS)
I	Induction (DIPS)
i	Interest (NTIO)
I	Introversion
IA	Immunoassay (ABAC)
IA	Import Administration
IA	Individual Assistance (DEMM)
IA	Iodine Absorber (ABAC)
IAARD	Integrated Avionics Architecture, Requirements, and Design (SPST)
IAB	Internet Activities Board (MLOA)
IAC	Integrated Avionics Computer (HLLA)
IADN	Integrated Atmospheric Deposition Network
IADRWG	Interagency Alternative Dispute Resolution Working Group
IAEGC	Inter-Agency Electronic Grants Committee
IAES	Interim Alternative Educational Setting
IAG	International Advisory Group
IAH	Internet Architect Holdrs. Tr. [AMEX symbol] (SG)
I&C	Instrumentation and Control (ABAC)
IAO	Individual Assistance Officer [Department of Emergency Management] (DEMM)
IAP	Incident Action Plan [Department of Emergency Management] (DEMM)
IAP	Inhibitor-of-Apoptosis
IAP	Internet Access Provider
IAQINFO	Indoor Air Quality Information Clearinghouse (AUEG)
IAR	Industrial All Risks (MARI)
IAR	Institute for Atmospheric Radioactivity [Feiberg, Germany] (CARB)
IAS	Index Amortizing Swap
IAS	Information and Advisory Services (HEAS)
IAS	Interdisciplinary American Studies
IASG	Internetwork Address Sub-Group
IASL	International Association of School Librarnship
IATAN	International Airlines Travel Agency Network (TRID)
IATAS	Interim Airborne Target Acquisition System (CCCA)
IATP	Institutional Admissions Testing Program
IAWT	International Association of World Tourism (TRID)
IBA	Interceptor Body Armor [Military]
IBB	Institute for British Business (COBU)
IBC	Institute Builders Risk Clause (MARI)
IBE	Institute of Biological Engineering
IBIS	Input Output Buffer Information Specification (AEBE)
IBMM	International Bluegrass Music Museum
IBM PC	International Business Machines Personal Computer (CARB)
IBN	ICICI Bank ADS [NYSE symbol] (SG)
IBNRPR	Incurred but Not Reported Properly [Insurance] (MARI)
IBOC	In-Band On-Channel
IBOMA	Inter-Bank Organisation and Methods Association (COBU)
IBP	International Biophysical Program (CARB)
IBPI	IntraBiotics Pharmaceuticals [NASDAQ symbol] (SG)
IBR	Incorporated by Reference (SARE)
IBS	Integrated Baseline System (ABAC)
IBSG	Internetwork Broadcast Sub-Group
IBSS	Institute of Biology of the Southern Seas
IBT	Illinois Bell Telephone (ROAS)
IBUFG	Internetwork Broadcast/Unknown Functional Group
IC	Incident Command (SARE)
i/c	Intercom (PIAV)
ICA	Independent Column Approximation (ARMP)
ICA	Independent Computing Architecture
ICAI	Intelligent Computer-Aided Instruction (IDAI)
ICALPE	International Centre for Alpine Environments [Chambery, France] (CARB)
ICAP	International Code Assessment and Applications Programme (HEAS)
ICAR	Intermediate-Size Car (TRID)
ICARUS	Imaging Cosmic and Rare Underground Signal
ICASVR	International Committee on Atmosphere-Soil-Vegetation Relations (CARB)
ICB	Interference Calibration Blank (ABAC)
ICBC	Insurance Corporation of British Columbia
ICBU	Intensive Care Baby Unit (ROAS)
ICBVI	Idaho Commission for the Blind and Visually Impaired (ROAS)
ICBW	I Could Be Wrong [Online dialog] (ROAS)
ICC	Institute Cargo Clauses (MARI)
ICC	International Communications Conference (CCCA)
ICCC	International Christian Chamber of Commerce (COBU)
ICCC	International Computer Communications Conference (CCCA)
ICCE	International Commission on Continental Erosion (CARB)
ICD	Interactive Call Distribution (ROAS)
ICDB	Ice Core Data Bank (CARB)
ICDP	Integrated Conservation and Development Project
Ice	Iceland (NTIO)
ICE	Illinois Computing Educators
ICE	Integrated Computer Environment (ABAC)
ICE	Interactive Collaborative Environment
ICE	Intrusion Countermeasures Electronics
ICEAR	International Centre for Equatorial Atmospheric Research [Indonesia] (CARB)
ICESS	Institute for Computational Earth System Science
ICFPM	International Centre for Fundamental Physics in Moscow
ICG	Institute of Careers Guidance (COBU)
ICG	Internet Capital Group
ICGW	International Commission on Ground Water (CARB)
ICH	International Countermeasures Handbook (CCCA)
ICI	Imperial Chemical Industries
ICL	Integrated Cloud Liquid (CARB)
ICM	Integrated Call Management
ICM	Internet Call Manager
ICMP	Internet Control Messaging Protocol (ITCA)
ICN	Infection Control Nurse (NUJO)
I/CO	Installation and Check Out (CTAS)
IConsA	Independent Consultants Association (COBU)
ICR	Image Character Recognition (IDAI)
ICRAF	International Centre for Research in Agroforestry
ICRC	International Committee of the Red Cross
ICS	Installation Control Specification [Computer science] (ITCA)
ICY	Packaged Ice [AMEX symbol]
Id	Idaho (NTIO)
ID	Identification (AEBE)
ID	Incapacitation Dose
ID	Inner Detector
id	Inner Diameter (NTIO)
ID	Integrated Demonstration (AUEG)
IDA	International Dark-Sky Association
IDAC	Internet Directory of Advisors and Consultants (COBU)
IDAL	Illinois Digital Academic Library
IDC	Integrated Demonstration Coordinator (ABAC)
IDD	Instrument Definition Document
IDD	Interface Design Document (CTAS)
IDE	Interior Design Engineering (SPST)
IDEA	International Institute for Democracy and Electoral Assistance
IDEAL	Initiating, Diagnosing, Establishing, Acting, Leveraging
IDELR	Individuals with Disabilities Education Law Report
IDH	IPI, Inc. [AMEX symbol] (SG)
IDI	Instrument Detection Limit (ABAC)
IDiagE	Institution of Diagnostic Engineers (COBU)
IDL	Interactive Data Language
IDR	Incremental Design Review (CTAS)
IDRD	Increment Definition Requirements Document (SPST)
IE	Individual Education (DIPS)
IEC	International Environmental Commitments
IECC	Integrated Electronic Control Centre (HEAS)
IECI	Independent Electrical Contractors, Inc. [An association]
IECQ	International Electronic Component Qualification
IED	Institution of Electrical Designers (COBU)
IEE	Independent Educational Evaluation
IEIC	Independent Engineering Insurers' Committee (HEAS)
IELTS	International English Language Testing System
IEM	Institute of Environmental Managers (COBU)
IEMA	Iowa Educational Media Association
IERI	Interagency Education Research Initiative
IES	Institute for Employment Studies (COBU)
IES	Institute of Employment Studies (HEAS)
IEUBK	Integrated Exposure Uptake Biokinetic Model (SARE)
IEV	Initial Entry Vehicle (ABAC)
IF	Infield [Baseball term] (NDBD)
IF	Infield Fly [Baseball term] (NDBD)
I/F	Interface (CTAS)
IF	Intermediate Facility (ARMP)
if	Intermediate Frequency (ABAC)
IFC	Institute Freight Clause (MARI)

IFCO............	IFCO Systems, NV [*NASDAQ symbol*] (SG)
IFD.............	Industrial Facilities Discharge (AUEG)
IFD.............	Instrument Flow Diagram (ABAC)
IFDC............	Interim Full Operating Capability (CCCA)
iff...............	If and Only If (NTIO)
IFF.............	Interrogate Friend or Foe (CCCA)
IFO..............	Intensive Field Observation (ARMP)
IFO..............	Intermediate Fuel Oil (RIMS)
IFTAA..........	International Forum of Travel and Tourism Advocates (TRID)
IFW.............	Inland Fisheries and Wildlife
IFX..............	Infineon Technologies ADS [*NYSE symbol*] (SG)
IG...............	Industry Group (HEAS)
IGA.............	Institute of Group Analysis (COBU)
IGasE...........	Institution of Gas Engineers (COBU)
IGETC..........	Intersegmental General Education Transfer Curriculum
IGRSS..........	International Geoscience and Remote Sensing Society (CARB)
IH&S...........	Industrial Hygiene and Safety (ABAC)
IHCP	Increment Hazard Control Plan (SPST)
IHIT............	Industrial Hygienist in Training (SARE)
IHospE	Institute of Hospital Engineering (COBU)
ihp..............	Indicated Horsepower (ABAC)
IHS.............	International Heliospheric Study (CARB)
IID..............	Interaural Intensity Differences
IIG.............	Indian Institute of Geomagnetism (CARB)
IIH.............	Internet Infrastruct Holdrs. Tr. [*AMEX symbol*] (SG)
IIID.............	International Institute of Information Design (CARB)
IIMR...........	Institute of Industrial Market Research (COBU)
IIMR...........	Institute of Investment Managers and Research (COBU)
IIP.............	Implementation and Integration Plan (CCCA)
IiP.............	Investors in People (HEAS)
IIPP............	Injury and Illness Prevention Program [*California*] (SARE)
IISX............	Integrated Information Sy. [*NASDAQ symbol*] (SG)
IITM...........	Indian Institute for Tropical Meteorology (CARB)
IL	Impact Level (ABAC)
ILA.............	Internet Learning Agent (IDAI)
ILB.............	Industry Lead Body (HEAS)
ILC.............	Independent Living Center
ILC.............	International Linear Collider
ILCI............	International Loss Control Institute (SARE)
ILETS..........	International Law Enforcement Telecommunications Seminar
ILIAD	IDEA Local Implementation by Local Administrators Partnership
ILL	Interlibrary Loan (AUEG)
ILMI...........	Interim Local Management Interface
ILOG	Institute of Logistics (COBU)
ILP.............	Inductive Logic Programming (IDAI)
ILRI............	International Livestock Research Institute
ILS.............	Industrial Law Society (HEAS)
ILS.............	Intermediate Level School
ILT.............	Industrial Language Training (HEAS)
ILT.............	Irish Law Times [*A publication*]
ILV.............	Indicative Limit Value (HEAS)
ILW.............	Integrated Liquid Water (ARMP)
IM-A1..........	Institute of Management (COBU)
IM-A1..........	Inorganic Monomeric Aluminum (CARB)
IMAPS	Integrated Military Airlift Planning System (CCCA)
IMB............	Information Management Branch (AUEG)
IMC............	Ice Mass Content (CARB)
IMC............	Intermediate Care Unit (NUJO)
IMDAA	Institute of Management Development Alumni Associates (COBU)
IME............	In My Experience [*Internet dialog*]
IMEO...........	In My Educated Opinion [*Internet dialog*]
IMEX...........	Inner Magnetosphere Explorer [*NASA*]
IMF............	Ice Mass Flux (CARB)
IMINT..........	Imagery Intelligence
IMIU...........	International Marine Insurance Union (MARI)
IML............	In My Life [*Internet dialog*]
IMLS...........	Institute of Museum and Library Services
IMMCL..........	Integrated Master Measurement and Command List (SPST)
immunol.........	Immunology (NTIO)
IMMV...........	Individual Mileage May Vary
IMNO	In My Noble Opinion [*Online dialog*]
IMO............	International Meteor Organization
IMP............	Ice Mass Path (CARB)
imp.............	Imported (NTIO)
IMPATT........	Impact Avalanche Transit Time (AEBE)
IMPT...........	IMPSAT Fiber Networks [*NASDAQ symbol*] (SG)
IMR............	Ice Mixing Ratio (ARMP)
IMS............	Instructional Management Systems
IMTA...........	International Mobile Telecommunications Association (CGWS)
IMW............	In My World [*Internet dialog*]
IN..............	Improvement Notice (HEAS)
IN..............	International (TRID)
INAD	Inadmissible Passenger [*Travel industry*] (TRID)
INADA	Investigational New Animal Drug Application
incl	Include
incldg	Including
incls............	Includes
INCPEC	Indonesian National Committee for Pacific Economic Cooperation
ind.............	Independence (NTIO)
Ind.............	Indian (NTIO)
indic............	Indicative (NTIO)
Ind LJ	Industrial Law Journal [*A publication*]
indus	Industrial (NTIO)
indus	Industry (NTIO)
Indus	Industry
INEEL..........	Idaho National Engineering and Environmental Laboratory
INFT...........	Inforte Corp. [*NASDAQ symbol*] (SG)
INKP...........	InKine Pharmaceutical
InLv	Independent Living
INRC...........	Identity, Negation, Reciprocal, and Correlative Transformations [*Developed by J. Piaget*] (DIPS)
ins	Inshell
INS.............	Involuntary Nervous System (DIPS)
INSAP	Inspiration of Astronomical Phenomena
INSN...........	InSilicon Corp. [*NASDAQ symbol*] (SG)
inst	Instant (NTIO)
inst	Instructional Manual
instr	Instructor (NTIO)
INTEGRAL....	International Gamma-Ray Astrophysics Laboratory [*Sponsored by European Space Agency*]
INTER	Interpolated Schedule of Reinforcement (DIPS)
Internic........	Internet Network Information Center
interrog........	Interrogative (NTIO)
intrans.........	Intransitive (NTIO)
INUR..........	Inventory Update Rule (SARE)
IOCP	Input/Output Configuration Program [*Computer science*] (ITCA)
IOE............	Initial Operating Experience (PIPO)
IOHS...........	International Occupational Hygiene Society (SARE)
IONL...........	International Organization of the Network Layer (ITCA)
IOP............	Increment Operations Plan (SPST)
IOP............	Intensive Operational Period (ARMP)
iop.............	Irrespective of Percentage (MARI)
IOTA...........	Infrared-Optical Telescope Array
IP..............	Independent Pixel (CARB)
IP..............	Industrial Plus (SARE)
IP..............	Input Port (CCCA)
IP..............	Integrated Program (ABAC)
IPA............	Independent Pixel Approximation (ARMP)
IPA............	Interaction-Process Analysis (DIPS)
IPA............	International Psychoanalytic Association
IPC............	Integrated Program Coordinator (ABAC)
IPC............	Inter Process Communication (CTAS)
IPCT...........	Industrial Process Cooling Towers
IPE............	Iris Pigmentepithelium
IPEI...........	Ionospheric Plasma and Electrodynamics Instrument (CARB)
IPET...........	Pets.com, Inc. [*NASDAQ symbol*] (SG)
IPhys	Institute of Physics (COBU)
IPI.............	Interested Party Information
IPK............	Imperial Parking Corp. [*AMEX symbol*] (SG)
IPL............	Inferior Parietal Lobule
IPL-V	Information Processing Language-V (DIPS)
IPM............	Initial Pretreatment Module (ABAC)
IPM............	Institute of Project Management (COBU)
IPM............	Instrument Performance Model (ARMP)
IPM............	Integrated Power Management
IPM............	Integrated Program Manager (ABAC)
IPO............	Integrated Provider Organization
IPP............	Integrated Program Plan (ABAC)
IPP............	Internet Presence Provider
IPQ............	Intellectual Property Quarterly [*A publication*]
IPR............	Institute of Population Research [*Beijing University*]
IPRC...........	Institute Port Risk Clause (MARI)
IPRM	Integrated Performance and Risk Management
IPS............	Inertial Pointing System
IPS............	Institute for Palestine Studies
IPS............	Iron Pipe Standard (SARE)
IPSSD	Integrated Program Scheduling Standard Document (SPST)
IPT............	Interpersonal Psychotherapy (DIPS)
IPT............	iParty Corp. [*AMEX symbol*] (SG)
ir..............	Infrared (CARB)
IR.............	Instrument Rating [*Aviation*] (PIAV)
IR.............	Irish Reports [*A publication*]
IRAA	Indoor Radon Abatement Act (AUEG)
IRAD	Internet Rapid Application Development (ITCA)
IRAF..........	Image Reduction and Analysis Facility
IRC............	Instrument Remote Controller (PIPO)
IRC............	International Route Charge [*Travel industry*] (TRID)
IRCA	Indiana Resource Center for Autism
IREA..........	Intermountain Rural Electrical Association
IRF............	Instantaneous Radiative Flux (ARMP)
IRF............	Instantaneous Radiative Transfer (CARB)
IRP............	Individual Retention Plan
IRP............	Integrated Resource Planning (ABAC)
IRR	Interest Rate Risk
IRS............	Investor Relations Society (COBU)
IRSS...........	Indian Remote Sensing Satellite (CARB)
IS-41..........	Interim Standard 41 for North American Inter-Switch Signaling (CGWS)
IS-54..........	Interim Standard 54 for the First North American Dual-Mode Time Division Multiple Access Cellular System (CGWS)
IS-88..........	Interim Standard 88 for the Narrowband Advanced Mobile Phone System Cellular System (CGWS)
IS-95..........	Interim STandard for Code Division Multiple Access Cellular Service (CGWS)
IS-136..........	Interim Standard 136 for North American Time Division Multiple Access Cellular Access (CGWS)
ISA............	Italian Space Agency (CARB)
ISA BUS.......	Industry Standard Architecture Bus
ISAG	Internet Security Advisors Group
ISB............	Incomplete Sentences Blank [*Psychology*] (DIPS)

ISB.............. Issues Screening Board [*NASA*] (SPST)
ISCNI.......... Institute for the Study of Contract with Non-Human Intelligence
ISDA .... Institutional Summary Data Service
ISDB .... Indirect Self-Destructive Behavior (DIPS)
ISDN-BRI ..... Integrated Services Digital Network-Basic Rate Interface (CGWS)
ISDN-PRI ..... Integrated Services Digital Network-Primary Rate Interface (CGWS)
ISDN-UP ...... Integrated Services Digital Network-User Part (CGWS)
ISDU .... Inertial System Display Unit (HLLA)
ISEH........... International Society for Ecosystem Health
ISH.............. In Situ Heating (ABAC)
ISI............... Inter-Symbol Interference (AEBE)
ISIL............. Intersil Holdings 'A' [*NASDAQ symbol*] (SG)
Isl .... Island (NTIO)
ISLVW .... Island View [*Travel industry*] (TRID)
ISMM.......... Institute of Sales and Marketing Management (COBU)
ISN............. Integrated Service Network
ISO............. International Standards Organization (CGWS)
ISOLDE ...... Isotype On-Line Separator
ISPP........... In-Situ Propellant Production
ISR............. In Situ Remediation (ABAC)
ISRTP .... International Society of Regulatory Toxicology and Pharmacology
ISS............. In Situ Sampling (ABAC)
ISSS........... Initial Sector Suite System (CTAS)
ISTE .... International Society for Technology in Education
isth .... Isthmus (NTIO)
IStructE....... Institution of Structural Engineers (COBU)
ISTTE.......... International Society of Travel and Tourism Educators (TRID)
ISVS........... In Situ Vapor Sampling (ABAC)
ISWC .... International Standard Work Code
IT .... Imitation Tiles
IT .... Inspection Time (DIPS)
IT .... Instrument Team (ARMP)
It .... Italian (NTIO)
ITA.............. Indiana Telecommunications Association (CGWS)
ITA.............. Integrated Truss Assembly [*NASA*] (SPST)
ITA.............. In Total Agreement [*Online dialog*]
ITA.............. I Totally Agree [*Online dialog*]
ITAG........... International Travel Agent Guild (TRID)
Ital .... Italic (NTIO)

ital .... Italicize (NTIO)
ITBS............ Iliotibial Band Syndrome [*Medicine*]
ITC.............. International Test Conference (AEBE)
ITCA............ Independent Television Contractors Association (COBU)
ITD.............. Intent to Deny
IT fare .... Inclusive Tour Fare [*Travel industry*] (TRID)
ITIR............. Infrared Thermal Imaging Radiometer (CARB)
ITM .... Incentive Travel and Meetings Association (COBU)
ITMN........... InterMune Pharmaceuticals [*NASDAQ symbol*] (SG)
ITO.............. Idiopathic Transient Osteoporosis [*Medicine*]
ITOH .... Idiopathic Transient Osteoporosis of the Hip [*Medicine*]
ITOY........... International Tropospheric Ozone Year (CARB)
ITP.............. Incidental Take Permit
ITTA .... Independent Travel Technology Association (TRID)
ITU.............. Integrated Terrain Unit (CARB)
ITU-R .... International Telecommunications Union-Radio Sector (CGWS)
ITVA .... Independent Television Association
ITWS........... Integrated Target Weather System (CTAS)
IU .... If Used (RIMS)
IUBMB .... International Union of Biochemistry and Molecular Biology (CARB)
IUE.............. International Union of Electrical Workers
IUGG .... International Union of Geodesy and Geophysics (CARB)
IUHTAUTC.... If Used, Half Time Actually to Count (RIMS)
IUM............. Interim Use Manual (SPST)
IUPAP .... International Conference on Few-Body Problems in Physics
IV .... Intervening Variable (DIPS)
IV&V .... Independent Validation and Verification
IVCD .... Initial Voice Channel Designation (CGWS)
IVRS .... Interim Voice Response System (PIPO)
IVSI............. Inertial Vertical Speed Indicator (PIPO)
IW .... Intentional Walk [*Baseball term*] (NDBD)
IWAV .... interWAVE Communic. Intl. [*NASDAQ symbol*] (SG)
IWF............. Inter-Working Function (MLOA)
IWGN .... Intermediate-Size Station Wagon (TRID)
IWMI........... International Water Management Institute
IWP............. Ice Water Path (ARMP)
IWV............. Integrated Water Vapor (ARMP)
IYC............. Institute Yacht Clause (MARI)
IYFP........... Iowa Youth and Families Project

J

By Acronym

J	Jammer (CCCA)
J	Jump (PIPO)
J/A	Joint Account (NTIO)
JACC	Journal of the American College of Cardiology [*A publication*] (ROAS)
JACM	Journal of the Association for Computing Machinery [*A publication*]
JACR	Joint Advisory Committee Report (HEAS)
JAD	Joint Analysis and Design (ABAC)
JAI	Journal of Artificial Intelligence [*A publication*]
Jam	Jamaica (NTIO)
JAM	Junction Adhesion Molecule
JANCPEC	Japan National Committee for Pacific Economic Cooperation
Jap	Japan (NTIO)
JAS	Japan Air System
JASWG	Joint Safety Assurance Working Group [*NASA*] (SPST)
JBFL&P	Journal of Banking and Finance Law and Practice [*A publication*]
JBIG	Joint Bi-Level Image Experts Group
JBL	Journal of Business Law [*A publication*]
jbo	Jumbo
JCF AWE	Joint Contingency Force Advanced Warfighting Experiment [*Army*]
JD	Juvenile Delinquent (NTIO)
JEOS	Japanese Earth Observing Satellite (CARB)
JEOS	Japanese Earth Observing System (CARB)
JET	Jitter Equivalent Target (CCCA)
JFK	John F. Kennedy International Airport (NTIO)
JFRO	Joint Fire Research Organisation (HEAS)
JHC	Joint Hulls Committee (MARI)
JHF	John Hancock Fin'l Svcs. [*NYSE symbol*] (SG)
JIB	Joint Industry Board for the Electrical Contracting Industry (HEAS)
JIN	Joint Implementation Network (CARB)
JK	Just Kidding [*Online dialog*]
Jkt	Jacket
JLD	Jammer Locator Detector (CCCA)
JLH	Journal of Legal History [*A publication*]
JLS	Journal of Law and Society [*A publication*]
JLT	Junior Leader Training [*Boy Scouts of America*]
JMO	Just My Opinion [*Online dialog*]
jnd	Just-Noticeable Difference (DIPS)
JNR	Jammer-to-Noise Ratio (CCCA)
jour	Journal (NTIO)
JPA	Job Performance Assistance (SPST)
JPOP	Japanese Polar-Orbiting Platform (CARB)
JRC	Joint Research Centre (HEAS)
JRO	J. Robert Oppenheimer
JRS	Joint Reconnaissance Structure (CCCA)
JRSTE	Junior Suite [*Travel industry*] (TRID)
JSCAS	Johnson Space Center Astronomical Society
JSCE	Joint Services Communications Element (CCCA)
JSCR	Joint Standing Committee Report (HEAS)
JSGPM	Joint Service General Purpose Mask [*Army*]
JSIPS	Joint Strategic Integrated Planning Staff (CCCA)
JSOW	Joint Statement of Work (ABAC)
JSTP	Joint Services Test Plan (CCCA)
JTP	Joint Technology Program (CCCA)
JTRS	Joint Tactical Radio System [*ARMY*]
JTSIN	Joint Transmission Services Information Network
jun	Junior (NTIO)
junc	Junction (NTIO)
JUSCADS	Joint United States Canadian Air Defense Study (CCCA)
juv	Juvenile (NTIO)
JVAP	Joint Vaccine Acquisition Program
JVMF	Joint Variable Message Format
JWL	Whitehall Jewellers [*NYSE symbol*] (SG)

K
By Acronym

K	Kilogram (NTIO)
K2	Coefficient of Nondetermination (DIPS)
KAE	Kinesthetic Aftereffect (DIPS)
KAIT	Kaufman Adolescent and Adult Intelligence Test (DIPS)
KamLAND	Kamioka Liquid Scintillator Anti-Neutrino Detector
KARMEN	Karlsruhe-Rutherford Medium-Energy Neutrino Experiment
KB	Knight Bachelor [British]
kbar	Kilobar (ABAC)
KBT	Kerry Blue Terrier (ROAS)
KC	Kilocycle (AEBE)
KC	Strikeout, Called [Baseball term] (NDBD)
Kcal	Kilcalorie (NTIO)
KCSI	Kansas City Southern Industries, Inc.
KCVL	Kentucky Commonwealth Virtual Library
KDCI	Key Display Call Indicator
KDD	Knowledge Discovery in Databases (IDAI)
KDT	Knowledge Discovery in Text (IDAI)
KE	Kroger Equity [NYSE symbol] (SG)
KEK	Koo Energy Ken
KeV	Kiloelectron Volt (ABAC)
KG	King Pharmaceuticals [NYSE symbol]
KGCHS	Knight Grand Cross of the Equestrian Order of the Holy Sepulchre of Jerusalem
KHLOS	Kilo High Level Language Operations per Second (CCCA)

KHPS	Kilo Hops per Second (CCCA)
Ki	Secret Identity Key (CGWS)
KIP	Keep Alone if Possible [Travel industry] (TRID)
KJ	Karaoke Jockey
KK	Knock-for-Knock (MARI)
KL	Kahunen-Loeve [Mathematics] (CCCA)
kn	Knot (ABAC)
KON	Kongcha [Publisher]
KOPEC	Korea National Committee for Pacific Economic Cooperation
KOSP	Kos Pharmaceuticals
KPFSM	King's Police and Fire Services Medal for Distinguished Service [British]
KPM	King's Police Medal for Distinguished Service [British]
KPM	King's Police Medal for Gallantry [British]
Kr	Krypton (ABAC)
KREM	Krispy Kreme Doughnuts [NASDAQ symbol] (SG)
KS	Kolmogorov-Smirnoff Tests (DIPS)
KS	Strikeout, Swinging [Baseball term] (NDBD)
KSMA	Kentucky School Media Association
KSOS	Kernelized Secure Operating System (CCCA)
kt	Karat (NTIO)
KT	Koopman's Theorem
KTM	Keep to Top of Mast (RIMS)
kw	Kilowatt (NTIO)
kwhr	Kilowatt-Hour (NTIO)

L
By Acronym

L .... Lambda Index (DIPS)
L .... Language Score (DIPS)
L .... Levorotatory [*Organic chemistry*] (DIPS)
L .... Line Drive [*Baseball term*] (NDBD)
L .... Losing Pitcher [*Baseball term*] (NDBD)
L .... Low Altitude (PIPO)
LA .... Lighter Than Air Airship (PIPO)
LAA .... Laboratory Animal Allergy (HEAS)
LAAS .... Local Area Augmentation System (HLLA)
LAAS .... Low Altitude Alert System [*Aviation*] (PIPO)
Lab .... Labrador (NTIO)
LAC .... Language Across the Curriculum
LAC .... Local Authority Circular (HEAS)
LACF .... Low Acid Canned Food
LACS .... Large Area Chemical Sensor (ABAC)
LAD .... Language-Acquisition Device (DIPS)
LAD .... Least Absolute Deviation (IDAI)
LAIS .... Local Automatic Intercept System
LAL .... Limulus Amebocyte Lysate [*Medicine*]
LAMA .... Large Array for Millimeter Astronomy
LAMS .... Light Aircraft Maintenance Schedule (PIAV)
LAO .... Location Administrative Officer (SARE)
LAP .... Learning Assistance Program
LAP-B .... Link Access Protocol-Balanced (MLOA)
LAQ STNS.... Laquer Stains
LAR .... Laboratory Animal Resources
LAS .... Laboratory Animal Sciences
LASER .... Light Amplification by Stimulated Emission of Radiation (HEAS)
LASS .... Leisure Accident Surveillance System (HEAS)
LASTCHP ..... Last Paging Channel (CGWS)
lat .... Latitude (NTIO)
LATA .... Local Area and Transport Area (CCCA)
LATCH .... Lower Anchors and Tethers for Children [*Car seat safety term*]
LAU .... Local Authority Unit (HEAS)
LAYCAN ...... Layday Cancelling Date (RIMS)
LB .... Long-Bout
LBC .... Little British Car
LBL .... Line by Line (ARMP)
LBO .... Line Build Out [*Telecommunications*] (MLOA)
L/C .... Land Cover (CARB)
L/C .... Letter of Credit (NTIO)
LC .... License Condition (HEAS)
LC .... Loading Capacity (RIMS)
LCAR .... Luxury Car (TRID)
LCCIEB........ London Chamber of Commerce and Industry Examinations Board
LCCIS......... Local Common Channel Interoffice Signaling (ROAS)
LCCIW .... Life Cycle Cost Impact Worksheet (SPST)
LCCM .... Lifo Cycle Cost Management (SPST)
lcd .... Least Common Denominator (NTIO)
LCD............. Loss of Cell Delineation (MLOA)
LCDC .... Licensed Chemical Dependency Counselor (NUJO)
LCDN .... Last Called Directory Number (ROAS)
LCDP .... Local Career Development Panels (HEAS)
LCIS........... Lobular Carcinoma in Situ
LCL .... Local (PIPO)
lcm .... Least Common Multiple (NTIO)
LCOS .... Liquid Crystal on Silicon (AEBE)
LCR............. Lowest Current Rate (RIMS)
LCS .... Laboratory Control Sample (ABAC)
LCT .... Last Compliance Time
LCTLs .... Less Commonly Taught Languages
LD .... Language Disordered
LD .... Learning Disabled (NTIO)
L/D............. Lift to Drag Ratio (PIPO)
LD .... Lymphocyte Depleted [*Medicine*]
LDA............. Localizer Type Directional Aid (PIPO)
Ldata .... Life Data (DIPS)
LDC .... Local Distribution Center (CCCA)
LD-CELP ..... Long Delay-Code Excited Linear Prediction
LDH .... Lactic Dehydrogenase
LDIN .... Lead in Lighting System (PIPO)
LDMWA........ Low Drag Multi/Wire Antenna (CCCA)
LDUA .... Light-Duty Utility Arm (ABAC)
LDW............. Loss Damage Waiver [*Travel industry*] (TRID)
LE .... Link Encapsulation (MLOA)
LEA .... Local Enforcement Agency (SARE)

LEAP........... Lasers and Electro-Optics Applications Program
LEC .... Local Emergency Coordinator (SARE)
leg .... Legato (NTIO)
legit .... Legitimate (NTIO)
LEIR............ Low Energy Ion Ring
LEP .... Low-Energy Photon (ABAC)
LEPS .... Low-Energy Photon Spectroscopy (ABAC)
LESC .... Lockheed Electronic Systems Company (SPST)
LEXG........... Lexicon Genetics [*NASDAQ symbol*] (SG)
lf .... Left Field [*Baseball term*] (NDBD)
LFC .... Lowest-Feasible Concentration (ABAC)
LFCDA .... London Fire and Civil Defence Authority (HEAS)
LFCM .... Liquid-Fed Ceramic Melter (ABAC)
LFMM .... Liquid-Fed Minimelter (ABAC)
LFP .... Life Point, Inc. [*AMEX symbol*] (SG)
LFS .... London Financial Studies
LFU Memory... Least Frequency Used Memory [*Computer science*] (ITCA)
L-G............. Lawson Gould [*Publisher*]
LGG .... Least General Generalization (IDAI)
LGH .... Launch Grapnel Hook
LGM .... Last Glacial Maximum
lgr............... Larger
lgt .... Light
LHB............. Left-Handed Batter [*Baseball term*] (NDBD)
LHMO .... Local Hazard Mitigation Officer [*Department of Emergency Management*] (DEMM)
LHS............. Lawrence Hall of Science
LHTL............ Luxury Hotel (TRID)
LHV............. Lower Heating Value (CARB)
LI .... Lifted Index (ARMP)
lib .... Liberal (NTIO)
lib .... Liberation (NTIO)
LIH .... Licensed Industrial Hygienist (SARE)
Limit Ed...... Limited Edition
LINEAR .... Lincoln Near-Earth Asteroid Research
ling............. Linguistics (NTIO)
LIPS............ Late-Inning Pressure Situation [*Baseball term*] (NDBD)
liq............... Liquid (NTIO)
liq............... Liquor (NTIO)
LIRAD .... Lidar/Radiometer (CARB)
LIS.............. Land Information System (CARB)
LIS.............. Lightning Imaging Sensor (CARB)
LISM........... Local Interstellar Medium
Lk .... Lake (NTIO)
LKS............. Landau-Kleffler Syndrome
LLC .... Local Liaison Committee (HEAS)
LLCM .... Low Level Control Module [*NASA*] (SPST)
LLD............. Language Learning Disorder
LLI .... Lower Large Intestine (ABAC)
LLRMW........ Low-Level Radioactive Mixed Waste (ABAC)
LLV............. Low Level Vault (ABAC)
LMD............. Linear Magnetic Drive (CCCA)
LMEP.......... Language MOS Evaluation Program [*Army*]
L/MF.......... Low/Medium Frequency (PIPO)
LMIN........... Lastminute.com plc ADS [*NASDAQ symbol*] (SG)
LMNX.......... Luminex Corp. [*NASDAQ symbol*] (SG)
LMP .... Late Middle Paleolithic
LMS .... Least Median Squares (ARMP)
LMSA.......... Large Millimetre and Submillimetre Array
LMWA......... Low-Molecular-Weight Organic Acid (ABAC)
LNC............. Legal Nurse Consultant (NUJO)
LNTE........... Lante Corp. [*NASDAQ symbol*] (SG)
LNTY........... L90, Inc. [*NASDAQ symbol*] (SG)
LO............... Left On [*Baseball term*] (NDBD)
Lo............... London Stock Exchange (SG)
LOB............. Legends of Batman
LOC............. Locator (PIPO)
LOCAE......... List of Classified and Authorised Explosives (HEAS)
LOEL........... Lowest Observed Effect Level (HEAS)
LOF .... Lloyd's Open Form (RIMS)
LOF .... Loss of Frame (MLOA)
Lo Ho.......... Lower Hold (RIMS)
LOI.............. Letter of Indemnity (RIMS)
LOIS............ Land-Ocean Interaction Study
LONDON SE... London Stock Exchange [*England*]
long............ Longitude (NTIO)

LOP.............	Loss of Pointer
LOQ	Lowest Obtainable Quantification (ABAC)
LOUD...........	Loudeye Tech [*NASDAQ symbol*] (SG)
LOW.............	Last Open Water (RIMS)
LP.................	Laboratory Port [*NASA*] (SPST)
LP.................	Little Person
LP.................	Lymphocyte Predominant [*Medicine*]
LPC.............	Loss and Prevention Council (HEAS)
LPC.............	Low Particle Concentration
LPCDF	Low Profile Combined Distributing Frame (ROAS)
lpd	Least-Perceptible Difference (DIPS)
LPGA	Liquefied Petroleum Gas Association (HEAS)
LPH.............	Landing Platform Helicopter (CCCA)
LPO.............	La Palma Observatory
LPO.............	Likely Preferred Options (ABAC)
LPT.............	Licensed Psychiatric Technician (NUJO)
LPV.............	Long Period Variable
LQG	Large Quantity Generator (AUEG)
LR................	Large Range (RIMS)
LR................	Laser Retroreflector (CARB)
L/R..............	Late Run
LR................	Lead Radial (PIPO)
lr.................	Living Room (NTIO)
LRA.............	Laser Retroreflector Array (CARB)
LRB.............	Liquid Rocket Booster
LRCP	Licensed Respiratory Care Practitioner (NUJO)
LRCT...........	Licensed Respiratory Care Technician (NUJO)
LRF.............	Leukaemia Research Fund [*British*]
LRF.............	Little Rubber Feet (MLOA)
LRGM	Long Range Guided Missile (CCCA)
LRI..............	Line Replaceable Item (CTAS)
LRM.............	Long Reach Manipulator (ABAC)
LRN.............	Learning Resource Interchange
LRPO	Location Radiation Protection Officer (SARE)
LRPT...........	Low-Resolution Picture Transmission (CARB)
LRTAP	Long-Range Transboundary Air Pollution
LS................	Light Shield (SPST)

LS...............	Liminal Sensitivity (DIPS)
LSA.............	Large Submillimeter Array
LSAC...........	Laboratory Studies in Atmospheric Chemistry
LSC.............	Learning Station.com
LSD.............	Lashed Secured Dunnage (RIMS)
LSE.............	Lincoln Space Experiment (CCCA)
lse	Loose
LSF.............	Local Selling Fare [*Travel industry*] (TRID)
LSM.............	Landing Ship Mechanized (CCCA)
LSM.............	Learning Subspace Method (IDAI)
LSPN	Lightspan Partnership [*NASDAQ symbol*] (SG)
LSS.............	Lightning Sensor System (HLLA)
LSS.............	Local Subscriber Switch (CCCA)
LTC.............	Local Time Clock
LTL.............	Low Temperature Loop (SPST)
LTP	Lunar Transient Phenomenon
LTRD	Lettered
LTS.............	Lights
LTSS............	Lotus Translation Services for Sametime
lu	Lute
LUFT...........	Leaking Underground Fuel Tank (SARE)
LVCS...........	Logility Value Chain Solution
LVEDd.........	Left Ventricular End-Diastolic Dimension [*Medicine*]
LVEL	Level 8 Systems
LVM.............	Literacy Volunteers of Massachusetts
LVQ.............	Learning Vector Quantization (IDAI)
LVS.............	Large-Volume Sampling (CARB)
LVS.............	Low-Volume Sampler (CARB)
LVSF............	Left Ventricular Shortening Fraction [*Medicine*]
L/W.............	Light Weathering
LWDF...........	Liquid Waste Disposal Facility (ABAC)
LWDII	Lost Workday Injury and Illness (SARE)
LWIN	Leap Wireless International
lwr	Lower
LWTS...........	Low-Level Waste Treatment System (ABAC)
Lx	Lumpectomy [*Medicine*]
lxb	Language Textbook
lyr	Layer

M	Mach (NTIO)
m	Masculine (NTIO)
m	Mean (DIPS)
m	Micrometer (ABAC)
m	Millimicron (DIPS)
M	Movement Response [*Used in Rorschach test scoring*] (DIPS)
MA	Malicious Damage (MARI)
ma	Milliamp (AEBE)
MA	Mobile Allocation (CGWS)
MAA	Mutual Aid Agreement (DEMM)
MAACE	Mississippi Association for Adult and Community Education
MAAL	Massachusetts Alliance of Adult Learners
MAAP	More Able Autistic Persons
MAAP	More Abled Autistic Persons
MAAPP	Manufacturing Assessment and Planning Package (SPST)
MAAS	Meet and Assist [*Travel industry*] (TRID)
MAC	Market Access and Compliance
MAC	Material Accounting Center (ABAC)
MAC	Media-Access Control (AEBE)
MACBS	Multi-Access Cable Billing System
MACDIS	Military Assistance for Civil Disturbance [*Department of Defense*] (DEMM)
MACE	Multipurpose Automatic Control Equipment (HEAS)
mach	Machine (NTIO)
MACI	Millon Adolescent Clinical Inventory (DIPS)
MACN	Mobile Allocation Channel Number (CGWS)
MACP	Marine Aviation Campaign Plan
MAD	Mutual Assured Destruction (CCCA)
MAF	Mineral Ash Free (ABAC)
MAF	Minimal Audible Field (DIPS)
MAFS	Management Arrangements Feasibility Study (HEAS)
mag	Magnetron
MAG	Metal Active Gas (HEAS)
MAGE	Marine Aerosol and Gas Exchange Experiment
maglev	Magnetic Levitation (TRID)
MAHO	Mobile Assisted Hand-Over (CGWS)
MAI	Mobile Allocation Index (CGWS)
MAIL	Mail.com
MAIO	Mobile Allocation Index Offset (CGWS)
Maj Gen	Major General (NTIO)
MAL	Malcolm Music [*Publisher*]
MALP	Master Alarm Light Panel [*NASA*] (SPST)
MALS	Multiangle Light Scattering
MALSP	Marine Aviation Logistics Support Program
MALTA SE	Malta Stock Exchange
MALTT	Massachusetts Adult Literacy and Technology Team
Mam	Mammoth
MAME	Michigan Association for Media in Education
man	Mandolin
MAN	Metropolitan Area Network
MANCPEC	Malaysia National Committee for Pacific Economic Cooperation
M&O	Management and Operating (AUEG)
M&O	Management and Operations (ABAC)
M&W	Marine and War Risks [*Insurance*] (MARI)
MANS	Michigan Association of Non-Public Schools
MANTRA	Middle Atmosphere Nitrogen Trend Assessment
manuf	Manufactured (NTIO)
MAP	Maximum Average Pressure
MAP	Minimal Audible Pressure (DIPS)
MAP	Mobile Access Part (CGWS)
MAPP	Model Accreditation Plan (AUEG)
MAPP	Major Accident Prevention Policy (HEAS)
MAPR	Multiple Antenna Profiler Radar (ARMP)
MAPS	Meteorological and Aeronautical Presentation System (CTAS)
MAPS	Miller Assessment for Preschoolers (DIPS)
MAPS	Modular Automated Parking System [*Developed by Robotic Parking*] (IDAI)
MAPS	Multiple Assessment Programs and Services
MAPTA	Metropolitan Association of Professional Travel Agents (TRID)
MAR	Major Acquisition Review (CTAS)
MAR	Major Area of Responsibility
MAR	Management and Administration Regulations (HEAS)
mar	Maritime (NTIO)
MAR	Missing at Random (IDAI)
MARAMA	Mid-Atlantic Regional Air Management Association
MarLIN	Marine Life Information Network for Britain & Ireland
MARS	Mobile Augmented Reality System
MARS	Multi-Access Reservations System [*Travel industry*] (TRID)
MARS	Multicast Address Resolution Server (MLOA)
MARS	Multivariate Adaptive Regression Spline (IDAI)
Mart	Martinique (NTIO)
MAS	Maximum Amount Subject (MARI)
MAS	Multi-Agent System (IDAI)
masc	Masculine (NTIO)
MASCAL	Mass Casualty [*Military*]
MASL	Missouri Association of School Librarians
Masnte	Maisonette
MAST	Marine Science and Technology
MAST	Midwest Agents Selling Travel (TRID)
math	Mathematics (NTIO)
MATSOL	Massachusetts Association of Teachers of English to Speakers of Other Languages
MaTSU	Marine Technology Support Unit (HEAS)
MAU	Modular Avionics Unit (HLLA)
MAWTS-1	Marine Aviation Weapons and Tactics Squadron 1
MB	Marker Beacon (PIPO)
MB	Merchant Broker (RIMS)
mba	Marimba
MBC	Machine Bath Collection
MBC	Mass Bias Correction (ABAC)
MBD	Machinery Breakdown (MARI)
MBLC	Massachusetts Board of Library Commissioners
MBM	Manual Berthing Mechanism [*NASA*] (SPST)
MBO	Million Barrels of Oil (ABAC)
MBS	Maximum Burst Size (MLOA)
MBT	Mobile Telesystems OJSC ADS [*NYSE symbol*]
MBT	Multimedia-Based Training
MBX	Mailbox (ROAS)
MC	Melter Cell (ABAC)
mc	Micro (NTIO)
MC	Multiple-Choice (DIPS)
MC4	Medical Communications for Combat Casualty Care [*Army*]
MC4-R	Melanocortin-4 Receptor (DIPS)
MCA	Maneuvering at Critically Slow Airspeed [*Aviation*] (PIPO)
MCAE	Massachusetts Coalition for Adult Education
MCAR	Missing Completely at Random (IDAI)
MCAVRET	Marine Corps Aviation Refresher Training
MCB	Manually Controlled Barrier (HEAS)
MCB	Memory Control Block (ROAS)
MCBH	Multiple Cloud Base Height (ARMP)
MCC	Mobile Country Code (CGWS)
MCC	Modulation Coding and Compression (CCCA)
MCCC	Mediacom Communic. 'A' [*NASDAQ symbol*] (SG)
MCCE	Modulation, Coding, Compression and Encryption (CCCA)
MCCs	Microclimate Cooling System (HEAS)
MCET	Massachusetts Corporation for Educational Telecommunications
MCH	Memory Controller Hub
MCIAS	Multi-Channel Intelligent/Intercept Announcement System [*Telecommunications*]
MCMC	Markov Chain Monte Carlo (IDAI)
MCMI-III	Millon Clinical Multiaxial Inventory-III (DIPS)
MCNP	Mobile Network Computing Protocol (AEBE)
MCNS	Multimedia Cable Networking Systems (AEBE)
MCO	Mars Climate Orbiter [*NASA*]
MCRG	Music Copyright Reform Group
MCS	Mining Certification Service (HEAS)
MCS	Multicast Server (MLOA)
MCSK	Multiple-Code-Shift Keying (CCCA)
MCU	Marine Corps University
MCU	Mechanism Control Unit (SPST)
MCWL	Marine Corps Warfighting Lab
MD	Malicious Damage (MARI)
M-D	Manic Depression
MD	Mental Deficiency (DIPS)
MDAU	Maintenance Data Acquisition Unit (HLLA)
MDB	Multichannel Distributed Bridge (CCCA)
Md D	Median Deviation (DIPS)
MDDB	Multidimensional Database (IDAI)
MDE	Middle East (CARB)
MDE	Multidisciplinary Evaluation
MDEA	Media 100
MDF	Minimum Detectable Flux

MDH .... Major Damage History [*Aviation*] (PIPO)
MDL .... Maximum Doping Limit
MDL .... Minimum Detectable Level
MDLP .... Minimum Description Length Principle (IDAI)
MDM .... Message Distribution Module (CCCA)
Mdn .... Median (DIPS)
MDN .... Mercury Deposition Network
MDP .... Markov Decision Problem (IDAI)
MDR .... Minimum Detectable Radiance (CARB)
mdr .... Minimum Detectable Radiance (ARMP)
MDR .... Multidrug-Resistant
MDS .... Milestone Description Sheet (ABAC)
MDSL .... Multi-Rate Digital Subscriber Line (AEBE)
MDSRS .... Morphology-Dependent Stimulated Raman Scattering (CARB)
MDTSA .... Methods for the Detection of Toxic Substances in Air (HEAS)
MDUA .... Mission Defined Unit Assemblage [*Army*]
MDWT .... Metric Deadweight Tons (RIMS)
MDZ .... MDZ, Inc. [*NYSE symbol*] (SG)
Me .... Maine (NTIO)
ME .... Marketing Education
ME .... Mediterranean
ME .... Mixture-of-Experts (IDAI)
ME .... Mobile Equipment (CGWS)
ME .... Molecular Emission (SARE)
MEA .... Mission Engagement Area [*Military*]
MEBU .... Minimum Essential Back Up (CCCA)
MEC .... Millennium Eco-Communities [*Canada*]
mech .... Mechanics (NTIO)
MECS .... Mining Equipment Certification Service (HEAS)
MECS .... Mobile Emergency Communication System (CCCA)
MECSLSI ...... Mission Equipment Cargo Support Launch Site Installation [*NASA*] (SPST)
MED .... e-MedSoft.com [*AMEX symbol*] (SG)
med .... Medical (NTIO)
Med .... Mediterranean (NTIO)
MEDA .... Military Emergency Diversion Airfield (PIAV)
medfly .... Mediterranean Fruit Fly (NTIO)
Medicaid ..... Medical Aid (NTIO)
Medicare ..... Medical Care (NTIO)
MedPAC .... Medicare Payment Assessment Commission
MEF .... Maximum Elevation Figure [*Aviation*] (PIPO)
MEI .... Multi-Engine Instrument (PIPO)
MELN .... Metropolitan Electrical League of New Jersey
MELV .... Medium Expendable Launch Vehicle (CARB)
MEM .... Manufacturing Enterprise Model
mem .... Membership (NTIO)
MEP .... Management Engineering Plan (CCCA)
mer .... Meridian (NTIO)
MERL .... Mobile Emergency Radiological Laboratory (DEMM)
MERS .... Medium Resolution Imaging Spectrometer (CARB)
MERS .... Mobile Emergency Response System (DEMM)
MES .... Medical Equipment Set [*Army*]
MESA .... Mathematics, Engineering, and Science Achievement (ABAC)
MESA .... Multi-Ethnic Study of Atherosclerosis
MESEC .... Multi-Cultural Environmental Science Education Centers (ABAC)
MESSENGER... Mercury Surface, Space Environment, Geochemistry and Ranging Mission [*NASA launch date proposed for March 2004*]
met .... Metallophone
Meteor .... Meteorology
meth .... Methamphetamine (NTIO)
metro .... Metropolitan (NTIO)
METT-T .... Mission, Enemy, Terrain, Troops, and Time [*Military*]
Mex .... Mexican (NTIO)
Mexamerican... Mexican-American (NTIO)
MF .... Meter Fix (CTAS)
mf .... Mezzo Forte (NTIO)
MF .... Multifactorial (DIPS)
MFAR .... Meter Fix Acceptance Rate (CTAS)
MFED .... Multifunctional Exercise Device (SPST)
MFMIS .... Metal Ferroelectric Metal Insulator Semiconductor
MFMMA .... Metal Forming Machinery Makers' Association (HEAS)
MFR .... Minimum Funding Requirement
MFR .... Multifilter Radiometer (ARMP)
MFRSR .... Multifilter Rotating Shadowband Radiometer (CARB)
MFT .... Melter Feed Tank (ABAC)
MFT .... Meter Fix Crossing Time (CTAS)
MG .... Margun Music [*Publisher*]
MG .... Mega-Gauss
Mg .... Milligram (DIPS)
MGB .... Medial Geniculate Body (DIPS)
MGCI .... Most General Common Instance (IDAI)
mgmt .... Management (NTIO)
MGO .... Main Geophysical Observatory [*Russia*] (CARB)
mgr .... Manager (NTIO)
MGU .... Most General Unifier (IDAI)
MH .... Medium Power Homing (PIPO)
mH .... Microhenry
mh .... Millihenry (AEBE)
MHA .... Multiple Hazard Analysis [*Department of Emergency Management*] (DEMM)
MHAU .... Major Hazards Assessment Unit (HEAS)
MHEC .... Midwestern Higher Education Commission
MHLOS .... Mega High Level Language Operations per Second (CCCA)
MHLW .... Major Hazards Legislation Working Party (HEAS)
MHO .... Modern Human Origins

MHRC .... Manitoba Health Research Council [*Canada*]
MHRS .... Modified Hazard Ranking System (ABAC)
MHS .... Microwave Humidity Sounder (CARB)
MI .... Mandatory Investigation (HEAS)
MI .... Mining Inspectorate (HEAS)
MIA .... Marine Insurance Act (MARI)
MIA .... Meetings Industry Association (COBU)
MIB .... Management Information Database (CGWS)
MICAP .... Multi-National Investigations Cooperative on Aerial Phenomena
microSQUID... Microscopy, Microscopic Superconducting Quantum Interference Devices
MID .... Missing Insects Department
MID .... Multinfarct Dementia (DIPS)
MIDEX .... Medium-Class Explorer
MIDI .... Musical Instrument Digital Interface (AEBE)
MIE .... Modal Identification Experiment [*NASA*] (SPST)
MIGE .... Missile Impact and Gaseous Explosions (HEAS)
mil .... Military
MILK .... Moments of Intimacy, Laughter and Kinship
MIMAC .... Measurement and Improvement of Manufacturing Capacity
MIMR .... Multifrequency Imaging Microwave Radiometer (CARB)
min .... Minor (NTIO)
Mini-POPs ... Mini Points of Presence
MIN/MAX .... Minimum/Maximum (RIMS)
MINR .... Minimum Rate [*Travel industry*] (TRID)
Mipad .... Multimodal, Interactive Note Pad
MIPS .... Million Instructions per Second (NTIO)
mips .... Millions of Instructions per Second
MIR .... Millimeter-Wave Imaging Radiometer (ARMP)
MIRA .... Massachusetts Immigrant and Refugee Advocacy Coalition
MIRSL .... Microwave Remote Sensing Laboratory (CARB)
MIS .... Master of Industrial Safety (SARE)
MISR .... Multiangle Imaging Spectroradiometer (ARMP)
MIST .... Metal-Insulator-Semiconductor Transistor (CCCA)
MIT .... Materials Interaction Test (ABAC)
MITA .... MetLife's Intelligent Text Analyzer [*Textual analysis of life insurance applications*] (IDAI)
MIX .... Mixed Schedule of Reinforcement (DIPS)
MJC .... Massachusetts Job Council
ML .... Middle Compass Locator (PIPO)
ML .... Milan Stock Exchange (SG)
ml .... Millilambert (DIPS)
ml .... Milliliter (AEBE)
MLBP .... Major League Baseball Properties (NDBD)
MLBPAA ...... Major League Baseball Players Alumni Association (NDBD)
MLCD .... Multi-Line Call Detail (ROAS)
MLP .... Monitored Line Program (SPST)
MLP .... Multiple Layer Perceptron (IDAI)
MLS .... Multiple Level Security (CCCA)
MLSAA .... Middle Level Student Activities Association
MLSC .... Multiple Loop Sidelobe Canceller (CCCA)
MM .... Man Machine (CGWS)
MMARS .... Military Middle Airspace Radar Service (PIAV)
MMC .... Maintenance Monitor Console (CTAS)
MMC .... Microsoft Management Console
MME .... Man Month Equivalents (SPST)
MMECT .... Multimonitored Electroconvulsive Treatment (DIPS)
MMFFS .... Multi-Modular Fluid Filtration System
MML .... Minimum Message Length (IDAI)
MMM .... Magnetism and Magnetic Materials
MMP .... Materials Management Plan (ABAC)
MMPI-2 .... Minnesota Multiphasic Personality Inventory-2 (DIPS)
MMPI-A ...... Minnesota Multiphasic Personality Inventory-Adolescent (DIPS)
MMR .... Mass Migration Response (DEMM)
MMR .... Mildly Mentally Retarded
MMR .... Moderate Mental Retardation (DIPS)
MMS .... Multi-Mission Spacecraft
MMT .... Multimodal Therapy [*Arnold Lazarus*] (DIPS)
MMT .... Multiple Mirror Observatory
MN .... Mansion
MNC .... Mobile Network Code (CGWS)
MNGIE .... Mitochrondrial Neurogastrointestinal Encephalomyopathy
MNPS .... Minimum Navigation Performance Specification Airspace (PIPO)
MNTA .... Minnesota Telephone Association (CGWS)
MO .... Management Operations (SPST)
MO .... Managing Owner (RIMS)
Mo .... Montreal Stock Exchange (SG)
MOBY .... Marine Optical Buoy (ROAS)
MOC .... Mars Observer Camera
MOC .... Mint on Card
MOC .... Mobile-Originated Call (CGWS)
MOCC .... Memory-Operating Characteristic Curve (DIPS)
MOD .... Moderate Room [*Travel industry*] (TRID)
mod .... Moderato (NTIO)
MODR .... Moderate Rate [*Travel industry*] (TRID)
mol .... Molecule (NTIO)
MOLA .... Mars Observer Laser Altimeter
MOLCHOP.... More or Less Charterer's Option (RIMS)
MOLIS .... Minority On-Line Information Service
MOLOO .... More or Less Owner's Option (RIMS)
MOMC .... Mint on Mint Card
MOMV .... Manned Orbital Maneuvering Vehicle
mon .... Monastery (NTIO)
MONE .... MatrixOne, Inc. [*NASDAQ symbol*] (SG)
Mong .... Mongolia (NTIO)

MOP............	Memorandum of Participation (ARMP)
MOPP..........	Military-Oriented Protective Posture
MOR	Marital Opportunity Ratio (DIPS)
Mor.............	Morocco (NTIO)
MOSAIC	Multifunctional on-the-Move Secure Adaptive Integrated Communications [*Military*]
MOT............	Monthly Overtime (RIMS)
MOU	Memorandum of Understanding
MOUT	Military Operations in Urban Terrain [*Army*]
MOUT	Military Operations on Urban Terrain
MOV............	Motor Oil Volatility
MP	Melrose Place [*Television program title*]
MP	Midpoint (DIPS)
M/P	Missing Parts
MPA............	Marine Protected Area
MPA............	Multiple Project Assurance
MPCA..........	Minnesota Pollution Control Agency
MPDS..........	Message Processing Display System (CCCA)
MPEC..........	Minor Planets Electronic Circular
MPF	Maximum Probably Flood (ABAC)
mpg	Miles per Gallon (NTIO)
MPL	Magneto Photo Luminescence
MPL	Mars Polar Lander
MPLS..........	Multi-Protocol Label Switching (MLOA)
MPP............	Material Processing Platform (SPST)
MPS............	Modular Power Subsystem
MPWP	Maximum Permissible Working Pressure (HEAS)
mpy	Mils per Year (ABAC)
MQE............	Managed Query Environment [*Computer science*] (ITCA)
MR..............	Mandatory Reporting (HEAS)
m/r..............	Mates' Receipt (HIMS)
MR..............	Methane Recovery (CARB)
MR..............	Motor Rifle (CCCA)
MRC............	Maracas
MRC............	Mid-Roll Change Capability
MRD	Maintenance Requirements Documents (CTAS)
MRF............	Meteorological Research Flight
MRL	Magnovox Research Laboratories (CCCA)
MRMC	Medical Research and Materiel Command [*Army*]
MRMDF	Multi-Use Remote Manipulator Development Facility [*NASA*] (SPST)
MRP............	Medical Removal Protection (SAHE)
MRP............	Multiple-Rate Processor (CCCA)
MRS............	Materials Research Society
MRT 6	Metropolitan Readiness Tests-Sixth Edition [*J. R. Nurss*] (DIPS)
MRU	Meteorological Research Unit
MRVL..........	Marvell Technology Group [*NASDAQ symbol*]
MS..............	Marine Stratus (ARMP)
MS..............	Marketing Society (COBU)
MS..............	Mass Spectroscopy
MS..............	Music Sales Corporation [*Publisher*]
MSA............	Minimum Sector Altitude [*Aviation*] (PIPO)
MSA............	Minimun Sector Altitude [*Aviation*] (PIAV)
MSAH	Michigan Sportsmen Against Hunger
MSC............	Maritime Surveillance Capability (CCCA)
MSCI...........	Military Science
MSCM	Mobile Station Class Mark (CGWS)
MSCN	Misconnection [*Travel industry*] (TRID)
MSCS..........	Microsoft Cluster Server
MSD............	Mass Spectral Detector (ABAC)
MSDD	Multi-Sensory Developmental Delays
MSDS	Mission Specific Data Set [*Army*]
MSER..........	Mental Status Examination Report (DIPS)
Msgr...........	Monsignor (NTIO)
M Sgt..........	Master Sergeant (NTIO)
MSH............	Mont Saint-Hilaire
mshsks	Mesh Sacks
MSI.............	Manufacturing Support Item
MSI.............	Medium Scale Integrated Circuit
MSI.............	Micorsoft Installer [*Computer science*]
MSIC...........	Mobile Subscriber Indentification Number (CGWS)
MSIN	Mail Stop Identification Number (ABAC)
MSISDN.......	Mobile Station Integrated Service Digital Network Number (CGWS)
MSL............	Maximum Street Load (CTAS)
msl.............	Mean Sea Level (PIAV)
MSP............	Munchausen Syndrome by Proxy [*Child abuse*] (DIPS)
MSR............	Management Summary Report (ABAC)

MSR............	Microwave Scanning Radiometer (CARB)
MSRE..........	Mir Sample Return Experiment [*NASA*] (SPST)
MSRN	Mobile Station Roaming Number (CGWS)
MSRT..........	Minnesota Spatial Relations Test (DIPS)
MSS............	Modulation Semiconductor Structure
MSSC..........	Multiple Sclerosis Society of Canada
MSSFA........	Michigan Steelhead and Salmon Fisherman's Association
MST............	McCarthy Screening Test [*Intended to diagnose academic potentials and disabilities*] (DIPS)
MST............	Therapeutic Massage Therapist (NUJO)
mstly	Mostly
MSU............	Medical Support Unit [*Department of Emergency Management*] (DEMM)
MSV............	Manufacturers Services [*NYSE symbol*]
MSW...........	Master's in Social Work
MT	Message Type (CGWS)
mt	Metric Ton (NTIO)
MT	Million Tonne (CARB)
mt	Mitochrondrial [*Medicine*]
MT	Mobile/Transportable (CCCA)
MTA............	Major Trading Area (CGWS)
MTBAP........	Mean Productive Time Between Assists
MTBFP........	Mean Productive Time Between Failures
MTBI...........	Mean Time Between Incident
MTBI...........	Mild Traumatic Brain Injury
MTC............	Mobile Terminated Call (CGWS)
MTCA..........	Military Terminal Control Area (PIAV)
MTCE..........	Million Tonnes of Carbon Equivalent (CARB)
MTCR..........	Million Tonnes of Coal Replacement (CARB)
MTE............	Missing Time Experience
MTFA..........	Modulation Transfer Function Area (DIPS)
MTI.............	Multispectral Thermal Imager
MTM...........	Metric Ton of Metal (ABAC)
MTONS	Metric Tonnes (RIMS)
MTP............	Message Transfer Protocol (CGWS)
MTP............	Microwave Temperature Profiler (ARMP)
MTS............	Microwave Temperature Sounder (CARB)
MTWV.........	Metawave Communications [*NASDAQ symbol*] (SG)
MTX............	Mobile Telephone Exchange (CGWS)
MU.............	Marvel Universe
MU.............	Microwave Unit (CARB)
MUA............	Military Utility Assessment
MUD...........	Multi-User Device (ABAC)
MUFON........	Mutual UFO Network, Inc.
MULT..........	Multiple Schedule of Reinforcement (DIPS)
mun	Municipal (NTIO)
muni	Municiple [*Bond*] (NTIO)
mus	Music (NTIO)
MUX...........	Multiplexer (PIPO)
mV..............	Microvolt
MVAK..........	Module Vertical Access Kit [*NASA*] (SPST)
MVBR..........	Motor Vehicle Body Repair (HEAS)
MVC............	meVC Draper Fisher Jurvest Fd. [*NYSE symbol*]
MVEA..........	Missouri Valley Electric Association
MVPE..........	Market Value of Portfolio Equity
MVR............	Monthly Variance Report (ABAC)
MVR............	Motor Vehicle Repair (HEAS)
mW.............	Microwatt
MWA...........	Midwest Area (SARE)
MWd...........	Megawatt-Day (ABAC)
MWL...........	Miniature Warning Light (HEAS)
MWNT	Multi-Walled Carbon Nanotube
MWP...........	Mixed Waste Project (ABAC)
MWR...........	Microwave Radiometer (CARB)
MWyr..........	Mogawatt Year (ABAC)
MXB............	Medix Resources [*AMEX symbol*] (SG)
MXCPEC	Mexico National Committee for Pacific Economic Cooperation
mxd	Mixed
MY	Motorized Yacht (TRID)
My	Myopia (DIPS)
MYE............	Man Year Equivalent (SPST)
MYHEC	Michigan Youth Hunter Education Challenge
Mz..............	Mezzo Soprano
MZ	Middle Zone (HEAS)
MZ	Monozygotic Twins (DIPS)
MZa	Monozygotic Twins Reared or Raised Apart (DIPS)
MZt	Monozygotic Twins Reared or Raised Together (DIPS)

N	Cranial Nerve (DIPS)
n	Need (DIPS)
N	Negative (PIPO)
N	Neuroticism
N	Nickel (NTIO)
N	Number Factor (DIPS)
N	Numerical Ability (DIPS)
NA	Net Absolutely (MARI)
NAA	North Atlantic Area (SARE)
NAACCR	North American Association of Central Cancer Registries
NAADMP	North American Air Defense Master Plan (CCCA)
NABBP	National Association of Base Ball Players (NDBD)
NABE	National Association for Business Economics
NABP	National Association of Boards of Pharmacy
NAC	Network Analysis Corporation (CCCA)
NAC	No Action Taken on Communication [*Travel industry*] (TRID)
NACD	National Association of Computer Dealers (ROAS)
nAch	Need for Achievement (DIPS)
NACHO	National Association of Chemical Hygiene Officers (SARE)
NACN	North American Cellular Network (CGWS)
NAD 27	North American Datum of 1927 (CARB)
NADC	North American Digital Cellular (CGWS)
NADOR	Notification of Accidents and Dangerous Occurrences Regulations 1980 (HEAS)
NAF	Naval Airfield (PIPO)
NAF	Northern Africa (CARB)
N Aff	Need for Affiliation (DIPS)
NAIC	National Air Intelligence Center
NAIT	National Association of Industrial Technologists
NAL	Negro American League [*Baseball*] (NDBD)
NALS	Neonatal Advanced Life Support (NUJO)
NAM	NASA Access Mechanism (ITCA)
NAM	New Account Memorandum
NAM	Number Assignment Module (CGWS)
NAMC	Northern Association of Management Consultants (COBU)
NAMPS	Narrowband Advanced Mobile Phone Service (CGWS)
NANC	North American Numbering Council (CGWS)
NANP	North American Numbering Plan (CGWS)
NAOAG	North American Official Airline Guide (TRID)
NAPAP	National Atmospheric and Precipitation Assessment Program
NAPIS	National Agricultural Pest Information System (AUEG)
NAPP	Non-Agricultural Pesticides Panel (HEAS)
NAR	New Arrival Information [*Travel industry*] (TRID)
NAR	Notification of Ammunition Reclassification [*Military*]
NARC	North Atlantic Route Chart (PIPO)
NARL	National Air and Radiation Laboratory (AUEG)
NARSID	Non-Avalanche-Related Snow-Immersion Death
NARSTO	North American Research Strategy for Tropospheric Ozone
NARUC	National Association of Regulatory Utility Commissioners (CGWS)
NAS	Network Attached Storage
NAT	North Atlantic Tracks (HLLA)
NAT	North Atlantic Traffic (PIPO)
NATESOL	National Association of Teachers of English for Speakers of Other Languages [*England*]
NAUN	Nearest Available Upstream Neighbor (MLOA)
NAVCOMSAT	Naval Communications Satellite
NAVCOMSTA	Naval Communications Station (CCCA)
NAVEUR	Naval Forces, Europe (CCCA)
NAVFAC	Naval Facility
NAVSSI	Navigation Sensor System Interface
NAVTA	North American Veterinary Technician Association
NAWC	Number of Additional Words Coming (CGWS)
NB	No Box
NBAC	National Bioethics Advisory Committee
NBCC	Nuclear, Biological, and Chemical Center
NBCi	NBC Internet Inc.
NBCWARN	Nuclear, Biological, and Chemical Warning
NBHA	National Barrel House Association
NBII	National Biological Information Infrastructure
NBL	Neutral Buoyancy Laboratory [*NASA*] (SPST)
NBMA	Non-Broadcast Multiple Access
NBY	NBC Capital [*AMEX symbol*] (SG)
NCA	National Cemetery Administration
NCA	Neutralized Current Acid (ABAC)
NCA	Non-Continuous Action (CCCA)
NCA	Northern Consultancy Association (COBU)
NCAW	Neutralized Current Acid Waste (ABAC)
NCB	Net Change of Biomass (CARB)
NCCDPHP	National Center for Chronic Disease Prevention and Health Promotion
NCCF	National Childhood Cancer Foundation
NCCU	Neurosurgical Critical Care Unit (NUJO)
NCD	No Computed Data (HLLA)
NCD	Non Coasting Drive
NCDA	North Carolina Department of Agriculture (ROAS)
NCEE	National Center on Education and the Economy
NCEEER	National Council for Eurasian and East European Research
NCEET	National Consortium for Environmental Education Training
NCEO	Non-Conforming End Office (CCCA)
NCID	Non-Cooperative Identification (CCCA)
NCL	Norwegian Cruise Lines (TRID)
NCLIS	National Commission on Libraries and Information Science
NCMHA	North Carolina Mobile Home Association
NCNT	Netcentives
NCO	Net Control Operator (CCCA)
NCPDI	National Coastal Pollutant Discharge Inventory (CARB)
NCPO	National Climate Program Office (CARB)
NCRP	National Committee for Responsive Philanthropy
NCRP	Non-Compulsory Reporting Point (PIPO)
NCRW	Neutralized Cladding Removal Waste (ABAC)
NCS	Network Clock Signal (CCCA)
NCS	Norwegian Continental Shelf (RIMS)
NCSA	National Strength and Conditioning Association
NCSBN	National Council of State Boards of Nursing, Inc.
NCSC	Neural Crest Stem Cell
NCTA	National Cable Television Association, Inc.
NCVG	National Council for Vocational Qualifications (COBU)
ND	Nhan Dan Newspaper [*A publication*]
ND	Notre Dame (NTIO)
NDA	Not Diagnosed with Anything
N Dak	North Dakota (NTIO)
NDB	Non-Directional Radio Beacon (PIPO)
NDC	Nondairy Cattle (CARB)
NDF	Narrative Data File (CARB)
NDH	No Damage History [*Aviation*] (PIPO)
NDSCS	National Duck Stamp Collectors Society
NE	Near Effect (DIPS)
NE	Network Element (MLOA)
NE	Not Entered (MARI)
ne	Not Exceeding (MARI)
NEA	Nurse Education Act
NEBS	Network Equipment-Building System
NEC	Nett Explosives Content (HEAS)
NEC	Network Emergency Co-Ordinator (HEAS)
NECCR	North of England Children's Cancer Research Unit
NEDB	National Exposure Data Base (HEAS)
NEDO	New Energy and Industrial Technology Development Organization
NEMRL	New England Marine Research Laboratory (ABAC)
NENA	National Emergency Number Association (CGWS)
NEOF	Neoforma.com, Inc. [*NASDAQ symbol*] (SG)
NEOP	New Earth Observation Projects
NEP	Net Earned Premiums [*Insurance*] (MARI)
NEPA	National Environmental Policy Act
NERSC	National Energy Research Scientific Computing Center
NESLI	National Electronic Site License Initiative
NET	Noise Equivalent Target (CCCA)
NETL	National Energy Technology Laboratory
NETS	National Educational Technology Standards
NETS	National Education Technology Standards
NETS	National Emergency Telecommunications System (CCCA)
neut	Neutral (NTIO)
Newf	Newfoundland (NTIO)
New Hebr	New Hebrides (NTIO)
New Test	New Testament (NTIO)
NEXRAD	Next-Generation Radar (ARMP)
NFCS	Nuclear Forces Communications Satellite (CCCA)
NFD	Network Flow Diagrams (CTAS)
NFERC	National Fertilizer and Environmental Research Center (CARB)
NFL	New Foreign Launch (CCCA)
NFR	National Finals Rodeo
NFR	National Fire Rating (SARE)
NFSC	Nuclear Fuel Services Corporation (ABAC)

NFSR	National Finals Steer Roping
NG	No Window Glazing
NGAD	Notice Given Arrival Date (MARI)
NGB	Nordic Gene Bank (CARB)
NHAP	National High-Altitude Photography Program (CARB)
NHBS	Natural History Book Service Ltd.
NHRC	National Hydrology Research Centre (CARB)
NHST	Null Hypothesis Significance Testing (DIPS)
NI	Notifiable Installation (HEAS)
NIAID	National Institute of Allergy and Infectious Diseases
NICE	National Institute of Clinical Excellence
NICMOS	Near-Infrared Camera and Multiobject Spectrometer
NID	Non-Interactive Display (CCCA)
NIDCR	National Institute of Dental and Craniofacial Research
NIDCR	National Institute of Dental Craniofacial Research
NIE	Natural and Induced Environment (SPST)
NIEP	Natural and Induced Environments Panel (SPST)
NIES	National Institute for Environmental Studies (CARB)
NIF	Network Interface Function (SPST)
NIG	National Interest Group (HEAS)
Nig.	Niger [African nation] (NTIO)
NIHHS	Notification of Installations Handling Hazardous Substances Regulations 1982 (HEAS)
NIKU	Niku Corp. [NASDAQ symbol] (SG)
NIPC	National Infrastructure Protection Center
N Ire	Northern Ireland (NTIO)
NIS	National Intelligence Scale (DIPS)
NIS	Norton Internet Security [Symantec Corp.]
NIS	Norwegian International Shipsregister (RIMS)
NISH	Naval Intelligence Support Headquarters (CCCA)
NISTIR	National Institute of Standards and Technology Interagency Report
NIT-MCS	Nippon Telephone and Telegraph-Mobile Cellular System (CGWS)
NIV	National Institute for Virology [South Africa]
NIWF	Network Interworking Function (MLOA)
NKCA	National Kidney Cancer Association
NL	National League (NTIO)
NLB	Network Load Balancing
NLD	Nonverbal Learning Disability
NLE	National Library of Education
NLLAP	National Lead Laboratory Accreditation Program
NLN	Navy Learning Network
NLO	Non-Linear Operator (CCCA)
NLP	Natural Language Parsing (IDAI)
NLPCA	Nonlinear Principal Components Analysis (IDAI)
NLR	Non-Linear Refraction
NLSY	National Longitudinal Survey of Youth
NLT	Non-Linear Time Sequence (ABAC)
NM	Nanometer (DIPS)
NM	Network Management (MLOA)
nm	Nuclear Magneton (ABAC)
NMB	Non-Maturing Balance
nmb	Number Book
NMD	Norwegian Maritime Directorate (RIMS)
NMDP	National Marrow Donor Program
NME	Network Management Entity (MLOA)
NME	Nonlinear Mesoscopic Elastic
N Mex	New Mexico (NTIO)
NMF	Non-Negative Matrix Factorization
nmi	No Middle Initial (NTIO)
NMIC	National Military Intelligence Center (CCCA)
NML	Network Management Layer (MLOA)
NMMPS	National Military Message Processor System (CCCA)
NMS	Network Management Station (MLOA)
NMTC	Numerical Technologies [NASDAQ symbol] (SG)
NMU	Navigation Management Unit (HLLA)
NMWP	National Mixed Waste Program (ABAC)
n N	Not North Of (RIMS)
NNAT	Naglieri Nonverbal Ability Test (DIPS)
NNF	Negation Normal Form (IDAI)
NNL	Negro National League [Baseball] (NDBD)
NNLS	Non-Negative Least Squares (ARMP)
NNM	Nasdaq National Market (SG)
NNRTC	Northwest Natural Resource Technologies Consortium
NNSF	National Natural Science Foundation
NNTAPS	National Nuclear Targeting Policy (CCCA)
no	North (NTIO)
NOAO	National Optical Astronomical Observatories
NOC	Notice of Commencement (SARE)
NOCN	No Connection [Travel industry] (TRID)
NOD	Not Otherwise Diagnosed
NODDY	Notions, Oddities, Doodads & Delights of Yesterday
NOI	Notice of Interest (DEMM)
NOIAN	National Operations Intelligence Analysis Net (CCCA)
nom	Nominative (NTIO)
NOMAD	Neutrino Oscillation Magnetic Detector
noncm	Non-Cumulative (SG)
Non-par	Non-Participating Provider
nonvtg	Non-Voting (SG)
Nor.	Norman (NTIO)
nor.	North (NTIO)
NORD	National Organization for Rare Disorders, Inc.
norm.	Normal (NTIO)
NOSC	Naval Oceanographic Systems Command (CCCA)
NOSH	No Show [Travel industry] (TRID)
NOSIC	Naval Ocean Surveillance Intelligence Command (CCCA)

NOSO	Not of Specific Origin
Notam	Notices to Airmen (PIAV)
NOTR	No Traffic Rights [Travel industry] (TRID)
NOV	Novello & Co. [Publisher]
NOVEL	New York Online Virtual Electronic Library
NP	Neutron Porosity (CARB)
NP	Number of Pitches [Baseball term] (NDBD)
NP	Nurse Prescriber (NUJO)
NPA	Network Performance Analyzer [Computer science] (ITCA)
NPA	North Plains Area (SARE)
N-PFPS	Navy Portable Flight Planning Software
NPI	Nuclear Propulsion Initiative (ABAC)
NPL	National Priority List (AUEG)
NPL	Zero Phonon Line
NPLI	Netpliance, Inc. [NASDAQ symbol] (SG)
NPN	Negative-Positive-Negative
NPO	Negative-Positive O Temperature Coefficient (AEBE)
NPPC	Nuclear Power Plant Consultant (IDAI)
NPR	National Partnership for Reinventing Government
NPRM	Notice of Proposed Rulemaking
NPT	National Pipe Thread (SARE)
NPTF	National Pipe Thread Fine (SARE)
NPTO	National Petroleum Technology Office
NR	No Rate [Travel industry] (TRID)
NRAL	No Risk after Landing (MARI)
nras	No Risk after Shipment (MARI)
NRB	Normalized Relative Backscatter (ARMP)
NRBF	Normalized Radial Basis Function (IDAI)
NRC	No Record [Travel industry] (TRID)
NRCC	National Registry of Clinical Chemists (SARE)
NRCF	Not Reconfirmed [Travel industry] (TRID)
NRCP	National Research Council for the Philippines (CARB)
NRCT	National Registry of Childhood Tumors [British]
NRCT	National Research Council of Thailand (CARB)
NRDP	National Rural Development Partnership
nREM	Nonrapid Eye Movement (DIPS)
NRGM	National Responsibility Group Minute (HEAS)
NRI	National Research Initiative
NRI	Non-Roster Invitee [Baseball term] (NDBD)
NRMWRP	Northern Rocky Mountain Wolf Recovery Plan
NRP	Non-Revenue Passenger [Travel industry] (TRID)
NRR	Nuclear Reactor Regulation (ABAC)
NRS	No Rate Specified [Travel industry] (TRID)
NRT	National Responsibility Team (HEAS)
nrtb	No Risk until on Board (MARI)
NRTOR	No Risk to Attach till on Rail (MARI)
nrtor	No Risk until Waterborne (MARI)
NRTWB	No Risk to Attach till Waterborne (MARI)
NRUS	Nonlinear Resonant Ultrasound Spectroscopy
NS	Nimbo Stratus (PIAV)
NSA	Northern Slope of Alaska (CARB)
NSA	Nuclear Science Abstracts (ABAC)
NSB	North Slope Borough (ARMP)
NS/BH	Neutron-Star/Black-Hole
NSC	Nasdaq Small Cap (SG)
NSC	Norwegian Space Center (CARB)
NSC	Nuclear Services Corporation (ABAC)
NSCMP	Non-Stockpile Chemical Material Program [Army]
NSCP	National Scalable Cluster Project [Computer science] (ITCA)
NSCP	National Soil Conservation Program [Canada]
NSCSS	National Society of Consulting Soil Scientists
NSD	National Security and Defense (ABAC)
NSFNet	National Science Foundation Network
NSI	Network Solutions
NSLA	Nova Scotia Library Association
NSM	Net-Shared Memory
NSM	Network Station Manager
NSN	New Substances Notification (SARE)
NSNA	No Stock Number Assigned
NSR	Non Significant Result [Medicine]
nss	Non-Sea-Salt (CARB)
NSSF	Near Surface Storage Facility (ABAC)
NSST	Non-Smoking Seat [Travel industry] (TRID)
NST	National Security Technology (ABAC)
NTBT	Nuclear Test Ban Treaty (CCCA)
NTG	Natco Group 'A' [NYSE symbol] (SG)
NTGX	net.Genesis Corp. [NASDAQ symbol] (SG)
NTI	National Toxics Inventory
NTI	Need Ticketing Information [Travel industry] (TRID)
NTKK	Net2000 Communications [NASDAQ symbol] (SG)
NTSAI	National Target Shooting Association of Ireland
NTSL	Nonintegrated Two-Stage Liquid (ABAC)
NTW	Navy Theater Wide
NU	Neurologically Unique
NUC	National Underseas Research Center (CARB)
NUFO	New Focus [NASDAQ symbol]
NuMI	Neutrinos at the Main Injector [Fermilab]
NUR	Not Under Repair (MARI)
NuTeV	Neutrinos at the Tevatron
NVCP	Network Voice Conferencing Protocol (CCCA)
NVI	No Value Indicated [Stamp collecting]
NVLD	Non-Verbal Learning Disability
NVP	Network Voice Protocol (CCCA)
NWEAMP	Nuclear Weapons Employment Acquisition Master Plan (CCCA)
NWLISN	Northwest Land Information System Network (CARB)

NWP .... Net Written Premiums [*Insurance*] (MARI)
NWPM .... Numerical Weather Prediction Model (CARB)
NWS .... Nuclear Weapon Site (CCCA)
NXTP .... Nextel Partners 'A' [*NASDAQ symbol*] (SG)
NXX .... End Office Code (CGWS)
NYBOT .... New York Board of Trade
NZPECC .... New Zealand Committee of the Pacific Economic Cooperation
           Council
NZSE .... New Zealand Stock Exchange

O
By Acronym

O................. Original Response (DIPS)
O................. Ovulation
OA.............. Open Access
OA.............. Over Aged (RIMS)
OAA .... Office of Academic Affairs
OAC .... Office of Antiboycott Compliance
OAIT .... Office of American Indian Trust
O&R .... Operations and Robotics (SPST)
O&S .... Operations and Service (CCCA)
OAR .... Oregon Administrative Rules (SARE)
OAS .... Option Adjusted Spread
OASIS .... Open Access Same-Time Information System
OATS .... Oxford Air Training School [*British*] (PIAV)
OB.............. Obligatory
OB.............. Operations Branch (HEAS)
OB.............. Order of Burma
OB.............. Organized Baseball (NDBD)
OBA .... On-Base Average [*Baseball term*] (NDBD)
OBL .... Office of Business Liaison
obo .... Or Best Offer (NTIO)
obs............. Obscene (NTIO)
obs............. Obstruction [*Baseball term*] (NDBD)
obst .... Obstruction (PIAV)
OC.............. Open Crossing (HEAS)
OC.............. Operational Circular (HEAS)
OCB .... Outgoing Calls Barred (CGWS)
occ............. Occasional
occ............. Occidental (NTIO)
OCCAM .... Ocean Circulation and Climate Advanced Modelling
occas .... Occasionally (NTIO)
OCEPA .... Office of Communications, Education, and Public Affairs (AUEG)
OCI............. Out of City Indicator
OCL .... Obstruction Clearance Limit [*Aviation*] (PIPO)
OCLC .... Online Computer Library Center
OCM .... Operator Console Monitor
OCN .... Oceania (CARB)
OCN .... Oncology Certified Nurse (NUJO)
OCNFT .... Oceanfront (TRID)
OCNVW....... Ocean View (TRID)
OCOKA........ Observation and Fields of Fire, Cover, and Concealment, Obstacles and Movement, Key Terrain, and Avenues of Approach [*Military*]
OCRE .... Optical Character Reader Equipment (CCCA)
OD .... Optical Detection (ABAC)
OD .... Outer Detector
od .... Outer Diameter (NTIO)
ODBMS .... Object-Oriented Database Management System
ODIN........... Onboard Data Interfaces and Network [*NASA*] (SPST)
ODS .... Operational Data Store [*Computer science*] (ITCA)
ODS .... Oxygen Depletion Sensor
ODT .... Order-Disorder Transition
OE .... Operating Environment (CTAS)
OEG .... Operational Exposure Guide
OEI............. Official Establishment Inventory
OEL............. Organic Electroluminescent (AEBE)
OEPA .... Vincristine, Etoposide, Prednisone, and Doxorubicin [*Medicine*]
OER .... Office of Environmental Restoration (AUEG)
OESM.......... Occupational and Environmental Safety Management
OETA .... Original Estimated Time of Arrival (CTAS)
OF.............. Outfielder [*Baseball term*] (NDBD)
OFA............ Ontario Federation of Agriculture [*Canada*]
OFA............ Other Federal Agencies (ABAC)
OFD .... Orofacial Dyskinesia (DIPS)
off .... Officer (NTIO)
OFM........... Open Frame Motor
OFX............ Outer Fix (CTAS)
OGCA .... Ohio Gun Collectors Association
OGD .... Other Government Departments (HEAS)
OGE .... Objective Grating Electronics (SPST)
OGLE .... Optical Gravitational Lensing Experiment
OGNC .... Organic, Inc. [*NASDAQ symbol*] (SG)
OGNP .... Obstetrical Gynecological Nurse Practitioner (NUJO)
OGS .... Oxford GlycoSciences
OHG .... Official Hotel Guide (TRID)
OHICU......... Open Heart Intensive Care Unit (NUJO)
OHMP .... Occupational Health Maintenance Program (SARE)

OICETS .... Optical Inter-Orbit Communications Engineering Test Satellite [*Sponsored by European Space Agency and Japan Space Agency*]
OILREC .... Oil Recovery (RIMS)
OJ .... Official Journal (HEAS)
OLC............. Occupation Level Crossing (HEAS)
OLC............. Overload Class (CGWS)
OLIPSE .... Optizon Liquid Phase Sintering Experiment [*NASA*] (SPST)
OLN .... Operator's License Number (SARE)
OLS .... Operational License Stage (CARB)
OLS .... Operational Line Scanner (CARB)
OM............. Operation Minute (HEAS)
OM............. Organometallic
OMA .... Ocular Motor Apraxia
OMAF.......... Ontario Ministry of Agriculture and Food [*Canada*]
OMAFRA...... Ontario Ministry of Agriculture, Food and Rural Affairs
OMC............ Operations Management Consultant [*Department of Emergency Management*] (DEMM)
OMCS .... Ozone Monitor Comparison System (CARB)
OMEE.......... Ontario Ministry of Environment and Energy [*Canada*]
OMEX.......... Ocean Margin Exchanges (CARB)
OMF............ Operations Management Forum (HEAS)
OML............ Ontology Markup Language (IDAI)
OMM........... Offshore Minerals Management Program
OMNR.......... Ontario Ministry of Natural Resources [*Canada*]
OMPLA .... Outer Membrane Phospholipase A
ONC .... Orthopaedic Nurse Certified (NUJO)
ONF .... Oncology Nursing Foundation
ONI .... Optical Networks, Inc.
ONIS .... ONI Systems [*NASDAQ symbol*]
ONIX .... Online Information Exchange [*Association of American Publishers*]
ONNN.......... SCG Holdings [*NASDAQ symbol*] (SG)
ONVI .... Onvia.com, Inc. [*NASDAQ symbol*] (SG)
ONW .... Onwards (RIMS)
OO .... Owner's Option (RIMS)
OODA.......... Observation, Orientation, Decision, Action
op .... Operation (NTIO)
OP.............. Other Person (TRID)
O/P .... Output (PIPO)
OP.............. Output Port (CCCA)
OPA .... Output and Performance Analysis (HEAS)
OPASTCO..... Organization for the Promotion and Advancement of Small Telephone Companies (CGWS)
OPC .... Other Project Costs (ABAC)
Opcode........ Operating Code [*Computer science*] (ITCA)
OPE............. Office of Planning and Environment (ABAC)
OpFor.......... Opposing Force
OPHM .... OraPharma, Inc. [*NASDAQ symbol*] (SG)
OPHS .... Office of Public Health and Science
OPI............. Office of Planning and Integration (ABAC)
OPK .... Ovulation Prediction Kit
OPM........... Output and Performance Measures (HEAS)
opn .... Open
opnwndo...... Open Window
OPS .... Optical Sensor (CARB)
opt .... Optical (NTIO)
OPTEMPO..... Operational Tempo [*Military*]
OPUS.......... Opus 360 Corp. [*NASDAQ symbol*] (SG)
OR .... Occurrence Report (ABAC)
o/r............. On Request (PIAV)
Or............. Oregon (NTIO)
ORA .... Operational Requirements Analysis (SPST)
ORACBA....... Office of Risk Assessment and Cost-Benefit Analysis
ORBF .... Ordinary Radial Basis Function (IDAI)
Orch............ Orchestra
ord............ Ordinal (NTIO)
ord............ Ordinary
org............ Nonprofit Organization
ORG............ Official Recreation Guide (TRID)
org............ Organic (NTIO)
ORHP .... Office of Rural Health Policy
orig............ Originally (NTIO)
ornith .... Ornithology (NTIO)
ORT .... Owner Requirements Table (HLLA)
orth........... Orthopedic (NTIO)
OS.............. Official Scorer [*Baseball term*] (NDBD)

55

OS............... Outer Segment
OS............... Outside Sales (TRID)
OS............... Overall Survival [*Medicine*]
OSA .... Office of Safety Assessment (ABAC)
OSAR.......... Operational Safety Analysis Report (ABAC)
OSBP.......... Office of Small Business Programs
OSCA.......... OSCA, Inc. [*NASDAQ symbol*]
OSCIA........ Ontario Soil and Crop Association [*Canada*]
OSD .... Open Shelter Deck (RIMS)
OSI.............. Other Service Information (TRID)
OSI.............. Outback Steakhouse [*NYSE symbol*]
OSP .... Online Service Provider
OSPI .... Office of Superintendent of Public Instruction
OSSN.......... Outside Sales Support Network (TRID)
OSTP .... Onboard Short Term Plan [*NASA*] (SPST)
OSU .... Operational Strategy Unit (HEAS)
OS/VS1 .... Operating System/Virtual Storage 1 [*Computer science*] (ITCA)
OS/VS2 .... Operating System/Virtual Storage 2 [*Computer science*] (ITCA)
O/T.............. Other Times (PIPO)
o/t .... Other Times (PIAV)

OTC.............. Orthogonal Transform Coding (CCCA)
OTD .... Official Tour Directory (TRID)
OTECH .... Oceaneering Technology Integration (ABAC)
OTFA........... Office of Technical Financial Assistance (ABAC)
OTGS .... OTG Software [*NASDAQ symbol*] (SG)
OTI.............. Office of Technology Integration (ABAC)
OTIS............. Oklahoma Telecommunications Interlibrary System (AUEG)
OTR .... Other-Total Ratio [*B. Mullen*] (DIPS)
OTS.............. Out of Service (PIPO)
OTSU .... Open Technology Support Unit (HEAS)
OTT............. Office of Transportation Technologies
OV................ Organic Variable (DIPS)
OV................ Organismic Variable (DIPS)
OVC .... Occupational Violent Crime (HEAS)
OW.............. Owners (RIMS)
OWL............ Optimal Waste Loading (ABAC)
OWW .... Organic Wash Waste (ABAC)
Oxbridge...... Oxford and Cambridge Universities (NTIO)
Oxfam.......... Oxford Committee for Famine Relief (NTIO)
OZ................ Outer Zone (HEAS)

P
By Acronym

P	Pacific Stock Exchange (SG)
p	Participle (NTIO)
P	Percentile (DIPS)
p	Peso (NTIO)
P	Pico
P	Pitcher (NTIO)
P	Poise [Unit of measure]
p	Practical Intelligence (DIPS)
P	Prime
p	Probability (DIPS)
P	Professor
P	Rank Correlation (DIPS)
P	Roll Rate
P2	Pollution Prevention
P2I	Planned Product Improvement
P3	Pacific Project Phoenix
P3P	Platform for Privacy Preferences
Pa	Paris Stock Exchange (SG)
PA	Pascal [Unit of measure]
PA	Pay and Allowances
PA	Pilotless Aircraft
PA	Planning Authority (HEAS)
PA	Plate Appearance [Baseball term] (NDBD)
PA	Polar to Analog
PA	Position Accuracy
PA	Post Award Contract [Department of Defense]
PA	Problem Analysis
PA	Program Announcement
PA	Protactinium
PAA	Primary Aromatic Amine (ABAC)
PAA	Priority Problem Areas
PAAAR	Pioneers Across America for Alzheimer's Research [An association]
PAAR	Pioneers Across America for Alzheimer's Research [An association]
PABST	Primary Adhesively Bonded Structure Techniques
PABX	Public-Area Branch Exchange (AEBE)
PAC	Pacific Airmotive Corporation
PAC	Personal Accident Coverage [Travel industry] (TRID)
PAC	Personal Analog Computer
PAC	Personnel Administrative Center
PAC	Polar Atmospheric Chemistry (CARB)
PAC	Polycylic Aromatic Hydrocarbons
PAC	President's Advisor for Science
PAC	Probably Approximately Correct (IDAI)
PAC	Professional Advisory Committee (DIPS)
PACE	Professional and Career Education for Early Childhood
PACE	Programs Advancing Citizenship Education [Institute]
PACE-LV	Preflight Acceptance Checkout Equipment-Launch Vehicle [NASA]
PACER	Post-Operational Analysis and Exercise Review [Program]
PACER	Programmed Automatic Communications Equipment Requirements
Pacif	Pacific (NTIO)
pack	Packed
PACS	Personal Access Communications System (CGWS)
PACT	Personal Air Communications Technology (CGWS)
PACT	Plasma Arc Centrifugal Treatment
PACT	Prisoners and Community Working Together [Institute]
PACT	Producers Alliance for Cinema & Television
PAD	Pseudoachondroplastic Spondyloepiphysial Dysplasia (DIPS)
PAD	Public Affairs Detachment
PADR	Product Assurance Discrepancy Report
PADS	Positioning Azimuth Determining System
PADS	Product Assurance Data System (SPST)
PAF	Pakistan Air Force
PAFTAD	Pacific Trade and Development Conference
PAG	Priorities Analysis Group
PAG	Program Advisory Group
PAGCH	Paging and Access Grant Channel (CGWS)
PAGEOS	Passive Geodetic Satellite
PAH	Polynuclear Aromatic Hydrocarbons (SARE)
PAHZ	Panzer Abwewp Hubschrauber [Attack Helicopter]
PAIV	Power as an Integral Variable
PA KEY	Program Extension Key [Computer science] (ITCA)
Pal	Palestine (NTIO)
PAL	Personal Answer Line
PAL	Phase Alternating Line [Telecommunications] (MLOA)
PAL	Process Assembly Languages
PAL	Process Asset Library
PAL	Publication Applicability List [Navy]
PALD	Phase Alternation Line Delay
PALM	Palm, Inc. [NASDAQ symbol] (SG)
PALS	Pediatric Advanced Life Support (NUJO)
PALS	Photographic Area and Location System
PALS	Preliminary Award Letter System
PAM	Performance Assessment Matrix (SARE)
PAMRI	Peripheral Adapter Module Replacement Item (CTAS)
PAMS	Parts Management System
PAMS	Photochemical Assessment Monitoring Stations
PAMS	Proceedings of the American Mathematical Society [A publication]
pan	Panorama
PAN	Personnel Advice Notes (HEAS)
PAN	Porte-Avion Nucleaire
P&A	Planning and Analysis (ABAC)
P&D	Performance and Demonstration
P&D	Production and Deployment
p&h	Postage and Handling (NTIO)
p & i	Principal and Interest (NTIO)
P&P	Preservation and Packing
P&RP	Production and Research Property [Department of Defense]
P&S	Panel and Shelf
P&SA	Payload and Servicing Accommodations [NASA] (SPST)
P&W	Particles and Waves (SPST)
P&Y	Pitch and Yaw
PANVALET	Direct Access Library Maintenance Package [Pansophic Systems]
PAO	Public Assistance Officer (DEMM)
PAPM	Pall Aircraft Porous Media
PAPS	Periodic Armaments Planning System
PAR	Parimeter Array Radar
PAR	Performance Analysis Report
PAR	Photosynthetically Available Radiation (CARB)
PAR	Preferred Arrival Route (CTAS)
PAR	Program Analysis Report
PAR	Progressive Airframe Rework
PAR	Protection Action Recommendation [Department of Emergency Management] (DEMM)
PARD	Protect as Restricted Data
PARENTS FLAG	Parents and Friends of Lesbians and Gays [An association]
PARFOX	Parapet Foxhole
PARI	Pre-Columbian Art Research Institute
parl	Parliament (NTIO)
PARL	Preferential Arrival Route [Aviation] (PIPO)
PARPRO	Peacetime Airborne Reconnaissance Program
PARREV	Paraglider Research Vehicle
part	Participle (NTIO)
PARTAS	Precision Asrania Range Target Acquisition and Control
PAS	Pioneer Aerodynamic Systems
PAS	Precategorical Acoustic Storage (DIPS)
PAS	Precision Acquisition System
PAS	Protocol Analysis System (ABAC)
PAS	Pseudo Aircraft Simulation (CTAS)
PAS	Public Affairs Specialist
PASC	Pan American Standards Committee
PASC	Polar Atmospheric and Snow Chemistry (CARB)
PASE	Polar Air-Snow Experiment (CARB)
PASEP	Pass Separately
pass	Passive (NTIO)
PASS	Passive Aircraft Surveillance System
PASS	Performance Assessment Scientific Support (ABAC)
PASS	Priority Academic Student Skills
PAT	Passive Angle Attack
PAT	Patersons [Publisher]
PAT	Preliminary Acceptance Tests
PAT	Program Activity Transmission
PAT	Prototype Adaptation Toolkit (CTAS)
PAT&E	Product Assurance Test and Evaluation
PAT&E	Production Acceptance Test and Evaluation
patd	Patented (NTIO)
PATE	Production Acceptance Test and Evaluation
PATRAM	Packaging and Transport of Radioactive Materials (HEAS)
PATRIOT ICC	Patriot Information Control Center
PAV	Pressure Ageing Vessel
PAVE-PAWS	Precision Acquisition of Vehicle Entry and Phased Array Warning System
PAX	Passengers

pax.............. Passengers (PIAV)
PAYGO......... Pay-As-You-Go
PB.............. Particle Beam
PB.............. Poor Box
P/B.............. Preburner
P/B.............. Push Button
P-BAND....... 225-390 Megacycles per Second
PBAX .... Private Automatic Branch Exchange [*Computer science*] (ITCA)
PBB............. Please Be Brief [*Internet dialog*]
PBCD.......... Packed Binary Coded Decimal (ROAS)
PBE............. Probability of Bit Error (CCCA)
PBM............. Peribacteriod Membrane (CARB)
PBM............. Pharmacy Benefits Manager
PBSC........... Packard BioScience [*NASDAQ symbol*] (SG)
PBSCT .... Peripheral Blood Stem Cell Transplant [*Medicine*]
PBT............. Portable Breathalyzer Test (SARE)
PBTB.......... Parsons Brinckerhoff-Tudor-Bechtel
PBX............. Private Branch Exchange
PBZ............. Personal Breathing Zone (HEAS)
Pc .... Chamber Pressure
pc .... Parallax Second (NTIO)
PC.............. PC Holdings ADS [*NYSE symbol*] (SG)
PC.............. Personal Computer (AUEG)
PC.............. Photoconductive
P/C.............. Pitch Control
PC.............. Port Charles [*Television program title*]
PC.............. Power Conversion
PC.............. Priority Control (MLOA)
PC.............. Program Coordinator
PC.............. Public Charter (TRID)
PCA............. Pharmacy Corporation of America
PCA............. Property Clearance Assessment (SARE)
PCAST .... President's Committee of Advisors on Science and Technology
PCATD .... Personal Computer Aircraft Training Device
PCB............. Printed Control Board
PCC............. Plastic Chip Carrier (AEBE)
PCC............. Procurement Coordination Committee
PCC............. Production Control Centers
PCCA .... Portable Computer and Communications Association (CGWS)
PCD .... Pioneer-Central Division [*Bendix*]
PCE............. Probability of Character Error (CCCA)
PCF............. Pacific Car and Foundry
PCFA.......... Fast Patrol Craft, Air Cushion [*Navy*]
PCFG .... Probabilistic Context Free Grammar (IDAI)
PCFH .... Fast Patrol Craft, Hydrofoil [*Navy*]
PCH .... Paging Channel (CGWS)
PCI............. Peripheral Connection Interface
PCI............. Precombat Checks and Inspections [*Army*]
PCI............. Product Configuration Item
PCI............. Production, Configuration, Integration
PCI............. Program Controlled Input
PCI............. Protocol Capability Indicator (CGWS)
PCL............. Positive Control Launch (CCCA)
PCL............. Process Control Laboratory (ABAC)
PCL............. Prodedure Change List
PCLN .... Priceline.com
PCL-R .... Psychopathy Checklist-Revised [*R. Hare*] (DIPS)
PCLS........... Passive Coherent Locating System (CCCA)
PCM............. Pulse Code Modulation [*Microwave System*]
PCM............. Pulse Code Modulation Microwave [*System*]
PCMC.......... Pirmasens Communications and Electronics Maintenance Center
PCMIA .... Personal Computer Manufacturer Interface Adaptor
PCMR .... Probability of Correct Message Receipt (CCCA)
PCO............. Polycystic Ovaries
PCO .... Program Control Output
PCO .... Program Counterpart Office
PCO/ACO..... Procuring Contracting Officer/Administrative Contracting Officer
PCOR.......... Purchase Change Order Request
PCOS........... Polycystic Ovarian Syndrome
PCP............. PeaCe Pill [*Slang for Phencyclidine*] (DIPS)
PCP............. Phencyclidine (NTIO)
PCP............. Processor Control Panel
PCPA .... Plan for Congressional and Public Affairs
PCPT........... Prostate Cancer Prevention Trial [*Medicine*]
PCR .... Peak Cell Rate (MLOA)
PCR .... Power Control Register
PCR .... Program Counter Register
PCR .... Punched Card Request
PCS............. Part Number Configuration Summary
PCS............. Public and Commercial Services Union (HEAS)
PCS............. Pulse Compression System
PCSFSK .... Phase Coherent Sinusoidal Frequency Shift Keying (CCCA)
PCSO .... Presidential Communications Support Office (CCCA)
pct .... Percent (NTIO)
PCT............. Product Consistency Test (ABAC)
PCT............. Prophyria Catanba Tarda [*Medicine*]
PCTAP .... Positive Control Turnaround Point (CCCA)
PCTOJ.......... Passive Correlation Track-On-Jam [*Department of Defense*]
PCU............. Power Convulsion Unit
PCU .... Procedure Change Unit
PCUD........... Peripheral Control Unit Diagnostic [*Program*]
PD.............. Pad
PD.............. Palladium
PD.............. Panic Disorder (DIPS)
PD.............. Payload Diameter

PD.............. Personal Disposition [*G. W. Allport*] (DIPS)
PD.............. Poor Decals
PD.............. Probability of Detection [*Department of Defense*]
PD.............. Project Development (ABAC)
PD.............. Project Director
PD.............. Promotion Dossier (HEAS)
PD.............. Propagation Delay (MLOA)
PDA .... Preliminary Damage Assessment [*Department of Emergency Management*] (DEMM)
PDA .... Probability Discrete Automation
PDA .... Process Design Analysis [*Program*]
PDA .... Property Disposal Agency
PD&C.......... Power Distribution and Control
PDB .... Parametric Data Base
PDB .... Primary Dispersal Base (CCCA)
PDC .... Pacific Digital Cellular (CGWS)
PDC .... Primary Domain Controller [*Computer science*]
PDC .... Project Data Coordinator
PDC .... Public Disclosure Commission
PD-CD Drive... Phase Change Dual Compact Disk Drive [*Computer science*] (ITCA)
PDCN .... Production Development Change Notice
PDD .... Physical Damage Division
PDD .... Program Design Document (CTAS)
PDDR.......... Product Definition Data Requirements (SPST)
PDG .... Precision Drop Glider
PDI............. Prise Ombilicale Derniers Instants
PDI............. Protein Disulphide Isomerase
PDIS .... Proceedings of the National Symposia [*A publication*]
PDL .... Procedure Description Language
PDM............. Possible Duplicate Message (TRID)
PDMFM....... Pulse-Duration Modulation-Frequency Modulation
PDMG .... Perspective Digital Map Generator
PDMS .... Plasma-Desorption Mass Spectrometry (ABAC)
PDO .... Property Disposal Organization
PDOS .... Professional Development of Officers Study
PDP .... Parallel Distributed Processing (DIPS)
PDP .... Programmable Display Pushbuttons
PDP .... Psychopharmacology Demonstration Project [*Department of Defense*] (DIPS)
PDPR .... Per Day Pro-Rata (RIMS)
PDR .... Preliminary Design Review
PDR .... Property Disposal Request (ABAC)
PDS .... Physician Data Services
PDS .... Plasma Display System
PDS .... Processing and Display System (CCCA)
PDS .... Professional Development Scheme (HEAS)
PDSI .... Professional Data Service, Incorporated
PDSS .... Payload Data Services System (SPST)
PDSS .... Post Deployment Software Support
PDSSC .... Post Deployment Software Support Center
PDT............. Pacific Daylight Time (AEBE)
PDU .... Packet Data Unit (MLOA)
PDW .... Personal Damage Waiver (TRID)
PE.............. Performance Evaluation (ABAC)
pe .... Photoelectron
P/E.............. Price-to-Earnings
PE.............. Probability of Error (CCCA)
pe .... Probable Error (DIPS)
PE.............. Propellants and Explosives
P/E.............. Purchase Enquiry (RIMS)
PEA .... Preliminary Endangerment Assessment (SARE)
PECL .... Positive Emitter-Coupled Logic (AEBE)
PECo........... Philadelphia Electric Company
PECS........... Picture Exchange Communication System
PED............. Platform Environment Deck
PEG............. Project Execution Guidelines (ABAC)
PEGS .... Pesticide Exposure Group of Sufferers (HEAS)
PEIRS .... Pathology Expert Interpretative Reporting System (IDAI)
PELP........... Poland Efficient Lighting Project
PEM............. Particle Modulator Radiometer (CARB)
pen .... Peninsula (NTIO)
PENAIDS..... Penetration Aids
PENGEM ..... Penetration of the Gray Electronics Market
PEO............. Pacific Economic Outlook
PEP............. Patient Environment Program [*Medicine*]
PEP............. Personal Financial Planner
PEP............. Physical Education for Progress [*Act*]
PEP............. Planner Epitaxiel Passivated
PEP............. Producibility Engineering Plan [*Air Force*]
PEP............. Proposal Evaluation Program
PEPS .... Plasma Electron Profiles, Symmetric
PEPS........... Priced Exhibit Processing System
per.............. Periodical
PER............. Periodic Evaluation Record (DIPS)
PERC .... Plasma Energy Recycle and Conversion
PERCS .... Preferred Equity Redemption Cumulative Stock
PERDDIMS... Personnel Deployment and Distribution Management System
perm........... Permanent (NTIO)
PERMINVAR... Permeability Invariable
PERSCOM.... Personnel Command [*Army*]
PERT COST... Program Evaluation and Review Techniques Costs
PERUPEC.... Peruvian National Committee for Pacific Economic Cooperation
PESD .... Post-Employment Services Demonstration
PESKI.......... Probabilities Expert Systems Knowledge and Inference (IDAI)

PET	Production Environmental Testing
PETB	Preflight Test Bus
PETC	Pet in Cabin [*Travel industry*] (TRID)
PF	Picofarad
PF	Poor Foam
P/F	Pre-Flight
PFA	Probability of False Alarm [*Department of Defense*]
PFADS	Physical Operators Foreign Area Data System
PFB	Patellofemoral Knee Brace [*Medicine*]
PFC	Post Flight Checklist
PFC	Power Factor Correction
Pfc	Private First Class [*Military*] (NTIO)
Pfd	Preferred (SG)
PFE	Portable Fire Extinguisher (SPST)
PFK	Program Function Keyboard
PF KEY	Program Function Key [*Computer science*] (ITCA)
PFM	Process Facility Modification (ABAC)
PFO	Pacific Food Outlook
PFOS	Perfluorooctane Sulfonate
PFRT	Preliminary Flight Rated Test
PFS	Progression Free Survival [*Medicine*]
PFTE	Portable Field Trainer/Evaluator
PFUND	Program for Understanding Neurological Diseases
PG	Patrol Escort [*Navy*]
PG	Patrol Vessel Gunboat [*Navy*]
PG	Program Management Assistance Group
PGB	Program Budget Guidance
PGF	Patrol Ship [*Navy*]
PGG	Guided Missile Patrol Combatant [*Navy*]
PGH	Per Geard Hatch (RIMS)
PGI	Power Generators, Incorporated
PGL	Partnership in Global Learning
PGL	Peter Group Leader
PGO	Pontine Geniculate Occipital (DIPS)
PGR	Reconnaissance Patrol Combatant [*Navy*]
PGRG	Potomac General Research Group
PGS	Power Generation Section
Ph	Hit Probability
PH	Pauling and Harrischfeger
PH	Pershing II
Ph	Philadelphia Stock Exchange (SG)
PHA	Peak Horizontal Acceleration
PHA	Pulse Height Analyzed
PHAROS	Phased Array Radar for Overland Surveillance
PHCP	Physically Handicapped Children's Program
PHI	Position Homing Indicator
PHIL	Philippians [*Biblical*]
phil	Philosphy (NTIO)
PHITAP	Priority High Interest Tactical Air Acoustic Forecast Prediction
PHM	Patrol Combatant Missile Hydrofoil [*Navy*]
PHM	Patrol Hydrofoil Missileship [*Navy*]
PHM	Philomon [*Biblical*]
PHO	Public Health Officer Inspector (HEAS)
PHOINT	Photographic Intelligence
phon	Phonetic (NTIO)
PHOTO	Photographic
photog	Photography (NTIO)
PHPD	Per Hatch per Day (RIMS)
phr	Phrase (NTIO)
phr	Phrase Book
PHR	Point-Hour Ratio (DIPS)
PHS&T	Packaging, Handling, Storage, and Transportability
PHV	Peak Horizontal Velocity
phys	Physical (NTIO)
PI	Paradoxical Intention [*V. E. Frankl*] (DIPS)
PI	Photographic Interpretation
PI	Premium Income (MARI)
PI	Product Improved
PI	Program Interrupter
PI	Public Involvement (ABAC)
PIA	Peril Insured Against (MARI)
PIAC	Printing Industry Advisory Committee (HEAS)
PIAP	Pesticides Incidents Appraisal Panel (HEAS)
PIAS	Precision Locator Strike System Intelligence Augmentation System
PIB	Publishing Information Bulletin
PIC	Particulate Inorganic Carbon (CARB)
PIC	Programmed Information Center
PIC	Project for Interface Compatibility
PICASSO-CENA	Pathfinder Instruments for Cloud and Aerosol Spacebourne Observations-Climatologie Etneduedes des Nuages et des Aerosols [*NASA's proposed launch date is March 2003*]
PICD	Primary Inventory Cutoff Data [*Supply*]
PID	Prime Input Development
PID	Process-Induced Defect
PID	Project Identification Code
PID	Proportional Integral Derivation
PID	Proportional Integration Derivation
PI/DE	Positive Indentification and Direction Finding Equipment
PIDG	Proportional, Integral, and Differential Gain (SPST)
PIE	Pulse Interference Elimination
PIE COST	Probability of Incurring Estimated Cost
PIF	Problem Identification Form (ARMP)
PIFA	Power Input Filter Assembly
PIG	Pendulous Integrating Gyroscope
PIGA	Pendulous Integrating Gyroscope Accelerometers

PIH	Poison Inhalation Hazard (SARE)
PIM	Position of Intended Movement
PIN	Pacific Island Nations
PIN	Pre-Invitation Notice
PIN	Prosthetic Intradithelial Neoplacia [*Medicine*]
PINRO	Polar Scientific Research Institute for Marine Fisheries and Oceanography [*Russian*]
PINS	Pipeline Inspection Notification System (PIAV)
PIO	Pioneer [*A publication*]
PI/O	Processor Input/Output
PIO	Provisioned Item Orders
PIP	Packaging and Industrial Polymers [*E.T. DuPont*]
PIP	Personal Injury Protection (TRID)
PIP	Picture-in-Picture
PIP	Pulsed Integrating Pendulum
PIPEFLEX	Pipe Flexibility [*Stress Analysis Program*]
PIPEMAID	Piping Program
PIPER	Pulsed Intense Plasma for Experimental Research
PIPI	Pipelines Inspectorate (HEAS)
PIR	Photographic Interpretation Report
PIR	Precision Infrared Radiometer (ARMP)
PIR	Publication Illustration Request
PIREP	Pilot Weather Report (PIPO)
PIRS	Personnel Information Retrieval System
PISC	Programme for the Inspection of Steel Components (HEAS)
PISE	Pneumatically Installed Stabilized Earth
PIT	Polaris Industrial Team [*Navy*]
PIT	Processing Index Terms
PIT	Project in Trouble (CCCA)
PITB	Poetry in the Branches [*Program*]
PIV	Particle Image Velocimeter (ABAC)
PIVT	Product Improvement Verification Test
Pixel	Picture Element [*Computer science*] (ITCA)
pixel	Picture Element (AEBE)
PIZ	Public Information Zone (HEAS)
PJL	Power Jets, Limited
Pk	Peak (NTIO)
Pk	Psychokinesis (DIPS)
PK	Soviet Light Machine Gun
pkd	Packed
PKG	Packaging Corp. America [*NYSE symbol*] (SG)
PKI	Public Key Infrastructure
pkt	Packet (NTIO)
P/L	Parts List
P/L	Payload
P/L	Post Landing
PI A	Polyactide [*Chemistry term*]
PLA	Programmable Link Adapter
PLANIT	Programming Language for Interactive Teaching
PLAT	Pilot Landing Air Television
PLAT	Pilot Landing Assistance Television
Plat	Plateau (NTIO)
PLAY	Participate in the Lives of America's Youth
PLCO	Prostate, Lung, Colorectal, and Ovarian [*Cancers*]
PLCP	Physical Layer Convergence Protocol (MLOA)
PLCT	Prelaunch Certification Test
PLFA	Primary Level Field Activities
PLLI	National Institute on Postsecondary Education, Libraries, and Lifelong Learning
PLMN	Public Land Mobile Network (CGWS)
PLMS	Periodic Leg Movements in Sleep (DIPS)
PLN	Private Line Network (CCCA)
PLO	Probability of Leakage through Overlay
PLOT	Plotter
PLS	Palletized Loading System
PLSO	Phonetic Letter Spell Out (CCCA)
PLT	Project Lead Time
PLU	Probability of Leakage through Underlay
PLU	Program Load Unit
PLUR	Photographics Laboratory Usage Reporting
plur	Plural (NTIO)
PLUTO	Programmed Logic for Automatic Teaching Operation
PLVW	Pool View (TRID)
PLY	Photolimited Yield
PLZT	Leading Lanthanum Zirconate Titanate
PM	Performance Measurement
PM	Photographic Master
PM	Physical Medium (MLOA)
PM	Post Meridian
PM	Primary Memory (DIPS)
PM	Probability of a Single Failure Causing Other Failures within a Three-Pack [*Department of Defense*]
pm	Project Management (ABAC)
PM	Promethium
PM	Purchase Memorandum
PMA	Preferred Machine Assist [*Computer science*] (ITCA)
PMA	Project Manager, Air
PMAA	Politico-Military Administrative Affairs [*Committee*]
PMAA	Propulsion Module Attach Assembly [*NASA*] (SPST)
PMAAH	Project Manager, Advanced Attack Helicopter
PMAC	Project Manager Allocation Chart
PMAS	Propulsion Module Attach Structure [*NASA*] (SPST)
PMASE	Project Manager, Aircraft Survivability Equipment
PMASH	Project Manager, Advanced Scout Helicopter
PMC	Partial Mission Capability [*Time*]

PMC............	Post Manufacture Checkout
PMC............	Precision Machinery Commercialization
PMC............	Pressure-Modulator Cell *(CARB)*
PMCB..........	Project Manager Control Board
PMCS..........	Partial Mission Capable-Supply
PMCS..........	Project Management Control System
PMD............	Power Management and Distribution Palmdale *[California]*
PMD............	Program Management Documents
PMDL..........	Post Mobilization Deployment List *[Department of Defense]*
PME............	Photomagnet Electric
PME............	Precision Measurement Equipment
PME............	Prime Mission Equipment
PME............	Profession Military Education *[Department of Defense]*
PMF............	Performance Monitoring Function
PMF............	Processeur Militaire Francais *[French]*
PMI............	Preliminary Maintenance Inspection *[Department of Defense]*
PMI............	Preliminary Marksmanship Instruction *[Army]*
PMI............	Premarksmanship Instruction *[Army]*
PMI............	Preventive Maintenance Instruction *[Department of Defense]*
PMI............	Programmable Machine Interface
PMI............	Program Management Instruction *[Department of Defense]*
PMIC..........	Payload Mission Integration Contract *[NASA]*
PMIC..........	Periodic Maintenance Information Cards
PMIR	Pressure Modulator Infrared Radiometer *(CARB)*
PML............	Perfectly Matched Layer *(ARMP)*
PML............	Possible Maximum Loss *(MARI)*
pmm............	Preventive Medicine Measures
PMM..........	Probability of Missed Message *(CCCA)*
PMML.........	Predictive Model Markup Language *(IDAI)*
PMNAVCON...	Project Manager, Navigation and Control
PMNUC.......	Project Manager for Nuclear *[Munitions]*
PMO............	Program Maintenance Office
PMO............	Program Management Organization *(HLLA)*
PMO............	Program Manager's Office
PMOM........	Project Manager's Office
PMOM........	Performance Management Operations Manager
P-MOS........	P-Channel Metal-Oxide Semiconductor
PMP............	Performance Monitoring Program *(CCCA)*
PMP............	Preventive Maintenance Periodic *[Inspection]*
PMP............	Program Master Plan *[Department of Defense]*
PMP............	Project Management Plan *(ABAC)*
PMR............	Private Mobile Radio *(CGWS)*
PMR............	Program Management Review
PMR............	Project Management Review
PMRP	Program Manager's Recommended Program
PMRPV	Project Manager, Remotely Piloted Vehicles *[Department of Defense]*
PMRS	Private Mobile Radio Service *(CGWS)*
PMS............	Performance Management System *(HLLA)*
PMS............	Planned Maintenance Subsystem
PMS............	Preventive Maintenance Services
PMS............	Project Manager System
PMS............	Project Master Schedule
PMS............	Property Management System *(TRID)*
PMSA..........	Project Management System Assessment
PM/SH	Preventive Maintenance and Self-Help *[Program]*
PM TRADE...	Project Manager, Training Devices
PMU..........	Personal Messaging Unit *(CGWS)*
PMUTTAS ...	Project Manager, Utility Tactical Transport Aircraft System
PN............	Parish Nurse *(NUJO)*
P/N............	Part Number
PN............	Plain
PN............	Positive Negative
PN............	Project de Norme
p/n	Promissory Note *(NTIO)*
PNA............	Polynuclear Aromatic Hydrocarbon *(ABAC)*
PNC............	Preferred Noise Criterion *[L. L. Beranek]* *(DIPS)*
PNDB..........	Perceived Noise Decibels
PNE............	Peaceful Nuclear Explosive
PNEC	Proceedings of the National Electronics Conference *[A publication]*
PNEUD........	Pneudraulic
PNF............	Partial Neutralization Feed *(ABAC)*
PNG	Proportional Navigation Guidance
PNI............	Paninternational
PNN............	Probabilistic Neural Network *(IDAI)*
PNP............	Paranitrophenal
PNP............	Probability of No Penetration *[NASA]* *(SPST)*
PNP............	Psychiatric Nurse Practitioner *(NUJO)*
PN-PRBS	Pseudo-Noise, Pseudo-Random Binary String/Stream *(CGWS)*
PNR............	Passenger Name Record *[Travel industry]* *(TRID)*
PNR............	Passenger Now Recorded *[Travel industry]* *(TRID)*
PNSC	Passenger Network Services Corporation *(TRID)*
PNT............	Paint Template
PNTR	Permanent Normal Trade Relations
PNUTS........	Possible Nuclear Underground Test Site
Po............	Polonium
PO............	Previous Owner
Po5............	Party of Five *[Television program title]*
POAR..........	Project Order Action Required
POBO..........	Project Office Business Operations
POC	Performance Operating Characteristic *(DIPS)*
POC	Productional Operational Capability
POEMS	Postoperative Expert Medical System *(IDAI)*
POF............	Parts Order Form
POG	Pediatric Oncology Group
POGO..........	Pogo Suppression System *[NASA]*

POI............	Parking Orbit Inspection *[NASA]*
POI............	Path Overhead Indicator *(MLOA)*
Pokeman	Pocket Monsters *[Nintendo Co., Ltd.]*
pol	Polite *(NTIO)*
pol	Politician *(NTIO)*
POL............	Polygram *[Publisher]*
POL............	Posterior Oblique Ligaments *[Medicine]*
POLSC	Political Science
POLYED	Polymer Education
POM............	Plan Objectives Memorandum *(CCCA)*
POME..........	Protect Our Mountain Environment *[Colorado]*
PONF	Paediatric Oncology Nurses Forum *[British]*
POP	Perpendicular to Orbital Plane
POP	Perpendicular-to-Orbit Plan
POPMail	Post Office Protocol Mail
POPS	Pyrotechnic Optical Plume Simulation
POR	Place of Receipt *(MARI)*
POR	Power-On Reset *(AEBE)*
PORSHE......	Project of Ocean Rafts System for Hydrogen Economy
PORT	Port Financial *[NASDAQ symbol]* *(SG)*
POS	Part-of-Speech *(IDAI)*
POS/NAV......	Positioning/Navigation
POT	Point of Turnaround *[Travel industry]* *(TRID)*
POV	Peak Operating Valve
PoW	Plan of Work *(HEAS)*
POW/MP	Prisoner of War/Missing Personnel
P-P............	Peak-to-Peak *[Value]*
p-p............	Peak-to-Peak *(AEBE)*
PP............	Pilot Pulse
P/P............	Print Punch
PP............	Program Performed
PP............	Purchased Part
PPA............	Performance Partnership Agreement *(SARE)*
PPA............	Photographic Peak Analysis
PPA............	Plane Parallel Approximation *(ARMP)*
PP&C..........	Program Planning and Control *(SPST)*
PPBS	Planning, Programming, and Budgeting Structure
PPBSO.........	Piping and Pipe Band Society of Ontario *[Canada]*
PPC............	Preservation and Packaging Committee
PPCO2	Partial Pressure Carbon Dioxide
PPD	Partial Packet Discard *(MLOA)*
PPD	Port Protection Device *[Computer science]* *(ITCA)*
PPD	Production Program, Douglas
PPD	Project Planning Document *(ABAC)*
PPDO..........	Per Person, Double Occupancy *[Travel industry]* *(TRID)*
PPDS	Purchase Parts Data Sheet
PPE............	Preparticipation Physical Examination
PPECC	Philippine Pacific Economic Cooperation Committee
PPG	Pittsburgh Paint and Glass *[Company]*
PPG	Prime Power Group
PPG	Priority Planning Grid *(ABAC)*
PPI............	Passe Partout International
PPI............	Precision Products, Incorporated
PPI............	Present Position Indicator
PPIF	Photographic Processing and Interpretation Facility
PPIR	Personal Property Inventory Report
PPIR	Personnel Planning Integration Report
PPM............	Pilot Pulse Missile
PPMP	Preliminary Program Management Plan
PPMR	Purchase Parts Material Request
PPN	Preferred Provider Network
PPO	Prototype Program Office
PPP	Package Processing Point
PPP............	Phased Program Planning
PPP............	Platoon Package Program
PPPoE.........	Point-to-Point Protocol over Ethernet
PPR	Passenger Profile Record *[Travel industry]* *(TRID)*
PPREP	Periodic Personnel Reports
pprm...........	Preprimer
PPS............	Pre-Processeur de Signal *[Computer]* *[French]*
PPS............	Program Peripheral Subsystems *(CCCA)*
PPS............	Pupil Personnel Services
PPSD	Personnel and Pay Services Division
PPS II	Payroll Personnel System
PPSS	President's Private Sector Survey
PPT............	Production Prototype Test
PPTC..........	Purchase Part Tab Card
PPTP..........	Personnel Performance and Training Program
pptv	Parts per Trillion by Volume *(CARB)*
PPU............	Primary Power Unit
PPW............	Patient Protective Wrap
PQA	Preliminary Qualification Analysis
PQA	Program Quality Acceptance *(SPST)*
PQE............	Project Quality Engineer
PQM............	Pilotless Drone Missile *[Department of Defense]*
PQQPRI.......	Preliminary Qualitative and Quantitative Personnel Requirements Information
PQT............	Production Qualification Testing
PQT............	Prototype Qualification Test
PR............	Partial Reinforcement *(DIPS)*
PR............	Partial Reward *(DIPS)*
PR............	Port Risks *(MARI)*
PR............	Praseodymium
PR............	Preflight
PR............	Pressure Regulation

Pr	Prior (SG)	PSB	Harbor Patrol Boat [Navy]
PR	Product Removal (ABAC)	PSB	Professional Staffs Branch (HEAS)
PR	Programmed Requirement	PSB	Public Safety Building (SARE)
PR	Proverb	PSC	Parallel to Series Converter
PR	Purchase Requisition	PSC	Plant Simulation Code (ABAC)
PRA	Precision Radar Approach (PIPO)	PSC	Prime Systems Contractor
PRAD	Pitch Radio Adjustment Device	PSC	Program Support Center
PRB	Probex Corp. [AMEX symbol] (SG)	PSCC	Packaging, Storage, and Containerization Center
PRB	Problem Review Board (ARMP)	PSCC	Power System Computation Conference
PRC	Pitch Radio Controller	PSCM	Pilot Scale Ceramic Melter (ABAC)
PRC	Player Relations Committee [Baseball] (NDBD)	PSCOE	Power Sources Center of Excellence
PRC	Precipitation (CARB)	PSD	Personal Smoke Device
PRC	Principal Reducing Credit	PSD	Prevent Significant Deterioration
PRC	Program Resources Catalog	PSDI	Presence Sensing Device Initiation (SARE)
PRC	Promotion Research Committee	PSDPC	Polar Satellite Data Processing Centre (CARB)
PRC	Propulsion Research Corporation	PSDU	Personnel Services Delivery Unit (HEAS)
PRCB	Program Review Change Board	PSE	Philippine Stock Exchange
PRCS	People's Republic of China Satellite	PSE	Programming Support Environment
PRD	Purdue Aeronautics Corporation	PSE	Psychological Stress Evaluation
PRE	Partial Reinforcement Effect (DIPS)	PSEAG	Physical Security Equipment Action Group
pred	Predicate (NTIO)	PSEL	Plant Specific Emission Limit (SARE)
pref	Preference (NTIO)	PS/FC	Power Supply/Fuel Cell
Pref	Preference (SG)	PSG	Permanent Steering Group
PREINSURV	President of Board for Inspection and Survey	PSG	Polysomnography (DIPS)
PRE-MOD	Premodulation	PSGE	Project Specification Group Engineer
PRE-OP	Pre-Operational	psgr	Passenger (TRID)
prep	Preparatory (NTIO)	PSHTM	Pilot Scale High Temperature Melter (ABAC)
pres	Present (NTIO)	PSI	Planned Speed Indicator
Presb	Presbyterian (NTIO)	PSI	Pollution Standards Index (SARE)
prev	Previous (NTIO)	PSI	Pulsepower Systems Incorporated
PRI	Performance Review Institutes	PSID	Panel Study of Income Dynamics
PRI	Photographic Radar Intelligence	PSIS	Pounds per Square Inch per Second
PRI	Potomac Research, Incorporated	PSIT	PSi Technologies Hldg. ADS [NASDAQ symbol] (SG)
prim	Primary (NTIO)	PSL	Parts Selection List (SPST)
PRIP	Product Reliability Improvement Program	PSL	Programming Support Library
PRIS	Publications Reliability Inspection Sheet	PSM	Pyrotechnic Substitute Monitor
PRL	Physical Research Laboratory (CARB)	PSMA	Prostate-Specific Membrane Antigen [Medicine]
PrL	Prolactin (DIPS)	PSNB	Public-Sector Net Borrowing
PRM	Partial Refund Message [Travel industry] (TRID)	P SNSR	Position Sensor
PRM	Partner Relationship Management	PSP	Police Service Pistol
prm	Primer	PSP	Pre-Stock Point
PRM	Pulse Ratio Modulator	PSP	Professional Scholarly Publishing
PRME	Prime Response [NASDAQ symbol] (SG)	PSPL Pre-Op	Prices Square Parts List-Pre-Operational
PRNET	Pocket Radio Network (CCCA)	PSPP	Preliminary System Package Program
PRO	Principal Reducing Option	PSR	Passenger Service Representative [Travel industry] (TRID)
PROB	Probability Percentage (PIAV)	PSRS	Patient Service Records System
prof	Professional (NTIO)	PSS	Performance Summary Sheet
PROM	Pockel's Readout Optical Memory	PSS	Protection Security Service
PROMIS	Problem Oriented Medical Guidance System	PSS	Pseudo-Sense Switch
pron	Pronoun (NTIO)	PSSEK	Probability of Single Shot Engagement Kill [Military]
prop	Proper (NTIO)	PSSP	Personnel Surety and Security Program
pros atty	Prosecuting Attorney (NTIO)	PST	Provincial Standard Time (TRID)
PROT	Protected Reservation [Travel industry] (TRID)	P-STATIC	Precipitation Static
Protect	Protection	PSW	Process Status Word
prov	Province (NTIO)	PSWMRL	Pasture Systems and Watershed Management Research Lab
PROV	Provisioning	psych	Psychology (NTIO)
PROVER	Procurement, Value, Economy, Reliability	PT	Personnel Training
PRP	Peer Review Panel (ABAC)	PT	Platinum
PRP	Presidential Reorganizational Project	Pt	Point (NTIO)
PRP	Product Requirements Plan	PT	Port Taxes (TRID)
PRPS	Programming Requirements Process Specifications	PT	Position Location Reporting System Terminal
PRR	Professional Rights and Responsibilities	PT	Propellant Injection Pressure
PRS	Peer Review Systems, Inc.	PT	Property Type
PRS	Pesticides Registration Section (HEAS)	PTA	Prepaid Ticket Advice [Travel industry] (TRID)
PRS	Placement Research Service	PTA	Procurement Technical Assistance
PRS	Power Reactant System	PTA	Profan Test Assessment [NASA]
PRS	Proportional Representation Society	PTAL	Payment Transaction Application Layer [Computer science] (ITCA)
PRS	Pure Resources [NYSE symbol]	PTC	Propeller Technical Committee
PRSD	Power Reactant Supply and Distribution	PTD	Program Test Director (CCCA)
PRSE	Precise Software Solutions [NASDAQ symbol]	PTD	Provisioning Technical Data
PRSS	Problem Report Squawk Sheet	PTD/E	Physical Teardown Evaluation
PRT	Patter Recognition Technique	PTE	Path Terminating Equipment
PRT	Pulse Repetition Time	PTF	Reengineering Task Force
PRTB	Soviet Mobile Rocket Technical Base	PTFD	Personnel, Training and Force Development
PRV	Pressure Reduction Valve	PTFMR	Peacetime Force Material Request
PRV	Pressure Regulation Valve	PTG	Planning and Tracking Group
PRV	Pressure Relief Valve	PTGS	Picosecond Transient Grating Spectroscopy
PRVT	Production Reliability Verification Test	PTHSE	Penthouse (TRID)
PRZ	Prize Energy [AMEX symbol] (SG)	PTI	Pacific Telecom, Incorporated
PS	Packet Send Sequence Number	PTI	Payload Type Identifier
PS	Picosecond	PTI	Practice Training Index
PS	Potentiometer Synchronometer	PTL	Phase Tracking Loop
Ps	Pressure (HLLA)	PTM	Priority Timing Module
PS	Problem Space	PTME	Physical Teardown/Maintenance Evaluation
PS	Propellant Seal	PTML	Positive Negative, Positive Negative Transistor Magnetic Logic
PS	Protective Structure	PTMR	Percutaneous Transmyocardial Revascularization [Medicine]
PS	Psalms	PTP	Peripheral Target Position (ABAC)
PS2	PlayStation 2 [Video game console]	PTR	Port Thermal Radiator (SPST)
PS2	Power Station Two	PTR	Problem Trouble Report (CTAS)
PSA	Passenger Service Agent [Travel industry] (TRID)	PTR	Processor Tape Reader
PSA	Personnel Support Agency	PTR	Program Technical Report (CTAS)
PSA	Potentiometric Stripping Analysis (ABAC)	PTT	Postal, Telephone, and Telegraph
PSA	Power and Servo Assembly	P-Tube	Pneumatic Tube
PSA	Preliminary Site Assessment (SARE)	PTVE	Propulsion and Terrain Vehicle Engineering [NASA]
Psa	Psychoanalysis (DIPS)	PTW	Permit to Work (HEAS)

PTWG .... Planning Tracking Working Group
pty .... Proprietary (NTIO)
PU .... Planning Unit (HEAS)
PU .... Plutonium
PU .... Pumps (RIMS)
PUBSAT ...... Publications Ships Assistance Team [*Navy*]
PUD .... Peri-Urethral Diathermy [*Medicine*]
PUK .... Prudential plc ADS [*NYSE symbol*]
PUMA .... Programmable Universal Machine for Assembly [*Robot*]
PUMS .... Public Use Micro Sample
PUP .... Peacetime Utilization Program
PUPO .... Pull-Up, Push-Out
PUSU .... Policy Unit Support Unit (HEAS)
PVC .... Permanent Virtual Channel
PVI .... Postage Validation Imprinter
PVMD .... Parallel Virtual Machine Daemon (CTAS)
PVST .... Premate Verification System Test [*NASA*]
PVT .... Production Validation Testing
PVT .... Protected Tube-Launched Optically Tracked Wire-Guided Anti-Tank
                    Missile Vehicle

PVT-G .... Product Verification Test-Government
PW .... Picowatts
PW .... Port-Wine Stain
PW .... Pratt and Whitney
PW .... Precipitable Water (CARB)
pw .... Pulse Width
PWCF .... Person with Cystic Fibrosis
PWCT .... Passenger Will Contact [*Travel industry*] (TRID)
PWE .... Present Working Estimate (ABAC)
PWH .... Per Workable Hatch (RIMS)
PWI .... Proximity Warning Instrument
PWM .... Probability of Wrong Message (CCCA)
PWP .... Personnel Work Plan (HEAS)
PWRA .... Professional Women's Rodeo Association
PWS .... Portable Work Station (SPST)
PWS .... Present Weather Sensor (ARMP)
PWWD .... Per Weather Working Day (RIMS)
PY .... Polygon
pyr .... Pyramid
pyrcrts .... Pyramid Cartons
PZEV .... Partial-Zero-Emission-Vehicle

Q
By Acronym

Q..................	Luminous Energy (DIPS)	QINB............	Quin with Bath (TRID)
Q..................	Quadrature	QINN............	Quin without Bath or Shower (TRID)
Q..................	Quantitative Test (DIPS)	QINS............	Quin with Shower (TRID)
Q..................	Qwest Communications Intl. [*NYSE symbol*] (SG)	QIT...............	Quality Improvement Team (ABAC)
Q/A.............	Quality Assurance	QK...............	Quick Flashing (PIPO)
QA&R...........	Quality Assurance and Revalidation	QL...............	Quantitation Limit (ABAC)
QAC	Quality Assurance Committee (HEAS)	Q/L...............	Quick Look
QACA	Quarters After Contract Award	QME............	Graduate Medical Education
QADB..........	Quad with Bath (TRID)	QME............	Quality Measurement Experiment (ARMP)
QADN...........	Quad without Bath or Shower (TRID)	QN	Quinoline (CARB)
QADS..........	Quad with Shower (TRID)	QNF	Quadruple Neuromuscular Facilitation (DIPS)
QAEO	Quick Action Engineering Order	QNH............	Altitude Indicated Above Sea Level
Q-alpha.......	Pitch Dynamic Pressure	QNIG...........	Quarries National Interest Group (HEAS)
QAMP.........	Quality Assurance Management Plan (ABAC)	QORC..........	Quadrature Overlapped Raised Cosine (CCCA)
QASAS........	Quality Assurance Specialist, Ammunition Specialist	QP...............	Quick Perusal
QAZ.............	Quasi-Alloy of Zirconium	QPM............	Queen's Police Medal for Distinguished Service [*British*]
Q-BAND	36,000 to 46,000 Megacycles per Second	QPOE	Quick Position Oriented Event
Q-beta	Yaw Dynamic Pressure	QR	Quality and Reliability
QC...............	Quality Check	QR	Quarterly Review
QCF.............	Quarterly Cost and Operational Effectiveness Analysis Forecast	QRA............	Quantitative Risk Assessment (SARE)
QCPP	Quality Control Program Plan (CTAS)	QRG............	Quarterly Return Group (HEAS)
QCW	Quadrature Phase Subcarrier	QRG............	Quiet Reliable Generators
qd	Quad (TRID)	QRIP	Quick Return on Investment Program
QD	Queue Difference (CCCA)	QRP	Quick Reaction Project
QD-IL...........	Quantity Distance-Interline Distance	QRR............	Qualitative Research Requirement
QDRI	Quality Development Requirements Information	QRR............	Quality Readiness Review
QE...............	Quantum Electronics [*A publication*]	QSCG..........	QS Communications ADS [*NASDAQ symbol*] (SG)
QEB.............	Quantitative Electrophysiological Battery (DIPS)	QT...............	Qualification Testing
QECA	Quantum Electronics and Applications Society	QTO	Quasi-Triennial Oscillation (CARB)
QED	Quick Erection Dome	QUADS........	1015 British Thermal Units/Year
QEDI	Quantum Effect Devices [*NASDAQ symbol*] (SG)	QUAL	Quality and Reliability Assurance Laboratory of the Marshall Space Flight Center [*NASA*]
qEEG..........	Quantitative Electroencephalograph (DIPS)	QUAL TEST...	Qualification Test
QELS...........	Quantum Electronics and Laser Science Conference	quar.............	Quarter (NTIO)
QFE.............	Altitude In Height Above Station	QUIC	Quadrupole-Ioffe-Configuration
QGIV	Quantized Gate Video	QUIDAS.......	Quick Look Data Assessment System
QH	Droned Helicopter	QuikTOMS ...	Quick Total Ozone Manning Spectrometer [*NASA*]
QIAET...........	Quartzsite Integrated Acoustic Engine Test	QV................	Queen Anne Villa

R
By Acronym

R................. Multiple Correlation (DIPS)
R................. Primary Reasoning (DIPS)
R................. Receive Only (PIPO)
R................. Regulation
R................. Rendered
R................. Resistance
R................. Yaw Rankin Rate
R2............... Coefficient of Multiple Determination (DIPS)
R4............... Recover, Reconstitute, Reload & Restrike [Military] (CCCA)
R/A.............. Radar Altimeter
RA............... Radio Altitude (HLLA)
RA............... Ranch
RA............... Research Assistant
RA............... Review and Analysis
RA............... Rural
RA............... Rural Area (CGWS)
RAAB............ Remote Amplifier and Adaptation Box
RAAWS.......... Range Antiarmor Antipersonnel Weapon System
RAB............. Random Access Burst (CGWS)
RAC............. Republic Aircraft Corporation
RACC........... Reverse Analog Control Channel (CGWS)
RACC........... Royal Armoured Corps Centre [British]
RACE........... Radioactive Containment Exclusion Clause [Insurance] (MARI)
RACH........... Random Access Channel (CGWS)
RACH........... Reynolds Army Community Hospital [Fort Sill]
RACK........... Remote Area Conflict Information Center
RAD............. Reactive Attachment Disorder
RAD............. Remote Antenna Driver (CGWS)
RAD............. Restructured Armored Division
RAD............. Retiree Activity Days
RadCon........ Radiological Control (ABAC)
RADES......... Realistic Air Defense Evaluation System
RAE............ Rotational Aftereffect (DIPS)
RAG............ Relay Assembly Group [Air Force]
RAG............ Requirements Assessment Group
RAG............ Review Advisory Group
RAI............. Rainfall Anomaly Index (CARB)
Raid............ Redundant Array of Inexpensive Disks [Computer science] (ITCA)
RAL............ Riverbed Acoustical Laboratory
RAI G.......... Risk Assessment Liaison Group (HFAS)
RAM............ Radiation Area Monitor (ABAC)
RAMP.......... Radar Action Message Processor
RAMPAT...... Reliability and Maintainability Prediction and Notification Tool (SPST)
RAN............ Resource Allocation Notice (SPST)
RAN............ Royal Australian Air Force
RANC.......... Radar Analysis of Noise and Clutter
RANC.......... Radar Attenuation, Noise and Clutter (CCCA)
RANDAM...... Random Access Indestructive Advanced Memory
r&cc........... Riot and Civil Commotion [Insurance] (MARI)
R&DPS....... Research and Development Planning Summary [Methodology]
R&K........... Ransom and Kidnap [Insurance] (MARI)
RANEL........ Royal Australian Navy Experimental Laboratory
RAO........... Retired Activities Offices [Navy]
RAO........... Revenue Accounting Office
RAoK.......... Random Acts of Kindness
RAP........... Response Analysis Processor
RAP........... Right Angle Program
RAPC.......... Review and Planning Conference
RAQ........... Reglements sur l'Assurance de la Quality [Quality Assurance Regulation] [French]
RAQCC........ Regional Air Quality Coordinating Committee
RAR............ Rendezvous and Recovery
RAR............ Runway Acceptance Rate (CTAS)
RAS............ Record Association System
RAS............ Reference Assembly Sequence (SPST)
RASA.......... Rochester Applied Science Association
RASC.......... Radio Atmospheric Study Centre (CARB)
RASERS...... Radio Amplification by Simulated Emission of Radiation System
RASP.......... Remote Antenna Signal Processor (CGWS)
RAT............ Remote Access Terminal [NASA]
RAWG......... Requirement Appraisal Work Group
RAWS......... Radar Altitude Warning System [Air Force]
RB............. Reactional Biography [A. Anastasi] (DIPS)
RB............. Rotating Beacon (PIPO)
R-BAR........ Radius Vector Axis
RBC........... Recognition by Components [I. Biederman] (DIPS)

RBCS.......... Remote Bar Code System
RBI............ Relative Bearing Indicator [Aviation] (PIAV)
rbis........... Biserial Coefficient of Correlation (DIPS)
RBMT.......... Rivermead Behavioral Memory Test [B. Wilson] (DIPS)
RBN........... Radio Beacon (PIPO)
RBRMI........ Review Board for Release of Materiel for Issue
RBS........... Refractive Backscattering
RBT........... Reliable Broadcast Toolkit (ROAS)
RC............ Conditioned Reflex (DIPS)
RC............ Radar Computer
RC............ Recorder Cycle
RC............ Research Council
RC............ Row Cottage
RCA........... Rural Cellular Association (CGWS)
RCAG......... Reserve Component Advisory Group
RCAR......... Retrofit Change Action Request
RCAS......... Reserve Component Allocation System
RCBF......... Regional Cerebral Blood Flow (DIPS)
RCC........... Radio Communications Coordinator (CCCA)
RCC........... Remote Communications Center
RCC........... Reverse Command Channel (ROAS)
RCCASP....... Reserve Component Civilian Acquired Skills Program
RCCS......... Remote Clinical Communications System
RCDS......... Retrofit Change Drawings
RCENGINE ... Rotating-Combustion Engine
RCGA......... Regional Commerce Growth Association
RCIS.......... Resource Center Information System (AUEG)
RCLDN........ Retrieval of Calling Line Directory Number
RCM........... Remote Carrier Module
RCOM......... Register.com, Inc. [NASDAQ symbol] (SG)
R Counter ... Receive Counter
RCP........... Radon Contractor Proficiency (AUEG)
RCRE......... Required Collaborative Research Experience (CARB)
RCS........... Remote Cloud Sensing (ARMP)
RCS........... Reports Control System
rCT........... Randomized Clinical Trial (DIPS)
RCTSR........ Radio Code Test Speed on Response
RD............ Reporting District (SARE)
R-D........... Resolver-to-Digital (AEBE)
RD............ Royal Naval and Royal Marine Forces Reserve Decoration [British]
RDA........... Research Development Associates (CCCA)
RDAC......... Research and Development Advisory Council
RDASC........ Research, Development, and Acquisition Specialties Committee
RDB........... Reply to Duplicate Booking Enquiry [Travel Industry] (TRID)
RDC........... Radar Data Converter
RDC........... Research and Development Center
RDCS.......... Radar Diagnostic Control System
RDDS......... Rigid Disk Drive System
RDI........... Radio Direction Indicator (HLLA)
RDI........... Remote Defect Indicator (MLOA)
RDMS......... Range Data Measurement System
RDO........... Radio Deployment Option [Department of Defense]
RDO........... Range Destruction Officer
RDOP......... Radar Diagnostic Operational Processor
RDOPP........ Research, Development, Test, and Evaluation Obligation Phase Plan [Department of Defense]
R DOT......... Range Rate to Target
RDP........... Radar Data Processor
RDP........... Remote Data Protocol [Computer science]
RDP........... Remote Desktop Protocol
Rdq........... Reading Quotient (DIPS)
rdr........... Reader
RDR........... Rejection and Disposition Request
RDR........... Ripple Down Rules (IDAI)
RDRAM........ Rambus Direct RAM
RDS........... Related Deviation Standard (ABAC)
RDTC......... Reverse Digital Traffic Channel (CGWS)
RDW........... Record Descriptive Word [Computer science] (ITCA)
RDX........... Cyclotrimethlenetramine
R/E........... Receiver/Exciter
RE............ Rediated Emission
RE............ Reproductive Endocrinologist
REACQ........ Reacquisition
REBT......... Rational Emotive Behavior Therapy [A. Ellis] (DIPS)
rec........... Recreation (NTIO)
REC........... Rural Electric Cooperative

RECCC	Reconstitutable and Enduring Command Control Communicatons (CCCA)
RECD	Rural Economic and Community Development
RECI	Reciprocal Electrical Council, Inc.
RED	Random Early Discard (MLOA)
Red	Redeemable (SG)
REDCAR	Readiness Capability
REDF	Rediff.com India ADS [*NASDAQ symbol*]
ref	Refer (NTIO)
REFORGER	Redeployment of Forces to Germany
REFTRA	Refresher Fleet Training [*Navy*]
reg	Regent (NTIO)
REGAL	Range and Evaluation Guidance for Approach and Landing
REGRE	Multiple Linear Regression Analysis
REHS	Registered Environmental Health Specialist (SARE)
REI	Request for Engineering Instructions
REINT	Reinitialization
REL	Radio Electronic [*Combat*]
rel	Religion (NTIO)
RELP	Residual Excited Linear Predictive (CGWS)
REMIDS	Remote Minefield Identification and Display System
REML	Reference My Letter (TRID)
REMOTS	Remote Ecological Monitoring of the Seafloor
REMS	Remote Sensor
REMT	Reference My Telegram (TRID)
rep	Republic (NTIO)
REPAIR	Random Path Infrared
REPLTR	Reply by Letter
REPOS	Repurchase Transactions
REPP	Redwood Employees Protection Program
REPSHIP	Report of Shipment
REP Test	Role Construct Repertory Test [*G. A. Kelly*] (DIPS)
req	Requirement (NTIO)
REQMTS	Requirements
RES	Radiation Exposure Status
RES	Reservation (NTIO)
res	Reservation (NTIO)
RESIST	Retirees to Eliminate Source Income State Tax
Resour	Resource
RESS	Radar Echo Simulation Subsystem
RET	Rational Emotive Therapy [*A. Ellis*] (DIPS)
RETAT	Requested That
RETMOD	Requirements for Total Mobilization
RETRANS	Return Transportation
rev	Revised (NTIO)
rew	Rewind (NTIO)
REYL	Reference Your Letter (TRID)
RF	Research Fellow
rf	Reticular Formation (DIPS)
rf	Right Field (NTIO)
rf	Right Fielder [*Baseball term*] (NDBD)
RFC	Radio Frequency Channel (CGWS)
RFC	Request for Check
RFDD	Regional Food and Drug Director
RFI	Radio Frequency Intelligence
RFP	Request for Plan
RFP	Request for Proposal (TRID)
RFP	Rocky Flats Publication [*Rockwell International*]
RFS	Radio Frequency Surveillance (CCCA)
RFSH	Rust Federal Services of Hanford, Inc. (ABAC)
RFSNW	Rust Federal Services Northwest (ABAC)
RG	Radar Group
RG	Registered Geologist (SARE)
RG	Retractable Gear [*Aviation*] (PIPO)
RGCI	Regent Communications [*NASDAQ symbol*] (SG)
RGD	Radiation Generating Device (ABAC)
RGPD	Range-Gated Pulse Doppler
RGR	Roger Received and Understood
RGS	Remote Ground Station (CCCA)
RHB	Right-Handed Batter [*Baseball term*] (NDBD)
RHBVAL	Radar Bomb Evaluation [*Air Force*]
rhet	Rhetoric (NTIO)
RHF	Ridiculously High Frequency (HLLA)
RHN	Rockwell Hardness Number (ABAC)
RHOGI	Radar Homing Guidance Intercept
RHP	Right Half Plane (CCCA)
RHP	Right-Handed Pitcher [*Baseball term*] (NDBD)
RHS	Rural Housing Service
RHYA	Release for Handling by Your Agency (TRID)
R/I	Receiving Inspection
RIBA	Regional Investment Bankers Association
RIC	Reportable Item Code
RICHS	Rural Information Center Health Service
RID	Range Instrumentation Division
rid	Riddles
RIEMA	Rhode Island Educational Media Association
RIH	Registered Industrial Hygienist (SARE)
RIL	Rhode Island Lines
RILST	Resident Integrated Logistics Support Team
RIMS	Research Institute for Mathematical Sciences [*Japan*]
RINT	Radiated Intelligence
RIOPr	Comp Vale do Rio Doca ADS [*NYSE symbol*]
RIP	Radar Improvement Proposal
RIP	Retired International Business Machine Program
RIP	Rodent Impact Program [*Detroit, MI*]

RIPR	Report on the In-Process Review
RIS	Reflector in Space (CARB)
RIS	Requirements Inventory Sheet
RISC	Radar Interface and Scheduling Control
RI/SD	Requisition and Invoice/Shipping Document
RISKAT	Risk Assessment Tool (HEAS)
RISOP	Red Integrated Strategic Operations Plan
RIT	Reinitialization Time
RIT	Royal Institute of Technology [*Sweden*]
Riv	River (NTIO)
RJMC	Rotary Joints Motor Controller [*NASA*] (SPST)
R/K	Radial Keratotomy
RK	Recharge
RKT	Registered Kinesiotherapist (NUJO)
RL	Registor Logic
RL	Reix Limen [*Absolute Threshold*] [*German*] (DIPS)
RL	Runway Edge Lights (PIPO)
RLC	Range Location in Correlator
RLC	Republican Leadership Council
RLCL	Range Location Clutter
RLCM	Remote Line Concentrating Module
RLE	Reservoir Level Sensor
RLFCM	Radioactive Liquid Fed Ceramic Melter (ABAC)
RLNG	Releasing (TRID)
RLO	Refugee Liaison Office
RLOC	Record Locator (TRID)
RLRIU	Routing Logic Radio Interface Unit
RLS	Range Location Skin
RLSE	Release (TRID)
RM	Reliability and Maintainability
RM	Risk Management (ABAC)
RM	River Mile (CARB)
RM	River Monitor [*Navy*]
RM	Road March [*Marine Corps*]
RMA	Risk Management Agency
RMAD	Register Memory Address
RMC	Radar Maintenance Control
RMC	Range Minimum Control
RMDE	Rapid Model Development Environment
RME	Risk Mitigation Experiment [*NASA*] (SPST)
RMERC	Rock Mechanics and Explosives Research Center
RMES	Relay Mirror Experimental Satellite (CARB)
RMI	Reaction Motors, Incorporated
RMINC	Range Minimum Commanded
RMK	Retrofit Modification Kit
RMKS	Remarks (TRID)
Rmon	Remote Monitoring [*Computer science*] (ITCA)
RMS	Range Measurement System
RMS	Remote Monitoring Subsystem (CTAS)
RMS	Resource Management System
RMS	Root Mean Squared (SARE)
RMSG	Raw Material Support Group
RMU	Radio Management Unit (PIAV)
RMU PWR	Remote Unit Power
RMW	Radioactive Mixed Waste (ABAC)
RN	Radon
Rnav	Area Navigation (PIAV)
RNAV	Random Area Navigation (PIPO)
RNB	Replacement New Box
RNCPEC	Russian National Committee for Pacific Economic Cooperation
RNF	Replacement New Foam
RNFA	Registered Nurse First Assistant (NUJO)
RNMI	Royal Netherlands Meteorological Institute (CARB)
RNP	Reduce Number in Party [*Travel industry*] (TRID)
RNR	Registered Nurse Recruiter (NUJO)
RNS	Radar Netting System
RO	Radiological Officer [*Department of Emergency Management*] (DEMM)
RO	Range Operator
RO	Rawlings Official [*Baseball term*] (NDBD)
R/O	Receive Only (PIPO)
Ro	Rome Stock Exchange (SG)
ROC	Reference Our Cable (RIMS)
ROC	Response Operating Characteristic (DIPS)
ROD	Rust, Oxidation, Discoloration [*Insurance*] (MARI)
ROG	Rogers Corp. [*NYSE symbol*] (SG)
ROH	Registered Occupational Hygienist (SARE)
ROHT	Registered Occupational Hygiene Technologist (SARE)
Rol	Retinol
ROLAP	Relational Online Analytic Processing (IDAI)
RON	Remain over Night (PIAV)
ROOM	Hotel Reservations Network 'A' [*NASDAQ symbol*] (SG)
RoR	Review of Regulation (HEAS)
ROS	Rosman [*North Carolina*]
ROTLX	Reference Our Telex (RIMS)
ROTSE	Robotic Optical Transient Search Equipment
ROTSE-I	Robotic Optical Transient Search Experiment I
ROV	Remote Operator Vehicle [*Nautical*]
RP	Radioplane [*Company*]
RP	Radio Port (CGWS)
RP	Red Poppy [*Publisher*]
RP	Repair Part
RP	Reporting Party (SARE)
RPA	Radiation Protection Adviser (HEAS)
RPA	Relative Percent Accuracy (ABAC)

RPA .... Remotely Piloted Aircraft (CARB)
RPB .... Roadstead Patrol Boat [*Navy*]
RPCU .... Radio Port Control Unit (CGWS)
RPD .... Radar Planning Device
RPD .... Relative Percent Difference (ABAC)
RPD .... Requirements and Product Design [*Phase*]
RPE .... Regular Pulse Excitation (CGWS)
RPE .... Respiratory Protective Equipment (HEAS)
RPFT........... Registered Pulmonary Function Technician (NUJO)
RPI .... Runway Point of Interception (PIPO)
RPIH .... Registered Professional Industrial Hygienist (SARE)
RPLL .... Radiation Protection Officer
RPN .... Registered Psychiatric Nurse (NUJO)
RPR .... Replacement Production Reactor (ABAC)
RPS .... Research Planning Section (HEAS)
RPSS .... Relative Partial Sum of Squares (CARB)
RPT............. Radiation Protection Technician (ABAC)
RPT............. Repeat Previous Transaction (TRID)
RQAC .... Receiving Quality Assurance Card
RQID........... Request is Desired (TRID)
RQL .... Reference Quality Level
RQR .... Request for Reply (TRID)
RQST .... Request Seat [*Travel industry*] (TRID)
RR .... Radio Resource (CGWS)
R/R .... Readout and Relay
RR .... Reconfirmed (TRID)
RR .... Respiration Rate
RRA .... Resource Recovery Act
RR&EO .... Race Relations and Equal Opportunity
RR&I .... Respective Rights and Interests (MARI)
RRCT .... Reflectance Ratio Cloud Test (CARB)
RRDCCC ...... Rapid Reaction Deployable Command Control Communications (CCCA)
RRF .... Risk Reduction Factor (ABAC)
RRI .... Rate Range Indicator
RRPT .... Registered Radiation Protection Technologist (SARE)
RRTM .... Rapid Radiative Transfer Model (ARMP)
RS .... Basket Range Stone
RS............... Radar Shelter
Rs .... Radius of Safety
R/S............. Range Safety
R/S............. Reconnaissance/Surveillance
RS............... Remote Sensing (CARB)
RS .... Request for Support
RS............... Research Student
RS............... Reserved Seat [*Travel industry*] (TRID)
RS............... Response Shock (DIPS)
RS............... Roadside
RSA .... Reliable Service Area (CGWS)
RSA .... Remote Station Automation [*System*] [*Air Force*]
RSA .... Republic of South Africa (CARB)
RSA .... Reservations Sales Agent (TRID)
RS&I .... Receipt, Storage, and Issue
RSA/RSL...... Rate Sensitive Assets/Rate Sensitive Liabilities
RSCEI .... Remote Station Communications Equipment Interface
RSDA .... Rough Set Data Analysis (IDAI)
RSFG .... Route Server Functional Group
RSIC .... Redstone Shielding Information Center [*NASA*]
RSL............. Radio Signaling Link (CGWS)
RSM............ Remote Storage Management [*Computer science*]
RSM............ Research Scale Meter (ABAC)
RSM............ Response Surface Matrix
RSMPS .... Romanian Society for Mathematical and Physical Sciences [*Romania*]

RSO .... Receptive Service Operator (TRID)
RSP .... Radial Structure Plot (ABAC)
RSP .... Recovery Support Plan
RSP .... Rendering Safe Procedures
RSRI .... Regional Science Research Institute
RSS .... Remote Subscriber Switch (CCCA)
RSSA .... Rockwell Ship Systems, Australia
RSSG.......... Royal Society Study Group (HEAS)
RSSI .... Received Signal Strength Indicator (CGWS)
RSTA .... Reconnaissance, Surveillance, and Target Acquisition [*Military*]
RSU .... Research Strategy Unit (HEAS)
RSV .... Rijn-Schelde-Verolme
RSVP .... Rapid Sequential Visual Presentation (DIPS)
R/T............. Radio Telephone
R/T............. Real Time
RT .... Receiver/Transmitter (PIPO)
R/T............. Receive-to-Transmit
RT .... Respiratory Technician (NUJO)
RT .... Right Turn
RTA .... Rocket Troops and Artillery
RTB............. Robotics Test-Bed [*Program*]
RTC............. Receiver Timing Counter
RTC............. Resolution Trust Company (NTIO)
RTC............. Reverse Traffic Channel Digital (CGWS)
RTC............. Rochester Theory Center
RTCC .... Real Time Computation Center [*NASA*]
RTG .... Radar Transmitter Group
RTG .... Radioisotopic Thermoelectric Generator
RTK............. Rentech, Inc. [*AMEX symbol*] (SG)
RTMC.......... Riverside Telescope Makers Conference [*California*]
RTP............. Records Turnover Package (ABAC)
RTP............. Rehabilitation Through Photography
RU .... Ruth
RU .... Ruthenium
RUBEN........ Re-Usable Benchmarking Environment (AEBE)
RUBIAC....... Rubber Industry Advisory Committee (HEAS)
RUN .... Reunion Industries [*AMEX symbol*] (SG)
RUS .... Rural Utilities Service
Rus .... Russian (NTIO)
R/V............. Recreational Vehicle
RV............... Research Volume (ABAC)
RV............... Return Verandah Villa
RVC .... Research Volume Cost (ABAC)
RVC .... Reverse Analog Voice Channel (CGWS)
RVDP.......... Reconnaissance Attack Squadron [*Air Force*]
RVDP.......... Riverdeep Group ADS [*NASDAQ symbol*] (SG)
RVHA.......... Reconnaissance Attack Squadron [*Navy*]
RVSM .... Reduced Vertical Separation Minimums (PIPO)
RVSN.......... RADVision, Ltd. [*NASDAQ symbol*] (SG)
R/W............ Runway
RWA .... Rotatable Wing Assembly
RWALK .... Random Walk
RWCT .... Radioactive Waste Collection Tank (ABAC)
RWP .... Radar Wind Profiler (ARMP)
RWRS .... Radar Warning System
rwy............. Runway (PIAV)
Rx............... Receiver (PIAV)
RX............... Report Crossing [*Aviation*] (PIPO)
RY............... Rydberg [*Unit of measure*]
RYC .... Reference Your Cable (RIMS)
RYD .... Responsible Young Drivers [*An association*]
RYT............. Reference Your Telegram (TRID)
RYTLX .... Reference Your Telex (RIMS)

S

By Acronym

S	Secret
s	Segment (SPST)
S	Simultaneous (PIPO)
s	Singular (NTIO)
S	Spatial Relations (DIPS)
s	Special Factor (DIPS)
s	Specific Factor (DIPS)
S	Standard Stimulus (DIPS)
S	Stimulus (DIPS)
S	Stone Undifferentiated
Sa	Saturday (NTIO)
S/A	Saturn/Apollo [NASA]
S/A	Schedule/Actual
SA	Seeker Antenna
SA	Self-Assessment (DIPS)
S/A	Shipalt [Navy]
S/A	Site Activation
SA	Social Age (DIPS)
S/A	Spacecraft Adaptor [NASA]
SA	Spectrum Analyzer
SA	Sponsoring Agency
SA	Springfield Arsenal
S/A	Subassembly
S/A	Subject to Acceptance (MARI)
s/a	Subject to Approval (MARI)
SA	Supervising Authority
SA	Supplemental Assembly (SPST)
SA	Supplies and Accounts
SA	Surface Air
S/A	Surface-to-Air
SA	System Analysis
SAAC	Simulated Air-to-Air Combat
SAAL	Single Address Assembly Machine Language
SAALC	San Antonio Air Logistic Center [Air Force]
SAAM	Special Assignment Airlift Mission [Air Force]
SAAM	Surface-to-Air Antimissile
SAAMI	Sporting Arms and Ammunition Manufacturers Institute
SAAS	Survivor Administration Assistance Service
SAAS II	Stress Analysis of Axisymmetric Solids Version II
Sab	Sabbath (NTIO)
SABA	Saba Software [NASDAQ symbol] (SG)
SABER	Situation Awareness Beacon with Reply
SABMIS	Sea Based Anti-Ballistic Missile Intercept System [Navy]
sac	Sacrifice [Baseball term] (NDBD)
SAC	Single Attachment Concentrator [Computer science] (ITCA)
SAC	Small Agency Council
SAC	Speaking Across-the-Curriculum
SAC	Stimulus as Coded (DIPS)
SAC	System Acquisition
SACA	Systemic Accident Cause Analysis (HEAS)
SACCS	Strategic Air Command Automated Command and Control System [Air Force]
SACDIN	Strategic Air Command Digital Network [Air Force]
SACLOS	Semiautomated Command-to-Line-of-Sight
SACP	Standing Advisory Committee on Pilot Licensing (PIAV)
SACTTYNET	Strategic Air Command Teletypewriter Network [Air Force]
SAD	Safety Arming Device
SADARM	Sense and Destroy Armor Missile
SADL	Sterilization Advance Development Laboratory
SADR	Satellite Data Relay
SADSAC	Seiler Algorithmic Oriented Language Digitally
SADSAC	Simulated Analog Computer
SADSAC	Small Acoustic Device Simulating an Aircraft Carrier [Navy]
SADT	Structured Analysis Design Technique
SAE	Serious Adverse Event [Medicine]
SAEDA	Subversion and Espionage Directed Against the Army
SAF	Safe, Arming, and Fuzing
SAF	Safeguard
SAF	Safety Approval Form (SARE)
SAF	Sample Analysis Form (ABAC)
SAF	Slovak Air Force
SAF	Stock Control Number Approval Form [Department of Defense]
SAF	System Authentication Facility [Computer science] (ITCA)
SAFE	Safe, Arm, Fuze, and Fire
SAFE	Spectronic Automatic Fire Extinguishing
SAFLOG	Safeguard Logistics Command

SAFPO	Safeguard Project Officer
SAFR	Source and Application of Funds Report
SAF/RD	Secretary of the Air Force for Research and Development
SAG	Space Astrophysics Group
SAG	System Advisory Group (CCCA)
SAGA	Spray Advisor Genetic Algorithm
SAGE	Semi-Automatic Ground Environment (CCCA)
SAGE	Solvent Alternatives Guide
SAH	Semiactive Homing
SAI	Safety Appliance Illustration (HEAS)
SAI	Science Applications International
SAI	Singapore Aircraft Industries
SAI	Social Accountability International
SAI	Standby Attitude Indicator
SAI	System Associates, Incorporated
SAIF	Standard Avionics Integrated Fusing
SAIL	Ship Alteration Inventory List [Navy]
SAIL	Shipboard Armament Inventory List [Navy]
SAILS	Standard Army Intermediate Level Supply
SAIMS	Supersonic Airborne Infrared Measurement Safety
SAIP	Spares Acquisition Improvement Program
SAIP	Spares Acquisition Integrated with End Item Production
SAIR	Service de la Surveillance Industrielle de'Armement [France]
SALF	Saudi Arabian Land Forces
SAL GP	Semi-Active Laser Guided Projectiles
SALSF	Short Approach Light System Sequenced Flashing Lights (PIPO)
SAM	School of Aviation Medicine [Air Force]
SAM	Search of Associative Memory [R. M. Shiffrin] (DIPS)
SAM	Standard Army Missile
SAM	Sterile Alpha Motif
SAM	System Actuation Monitoring
SAMBA	Systems Approach to Managing Bureau of Ships Acquisition [Navy]
SAMBO	Simultaneous Auroral Multi-Balloons Observations (CARB)
SAM-D	Surface to Air Missile Development
SAMOS	Satellite and Missile Observation System
SAMPAM	System of Automation of Material Plans for Army Material
SAMS	Saudia Air Force Material Study
SAMSI	Spacecraft Array for Michelson Spatial Interferometer
SAMSON	Support Availability Multi System Operational Model
SAMSOT	Ships Anti-Missile Systems Operability Test
SANCOR	South African National Committee for Oceanographic Research
S&A	Safety and Arming
S&C	Switches and Crossings (HEAS)
s&h	Shipping and Handling (NTIO)
S&I	Standardization and Interoperability
S and LP	Safety and Loss Prevention (HEAS)
S&M	Structures and Materials
S&T	Signal and Telecommunications (HEAS)
S&T	Supply and Transportation
S&TI	Scientific and Technical Information
sanr	Subject to Approval No Risk (MARI)
SAO	System Analysis Organization
SAP	Self-Amortizing Project
SAP	Service Assessment Pool (ABAC)
SAPIR	System of Automatic Processing and Indexing Reports
SAP IV	Structural Analysis Program Version 4
SAPOC	Special Access Program Oversight Committee
SAPVERSION 4	Structural Analysis Program Version 4
SAR	Search and Reserve (CCCA)
SAR	Selected Acquisition Review
SAR	Software Architecture Review (SPST)
SAR	Special Astronautical Requirement
SAR	Synthetic Operative Radar
SAR	Systems Analysis Recording (CTAS)
SARAH	Search and Rescue Homing
SARAH	Semi-Automated Range, Azimuth, and Height
SARC	Service Acquisiton Review Council
SARCC	Search and Rescue Coordination [FAA]
SARD	Site Activation Requirements Documents
SARMOTI	Siegfried and Roy Masters of the Impossible
SARP	Scheduling and Review Procedures
SARPF	Strategic Air Relocatable Processing Facility
SARUC	Southeastern Association of Regulatory Utility Commissioners
SAS	Sub-Arctic Summer (ARMP)
SASA	Security Affairs Support Association
SASC	Semi-Automatic Switch Center (CCCA)

SASE............ Specific Application Software Elements (SPST)
SASO .... Stability and Support Operation [*Army*]
SASP .... Special Ammunition Storage Point
SASS .... Society for the Social Sciences
SASSTIXS .... Satellite, Air, Surface, Subsurface Tactical Information Exchange Subsystem
SASSTO ...... Single-Stage-to-Orbit
SAT............ School Ability Tests (DIPS)
SAT............ School Achievement Test (DIPS)
SAT............ Site Acceptance Test (CTAS)
SAT............ Societe Anonyme Telecommunication [*French*]
SAT............ Supervisory Audio Tone (CGWS)
SAT............ System Approach to Training
SATCAP ...... Sol-Air Tres Courte Portee [*Very Short Range Ground to Air*]
SATCOM ...... Scientific and Technical Communications Committee
satcoms ...... Satellite Communications (PIAV)
SATRAK ...... Short Airfield Tactical
SATRAK ...... Small Airfield Tactical
SATS........... System Architectural and Trade Study
SATSHEX .... Saturdays, Sundays, Holidays Excepted (RIMS)
SATSHINC .... Saturdays, Sundays, Holidays Included (RIMS)
SAU .... Single Acquisition Unit
SAVA .... Society for Accelerator and Velocity Apparatus
SAVIM .... Survivability and Vulnerability Improvement
SAW............ Sawlog Harvest (CARB)
SAW............ Sub-Arctic Winter (ARMP)
SAWG .... Smoke/Aerosol Working Group
Sax .... Saxon (NTIO)
SB............... Saddle Bronc Riding [*Rodeo term*]
SB............... Science Budget
SB............... Sea Based [*Navy*]
SB............... Short-Bout
S/B............. Standby
SB............... Stanford-Binet Intelligence Scale (DIPS)
SBA............. Summary Basis of Approval
SBCC .... Santa Barbara Community College [*California*] (ROAS)
SBD............. Science Baseline Document
SBDP .... Soviet Battlefield Development Plans
SBEMF........ Surface Burst Electromagnetic Pulse
SBI............. Signal Band Indication
SBIR .... Space-Based Infrared [*Missile system*]
SB-IV .... Stanford-Binet IV [*Test*] (DIPS)
SBLC........... S-Band Linear Collider
SBML........... Signal Band Energy in the Main Lobe
SBMS.......... Southwestern Bell Mobile Service
SBS............. Submerged Bed Scrubber (ABAC)
SBSA .... Small Business Set Aside
SBSIM .... Space-Based System Simulation
SBSS .... Space Based Surveillance System (CCCA)
SBT............ Screen-Based Telephone (ROAS)
SBUS .... School Bus (ROAS)
SC.............. Conditioned Stimulus (DIPS)
SC.............. Safety Coordinator
SC.............. Schedule Change (TRID)
SC.............. Science Committee
SC.............. Self-Containing
SC.............. Service Coordinator
SC.............. Signaling Controller (CGWS)
SC.............. Skillcentre (HEAS)
SC.............. Statement of Charges
SC.............. Stick and Click (MLOA)
SC.............. Strategic Connectivity (CCCA)
SC.............. Stream Class (CTAS)
SC.............. Subcommunity
SC.............. Support Concept
SCA............ Snow-Covered Area (CARB)
SCA............ Subcarrier Adapter (AEBE)
SCADA .... System Control and Data Acquisition
SCADS .... Superfund Chemical Analysis Data System (AUEG)
SCB............ System Control Block (ROAS)
SCC............ Strategic Connectivity Communications (CCCA)
SCCS .... Selective Class of Call Screening (CGWS)
SCCS .... Software Configuration Control System (ROAS)
SCCS .... Specialized Common Carrier Service (ROAS)
SCD............ Standard Color Display (ROAS)
SCDS .... Superior Canal Dehiscence Syndrome [*Medicine*]
SCEAP .... Student/Community Enrichment Activity Program
SCF............ Selective Call Forwarding
SCF............ System Control Facility
scfm........... Standard Cubic Feet per Minute (ABAC)
S-CHIP........ State Children's Health Insurance Program
SCIC........... Suppressed-Conductivity Ion Chromatography (ABAC)
sci-fi........... Science Fiction (NTIO)
SCL............ Strategic Configured Load [*Military*]
SCLP........... Signalling Channel Link Protocol
SCM............ Station Class Mark (CGWS)
SCMOH........ Since Chrome Major Overhaul [*Aviation*] (PIPO)
SCO .... Scorpio (NTIO)
SCORM........ Shareable Courseware Object Reference Model [*Computer science*]
SCOT .... Single Channel Objective Terminal (CCCA)
SCP............ Site Characterization Plan (ABAC)
SCPMP .... Station Crew Procedures Management Plan [*NASA*] (SPST)
SCR .... Site Characterization Report (ABAC)
SCR .... Sustainable Cell Rate (MLOA)

SCRIPPS...... Scripps Institution of Oceanography [*University of California at San Diego*] (CARB)
SCS............ Strategic Communications System (CCCA)
SCSI........... Small Computer Standard Interface
SCSN .... Southern California Seismograph Network
SCT............ Same Clock Timing (MLOA)
SCT............ Short Contact Time (ABAC)
SCTIS.......... Single Channel Transponder Injection System (CCCA)
sctx........... Science Textbook
SCVICU....... Surgical and Cardiovascular Intensive Care Unit (NUJO)
SCVPH .... Scientific Committee for Veterinary Measures Relating to Public Health
SCW........... Special Case Waste (ABAC)
SCWG .... Security Certification Working Group (CCCA)
SD.............. School District
SD.............. Secure Digital
SD.............. Software Development (CTAS)
SD.............. Student Development
S-D............ Synchro-to-Digital (AEBE)
SD.............. Systematic Desensitization (DIPS)
SDA............ Strategic Defensive Architecture (CCCA)
SDAY .... Sunday Communic. ADS [*NASDAQ symbol*] (SG)
SDB .... Single-Channel Distribution Bridge (CCCA)
SDCCH........ Standalone Dedicated Control Channel (CGWS)
SDE............ Senior District Executive [*Boy Scouts of America*]
SDH .... Synchronous Data Hierarchy (AEBE)
SDHF .... Standard Dutch Hull Form (MARI)
SDI............. Silt Density Index
SDIL........... Software Development Integration Laboratory (SPST)
SDL............ Service Data Link [*Computer science*] (ITCA)
SDM............ Secure Digital Modem (CCCA)
SDMA .... Spacial Division Multiple Access (CGWS)
SDMC .... Scratching, Denting, Marring, Chipping [*Insurance*] (MARI)
SDO............ Solenoid Driver Output (SPST)
SDRI .... Sealed Double-Ring Infiltrometer (ABAC)
SDSI........... Synchronous Data-Link Control
SDT............ System Design Team (CTAS)
SDT............ Systems Development Team (CTAS)
SDTN .... Synchronous Digital Transmission Network (CCCA)
SDW .... Southdown
SE.............. Scout Executive [*Boy Scouts of America*]
SE.............. Seed End
S/E............. Survivable and Endurable (CCCA)
SE.............. System Engineer (CTAS)
SE1............ System Extension Release 1 [*Computer science*] (ITCA)
SE2............ System Extension Release 2 [*Computer science*] (ITCA)
SEA............ Bio-Aqua Systems 'A' [*AMEX symbol*] (SG)
SEAD .... Suppress Enemy Air Defense [*Army*]
SEAL.......... Scribner Encyclopedia of American Lives [*A publication*]
SEC............ Solvent Extract Conductivity
SECB .... Severely Errored Cell Block
SECID .... South-East Consortium for International Development [*Washington, D.C.*]
sec'y.......... Secretary (NTIO)
SED............ Safety Evaluation Document (ABAC)
SED............ Severely Emotionally Disturbed
SED............ Spherical Equilvalent Diameter (ABAC)
SEDAC .... Socioeconomic Data and Applications Center
SEDB .... Support Equipment Data Base (SPST)
SEDM.......... Schedule Exchange Data Message (TRID)
SEE............ Sample Exchange Evaluation (ABAC)
SEE............ Single Event Effect (SPST)
SEI............. Safety Environment Institute (HEAS)
SEI............. Systems Engineering and Integration (CTAS)
SELD.......... Severe Expressive Language Delay
SELFDISCH... Self Discharger (RIMS)
sem............ Seminary (NTIO)
Sem............ Semitic (NTIO)
SEN........... SEMCO Energy [*NYSE symbol*] (SG)
sen............ Senate (NTIO)
SEO........... Special Exemption Order (HEAS)
Sep............ September (NTIO)
SERMS .... Selective Estrogen Receptor Modulator [*Medicine*]
SERS .... Selective Equipment Removal System (ABAC)
SES .... Safety and Enforcement Statistics (HEAS)
SES .... School of Environment Studies
SES .... Severely Errored Seconds (MLOA)
SES .... Surface Environmental Surveillance (ABAC)
SET............ Self-Instructional Training (DIPS)
SET............ Students' Evaluation of Teaching (DIPS)
SEVP.......... Senior Executive Vice President
sf.............. Sforzando (NTIO)
SF............. Single Fronted
sf.............. Square Feet (NTIO)
SF............. Subject File (HEAS)
SF............. Superficial Feet (RIMS)
SF............. Switch Fabric (MLOA)
SFAI .... San Francisco Art Institute
sfc............. Specific Fuel Consumption [*Aviation*] (PIAV)
SFL............ Sequenced Flashing Lights (PIPO)
SFML.......... Sea Food Meal (TRID)
SFRD .... System Functional Requirements Description (CCCA)
SFRM.......... Since Factory Remanufacture [*Aviation*] (PIPO)
SFWMD .... South Florida Water Management District
S:G............. Straw:Grain

SGC	Server-Gated Cryptography [*Computer science*]
sgl	Single (TRID)
SGLB	Single Room with Bath (TRID)
SGLN	Single Room without Bath (TRID)
SGLS	Single Room with Shower (TRID)
SGMRS	Semiconductor Generic Manufacturing Requirements Specification
SGMT	Segment (TRID)
SGP	Single Gauss Point (CARB)
SGR	Specific Growth Rate (CARB)
SH	Shack
SHA	Shawnee Press [*Publisher*]
SHG	Self-Help Group (DIPS)
SHLW	Solidified High-Level Waste (ABAC)
SHLWS	Simulated High-Level Waste Slurry (ABAC)
ShO	Shutout [*Baseball term*] (NDBD)
SHPM	Scanning Hall Probe Microscope
shs	Shares (SG)
SHS	Since Hot Section (PIPO)
SHSG	Spherical Harmonic Spatial Grid (CARB)
SHTL	Second-Class Hotel (TRID)
SI	Senior Inspector (HEAS)
SI	Service Information (TRID)
SI	Solar Influence (CARB)
SI	Speech Impairment
SI	Statutory Instrument (HEAS)
SIAM	Speech Interface Assessment Method (DIPS)
SI&A	Systems Integration and Avionics (SPST)
SI&T	Software Integration and Test (SPST)
SIB	Safety Information Bulletin (HEAS)
SIC	Second in Command [*Aviation*] (PIPO)
SID	Sensory Integration Dysfunction
SID	Sensory Integrative Dysfunction
SID	Single Deck (RIMS)
SID	System Identification (CGWS)
SIDS	Sustainable Development of Small Island Developing States (CARB)
SIDS	System Integration Design Specification (CCCA)
SIE	Selective Ion Electrode (ABAC)
SIES	Office of Strategic Industries & Economic Security
SII	Strong Interest Inventory (DIPS)
SIIA	Software & Information Industry Association
SILW	Solidified Intermediate-Level Waste (ABAC)
sim	Selected Ion Monitoring (ABAC)
SIM	Space Interferometry Mission [*NASA*]
SIM	Subscriber Identity Module (CGWS)
SIMEG	Subscriber Identity Module Export Group (CGWS)
sin	Sine (NTIO)
SINCPEC	Singapore National Committee for Pacific Economic Cooperation
SIRMO	Senior Information Resource Management Officer (AUEG)
SIS	Sensory-Information Store (DIPS)
SIS	Shaken Infant Syndrome
SIT	Stress-Innoculation Training (DIPS)
sitcom	Situation Comedy (NTIO)
SITL	Sold Inside, Ticketed Inside [*Travel industry*] (TRID)
SITO	Sold Inside, Ticketed Outside [*Travel industry*] (TRID)
SJ	Sample Job (ABAC)
S/J	Signal to Jam (CCCA)
SK	Super Kamiokande
sl	Sea Level (PIAV)
SL	Senior Lecturer
SL	Sensation Level of Sound (DIPS)
SLA	Service Level Agreement (HEAS)
SLAB	Silicon Labs [*NASDAQ symbol*] (SG)
SLAP	Superior Labral Anterior and Posterior [*Medicine*]
Slav	Slavic (NTIO)
SLAVE	Symbolic Language for Automated Verification and Execution [*Computer science*] (ITCA)
SLBM	Submarine Launched Ballistic Missile
SLCC	Subscriber Line Control Circuit (AEBE)
SLD	Second Level Domain
SLI	Speech and Language Impaired
SLIES	Stratospheric Limb Infrared Emission Spectrometer (CARB)
SLIG	Student Learning Improvement Grant
SLIP	Serviceability Level Indication Processing [*Computer science*] (ITCA)
SLM	Short Life Memorandum (HEAS)
SLPTA	Slop Tanks (RIMS)
SLR	State and Local Relations (AUEG)
SLS	Satellite Landing System (HLLA)
SLS	Search Look Strategy (CCCA)
SLS	System Level Specification (CTAS)
SLT	Silverline Technologies 'A' [*NYSE symbol*]
SLT	Slight Tarnish
SLTC	Selectica, Inc. [*NASDAQ symbol*] (SG)
SM	Sadomasochism (DIPS)
SM	Sadomasochistic (DIPS)
SM	Scoutmaster [*Boy Scouts of America*]
SMAIT	Subcontractor Management Analysis and Integration Team (SPST)
SMAP	Software Management and Assurance Program (SPST)
SMART-1	Small Mission for Advanced Research in Technology [*Sponsored by European Space Agency*]
SMBS	Stripped Mortgage-Backed Security
SMC	System Maintenance Console (CTAS)
SMC	System Manager Console (CTAS)
SMCC	Sun Microsystems Computer Corporation (ROAS)
SMC-GUI	System Manager's Console Graphical User Interface (CTAS)
SMDA	Safe Medical Devices Act [*Food and Drug Administration*]
SME	Small and Medium Enterprise
SME	Software Maintenance Engineer
SME&T	Science, Mathematics, Engineering, and Technology
SMF	Standardized Monitoring Framework (AUEG)
SMFA	Systems Management Functional Area [*Computer science*] (ITCA)
SMG	Special Mode Group (CGWS)
SMI	Supplementary Medical Insurance
S/MIME	Secure Electronic Mail
SML	Single-Major-Locus Model (DIPS)
SMMC	System Maintenance Monitoring Console (CTAS)
SMO	Samoa Observatory (CARB)
SMO	Sample Management Office (AUEG)
SMP	Sheet Metal and Plastics
SMP	Survey of Management Practices [*C. L. Wilson*] (DIPS)
SMR	Selective Message Routing (CCCA)
SMR	Senior Management Review (HEAS)
SMR	Supply of Machinery Safety Regulations (HEAS)
SMS	Site Management System (ABAC)
SMS	Smith-Magenis Syndrome
SMSCB	Short Message Service Call Broadcast (CGWS)
SMSS	Surviving Missile Surveillance Study (CCCA)
SMST	Smoking Seat (TRID)
SMTF	Shuttle Mission Training Facility [*NASA*] (SPST)
S/N	Serial Number (PIPO)
s/n	Signal to Noise Ratio (DIPS)
SN	Space Network (CARB)
SNA	State Nurses Association
SNARE	Sulphur Nitrogen Aerosol Regional Experiment
SNCA	Solaris Network Cache and Accelerator
SND	Sound Installed
SNG	Special Needs Gifted
SNH	Scottish Natural Heritage
SNLG	Scottish and Newcastle Lymphoma Group
SNMER	Society of Nuclear Medicine Education and Research Foundation
SNMOC	Speciated Non-Methane Organic Compound
SNO	Selected Nuclear Option (CCCA)
SNP	Solar Neutrino Problem
SO	Solicitor's Office (HEAS)
so	Southern (NTIO)
so	Strike Out (NTIO)
SoA	Society of Authors
soc	Social (NTIO)
SOCC	Satellite Operation Command and Control (CARB)
SOD	Sexual-Orientation Disturbance (DIPS)
SOD	Small Outline Diode
SODALS	Simplified Omnidirectional Approach Light System (PIPO)
SODD	Silencer of Death Domains
SOF	Statement of Facts (RIMS)
SOH	Since Overhaul [*Aviation*] (PIPO)
SOI	Southern Oscillation Index (CARB)
SOL	Site Operations Log (ARMP)
SOL	Solicitation
sol	Soliloquy (NTIO)
SOL	Standards of Learning
SOLIS	Synoptic Optical Long-Term Investigations of the Sun
Som	Somalia (NTIO)
SOM	Start of Message (CCCA)
SOM	Sulfuric Acid-Ozone Mixture
SOM	Swedish Official Measure (RIMS)
son	Song Book
SONE	S1 Corp.
SOP	Safe Operating Practice
SOP	Small Outline Package
soph	Sophomore (NTIO)
SoR	Society of Rheology
SOR	Stimulus-Organism-Response (DIPS)
SORTI	Solar Radiance Transmittance Interferometer (ARMP)
SOS	Schedule Optimization Study (ABAC)
SOSER	Social Services
SOTI	Sold Outside, Ticketed Inside [*Travel industry*] (TRID)
SOTO	Sold Outside, Ticketed Outside [*Travel industry*] (TRID)
Sov	Soviet (NTIO)
Soweto	Southwest Townships [*South Africa*] (NTIO)
SP	Safe Ports (RIMS)
S/P	Science Payload
SP	Signaling Point (CGWS)
SP	Spanish
SP	Starting Pitcher [*Baseball term*] (NDBD)
SP	Strictly Private (ABAC)
SP	Systems Product [*Computer science*] (ITCA)
SPA	System-Programmable Gate Array (AEBE)
SPAD	Signal Passed at Danger (HEAS)
SPA-LEED	Spot Profile Analysis Low Energy Electron Diffraction
Span	Spanish (NTIO)
SPB	St. Petersburg (RIMS)
SPBA	Senior Professional Baseball Association (NDBD)
SPC	Society of Pension Consultants (COBU)
SPC	Sulfur Polymer Cement (ABAC)
SPC	Surface Photoconductivity
SPC	Systems Planning Corp. (CCCA)
SPCC	Self-Perceived Communication Competence
SPD	Semantic Pragmatic Disorder
S/PDIF	Sony/Philips Digital Interface
SPEAR	Stanford Positron Electron Accelerating Ring

SPEBSQUA...	Society for the Preservation and Encouragement of Barber Shop Quartet Singing in America	
spec............	Special (NTIO)	
Spec Ed	Special Edition	
SPECT..........	Single Photon Emission Computerised Tomography	
SPEEA..........	Society of Professional Engineering Employees in Aerospace	
SPEM............	Smooth-Pursuit Eye Movements (DIPS)	
SPEWG........	System Planning and Engineering Working Group (CCCA)	
SPGA	System Programmable Gate Array	
SPIE.............	International Society for Optical Engineering	
SPILA...........	Siliconware Precision ADS [NASDAQ symbol]	
SPIN	Stop Pirating Internationally Now [An association]	
SPL	Senior Patrol Leader [Boy Scouts of America]	
SPL	Student Performance Level	
SPLD	Simple Programmable Logic Device (AEBE)	
SPM.............	Site Program Manager (ARMP)	
SPO	Sonicport.com, Inc. [AMEX symbol] (SG)	
SPOH	Since Prop Overhaul [Aviation] (PIPO)	
SPOT	Space Station Proximity Operations Trainer [NASA] (SPST)	
SPP&A..........	Strategic Project Planning and Assessment (SPST)	
SPPF............	Site Platform Processing Facility (SPST)	
SQ	Space Requested (TRID)	
SQA	Semiquantitative (ABAC)	
SQNM............	Sequenom, Inc. [NASDAQ symbol] (SG)	
SQUID..........	Standard Quick Release Universal Interface Device (SPST)	
Sr................	Sister (NTIO)	
SR................	Size-Resolving (CARB)	
SR................	Software Review (CTAS)	
SR................	Steer Roping [Rodeo term]	
SRA	Strategic Rail Authority [London, England]	
SR&CC..........	Strikes, Riots, and Civil Commotions [Insurance] (MARI)	
SR&CC&MD...	Strikes, Riots, Civil Commotions, and Malicious Damage [Insurance] (MARI)	
SRB	Source Routing Bridging [Telecommunications] (MLOA)	
S/R B/L........	Signing and Releasing Bill of Lading (RIMS)	
SRC	Sexual-Response Cycle (DIPS)	
SRES	System Response (CGWS)	
SRF.............	Satellite Ranging Facility	
SRF.............	Senior Research Fellow	
SRI	Serotonin Reuptake Inhibitor [Medicine] (DIPS)	
SRIC	Short-Rotation Intensive Culture (CARB)	
SRL	Ship Repairer's Liability [Insurance] (MARI)	
SRO	Spigadoro, Inc. [AMEX symbol] (SG)	
SRO	Statutory Regulation Order (HEAS)	
SrR	Strontium Recovery (ABAC)	
SRR	Systematic Rational Restructuring (DIPS)	
SRRP	Source Reduction Review Project	
SRTS	Synchronous Residual Time Stamp	
SRUFO..........	Scottish UFO Research	
SRVS	Serves (TRID)	
SS................	Sample Stabilizer (ABAC)	
SS................	Short Supply	
SS................	Staff Side (HEAS)	
SS................	Stainless Steel (ABAC)	
SS................	Supplementary Service (CGWS)	
SS................	Switching System [Telecommunications] (MLOA)	
SSA	Smallest Space Analysis (DIPS)	
SSALF..........	Simplified Short Approach Light System with Sequenced Flashing Lights (PIPO)	
SSB.............	Substitute Senate Bill	
SSB.............	Subsurface Barrier (ABAC)	
SSC.............	Sealed Storage Cask (ABAC)	
SSC.............	Space Surveillance Center (CCCA)	
SSC.............	Super Stream Class (CTAS)	
SSCC	Space Station Control Center [NASA] (SPST)	
SSCF............	Service Specific Coordination Function	
SSCI............	Social Science	
SSCOP..........	Service Specific Connection Oriented Protocol	
SSCS	Service Specific Convergence Sublayer	
SSCS/VSE	Small System Executive/Virtual Storage Extended [Computer science] (ITCA)	
SSD	Software Specification Document	
SSDM	Second Stage Digital Multiplexer (CCCA)	
SSE.............	Space Station Element [NASA] (SPST)	
SSE.............	Space Support Equipment [NASA] (SPST)	
SSE.............	Stationary Source Enforcement (SARE)	
SSE.............	Streaming SIMD Extension	
SSE.............	System Support Element (CCCA)	
SSFF............	Space Station Furnace Facility [NASA] (SPST)	
SSHEX..........	Saturdays, Sundays, Holidays Excepted (RIMS)	
SSHINC..........	Saturdays, Sundays, Holidays Included (RIMS)	
SSHT	Sea Surface Height (CARB)	
SSHTM..........	Small Scale High Temperature Melter (ABAC)	
SSI	Superintending Specialist Inspector (HEAS)	
SSM.............	Segment Status Message (TRID)	
SSM.............	Small Scale Melter (ABAC)	
SSM.............	Special Sensor Microwave (CARB)	
SSM.............	Standard Solar Model	
SSN	Signaling System Number (CGWS)	
SSO	Struck Submerged Object [Insurance] (MARI)	
SS or B.........	Stranded, Stunk, or Burnt [Insurance] (MARI)	
SSP.............	Scanning Spectral Polarimeter (CARB)	
SSP.............	Service Switching Point (CGWS)	
SSPM............	Space Station Pricing Model [NASA] (SPST)	
SSQ	Space Station Quality [NASA] (SPST)	

SSR	Satellite Signal Receiver (CCCA)	
SSR	Special Service Requirement (TRID)	
SSRFAR.........	Space Station Research Facility Assessment Review [NASA] (SPST)	
SST.............	Self-Statement Training (DIPS)	
SST.............	Social-Skills Training (DIPS)	
sst...............	Social Studies	
SST.............	Stimulus Sampling Theory (DIPS)	
SSTL............	Stub-Series Terminated Logic (AEBE)	
SSUAS	Space Station Utilization Advisory Subcommittee [NASA] (SPST)	
SSUPS	Solid State Uninterruptible Power Source (CCCA)	
ST................	Signaling Tone (CGWS)	
ST................	Special Topic	
ST................	Speech Therapy	
ST................	Star Trek	
ST................	Stick and Turn (MLOA)	
STA	Scheduled Time of Arrival (CTAS)	
STAR	Science to Achieve Results	
STaRS	Science Teacher and Research Scientist [Fellowships]	
STARS	Science, Technology, and Research Students [Program]	
STARS	Strategic Targeting Activities Reporting System (AUEG)	
STAS...........	Superman, the Animated Series	
STAT	Sternberg Triarchic Abilities Test (DIPS)	
stats...........	Statistics (NTIO)	
STAWRS	Simplified Tax and Wage Reporting System	
STB	Set-Top Box (AEBE)	
STC.............	School-to-Career	
STCCS	Strategic and Theater Command and Control Systems (CCCA)	
STCS	Software Technologies [NASDAQ symbol] (SG)	
STD.............	Saigon Times Daily [A publication]	
STD.............	Scheduled Time of Departure (CTAS)	
STEM	Subject to Enough Merchandise (RIMS)	
STEPS..........	Science Technology & Engineering Preview Summer [1997]	
STEX...........	Simulation Test and Exercise (CCCA)	
STG.............	System Time Generator (CCCA)	
STI	Stanford Telecommunications, Inc. (CCCA)	
STLW...........	Stratos Lightwave [NASDAQ symbol]	
STM.............	Scanning Tunneling Microscopy	
STO.............	Studio (TRID)	
STOH	Since Top Overhaul [Aviation] (PIPO)	
STOM...........	Ship-to-Objective Maneuver	
STOR	Storage Networks, Inc. [NASDAQ symbol]	
STPN	Satellite Ticket Printer Network (TRID)	
Str...............	Strait (NTIO)	
STREAMS	Science Teams in Rural Environments for Aquatic Management Studies	
STRIKWARN...	Strike Warnings [Military]	
STRM...........	Star Media Network	
STTI	Sigma Theta Tan International	
stud	Student (NTIO)	
STVR	Stopover (TRID)	
STW.............	Saigon Time Weekly [A publication]	
STW.............	School-to-Work	
SU................	Sensation Unit (DIPS)	
Su................	Sunday (NTIO)	
sub.............	Submarine (NTIO)	
sub.............	Suburb (NTIO)	
subj	Subjunctive (NTIO)	
SUD	Safe Use Determination (SARE)	
SUD	Subjective Units of Distress (DIPS)	
Sud	Sudan (NTIO)	
SUE.............	Standardized Unexpected Earnings	
suff	Suffix (NTIO)	
SUI.............	Sound User Interface	
SULEV	Super Ultra-Low Emission Vehicle	
SUN	Sunset Beach [Television program title]	
SUP	Soluble Unreactive Phosphorus (CARB)	
SUP	Superior Room (TRID)	
sup.............	Superlative (NTIO)	
super	Superintendent (NTIO)	
supl info	Supplementary Information (TRID)	
sur	Surplus (NTIO)	
SURF	Surface Storage Facility (ABAC)	
SURR............	Stage Unique Requirements Report (SPST)	
SURTASS.....	Surface Towed Array Sensor System (CCCA)	
SV................	Stilwell Financial [NYSE symbol]	
SVC.............	Saab Variable Compression	
SVE.............	Secure Voice Element (CCCA)	
SVF.............	Software Verification Facility (SPST)	
SVIB-SCII.....	Strong-Campbell Interest Inventory Form of the Strong Vocational Interest Blank (DIPS)	
SVNX...........	724 Solutions [NASDAQ symbol] (SG)	
SVS.............	State Veterinary Service	
SVVS	Savvis Communications [NASDAQ symbol] (SG)	
SVW.............	Sea View (TRID)	
SW.............	Star Wars	
SW.............	Steer Wrestling [Rodeo term]	
SW.............	Surface Water (AUEG)	
SW.............	Surveillance and Warning (CCCA)	
SWA	Solid Waste Act (SARE)	
SWAD	Salt Water Arrival Draft (RIMS)	
SWAG	Simulated Waste Access to Ground Water (AUEG)	
SWAP	Severe Weather Avoidance Procedures (CTAS)	
SWAT...........	Special Weapons Attack Team (NTIO)	
Swaz...........	Swaziland (NTIO)	
SWBD	Switchboard, Inc. [NASDAQ symbol] (SG)	

SWBT........... South Western Bell Telephone (ROAS)
SWD .... Sea Water Damage [*Insurance*] (MARI)
SWDD.......... Salt Water Departure Draft (RIMS)
SWE............. Shallow-Water Equations (CARB)
SWEDAC...... Swedish Board for Technical Accreditation (CARB)
SWEDC....... Southwest Washington Educational Development Consortium
SWIG .... Sensors for the Water Industry Group
SWIRLS....... Stratospheric Wind Infrared Limb Sounder (CARB)
SWIS .... Solid Waste Information System (SARE)
SWIT........... Structured Written Interview Technique (DIPS)
SWITS .... Solid Waste Information and Tracking System (ABAC)
SWMP .... Stormwater Monitoring Program (SARE)
SWO .... Staff Welfare Officer (HEAS)
SWOG.......... Southwest Oncology Group

SWP............ Special Work Permit (ABAC)
SWP3.......... Storm Water Pollution Prevention Plan
SWR .... Shortwave Radiation (ARMP)
SWS............ Shortwave Spectroradiometer (ARMP)
SWSS .... Southern Weed Science Society
SWTS.......... Solid Waste Technology Support (ABAC)
SWX............ Swiss Exchange
SY.............. Seasonal Year (CARB)
Sym .... Symphony
syn.............. Synonym (NTIO)
sync............ Synchronize
SYNC .... Synchronous
SysPrep .... System Preparation
SysPrep .... System Preparation Tool

T

By Acronym

T	Takeoff Minimum [*Aviation*] (PIPO)
T	Toxic (HEAS)
T	Tutor
T3	Transurethral Thermo-Ablation Therapy [*Medicine*] (DAVI)
TA	Tanks (RIMS)
Ta	Tonometry Applanation [*Medicine*] (DAVI)
TA	Total Average [*Baseball term*] (NDBD)
TA	Travel Agent (TRID)
TAA	Therapeutic Activities Aide (DAVI)
TAAD	Travel Agent Automated Deduction (TRID)
TAC	Technical Assistance Contractor (CTAS)
TAC	Travel Agency Commission (TRID)
TA/CE	Technical Analysis/Cost Estimate (CCCA)
TACH	Traffic and Associated Channel (CGWS)
TACMS	Theater Army Command Multichannel System (CCCA)
TACOM	Tank-Automotive and Armaments Command [*Army*]
TACP	Tactical Air Control Post (CCCA)
TACS	Terminal Access Control System (CCCA)
TADD	Taskforce on Amphibian Declines and Deformities
TAF	Terminal Area Forecast (PIAV)
TA-GVHD	Transfusion-Associated Graft-Versus-Host Disease (DAVI)
TAHL	Thick Ascending Limb of Henle's Loop [*Medicine*] (DAVI)
TAIS	Tactical Airspace Integration System [*Army*]
TAIS	Total Aircraft Information System (HLLA)
TALCE	Transportable Air Lift Control Element (CCCA)
TAM	Teletype Adaptor Module (CCCA)
TAML	Therapy-Related Acute Myelogenous Leukemia [*Medicine*] (DAVI)
TAMS	Total Airport Management System (HLLA)
TAN	Treatment Authorization Number (DAVI)
TAND	Tandem Schedule of Reinforcement (DIPS)
T&C	Type and Crossmatch [*Medicine*] (DAVI)
T&D	Training and Development (TRID)
T&DA	Tracking and Data Acquisition (SPST)
T&E	Transverse Electric (CCCA)
T&E	Traversing and Elevating
T&H	Transportation and Handling (SPST)
T&H	Type and Hold (DAVI)
T&L	Transform and Lighting
T&M	Type and Crossmatch (DAVI)
T&N	Tension and Nervousness (DAVI)
T&P	Temperature and Pulse (DAVI)
t&s	Touch and Stay (MARI)
T&S	Turn and Slip Indicator [*Aviation*] (PIPO)
T&T	Tobramycin and Ticarcillin [*Medicine*] (DAVI)
TAP	Tank Advisory Panel (ABAC)
TAP	Tonometry by Applanation [*Medicine*] (DAVI)
TAP	Transesophageal Atrial Paced [*Medicine*] (DAVI)
TAP	Transportation Adjudication Panel
TAR	Total Anorectal Reconstruction [*Medicine*] (DAVI)
TART	Tenderness, Asymmetry, Restricted Motion, and Tissue Texture Changes [*Medicine*] (DAVI)
TAS	Turning Against Self (DAVI)
TAS	Typical Absence Seizures [*Medicine*] (DAVI)
TASA	Telecommunication Alarm-Sequence Analyzer (IDAI)
TASC	Transportation Administrative Service Center
TASC	Travel Agents of Suffolk County [*New York*] (TRID)
TAT	Tandem Auto-Transplants [*Medicine*] (DAVI)
TAT	Theoretical Arrival Time (MLOA)
TAT	Total Air Temperature (HLLA)
TAT	Transitional Automated Ticket [*Travel industry*] (TRID)
TAUC	Time-Averaged Urea Concentration [*Medicine*] (DAVI)
TAWS	Terrain Awareness and Warning System
TAWS	Terrain Awareness System
TB	Taco Bell
TB	Twisting and Bending (MARI)
TBAGA	Term Birth Appropriate for Gestational Age (DAVI)
T-bar	Tracheotomy Bar (DAVI)
TBD	To Be Documented (CTAS)
T-berg	Trendelenburg (DAVI)
TBEV	Tick-Borne Encephalitis Virus (DAVI)
Tbili	Total Bilirubin (DAVI)
TBLF	Term Birth, Living Female (DAVI)
TBLM	Term Birth, Living Male (DAVI)
TBM	Tracheobronchomalacia [*Medicine*] (DAVI)
TBMg	Total-Body Magnesium (DAVI)
TBN	To Be Named (RIMS)

TBOCS	Tale-Brown Obsessive-Compulsive Scale (DAVI)
TBP	Total-Body Phosphorus (DAVI)
TBP	Total-Body Protein (DAVI)
Tbps	Terabits per Second
TBR	To-Be-Remembered (DIPS)
TBR	To Be Renamed (RIMS)
TB/S	Time Code Bits per Sample (CCCA)
tbsp	Tablespoon (NTIO)
TBT	Transbronchoscopic Balloon Tipped [*Medicine*] (DAVI)
TBV	Thiotepa, Bleomycin, and Vinblastine [*Medicine*] (DAVI)
TC	Tar Creosote (HEAS)
TC	Team Conference (DAVI)
TC	Terminal Cancer (DAVI)
TC	Terrace House
TC	Testicular Cancer (DAVI)
TC	Therapeutic Community (DIPS)
TC	Thioguanine and Cytarabine [*Medicine*] (DAVI)
TC	Thoracic Circumference (DAVI)
TC	Tiger Cub [*Boy Scouts of America*]
TC	Tolonium Chloride (DAVI)
TC	Tracheal Collar [*Medicine*] (DAVI)
TC	Transmission Convergence [*Telecommunications*] (MLOA)
TC	Trauma Center (DAVI)
TC	Turn Coordinator (PIPO)
TCA	Terminal Control Area (PIAV)
TCA	Thioguanine and Cytarabine [*Medicine*] (DAVI)
TCA	Tumor Chemosensitivity Assay [*Medicine*] (DAVI)
TCAD	Traffic Collision Alerting Device
TCAD	Transplant-Related Coronary-Artery Disease (DAVI)
TC-AIMS II	Transportation Coordinators'-Automated Information Movements System II [*Army*]
TCAR	Tiazofurin (DAVI)
TC/CL	Ticarcillin-Clavulanate [*Medicine*] (DAVI)
TCD	Transcerebellar Diameter [*Medicine*] (DAVI)
TCD	Transcranial Doppler (DAVI)
TCD	Transcystic Duct [*Medicine*] (DAVI)
TCD	Transverse Cardiac Diameter [*Medicine*] (DAVI)
TCE	Total Colon Examination (DAVI)
TCH/FS	Traffic Channel/Full Rate Speech (CGWS)
TCH/HS	Traffic Channel/Half Rate Speech (CGWS)
TCP	Time Charter Party (RIMS)
TCR	Tagged Cell Rate (MLOA)
TCR	T-Complex Responder [*Medicine*]
TCS	Tethered Cord Syndrome
TCT	Time Charter Trip (RIMS)
TCT	Trans Canada Trail
TCTA	Transcontinental Control Area (PIPO)
TCU	Transitional Care Unit (DAVI)
TD	Technology Development (AUEG)
TD	Test Dose (DAVI)
Td	Tetanus-Diphtheria Toxoid [*Medicine*] (DAVI)
TD	Ticket Designator (TRID)
TD&D	Technical Data and Documentation (SPST)
TDC	Total Direct Cost
TDD	Time Division Duplex (CGWS)
TDD	Total Daily Dose [*Medicine*] (DAVI)
TDDR	Total Direct Diffuse Radiometer (CARB)
TDF	Total-Dietary Fiber (DAVI)
TDI	Turbo Direct Injection
TDLS	Tunable Diode Laser Spectroscopy (CARB)
TDO	Temporary Denial Order
TDOR	Two-Door Car (TRID)
TDR	Time Distribution Record (ABAC)
TDRSS	Tracking Data Relay Satellite System
TDS	Totally Dissolved Solid (SARE)
TDT	Trieger Dot Test (DAVI)
TDUS	Task-Oriented Dialogue Understanding System (DIPS)
TDW	Target Dry Weight (DAVI)
TDZ	Touchdown Zone [*Aviation*] (PIPO)
TDZ/CL	Touchdown Zone and Centerline Lighting [*Aviation*] (PIPO)
TDZL	Touchdown Zone Lighting [*Aviation*] (PIPO)
TE	Terminal Extension (DAVI)
T/E	Testosterone to Epitestosterone Ratio (DAVI)
TE	Transesophageal Echocardiography [*Medicine*] (DAVI)
TE	Transmitted Electron
TE	Transrectal Electroejaculation [*Medicine*] (DAVI)

TEA .... Temperate East Asia (CARB)
TEB .... Thoracic Electrical Bioimpedance
TEC .... Test and Electrical Characterization
TECAP .... Transistor Electrical Characterization and Analysis Program
TECO........... Terrestrial Ecosystems (CARB)
TED .... Thermal Expansion Difference (ABAC)
TED .... Transmitted Electron Detection
TEDF .... Treated Effluent Disposal Facility
TEE .... Total Energy Expended [*Medicine*] (DAVI)
TEE .... Trans-European Express (TRID)
TEE .... Transnasal Endoscopic Ethmoidectomy [*Medicine*] (DAVI)
TEHOF .... Thermal Electric Holding Facility [*NASA*] (SPST)
TEI .... Terminal End Point Indentifier [*Computer science*] (ITCA)
TEI .... Terminal Equipment Identifier (CGWS)
TEI .... Total Episode of Illness (DAVI)
TEJ .... Tropical Easterly Jet (ARMP)
Telecomm ... Telecommunications
TELEX .... Telephone Exchange (PIPO)
TEM .... Transanal Endoscopic Microsurgery (DAVI)
TEM .... Transmission Electron Microscopy
TEM .... Tunneling Electron Microscopy
TEMI .... Transient Episodes of Myocardial Ischemia [*Medicine*] (DAVI)
TEN .... Tension (DAVI)
TEN .... Ticket Exchange Notice [*Travel industry*] (TRID)
TEOAE......... Transient Evoked Otoacoustic Emission [*Medicine*] (DAVI)
TEP .... Total Extraperitoneal [*Medicine*] (DAVI)
TEPS........... Telerobotic Electrical Power Subsystem [*NASA*] (SPST)
TER .... Terlipressin [*Medicine*] (DAVI)
TERC .... Test of Early Reading Comprehension (DAVI)
TERPS .... Terminal Instrument Approach Procedures (PIPO)
TES .... Tropospheric Emission Spectrometer (ARMP)
TESLA......... TeV-Energy Superconducting Linear Accelerator
TEUR .... Tele 1 Europe ADS [*NASDAQ symbol*] (SG)
TF .... Throughfall (CARB)
TFCC .... Tactical Force Command Center (CCCA)
TFF .... Technology Flavors and Fragrances [*AMEX symbol*] (SG)
TFT .... Trifluorotoluene
TGB............. Tiagabine (DAVI)
TGD .... Thyroglossal Duct [*Medicine*] (DAVI)
TGM .... Thesaurus of Graphics Materials
TGTL........... Total Glottic Transverse Laryngectomy [*Medicine*] (DAVI)
TGU .... Time Generation Unit (SPST)
TGUI .... Timelife Graphical User Interface (CTAS)
TGXT........... Thallium-Graded Exercise Test (DAVI)
TGZ............. Troglitazone [*Medicine*] (DAVI)
TH .... Time Hopped (CCCA)
T/H.............. Track and Hold (AEBE)
THC .... Terminal Handling Charge (MARI)
THC .... Terminal Handling Cost (RIMS)
THNB .... Time Hopped Narrow Beam (CCCA)
THR .... Thruster (RIMS)
THTL........... Tourist Hotel (TRID)
TIA............. Travel Industry Association (TRID)
TIAG........... Travel Industry Association of Georgia (TRID)
TICE .... Training Information and Communication Enhancement
TID............. Total Ionizing Dose (CCCA)
TIDS........... Travel Intermediary Designator Service (TRID)
TIE .... Total Ion Electropherogram
TIF .... Technical Integration Forum
TIH............. Tumor-Inducing Hypercalcemia (DAVI)
TIIF .... Telecommunications and Information Industry Forum
TIMED .... Thermosphere-Ionosphere-Mesosphere Energetics and Dynamics
TIME-GCM ... Thermosphere Ionosphere-Mesosphere-Electrodynamics General Circulation Model
tinct .... Tincture (DAVI)
TIND .... Treatment Investigational New Drug (DAVI)
TINEM......... There is No Evidence of Malignancy (DAVI)
TIP............. Taking Inward Pilot (RIMS)
TIP............. Threat-Image Projection
TIP............. Tool Interface Plate
TIP............. Toxic Interstitial Pneumonitis [*Medicine*] (DAVI)
TIP............. Treatment Improvement Protocol (DIPS)
TIPI .... Tactical Intelligence Photo Interpretation (CCCA)
TIPSS........... Transjugular Intrahepatic Portosystemic Shunt [*Medicine*] (DAVI)
TIRS........... Transient Infrared Emission Spectroscopy
TIVA........... Total Intravenous Anethesia [*Medicine*] (DAVI)
TJA .... Total Joint Arthroplasty [*Medicine*] (DAVI)
TJN .... Tongue Jaw Neck (DAVI)
Tk .... Tool Kit (CTAS)
TK .... Toxicokinetics (DAVI)
TKA .... Tyrosine Kinase Activity (DAVI)
TKE .... Terminal Knee Extension (DAVI)
TKG............. Trunk Key Generator (CCCA)
TKIC........... True Knot in Cord [*Medicine*] (DAVI)
TKNO .... Ticket Number [*Travel industry*] (TRID)
TKP............. Total Knee Prosthesis (DAVI)
TKRL........... Total Knee Replacement Left (DAVI)
TKRR........... Total Knee Replacement Right (DAVI)
TKTL........... Ticket Time Limit [*Travel industry*] (TRID)
TL .... Speech Tolerance Level (DIPS)
TL .... Tolerance Level (DIPS)
TLA .... Texas Library Association
TLC .... Thornton Leadership Council
TLC .... Total Linux Coverage
TLCF .... Technology Literacy Challenge Fund

TLCT .... Telocity, Inc. [*NASDAQ symbol*] (SG)
TLI .... Training Liaison Inspector (HEAS)
TLM .... Transition Line Model
TLP .... Time-Limited Psychotherapy (DIPS)
TLR .... Tonic Labyrinthine Reflex [*Medicine*] (DAVI)
TLS .... Tumor Lysis Syndrome [*Medicine*] (DAVI)
TLSO........... Thoracic Lumbar Sacral Orthosis [*Medicine*] (DAVI)
TLSSO .... Thoracolumbosacral Spinal Orthosis [*Medicine*] (DAVI)
TLT .... Tonsillectomy (DAVI)
TLV .... Threshold Limit Value (CARB)
TLV .... Transition Level (PIPO)
TLVO .... Total Loss of Vessel Only [*Insurance*] (MARI)
TLXS .... Telaxix Communications [*NASDAQ symbol*] (SG)
TM .... Temperature by Mouth (DAVI)
TM .... Testing Memorandum (HEAS)
tm .... Trademark
TM .... Training Manager (HEAS)
TM .... Typing Manager (HEAS)
TMA .... Telephone Managers Association (COBU)
T/MA .... Tracheostomy Mask [*Medicine*] (DAVI)
TMA .... Transcortical Motor Aphasia (DIPS)
TMC .... Traffic Management Coordinator (CTAS)
TMC .... Transfer Module Controller
TMC-GUI ...... Traffic Management Coordinator-Graphical User Interface (CTAS)
TMCN........... Triamcinolone (DAVI)
TMD .... Temporomandibular Dysfunction [*Medicine*] (DAVI)
TMD .... Trainable Mental Defective (DIPS)
TME .... Thermolysin-Like Metalloendopeptidase [*Medicine*] (DAVI)
TMG .... Thermal Model Generator (SPST)
TMI .... Traffic Management Systems Interface (CTAS)
TMS .... Traffic Management Station (CTAS)
TMSI........... Temporary Mobile Service Identity (CGWS)
TMZ............. Temazepam [*Medicine*] (DAVI)
TNB .... Term Newborn (DAVI)
TNBP .... Transurethral Needle Biopsy of Prostate [*Medicine*] (DAVI)
TNCPEC ...... Thailand National Committee for Pacific Economic Cooperation
TND .... Traditional Neighborhood Development
TNDM .... Transient Neonatal Diabetes Mellitus [*Medicine*] (DAVI)
TNFSS .... Tactical Nuclear Force Security & Survivability (CCCA)
TNI .... Targeted Nutritional Intervention
TNMOC .... Total Non-Methane Organic Compound
TNO .... Trans-Neptunian Object
TNO .... Trans-Neptunian Objects
TNOX .... Tanox, Inc. [*NASDAQ symbol*] (SG)
TNR .... Trap, Neuter, and Return
TNRS........... Time of Non-Redundant Sample (CCCA)
TNS .... Training Needs Statement [*Military*]
TNS .... Transient Neurologic Symptoms (DAVI)
TNT .... Tramcinolone and Nystatin [*Medicine*] (DAVI)
TNW .... Thermo-Nuclear War (CCCA)
T/O.............. Take-Off (PIPO)
To .... Toronto Stock Exchange (SG)
TO .... Tour Order [*Travel industry*] (TRID)
TO .... Training Officer (DEMM)
TOA .... Tropical Ocean-Atmosphere (CARB)
TOBENA...... To Be Named (RIMS)
TOC .... Take-Off Configuration (PIPO)
TOCE........... Transcatheter Oily Chemoembolization [*Medicine*] (DAVI)
TOCO........... Tocodynamometer (DAVI)
TODAM .... Theory of Distributed Associative Memory [*B. B. Murdock*] (DIPS)
TOE .... Ticket Order Exception [*Travel industry*] (TRID)
TOF .... Theoretical Orthogonal Function (CARB)
TOG .... Total Organic Gas
TOH .... Throughout Hospitalization (DAVI)
Tol .... Toluene
TOM .... Theory of Mind
TOM .... Therapeutic Outcomes Monitoring (DAVI)
TON .... Total Organic Nitrogen (CARB)
TOP............. Taking Outward Pilot (RIMS)
TOP............. Thematic Organization Point (DIPS)
TOP............. Tour Operator Program (TRID)
TOPCAT :...... Total Program Cost Analysis Tool (SPST)
TOPSSWG..... Toward Other Planetary Systems Science Working Group
TOR .... Tropospheric Ozone Research (CARB)
TOT BILI ...... Total Bilirubin [*Medicine*] (DAVI)
TOTL.......... Total (TRID)
TOV............. Trial of Void (DAVI)
TOVA .... Test of Variable Attention
TOVE........... Toronto Virtual Enterprise [*Project*] (IDAI)
TOX............. Toxaphene
TOXNET .... Toxicology Network (AUEG)
TP .... Temperature Profiling (ARMP)
TP .... Temporoparietal (DAVI)
TP .... Therapeutic Pass (DAVI)
TP .... Thought Process (DAVI)
TP .... Todd's Paralysis (DAVI)
TP .... Treating Physician (DAVI)
TPA .... Temporary Portacaval Anastomosis [*Medicine*] (DAVI)
TPC .... Target Plasma Concentration [*Medicine*] (DAVI)
TPCA........... Toxic Pits Cleanup Act (SARE)
TPE .... Total Placental Estrogens [*Medicine*] (DAVI)
TPF .... Trade Policy Forum
TPF .... Trained Participating Father (DAVI)
TPITS........... Two-Phase Integrated Thermal System (SPST)
TPL .... Templeton [*Publisher*]

TPL............	Total Path Length (CTAS)
tpl..............	Triple (TRID)
TPM............	Ticketed Point Mileage [*Travel industry*] (TRID)
TPM............	Total Productive Manufacturing
TPO............	Tempo Music [*Publisher*]
TPO............	Temporary Protection Order (SARE)
TPS............	Technical Performance Specification (CCCA)
TPS............	Textured Particle System
TPS............	Theorem Proving System (IDAI)
TPU............	Tropical Phagedenic Ulcer [*Medicine*] (DAVI)
T putty........	Theraputty (DAVI)
TPZ............	Tirapazamine (DAVI)
TQ..............	Cash Technologies [*AMEX symbol*] (SG)
TQFP..........	Thin Quad Flat-Pack (AEBE)
TR..............	Team Roping [*Rodeo term*]
TR..............	Therapeutic Recreation (DAVI)
T/R..............	Thrust Reverser [*Aviation*] (PIPO)
TRASYS........	Thermal Radiation Analyzer System (SPST)
TRD	Total-Retinal Detachment (DAVI)
TRDN..........	Transient Respiratory Distress of the Newborn (DAVI)
TRDR..........	Trader.com NV 'A' [*NASDAQ symbol*] (SG)
TRDS	Text Retrieval Data System (AUEG)
TRF.............	Teaching Research Fellow
TRI.............	Transient Radicular Irritation [*Medicine*] (DAVI)
TRIC...........	Time-Resolved Ion Correlation
TRIG	Triglycerides (DAVI)
TRIPS	Trade-Related Aspects of Intellectual Property
TRIPS	Trade-Related Intellectual Property Rights
TRISS	Trauma Related Injury Severity Score (DAVI)
TRM............	Treatment Related Mortality (DAVI)
trmt............	Treatment
TRNBP	Transrectal Needle Biopsy Prostate (DAVI)
TRND	Trendelenburg (DAVI)
TROFO	Trofosfamide (DAVI)
TROM	Total Range of Motion (DAVI)
TROSY........	Transverse Relaxation-Optimized Spectroscopy
TRP............	Toxicology Review Panel
TRPB	Triple with Bath (TRID)
TRPN	Triple without Bath (TRID)
trprm..........	Transition Primer
TRPS	Triple with Shower (TRID)
TRS.............	Therapeutic Recreation Specialist (DAVI)
TRT.............	Tangential Radiation Therapy (DAVI)
TR/TE..........	Time to Repetition and Time to Echo in Spin (DAVI)
TRUSP	Transrectal Ultrasonography of the Prostate [*Medicine*] (DAVI)
TRW............	Thompson Ramo Wooldridge, Inc. (CCCA)
TS..............	Telomerase (DAVI)
TS..............	Traffic Shaping [*Telecommunications*] (MLOA)
TS..............	Trajectory Synthesis (CTAS)
TSA............	Temperate South America (CARB)
TSA............	Transcortical Sensory Aphasia (DIPS)
TSB............	Technical Staffs Branch (HEAS)
TSB............	Total Serum Bilirubin [*Medicine*] (DAVI)
TSC............	Theophylline Serum Concentration (DAVI)
TSDP	Tapered Steroid Dosing Package [*Medicine*] (DAVI)
TSE............	Transmissible Spongiform Encephalopathy
T set	Tracheotomy Set (DAVI)
TSI.............	Titan Systems Corp. (CCCA)
TSI.............	Travel Service Intermediary (TRID)
TSIX...........	36Onetworks, Inc. [*NASDAQ symbol*] (SG)
T Skull........	Trauma Skull (DAVI)
TSMA..........	Technical Support Management Assistance (CCCA)
TSM-Soldier...	TRADOC System Manager-Soldier
TSP............	Technical Steering Panel
TSPA..........	Thiotepa (DAVI)
TSR.............	Technical Safety Requirement (SARE)

TSR.............	Test Status Review (CTAS)
TSS............	Tangential Sensitivity Signal (CCCA)
TSS............	Total Serum Solids (DAVI)
TST............	Transitional Stored Ticket [*Travel industry*] (TRID)
TSTN..........	Turnstone Systems [*NASDAQ symbol*] (SG)
TSWG	Track Safety Working Group (HEAS)
TT	Test Tape (DAVI)
TT	True Track (PIAV)
TTAE	Total Time Aircraft and Engine (PIPO)
TTAT	Thompson Thematic Apperception Test [*C. E. Thompson*] (DIPS)
TTAT	Toe Touch as Tolerated (DAVI)
TTC............	Transtracheal Catheter (DAVI)
TTD............	Tarsal Tunnel Decompression [*Medicine*] (DAVI)
TTDM	Thallim Threadmill (DAVI)
TTE	Transthoracic Echocardiography [*Medicine*] (DAVI)
TTF	Time to Treatment Failure (DAVI)
TTII	Thyrotopin-Binding Inhibitory Immunoglobulins [*Medicine*] (DAVI)
TTJV	Transtracheal Jet Ventilation [*Medicine*] (DAVI)
TTM	Total Tumor Mass (DAVI)
TTP	Technical Task Plan
TTP	Technical Task Plans (AUEG)
TTSN..........	Total Time Since New [*Aviation*] (PIPO)
TTW	Time to Waypoint (HLLA)
TU..............	Technology Unit (HEAS)
TU..............	Transrectal Ultrasound [*Medicine*] (DAVI)
TUAV	Tactical Unmanned Aerial Vehicle [*Military*]
TUCD	Total User Cell Difference (MLOA)
TUE............	Transurethral Extraction [*Medicine*] (DAVI)
TUF	Total Ultrafiltration [*Medicine*] (DAVI)
TUIBN	Transurethral Incision of Bladder Neck [*Medicine*] (DAVI)
TUMT..........	Transurethral Microwave Thermotherapy [*Medicine*] (DAVI)
TUN	Total Urinary Nitrogen [*Medicine*] (DAVI)
TUNA	Transurethral Needle Ablation [*Medicine*] (DAVI)
TUP............	Tupperware
TUPR..........	Transurethral Prostatic Resection [*Medicine*] (DAVI)
TURVN........	Transurethral Resection of Vesical Neck [*Medicine*] (DAVI)
TUS............	Trade Union Side (HEAS)
TUS............	Trailing Umbilical System (SPST)
TUU	Transureteroureterostomy [*Medicine*] (DAVI)
TUV	Transurethral Valve [*Medicine*] (DAVI)
TUVP	Transurethral Vaporization of the Prostate [*Medicine*] (DAVI)
TV..............	Temporary Visit (DAVI)
T/V..............	Touch-Verbal (DAVI)
TV..............	Turbine Vessel (TRID)
TVCS...........	Trend Virus Control System
TVF............	True Vocal Fold (DAVI)
TW.............	Thames Water (HEAS)
TWA............	Theater War Architecture (CCCA)
TWAG	Time Weighted Average Gap
TWAV..........	Therma-Wave, Inc. [*NASDAQ symbol*] (SG)
TWCP	Tank Waste Characterization Plan
TWDL..........	Two-Way Data Link (HLLA)
TWI.............	Two-Way Interface (CTAS)
TWINS	Two Wide-Angle Imaging Neutral-Atom Spectrometers [*NASA*]
TWNB	Twin Room with Bath (TRID)
TwnHse........	Townhouse
TWNN	Twin Room without Bath (TRID)
TWNS	Twin Room with Shower (TRID)
TWPO	Tropical Western Pacific Ocean (CARB)
TWRA	Tennessee Wildlife Resources Agency (CARB)
TWRI	Trendwest Resorts [*NASDAQ symbol*] (SG)
TWRS	Tank Waste Remediation System
Tx	Transcription [*Medicine*] (DAVI)
Tx	Transmitter (PIAV)
txt	Text File Extension
TZ	Temozolomide [*Medicine*] (DAVI)

U

By Acronym

U	Unassisted Putout [*Baseball term*] (NDBD)
U	Unicom (PIPO)
UA&M	Urinalysis and Microscopy (DAVI)
UADT	Upper Aerodigestive Tract [*Medicine*] (DAVI)
U&O	Utilization and Operations (SPST)
UAOB	Upper Air Observation (CARB)
UAP	Unidentified Atmospheric Phenomenon
UAP	Unlicensed Assistive Personnel
UAPA	United Aerial Phenomenon Agency
UAPF	Upon Arrival Patient Found (DAVI)
U ARM	Upper Arm (DAVI)
UASA	Upper Airway Sleep Apnea (DAVI)
UATMP	Urban Air Toxics Monitoring Program
UAV	Unmanned Aerospace Vehicle (CARB)
UAV	Unmanned Automated Vehicle
UAXS	Univl Access [*NASDAQ symbol*] (SG)
UBD	Universal Blood Donor
UBI	Ubrandit.com [*AMEX symbol*] (SG)
UBL	United Baseball League (NDBD)
UBM	Unpressurized Berthing Mast [*NASA*] (SPST)
UBT	Urea Breath Test (DAVI)
UBW	Usual Body Weight (DAVI)
UC	Unconscious (DAVI)
UCB	Umbilical Cord Blood [*Medicine*] (DAVI)
UCBT	Unrelated Cord Blood Transplant [*Medicine*] (DAVI)
UCCCF	Universal Credit Card Charge Form (TRID)
UCD	User Code Document (ROAS)
UCE	Urea Cycle Enzymopathy [*Medicine*] (DAVI)
UCEA	Universities and Colleges Employers Association
UCH	User Channel (CGWS)
UCHS	Uncontrolled Hemorrhagic Shock [*Medicine*] (DAVI)
UCITA	Uniform Computer Information Transactions Act
UCL	Universal Communications Language
UCLES	University of Cambridge Local Examinations Syndicate
UCO	Use Classes Order (HEAS)
UCP	Umbilical Cord Prolapse [*Medicine*] (DAVI)
UCs	Unconscious (DIPS)
UCS	Union of Concerned Scientists
UCWA	Urgent Center Weather Advisory (PIPO)
UD	Ulster Defence Regiment Medal
UDP	Unassisted Diastolic Pressure (DAVI)
UDS	Unconditioned Stimulus (DAVI)
UDS	User Display Segment (CCCA)
UE	Under Elbow (DAVI)
UEL	Upper Exposure Limit (HEAS)
UES	Undifferentiated Embryonal Sarcoma [*Medicine*] (DAVI)
UESEP	Upper Extremity Somatosensory Evoked Potential (DAVI)
UF	University Fellow
UFC	Uniform Fire Code (SARE)
UFCW	United Food & Commercial Workers
UFF	Unusual Facial Features (DAVI)
UFH	Unfractionated Heparin [*Medicine*] (DAVI)
UFOIRC	UFO Information Retrieval Center
UFONS	UFO Newsclipping Service
UFORA	UFO Research Australia
UFORIC	UFO Research Institute of Canada
UFOROM	Ufology Research of Manitoba [*Canada*]
UFT	Uracil and Tegafur [*Medicine*] (DAVI)
UFV	Ultrafiltration Volume (DAVI)
UG	Universal Grammar (DIPS)
UG	Until Gone (DAVI)
UG	Urinary Glucose (DAVI)
UGA	Urogenital Atrophy [*Medicine*] (DAVI)
UGC	United Global Com
UGCR	Ultrasound-Guided Compression Repair (DAVI)
UGI	Upper Gastrointestinal with Small Bowel Follow Through (DAVI)
UGIT	Upper Gastrointestinal Tract (DAVI)
UGK	Urine, Glucose, and Ketones (DAVI)
UGP	Urinary Gonadotropin Peptide (DAVI)
UGST	Underground Storage Tank (SARE)
UGVA	Ultrasound-Guided Vascular Access (DAVI)
UH	Umbilical Hernia (DAVI)
UH	Unfavorable History (DAVI)
UHCL	University of Houston-Clear Lake [*Texas*]
UHF	Ultra High Frequency (HLLA)
UHMRA	Upper Heyford Mandatory Radio Area [*British*] (PIAV)
UHTS	Ultra-High-Throughput Screening
U/I	Urban/Industrial (CCCA)
UIB	Unemployment Insurance Benefits (DAVI)
UIE	User Interface Environment (SPST)
UIEP	Urine Immunoelectrophoresis [*Medicine*] (DAVI)
UIR	Upper Flight Information Region (PIPO)
UJ	Universal Joint [*Medicine*] (DAVI)
UKHIS	United Kingdom Hazard Information System (HEAS)
UKIC	Urokinase Intracoronary [*Medicine*] (DAVI)
UL	University Lecturer
U/L	Upper and Lower (DAVI)
UL	Upper Lid (DAVI)
ULIRG	Ultraluminous Far Infrared Galaxies
ULLE	Upper Lid, Left Eye (DAVI)
ULPA	Ultra-Low Penetration Air (SARE)
ULRE	Upper Lid, Right Eye (DAVI)
ULSB	Upper Left Sternal Border (DAVI)
UM	Uniform Manifest (SARE)
UM	University of Montana
UML	Unified Modeling Language [*Computer science*] (ITCA)
UMLS	Unified Medical Language System (IDAI)
UNC	Uncrossed (DAVI)
UNCITRL	United Nations Commission on International Trade Law (MARI)
UnCR	Unconditioned Response (DIPS)
UNCSB-JSA	United Nations Command Security Battalion-Joint Security Area
UNDEL	Undelivered (DAVI)
UNEC	United Nations Economic Committee (CARB)
UNGCRP	United Nations Global Change Research Program (CARB)
UNI	User-to-Network Interface (MLOA)
UNICOM	Universal Communications (PIPO)
UNICON	Uncontainerable Goods (MARI)
UNL	Upper Normal Levels [*Medicine*] (DAVI)
UNLTRD	Unlettered
UNOPS	United Nations Office for Project Services
UNP	United Nations Political Affairs (CARB)
UNS	United Nations Sanctions
UNTAB	United Nations Technical Assistance Board (CARB)
UO	Undetermined Origin (DAVI)
UO	University of Oregon
UOP	Urinary Output (DAVI)
UOPX	University of Phoenix Online
UOR	Under One Roof (MARI)
Uosm	Urinary Osmolality [*Medicine*] (DAVI)
UP	Unipolar (DAVI)
U/P	Unpainted
UPC	United Pan-European Communications [*Amsterdam*]
UPC	United Pan-Europe Communications
UPC	Unknown Primary Carcinoma (DAVI)
UPCS	UbiQui Tel, Inc. [*NASDAQ symbol*]
UPIN	Unique Physician Identification Number (DAVI)
UPLIF	Unilateral Posterior Lumbar Interbody Fusion [*Medicine*] (DAVI)
UPOV	Useful Field of View (DAVI)
UPR	User Performance Requirements (CGWS)
UPR	User Preferred Routing (CTAS)
UPRO	Uproar, Inc. [*NASDAQ symbol*] (SG)
UPS	Unattended Power Source (CCCA)
UPSC	Uterine Papillary Serous Carcinoma [*Medicine*] (DAVI)
UPT	Universal Personal Telecommunications (CGWS)
UPT	Uptake (DAVI)
U/R	Under Repair (MARI)
UR	Urinary Retention (DAVI)
UR AC	Uric Acid (DAVI)
URD	Undifferentiated Respiratory Disease (DAVI)
URGENT	Urban Regeneration of the Environment
URI	Uniform Resource Indicator
URIC A	Uric Acid (DAVI)
url	Unrelated (DAVI)
URL	Upper Range Limit (CARB)
UROB	Urobilinogen (DAVI)
UROD	Ultra-Rapid Opiate Detoxification [*Medicine*] (DAVI)
UROL	Urologist (DAVI)
U/S	Ultrasonic
u/s	Unserviceable [*Aviation*] (PIAV)
U/S	Unserviceable (PIPO)
USA	Unconventional Stellar Aspect

USAR........... Urban Search and Rescue [*Department of Emergency Management*] (DEMM)
USATA .... United States Air Tour Association
USC .... Unless Sooner Commenced (RIMS)
USCSOI........ United States Service Office of Investigation
USFDA .... United States Food and Drug Administration (SARE)
USGCRPO .... United States Global Change Research Program Office (CARB)
USH .... United Services for Handicapped (DAVI)
USL.............. Underwater Sound Laboratory
USL.............. United States League [*Baseball*] (NDBD)
USM............ Ultrasonic Mist (DAVI)
US/NATO..... United States/North Atlantic Treaty Organization
USNCPEC..... United States National Committee for Pacific Economic Cooperation
USNMAS...... United States National Map Accuracy Standard (CARB)
USOC........... U.S. Science Operations Center (SPST)
USOGH .... Usual State of Good Health (DAVI)
USOH........... Usual State of Health (DAVI)
USOS........... U.S. On-Orbit Segment (SPST)
USP .... Unassisted Systolic Pressure [*Medicine*] (DAVI)
USPL .... U.S. Plastic Lumber [*NASDAQ symbol*] (SG)
USPPS .... United States Possessions Possessions Society [*Founded in 1978*]
USQ .... Unreviewed Safety Question
USQD........... Unreviewed Safety Question Determination
USR .... Upwelling Solar Radiation (ARMP)
USS .... Undersea Surveillance System (CCCA)
USSEE .... United States Society of Ecological Economics
USTAR .... United States Travel Agent Registry (TRID)
USUC........... United States Unilateral Control (CCCA)
USYNR/T...... Universal Synchronous Receive/Transmit (CCCA)

UT1............. Unit Telescope 1
UTC............. United Telecommunications Council (CGWS)
UTC............. Universal Time Coordinates (ARMP)
UTD .... Unable to Determine (DAVI)
UTDN.......... Unattended Ticket Delivery Network (TRID)
UTE............. User Terminal Element (CCCA)
UTL............. Unable to Locate (DAVI)
UTLS........... Upper Troposphere-Lower Stratosphere
UTM............ Urinary-Tract Malformation [*Medicine*] (DAVI)
UTO .... Unable to Obtain (DAVI)
uTOK........... Users' Tree of Knowledge [*Computer science*]
UTR .... Unable to Reach (TRID)
UTRCA .... Upper Thames River Conservation Authority [*Canada*]
UTSI............ UTStarcom, Inc. [*NASDAQ symbol*] (SG)
UTV............. Universal Travel Voucher (TRID)
UU .... Unless Used (RIMS)
UUIWCTAUTC... Unless Used in Which Case Time Actually Used to Count (RIMS)
UUO .... Underwater Unidentified Objects
uv-A............. Ultraviolet Type A (CARB)
uv-B............. Ultraviolet Type B (CARB)
UVL............. Ultraviolet Lithography
UVSR .... Ultraviolet Spectral Radiometer (ARMP)
uv-vis........... Ultraviolet-Visible [*Spectroscopy*] (CARB)
UV/vis.......... Ultra Violet/Visible
U/W............. Underwriter (MARI)
UWC .... User Worked Crossing (HEAS)
UWCC........... United Wireless Communications Consortium (CGWS)
UWED.......... Use of Work Equipment Directive (HEAS)
UWTF.......... Underwater Test Facility (SPST)
UWWD........ Urban Wastewater Directive

V	Variable Stimulus	(DIPS)
V	Variance	(DIPS)
V	Variation Coefficient	(DIPS)
V	Ventricular	(DAVI)
V	Verbal Ability	(DIPS)
V	Vertebral	(DAVI)
V	Viral	(DAVI)
V	Vista Response	(DIPS)
V	Visual Descent Point	(PIPO)
v	Volt	
VA	Ventriculoatrial Shunt [Medicine]	(DIPS)
VAcc	Distance Visual Acuity with Correction	(DAVI)
VAccl	Near Visual Acuity with Correction	(DAVI)
VAC EXT	Vacuum Extractor	(DAVI)
VaD	Vascular Dementia [Medicine]	(DAVI)
VAD	Vascular Dementia	(DIPS)
VAD	Voice Activity Detection	(CGWS)
VADCS	Ventricular Atrial Distal Coronary Sinus [Medicine]	(DAVI)
VADRIAC	Vincristine, Doxorubicin, and Cyclophosphamide [Medicine]	(DAVI)
VAE	Vertical Assault Element [Military]	
VAFD	Vascular Access Flush Device [Medicine]	(DAVI)
VAHBE	Ventricular Atrial His Bundle Electrocardiogram [Medicine]	(DAVI)
VAHRA	Ventricular Atrial Height Right Atrium [Medicine]	(DAVI)
VAIT	Vehicle Analysis and Integration Team [NASA]	(SPST)
VAL	Voice Application Language [Computer science]	
VALS	Values Lifestyle Groups	(DIPS)
VANCO/P	Vancomycin-Peak [Medicine]	(DAVI)
VANCO/T	Vancomycin-Trough [Medicine]	(DAVI)
V&A	Vagotomy and Antrectomy [Medicine]	(DAVI)
V&C	Vertical and Centric	(DAVI)
V&D	Vomiting and Diarrhea	
V&G	Vagotomy and Gastroenterotomy [Medicine]	(DAVI)
VAOD	Visual Acuity, Right Eye	(DAVI)
VAOS	Visual Acuity, Left Eye	(DAVI)
VAP	Value Added Procedure	(ARMP)
VAP	Venous Access Port [Medicine]	(DAVI)
VAPCS	Ventricular Atrial Proximal Coronary Sinus [Medicine]	(DAVI)
var	Variation	(PIAV)
VAR	Varicella Vaccine	(DAVI)
VASPI	Visual Analogue Self Assessment Scales for Pain Intensity	(DAVI)
VAT	Video-Assist Thoracoscopy [Medicine]	(DAVI)
VAT	Visual Audio Tool	(MLOA)
VATA	Versata, Inc. [NASDAQ symbol]	(SG)
VB	Vacuum Bottom	
VBG	Venous Blood Gas	(DAVI)
VBGP	Vertical Banded Gastroplasty [Medicine]	(DAVI)
vBNS	Very High Performance Backbone Network System	
VBP	Vinblastine, Bleomycin, and Cisplatin [Medicine]	(DAVI)
VBScript	Visual Basic Syntax	
Vc	Vancouver Stock Exchange	(SG)
VC	Virtual Channel	
VC	Visteon Corp. [NYSE symbol]	
VCA	Vasoconstrictor Assay [Medicine]	(DAVI)
VCC	Voltage Common-Collector	(AEBE)
VCCA	Velocity Common Carotid Artery [Medicine]	(DAVI)
VCD	Virtual Communications Driver	(ROAS)
VCD	Vocal Cord Dysfunction	(DAVI)
VCE	Virtual Collaborative Environment	
VCFC	Virtual Channel Flow Control	(MLOA)
VCFS	Velo-Cardio-Facial-Syndrome	
vCJD	Variant Creutzfeldt-Jakob Disease [Medicine]	
VCL	Vegetation Canopy Lidar Mission [NASA]	
VCLK	ValueClick, Inc. [NASDAQ symbol]	(SG)
VCM	Voice-Coil Motor	(AEBE)
VCNT	Vicinity Corp. [NASDAQ symbol]	(SG)
VCP	Votorantim CeluLose ADS [NYSE symbol]	(SG)
VCS	Virus Control System	
VCS	Voice Controlled Switch	(CGWS)
VCTS	Vitreal Corneal Touch Syndrome	(DAVI)
VD	Venereal Disease [Medicine]	(DIPS)
VDAC	Voltage Dependent Anion Channel	
VDC	Vincristine, Doxorubicin, and Cyclophosphamide [Medicine]	(DAVI)
VDDR I	Vitamin D Dependency Rickets Type I	(DAVI)
VDDR II	Vitamin D Dependency Tickets Type II	(DAVI)
VDO	Varus Derotational Osteotomy [Medicine]	(DAVI)
VDRF	Ventilator Dependent Respiratory Failure [Medicine]	(DAVI)
VDS	Vasodepressor Syncope [Medicine]	(DAVI)
VDS	Video Distribution System	(CCCA)
VE	Vertex	(DAVI)
V/E	Violence and Eloper	(DAVI)
VE	Visual Exempted	(PIPO)
VEC	Vecuronium [Medicine]	(DAVI)
VED	Vacuum Extraction Delivery [Medicine]	(DAVI)
VEGF-2	Vascular Endothelial Growth Factor-2	
VEMA	Virginia Educational Media Association	
VEN	Vietnam Economic News [A publication]	
VEO	Visible Emissions Observation	(SARE)
VES	Ventricular Extrasystoles	(DAVI)
VESL	Vocational English as a Second Language	
VFC	Vaccines for Children	(DAVI)
VFFC	Visual Fields Full to Confrontation	(DAVI)
VFI	Visual Fields Intact	(DAVI)
VFL	Vinflunine	(DAVI)
vfr	Very Far Radiation	(CARB)
VFT	Venous Filling Time	(DAVI)
VG	Viasystems Group [NYSE symbol]	(SG)
VGAD	Vein of Galen Aneurysmal Dilatation [Medicine]	(DAVI)
VGAM	Vein of Galen Aneurysmal Malformation [Medicine]	(DAVI)
VGM	Vein Graft Myringoplasty [Medicine]	(DAVI)
VGPO	Volume-Guaranteed Pressure Option [Medicine]	(DAVI)
VHA	Veterans Health Administration	
vhf	Very High Frequency	(CARB)
VHF	Viral Haemorrhagic Fever [Medicine]	(HEAS)
VHSA	Variable Hydrologic Source Area	(CARB)
VI	Villa	
VI	Visually Impaired	
VIA	Versatile Integrated Avionics	(HLLA)
vib	Vibration	(DAVI)
VIB	Vibration	(PIPO)
VIBS	Victim's Information Bureau Service	(DAVI)
VIC	Video Conferencing	(MLOA)
VICA	Velocity Internal Carotid Artery [Medicine]	(DAVI)
VICE	Visual C Environment [Computer science]	(ITCA)
VIE-PNN	Vienna Expert System for Parental Nutrition of Neonates [Design of nutritional feeding regimens for newborn infants]	(IDAI)
VIMS	Visually Induced Motion Sickness	
VIQ	Vehicle in Question	
VIR	Vietnam Investment Review [A publication]	
VIRS	Visible Infrared Scanner	(CARB)
VIRSR	Visible Infrared Scanning Radiometer	(CARB)
VIS	Visual Impairment Service	(DAVI)
VISC	Vitreous Infusion Suction Cutter	(DAVI)
VISI	Volar Intercalated Segmental Instability	(DAVI)
VIT CAP	Vital Capacity	(DAVI)
VITS	Video Teleconferencing System	(SPST)
VIU	Visual Internal Urethrotomy [Medicine]	(DAVI)
VIVID	Video, Voice, Image, and Data	
VIVO	Voice-In/Voice-Out	
VKDB	Vitamin K Deficiency Bleeding	(DAVI)
VL	Vacant Land	
VLA	Verification Loads Analysis	(SPST)
VLA	Very-Late Antigen	(DAVI)
VLAD	Variable Life-Adjusted Display	
VLAP	Vaporization Laser Ablation of the Prostate [Medicine]	(DAVI)
VLBWPN	Very Low Birth Weight Preterm Neonate	(DAVI)
VLE	Vision Left Eye	(DAVI)
VLHC	Very Large Hadron Collider	
VLL	Video Lead Locator	
VLN	Verification Logic Network	(SPST)
VLR	Vastus Lateralis Release [Medicine]	(DAVI)
VLR	Visited Location Register	(CGWS)
VLSA	Very Large Submillimeter Array	
VLSI	Very Large Scale Integration	(CCCA)
VM	Ventilated Mask [Medicine]	(DAVI)
VMAC	Voice Mobile Attenuation Code	(CGWS)
vman	Veterinary Manual	
VME	Versa Module Europe	
VM/E	Virtual Machine Entry [Computer science]	(ITCA)
VME	Virtual Manufacturing Enterprise	
VMH	Ventromedial Nucleus of the Hypothalamus [Medicine]	(DIPS)
VMS	Vanilla Milkshake	(DAVI)
VM/XA	Virtual Machine/Extended Architecture [Computer science]	(ITCA)

VN	Vietnam News [*A publication*]
VNAV	Vertical Navigation (PIPO)
Vnav	Vertical Navigation (PIAV)
VNB	Vinorelbine (DAVI)
VNC	Vesicle Neck Contracture (DAVI)
VNCPEC	Vietnam National Committee for Pacific Economic Cooperation
VOA	Volatile Organic Analyzer (SPST)
voc	Vocabulary
VOCOR	Void On-Call to Operating Room (DAVI)
VoD	Video on Demand (MLOA)
VOE	Vascular Occlusive Episode [*Medicine*] (DAVI)
VOM	Volt Ohm Milliameter
VOX	Voice Control (CGWS)
VOX	Voice Operated (PIPO)
voxel	Volume Picture Element (AEBE)
VP	Visual Perception (DAVI)
VPA	Ventricular Premature Activation (DAVI)
VPCI	Virtual Path Connection Identifier
VPD	Ventricular Premature Depolarization [*Medicine*] (DAVI)
VPD	Vessel Pay Dues (RIMS)
VPDC	Ventricular Premature Depolarization Contraction [*Medicine*] (DAVI)
VPDF	Vegetable Protein Diet Plus Fiber (DAVI)
VPI	Velopharyngeal Incompetence [*Medicine*] (DAVI)
VPLS	Ventilation-Perfusion Lung Scan [*Medicine*] (DAVI)
VPM	Venous Pressure Module [*Medicine*] (DAVI)
vppm	Volume Parts per Million
VPR	Volume Pressure Response (DAVI)
VPT	Vascularized Patellar Tendon [*Medicine*] (DAVI)
VR	Venous Resistance
VRA	Viragen, Inc. [*AMEX symbol*] (SG)
VRA	Visual Reinforcement Audiometry (DAVI)
VRC	Vaccine Research Center [*National Institutes of Health*]
VRC	Vocational Rehabilitation Counselor (DAVI)
VRG	Virtual Rain Gauge (DEMM)
VRP	Vocational Rahabilitation Program (DAVI)
VRS	Viral Rhinosinusitis [*Medicine*] (DAVI)
VRT	Variance of Resident Time (DAVI)
VRTA	Vocational Rehabilitation Therapy Assistant (DAVI)
VRTL	Vertel
VRTM	Verification Requirements Traceability Matrix (CTAS)
VRU	Ventilator Rehabilitation Unit (DAVI)
VS	Virtual Subnet (MLOA)
VSADP	Vocational Skills Assessment and Development Program (DAVI)
VSBE	Very Short Below Elbow (DAVI)
VSC	Vocational Skills Center
VSC	Voluntary Safety Cases (HEAS)
VSI	Visual Motor Integration (DAVI)
VSI/TRA	Vertical Speed Indicator/Traffic, Resolution Advisory [*Honeywell*] (HLLA)
VSN	Vital Signs Normal (DAVI)
VSO	Vertical Subcondylar Oblique [*Medicine*] (DAVI)
VSQOL	Visual Signs Quality of Life (DAVI)
VSS	Vapor Sampling System
VSS	Vehicle Sampling System
VSSAF	Vital Signs Stable, Afebrile [*Medicine*] (DAVI)
VST	Visual Search Task (DAVI)
VSTL	Vertical Short Takeoff and Landing (PIPO)
VT	Validation Therapy (DAVI)
VTBI	Volume to be Infused (DAVI)
vtc	Voting Trust Certificates (SG)
VTED	Venous Thromboembolic Disease [*Medicine*] (DAVI)
VT-NS	Ventricular Tachycardia Non-Sustained [*Medicine*] (DAVI)
VTOP	Voluntary Termination of Pregnancy (DAVI)
VT-S	Ventricular Tachycardia Sustained [*Medicine*] (DAVI)
VTS	Volunteer Transport Service (DAVI)
VT/VF	Ventricular Tachycardia/Fibrillation [*Medicine*] (DAVI)
V/U	Verbalize Understanding (DAVI)
VU	Vesicoureteral [*Medicine*] (DAVI)
VUFORS	Victorian UFO Research Society [*Australia*]
VUJ	Vesico Ureteral Junction [*Medicine*] (DAVI)
V-V	Vulva and Vagina [*Medicine*] (DAVI)
VVB	Venovenous Bypass [*Medicine*] (DAVI)
VVC	Vulvovaginal Candidiasis [*Medicine*] (DAVI)
VVN	Vitran Corp. [*AMEX symbol*] (SG)
VVYO	Vyyo, Inc. [*NASDAQ symbol*] (SG)

W

By Acronym

W	Coefficient of Concordance (DIPS)
W	Coefficient of Stability (DIPS)
W	Wash (DAVI)
W	Winning Pitcher [*Baseball term*] (NDBD)
WA	Webelos Assistant [*Boy Scouts of America*]
W-A	Wyeth-Ayerst Laboratories (DAVI)
WAC	Writing Across the Curriculum
WACP	Wide Area Calling Plan (CGWS)
WACS	Wireless Access Communications System (CGWS)
WADA	World Anti-Doping Agency
WAF	Weakness, Atrophy, and Fasciculation [*Medicine*] (DAVI)
WAHM	Work at Home Mom
WAISIII	Wechsler Adult Intelligence Scale-Third Edition [*Test*] (DIPS)
WAL	Weighted-Average Life
WALK	Weight Activated Locking Knee (DAVI)
WAME	Washington Association of Marketing Educators
W&S	Wound & Skin (DAVI)
WAP	Western Antarctic Peninsula
WAP	Wireless Application Protocol
WASA	Washington Association of School Administrators
WASSP	Washington Association of Secondary School Principals
WAT	Weight and Temperature (PIAV)
WAV	Sound Wave File
WAVA	Washington Association of Vocational Administrators
WAVESNP	Washington Association of Vocational Education Special Needs Personnel
WAWS	Washington Area Wideband System (CCCA)
WB	Welcome Back [*Internet dialog*]
WB	Wood Badge [*Boy Scouts of America*]
WB	Wrong Box
WBC	Whole-Body Count
WB-CDMA	Wideband Code Division Multiple Access (CGWS)
WBLT	Watson-Barker Listening Test
WBM	Web-Based Management
WBSN	Websense, Inc. [*NASDAQ symbol*] (SG)
WBT	Web Based Training
WBUS	Weeks by Ultrasound (DAVI)
WBV	Whole Blood Volume (DAVI)
WBV	Whole Body Vibration (HEAS)
WC	Ward Confinement (DAVI)
WC	Wireless Carrier (CGWS)
WCA	Work Capacity Assessment (DAVI)
WCC	Well Child Care (DAVI)
WCDMA	Wideband Code Division Multiple Access
WCE	White Coat Effect (DAVI)
WCELA	West Coast Environmental Law Association
WCELRF	West Coast Environmental Law Research Foundation
WCF	Winchester Center-Fire
wch	Wall Chart
WCH	White Coat Hypertension (DAVI)
WCHC	Wheelchair Passenger Immobile (TRID)
WCHR	Wheelchair (TRID)
WCHS	Wheelchair Passenger Cannot Negotiate Stairs (TRID)
WC/LC	Warm Compresses and Lid Scrubs (DAVI)
WCO	Workplace Contact Officer (HEAS)
WCP	Waste Compliance Plan
WCR	Wyoming Cloud Radar (ARMP)
WCS	Work Capacity Specialist (DAVI)
W/D	Warm and Dry (DAVI)
WDA	Wireless Dealers Association (CGWS)
WDF	White Divorced Female (DAVI)
WDF	Wireless Data Forum (CGWS)
WDL	Webelos Den Leader [*Boy Scouts of America*]
WDM	White Divorced Male (DAVI)
WDR	Waste Discharge Requirements (SARF)
WEA	Washington Education Association
WEBM	Web Methods, Inc. [*NASDAQ symbol*] (SG)
WEBS	World Equity Benchmarks
WEC	Work of Engineering Construction (HEAS)
WECA	Wireless Ethernet Compatibility Alliance
WELD	Web-Based Electronic Design (AEBE)
WEMA	Wisconsin Educational Media Association
WER	Word Error Rate (IDAI)
WESR	Westergren Erythrocyte Sedimentation Rate (DAVI)
WestPac	Western Pacific
WEX	Winland Electronics [*AMEX symbol*] (SG)
W/F	Weakness and Fatigue (DAVI)
WFH	White-Faced Hornet (DAVI)
WFLC	White Female Living Child (DAVI)
WFOM	Wait for Overhead Message (CGWS)
WFP	Windows File Protection [*Computer science*]
WFQ	Weighted Fair Queuing (MLOA)
WGA	Waste Gas Assembly (SPST)
WGA	Western Governors' Association (AUEG)
WGIR	Working Group on Ionising Radiations (HEAS)
WH	Walking Heel (DAVI)
WHCNP	Women's Health Care Nurse Practitioner (NUJO)
WHEP	White House Emergency Plan (CCCA)
WHNP	Women's Health Nurse Practitioner (NUJO)
WHP	Wellhead Protection (AUEG)
WHPB	Whirlpool Bath (DAVI)
WHZ	Wheezes (DAVI)
WIA	Wireless Industry Association (CGWS)
WIBON	Whether in Berth or Not (RIMS)
WIED	Walk-In Emergency Department (DAVI)
WIMP	Window, Icon, Menu, Pointer
WIN	Watershed Initiative Network
WIPON	Whether in Port or Not (RIMS)
WIPT	Working Integrated Product Team
WIRRS	Waste Ice Release and Removal System (SPST)
WISCIII	Wechsler Intelligence Scale for Children-Third Edition [*Test*] (DIPS)
WITC	World Travel and Tourism Council (TRID)
WITS	Witness Systems [*NASDAQ symbol*] (SG)
wkb	Workbook
WKI	Wakefield Inventory (DAVI)
WL	Weight Loss (DAVI)
WLA	Wireless LAN Alliance (CGWS)
WLE	Wide Local Excision [*Medicine*] (DAVI)
WLL	Wireless Local Loop (CGWS)
WLMA	Washington Library Media Association
WLOT	Webelos Leader Outdoor Training [*Boy Scouts of America*]
WLS	Wave Length Shifter
WM	Warm, Moist (DAVI)
WM	Window Manager (SPST)
WMA	Windows Media Audio
WMD	Warm Moist Dressings (DAVI)
WMI	Wall Motion Index (DAVI)
WMI	Windows Management Instrumentation
WML	White Matter Lesions (DAVI)
WMLC	White Male Living Child (DAVI)
WMP	Warm Moist Packs (DAVI)
WMP	Windows Media Player
WMS	Warehouse Management System
WNFT	Women's Network for Entrepreneurial Training
WNF	West Nile Fever (DAVI)
WNLS	Weighted Nonlinear Least Squares (DAVI)
WO	Wide Open (DAVI)
WOAG	Worldwide Official Airline Guide (TRID)
WOD	Word of Day (CCCA)
WOG	Without Guarantee (RIMS)
WOR	Worthington Indus. [*NYSE symbol*] (SG)
WOS	Weather Observing Station (PIPO)
WOTS	Wireless Office Telephone System (CGWS)
WPA	White Paper Account (HEAS)
WPI	World Precision Instruments
WPS	Wisconsin Public Service
WPSSIR	Wechsler Preschool and Primary Scale of Intelligence-Revised [*Test*] (DIPS)
WQAS	Water Quality Analysis System (AUEG)
WQNI	World Quest Networks [*NASDAQ symbol*] (SG)
WQP	Water Quality Parameters (AUEG)
WRBU	Walter Reed Biosystematics Unit (ROAS)
WRC	World Radiation Center (CARB)
WRD	Wide Range Destillate (RIMS)
WRIC	Wire Rods in Coils (RIMS)
WRM	Water Recovery Management (SPST)
WRT	Weekly Radiation Therapy (DAVI)
wrtg	Writing Book
WRUED	Work-Related Upper-Extremity Disorder (DAVI)
WRULD	Work Related Upper Limb Disorders [*Medicine*] (HEAS)
WS	Walking Speed (DAVI)
WS	Work Simplification (DAVI)

WS..............	Work Status (DAVI)
WS..............	Work Stimulation (DAVI)
WS..............	World Series [*Baseball term*] (NDBD)
WSAAG........	Western Sydney Amateur Astronomical Group
WSBEA	Washington State Business Education Association
WSC.............	Wireless Switching Center (CGWS)
WSCA	Washington School Counselor Association
WSE.............	Word Superiority Effect [*J. M. Cattell*] (DIPS)
WSepF.........	White Separated Female (DAVI)
WSepM........	White Separated Male (DAVI)
WSF.............	White Single Female (DAVI)
WSFT...........	Washington State Federation of Teachers
WSH	Windows Script Host [*Computer science*]
WSIWYG......	What You See is What You Get (ITCA)
WSLC	Washington State Labor Council
WSM............	Watershed Model (AUEG)
WSP.............	Wearable Speech Processor (DAVI)
WSP.............	Wireless Service Provider (CGWS)
WSPEP	Washington State Parent/Educator Partnership Project
WSSDA........	Washington State School Directors' Association
WSWS	Western Society of Weed Science
WT	Walking Tank (DAVI)

WTC.............	Willingness to Communicate
W-T-D..........	Wet to Dry (DAVI)
WTH.............	Whole-Tree Harvest (CARB)
WTI.............	Weapons and Tactics Instructor [*Military*]
WTM............	Word-Tag Model (IDAI)
WTO/WTOR...	Write to Operator/Write to Operator with Reply [*Computer science*] (ITCA)
WTPT..........	Walk-Through Performance Testing (DIPS)
WTRVW	Water View (TRID)
WTS.............	Whole Tomography Slice (DAVI)
WUA	Weighted Usable Area (CARB)
WUF............	Water User Fee
WV..............	Water Vapor (ARMP)
WVA.............	Washington Vocational Association
WVATA	Washington Vocational Agriculture Teachers Association
WVP.............	Water Vapor Profiling (ARMP)
WVR	Water Vapor Radiometer (CARB)
WW..............	Wheeled Walker (DAVI)
WWBrd.........	Whole Wheat Bread (DAVI)
WWCL	World Wide Christian Literature
WWO	Waste Water Outflow (CARB)
WWR	When, Where Ready (RIMS)
WWT............	Wastewater Treatment (AUEG)

X-Y-Z

By Acronym

XBAG	Excess Baggage	(TRID)
XBT	Xylose Breath Test	(DAVI)
XC	Cross Connect	(MLOA)
XCAR	XCare.net, Inc. [*NASDAQ symbol*]	(SG)
XeCT	Xenon-Enhanced Computed Tomography	(DAVI)
XEM	Xonics Electron Mammography	(DAVI)
XIE	X-Ray Imaging Experiment	(CARB)
XLD	Cancelled [*Travel industry*]	(TRID)
XLFDP	Cross-Linked Fibrin Degradation Products	(DAVI)
XML	Extension Markup Language [*Computer science*]	(ITCA)
xmsn	Transmission	(PIAV)
XN	Cancelled Name [*Travel industry*]	(TRID)
XO	Exchange Order [*Travel industry*]	(TRID)
XOM	Extraocular Movements	(DAVI)
XPDR	Transponder	(HLLA)
xpdr	Transponder	(PIAV)
XR	Cancellation Recommended [*Travel industry*]	(TRID)
XRT	Radiation Therapy	(DAVI)
XS	Cancelled Segment [*Travel industry*]	(TRID)
XTLE	Extratemporal-Lobe-Epilepsy	(DAVI)
XTN	Extension	(TRID)
X/WIND	Crosswind	(HLLA)
XX	Cancelled	(TRID)
Y&R	Young and the Restless [*Television program title*]	

YAS	Youth Action Section	(DAVI)
YC	Yield Curve	
Y/D	Yaw Damper	(PIPO)
Yel	Yellow	(DAVI)
YFH	Yellow-Faced Hornet	(DAVI)
YFI	Yellow Fever Immunization	(DAVI)
YHL	Years of Healthy Life	(DAVI)
YLD	Years of Life with Disability	(DAVI)
YLL	Years of Life Lost	(DAVI)
YMC	Young Male Caucasian	(DAVI)
YMRS	Young Mania Rating Scale	(DAVI)
YODA	Your Own Disk Access	
Z	Zillion	(HLLA)
Z	Zulu	(PIPO)
ZEEI	Exclusive Economic Zone of Indonesia	(CARB)
ZnOE	Zinc Oxide and Eugenol	(DAVI)
ZnPc	Zinc Phthalocyanine	(DAVI)
ZNS	Zonisamide	(DAVI)
ZOT	Zonula Occludens Toxin	(DAVI)
ZPC	Zero Point of Change	(CARB)
ZPC	Zopiclone	(DAVI)
ZPS	Zero-Prebreathe Spacesuit [*NASA*]	(SPST)
ZSB	Zero Stools Since Birth [*Medicine*]	(DAVI)
ZWD	Zenith Wet Delay	(ARMP)

Numerics
By Meaning

5-Fluorouracil [*Medicine*] 5-FU
6-Mercaptopurine [*Medicine*] 6-MP
6-Thioguanine [*Medicine*] 6-TG
36Onetworks, Inc. [*NASDAQ symbol*] (SG) .... TSIX
724 Solutions [*NASDAQ symbol*] (SG) .... SVNX
1015 British Thermal Units/Year .... QUADS
36,000 to 46,000 Megacycles per Second .... Q-BAND
225-390 Megacycles per Second .... P-BAND

A

By Meaning

Abandoned Site Program Information System (SARE) .... ASPIS
Abbess (ADWA) .... Abb
Abbreviate (ADWA) .... abbr
Abbreviate (ADWA) .... abbrev
Abbreviated New Animal Drug Application [Food and Drug
   Administration] .... ANADA
Abbreviation (ADWA) .... ab
Abdicated (ADWA) .... abd
Abdominal (ADWA) .... adbom
Abdominal Muscles (ADWA) .... abs
Ablative Absolute (ADWA) .... abl absol
Ableauctions.comInc. [AMEX symbol] .... AAC
Abnormal (ADWA) .... ABN
Abnormal End of Task (ADWA) .... ABEND
Abnormal Spindle .... asp
Aboriginal (ADWA) .... Aborg
About.com .... BOUT
Above (ADWA) .... abv
Above Aerodrome Elevation [Aviation] (PIAV) .... aae
Above Field Height (PIPO) .... AFH
Above Ground Level (PIAV) .... agl
Above Mean Sea Level (PIAV) .... amsl
Above Named (ADWA) .... an
Absent (ADWA) .... a
Absent (ADWA) .... abs
Absolute (ABAC) .... abs
Absolute (ADWA) .... absol
Absolute Global Warning Potential (CARB) .... AGWP
Absolute Radio Frequency Channel Number (CGWS) .... ARFCN
Absolute Solar Transmittance Interferometer (ARMP) .... ASTI
Absorptive Stripping Voltametry (ABAC) .... ASV
Abstract (ADWA) .... abstr
Abstract Data Type (AUEG) .... ADT
Abstract Syntax Notation (MLOA) .... ASN
Abused Deaf Women's Advocacy Services (ADWA) .... ADWAS
Academic (ADWA) .... acad
Academic Operating System .... AOS
Academy of Health Information Professionals (NUJO) .... AHIP
Accelerated Networks [NASDAQ symbol] .... ACCL
Acceleration (NTIO) .... a
Acceleration of Gravity Force (PIPO) .... G
Accelerator Globulin (ADWA) .... ac-q
Acceptance and Commitment Therapy [Developed by Steven Hayes]
   (DIPS) .... ACT
Acceptance Test Review (CTAS) .... ATR
Acceptor of Action Results (DIPS) .... AAR
Access Control Machine .... ACM
Access Michigan Periodical List-Full Text .... AMPL-FT
Access Overload Class (CGWS) .... ACCOLC
Access Pharmaceuticals [AMEX symbol] (SG) .... AKC
Access to Voluntary and Safe Contraception (ADWA) .... AVSC
Accessory .... Access
Accident and Health (ADWA) .... a&h
Accident Investigator (SARE) .... AI
Accident Prevention Advisory Unit (HEAS) .... APAU
Accident Prevention Council (ABAC) .... APC
Accidental Death Benefit (ADWA) .... adb
Accommodative Convergence/Accommodation (ADWA) .... AC/A
Accompaniment (ADWA) .... accomp
According (ADWA) .... acc
Accordion .... acn
Account Current (ADWA) .... a/c
Account Paid (ADWA) .... A/P
Accountant (ADWA) .... acct
Accounts Receivable (ADWA) .... A/cs rec
Accounts Receivable (NTIO) .... A/R
Accredited Safety Auditor [International Loss Control Institute] (SARE) .... ASA
Accrued (ADWA) .... accrd
Accrued Rights Premium (MARI) .... ARP
Accumulate (ADWA) .... accum
Accusative (NTIO) .... accus
Acetone (ADWA) .... acet
Acetylchlorine (DIPS) .... Ach
Acetylcholine .... ACH
Achievement (ADWA) .... achiev
Achieving the Competitive Edge (ABAC) .... ACE

Acid Deposition Data Network [Environmental Protection Agency]
   (CARB) .... ADDNET
Acid Deposition System [EPA] (AUEG) .... ADS
Acknowledge (ADWA) .... ack
Aclara BioSciences [NASDAQ symbol] (SG) .... ACLA
Acoustic (ADWA) .... acst
Acoustic Variable Density (CARB) .... AVD
Acquire (ADWA) .... acq
Acquired Brain Injury (ADWA) .... ABI
Acquisition Career Record Brief [Army] .... ACRB
Acquisition Career Record Briefs [Army] .... ACRD
Acquisition Education and Training Program [Army] .... AETP
Acquisition Management Branch [Army] .... AMB
Acquisition Reform Communications Center .... ARCC
Acquistion Reform Network .... ARNet
Acre-Feet (ADWA) .... AF
Acre-Feet per Year (ADWA) .... AFY
Acridine Orange Direct Count (CARB) .... AODC
Across (ADWA) .... A
Acting (ADWA) .... actg
Acting Bureau Chief (DEMM) .... ABC
Action Figure .... AF
Action Item System .... AIS
Activ Card SA ADS [NASDAQ symbol] (SG) .... ACTI
Activation and Checkout [NASA] (SPST) .... A&C
Active Galactic Nuclei .... AGN
Active Instability Control (HEAS) .... AIC
Active Isolated Stretching .... AIS
Active List (NDBD) .... AL
Active Thermal System (SPST) .... ATS
Activities for Daily Living .... ADL
Activity Based Risk Evaluation Model of Auditing .... ABREMA
Actual Cash Value (ADWA) .... acv
Actual Flying Time [Travel industry] (TRID) .... AFT
Actual Navigation Performance (HLLA) .... ANP
Actually Time Used to Count (RIMS) .... ATUTC
Acute Care Nurse Practitioner .... ACNP
Acute Physiology and Chronic Health Evaluation (IDAI) .... APACHE
Ad Valorem [According to Value] [Latin] (NTIO) .... A/V
Adaptation (ADWA) .... adapt
Adaptation Controlled Environment System (ADWA) .... ACES
Adapter (ADWA) .... ad
Adapter Interface (ADWA) .... AI
Adaptive Fuzzy Associative Memory (IDAI) .... AFAM
Adaptive Learning Environments Program .... ALEP
Adaptive Physical Education .... APE
Adaptive Predictive Correction (CGWS) .... APC
Added Name [Travel industry] (TRID) .... AN
Added Segment (TRID) .... AS
Addition (ADWA) .... add
Addition (ADWA) .... addn
Additional (ADWA) .... addnl
Additional Collection [Travel industry] (TRID) .... add/col
Additivity and Variance Stabilization (IDAI) .... AVAS
Address Commission (RIMS) .... ADCOM
Address Information System (AUEG) .... AIS
Adecco SA ADS [NYSE symbol] (SG) .... ADO
Adenoidal-Pharyngeal-Conjunctival (ADWA) .... A-P-C
Adjacent Arctic Ocean (ARMP) .... AAO
Adjacent Carrier Interference Protection Ratio (CGWS) .... ACIPR
Adjectival (ADWA) .... adj
Adjustable Premium Policy (MARI) .... APP
Adjusted Community Rate Proposal .... ACRP
Adjusted Interest-Bearing Liabilities .... ADJ IBL
Adjusting Schedule of Reinforcement (DIPS) .... ADJ
Adlai E. Stevenson (ADWA) .... AES
Administering Agency (SARE) .... AA
Administration (NTIO) .... adm
Administration Manager (HEAS) .... AM
Administration of Justice .... AJ
Administration Planning Group (HEAS) .... APG
Administrative Authority Identifier [Computer science] .... AAI
Administrative, Executive, and Clerical (HEAS) .... AEC
Administrator (ADWA) .... admin
Administrators in Oncology/Hematology Assembly (ADWA) .... AOHA
Adolescence Directory Online (ADWA) .... ADOL

Adolescent Argumentativeness Scale [*Roberto and Finucane, 1997*] .... ADARG
Adolescent Verbal Aggressiveness Scale [*Roberto and Finucane, 1997*] ..... ADVA
Adrenergic Blocking Agent (DIPS) .... ABA
Adrenergic Blocking Agent (DIPS) .... aba
Adult and Community Learning Services .... ACLS
Adult Children of Alcoholics (DIPS) .... ACOA
Adult Diploma Program .... ADP
Adult Education Act .... AEA
Adult Independent Living Center (ADWA) .... AILC
Adult Literacy Initiative .... ALI
Adult Literacy Resource Institute .... ALRI
Adult Numeracy Practitioners Network .... ANPN
Adult Performance Level .... APL
Adult Secondary Education .... ASE
Advance (ADWA) .... adv
Advance Informed Agreement .... AIA
Advanced Along Track Scanning Radiometer .... AATSR
Advanced Booking Charters [*Travel industry*] (TRID) .... ABC
Advanced Breast Cancer [*Medicine*] .... ABC
Advanced Cell Technology .... ACT
Advanced Communications Function for the Telecommunications Access
  Method (ITCA) .... ACF/TCAM
Advanced Communications Function for the Virtual Telecommunications
  Access Method Entry (ITCA) .... ACF/VTAME
Advanced Communications Function/Network Control Program
  (ITCA) .... ACF/NCP
Advanced Computer Applications (CARB) .... ACA
Advanced Conceptual Design (ABAC) .... ACD
Advanced Controls Technology for Integrated Vehicles (ADWA) .... ACTIVE
Advanced Data Dictionary System (ITCA) .... ADDS
Advanced Developing Country (ADWA) .... ADC
Advanced Development Laboratory (CCCA) .... ADL
Advanced Earth Location Data System (ADWA) .... AELDS
Advanced Electro-Optical System (ADWA) .... AEOS
Advanced Imagery Exploitation System (CCCA) .... AIES
Advanced Infrared Search and Track (ADWA) .... AIRST
Advanced Inventory Management System .... AIMS
Advanced Laminate Analysis Code (SPST) .... ADVLAM
Advanced Land Observation Satellite (ARMP) .... ALOS
Advanced Land Observing Satellite [*Sponsored by Japan Space Agency*] .... ALOS
Advanced Liquid Hydrogen (ADWA) .... ALH
Advanced Microwave Scanning Radiometer (ARMP) .... AMRS
Advanced Mobile Phone System .... AMPS
Advanced Moisture and Temperature Sounder (CARB) .... AMTS
Advanced Navigation System Inertial Reference (HLLA) .... ANSIR
Advanced Nuclear Fuels Corp. (ABAC) .... ANF
Advanced Nucleic Acid Analyzer .... ANAA
Advanced Pediatric Life Support (NUJO) .... APLS
Advanced Personnel Testing (ADWA) .... APT
Advanced Practice Nurse (NUJO) .... APN
Advanced Processing Technology (ABAC) .... APT
Advanced Processing Technology Institute (ABAC) .... APTI
Advanced Radar Altimeter (CARB) .... ADALT
Advanced Radio Interferometry Between Space and Earth .... ARISE
Advanced Radio Technology Subcommittee (CGWS) .... ARTS
Advanced Reasoning Tool (IDAI) .... ART
Advanced Relay Technology Mission .... ARTEMIS
Advanced Research and Global Observation Satellite (ADWA) .... ARGOS
Advanced Research Projects Agency Network .... ARPANet
Advanced Research Testbed for Medical Informatics (ADWA) .... ARTEMIS
Advanced Scatterometer (CARB) .... A-SCAT
Advanced Scatterometer (CARB) .... ASCATT
Advanced Schottky (AEBE) .... AS
Advanced Small Computer Systems Interface (ADWA) .... ASPI
Advanced Solid State Array Sensor (CARB) .... ASAS
Advanced Spaceborne Computer Module .... ASCM
Advanced Strip Processor .... ASP
Advanced Technology Anti-G Suit (ADWA) .... ATAGS
Advanced Technology Attachment Interface with Extensions [*Computer
  science*] (ITCA) ATA-2
Advanced Threat Infrared Countermeasures (ADWA) .... ATIRCM
Advanced Tracking and Data Relay Satellite (ADWA) .... ATDRS
Advanced Trauma Management [*Army*] .... ATM
Advanced Wastewater Treatment (ADWA) .... AWT
Advances in Osteoporosis (ADWA) .... AIO
Advent (ADWA) .... Adv
Adventure .... Adv
Adventure Activities Industry Advisory Committee (HEAS) .... AAIAG
Adventures of Batman and Robin .... AB&R
Adverbial (ADWA) .... advb
Adverbs (ADWA) .... advs
Adverse Drug Reaction (DIPS) .... ADR
Adverse Event .... AE
Advise as to Names [*Travel industry*] (TRID) .... ADVN
Advise as to Rate [*Travel industry*] (TRID) .... ADVR
Advise if Duplicate Booking [*Travel industry*] (TRID) .... ADB
Advise if Not Okay [*Travel industry*] (TRID) .... ADNO
Advise if Ticketed [*Travel industry*] (TRID) .... ADTK
Advise on Arrival [*Travel industry*] (TRID) .... ADOA
Advising Schedule Change [*Travel industry*] (TRID) .... ASC
Advisory Committee on Agricultural and Veterinary Chemicals
  (AUEG) .... ACAVC
Advisory Committee on Conservation of Biological Diversity (AUEG) ..... ACCBD
Advisory Committee on Construction Safety and Health (SARE) .... ACCSH
Advisory Committee on Environmental Resources (AUEG) .... ACER

Advisory Council on the Misuse of Drugs (HEAS) .... ACMD
Advisory Map Display (HLLA) .... AMD
Advisory Review Panel .... ARP
Aerial Photo Interpretation (AUEG) .... API
Aeroballistic Rocket (ADWA) .... ABR
Aerodrome (PIAV) .... A/D
Aerodrome Advisory Area (PIPO) .... ADA
Aerodrome Control Zone [*Aviation*] (PIAV) .... ACZ
Aerodrome Information Zone [*Aviation*] (PIAV) .... AIZ
Aerodrome Reference Point [*Aviation*] (PIAV) .... ARP
Aerodrome Traffic Frequency (PIPO) .... ATF
Aerodromes Environmental Federation (PIAV) .... aef
Aerodromes Protection Agency [*British*] (PIAV) .... APA
Aerodynamics (ADWA) .... aerodyn
Aerojet Nuclear Company (ABAC) .... ANC
Aeronautical (ADWA) .... aero
Aeronautics (ADWA) .... aeron
Aeronautics .... Aeron
Aeronautics (ADWA) .... aeronaut
Aeronautics Maintenance .... AERO
Aerosol Extinction-to-Backscatter Ratios (ARMP) .... AEBR
Aerosol Observing System (ARMP) .... AOS
Aerosol Photoemission (HEAS) .... APE
Aerosol Radiative Forcing (ARMP) .... ARF
Aerosol Scattering Ratio (ARMP) .... ASR
Aerospace Defense Command (CCCA) .... ADCOM
Affairs (ADWA) .... aff
Affidavit (ADWA) .... afft
Affiliated Data Center (CARB) .... ADC
Affirmed (ADWA) .... affd
Affirming (ADWA) .... affg
Affix (ADWA) .... af
Afghan (ADWA) .... Af
Afghanistan (ADWA) .... Afg
A-Frame .... AF
African (NTIO) .... Afr
Afrikaans (ADWA) .... Afk
Afrikaans (ADWA) .... Afrik
After Arrival (MARI) .... aa
Against (ADWA) .... agst
Agency for Health Care Administration (DEMM) .... AHCA
Agency for Healthcare Research and Quality .... AHRQ
Agent's Discount (TRID) .... AD
Agricultual Machinery Advisory Group (HEAS) .... AMAG
Agricultural (ADWA) .... ag
Agricultural (ADWA) .... agr
Agricultural (ADWA) .... agri
Agricultural (ADWA) .... agric
Agricultural Safety (HEAS) .... AS
Agricultural Training Board (COBU) .... ATB
Agriculture (NTIO) .... agr
Agriculture .... Agric
Agriculture and Agri-Food Canada .... AAFC
Agriculture Industry Advisory Committee (HEAS) .... AIAC
Agriculture Network Information Center .... AgNIC
Agri-Food Development Branch [*Canada*] .... AFDB
Agronomy (ADWA) .... agron
AIDS Coalition to Unleash Power [*An association*] (NTIO) .... ACT-UP
AIDS Education Global Information System (ADWA) .... AEGIS
Air Combat Command Intelligence Network (ADWA) .... ACCINTNET
Air Conditioned (TRID) .... ACON
Air Data Module (HLLA) .... ADM
Air Data Reference (HLLA) .... ADR
Air Data Tester (HLLA) .... ADT
Air Defense Master Plan (CCCA) .... ADMP
Air Discount Bulletin [*Travel industry*] (TRID) .... ADB
Air Force Electronic Warfare Effectiveness Simulator (ADWA) .... AFEWES
Air Force Geographic Information Handling System (ADWA) .... AFGIHS
Air Force Intelligence (CCCA) .... AFIN
Air Force Intelligence Officer (CCCA) .... AFIO
Air Force Research Laboratory .... AFRL
Air Force Reserve Command .... AFRC
Air Force Satellite (CCCA) .... AFSAT
Air Force Satellite Communications System (CCCA) .... AFSCF
Air Force Space Forecasting Center (ADWA) .... AFSFC
Air Heater (CARB) .... AH
Air Launched Anti-Satellite (CCCA) .... ALASAT
Air Line Pilots Association .... ALPA
Air Operating Base (CCCA) .... AOB
Air to Air (PIPO) .... A/A
Air Toxics Control Measure (SARE) .... ATCM
Air Traffic Navigation, Integration and Coordination System [*Army*] .... ATNAVICS
Air Traffic Operations (CTAS) .... ATO
Air Traffic Plans and Requirements Service (CTAS) .... ATR
Air Traffic Requirements (CTAS) .... ATR
Air Transport Indicator (HLLA) .... ATI
Air Transport Systems (HLLA) .... ATS
Airborne (ADWA) .... abn
Airborne Battalion Combat Team [*Army*] .... ABCT
Airborne Cloud-Radiation Observing System (ARMP) .... ACROS
Airborne Command and Control Center (ROAS) .... ABCCC
Airborne Command Control Squadron (CCCA) .... ACCSQ
Airborne Emission Spectrometer (ARMP) .... AES
Airborne Flight Information Service (HLLA) .... AFIS
Airborne Intercept (ADWA) .... ai

Airborne Synthetic Aperture Radar System (CCCA) ... ASARS
Airborne Turnable Laser Absorption Spectrometer (CARB) ... ATLAS
Air-Cool (ADWA) ... ac
Aircraft (ADWA) ... acft
Aircraft Battle Damage Repair (ADWA) ... ABDR
Aircraft Communication and Recording System (CARB) ... ACARS
Aircraft Identifier (CTAS) ... AID
Aircraft Indentification (CTAS) ... AID
Aircraft Laser Infrared Absorption Spectrometer (CARB) ... ALIAS
Aircraft Maintenance Officer ... AMO
Aircraft on Ground (PIAV) ... AOG
Aircraft per Hour (CTAS) ... AC/HR
Aircraft Radio Control of Aerodrome Lighting (PIAV) ... ARCAL
Aircraft Situational Display (CTAS) ... ASD
Aircraft Weather Report (CARB) ... AIREP
Aircraft-to-Satellite Data Relay System (ADWA) ... ASDAR
Air-Ground Radiotelephone Automated Service (CGWS) ... AGRAS
Air-Ground Radiotelephone Automated Service Credit Card Number (CGWS) ... AGRASCCN
Airline Inventory Redistribution System ... AIRS
Airline Maintenance and Operation Support System (HLLA) ... AMOSS
Airline Modifiable Information (HLLA) ... AMI
Airline Operations Center (CTAS) ... AOC
Airline Passenger Tariff [*Travel industry*] (TRID) ... APT
Airlines Reporting Corporation (TRID) ... ARC
Airline-Selected Equipment (HLLA) ... ASE
Airman (ADWA) ... Amn
Airplane Multi-Engine Land (PIPO) ... AMEL
Airplane Multi-Engine Sea (PIPO) ... AMES
Airplane Single-Engine Sea (PIPO) ... ASES
Airport (PIAV) ... A/P
Airport Area (PIPO) ... A
Airport Facilities Directory (PIPO) ... A/FD
Airport of Entry (PIAV) ... AoE
Airport Operators' Association (PIAV) ... AOA
Airport Ticket Office (TRID) ... ATO
Air-Speed (PIPO) ... A/S
Air-to-Ground (PIAV) ... A/G
Airway (PIAV) ... Awy
Airworthiness Review Board (PIAV) ... ARB
Alabama (ADWA) ... Ala
Alain Boublil Music Limited [*Publisher*] ... BOU
Alarm (ADWA) ... alm
Alaska (NTIO) ... Alas
Alaska-Canada (ADWA) ... Alcan
Alaskan AIDS Assistance Association ... AAAA
Albanian (ADWA) ... Alb
Alberta (ADWA) ... Alba
Alberta Environmental Protection and Enhancement Act [*Canada*] ... AEPA
Albumen (ADWA) ... alb
Albumin-Globulin Ratio (ADWA) ... A/G ratio
Alcohol (ADWA) ... al
Alcohol (ADWA) ... alc
Alcohol and Drug Services Study (ADWA) ... ADSS
Alderwoman (ADWA) ... Ald
Alert Severe Weather Watch (PIPO) ... AWW
Algebra (ADWA) ... alg
Algerian (ADWA) ... Alg
Algorithmic-Oriented Language (ADWA) ... ALGOL
Alive No Evidence of Disease [*Medicine*] ... ANED
Alkali (ADWA) ... alk
Alkalinity (ADWA) ... alky
All Electrical Kitchen (ADWA) ... AEK
All England Law Reports [*A publication*] ... All ER
All Going Well (RIMS) ... AGW
All My Children [*Television program title*] ... AMC
All Other Contents (MARI) ... AOC
All-Around [*Rodeo term*] ... AA
Allegheny International ... AI
Alliance of Business Consultants (COBU) ... ABC
Allied and Alternative Medicine (ADWA) ... AMED
Allied Command Europe Command Control Information System (CCCA) ... ACECCIS
All-Important Box Score [*Baseball term*] (NDBD) ... AIBS
All-Important Loss Column [*Baseball term*] (NDBD) ... AILC
Alloisoleucine (ADWA) ... alle
Allos Therapeutics [*NASDAQ symbol*] (SG) ... ALTH
Allou Health & Beauty Care ... ALU
Allowable Limit of Intake (ABAC) ... ALI
Allowance (ADWA) ... alw
All-Trans-Retinylester ... atRY
Allusion (ADWA) ... allus
Along the Same Line (ADWA) ... ATSL
Alpha Energy Analysis (ABAC) ... AEA
Alpha/Numeric Wall Display (CCCA) ... ANWD
Alpha Particle (ADWA) ... A-part
Alpha Track Detector (ABAC) ... ATD
Alphabetical and Numerical (ADWA) ... alphanumeric
Alphafetoprotein Test ... AFP
Alphaglucosylrutin [*Antioxidant*] ... AGR
Alpine (ADWA) ... alp
Also Printed As (ADWA) ... APA
Alteration (ADWA) ... alt
Alteration (ADWA) ... alter
Alternate Concentration Limits (ADWA) ... ACLs
Alternate Reconstitution Base (CCCA) ... ARB
Alternating Current/Direct Current (NTIO) ... AC/DC
Alternating Hemiplegia of Childhood ... AHC
Alternative Agricultural Research and Commercialization Center ... AARC
Alternative Billing Service ... ABS
Alternative Internet Resource ... AIR
Alternative Local Exchange Carrier (CGWS) ... ALEC
Alternative Schedule of Reinforcement (DIPS) ... ALT
Altimeter (ADWA) ... altm
Altitude Compensation Induction System ... ACIS
Altitude in Height Above Station ... QFE
Altitude Indicated Above Sea Level ... QNH
Altitude Select [*Aviation*] (PIPO) ... ASEL
Alto ... a
Alto Clarinet ... acl
Alto Flute ... afl
Alto Saxophone ... asx
Aluminum (ABAC) ... Al
Aluminum Gallium Nitride ... AlGaN
Alumna (NTIO) ... alum
Alumnae (ADWA) ... alum
Always Afloat Always Accessible (RIMS) ... AAAA
Alzheimer Disease and Associated Disorders (ADWA) ... ADAD
Amateur Athletic Union (NTIO) ... AAU
Amateur Radio on the International Space Station ... ARISS
Amateur Telescope Maker ... ATM
Ambassador (ADWA) ... amb
Ambulatory Care Quality Improvement Program (ADWA) ... ACQIP
Ambulatory Patient Group (ADWA) ... APG
Amended (ADWA) ... amd
America (ADWA) ... Ame
American Accreditation Health Care Commission (ROAS) ... AAHCC
American Association for Counseling (DIPS) ... AAC
American Association of Applied and Preventive Psychology (DIPS) ... AAAPP
American Association of Bovine Practitioners ... AABP
American Association of Clinical Psychologists (DIPS) ... AACP
American Association of Critical-Care Nurses ... AACN
American Association of Geographers (CARB) ... AAG
American Association of Independent Architects ... AAIA
American Canadian Caribbean Line (TRID) ... ACCL
American Car Buying Service ... ACS
American Center for Social Awareness (ADWA) ... ACSA
American College of Cardiology Extended Learning (ADWA) ... ACCEL
American College of Childbirth Educators (NUJO) ... ACCE
American College of Physicians-American Society of Internal Medicine ... ACP-ASIM
American College of Poultry Veterinarians ... ACPV
American College Test (NTIO) ... ACT
American College Testing Program (DIPS) ... ACTP
American Council for Collaboration in Education and Language Studies ... ACCELS
American Depository Receipts ... ADR
American Digestive Health Foundation ... ADHF
American Disabled for Attendant Programs Today (ADWA) ... Adapt
American English (ADWA) ... AE
American Express (NTIO) ... AmEx
American French (ADWA) ... AmerF
American Genetic Resources Alliance ... AGRA
American Home Products ... AHP
American Horticultural Society ... AHS
American Hotel and Motel Association (TRID) ... AHMA
American Hull Form (MARI) ... AHF
American Hyperlexia Association ... AHA
American Indian (ADWA) ... AmerInd
American Industrial Hygiene Conference and Exposition (ADWA) ... AIHCE
American Institute of Hypnotherapy ... AIH
American Journal of Comparative Law [*A publication*] ... AJCL
American Junior Rodeo Association ... AJRA
American Museum of Natural History (AUEG) ... AMNH
American Oil Company (NTIO) ... Amoco
American Organization of Analytical Chemists (ABAC) ... AOAC
American Petroleum Institute (HEAS) ... API
American Public Power Association (HEAS) ... APPA
American Segment Trainer [*NASA*] (SPST) ... AST
American Sign Language (NTIO) ... Ameslan
American Society for Cell Biology ... ACSB
American Society of Hospital Pharmacists Research and Education Foundation ... ASHPRF
American Spanish (ADWA) ... AmerSp
American Special Interest Group (ADWA) ... ASIG
American Speech-Language-Hearing Foundation ... ASLH
American Standard Language for Information Interchange ... ASCII
American Standards Committee for Information Interchange (ARMP) ... ASCII
American Stock Exchange (SG) ... AS
American Studies ... AMST
American Textile Industry (ABAC) ... AMTEX
American Track (NTIO) ... Amtrak
American Veterans (ADWA) ... AMVETS
American Vocational Information Association ... AVIA
American-Israeli Political Action Committee ... AIPAC
Americans for Technology Leadership ... ATL
AmeriVest Properties [*AMEX symbol*] (SG) ... AMV
Ames Airborne Tracking Sunphotometer (ARMP) ... AATS
Ames Laboratory ... AMES
Ames-Dryden Flight Research Facility [*NASA*] ... ADFRF

Ammeter (ADWA)	am
Ammunition (ADWA)	ammo
Amortization (ADWA)	amort
Amount of Invested Mental Effort	AIME
Ampere-Hour (ADWA)	A-h
Ampere-Hour (NTIO)	ah
Ampere-Turn (ADWA)	At
Amplitude (DIPS)	a
Amplitude and Phase Modulation (CCCA)	APM
Amplitude Modulated (PIPO)	AM
Amsterdam Exchanges N.V. [Netherlands]	AEX
Amsterdam Stock Exchange (SG)	Am
Amsterdam-Antwerpen-Rotterdam Area (RIMS)	AARA
Amsterdam-Rotterdam-Antwerp-Gent Range (RIMS)	ARAG
Analog Hardware Description Language (AEBE)	AHDL
Analog Hardware Descriptive Language (ADWA)	AHDL
Analog Quantum Computers	AQC
Analog Simultaneous Voice/Data Technology (ITCA)	ASVD
Analog to Digital (CGWS)	A/D
Analogous (ADWA)	anal
Analog-to-Digital (AEBE)	A2D
Analog-to-Time Module	ATM
Analysis	Anal
Analytical (ADWA)	analyt
Analytical Laboratory Operations (ABAC)	ALO
Analytical Quality Assurance (HEAS)	AQUA
Analytical Reagent (ABAC)	AR
Analytical Spectral Devices (ARMP)	ASD
Anaplastic Anaemia [Medicine]	AA
Anatomical (ADWA)	anat
Anchor Handling (RIMS)	A/H
Andante (ADWA)	and
Andorran (ADWA)	And
Androgynous Peripheral Attachment System [NASA] (SPST)	APAS
Anesthesia (ADWA)	anes
Angiogram (ADWA)	ang
Angle of Attack [Aviation] (PIPO)	AGA
Anglican (ADWA)	Angl
Anglo-Indian (ADWA)	Anglo-Ind
Anglo-Irish (ADWA)	Anglo-Ir
Anglo-Saxon (NTIO)	AS
Angola (ADWA)	Ang
Angstrom (ADWA)	angst
Angular Dependence Model (ARMP)	ADM
Anhydrous (ADWA)	anhyd
Animal Welfare Officer (SARE)	AWO
Animal-Assisted-Therapy (ADWA)	AAT
Anionic Neutrophil Activating Peptide (ADWA)	ANAP
Annals (ADWA)	ann
Anniversary (ADWA)	anniv
Anniversary	Anniv
Annotated (ADWA)	annot
Annual Activities Summary (ABAC)	AAS
Annual Digest and Reports of Public International Law Cases [A publication]	ADIL
Annual Effective Dose Equivalent (ABAC)	AEDE
Annual Premium (MARI)	AP
Annular Beam Oscillator (ADWA)	ABO
Anomalous Diffraction Approximation (ARMP)	ADA
Another World [Television program title]	AW
Anoxic Limestone Drains	ALD
Antarctic Circumpolar Wave	ACW
Antarctic Reception Imagery for Environmental Studies	ARIES
Antarctica (ADWA)	Ant
Antecedent Moisture Condition (ADWA)	AMC
Antenna Group Interface Tube (SPST)	AGIT
Antenna Pointing Mechanism (ADWA)	APM
Antenna Subsystem (ADWA)	ANTS
Antenna Test Bed (SPST)	ATB
Anthology (ADWA)	anthol
Anthropological (ADWA)	anthrop
Anthropological (ADWA)	anthropol
Anthropology	ANTH
Anthropology (ADWA)	anthro
Anticipatory Account (ABAC)	AA
Antiferroelectric	AFLC
Anti-Ice (PIPO)	A/I
Antilogarithm	antilog
Antimatter Decelerator	AD
Antiovarian Antibody (ADWA)	AVA
Antiphospholipid Syndrome (ADWA)	APLS
AntiProton Experiments	APEX
Antiquarian (ADWA)	antiq
Antiquity (ADWA)	ant
Antwerp-Hamburg Range (RIMS)	ANTHAM
Anvil Stratus (ARMP)	AS
Any (ADWA)	AY
Any Day Now (ADWA)	ADN
Any One Accident (MARI)	aoa
Any One Bottom (MARI)	aob
Any One Event (MARI)	aoe
Any One Loss (MARI)	aol
Any One Occurrence (MARI)	aoo
Any One Vessel (MARI)	aov
Any One Voyage (MARI)	aovov

Any Safe Port in the World (RIMS)	ASPW
Any Time Day/Night Sundays and Holidays Included (RIMS)	ATDNSHINC
Any Will Provider (ADWA)	AWP
Any Willing Provider	AWP
Anything (ADWA)	AYG
Aorist (ADWA)	aor
Aorta (ADWA)	AO
Aorticopulmonary (ADWA)	AP
Aperture (ADWA)	aper
Aphetized (ADWA)	aphet
Apoenzyme (ADWA)	apo
Apolipoprotein-E (ADWA)	apo-E
Apostle (ADWA)	Ap
Apothecary (ADWA)	ap
Appalachian Cooperative Economics Network	AceNET
Apparent (ADWA)	appar
Apparently (ADWA)	app
Appendix (ADWA)	apx
Apple Print Recognizer [Handwriting recognition system] (IDAI)	APR
Appliances (ADWA)	appl
Applicable, Revelant, or Appropriate Requirements (ADWA)	ARARs
Application Identification (ADWA)	APID
Application Launching and Embedding [Computer science]	ALE
Application Service Provider	ASP
Application-Specific-Integrated Chip (ADWA)	ASTC
Applied Computational Electromagnetics Society	ACES
Applied Space Resources	ASR
Appoint (ADWA)	appt
Appointment (ADWA)	appmt
Approach Lighting System [Aviation] (PIPO)	ALS
Approved (CTAS)	APP
Approved (MARI)	Appd
Approved Carriage List (HEAS)	ACL
Approved Dosimetry Service (HEAS)	ADS
Approved Regulations for Transportable Pressure Receptacles (HEAS)	ARTPR
Approved Tank Requirements (HEAS)	ATR
Approximate (ADWA)	appr
Approximate (ADWA)	approx
Approximate Vertical Profile (CTAS)	AVP
April (ADWA)	Apl
April (ADWA)	Apr
Aquarius (ADWA)	AQR
Aquatic Effects Research Program (AUEG)	AERP
Arabian (ADWA)	Arab
Arabic (NTIO)	Arab
Aramaic (ADWA)	Ar
Aramaic (ADWA)	Aram
Arbitrageur (ADWA)	arb
Arc Cosecant (ADWA)	arc csc
Arc Secant (ADWA)	arc sec
Arc Sine (ADWA)	arc sin
Arc Tangent (ADWA)	arc tan
Arcade (ADWA)	Arc
Archaeological Fieldwork Opportunities Bulletin [A publication]	AFOB
Archaism (ADWA)	arch
Archbishop (ADWA)	ABP
Architectural and Transportation Barriers Compliance Board (ADWA)	ACCESS
Architecture	archit
Architecture Description Document (SPST)	ADD
Arctic Atmospheric Radiation and Cloud Station (ARMP)	A-ARCS
Arctic Ice Thickness Project (CARB)	AITP
Arctic Monitoring and Assessment Program (ARMP)	AMAP
Arctic Oscillation	AO
Arctic Regional Climate System Model (ARMP)	ARCSYM
Arctic Stratus Cloud (ARMP)	ASC
Area Control Operation Center (CCCA)	ACOC
Area Coordinator (DEMM)	AC
Area Director (HEAS)	AD
Area Executive (HEAS)	AE
Area Navigation (PIAV)	Rnav
Area of Emphasis (SPST)	AOE
Area of Intense Aerial Activity [Aviation] (PIAV)	AIAA
Area Settlement Plan (TRID)	ASP
Areas Requiring Corrective Action [Department of Emergency Management] (DEMM)	ARCA
Argent (ADWA)	arg
Argentinean (ADWA)	Arg
Argonne Boundary Layer Experiment (ARMP)	ABLE
Argonne Remote Manipulator	ARM
Arid Integrated Demonstration (ABAC)	arid ID
Aries (NTIO)	ARI
Aristocrat (ADWA)	aristo
Arithmetic (NTIO)	arith
Arizona (ADWA)	Ariz
Arkansas (ADWA)	Ark
Arkansas Basin Red River Forecast Center (ARMP)	ABRFC
Armenian (ADWA)	Arm
Army Command Control Master Plan (CCCA)	ACCMP
Army Communications and Control System (ROAS)	ACCS
Army Experimentation Campaign Plan	AECP
Army Medical Department Center and School	AMEDDC&S
Army of the Republic of North Vietnam (NTIO)	ARVN
Army Reserve Personnel Command	ARPERSCOM
Army Review Boards Agency	ARBA

Army Tactical Command and Control System (ROAS) ... ATCCS
Army Tactical Operations Center (CCCA) ... ATOC
Around the World (TRID) ... ATW
Arranged (ADWA) ... arr
Arranged Total Loss (MARI) ... Arr Tl
Array Drive Electronics (ADWA) ... ADE
Array of Low Energy X-Ray Imaging Sensors (ADWA) ... ALEXIS
Arrival (ADWA) ... ar
Arrival/Departure (CTAS) ... A/D
Arrival First Sea Pilot Station (RIMS) ... AFSPS
Arrival Pilot Station (RIMS) ... APS
Arrival Sequencing Program (CTAS) ... ASP
Arrow of Light [*Boy Scouts of America*] ... AOL
Arrow Point Communications [*NASDAQ symbol*] (SG) ... ARPT
Art Deco ... AD
Arteries (ADWA) ... aa
Arteriosclerotic Cardiovascular Disease (ADWA) ... ACVD
Arteriovenous (ADWA) ... A-V
Arteriovenous Shunt (ADWA) ... A-V Shunt
Arthritis and Rheumatism Branch ... ARB
Article (NTIO) ... art
Artificial Intelligence Advisory Committee (AUEG) ... AIAC
Artificial Neural Network (IDAI) ... ANN
Artillery (ADWA) ... art
Artillery (ADWA) ... arty
Artists and Repertory (ADWA) ... A and R
Arts and Entertainment (ADWA) ... A&E
Aruba, Bonaire, and Curacao Islands (NTIO) ... ABC Islands
Aryl Hydrocarbon Receptor-Interacting Protein ... AIP
As a Matter of Fact (ADWA) ... AAMOF
As Far as I Can Recall (ADWA) ... AFAICR
As Far As I Can See [*Online dialog*] ... AFAICS
As Far as I Can Tell (ADWA) ... AFAICT
As Far As I Know [*Online dialog*] ... AFAIR
As Far As I Know Today [*Online dialog*] ... AFAIKT
As Far as I Recall (ADWA) ... AFAIR
As Late as Reasonably Achievable (ADWA) ... ALARA
As Low as Technically and Economically Praticable (ABAC) ... ALATE
As per List (MARI) ... apl
Asbestos Containing Material ... ACM
Asbestos Insulation Board (HEAS) ... AIB
Asbestos Licensing Principal Inspector (HEAS) ... ALPI
Asbestos Licensing Regulations (HEAS) ... ASLIC
Asbestos Licensing Unit (HEAS) ... ALU
Asbestos Safety Equipment Manufacturer's Association (HEAS) ... ASEMA
Asbestos Shingles ... AS
Ascending (ADWA) ... asc
Ascending Activating System (DIPS) ... AAS
Asia Info Holdings [*NASDAQ symbol*] (SG) ... ASIA
Asian (ADWA) ... As
Asian and Pacific Islander (ADWA) ... API
Asian Christian Male (ADWA) ... ACM
Asian Network of Biological Sciences (CARB) ... ANBS
Asian Professional Female (ADWA) ... APF
Asian Standards Advisory Committee (HEAS) ... ASAC
Asian-American Christian Fellowship ... AACF
Asian-American Donor Program (NUJO) ... AADP
Asia-Pacific Economic Cooperation (ARMP) ... APEC
Asia-Pacific Network (ARMP) ... APN
Asked Price (SG) ... A
Aspartame Consumer Safety Network (ADWA) ... ACSN
Aspartate Transaminase ... AST
Aspect Medical Systems [*NASDAQ symbol*] (SG) ... ASPM
Asperger's Syndrome ... AS
Assembly (ADWA) ... asm
Assembly (ADWA) ... assem
Assembly (ADWA) ... assy
Assembly Contingency Radio Frequency Group (SPST) ... ACRFG
Assembly Implementation Requirements Document [*NASA*] (SPST) ... AIRD
Assembly, Integration, and Test (ADWA) ... AIT
Assembly of Surgical Group Practice Administrators (ADWA) ... ASGPA
Assembly-Integration-Verification (ADWA) ... AIV
Assigned (ADWA) ... asg
Assigned Protection Factor (SARE) ... APF
Assimilated (ADWA) ... assim
Assistant Chief Inspecting Officer (HEAS) ... ACIO
Assistant Director of Nursing (NUJO) ... ADON
Assistant Manager of Facility Transition (ABAC) ... AMF
Assistant Nurse Manager (NUJO) ... ANM
Assistant Principal ... AP
Assistant Scientific Officer (HEAS) ... ASO
Assistant Scoutmaster [*Boy Scouts of America*] ... ASM
Assistant Secretary of the Army for Acquisition, Logistics and Technology ... ASAALT
Assisted (ADWA) ... asstd
Assistive Technology ... AT
Assistive Technology Resource Alliance (ADWA) ... ATRA
Associate Administrator for Airway Facilities (CTAS) ... AFF
Associate Advisor ... AA
Associate Fellow of the British Psychological Society ... AFBPS
Associate of the Institute of Occupational Safety and Health (HEAS) ... AIOSH
Associate of the Library Association of Australia ... ALAA
Associate Program Manager (CTAS) ... APM
Associate Program Manager for Contracting (CTAS) ... APMC
Associate Program Manager for General Counsel (CTAS) ... APMGC
Associate Program Manager for Logistics (CTAS) ... APML
Associate Program Manager for Operations (CTAS) ... APMO
Associate Program Manager for Procedures (CTAS) ... APMP
Associate Program Manager for Quality (CTAS) ... APMQ
Associate Program Manager for Requirements (CTAS) ... APMR
Associate Program Manager for System Engineering (CTAS) ... APMSE
Associate Program Manager for Test (CTAS) ... APMT
Associated Control Channel (CGWS) ... ACCH
Associated Manufacturing and Design [*Alexandria, Virginia*] (ABAC) ... AMD
Associated Offices Technical Committee (HEAS) ... AOTC
Associated Western Universities-Northwest (ABAC) ... AWUNW
Association (NTIO) ... assoc
Association for Database Services (COBU) ... ADSET
Association for Energy Systems, Operations, and Programming (ABAC) ... AESOP
Association for Environmental Education (AUEG) ... AEE
Association for Neuro-Linguistic Programming (COBU) ... ANLP
Association for Rational Emotive Therapists (COBU) ... ARET
Association for the Advancement of Computing in Education ... AACE
Association Health Plan ... AHP
Association of Applied Psychologists (DIPS) ... AAP
Association of British Healthcare Industries (COBU) ... ABHI
Association of British Professional Conference Organisers (COBU) ... ABPCO
Association of Building Services Agencies (COBU) ... ABSA
Association of Business Schools (COBU) ... ABS
Association of Centres of Excellence in Foreign Language Training (COBU) ... ACCENT
Association of Certified Social Workers ... ACSW
Association of Chief Executives of National Voluntary Organisations (COBU) ... ACENVO
Association of Coffee Producing Countries ... ACPC
Association of Conference Executives (COBU) ... ACE
Association of Consulting Science and Technology (COBU) ... ACST
Association of Consulting Scientists (COBU) ... ACS
Association of Local Television Stations, Inc. ... ALTV
Association of London Authorities (HEAS) ... ALA
Association of Medical Expenses Insurers (COBU) ... AMEI
Association of Personal Injury Lawyers ... APIL
Association of Physical Plant Administrators (SARE) ... APPA
Association of Professional Hygienists (SARE) ... APIH
Association of Qualitative Research Practitioners (COBU) ... AQRP
Association of Sales Professionals (COBU) ... ASP
Association of Temporary and Interim Executive Services (COBU) ... ATIES
Associations of Service Providers Implementing IDEA Reforms in Education ... ASPIIRE
Assumption Based System [*Logic system*] (IDAI) ... ABS
Assyrian (ADWA) ... Assyr
Astrological (ADWA) ... astrol
Astrology (NTIO) ... astrol
Astronaut Crew Rescue Vehicle [*NASA*] ... ACRV
Astronaut Positioning Mechanism [*NASA*] (SPST) ... APM
Astronautics (ADWA) ... astronaut
Astronomer (ADWA) ... astron
Astronomical Journal [*A publication*] ... AJ
Astronomical Observation Template (ADWA) ... AOT
Astronomical Society of the Atlantic ... ASA
Astronomy and Astrophysics ... A&A
Astrophysical Data Program [*NASA*] ... ADP
Astrophysical Journal [*A publication*] ... ApJ
Astrophysics Data System [*NASA*] ... ADS
Asymmetric (ADWA) ... asym
Asynchronous Transfer Mode Adaptation Layer (ITCA) ... AAL
Asynchronous Transmission Mode (AEBE) ... ATM
At All Times (PIPO) ... AATM
At Sight (ADWA) ... A/S
Atacama Large Millimeter Array ... ALMA
AT&T Corp-Wireless Grp. [*NYSE symbol*] (SG) ... AWE
Athlete (ADWA) ... athl
Athletic (ADWA) ... ath
Atlantic Frontier Environmental Network ... AFEN
Atlantic Isopycnic Model ... AIM
Atlantic Southeast Airlines ... ASA
Atlantic Time (ADWA) ... AT
Atlas Pipeline Ptnrs. LP [*AMEX symbol*] (SG) ... APL
Atmosphere (ADWA) ... at
Atmosphere (ADWA) ... atm
Atmosphere Absolute (ADWA) ... ata
Atmosphere Radiation and Cloud Station (ARMP) ... ARCS
Atmosphere Spectroscopy Applications (CARB) ... ASA
Atmosphere-Ocean (CARB) ... AO
Atmospheric ... Atmos
Atmospheric (ADWA) ... atmos
Atmospheric Chemical Transport Model (CARB) ... ACTM
Atmospheric Chemistry Modelling Support Unit ... ACMSU
Atmospheric Chemistry Studies in the Oceanic Environment ... ACSOE
Atmospheric Convergence Line ... ACL
Atmospheric Emitted Radiance Interferometer (ARMP) ... AERI
Atmospheric Environmental Research, Inc. (ARMP) ... AER
Atmospheric General Circulation Model (CARB) ... ACCM
Atmospheric Radiation Measurement Satellite (CARB) ... ARMSAT
Atmospheric Radiative Heating (ARMP) ... ARH
Atmospheric Science ... AS
Atmospheric Stabilization Framework (AUEG) ... ASF
Atmospheric Trace Spectroscopy (ARMP) ... ATMOS
Atmospheric Transmission Factor (CARB) ... ATF

By Meaning

Atomic Energy Commission (AUEG)	AEC
Atomic Mass Unit (ABAC)	amu
Atrial Fibrillation (ADWA)	A-Fib
Attach (ADWA)	atch
Attached Resupply Carrier [*NASA*] (SPST)	ARCA
Attachment (ADWA)	att
Attachment Disorder	AD
Attention-Deficit Disorder with Hyperactivity (DIPS)	ADDH
Attention-Deficit Hyperactivity Disorder (DIPS)	AHD
Attitude and Orbit Control Measurement System (ADWA)	AOCMS
Attitude Anomaly Detector (ADWA)	AAD
Attitude Calibration Module [*NASA*] (SPST)	ACM
Attitude, Control, and Stabilization [*NASA*] (SPST)	AC&S
Attitude Control Unit (ADWA)	ACU
Attitude Determination and Control Subsystem (ADWA)	ADACS
Attitude Director Indicator (PIPO)	ADI
Attitude Pointing Mechanism Electronics (ADWA)	APME
Attitude Toward Disabled Persons Scale (DIPS)	ATDPS
Attotesla (ADWA)	aT
Attractive (ADWA)	attr
Attributively (ADWA)	attrib
Audience (ADWA)	aud
Audio Automatic Switch (CCCA)	AAS
Audio Communications Controller (ROAS)	ACC
Audio Frequency (ABAC)	af
Audio Interchange Format	AIF
Audio Interface Format	AIFF
Audio-Visual Service Specific Convergence Sublayer	AVSSCS
Auditor (ADWA)	aud
Auditory Integrated Training	AIT
Auditory Integration Training	AIT
Auditory Processing Disorder	APD
Augmentative (ADWA)	aug
Augmentative (ADWA)	augm
Augmented Materials Production (ABAC)	AMP
August (ADWA)	Ag
August (ADWA)	Aug
Aural Warning System [*Aviation*] (PIPO)	AWS
Auroral Imaging Observatory (CARB)	AURIO
Austerity	AU
Australia (ADWA)	Aus
Australia (ADWA)	Aust
Australia (ADWA)	Austl
Australia (NTIO)	Austral
Australia and New Zealand Army Corps (ADWA)	Anzac
Australia School Library Association	ASLA
Australian Boxing Federation	ABF
Australian Centre for UFO Studies	ACUFOS
Australian Institute of Cartographers	AIC
Australian National Antarctic Research Establishment (CARB)	ANARE
Australian Pacific Economic Cooperation Committee	AUSPECC
Australian Radiation Laboratory (CARB)	ARL
Australian Stock Exchange (SG)	Au
Authentication Center (CGWS)	AC
Authentication Center (CGWS)	AuC
Authentication Request (ADWA)	ARq
Authentication Response (ADWA)	ARs
Authority (ADWA)	auth
Authorized User Key [*Computer science*] (ITCA)	AUK
Authorized Version (ADWA)	Auth Ver
Author's Alteration (ADWA)	aa
Authors' Registry	AR
Autism National Committee	AutCom
Autism Research Institute	ARI
Autistic Spectrum	AS
Autistic Spectrum Disorder	ASD
Auto Body Repair and Painting	ABRP
Autologous Blood and Marrow Transplant Registry (ADWA)	ABMTR
Autologous Bone Marrow Transplantation (ADWA)	ABMT
Automated Aircraft Reporting System (ADWA)	AARS
Automated Calling Card Service (ROAS)	ACCS
Automated Data Processing Equipment (CTAS)	ADPE
Automated External Defibrillator	AED
Automated Health Research Information System (ADWA)	AHRIS
Automated Information Security (ADWA)	AIS
Automated Information Systems Security Program	AISSP
Automated Interaction Detector (AUEG)	AID
Automated Large Panel Display (CCCA)	ALPD
Automated Meteorological Station (AUEG)	AMS
Automated Nautical Charting System (ADWA)	ANCS
Automated Regression Tester [*Computer science*] (ITCA)	ART
Automated Remediation Assessment Methodology (ABAC)	ARAM
Automated Surface Observation System [*Aviation*] (PIPO)	ASOS
Automated Ticket and Fare Determination System [*Travel industry*] (TRID)	ATFDS
Automated Transportation Management System (ABAC)	ATMS
Automated Weather Station (ARMP)	AWS
Automatic Barrier Crossing, Locally Monitored (HEAS)	ABCL
Automatic Bit Rate	ABR
Automatic Calibration and Equalization	ACE
Automatic Communications Monitor (CCCA)	ACM
Automatic Data Processing Standards Policy Group (CCCA)	ASPG
Automatic Data Transition (CCCA)	ADT
Automatic Flow Controller	AFC
Automatic Flue Closing Device (HEAS)	AFCD
Automatic Intercept Communications Controller (ROAS)	AICC
Automatic Key Distribution Center (CCCA)	AKDC
Automatic Message Processing Equipment (CCCA)	AMPE
Automatic Observing Station (PIPO)	AUTOB
Automatic Open Crossing Locally Monitored (HEAS)	AOCL
Automatic Open Crossing, Remotely Monitored (HEAS)	AOCR
Automatic Phase Control	apc
Automatic Power Boom Lowering (HEAS)	APBL
Automatic Radial Centering [*Aviation*] (PIPO)	ARC
Automatic Safe Load Indicator (HEAS)	ASLI
Automatic Surface Observing System (ARMP)	ASOS
Automatic Teller Machine (NTIO)	ATM
Automatic Test Generation	ATG
Automatic Tracking System (ABAC)	ATS
Automatic Transmission (NTIO)	AT
Automatic Weather Reporting Station (PIPO)	AWRS
Automobile (ADWA)	auto
Automotive Technology	AMT
Autosomal Dominant-Progressive External Ophthalmoplegia	AD-PEO
Auxiliary Aviation Weather Facility (PIPO)	AAWF
Auxiliary Power Unit (ADWA)	apu
Auxiliary Verb (ADWA)	AUX
Auxilliary Operator Service System	AOSS
Availability Status Messages [*Travel industry*] (TRID)	AVS
Available (ADWA)	AVL
Available (ADWA)	avlbl
Available Cell Rate (MLOA)	ACR
Available for Sale	AFS
Available Solar Energy (ADWA)	ASE
Available Solar Radiation (ADWA)	ASR
Avalanche Photon Device	APD
Avanir Pharmaceuticals 'A' [*AMEX symbol*] (SG)	AVN
Average (ADWA)	av
Average (MARI)	Av
Average (ABAC)	avg
Average Busy Season Busy Hour	ABSBH
Average Emission Factor (CARB)	AEF
Average Evoked Response Technique (DIPS)	AERT
Avestan (ADWA)	Avest
Aviation (ADWA)	avn
Aviation Development Tactics and Evaluation Department [*Military*]	ADTE
Aviation Gasoline (ADWA)	avgas
Aviation Supplies & Academics	ASA
Aviation Training Association (COBU)	ATA
Aviation Turbine Fuel (PIAV)	avtur
Aviation Week & Space Technology (CCCA)	AWST
Avitar, Inc. [*AMEX symbol*] (SG)	AVR
Avoirdupois (NTIO)	avdp
Awake-Alert-Oriented (ADWA)	A-A-O
Award of Merit [*Boy Scouts of America*]	AOM
Awareness and Preparedness for Emergencies at Local Level (HEAS)	APELL
Awkward (ADWA)	awk
Axiom (ADWA)	ax
Axis (DIPS)	Ax
Azerbaijan (ADWA)	AZE
Azimuth Angle (ARMP)	AZA
Azure (ADWA)	az

B
By Meaning

Babcock & Wilcox Co. (ABAC) .... B&W
Babcock & Wilcox Hanford Co. (ABAC) .... BWHC
Bachelor of Science Degree in Computer Science .... BSCS
Bachman Turner Overdrive (ROAS) .... BTO
Back Trajectory (ARMP) .... BT
Background (ADWA) .... bkgd
Backhaul Check (TRID) .... BHC
Backplane Transceiver Logic (AEBE) .... BTL
Backup Computational Facility (CCCA) .... BCF
Bacterial (ADWA) .... bact
Bacteriology (ADWA) .... bacteriol
Balanced Force Requirements Analysis Model (CCCA) .... BALFRAM
Balcony (NTIO) .... bal
Balcony (ADWA) .... balc
Balcony [Travel industry] (TRID) .... BLCY
Bale (ADWA) .... bl
Baled .... Bld
Bales (MARI) .... Bls
Ballistic Electron Emission Microscopy .... BEEM
Ballistic Missile Defense Systems Command (CCCA) .... BMDSC
Ballistic Missile Technology (ADWA) .... BMT
Balloon-Borne Sounding System (ARMP) .... BBSS
Baltic (ADWA) .... Balt
Baltimore and Ohio (ADWA) .... B&O
Band Interleaved by Pixel (ADWA) .... BIP
Bandwidth Compression (ROAS) .... BWC
Bandwidth Demand Assignment (CCCA) .... BDA
Bandwidth Efficient Zero Suppression (ADWA) .... BEZS
Bandwidth Test Set (ROAS) .... BWTS
Bandwidth Time (CCCA) .... BT
Banjo .... bjo
Bank Angle [Aviation] (PIPO) .... B/A
Bank Buying Rate (TRID) .... BBR
Bank of Scotland .... BOS
Baptist (NTIO) .... Bap
Baptist Union of Western Canada (ROAS) .... BUWC
Baptized (ADWA) .... bapt
Bar (ABAC) .... b
Barbados (ADWA) .... Bds
Bareback Riding [Rodeo term] .... BB
Bareboat (RIMS) .... Bb
Bargain Purchase Option (ADWA) .... BPO
Baritone Saxophone .... barsx
Barometer (NTIO) .... bar
Barracks (ADWA) .... bks
Barrel (ADWA) .... brl
Barrel Racing [Rodeo term] .... GB
Barrels per Day (ADWA) .... bpd
Barrier Development Program Plan (ABAC) .... BDPP
Barrier Injected Transit Time (CCCA) .... BARRITT
Barrier Technical Advisory Board (ABAC) .... BTAB
Barring of All Incoming Calls (CGWS) .... BAIC
Barring of All Outgoing Calls (CGWS) .... BAOC
Basal (ADWA) .... bas
Basal Metabolism Rate (NTIO) .... BMR
Basalt Waste Isolation Project (ABAC) .... BWIP
Base Catalyzed Destruction (ABAC) .... BCD
Base Communications Processor (CCCA) .... BCP
Base Flood Elevation (DEMM) .... BFE
Base Network Control Center .... BNCC
Baseball (NDBD) .... BB
Baseball Assistance Team (NDBD) .... BAT
Baseband Processor .... BBP
Baseline Air Pollution Station (AUEG) .... BAPS
Baseline Change Request (ARMP) .... BCR
Baseline Information Tracking System (ABAC) .... BITS
BASF AG ADS [NYSE symbol] .... BF
Basic Commercial Pilot's License (PIAV) .... BCPL
Basic Education Act [1977] .... BEA
Basic English in the Native Language .... BENL
Basic English Skills Test .... BEST
Basic Ground Instructor [Aviation] (PIPO) .... BGI
Basic Health Management .... BHM
Basic Helix-Loop-Helix .... bHLH
Basic Inspection (HEAS) .... BAS
Basic Ordering Agreement (ADWA) .... BOA

Basic Oxygen Demand (SARE) .... BOD
Basic Rate Access .... BRA
Basic Rate Service .... BRS
Basic Reference Model .... BRM
Basic Research and Human Resources (ADWA) .... BRHR
Basic Safety Standards Directive (HEAS) .... BSS
Basic Services Terminal .... BST
Basic Sine In (TRID) .... BSI
Basic Sine Out (TRID) .... BSO
Basket .... bast
Basket .... bkt
Basket (ADWA) .... bsk
Basket Range Stone .... RS
Basking in Reflected Glory (DIPS) .... BIRG
Bass Clarinet .... bcl
Bass Guitar .... bgtr
Bass Trombone .... btbn
Basset Horn .... bthn
Bassoon .... bn
Batboy (NDBD) .... BB
Batch Command Language [Computer science] .... BCL
Batch Message Processing Program [Computer science] (ITCA) ..... BMP
Batelle Development Corporation (ABAC) .... BDC
Batelle Project Management Division (ABAC) .... BPMD
Bates Large Acceptance Spectrometer Toroid .... BLAST
Bathroom (ADWA) .... ba
Batman and Robin .... B&R
Batman Forever .... BF
Batman Returns .... BR
Batman, the Animated Series .... BAS
Batman, the Animated Series .... BTAS
Battalion (ADWA) .... bat
Battalion (ADWA) .... batt
Battelle Europe (ABAC) .... BE
Battelle Portland Operations (ABAC) .... BPO
Battelle Seattle Research Center (ABAC) .... BSRC
Battelle Washington Office (ABAC) .... BWO
Battery (ADWA) .... btty
Battery Discharge Regulator (ADWA) .... BDR
Battery Reconditioning Unit (ADWA) .... BRU
Battle Staff Training Facility [Marine Corps] .... BSTF
Baud (ABAC) .... bd
Bay Window Villa .... BV
Bayesian Information Criteria (IDAI) .... BIC
Bayesian Network [Graphical Model] (IDAI) .... BN
Bayesian Network Interchange Format (IDAI) .... BNIF
Be Back Soon [Online dialog] .... BBS
Beachfront [Travel industry] (TRID) .... BCHFT
Beacon (ADWA) .... bcn
Beacon Available [Aviation] (PIPO) .... B
Beacon Transmitter (ADWA) .... BTX
Beam (ADWA) .... bm
Beam Forming & Switching Network (CCCA) .... BFSN
Beam Line Operations and Safety Awareness (SARE) .... BLOSA
Beam Management Terminal .... BMT
Bearing (ADWA) .... brg
Beat Frequency Oscillator (AEBE) .... bfo
Beaume Scale (ADWA) .... Be
Because (ADWA) .... bec
Because (ADWA) .... BK
Bechtel Hanford Incorporated (ABAC) .... BHI
Becquerel (ABAC) .... bq
Bed and Breakfast (TRID) .... B&B
Bed Volume (ABAC) .... BV
Bedroom (ADWA) .... br
Been There, Done That [Internet dialog] .... BTDT
Before Breaking Bulk (RIMS) .... BBB
Begin (ADWA) .... beg
Behavior Based Safety (SARE) .... BBS
Behavior Intervention Plan .... BIP
Behavior Management Plan .... BMP
Behavior Management Plan .... BMT
Behavioral Activation System .... BAS
Behavioral Approach System (DIPS) .... BAS
Behavioral Inhibition System .... BIS

Behavioral Neurogenetics and Neuroimaging Research Center (ADWA) ... BNNRC
Behaviorally/Emotionally Handicapped ... BEH
Behaviorally Handicapped ... BH
Behavioural Sciences Research Division (HEAS) ... BSRD
Belfort Laser Ceilometer (ARMP) ... BLC
Belgian (ADWA) ... Belg
Bell Industries [*AMEX symbol*] (SG) ... BI
Bell Labs Layered Space-Time ... BLAST
Bell Systems Technical Journal [*A publication*] (CCCA) ... BSTJ
Ben R. Oppenheimer [*California Institute of Technology*] ... BRO
Bengal (ADWA) ... Beng
Benign Asbestos Pleural Effusion (HEAS) ... BAPE
Bent Up Trailing Edge [*Aviation*] (PIPO) ... BUTE
Benzene (ABAC) ... Bz
Berkeley Internet Name Domain [*Computer science*] (ITCA) ... BIND
Berkshire Hills Bancorp [*AMEX symbol*] ... BHL
Bermuda Stock Exchange Ltd. ... BSX
Best of Both Worlds (ADWA) ... BOBW
Best Offer (ADWA) ... B/O
Better ... btr
Between (ADWA) ... betw
Beverly Hills 90210 [*Television program title*] ... 90210
Bible (NTIO) ... Bib
Biblical (ADWA) ... bib
Biblical (ADWA) ... bibl
Bibliographer (ADWA) ... bibliog
Bibliography (ADWA) ... bibliogr
Bid Price (SG) ... B
Bidirectional Surface-Scattering Distribution Function [*Computer graphics*] ... BSSDF
Bilateral (ADWA) ... bil
Bilateral Lung Transplantation (ADWA) ... BLT
Bilateral Program Review (SPST) ... BPR
Bill of Lading Ton (MARI) ... B/L Ton
Bill of Sale (ADWA) ... b/s
Billed Number Screening ... BNS
Billing Validation Center (ROAS) ... BVC
Billion Cubic Feet (ADWA) ... bcf
Billion Electron Volts (AEBE) ... BEV
Bills Discounted (ADWA) ... B/D
Bills of Lading (ADWA) ... Bs/L
Bills Receivable (ADWA) ... B/R
Binary Frequency Shift Keying (CCCA) ... BFSK
Binary Information File [*Computer science*] ... BIF
Binary Input-Output Fuzzy Adaptive Memory (IDAI) ... BIOFAM
Binary Non-Consecutive Ones (CCCA) ... BNO
Binary Reflected Gray Code ... BRGC
Binary Symmetric Erasure Channel (CCCA) ... BSEC
Binary Universal Form for Representation (ADWA) ... BUFR
Binding (ADWA) ... bdg
Bio-Aqua Systems 'A' [*AMEX symbol*] (SG) ... SEA
Bioconcentration Potential (ADWA) ... BCP
Biodegradation of Environmental Chemicals Modeled with Aquatic, Relative-Rate Coefficients (AUEG) ... BENCHMARC
Bioelectric Impedance Analysis (DIPS) ... BIA
BioInformatics Molecular Analysis Section ... BIMAS
Biologic License Application ... BLA
Biological Defense ... BD
Biological Exposure Limits (HEAS) ... BELS
Biological Resource Division ... BRD
Biological Sciences Center (ADWA) ... BSC
Biological Synoptic Ocean Prediction (CARB) ... BIOSYNOP
Biological Tolerance Value (HEAS) ... BAT
Biologist (ADWA) ... biol
Biology (NTIO) ... bio
Bioluminescence Immunoassay ... BIA
Biomass and Biofuels Association (COBU) ... BABA
Biomass Burned (CARB) ... BB
Biomass Production Chamber (ADWA) ... BPC
Biopsy [*Medicine*] ... Bx
Bioscience ... Biosci
Biosphere-Atmosphere Trace Gas Exchange (CARB) ... BATGE
Biotechnology (ADWA) ... biotech
Bipolar Field Effect Transistor (ADWA) ... BIFET
Birthplace (ADWA) ... bp
Birthplace (ADWA) ... bpl
Birthweight (NTIO) ... bw
Biserial Coefficient of Correlation (DIPS) ... rbis
Bisexual (ADWA) ... Bi
Bisexual Asian Female (ADWA) ... BIAF
Bisexual Asian Male (ADWA) ... BIAM
Bisexual Black Female (ADWA) ... BIBF
Bisexual Black Male (ADWA) ... BIBM
Bisexual Hispanic Female (ADWA) ... BIHF
Bisexual Hispanic Male (ADWA) ... BIHM
Bisexual Jewish Female (ADWA) ... BIJF
Bisexual Jewish Male (ADWA) ... BIJM
Bishop (NTIO) ... Bish
Bit Error Rate (CGWS) ... BER
Bit Error Rate Test ... BERT
Bit Test (ROAS) ... BT
Bit Test and Complement (ROAS) ... BTC
Bit Test and Reset [*Telecommunications*] (ROAS) ... BTR
Bit Test and Set (ROAS) ... BTS
Bit-Block Transfer (ADWA) ... BitBit
Bit-Mapped File ... BMP
Black (ADWA) ... bk
Black (ADWA) ... blk
Black, Brown, Red, Orange, Yellow, Green, Blue, Violet, Grey, White [*Electronic component color codes*] (ROAS) ... BBROYGBVGW
Black Carbon (CARB) ... BC
Black Christian Female (ADWA) ... BCF
Black Christian Male (ADWA) ... BCM
Black Hole ... BH
Black Letter (ADWA) ... bklr
Black Professional Female (ADWA) ... BPF
Black Professional Male (ADWA) ... BPM
Blatant Self-Promotion (ADWA) ... BSP
Blaze Software [*NASDAQ symbol*] (SG) ... BLZE
Blind Copy (NTIO) ... bc
Blind Passenger [*Travel industry*] (TRID) ... BLND
Block Acceptance Reporting Mechanism (ADWA) ... BARM
Block Acquisition Sequence (ADWA) ... BAS
Block Data Message (CTAS) ... BDM
Block Descriptive Word [*Computer science*] (ITCA) ... BDW
Block Sequence Number (CCCA) ... BSN
Blocked Asynchronous Transmission [*Computer science*] (ITCA) ... Blast
Blond (ADWA) ... Blnd
Blood Lead Laboratory Reference System (ADWA) ... BLLRS
Blood Monitoring [*Medicine*] ... BM
Blood Pressure ... BP
Blood Pressure (NTIO) ... bp
Blood Volume Pulse (ADWA) ... BVP
Bloodborne Pathogen (SARE) ... BBP
Blood-Brain Barrier (DIPS) ... BBB
Blown Save [*Baseball term*] (NDBD) ... BS
Blue (ADWA) ... Blu
Blue Cone Pigment ... BCP
Blue Light Radiation (HEAS) ... BLR
Blueprint Reading ... BLPRT
Board (ADWA) ... brd
Board Foot (ABAC) ... bd ft
Board of Chief Inspectors (HEAS) ... BCI
Board of Regents (DEMM) ... BOR
Board Tracking System (ROAS) ... BTS
Boarding Pass Reserve [*Travel industry*] (TRID) ... BPR
Boat (ADWA) ... bt
Body Centered Cubic (ABAC) ... bcc
Boeing Commercial Airplanes (HLLA) ... BCA
Boeing Computer Services Richland, Inc. (ABAC) ... BCSR
Bohmian Quantum Mechanics I [*Physics*] ... BQMI
Boiler and Pressure Vessel Code (ABAC) ... BPVC
Bold and the Beautiful [*Television program title*] ... B&B
Boldface (ADWA) ... bld
Bold-Type Headings ... BTH
Bolivian (ADWA) ... Bol
Bolsa de Valores do Sao Paulo [*Sao Paulo Stock Exchange*] [*Brazil*] ... BOVESPA
Bolt Motor Actuator (SPST) ... BMA
Bolus (ADWA) ... bol
Bomb Disposal Squad (ADWA) ... BDS
Bond-Equivalent Effective Margin ... BEEM
Bone Marrow Edema Syndrome [*Medicine*] ... BMES
Bone-Marrow-Derived Cell (ADWA) ... B cell
Book Club Edition (ADWA) ... BCE
Bookbinder (ADWA) ... bkbndr
Bookham Technology plc ADS [*NASDAQ symbol*] (SG) ... BKHM
Booking Note (RIMS) ... B/N
Bookkeeper (ADWA) ... bkpr
Bookkeeping (ADWA) ... bkg
Bookkeeping (ADWA) ... bkpg
Book-of-the-Month Club (ADWA) ... BOMC
Books (ADWA) ... bb
Booktech.com, Inc. [*AMEX symbol*] (SG) ... BTC
Boomerang ... BO
Boot Parameters Protocol [*Computer science*] (ITCA) ... BOOTP
Bordeaux (ADWA) ... Bdx
Bordeaux/Hamburg Limits (MARI) ... B/H
Border Intermediate System ... BIS
Boron Experiment ... BOREXINO
Borough (ADWA) ... Bor
Borough President (ADWA) ... Beep
Borough President (ADWA) ... BP
Bose-Einstein Condensate ... BEC
Boston Consulting Group ... BCG
Boston Stock Exchange (SG) ... B
Botanical (ADWA) ... bot
Both Ends (RIMS) ... BE
Both Inclusive (RIMS) ... BI
Bottle (ADWA) ... btl
Bottoms Recycle (ABAC) ... BR
Bouffees Delirantes [*An acute delusional disorder*] (DIPS) ... BD
Bought (ADWA) ... bgt
Boulevard (NTIO) ... Boul
Bound (ADWA) ... bnd
Boundary (ADWA) ... bdry
Boundary (ADWA) ... bdy
Boundary Facility (ARMP) ... BF
Boundary Layer Experiment (ARMP) ... BLX
Boundary Scan Descriptor Language [*Computer science*] ... BSDI

Bourbon and Soda (ADWA) ..... B and S
Boxed (ADWA) ..... bxd
Boyce Thompson Institute [*Cornell University*] ..... BTI
Brackish Water Arrival Draft (RIMS) ..... BWAD
Brain Response Interface ..... BRI
Brass ..... br
Brassiere (ADWA) ..... bra
Bratwurst (ADWA) ..... brat
Brazilian (ADWA) ..... Braz
Brazilian Portuguese (ADWA) ..... BrazPg
Breacher's Explosive Access Selectable Tool ..... BEAST
Breadth (ADWA) ..... b
Breadth (RIMS) ..... Br
Break Cloud Procedure [*Aviation*] (PIAV) ..... BCP
Break Load (RIMS) ..... Brld
Breakfast (ADWA) ..... brkfst
Breakfast Plan [*Travel industry*] (TRID) ..... BP
Breaking and Entering (ADWA) ..... B and E
Breast Feeding ..... BF
Breast-Conserving Therapy (ADWA) ..... BCY
Breton (ADWA) ..... Bret
Brevet (ADWA) ..... brev
Brick or Stone Built, Slated or Tiled (MARI) ..... bsst
Bridge (NTIO) ..... br
Brief-Stimuli Technique (DIPS) ..... BST
Brigade (ADWA) ..... bde
Brigade ..... BDG
Brigade (ADWA) ..... brig
Brigade Aid Station [*Military*] ..... BAS
Brigade Force Initiative [*Army*] ..... BFI
Bright (ADWA) ..... brt
Brightness Temperature (ARMP) ..... BT
Brightness Temperature Difference (ARMP) ..... BTD
British (ADWA) ..... Br
British Association of Educational Supplies (COBU) ..... BESA
British Association of Print and Copyshops (COBU) ..... BAPC
British Association of Psychological Types (COBU) ..... BAPT
British Association of State English Language Teaching ..... BASELT
British Civil Air Requirements (PIAV) ..... BCAR
British Columbia Trade Development Corporation (ABAC) ..... BCTDC
British Committee on Radiological Units (HEAS) ..... BCRU
British Company Law Cases [*A publication*] ..... BCC
British Digest of International Law [*A publication*] ..... BDIL
British Elastic Rope Sports Association (HEAS) ..... BERSA
British Hang-Gliding and Paragliding Association (PIAV) ..... BHPA
British Health and Safety Society (HEAS) ..... BHSS
British Institute of Facilities Management (COBU) ..... BIFM
British Institute of Occupational Hygiene (HEAS) ..... BIOH
British Insurers' International Committee (MARI) ..... BIIC
British Journal of Criminology [*A publication*] ..... BJ Crim
British Journal of Industrial Relations [*A publication*] ..... BJIR
British Journal of Law & Society [*A publication*] ..... BJLS
British Literary and Artistic Copyright Association ..... BLACA
British Marine Mutual (RIMS) ..... BMM
British Marine Underwriters Associations (MARI) ..... BMUA
British Materials Handling Board (HEAS) ..... BMHB
British National Lymphoma Investigation ..... BNLI
British Nuclear Fuels ..... BNFL
British Rail Privatisation Safety Unit (HEAS) ..... BRPSU
British Railway (TRID) ..... BritRail
British Sitcom (ADWA) ..... Britcom
British Tax Review [*A publication*] ..... BTR
British Thermal Unit (NTIO) ..... btu
British Transport Police (HEAS) ..... BTP
British West Indies (TRID) ..... BWI
British Yearbook of International Law [*A publication*] ..... BYBL
Broad Agency Announcement ..... BAA
Broad Area Review ..... BAR
Broadband Hemispherical in Flux Radiometer (CARB) ..... BBHIR
Broadband Hemispherical Solar Radiometer (CARB) ..... BBHSR
Broadband Outdoor Radiometer Calibration (ARMP) ..... BORCAL
Broadband-Low Layer Information [*Telecommunications*] (MLOA) ..... B-LLI
Broadcast Channel (CGWS) ..... BCH
Broadcast Interrupt (CCCA) ..... B/I
Broadcast Station (PIPO) ..... BS
Broadcast Warning Message (ROAS) ..... BWM
Broadway (NTIO) ..... Bway
Bromoflurobenzene (ABAC) ..... BFB
Brother (NTIO) ..... Br
Brother (ADWA) ..... Bro
Brothers (ADWA) ..... bros
Brought Forward (ADWA) ..... B/F
Brown (ADWA) ..... Br
Brown (ADWA) ..... Brn
Brownstone (ADWA) ..... brwnstn
Brunei Darussalam National Committee for Pacific Economic Cooperation ..... BDCPEC
Brushed ..... Brshd
Bubble Jet Color ..... BJC
Buccal Epithelial Cells ..... BEC
Buccolingual Masticatory Syndrome (DIPS) ..... BLM
Budgeting and Reporting (ABAC) ..... B&R
Budweiser (ADWA) ..... Bud
Buffering in Progress ..... BIP
Buffet Breakfast [*Travel industry*] (TRID) ..... BB
Build Absolutely Nothing Anywhere Near Anybody (ADWA) ..... Banana
Building and Loan (ADWA) ..... B and L
Building Energy Standards Program (ABAC) ..... BESP
Building Operation (HEAS) ..... BO
Building Systems Program (ABAC) ..... BSP
Buildings and Utilities (ABAC) ..... B&U
Build-to-Order Software Selector ..... BOSS
Built-In (ADWA) ..... BI
Bulgarian (ADWA) ..... Bulg
Bulk Encryption (CCCA) ..... BE
Bulk Volume (ROAS) ..... BV
Bulk Water (CARB) ..... BW
Bulkhead (ADWA) ..... bhd
Bull Riders Only [*An association*] ..... BRO
Bull Riding [*Rodeo term*] ..... BR
Bulletin (ADWA) ..... bul
Bulletin of the American Meteorological Society [*A publication*] (ARMP) ..... BAMS
Bullfighting [*Rodeo term*] ..... BF
Bunched ..... bchd
Bundle (ADWA) ..... bdl
Bundle (ADWA) ..... bdle
Bungalow ..... BU
Bunker on Board (RIMS) ..... BOB
Bunkers Remaining on Board (RIMS) ..... BROB
Bunt [*Baseball term*] (NDBD) ..... B
Bureau (ADWA) ..... bu
Bureau Chief (DEMM) ..... BC
Bureau of Compliance Planning and Support [*Department of Emergency Management*] (DEMM) ..... BCPS
Bureau of Preparedness and Response [*Department of Emergency Management*] (DEMM) ..... BPR
Bureau of Primary Health Care ..... BPHC
Bureau of Recovery and Mitigation [*Department of Emergency Management*] (DEMM) ..... BRM
Burger King ..... BK
Burgundy (ADWA) ..... Bdy
Buried (ADWA) ..... bur
Buried Waste Integrated Demonstration (ABAC) ..... BWID
Burlap (ADWA) ..... brlp
Burma (ADWA) ..... Bur
Burmese (ADWA) ..... Burm
Burned in Time Codes ..... BITC
Burst Out Laughing [*Internet dialog*] ..... BOL
Bursting with Laughter [*Internet dialog*] ..... BWL
Bushel (ADWA) ..... bsh
Bushel ..... bu
Business Administration Manager (ABAC) ..... BAM
Business and Professional Women (ADWA) ..... BPW
Business Education ..... BE
Business Efficiency Unit (HEAS) ..... BEU
Business Law Review [*A publication*] ..... BLR
Business Lawyer [*A publication*] ..... Bus Law
Business Process Reengineering ..... BPR
Business Professionals of America ..... BPA
Business Reply Card ..... BRC
Business Residence Custom Service ..... BRCS
Business Sensitive (ABAC) ..... BS
Business Service Centers (ADWA) ..... BSCs
Business Services Branch (HEAS) ..... BSB
Business Services Division (HEAS) ..... BSD
Business Telephony on Passive Optical Network [*Telecommunications*] (ROAS) ..... BTPON
Business Travel Department (TRID) ..... BTD
Business Unit (ROAS) ..... BU
Business Wire (ROAS) ..... BW
Business-to-Business B2B
Butterworths Company Law Cases [*A publication*] ..... BCLC
Butterworths Journal of International Banking & Financial Law [*A publication*] ..... BJIB & FL
Butterworths Medico-Legal Reports [*A publication*] ..... BMLR
Button (ADWA) ..... btn
Bye Bye for Now [*Internet dialog*] BB4N
Bye for Now (ADWA) ..... BFN
Bye-Bye for Now (ADWA) ..... BBFN
Bypass (ADWA) ..... byp
Bytes per Second (ADWA) ..... bps
Bytes per Second (AEBE) ..... Bps

C
By Meaning

Cabin Baggage [*Travel industry*] (TRID) .... CBBG
Cabinet Office Deregulation Unit (HEAS) .... CORU
Cable Management Software .... CMS
Cable Modem Termination System .... CMTS
Cable News Financial Network (ADWA) .... CNFN
Cabletelevision Advertising Bureau, Inc. .... CAB
Cabot Microelectronics [*NASDAQ symbol*] (SG) .... CCMP
Caesarean Section (NTIO) .... C section
Caitlin Raymond International Registry (ADWA) .... CRIR
Calcium Pyrophosphate Deposition Disease (ADWA) .... CPPD
Calcium-Calmodulin-Dependent Protein Kinase II .... CaMKII
Calculate (ADWA) .... calc
Calculus (NTIO) .... calc
Caldera Systems [*NASDAQ symbol*] (SG) .... CALD
Calendar Year to Date (ABAC) .... CYTD
Calf Roping [*Rodeo term*] .... CR
Calfskin (ADWA) .... cf
Caliber (ADWA) .... cal
Calibrated Ancillary System [*NASA*] (SPST) .... CAS
Calibration (ADWA) .... cal
California (NTIO) .... Cal
California Basic Education Skills Test (ROAS) .... CBEST
California Clean Air Act (SARE) .... CCAA
California Clearinghouse for Library Instruction CCLI
California Coalition for Ethical Mental Health Care .... CCEMHC
California Department of Transportation (SARE) .... CalTrans
California Division of Occupational Safety and Health (SARE) .... Cal-OSHA
California Education and Research Federation .... CERF
California Education and Research Federation Network .... CERFNET
California Energy Commission (ABAC) .... CEC
California Environmental Resources Evaluation System (AUEG) .... CERES
California Law Review [*A publication*] .... Cal LR
California Psychological Inventory Test (DIPS) .... CPIT
California School Library Association .... CSLA
California State Fire Marshall (SARE) .... CSFM
Call Control (CGWS) CC
Call Control Module (CCCA) .... CCM
Call Data Transmitter (ROAS) .... CDT
Call Forward Busy .... CFB
Call Sign (PIAV) .... c/s
Call-for-Fire-Zone [*Army*] .... CFFZ
Calling Card Validation (ROAS) CCV
Calling Line Directory Number .... CLDN
Calling Party Pays (CGWS) .... CPP
Calnexin .... Cnx
Calorie (NTIO) .... Cal
Calories from Fat .... CFF
Calreticulin .... Crt
Cambridge (ADWA) .... Cam
Cambridge Antibody Technology .... CaT
Cambridge Examination in English for Language Teachers .... CEELT
Cambridge Law Journal [*A publication*] .... CLJ
Caminus Corp. [*NASDAQ symbol*] (SG) .... CAMZ
Camouflage (ADWA) .... cam
Campanology (ADWA) .... campanol
Campus Custom Publishing (ADWA) .... CCP
Campus Improvement Council CIC
Campus Safety, Health, and Environmental Management Association (SARE) .... CSHEMA
Campus-Wide Information Server .... CWIS
Canada-Ontario Environmental Sustainability Agreement .... COESA
Canadian (ADWA) .... Canad
Canadian Air Defense Zone (PIPO) .... CADIZ
Canadian Bar Journal [*A publication*] .... Can BJ
Canadian Cystic Fibrosis Foundation .... CCF
Canadian Defense System (CCCA) .... CDS
Canadian Electrical Distributors Association .... CEDA
Canadian Global Change Program (CARB) .... CGCP
Canadian High Acceptance Orbit Spectrometer .... CHAOS
Canadian Hyperlexia Association .... CHA
Canadian Institutes of Health Research .... CIHR
Canadian International Trade Tribunal .... CITT
Canadian Light Source .... CLS
Canadian Memorial Chiropractic College .... CMCC
Canadian National Committee for Pacific Economic Cooperation .... CANCPEC
Canadian Oncology Society .... COS

Canadian Professional Rodeo Association .... CPRA
Canadian Registration Board of Occupational Hygienists (SARE) .... CRBOH
Canadian Society for Engineering in Agriculture, Food, and Biological Systems .... CSAE
Canadian Television and Radio Commission (CGWS) .... CTRC
Canadian Transport Emergency Center (HEAS) .... CANUTEC
Canadian UFO Research Network .... CUFORN
Canadian Wireless Telecommunications Association (CGWS) .... CWTA
Canal (NTIO) .... Can
Cancel Former Order (ADWA) .... CFO
Canceled (NTIO) .... canc
Cancellation (ADWA) .... can
Cancellation Ratio (CCCA) .... CR
Cancellation Recommended [*Travel industry*] (TRID) .... XR
Cancelled [*Travel industry*] (TRID) .... XLD
Cancelled (TRID) XX
Cancelled Name [*Travel industry*] (TRID) .... XN
Cancelled Segment [*Travel industry*] (TRID) .... XS
Cancelling of Policy Returns Only [*Insurance*] (MARI) .... CRO
Cancer and Steroid Hormonal Study (ADWA) .... CSHS
Cancer Biotherapeutics Newsletter [*A publication*] (ADWA) .... CBN
Cancer Research Foundation of America (ADWA) .... CRFA
Cancer Research Institute .... CRI
Canned Ration (ADWA) .... C ration
Can't Play and No Chance [*Baseball term*] (NDBD) .... cp and nc
Can't Remember Stuff (ADWA) .... CRS
Canyon Forest Village .... CFV
Capability Performance .... CP
Capacitive Deionization (ADWA) .... CDI
Capacitive Feedback Transimpedance Amplifier (ADWA) .... CTIA
Cape Cod CC
Capital Asset Management Process (ABAC) .... CAMP
Capitation .... Cap
Capitol Emergency Response Plan (DEMM) .... CERP
Capricorn (NTIO) .... CAP
Capstone Turbine [*NASDAQ symbol*] .... CPST
Capsule (NTIO) .... Caps
Capsule/Tablet (NTIO) .... caplet
Captain (NTIO) .... Cpt
Captioned Media Program .... CMP
Capture the Flag (ADWA) .... CTF
Carat (NTIO) .... Ct
Carbine (ADWA) .... cbn
Carbo Ceramics [*NYSE symbol*] .... CRR
Carbohydrate (ADWA) .... carbo
Carbohydrate Deficient Glycoprotein Syndrome .... CDGS
Carbon Fraction (CARB) .... CF
Carbon Fraction of Above Ground Biomass (CARB) .... CFAGB
Carbon Released from Living Biomass (CARB) .... CRL
Carbon Stored (CARB) .... CS
Carcinoma (ADWA) .... ca
Cardiac Thoracic Intensive Care Unit .... CTICU
Cardiovascular Intensive Care Unit (NUJO) .... CVICU
Cardiovascular/Thoracic Surgery and Cardiology Assembly (ADWA) .... CSCA
Care at Home .... CAH
Care Of (NTIO) .... c/o
Care of the Body Surface (DIPS) .... COBS
Career Development and Outplacement Association (COBU) .... CDOA
Career-Limiting Maneuver (ADWA) .... CLM
Cargo Remaining on Board (RIMS) .... CROB
Caribbean Community (ADWA) .... Caricom
Carlanita Music [*Publisher*] .... CMC
Carolina Bird Club (ROAS) .... CBC
Carolina Brown Lung Association (ROAS) .... CBLA
Carpentry .... CARP
Carpentry (ADWA) .... carp
Carpeted (ADWA) .... cptd
Carport (ADWA) .... crpt
Carriage of Dangerous Goods by Rail Regulations (HEAS) .... CDG Rail
Carriage Return/Line Feed (ADWA) .... cr/lf
Carrier (ADWA) .... carr
Carry Back (ADWA) .... c/b
Carry Over (ADWA) .... c/o
Cartage (ADWA) .... ctge
Cartilage-Derived Morphogenic Proteins [*Medicine*] .... CDMP
Cartridge (ADWA) .... ctg

Cascading Style Sheets Level 1 ... CSS1
Case Tool for Knowledge Engineering (IDAI) ... CAKE
Cash Refund Notice (TRID) ... CRN
Cash Technologies [*AMEX symbol*] (SG) ... TQ
Cassette (ADWA) ... cas
Casting (ADWA) ... csg
Castle (ADWA) ... cas
Catalan (ADWA) ... Catal
Catalyst Bed Heater (ADWA) ... CBH
Catalyzed Electrochemical Oxidation (ABAC) ... CEO
Catapult (ADWA) ... cat
Cataract (ADWA) ... cat
Catastrophic Disaster Response Group (DEMM) ... CDRG
Catch You Later (ADWA) ... CUL
Catcher's Earned Run Average [*Baseball term*] (NDBD) ... CERA
Catecholamines (DIPS) ... CAs
Cathedral (NTIO) ... Cath
Catheter (ADWA) ... cath
Cathode (DIPS) ... Ca
Cathode (ADWA) ... cath
Catholic Women of the Chapel ... CWOC
Cathotic Annodic Filaments ... CAF
Caucasian (NTIO) ... cauc
Caudality (DIPS) ... CA
Caulking (ADWA) ... clkg
Causative (ADWA) ... caus
Cause-and-Effect Analysis (CARB) ... CEA
Caustic Slurry Waste (ABAC) ... CSW
Caveat (ADWA) ... cav
Cavity-Ringdown Spectrometer (CARB) ... CRS
Ceiling (ADWA) ... clg
Ceiling and Visibility [*Aviation*] (PIAV) ... CAVOK
Celebrity (ADWA) ... celeb
Celesta ... cel
Cell Broadcast Channel (CGWS) ... CBCH
Cell Crates ... celcrts
Cell for Voting (ADWA) ... CFV
Cell Pack ... Clpk
Cell Relay Function (MLOA) ... CRF
Cell-Based Array (AEBE) ... CBA
Cell-Loc, Inc. [*Alberta Stock Exchange*] ... CLQ
Cellsite on Wheels (ADWA) ... COW
Celltech Group ADS [*NYSE symbol*] (SG) ... CLL
Cellular (ADWA) ... cell
Cellular Anti-Fraud (CGWS) ... CAF
Cellular Message Information Block ... CMIB
Cellular Provider (CGWS) ... CP
Cellular Provider Equipment (CGWS) ... CPE
Cellular Subscriber Station (CGWS) ... CSS
Cellular Telephone-2nd Generation (CGWS) ... CT2
Celluloid (ADWA) ... cel
Celsion Corp. [*AMEX symbol*] ... CLN
Cement Manufacturers' Association (CARB) ... CMA
Cemetery Net (CCCA) ... CN
Cenozoic (NTIO) ... Cen
Centavo (ADWA) ... ctvo
Center Field [*Baseball term*] (NDBD) ... cf
Center for Advanced Aviation System Development (CTAS) ... CAASD
Center for Advanced Research on Language Research ... CARLA
Center for Astrophysics ... CfA
Center for Astrophysics [*Harvard-Smithsonian*] ... CFA
Center for Earth and Planetary Studies ... CEPS
Center for Global Environmental Studies (CARB) ... CGES
Center for Group Learning ... CGL
Center for Imaging and Pharmaceutical Research (ADWA) ... CIPR
Center for Inherited Disorders of Energy Metabolism (ADWA) ... CIDEM
Center for Innovative Learning Technologies ... CILT
Center for International Earth Sciences Information Network (ARMP) ... CIESIN
Center for International Economics (AUEG) ... CIE
Center for International Health Information (ADWA) ... CIHI
Center for Naval Research (CCCA) ... CNR
Center for Orthopaedic Research (ADWA) ... COR
Center for Research and Lessons Learned [*Army*] ... CENTRALL
Center for Scientific Review [*National Institutes of Health*] ... CSR
Center for Social Epidemiology (ADWA) ... CSE
Center for Subatomic Structure of Matter [*Australia*] ... CSSM
Center for the Advancement of Electronic Health Records (ADWA) ... CAEHR
Center for the Improvement of Student Learning ... CISL
Center for the Study of American Business ... CSAB
Center for the Study of Environmental Endocrine Effects (ADWA) ... CSEEE
Center for the Study of Extraterrestrial Intelligence ... CSETI
Center for the Study of Intelligence ... CSI
Center for Violence and Injury Control (ADWA) ... CVIC
Center Tank (RIMS) ... ce Ta
Center to Protect Workers' Rights (SARE) ... CPWR
Centerfold ... Cent
Centibar (ADWA) ... cb
Centigram (NTIO) ... cg
Centiliter (ADWA) ... cl
Centillium Communic. [*NASDAQ symbol*] ... CTLM
Centimo (ADWA) ... ctmo
Centipoise (ABAC) ... cP
Central (NTIO) ... cent
Central Arid Asia (CARB) ... CAA
Central Auditory Processing Disorder ... CAPD
Central Auditory Processing Disorder ... CAPD
Central Canada Broadcast Engineers (ROAS) ... CCBE
Central Computer and Telecommunications Authority (COBU) ... CCTA
Central Control Terminal (ROAS) ... CCT
Central Customer Manager ... CCM
Central Data Handling Facility (ADWA) ... CDHF
Central Data Processor (CCCA) ... CDP
Central Detector ... CD
Central Eastern Pacific Routes (PIPO) ... CEPAC
Central Facility (ARMP) ... CF
Central Index of Dose Information (HEAS) ... CIDI
Central Institute for Molecular Biology [*East Berlin*] ... CIMB
Central Issuing Facility [*Army*] ... CIF
Central Missouri Astronomical Association ... CMAA
Central Nervous System (DIPS) ... cns
Central Nevada Seismic Zone ... CNSZ
Central on Board Softwear (ADWA) ... COBS
Central Science Laboratory ... CSL
Central Standard Time (AUEG) ... CST
Central States Communication Association ... CSCA
Central Technical Operations (HLLA) ... CTO
Central Valley Trucks ... CV
Centralized Fault Display System (HLLA) ... CFDS
Centralized Maintenance and Administration Center ... CMAC
Centralized Message Distribution [*Computer science*] ... CMD
Centrally Planned Asia (CARB) ... CPA
Centre for Coastal & Marine Sciences ... CCMS
Centre for Earth Observation Science ... CEOS
Centre for Electrical Power Engineering [*Glasgow*] ... CEPE
Centre for Global Atmospheric Modelling ... CGAM
Centre for Land and Biological Resource Research [*Canada*] ... CLBRR
Centre of Gravity [*Aviation*] (PIAV) ... c of g
Centre of Pressure [*Aviation*] (PIAV) ... C of P
Centre on Addiction and Substance Abuse [*Columbia University*] ... CASA
Centre-Line [*Aviation*] (PIAV) ... C/L
Ceramic Ball Grid Array ... CBGA
Ceramic Chip Carrier ... CCC
Ceramics Industry Advisory Committee (HEAS) ... CERIAC
Cerebral Electrotherapy (DIPS) ... CET
Certainly (ADWA) ... cert
Certificate (ADWA) ... cert
Certificate (ADWA) ... ct
Certificate (NTIO) ... ctf
Certificate Authority ... CA
Certificate in English Language Teaching for Adults ... CELTA
Certificate in Social Work (ADWA) ... CSW
Certificate in the Teaching of English as a Foreign Language to Adults ... CTEFLA
Certificate of Airworthiness [*Aviation*] (PIAV) ... C of A
Certificate of Authenticity (ADWA) ... COA
Certificate of Experience [*Aviation*] (PIAV) ... C of E
Certificate of Origin (ADWA) ... C/O
Certificate of Public Convenience (CGWS) ... CPC
Certificate Trust Lists ... CTL
Certificated (ADWA) ... certif
Certificates (SG) ... Ctf
Certification of Electrical Equipment for Mining Advisory Council (HEAS) ... CEEMAC
Certification of Flight Readiness [*NASA*] (SPST) ... CoFR
Certification of Proposal ... COP
Certified (ADWA) ... ctf
Certified Addictions Registered Nurse (NUJO) ... CARN
Certified Ballasts Manufacturers [*An association*] ... CBM
Certified Breastfeeding Educator (NUJO) ... CBE
Certified Case Manager (NUJO) ... CCM
Certified Computer Programmer (ROAS) ... CCP
Certified Critical Care Registered Nurse (NUJO) ... CCRN
Certified Deposit (ROAS) ... CD
Certified Developmental Disabilities Nurse (NUJO) ... CDDN
Certified Disability Management Specialist (NUJO) ... CDMS
Certified Drug and Alcohol Counselor (NUJO) ... CDAC
Certified Employee Assistance Professional ... CEAP
Certified Enterostomal Therapy Nurse (NUJO) ... CETN
Certified Family Life Educator ... CFLE
Certified Fragrance Sales Specialist (ADWA) ... CFSS
Certified Gastroenterological Registered Nurse (NUJO) ... CGRN
Certified Health Education Specialist (ADWA) ... CHES
Certified Health Physicist (SARE) ... CHP
Certified Health Professional (SARE) ... CHP
Certified Hemodialysis Technician (NUJO) ... CHT
Certified Hospice and Palliative Care Nurse (NUJO) ... CHPN
Certified Insurance Rehabilitation Specialist (NUJO) ... CIRS
Certified Legal Nurse Consultant (NUJO) ... CLNC
Certified Licensed Evaluation Facility ... CLEF
Certified Life Care Planner (NUJO) ... CLCP
Certified Master Locksmith ... CML
Certified Medical Practice Executive (ADWA) ... CMPE
Certified Meeting Professional (TRID) ... CMP
Certified Nephrology Nurse (NUJO) ... CNN
Certified Niche Specialist (TRID) ... CNS
Certified Nutrition Support Dietitian (NUJO) ... CNSD
Certified Occupational Health Nurse (NUJO) ... COHN
Certified Occupational Health Nurse Specialist (NUJO) ... COHN-S
Certified Ophthalmic Assistant (NUJO) ... COA
Certified Ophthalmic Medical Technologist (NUJO) ... COMT

Certified Ophthalmic Technician (NUJO)	COT
Certified Pain Practitioner (NUJO)	CPP
Certified Pediatric Oncology Nurse (NUJO)	CPON
Certified Professional in Healthcare Quality (NUJO)	CPHQ
Certified Pulmonary Function Technician (NUJO)	CPFT
Certified Registered Nurse First Assistant (NUJO)	CRNFA
Certified Registered Nurse Hospice (NUJO)	CRNH
Certified Registered Nurse in Ophthalmology (NUJO)	CRNO
Certified Reporting Limit (ABAC)	CRL
Certified Specialist in Poison Information	CSPI
Certified Surgical Assistant (NUJO)	CSA
Certified Transplant Nurse (NUJO)	CTN
Certified Wound Care Nurse (NUJO)	CWCN
Cervical Spine (ADWA)	C-spine
Cervix (ADWA)	cx
Cesarean Section (ADWA)	cs
Cesarean Section (ADWA)	C-section
Cesium Demonstration Unit (ABAC)	CDU
Chained Schedule of Reinforcement (DIPS)	CHAIN
Chairperson (ADWA)	chpn
Chajnantor Observatory Sub-Millimeter International Collaboration	COSMIC
Chaldean (ADWA)	Chal
Chaldean (ADWA)	Chald
Chamber Pressure	Pc
Champion (ADWA)	Champ
Chancellor (NTIO)	Chanc
Change (ADWA)	chg
Change Group	CHGRP
Change Management Programme (HEAS)	CHAMP
Change Mode	CHMOD
Change Name To [Travel industry] (TRID)	CHNT
Change Over Point [Aviation] (PIPO)	COP
Change Owner	CHOWN
Change Record (TRID)	CR
Channel (NTIO)	Ch
Channel (ADWA)	Chan
Channel Check	CHCK
Channel Quality Measurement (CGWS)	CQM
Channel Queue Table (CCCA)	CQT
Channel Terminating Unit (CCCA)	CTU
Channel Tunnel Safety Authority (HEAS)	CTSA
Chaplain (ADWA)	Chap
Character Error Rate (CCCA)	CER
Characteristic (ADWA)	char
Chardonnay (ADWA)	chard
Charge Sensitive Amplifier	CSA
Charge Time-of-Flight (ADWA)	CTOF
Charged (ADWA)	chgd
Charged Coupled Device	CCD
Charged Liquid Cluster Beam (ROAS)	CLCB
Charles G. Chandler	CGC
Charles River Labs. [NYSE symbol]	CRL
Charm (ADWA)	C
Charted Visual Flight Procedure (PIPO)	CVFP
Charter [Travel industry] (TRID)	CHTR
Charter Yacht Brokers Association (TRID)	CYBA
Chartered Association of Certified Accountants (COBU)	ACCA
Chartered Psychologist	CPsychol
Chartered Quantity Surveying Association (COBU)	CQSA
Charterers' Option (RIMS)	CHOPT
Charting by Exception	CBE
Cheap Personal Computer (ADWA)	CPC
Cheapest to Deliver (ADWA)	CTD
Check Visit (HEAS)	CV
Checkmate (ADWA)	chm
Chemical and Biological Medical Treatment Symposia (ADWA)	CBMTS
Chemical Assessments and Related Activities (AUEG)	CARA
Chemical, Biological and Radiological Integrated Reconnaissance System [Army]	CBRIDS
Chemical, Biological, Protected Shelter	CBPS
Chemical Demilitarization Program [Army]	CDP
Chemical Engineering Laboratory (ABAC)	CEL
Chemical Field Emission Transistor (ABAC)	Chem-FET
Chemical Hazard Alert Notices (HEAS)	CHAN
Chemical Hazards Communications Society (HEAS)	CHCS
Chemical Hygiene Officer (SARE)	CHO
Chemical Industry Institute of Technology (SARE)	CIIT
Chemical Industry Scheme for Assistance in Freight (HEAS)	CHEMSAFE
Chemical Management System (ABAC)	CMS
Chemical Safety and Hazard Investigation Board	CSB
Chemical Stockpile Emergency Preparedness Program (ABAC)	CSEPP
Chemical Transport Model	CTM
Chemical Warfare Agent (ABAC)	CWA
Chemical Warning	CHEMWARN
Chemical Wavelength (CCCA)	CW
Chemical Wavelength Laser (CCCA)	CWL
Chemicals in Agriculture Advisory Group (HEAS)	CHEMAG
Chemistry (NTIO)	chem
Chemistry and Materials Science	C&MS
Chemistry Division (CARB)	CD
Chemotherapy (NTIO)	chemo
Chester Music [Publisher]	CH
Chicago (NTIO)	Chgo
Chicago (ADWA)	Chi
Chicago Board of Options Exchange (ROAS)	CBOE
Chief Financial Officers Council	CFOC
Chief Inspector of Agriculture (HEAS)	CIAg
Chief Inspector of Factories (HEAS)	CIF
Chief Inspector's Management Meeting (HEAS)	CIMM
Chief Inspector's Memo (HEAS)	CIM
Chief Inspector's Specialist Management Meeting (HEAS)	CISMM
Chief Privacy Officer	CPO
Child Abuse (DIPS)	CA
Child Exploitation and Obscenity Section	CEOS
Child Online Protection Act	COPA
Children's Cancer Research Group [England]	CCRG
Children's Environmental Health Network (ADWA)	CEHN
Children's Liver Alliance	CLA
Children's Memory Scale [M. Cohen] (DIPS)	CMS
Children's Online Privacy Protection Act	COPPA
Children's Safety Network (ADWA)	CSN
Child's Meal [Travel industry] (TRID)	CSML
Chilean National Committee for Pacific Economic Cooperation	CHILPEC
Chimes	chm
China, Burma, India (ADWA)	CBI
China National Committee for Pacific Economic Cooperation	CNCPEC
China National Petroleum Corp.	CNPC
China Unicom ADS [NYSE symbol]	CHU
Chinese Ecological Research Network (CARB)	CERN
Chinese Hamster Ovary	CHO
Chinese Institute of Electronics (CARB)	CIE
Chinese Society of Astronautics (CARB)	CSA
Chinese Taipei Pacific Economic Cooperation Committee	CTPECC
Chips per Second (CCCA)	CPS
Chiropractic Library Consortium (ADWA)	CLIBCON
Chlamydia Trachomatis [Medicine]	CT
Chlorinated Hydrocarbon Solvents	CHS
Chlorine	CL
Chlorine (ABAC)	Cl
Chloroform (ADWA)	chl
Cholesterol (ADWA)	chol
Choreographed By (ADWA)	chor
Chorionic Villus Sampling (ADWA)	CVS
Chris-Craft Industries	CCN
Chronic Freshwater Toxicity Level (ABAC)	CFWTL
Chronic Lyme Disease	CLD
Chronic Respiratory Questionnaire (ADWA)	CRQ
Chronological (ADWA)	chron
Chronological (ADWA)	chronol
Churn Analysis, Modeling, and Prediction (IDAI)	CHAMP
Climate Dynamics and Experimental Prediction (ARMP)	CDEP
Cimbalom	cimb
Cincinnati Bell Information Systems (ROAS)	CBIS
Cinematography (ADWA)	cinemat
Circle Trip [Travel industry] (TRID)	CT
Circle Trip Minimum [Travel industry] (TRID)	CTM
Circuit (NTIO)	cir
Circuit (ADWA)	circ
Circuit (ADWA)	ckt
Circuit Mode Voice	CMV
Circular Mail (NTIO)	cm
Circular Mil	cmil
Circular Minute (HEAS)	CM
Circulation (NTIO)	circ
Circumcised (ADWA)	c
Circumference (ADWA)	c
Circumference (NTIO)	circum
Circumstellar Imaging Telescope	CIT
Cirrus Test (CARB)	CIRT
Citizen (NTIO)	cit
Citizens Against Nuclear Trash [An association]	CANT
City Ticket Office [Travel industry] (TRID)	CTO
Civil Aviation Authorities (CTAS)	CAA
Civil Aviation Authority Flying Unit (PIAV)	CAAFU
Civil Aviation Notification Procedure (PIAV)	CANP
Civil Justice Quarterly [A publication]	CJQ
Civilian (NTIO)	civ
Civilian Personnel Advisory Center [Army]	CPAC
Civilian Personnel Management Services	CPMS
Cladding Hull Waste (ABAC)	CHW
Cladding Removal Waste (ABAC)	CRW
Claims Payable Abroad [Insurance] (MARI)	CPA
Clarinet	cl
Class (SG)	Cl
Class Interval (DIPS)	ci
Classification of Mental Disorders (DIPS)	CMD
Clause (MARI)	Cl
Clean (ADWA)	cln
Clean Air	CA
Clean Air Facility (CARB)	CAF
Clean Air Status and Trends Network	CASTNet
Clean Lakes Clearinghouse (AUEG)	CLC
Clearance Delivery [Aviation] (PIPO)	CD
Clearance Delivery (PIPO)	CLNCDEL
Cleared As Filed [Aviation] (PIPO)	CAF
ClearWorks.net, Inc. [AMEX symbol]	CLW
Cleft Palate Foundation (ADWA)	CPF
Clerkship Directors in Internal Medicine (ADWA)	CDIM
Click Commerce [NASDAQ symbol]	CKCM
Climate Applications Referral System (CARB)	CARS

Climate Modeling, Analysis, and Prediction Program (ARMP) ... CMAP
Climate Research Committee (CARB) ... CRC
Climate Research Institute [*Oklahoma State University*] (CARB) ... CRI
Climate Simulation Laboratory (ARMP) ... CSL
Climate Variability and Predictability (ARMP) ... CLIVAR
Climatic ... Clim
Clinic Without Walls (ADWA) ... CWW
Clinical (ADWA) ... clin
Clinical Administrative Data Service (ADWA) ... CADS
Clinical Bulletin of Myofascial Therapy [*A publication*] (ADWA) ... CBMT
Clinical Magnetic Resonance Society (ADWA) ... CMRS
Clinical Micro Sensors ... CMS
Clinical Microbiology Procedures Handbook [*A publication*] (ADWA) ... CMPH
Clinical Nurse Consultant (NUJO) ... CNC
Clinical Nutrition Certification Board (ADWA) ... CNCB
Clinical Orthopaedics and Related Research (ADWA) ... CORR
Clinical Pathway Database (ADWA) ... CPDB
Clinical Research Unit for Anxiety Disorders (ADWA) ... CRUFAD
Clinical Trials Office [*Medicine*] ... CTO
Clinical Trials Supplies ... CTS
Clockwise (ADWA) ... ckw
Clomiphene Challenge Test (ADWA) ... CCT
Clomiphene Citrate Challenge Test (ADWA) ... CCCT
Close Combat Leadership Exercise [*Military*] ... CCLEx
Close Combat Optics ... CCO
Closed Loop Television Camera (SPST) ... CTVC
Closet (ADWA) ... CLST
Closing of Business London (RIMS) ... COBLDN
Cloud Base Height (ARMP) ... CBH
Cloud Cover Radiometer (ADWA) ... CCR
Cloud Detection Lidar (ARMP) ... CDL
Cloud Drop Number Concentration (CARB) ... CDNC
Cloud Ensemble Model (ARMP) ... CEM
Cloud Layer Experiment (ARMP) ... CLEX
Cloud Photopolarimeter (CARB) ... CPP
Cloud Profiling Radar System (ARMP) ... CPRS
Clouds, Storms, and Regional Meteorology ... CSRM
Cloudscope (ARMP) ... CS
Cloud-Topped Boundary Layer (ARMP) ... CTBL
Cloudy (ADWA) ... cldy
Cluster Environmental Protection Specialist (SARE) ... CEPS
CNN Financial News ... CNNFn
Coal Energy Research Committee ... CERC
Coal India Limited (CARB) ... CIL
Coal Industry National Consultative Council (HEAS) ... CINCC
Coalition for Energy Efficiency and Renewable Technologies ... CEERT
Coalition for Travel Industry Parity (TRID) ... CTIP
Coarse Sun Pointing Attitude Anomaly Detection (ADWA) ... CSPAAD
Coastal Building Zone (DEMM) ... CBZ
Coastal Change Analysis Program (ROAS) ... CCAP
Coastal Construction Control Line (DEMM) ... CCCL
Coastal Coordination Council [*Texas*] ... CCC
Coastal High Hazard Area (DEMM) ... CHHA
Coasting Drive ... CD
Coaxial Cable (ADWA) ... coax
Cochrane Controlled Trials Register (ADWA) ... CCTR
Cockpit Display System ... CDS
Code Division Multiple Access Development Group (CGWS) ... CDG
Code Violations (ADWA) ... CV
Code Walk-Through (CTAS) ... CWT
Coded Block Pattern (ROAS) ... CBP
Coefficient (ADWA) ... coef
Coefficient (ADWA) ... coeff
Coefficient Association (DIPS) ... CA
Coefficient of Concordance (DIPS) ... W
Coefficient of Contingency (DIPS) ... C
Coefficient of Mean Square Contingency (DIPS) ... C
Coefficient of Multiple Determination (DIPS) ... R2
Coefficient of Nondetermination (DIPS) ... K2
Coefficient of Stability (DIPS) ... W
Cognate (ADWA) ... cog
Cognitive Processing Therapy (DIPS) ... CPT
Coherent Digital Exciter (ADWA) ... CoDE
Coin-Operated (ADWA) ... coin-op
Cold Crucible Melter (ABAC) ... CCM
Collaboration Planning Forecasting Replenishment ... CPFR
Collaborative Arrival Planning (CTAS) ... CAP
Collaborative Longitudinal Evaluation of Keratoconus (ADWA) ... CLEK
Collaborative Solar-Terrestrial Research (ADWA) ... COSTR
Collateral (ADWA) ... collat
Collective Protection Shelter [*Army*] ... CPS
Collective Routing Indicator (CCCA) ... CRI
Collector's Edition ... Coll Ed
College Admission Test (DIPS) ... CAT
College and University Affiliations Program ... CUAP
College Entry Examination Board (ADWA) ... CEEB
College Student Experinces Questionnaire ... CSEQ
College World Series [*Baseball*] (NDBD) ... CWS
College-Level and State Services ... CLSS
CollegeLink.com, Inc. [*AMEX symbol*] (SG) ... APS
Collegiate Pacific [*AMEX symbol*] ... BOO
Colliery Information System (HEAS) ... CIS
Collision and Contamination Avoidance Maneuver (ADWA) ... CCAM
Colloquial (NTIO) ... colloq
Cologarithm (ADWA) ... colog
Colombia (NTIO) ... Col
Colombia National Committee for Pacific Economic Cooperation ... COLPECC
Colonial ... CL
Colonial (ADWA) ... Col
Colonial Police Meritorious Service Medal [*British*] ... CPMSM
Colony (NTIO) ... col
Color Display (ROAS) ... CD
Color Graphics Workstation ... CGW
Color Response [*Used in Rorschach tests*] (DIPS) ... C
Colorado Association of Research Libraries (AUEG) ... CARL
Colorado Educational Media Association ... CEMA
Colorado Springs Mineralogical Society ... CSMS
Coloratura ... col
Coloring Book ... clrb
Colossal ... Col
Columbia Law Review [*A publication*] ... Col LR
Columbia River Comprehensive Impact Assessment (ABAC) ... CRCIA
Column Grid Array ... CGA
Column Volume (ABAC) ... cv
Columnar Water Vapor (ARMP) ... CWV
Comarco ... CMRO
Combat Infantry Badge [*Army*] ... CIB
Combat Lifesaver [*Army*] ... CLS
Combat Stress Control [*Army*] ... CSC
Combination Job Analysis Method (DIPS) ... C-JAM
Combined (NTIO) ... comb
Combined Cycle (CARB) ... CC
Combined Main Distributing Frame ... CMDF
Combined Paging and Access (CGWS) ... CPA
Combined Sensor Program (ARMP) ... CSP
Combined Sewer System (ADWA) ... CSS
Combined Transcortical Aphasia (DIPS) ... CTA
Combining (ADWA) ... comb
Combustion (ADWA) ... com
Combustion Efficiency (CARB) ... CE
Comedy Central (ADWA) ... COM
Comet Nucleus Sample Return ... CNSR
Comet Nucleus Tour [*NASA's study of photochemical processes in comet comas*] ... CONTOUR
Comfortable Interpersonal Distance Scale (DIPS) ... CIDS
Command (ADWA) ... cmd
Command & Control (CCCA) ... CC
Command and Control Warfare (ADWA) ... CCW
Command Control & Communications (CCCA) ... CCC
Command, Control, Communications, Computers, Intelligence, Surveillance, and Reconnaissance [*Military*] ... C4ISR
Command Link Control Word (ADWA) ... CLCW
Command List [*Computer science*] (ITCA) ... CLIST
Command Management Systems Engineer (ADWA) ... CMSE
Command Post Modern Processor (CCCA) ... CPMF
Command Selection List [*Army*] ... CSL
Commander (ADWA) ... comb
Commander Carrier (CCCA) ... COMC
Commander Naval Air, Atlantic ... ComNavAirLant
Commander Naval Task Force (CCCA) ... CNTF
Commander-in-Chief Aerospace Defense Command (CCCA) ... CINCAD
Commander-in-Chief, Atlantic Command (DEMM) ... CINCLANT
Commanding (ADWA) ... cdg
Commanding (ADWA) ... cmdg
Commerce (NTIO) ... comm
Commercial ... com
Commercial (ADWA) ... comm
Commercial Asset Funding Company ... CAFCO
Commercial Generic Bioprocessing Apparatus (SPST) ... CGBA
Commercial Industrial Trade Receivables ... CIESCO
Commercial Interest Reference Rate (RIMS) ... CIRR
Commercial Internet Exchange ... CIE
Commercial Mail Relay ... CMR
Commercial Materials Processing Laboratory (SPST) ... CMPL
Commercial Satellite Terminal (CCCA) ... CST
Commercial Spent Fuel Management (ABAC) ... CSFM
Commercial Waste Management Statement (ABAC) ... CWMS
Commercialization Model for Environmental Technologies (ABAC) ... ComMet
Commission on Ecology (AUEG) ... COE
Commission on Narcotic Drugs (ADWA) ... CND
Commission on New Minerals and Mineral Names [*Mineralogical Association*] ... CNMMN
Commission on Student Learning ... CSL
Commissioned Research ... CR
Commissioner (ADWA) ... Comr
Committee for Electrical Equipment for Use in Flammable Atmospheres (HEAS) ... CEFFA
Committee for Library Advocacy and Student Success ... CLASS
Committee for the Advancement of Professional Practice (DIPS) ... CAPP
Committee for the Elimination of Racial Discrimination ... CERD
Committee of Ten Thousand (ADWA) ... COTT
Committee on Science and Technology in Developing Countries (ADWA) ... COSTED
Committee on Special Education ... CSE
Committee on the Status of Women in the Profession ... CSWP
Commodity Classification Automated Tracking System ... CCATS
Commodore (ADWA) ... commo
Common (SG) ... Com
Common Aviation Weather Sub-System (PIPO) ... CAWS
Common Channel Signaling System No. 7 (CGWS) ... C7

Common Channel Signaling System Number 7 (CGWS) CCS7
Common Control Channel (CGWS) .... CCH
Common Display System (HLLA) .... CDS
Common Equipment Card [*Telecommunications*] (MLOA) .... CEC
Common Equipment Voltage Indicator .... CEVI
Common Flash-Memory Interface .... CFI
Common Market (ADWA) .... CM
Common Missile Approach Warning System (ADWA) .... CMAWS
Common Missile Warning System (ADWA) .... CMWS
Common Occupational Classification System (ABAC) .... COCS
Common Toxicity Criteria [*Medicine*] .... CTC
Common User Installation Transport Network .... CUITN
Commonwealth (ADWA) .... Com
Commonwealth Law Reports [*A publication*] .... CLR
Commonwealth of Independent Republics .... CIR
Communicable Disease Report (HEAS) .... CDR
Communication (NTIO) .... com
Communication Apprehension .... CA
Communication Arts .... CA
Communication Deviance (DIPS) .... CD
Communications (PIPO) .... COMM
Communications Access Processor (CCCA) .... CAP
Communications and Data Processing Exhibition (ADWA) .... Comdex
Communications Control and Management Processor .... CCMP
Communications Electronics Security Department (HEAS) .... CESD
Communications Improvement Plan (CCCA) .... CIP
Communications Maintenance Terminal .... CMT
Communications Operating Requirement (CCCA) .... COR
Communications Outage Recorder [*NASA*] (SPST) .... COR
Communications Output Processor (CCCA) .... COP
Communications Satellite Corporation (ITCA) .... COMSTAT
Communications Selector Switch (CCCA) .... CSS
Communications Signal Processor (CCCA) .... CSP
Communications Society (CCCA) .... COMSOC
Communications Technology Laboratory (CCCA) .... CTL
Communist (NTIO) .... com
Community (ADWA) .... Comm
Community Assistance Consultant (DEMM) .... CAC
Community Assistance Visit (DEMM) .... CAV
Community Breast Health Project (ADWA) .... CBHP
Community Education .... CE
Community Emergency Exposure Level (SARE) .... CEEL
Community Health Accreditation Program (ADWA) .... CHAP
Community Health Information Network .... CHIN
Community Health Information Partnerships (ADWA) .... CHIP
Community Health Information Technology Alliance (ADWA) .... CHITA
Community Health Management Information Systems (ADWA) .... CHMIS
Community Health Nurse (NUJO) .... CHN
Community Integrated Service Systems (ADWA) .... CISS
Community Oriented Intelligence Network System (CCCA) .... COINS
Community Outreach Program (DIPS) .... COP
Community Program Administrator (DEMM) .... CPA
Community Research Project .... CRP
Community Wholistic Health Center (ADWA) .... CWHC
Comp Vale do Rio Doca ADS [*NYSE symbol*] .... RIOPr
Compact Car (TRID) .... CCAR
Compact Disc Interactive (AEBE) .... CD-I
Compact Disk-Extended Architecture (ROAS) .... CD-XA
Compact Disk-Read Only Memory Data Exchange Standard (ROAS) .... CD-RDx
Compact Disk-Read or Write .... CD-RW
Compact Muon Solenoid .... CMS
Company (NTIO) .... co
Comparative (ADWA) .... comp
Comparative (ADWA) .... compar
Comparison Level (DIPS) CL
Comparison Level for Alternatives (DIPS) .... CLAlt
Comparison Stimulus (DIPS) .... Co
Compartment (ADWA) .... compt
Compass Diagnostic Test of Arithmetic (DIPS) .... CDTA
Compatibility Modification Inference (IDAI) .... CMI
Compensation (NTIO) .... comp
Competitive Impulse, Non-Carcinogenic Hypergol .... CINCH
Competitive Long Distance Coalition .... CLDC
Comple Tel Europe NV [*NASDAQ symbol*] (SG) .... CLTL
Complement (ADWA) .... compl
Complementary Heterostructure Field Effect Transistor (ADWA) .... C-HFET
Complementary Ribonucleic Acid (ADWA) .... cRNA
Complete (NTIO) .... comp
Complete (ADWA) .... cpl
Complete Health and Safety Evaluation Scheme (HEAS) .... CHASE
Complex Node Representation .... CNR
Complex Programmable Logic Device (AEBE) .... CPLD
Complexant Concentrate (ABAC) CC
Compliance Cost Assessments (HEAS) .... CCA
Composite Observing System for the North Atlantic (ADWA) .... COSNA
Composite Variability Study (ABAC) .... CVS
Composition (ADWA) .... comp
Composition Material (ADWA) .... compo
Compositional Rule of Inference (IDAI) .... CRI
Compound (ADWA) .... cpd
Comprehensive Aerological Reference Data Set (ARMP) .... CARDS
Comprehensive Capitol Complex Security Plan (DEMM) .... CCCSP
Comprehensive Emergency Assistance System .... CEAS
Comprehensive Emergency Management Plan (DEMM) .... CEMP
Comprehensive Epidemiologic Data Resource (ADWA) .... CEDR

Comprehensive Integrated Planning Process (ABAC) .... CIPP
Comprehensive Loss Management, Inc., of Minneapolis (SARE) .... CLMI
Comprehensive Risk Evaluation and Management (ABAC) .... CREAM
Comprehensive Spending Review .... CSR
Comprehensive Supra Thermal and Energetic Particle (ADWA) CO3TEP
Comprehensive Test Ban Treaty (AUEG) .... CTBT
Compressor-Expander (ADWA) .... compander
Compromised Container Caps [*Jerry Mason, 1995*] (SARE) CCC
Compute (ADWA) .... cmpt
Computer Aided Planning System (HEAS) .... CAPS
Computer Assisted New Drug Application [*Food and Drug Administration*] .... CANDA
Computer Bulletin Board System .... CBBS
Computer Control Center CCC
Computer, Electronics, and Networking Technology .... CENT
Computer Graphics World .... CGW
Computer Law & Security Report [*A publication*] .... CLSR
Computer Management and Development Services .... CMDS
Computer Program Functional Specification (CTAS) .... CPFS
Computer Security Officials (ADWA) .... CSO
Computer UFO Network .... CUFON
Computer-Aided Data Retrieval and Evaluation Software (AUEG) .... CADRE
Computer-Aided Design and Computer-Aided Manufacture (NTIO) .... CAD-CAM
Computer-Aided Engineering Network (ADWA) .... CAEN
Computer-Aided Manufacture (NTIO) .... CAM
Computer-Aided Testing and Implementation (ITCA) .... CATI
Computerized Needs-Oriented Quality Measurement Evaluation System (ADWA) .... CONQUEST
Concentration (ADWA) .... concn
Concentrator and Feed Make-Up-Tank (ABAC) .... CFMT
Concentrator Group Number .... CGN
Concept Integration and Verification Laboratory [*NASA*] (SPST) CIVL
Conceptual Design (ABAC) .... CD
Conceptual Design and Cost Review (CARB) .... CDCR
Conceptual Design Plan (ABAC) .... CDP
Conceptual Design Report (ABAC) .... CDR
Conceptual Design Review (ABAC) .... CDR
Conceptual Knowledge Markup Language (IDAI) .... CKML
Concerning (ADWA) .... conc
Concerto (ADWA) .... con
Concerto .... Conc
Concerto (ADWA) .... cto
Conclusion (NTIO) .... con
Conclusion (ADWA) .... concl
Concurrent Disk Operating System (ROAS) .... CDOS
Concurrent Product Development .... CPD
Concurrent Schedule of Reinforcement (DIPS) .... CONC
Concurrent Semiconductor Production and Equipment Development .... CSPED
Condensation Trail (ADWA) .... contrail
Condenser (ADWA) .... cond
Condition Assessment Programme (RIMS) .... CAP
Conditioned Reflex (DIPS) .... RC
Conditioned Stimulus (DIPS) .... SC
Condominium Travel Associates (TRID) .... CTA
Conduct Disorder (DIPS) .... CD
Conduct of Operations (SARE) .... COO
Conducted Electromagnetic Interference .... CEI
Conduction Time (DIPS) .... CT
Conductor (NTIO) .... Cond
Cone of Influence (ADWA) .... COI
Cone Penetrometer (ABAC) .... CPT
Confabulation (ADWA) .... confab
Confederate (NTIO) .... Confed
Confederation (ADWA) .... confed
Conference Control Protocol (CCCA) .... CCP
Conference Control Unit (CCCA) .... CCU
Conference Director (CCCA) .... CD
Conference Order Wire (CCCA) .... COW
Confidence (NTIO) .... con
Confidence Game (ADWA) .... con
Confidence Game (ADWA) .... con game
Confidence Man (ADWA) .... con man
Confidential (ADWA) .... conf
Configurable Logic Block (AEBE) .... CLB
Configuration (ADWA) .... config
Configuration Coordinate Diagram .... CCD
Configuration Engineering Office (SPST) .... CEO
Configuration Management Board .... CMB
Configuration Management Facility (CTAS) .... CMF
Configuration Management Information System .... CMIS
Configuration Management Organization (CTAS) .... CMO
Confirmed (TRID) .... CFMD
Conga .... cga
Congenital Hip Dysplasia .... CHD
Congo (NTIO) .... Con
Congregation .... cong
Congregational (NTIO) .... cong
Congressionally Directed Medical Research Programs .... CDMRP
Conjunctive (ADWA) .... conj
Conjunctive Normal Form (IDAI) .... CNF
Conjunctive Schedule of Reinforcement (DIPS) .... CONJ
Connecticut Educational Media Association .... CEMA
Connecticut Educators Computer Association .... CECA
Connotation (ADWA) .... conn
Conscious (DIPS) .... Cs

By Meaning

ConSeal Private Desktop ... CPD
Consecutive (ADWA) ... consec
Consequence Management (DEMM) ... CoM
Consequential Loss Committee [*Insurance*] (MARI) ... CLC
Conservation Authority [*Canada*] ... CA
Conservation Reserve Enhancement Program [*Michigan*] ... CREP
Conservative (ADWA) ... Cons
Consigned (ADWA) ... cons
Consistent With (ADWA) ... c/w
Consolidated Communications Facilities [*NASA*] (SPST) ... CCF
Consolidated Operating Base (CCCA) ... COB
Consolidated Satellite Operations Center (CCCA) ... CSOC
Consolidated Satellite Test Center (ADWA) ... CSTC
Consolidated Space Test Center ... CSTC
Consolidated Theater Target Services [*Military*] ... CTTS
Consonant (NTIO) ... cons
Consortium of North American Veterinary Interactive New Concept Education (ADWA) ... CONVINCE
Consortium Research on Indicators of System Performance (ADWA) ... CRISP
Constable (NTIO) ... Cons
Constable (ADWA) ... const
Constant Air Volume (SARE) ... CAV
Constant Level Signalling (CCCA) ... CLS
Constant-Speed [*Propeller*] (PIAV) ... CS
Constitution (NTIO) ... cons
Constitution (ADWA) ... Const
Constraint Based Diagnostic System (ROAS) ... CBDS
Constructed (NTIO) ... cons
Construction Central Operations Unit (HEAS) ... CCOU
Construction Design and Management (HEAS) ... CDM
Construction Design and Management Regulations (HEAS) ... CONDAM
Construction Forces (ABAC) ... CF
Construction Health and Safety Group (HEAS) ... CHSG
Construction Industry Advisory Committee (HEAS) ... CONIAC
Consul (ADWA) ... cos
Consultation Distance (HEAS) ... CD
Consultation Zone (HEAS) ... CZ
Consultative Board for Diver Training (HEAS) ... CBDT
Consultative Document (HEAS) ... CD
Consumer Electronics Show ... CES
Consumer Health Information (ADWA) ... CHI
Consumer Information Catalog (AUEG) ... CIC
Consumer Safety Inspector [*Food and Drug Administration*] ... CSI
Consumer Safety Officer [*Food and Drug Administration*] ... CSO
Consumer-to-Consumer ... C2C
Contact's Business Phone (TRID) ... CTCB
Contact's Home Phone (TRID) ... CTCH
Container Vessel (TRID) ... CV
Containers ... cntrs
Containing (ADWA) ... contg
Contaminated Surface Soil (ABAC) ... CSS
Contemporary (NTIO) ... contemp
Contemptuous (ADWA) ... contempt
Content Vectoring Protocol ... CVP
Content-Based Retrieval ... CBR
Continent (ADWA) ... cont
Continental Stratus Archive (ARMP) ... CSA
Continental United States Army (DEMM) ... CONUSA
Contingency Coefficient (DIPS) ... C
Continuation (ADWA) ... contn
Continue With [*Medicine*] ... C/W
Continuing Medical Education Information Services (ADWA) ... CMEIS
Continuing Nursing Education (ADWA) ... CNE
Continuity of Operations (CCCA) ... COO
Continuous Hyperfractionated Accelerated Radiotherapy (ADWA) ... CHART
Continuous Improvement Team ... CIT
Continuous Schedule of Reinforcement (DIPS) ... CRF
Continuous Veno-Veno Hemodialysis (NUJO) ... CVVHD
Continuous Veno-Venous Hemofiltration (NUJO) ... CVVH
Continuously Operating per Fluorocarbon Sniffer (CARB) ... COPS
Contrabass Clarinet ... cbcl
Contrabassoon ... cbn
Contract ... CNT
Contract (ADWA) ... contr
Contract Direction (SPST) ... CD
Contract of Affreightment Charter Party (RIMS) ... COACP
Contractions (ADWA) ... Ctx
Contractor and Government Entity Code ... CAGE
Contractor Depot Logistics Support (CTAS) ... CDLS
Contractor Maintenance and Logistics Support (CTAS) ... CMLS
Contractor's Current Fiscal Year (ROAS) ... CCFY
Contract-Research Organisations ... CROS
Contributing (NTIO) ... contrib
Contribution-Based Compensation and Appraisal System [*Army*] ... CCAS
Control (ADWA) ... ctrl
Control and Switching Element (CCCA) ... CSE
Control Architecture (SPST) ... CA
Control Bus (SPST) ... CB
Control Center Operations Manager (ADWA) ... CCOM
Control Center Systems Manager (ADWA) ... CCSM
Control Interval [*Computer science*] (ITCA) ... CI
Control of Asbestos at Work Regulations (HEAS) ... CAWR
Control of Communicable Diseases in Man (ADWA) ... CCDM
Control of Electromagnetic Radiation (NTIO) ... Conelrad
Control of Industrial Major Accident Hazards Regulations (HEAS) ... CIMAH
Control of Major Accident Hazards (HEAS) ... COMAH
Control of Work in Confined Spaces (HEAS) ... CWCS
Controlled Ecological Life Support System ... CELSS
Controlled Manual (ABAC) ... CM
Controlled Vortex Combustion Chamber (ROAS) ... CVCC
Controller (ADWA) ... Contr
Convective Inhibition (ARMP) ... CIN
Convective Precipitation Over Land (ARMP) ... CL
Convective Precipitation Over Water (ARMP) ... CW
Convention (NTIO) ... conv
Convention and Visitors Bureau (TRID) ... CVB
Convention of Scottish Local Authorities ... CoSLA
Conventional ... CO
Conventional Core-Barrel Sampling (ABAC) ... CCBS
Conventual (ADWA) ... Conv
Convert (ADWA) ... cnvt
Convertible (ADWA) ... CNVRT
Convertible (ADWA) ... CNVRTBL
Convertible (ADWA) ... cv
Convertible (ADWA) ... cvt
Conveyancer, Conveyancer & Property Lawyer [*A publication*] ... Conv
Convocation (ADWA) ... conv
Convulsant Antidote for Nerve Agent ... CANA
Cookbook ... ckb
Cooled (ADWA) ... cld
Cooperative (ADWA) ... co-op
Cooperative (NTIO) ... Co-op
Cooperative Agreement Notice ... CAN
Cooperative Astrophysics and Technology Satellite [*Sponsored by the University of New Hampshire*] ... CATsat
Cooperative Compliance Program (SARE) ... CCP
Cooperative Engagement Capability [*Military*] ... CEC
Cooperative Robot (ADWA) ... cobot
Coordinate (ADWA) ... coord
Coordinated Interagency Partnership Regulating International Students ... CIPRIS
Co-Ordinating Committee on Health Aspects of Radiation Research (HEAS) ... CCHARR
Coordinating Group ... CG
Coordination Group for Meteorological Satellites (ADWA) ... CGMS
Co-Ordinator of Health Education (HEAS) ... CHE
Coping Strategies Questionnaire (DIPS) ... CSQ
Coptic (ADWA) ... Cop
Copy (ADWA) ... cop
Copyright (ADWA) ... c
Copyright Licensing Agency Rapid Clearance Service ... CLARCS
Cordless Telephone-1st Generation (CGWS) ... CT1
Core and Payload Control Centers [*NASA*] (SPST) ... C&PCC
Corinthian Colleges [*NASDAQ symbol*] (SG) ... COCO
Cornell Institute for Research in Chemical Ecology ... CIRCE
Cornerstone Internet Solutions ... CNRS
Cornet ... cnt
Cornet (ADWA) ... cor
Cornwall (ADWA) ... Corn
Corollary (ADWA) ... corol
Corollary (NTIO) ... coroll
Coronary Artery Bypass Grafting [*Medicine*] ... CABG
Corporal (ADWA) ... Corp
Corporal (ADWA) ... Corpl
Corporate Asset Funding Unit ... CAF
Corporate Bureaucrat (ADWA) ... corprcrat
Corporate Hospitality Association (COBU) ... CHA
Corporate Travel Department (TRID) ... CTD
Corporation (NTIO) ... corp
Correct Me If I'm Wrong (ADWA) ... CMIIW
Corrective Action Reporting System (AUEG) ... CARS
Correlative (ADWA) ... correl
Correspondence (ADWA) ... corresp
Corrugated (ADWA) ... corr
Corrugated Asbestos ... CA
Corruption (ADWA) ... corrupt
CORUS Entertainment 'B' [*NYSE symbol*] ... CJR
Cosecant (ADWA) ... cosec
Cosecant (NTIO) ... csc
Cosine (ABAC) ... cos
Cosmic Hot Interstellar Plasma Spectrometer [*Developed to study a gas cloud surrounding the solar system*] ... CHIPS
Cosmic X-Ray Background Radiation ... CXBR
Cost Accounting Work Plan (ABAC) ... CAWP
Cost Benefit Analysis (ROAS) ... CBA
Cost of Ownership Luminator ... COOL
Cost/Quality Management Assessment (ABAC) ... CQMA
Cost-of-Living Adjustment (NTIO) ... cola
Cotangent (NTIO) ... cot
Cotangent (ADWA) ... ctn
Cottage [*Travel industry*] (TRID) ... cot
Cottage ... CT
Cotton and Allied Textiles Industry Advisory Committee (HEAS) ... CATIAC
Council for Higher Education Accreditation ... CHEA
Council for National Research Initiatives ... CNRI
Council of Emergency Medicine Residency Directors (ADWA) ... CORD
Council of Musculoskeletal Specialty Societies (ADWA) ... COMSS
Council on Vocational Education ... COVE
Counsel (ADWA) ... coun
Count (NTIO) ... Ct

Counter Force/Counter Value (CCCA) .... CF/CV
Counter Rotating [*Aviation*] (PIPO) .... C/R
Counter Value (CCCA) CV
Counterclockwise (NTIO) .... cckw
Oounterpoint (ADWA) .... cpt
Countersink (ADWA) .... csk
Countertenor .... Ct
Country Damage (MARI) .... C/D
Country of Commencement [*Travel industry*] (TRID) ..... COC
Country Western (ADWA) .... C/W
Counts per Minute (ABAC) .... cpm
County (ADWA) .... Co
County (ADWA) .... Cty
County (ADWA) .... Cy
County Designated Mental Health Professional (ROAS) .... CDMHP
County Education Authority .... CEA
County Emergency Operations Center (DEMM) .... CEOC
County Public Health Unit (DEMM) .... CPHU
County Situation Report [*Department of Emergency Management*]
  (DEMM) .... Co-SITREP
County Solid Waste Management Plan [*California*] (SARE) .... CSWMP
County Warning Area [*Department of Emergency Management*] (DEMM) ...... CWA
Coupled Ocean-Atmosphere Processes and their Effect on Climate ...... COAPEC
Coupon (ADWA) .... cp
Course Heading [*Aviation*] (PIPO) .... CH
Course of Action Analysis [*Military*] .... COAA
Court (ADWA) .... crt
Court of Honor [*Boy Scouts of America*] .... COH
Covenants, Conditions, and Restrictions (ROAS) .... CCR
Cover (ADWA) .... cvr
Crane (RIMS) .... Cr
Cranial Nerve (DIPS) .... N
Crate .... crt
Cray Fish Co. ADS [*NASDAQ symbol*] (SG) .... CRFH
Creatine Kinase Myocardial Band .... CK-MB
Creating a More Efficient Office (HEAS) .... CAMEO
Creators' Copyright Coalition CCC
Credentials Verification Organization (ADWA) .... CVO
Credit (NTIO) .... cr
Credit Card Return Notice (TRID) .... CCRN
Credit Note (ADWA) .... C/N
Creek (NTIO) .... Cr
Creek (ADWA) .... cr
Crepitation (ADWA) .... crep
Crew and Equipment Translation Techniques and Routing [*NASA*]
  (SPST) .... CETTR
Crew Loads Instrumental Panel [*NASA*] (SPST) .... CLIP
Crew Requirements Data Base [*NASA*] (SPST) .... CRDB
Crime Control CC
Criminal (ADWA) .... crim
Criminal Law Quarterly [*A publication*] .... Crim LQ
Criminal Law Review [*A publication*] .... Crim LR
Criminologist (ADWA) .... criminol
Crisis Management (DEMM) .... CrM
Critic (NTIO) .... crit
Critical Care Nurse (NUJO) .... CCN
Critical Flicker Frequency (DIPS) .... cff
Critical Incident Debriefing for General Aviation Pilots ...... CIDGAP
Critical Incident Detection (HEAS) .... CID
Critical Infrastructure Assurance Office .... CIAO
Critical Infrastructure Protection (DEMM) .... CIP
Critical Line Item (CCCA) CLI
Critical Micelle Concentration (ADWA) .... cmc
Critical Oxygen Index (HEAS) .... COI
Critically Alarm Annunciators (ABAC) .... CAA
Criticism (NTIO) .... crit
Criticized (ADWA) .... crit
Croatian (ADWA) .... Croat
Crocodile (ADWA) .... croc
Crop Reserve Program (ADWA) .... CRP
Cross Connect (MLOA) XC
Crossing Restrictions (CTAS) .... CR
Cross-Linked Fibrin Degradation Products (DAVI) ...... XLFDP
Crosswind (HLLA) .... X/WIND

Crown Office Digest [*A publication*] .... COD
Crown-Heel Length (ADWA) .... CHL
Crustal Dynamics Data Information System (ARMP) ...... CDDIS
Crying My Eyes Out [*Online dialog*] .... CMEO
Cryogen Tank (SPST) .... CRYT
Cryogenic Infrared Radiance Instrument for Shuttle [*NASA*] ...... CIRRIS
Crypto Interface Unit (CCCA) .... CIU
Cryptograph Ancillary Unit (CCCA) .... CAU
Cryptographic Net Control Station (CCCA) .... CNCS
Cryptographic Unit (CCCA) .... CU
Cryptography (ADWA) .... crypto
CT Communications [*NASDAQ symbol*] (SG) .... CTCI
Cubic (NTIO) c
Cubic Feet (RIMS) .... CBFT
Cubic Feet per Day (ADWA) .... cfd
Cubic Feet per Minute (ABAC) .... cfm
Cubic Feet per Second per Square Mile (ADWA) .... cfsm
Cubicle (ADWA) .... cube
Culinary (ADWA) .... cul
Culminating Demonstration .... CD
Cultural Practices (ADWA) .... CP
Culture (ADWA) .... cult
Culture-Fair Intelligence Test (DIPS) .... CFIT
Culture-Free Intelligence Test (DIPS) .... CFIT
Cumbria (ADWA) .... Cumb
Cumulative (SG) .... cm
Cumulative (ADWA) .... cum
Cumulative Discounted Cash Flow .... CDCF
Cumulative Probability Density Function (CCCA) .... CPDF
Cumulus (ADWA) .... Cu
Cumulus Kinetic Energy (CARB) .... CKE
Currency (NTIO) .... cur
Currency (ADWA) .... curr
Currency Forwards Contract .... CFC
Current Acid Waste (ABAC) .... CAW
Current Bibliographies in Medicine [*A publication*] (ADWA) ...... CBM
Current Injection Test (CCCA) .... CIT
Current Law [*A publication*] CL
Current Law Year Book [*A publication*] .... CLYB
Current Legal Information [*A publication*] CLI
Current Legal Problems [*A publication*] .... CLP
Current Model Logic .... CML
Curriculum (ADWA) .... curric
Custodian (ADWA) .... cust
Custom Defense Package .... CDP
Custom Finished .... C/F
Custom Painted .... C/P
Customer Care Consultant (ROAS) CCC
Customer Furnished Equipment .... CFE
Customer Relationship Management .... CRM
Customer Service Administration Control Center (ROAS) ...... CSACC
Customer Service Unit/Data Service Unit [*Computer science*] (ITCA) ... CSU/DSU
Customer Support Room (SPST) .... CSR
Customer Waste Solidification Facility (ABAC) .... CWSF
Cyanide (ABAC) .... CN
Cyanide (ADWA) .... Cy
Cyan-Yellow-Magenta (AEBE) .... CYM
Cyber Sentry, Inc. [*AMEX symbol*] .... CYR
Cybernetic (ADWA) .... cyber
Cycle (ADWA) .... cy
Cycle Day (ADWA) .... CD
Cyclic Uridine 3c, 5c-Monophosphate (ADWA) .... cUMP
Cyclooxygenase-2 .... COX-2
Cyclopedia (ADWA) .... cyc
Cyclopedia (ADWA) .... cycl
Cyclophosphamide, Vincristine, Procarbazine, and Prednisone
  [*Medicine*] .... COPP
Cyclotrimethlenetramine .... RDX
Cylinders (RIMS) .... Cy
Cymbals .... cym
Cymric (ADWA) .... Cym
Cyrstallography (ADWA) .... cryst
Cytidine 5c-Triphosphate (ADWA) .... CTP
Cytological (ADWA) .... cytol
Czechoslovakia (NTIO) .... Czech

D
By Meaning

Daily Historical Climate Network (CARB) .... DHCN
Daily Sum Insured [*Insurance*] (MARI) .... DSI
Damage Received in Collision [*Insurance*] (MARI) ..... DRC
Damage Survey Report [*Department of Emergency Management*] (DEMM) ..... DSR
Damp Basement (ADWA) .... DB
Dandy-Walker Syndrome Network (ADWA) .... DWSN
Danger Area Activity Information Service (PIAV) ..... DAAIS
Danger Area Crossing Service (PIAV) .... DACS
Dangerous Occurrence (HEAS) .... DO
Dangerous Pathogen Advisory Group (HEAS) .... DPAG
Dangling Construction (ADWA) .... dgl
Danish (ADWA) .... Da
Danish (ADWA) .... Dan
Darkness Emitting Diode (AEBE) .... DED
Darling Husband (ADWA) .... DH
Darling Wife (ADWA) .... DW
Data Acquisition and Control Subsystems (ADWA) ..... DACS
Data Acquisition Glove (ADWA) .... DAG
Data Active Archive Center (CARB) .... DAAC
Data Availability Acknowledgment (ADWA) .... DAA
Data Capture Facility (ADWA) .... DCF
Data Delivery Acknowledgment (ADWA) .... DDA
Data Delivery Notice (ADWA) .... DDN
Data Distribution Facility (ADWA) .... DDF
Data Evaluation Laboratory (ADWA) .... DEL
Data Format Control Documents (ADWA) .... DFCD
Data Group (SPST) .... DG
Data Integration and Collection Environment (ADWA) ..... DICE
Data Link Control/Logical Link Control (ADWA) ..... DLC/LLC
Data Management Team (ARMP) .... DMT
Data Manager (CTAS) .... DM
Data Message Handler (CGWS) .... DMH
Data Mining Query Language (IDAI) .... DMQL
Data Mobile Channel (CGWS) .... Dm
Data Processing Engineer (ADWA) .... DPE
Data Product Code (ADWA) .... DPC
Data Quality Assessment (ABAC) .... DQA
Data Quality Message (ADWA) .... DQM
Data Record/Playback (CTAS) .... DRP
Data Recovery Unit (ADWA) .... DRU
Data Relay Test Satellite [*Sponsored by Japan Space Agency*] ..... DRTS
Data Requirements, Evaluation, and Management (ABAC) ..... DREAM
Data Servicing Unit (CTAS) .... DSU
Data Storage and Distribution System (ADWA) ..... DSDS
Data Summary (ADWA) .... DSUM
Data Support Section (ARMP) .... DSS
Data Terminal Equipment .... DTE
Data Transfer Module .... DTM
Data Transmission Subsystem (CCCA) .... DTS
Data Voice Digital Multiplexer (CCCA) .... DVDM
Data-Assimilation System (CARB) .... DAS
Database Management Environment .... DBME
Dataram .... DRAM
Date Last Seen [*Medicine*] .... DLS
Date to Be Advised (MARI) .... DTBA
Dative (ADWA) .... dat
Dawson's Creek [*Television program title*] .... DC
Day Optical Scope .... DOS
Days All Purposes (RIMS) .... DAP
Days Post-Ovulation [*Medicine*] (ADWA) .... DPO
DDi Corp. [*NASDAQ symbol*] (SG) .... DDIC
Dead-End User (ADWA) .... DEU
Deadweight (MARI) .... D/w
Deadweight Tonnage (ADWA) .... DWT
Deaf .... DEF
Deaf Passenger [*Travel industry*] (TRID) .... DEAF
Dear Husband .... DH
Death-Effector Domain .... DED
Debtor (ADWA) .... dr
Debutante (ADWA) .... deb
Decaffeinated Coffee (ADWA) .... decaf
Decagram (ADWA) .... dag
Decal Film .... DF
Decayed, Missing, and Filled Teeth (ADWA) .... DMF
Deceased (ADWA) .... decd
Decibel (DIPS) .... Db

Decibels Above or Below 1 Milliwatt (AEBE) .... dBm
Decibels per Milliwatt (ADWA) .... dBm
Decibels Referenced to Isotropic Gain (ADWA) .... dBI
Decibels Referenced to One Watt (ADWA) .... dBW
Decided Cases Index (HEAS) .... DCI
Decimeter (ABAC) .... dm
Decision (ADWA) .... decn
Decision Feedback Equalization (AEBE) .... DFE
Decision Level Concentration (ABAC) .... DLC
Declaration (ADWA) .... dec
Declension (NTIO) .... decl
Decoherent Histories .... DH
Decontamination .... decon
Decontamination and Decommissioning (ABAC) .... D&D
Decoration (ADWA) .... dec
Decryption Authentication Unit (ADWA) .... DAU
Dedicated Short Range Communications .... DSRC
Deduct (ADWA) .... ded
Deductive Database (IDAI) .... DDB
Deep Monitoring (CARB) .... DM
Deep Near-Infrared Survey .... DENIS
Default Protection Plan [*Travel industry*] (TRID) .... DPP
Defendant (ADWA) .... dft
Defense Against Ballistic Missiles (CCCA) .... DABM
Defense & Space Systems Group (CCCA) .... DSSG
Defense Automated Warning System (ADWA) .... DAWS
Defense Contract Management District East .... DCMDE
Defense Contract Management District International .... DCMDI
Defense Coordinating Executive [*Department of Defense*] (DEMM) ..... DCE
Defense Coordinating Officer [*Department of Defense*] (DEMM) ..... DCO
Defense Distribution Center .... DDC
Defense Energy Support Center .... DESC
Defense Federal Acquisition Regulations .... DFAR
Defense Intelligence Service (CCCA) .... DIS
Defense Logistics Information Service .... DLIS
Defense Nuclear Facilities Safety Board .... DNSC
Defense Prisoner of War/Missing Personnel Office .... DPMO
Defense Security Service .... DSS
Defense Threat Reduction Agency .... DTRA
Defensive Aid System .... DAS
Defensive System Technology Study (CCCA) .... DSTS
Deficiency Love [*A. Maslow*] (DIPS) .... Dlove
Deficiency Needs [*A. Maslow*] (DIPS) .... Dneeds
Deficit Reduction Act (ADWA) .... DRA
Definite (ADWA) .... def
Definitely (ADWA) .... def
Definitive Design (ABAC) .... DD
Degree (NTIO) .... deg
Degree of Sensitization (ABAC) .... DOS
Deionized Water (ABAC) .... DIW
Dekagram (NTIO) .... dag
Dekagram (ADWA) .... dkg
Dekaliter (ADWA) .... dkl
Dekameter (ADWA) .... dkm
Delegation (ADWA) .... del
Delete (NTIO) .... Del
Delicatessen (ADWA) .... deli
Delicious .... delic
Delirium Tremens (DIPS) .... dts
Delivered (MARI) .... Dd
Delivered Ex Quay (RIMS) .... DEQ
Delivered Ex Ship (RIMS) .... DES
Delivery (ADWA) .... dlvy
Delta Clipper .... DC
Delta Clipper Experimental .... DCX
Delta Luminance Color Difference .... DYUU
Deltoid Muscles (ADWA) .... delts
Deluxe Room [*Travel industry*] (TRID) .... DLX
Demand Planning Module .... DPM
Demobilize (ADWA) .... demob
Democratic (ADWA) .... DEM
Democratic (NTIO) .... Dem
Demodulator (ADWA) .... dem
Demolition Proceeding (ADWA) .... DP
Demonstration (ADWA) .... demo
Demonstrative (NTIO) .... dem

Demonstrative (ADWA) .... demon
Demonstrative (ADWA) .... demonstr
Demurrage (ADWA) .... dem
Den Leader [*Boy Scouts of America*] .... DL
Denial of Service (ADWA) .... DOS
Denied Persons List .... DPL
Denomination (NTIO) .... denom
Denotation (ADWA) .... den
Dental (NTIO) .... dent
Dental Education Resources on the Web (ADWA) .... DERWeb
Dental Treatment Facility .... DTF
Dentistry (ADWA) .... dent
Denver Museum of Natural History .... DMNH
Deoxyadenosine (ADWA) .... dAdo
Deoxycytidylic Acid (ADWA) .... dCMP
Deoxyguanylic Acid (ADWA) .... dGMP
Deoxyribonuclease (ADWA) .... DNase
Department (NTIO) .... dpt
Department of Agriculture and Consumer Services (DEMM) .... DACS
Department of Banking and Finance (DEMM) .... DBF
Department of Business and Professional Regulation (DEMM) .... DBPR
Department of Children and Families (DEMM) .... DCF
Department of Community Affairs (DEMM) .... DCA
Department of Corrections (DEMM) .... DOC
Department of Defense Intelligence Information System (ADWA) .... DoDIIS
Department of Elder Affairs (DEMM) .... DOEA
Department of Environmental Protection (AUEG) .... DEP
Department of Fisheries Research (HEAS) .... DFR
Department of Health Services (SARE) .... DOHS
Department of Highway Safety & Motor Vehicles (DEMM) .... DHSMV
Department of Insurance (DEMM) .... DOI
Department of Labor and Employment Security (DEMM) .... DLES
Department of Management Services (DEMM) .... DMS
Department of Military Affairs (DEMM) .... DMA
Department of Natural Resources and Conservation (AUEG) .... DNRC
Department of Pesticide Regulation [*California*] (SARE) .... DPR
Department of Revenue (DEMM) .... DOR
Department of Social and Health Services .... DSHS
Department of Special Services .... DSS
Department of Transport (PIAV) .... DoT
Departure (NTIO) .... dep
Departure (TRID) .... dptr
Dependent Care Connection (ADWA) .... DCC
Deponent (ADWA) .... dpt
Deposed (ADWA) .... dep
Depositary Receipts .... ADR
Depositary Receipts (SG) .... Dep
Depreciation (ADWA) .... depr
Deputy (ADWA) .... dept
Deputy Assistant Secretary (ABAC) .... DAS
Deputy Borough Environmental Health Officer (HEAS) .... DBEHO
Deputy Chief Environmental Health Officer (HEAS) .... DCEHO
Deputy Chief Inspecting Officer (HEAS) .... DCIO
Deputy Chief Inspector (HEAS) .... DCI
Deputy Chief Inspector of Factories (HEAS) .... DCIF
Deputy Director of Public Health (HEAS) .... DDPH
Deputy Federal Coordinating Officer (DEMM) .... DFCO
Deputy State Coordinating Officer [*Department of Emergency Management*] (DEMM) .... DSCO
Deputy Superintending Inspector (HEAS) .... DSI
Deregulation Unit (HEAS) .... DU
Derivation (ADWA) .... deriv
Derivative (ADWA) .... der
Dermatology (ADWA) .... derm
Derogatory (ADWA) .... derog
Descant Recorder .... drec
Descending (ADWA) .... desc
Descending Reticular Activating System (DIPS) .... DRAS
Desert (NTIO) .... Des
Design Analysis Cycle (SPST) .... DAC
Design Business Association (COBU) .... DBA
Design, Development, Test, and Evaluation (ADWA) .... DDTE
Design Qualification Test (CTAS) .... DQT
Design Requirements Agreement (SPST) .... DRA
Design, Testing, and Evaluation (ABAC) .... DT&E
Designated Player [*Baseball term*] (NDBD) .... DP
Designated Transit List (MLOA) .... DTL
Designated Transit List Information Ethernet (MLOA) .... DTL IE
Designation (ADWA) .... des
Designers and Artists Copyright Society .... DACS
Desktop Color Imaging .... DCI
Despatch Half Demurrage on All Time Saved Both Ends (RIMS) .... DHDATSBE
Despatch Half Demurrage on Working Time Saved Both Ends (RIMS) .... DHDWTSBE
Destination (ADWA) .... destn
Destination End System [*Telecommunications*] (MLOA) .... DES
Destination Marketing Organization (TRID) .... DMO
Detachment (ADWA) .... det
Detailed Design Data Package (ABAC) .... DDDP
Detailed Mission Requirements (ADWA) .... DMR
Detailed Time Line (SPST) .... DTL
Determination (ADWA) .... detn
Determination, Integrity, Vitality, and Aspiration [*Self-esteem plan devised by fitness instructor Terri Walsh*] .... DIVA
Detroit Public Schools [*Michigan*] .... DPS
Deuteron (ADWA) .... d
Development .... Develop
Development Disorder .... DD
Development Integration Test (SPST) .... DIT
Developmental Apraxia of Speech .... DAS
Developmental Verbal Dyspraxia .... DVD
Developmentally Disabled Service Office .... DDSO
Developmentally Handicapped .... DH
Deviation (DIPS) .... d
Device for Automated Desensitization (DIPS) .... DAD
Device Support Processor [*Computer science*] (ITCA) .... DSP
Device Test Module .... DTM
Dexterous Robotics System [*NASA*] (SPST) .... DRS
Diabetic (ADWA) .... diab
Diagnosis (ADWA) .... dx
Diagnosis .... DX
Diagnostic Accreditation Program (ADWA) .... DAP
Diagnostic Processor (CCCA) .... DP
Diagnostic Statistical Manual .... DSM
Diagonally (ADWA) .... diag
Diagram (NTIO) .... diag
Dial Tone Multiple Frequency [*Telecommunications*] (MLOA) .... DTMF
Dialectal (ADWA) .... dial
Diamond-Pyramid Hardness (ABAC) .... dph
Dictation (ADWA) .... dict
Dideoxyinosine (ADWA) .... DDI
Didymium (ADWA) .... Di
Diesel Mechanics .... DIMCH
Dietary (ADWA) .... diet
Dietary Approaches to Stop Hypertension .... DASH
Dietetic Technician Registered (NUJO) .... DTR
Dietitian (ADWA) .... Diet
Difference (NTIO) .... dif
Difference (ADWA) .... diff
Difference in Perils (MARI) .... DIP
Differential Ability Scales [*C. D. Elliott*] (DIPS) .... DAS
Differential Detection (CCCA) .... DD
Differential Optical Absorption Spectroscopy (SARE) .... DOAS
Differential Pressure (ABAC) .... dp
Differential Quadrature Phase-Shift Keying (AEBE) .... DQPSK
Differential Quadri-Phrase Shift Keying (CCCA) .... DQPSK
Differential Reinforcement of High Rate [*B.F. Skinner*] (DIPS) .... drh
Differential Reinforcement of Low Rate [*B.F. Skinner*] (DIPS) .... drl
Diffuse Thalamic Projection System (DIPS) .... DTPS
Diffuse Viewing Only (SARE) .... DVO
DiGeorge Syndrome .... DiG
Digestive Disease Week (ADWA) .... DDW
Digit (ADWA) .... dgt
Digital Aeronautical Chart Supplement (CTAS) .... DACS
Digital Audio Video Broadcasting .... DAVB
Digital Cellular Communications-1800 (CGWS) DCT-1800
Digital Communications Corp. (CCCA) .... DCC
Digital Communications System on 1800 MHz Band (CGWS) DCS-1800
Digital Conference Unit (CCCA) .... DCU
Digital Cordless Telephone (CGWS) .... DCT
Digital Distance Radio Magnetic Indicator (HLLA) .... DDRMI
Digital Electronic Engine Control System (ADWA) .... DEECS
Digital Flight Guidance Computer (HLLA) .... DFGC
Digital Interactive Business Oriented Language [*Computer science*] (ITCA) .... DIBOL
Digital Line Graph-Enhanced (CARB) .... DLG-E
Digital Multimeter (AEBE) .... DMM
Digital Radio Frequency Memory (ADWA) .... DRFM
Digital Radio System (CCCA) .... DRS
Digital Rights Management .... DRM
Digital Secure Voice Terminal (CCCA) .... DSVT
Digital Service Cross-Connect (MLOA) .... DSX
Digital Signal Processing .... DSP
Digital Source Collector .... DSC
Digital Subscriber Line Access Multiplexer (MLOA) .... DSLAM
Digital Television Element (CCCA) .... DTVE
Digital Think, Inc. [*NASDAQ symbol*] (SG) .... DTHK
Digital Transportation Marketplace .... DTM
Digital Universe (ADWA) .... digiverse
Digital Versatile Disk-Random Access Memory (ADWA) .... DVD-RAM
Digital Versatile Disk-Read Only Memory (ADWA) .... DVD-ROM
Digital Versatile Disk-Read-Write (ADWA) .... DVD-RW
Digital Versatile Disk-Recordable (ADWA) .... DVD-R
Digitally Connected Private Branch Exchange [*Telecommunications*] (ROAS) .... DCPBX
Digital-to-Analog (AEBE) D2A
Digital-to-Analog Conversion .... DAC
Digitas, Inc. [*NASDAQ symbol*] (SG) .... DTAS
Digraph Matrix Analysis (SPST) .... DMA
Dihydroeplandrosterone (ADWA) .... DHEA
Dihydroeplandrosterone (ADWA) .... DHEAS
Dihydrofolic Acid (ADWA) .... DHF
Dihydroxyphenylalanine (ADWA) .... dopa
Diisopropyl Iminodiacetic Acid (ADWA) .... DISIDA
Dilation and Extraction (ADWA) .... D&E
Dilation and Extraction (ADWA) .... D&X
Dilute (ADWA) .... dil
Dimethylglyoxide (ABAC) .... DMG
Dining Area (ADWA) .... DA
Dining Room (ADWA) .... din

Dining Room (NTIO) ... dr
Diocesan (ADWA) ... dioc
Diphtheria (ADWA) ... diph
Diphtheria (ADWA) ... dT
Diphtheria, Tetanus, and Acellular Pertussis (ADWA) ... DTaP
Diploma (ADWA) ... dip
Diploma (ADWA) ... dipl
Diploma in English Language Teaching for Adults ... DELTA
Diploma in the Teaching of English as a Foreign Language to Adults ... DTEFLA
Direct Access Library Maintenance Package [*Pansophic Systems*] ... PANVALET
Direct Access System (CARB) ... DAS
Direct Aqueous Injection (ABAC) ... DAI
Direct Aqueous Injection/Gas Chromatography (ABAC) ... DAI/GC
Direct Broadcast (CARB) ... DB
Direct Chill (HEAS) ... DC
Direct Cost ... DC
Direct Costs (MARI) ... DC
Direct Credits Society (ADWA) ... DCS
Direct High Power (ADWA) ... DHP
Direct Hydrophilic Conjugation ... DHC
Direct Intraperitoneal Insemination [*Medicine*] (ADWA) ... DIPI
Direct Link for the Disabled, Inc. (ADWA) ... DLD
Direct Memory Access ... DMA
Direct Memory Load (ADWA) ... DML
Direct Observation of the Nu Tau ... DONUT
Direct Oocyte-Sperm Transfer [*Medicine*] (ADWA) ... DOST
Direct Receiving Station (ADWA) ... DRS
Direct Reference System (TRID) ... DRS
Direct Sampling Ion Trap Mass Spectrometry (ABAC) ... DSITMS
Direct Solar Radiation (ARMP) ... DSR
Direct Stream Digital (ADWA) ... DSD
Direct User Access Terminal System (PIPO) ... DUAT
Directed Infrared Countermeasures (ADWA) ... DIRCM
Directed Scattering Coefficients (ARMP) ... DSC
Direction (ADWA) ... dir
Directional Gyro (PIPO) ... D/G
Directional Minimum Check [*Travel industry*] (TRID) ... DMC
Direction-Finding (PIAV) ... DF
Direct-Normal Solar Irradiance (ARMP) ... DNSI
Director of Environmental Health (HEAS) ... DEH
Director of Environmental Health Services (HEAS) ... DEHS
Director of Hazardous Materials Management (SARE) ... DHMM
Director of Military Support [*Army*] (DEMM) ... DOMS
Director of Studies ... DOS
Directorate Controlled Project ... DCP
Directorate General (HEAS) ... DG
Directorate of Science and Technology (HEAS) ... DST
Directors' & Producers' Rights Society ... DPRS
Director's Cut ... Dir Cut
Directory Assistance Call Completion (CGWS) ... DACC
Directory Client Agent ... DCA
Directory of Biotechnology Resources (ADWA) ... DBIR
Directory Server Agent ... DSA
Disability (ADWA) ... disab
Disaster Application Center [*Department of Emergency Management*] (DEMM) ... DAC
Disaster Assistance Programs (DEMM) ... DAP
Disaster Legal Services (DEMM) ... DLS
Disaster Medical Assistance Team (ADWA) ... DMAT
Disaster Mortuary Response Team (DEMM) ... DMORT
Disaster Preparedness Improvement Grant (DEMM) ... DPIG
Disaster Recovery Center (DEMM) ... DRC
Disaster Recovery Manager (DEMM) ... DRM
Disaster Recovery Operations (DEMM) ... DRO
Disbursement Account (RIMS) ... D/A
Discharge (ADWA) ... d/c
Discharge (ADWA) ... disch
Discharge Capacity (RIMS) ... DC
Discomfort-Relief Quotient (DIPS) ... drq
Discontinue (ADWA) ... dc
Discontinued (TRID) ... dis
Discotheque (ADWA) ... disco
Discovered (ADWA) ... disc
Discovery Channel (ADWA) ... DSC
Discrete Ordinate Radiative Transfer (ARMP) ... DISORT
Discrete Trial Training ... DIT
Discussed With [*Medicine*] ... D/W
Disinfectant and Disinfection Byproduct (ADWA) ... D/DBP
Disintegration (ABAC) ... dis
Disintegration per Minute (ABAC) ... dis/min
Disintegrations per Second (ABAC) ... dis/sec
Disintegrations per Second (ABAC) ... dps
Disjunctive Normal Form (IDAI) ... DNF
Disk Control Block (ROAS) ... DCB
Disk Transfer Address (ADWA) ... DTA
Disney Channel (ADWA) ... DIS
Dispatch Applications Processor (CGWS) ... DAP
Dispensary (ADWA) ... disp
Displacement (ADWA) ... displ
Displacements per Atom (ABAC) ... dpa
Display Remoting Enhancement (CCCA) ... DRE
Display Screen Equipment (HEAS) ... DSE
Disqualify (ADWA) ... DQ
Dissertation (ADWA) ... diss
Dissimilar Iron Reducing Bacteria (ABAC) ... DIRB
Dissolved Organic Macromolecules (CARB) ... DOM
Dissolved Oxygen Demand ... DoD
Distance Learning (HEAS) ... DL
Distance to Cell Radius Ratio (CGWS) ... D/R
Distance Visual Acuity with Correction (DAVI) ... VAcc
Distant (ADWA) ... dis
Distant Early Warning System (CCCA) ... DEWS
Distant Radio Reception (AEBE) ... DX
Distillation (ADWA) ... distn
Distress and Diversion Cells at Air Traffic Control Centres [*British*] (PIAV) ... D & D
Distributed Call Measurement System ... DCMS
Distributed Communications Grid Network (CCCA) ... DCGN
Distributed File System [*Computer science*] ... Dfs
Distributed Problem Solving (IDAI) ... DPS
Distribution From (CCCA) ... DF
Distribution Requirements Module ... DRM
Distribution Uniformity (ADWA) ... DU
Distributive (ADWA) ... distrib
Distributor (ADWA) ... distr
District Environmental Health Officer (HEAS) ... DEHO
District Executive [*Boy Scouts of America*] ... DE
Ditech Communications ... DITC
Dive Travel Industry Association (TRID) ... DTIA
Diversa Corp. [*NASDAQ symbol*] (SG) ... DVSA
Division Medical Supply Office [*Army*] ... DMSO
Division of Cancer Control and Population Sciences (ADWA) ... DCCPS
Division of Cancer Epidemiology and Genetics (ADWA) ... DCEG
Division of Cancer Prevention (ADWA) ... DCP
Division of Capital Police (DEMM) ... DCP
Division of Emergency Management (DEMM) ... DEM
Division of Forestry (DEMM) ... DOF
Divorced Asian Female (ADWA) ... DAF
Divorced Asian Male (ADWA) ... DAM
Divorced Hispanic Male (ADWA) ... DHM
Divorced Professional Female (ADWA) ... DPF
Divorced Professional Male (ADWA) ... DPM
Do All Possible [*Travel industry*] (TRID) ... DAPO
Do Your Own Homework (ADWA) ... DYOH
Doberman Pinscher (ADWA) ... dobe
Dobson Communic. 'A' [*NASDAQ symbol*] (SG) ... DCEL
Dock (ADWA) ... dk
Dock Owner's Liability [*Insurance*] (MARI) ... DOL
Docket (ADWA) ... dkt
Docking Compartment [*NASA*] (SPST) ... DC
Doctor (NTIO) ... Doc
Doctrine, Organization, Training, Equipment, and Supporting Facilities [*Military*] ... DOTES
Doctrine, Organization, Training, Materiel, Personnel and Leader Development [*Army*] ... DOTMPL
Document Style Language (ADWA) ... DSL
Documentary Sight Draft (MARI) ... DSD
Documenting Aerosol Electromagnetics, Defining Aerosol Lifetimes, and Understanding Sources [*Research station*] (CARB) ... DAEDALUS
Document-Like Objects ... DLO
Doing Business As (NTIO) ... d/b/a
Doing His Job (ADWA) ... DHJ
Domain Dynamics Ltd. ... DDL
Domestic (TRID) ... dom
Domestic Emergency Support Team [*Federal Bureau of Investigation*] (DEMM) ... DEST
Dominant (ADWA) ... dom
Domination and Submission (ADWA) ... D&S
Dominican (NTIO) ... Dom
Dominion (NTIO) ... dom
Donegal (ADWA) ... Don
Donor Eggs (ADWA) ... DE
Doppler Weather Radar (ADWA) ... DWR
Doric (ADWA) ... Dor
Dose Limiting Toxicity [*Medicine*] ... DLT
Dot Pitch (ADWA) ... dp
Double (ADWA) ... dble
Double Annular Factory for Nice Experiments ... DAFNE
Double Extended Three-Letter Abbreviation (ADWA) ... DETLA
Double Room with Bath (TRID) ... DBLB
Double Room with Shower (TRID) ... DBLS
Double Room without Shower or Bath (TRID) ... DBLN
Double Skinned (RIMS) ... DBL SKIN
Doublebass ... db
Double-Crossing (ADWA) ... doublexing
Double-Data-Rate Synchronous Dynamic Random Access Memory (AEBE) ... DDRSDRAM
Doubleheader [*Baseball term*] (NDBD) ... DH
Double-Shell Slurry (ABAC) ... DSS
Double-Shell Slurry Feed (ABAC) ... DSSF
Double-Simultaneous Stimulation (DIPS) ... DSS
Dow Jones Industrial Average ... DIA
Down (ADWA) ... D
Down Under the Manhattan Bridge Overpass [*New York*] ... DUMBO
Downstairs (ADWA) ... dwnstrs
Dozen ... dz
Drachma (ADWA) ... d
Dramatic (NTIO) ... dram
Dramatist (ADWA) ... dram
Drawing Interchange File (ADWA) ... DXF

Drawing Interchange Format .... DXF
Dreaded Abbreviation Syndrome .... DAS
Dressing (ADWA) .... drsg
Drive Stimuli (DIPS) .... d
Drive Strength (DIPS) .... D
Driver's License (SARE) .... DL
Driving under Revocation (SARE) .... DUR
Driving under Suspension (SARE) .... DUS
Droned Helicopter .... QH
Drop Size Distribution (ARMP) .... DSD
Dropping Last Outwards Sea Pilot (RIMS) .... DLOSP
Dropping Outward Pilot (RIMS) .... DOP
Dropping Zone (PIAV) .... DZ
Drug and Disease Free (ADWA) .... D/DF
Drug and Disease Free (ADWA) .... D&D
Drug History .... D/H
Drug Product Database (ADWA) .... DPD
Drug Services Research Survey (ADWA) .... DSRS
Drum .... dm
Drum Kit .... dmkit
Dry Chemical (PIPO) .... DC
Dry Well Storage Facility (ABAC) .... DWSF
Dual Address Space [*Computer science*] (ITCA) .... DAS
Dual Irradiance Absolute Radiometer (ADWA) .... DIARAD
Dual Valuation [*Insurance*] (MARI) .... D/V
Dual Wavelength Ratio (ARMP) .... DWR
Dual-Double Tandem Axle (PIPO) .... DDT

Dual-Mode Advanced Mobile Phone System (CGWS) .... D-AMPS
DualStar Technologies .... DSTR
Dublin (ADWA) .... Dub
Dublin (ADWA) .... Dubl
Duchy (NTIO) .... Du
Duck Embryo Origin Vaccine (ADWA) .... DEV
Duck Head Apparel [*AMEX symbol*] .... DHA
Ductal Carcinoma in Situ [*Medicine*] (ADWA) .... DCIS
Dummy Section [*Computer science*] (ITCA) .... DSECT
Dunvagen [*Publisher*] .... DVG
Duplex (TRID) .... DPLX
Duplication of Benefits (DEMM) .... DOB
Durham (ADWA) .... Dur
Dust and Mist (SARE) .... DM
Dust, Fume and Mist (HEAS) .... DFM
Dutch (ADWA) .... Du
Duty Officers Procedure Guide [*Department of Emergency Management*]
   (DEMM) .... DOPG
Dying with Dignity (ADWA) .... D/W
Dynamic Integrated Climate Economy (CARB) .... DICE
Dynamic Mechanical Spectroscopy .... DMS
Dynamic Planner (CTAS) .... DP
Dynamic Positioning (RIMS) .... DYNPOS
Dynamic Probabilistic Network (IDAI) .... DPN
Dynamic Simulator (CTAS) .... DYSIM
Dynamic Systems Development Method [*Computer science*] (ITCA) .... DSDM
Dyne (NTIO) .... dy
Dystrophic Epidermolysis Bullosa Research Association (ADWA) .... DEBRA

E

By Meaning

Each (NTIO) .... ea
Each and Every Accident (MARI) .... e&ea
Each and Every Loss (MARI) .... e&el
Each and Every Occurrence (MARI) .... e&eo
Eagle Wireless Intl. [AMEX symbol] (SG) .... EAG
Early Childhood Direction Center .... ECDC
Early Childhood Education Assistance Program .... ECEAP
Early Childhood Special Education .... ECSE
Early Deployment System (ABAC) .... EDS
Early External Active Thermal Control System [NASA] (SPST) ...... EEATCS
Early Morning Urine Osmolality [Medicine] .... EMUO
Early Mortality Syndrome .... EMS
Early Psychosis Assessment Team (ADWA) .... EPAT
Early Run .... E/R
Early Termination of Pregnancy (ADWA) .... ETP
Early Upper Paleolithic .... EUP
Earned Value Management System [Army] .... EVMS
Earnings after Taxes (ADWA) .... EAT
Earnings Before Interest, Taxes, Depreciation, and Amortization ..... EBITDA
Earth & Magnet (MLOA) .... E&M
Earth Attitude Angle (ADWA) .... FAA
Earth Coverage (CCCA) .... EC
Earth Observation Center (CARB) .... EOC
Earth Observation Initiative .... EOI
Earth Observation Science Initiative .... EOSI
Earth Observing One [NASA] EO-1
Earth Observing Satellite-Chemistry [NASA] .... EOS-Chem
Earth Observing Scanning Polarimeter (CARB) .... EOSP
Earth Radiation Budget Explorer Satellite (CARB) .... ERBES
Earth Relative Time (ADWA) .... ert
Earth Resource Data Analysis .... ERDAS
Earth Science Data and Information System (CARB) .... ESDIS
Earth Terminal Facility (CCCA) .... ETF
Earthquake Research Institute .... ERI
East Asia and Western Pacific (CARB) .... EAWEP
East Frisian (ADWA) .... EFris
East Germanic (ADWA) .... EGmc
Eastern Canada Cat Institute (ROAS) .... ECCI
Eastern Cereal and Oilseed Research Centre [Ottawa, Canada] ..... ECORC
Eastern Ontario Trails Alliance [Canada] .... EOTA
Eastern Pacific (CCCA) .... EPAC
Eastern Standard Time (TRID) .... EST
Eating Disorders Shared Awareness (ADWA) .... EDSA
Ebola Virus, Zaire Strain (ADWA) .... EBOZ
Ecclesiastical (NTIO) .... eccl
Ecclesiastical Greek (ADWA) .... Eccl Gk
Ecological Risk Assessment (ABAC) .... ERA
Ecology (ADWA) .... ecol
Economics (ADWA) .... econ
Economist (ADWA) .... econ
Economy Car (TRID) .... ECAR
Economy Car with Manual Transmission (TRID) .... EMAN
Ecuador (ADWA) .... Ec
Ecuador (ADWA) .... Ecua
Ecuadorian Committee of the Pacific Economic Cooperation Council ..... ECPECC
e-Customer Relationship Management .... eCRM
Edge Device Functional Group .... EDFG
Editor (ADWA) .... edit
Educable Mentally Impaired (ADWA) .... EMI
Education (ADWA) .... ed
Education and Career Opportunities System .... ECOS
Education for All Handicapped Children [1975] (DIPS) .... EAHCA
Education of All Handicapped Children Act .... EAHCA
Educational (ADWA) .... educ
Educational Leave of Absence (ABAC) .... ELOA
Educational Media Association of New Jersey .... EMAnj
Educational Recording Agency .... ERA
Educational Theorem Proving System (IDAI) .... ETPS
Edwards Lifesciences [NYSE symbol] (SG) .... EW
Edwin Ashdown [Publisher] .... ASH
Effective (TRID) .... eff
Effective Cleaning Radius (ABAC) .... ECR
Efficiency (ADWA) .... EF
Efficiency (ADWA) .... eff
Efficiency (ADWA) .... effic
Efficiency (ADWA) .... EFFNCY

Efficient Water Management Practice (ADWA) .... EWMP
Effluent Charge Law [1976] .... ECL
eFunds Corp. [NASDAQ symbol] .... EFDS
Egg White .... EW
Egypt (NTIO) .... Eg
Egyptian (ADWA) .... Eg
Egyptian (ADWA) .... Egypt
Egyptology (ADWA) .... egyptol
Eisenhower National Clearinghouse .... ENC
Elaboration-Likelihood Model [R.E Petty & J. T. Cacioppo] (DIPS) ..... ELM
Electric .... e
Electric Bass .... eb
Electric Counter Measure (CCCA) .... ECM
Electric Flow in Amperes (NTIO) I
Electric Guitar .... egtr
Electric Surface Heating (HEAS) .... ESH
Electric Violin .... evn
Electrical Apparatus Service Association, Inc. .... EASA
Electrical Brain Stimulation (DIPS) .... EBS
Electrical Certification Support Unit (HEAS) .... ECSU
Electrical Damage (ADWA) .... ED
Electrical Equipment Certification Management Board (HEAS) ..... EECMB
Electrical Load Management Center (ADWA) .... ELMC
Electrical Power Consuming Equipment (SPST) .... EPCE
Electrical Power Subsystem (ADWA) .... EPSS
Electrical Self-Stimulation of the Brain (DIPS) .... ESSB
Electrical Transcranial Stimulation (DIPS) .... ETS
Electrically Erasable Programmable Read Only Memory (AEBE) E2PROM
Electrically Eraseable Programmable Read Only Memory (CGWS) E2PROM
Electrically Powered Actuation Device (ADWA) .... EPAD
Electricity (NTIO) .... elec
Electricity (ADWA) .... electr
Electroconvulsive Shock Therapy (DIPS) .... EST
Electrocorticogram (DIPS) .... ECoG
Electrodialysis Reversal (ADWA) .... EDR
Electroencephalograph (DIPS) .... EEG
Electroencephalographic (DIPS) .... EEG
Electrohydraulic Shock Wave Lithotripsy (ADWA) .... ESWL
Electromagnetic Unit (ADWA) .... emu
Electromagnetic Units (ABAC) .... emu
Electromigration .... EM
Electromyograph (DIPS) .... EMG
Electromyographic .... EMG
Electron Affinity (ABAC) .... EA
Electron Beam High Throughput Lithography .... EBHT
Electron Capture-Gas Chromatograph (ADWA) .... EC-GC
Electron Impact (ABAC) .... EI
Electron Multiplier Voltage (ABAC) .... EMV
Electron Proton Helium Instrument (ADWA) .... EPHIN
Electron Volt (ABAC) .... eV
Electronic (ADWA) .... elect
Electronic Address (ADWA) .... E-dress
Electronic Arts, Inc. .... EA
Electronic Auditory Stimulation Effect .... EASe
Electronic Bill Presentment and Payment .... EBPP
Electronic Business (ADWA) .... e-business
Electronic Calibration (ADWA) .... ECAL
Electronic Cash (ADWA) .... e-cash
Electronic Cash (ITCA) .... E-cash
Electronic Catalogs .... ecx
Electronic Check (ITCA) .... E-Check
Electronic Commerce (ITCA) .... E-com
Electronic Commerce (ADWA) .... e-commerce
Electronic Dictionary Research (IDAI) .... EDR
Electronic Entertainment Expo (ADWA) E3
Electronic Fetal Monitor (ADWA) .... EFM
Electronic Health Economics Analysis Letters (ADWA) .... eHEAL
Electronic Health Economics Letters (ADWA) .... eHEL
Electronic Image Management (ITCA) .... EIM
Electronic Information Standards (ADWA) .... EIS
Electronic Ink (ADWA) .... e-ink
Electronic Journal of the Astronomical Society of the Atlantic
    [A publication] .... EJASA
Electronic Licensing & Security Initiative (ITCA) .... ELSI
Electronic Liquor Dispenser (TRID) .... ELD
Electronic Mail (AUEG) .... E-Mail

Electronic Medical Record System (ADWA) .... EMRS
Electronic Money (ADWA) .... e-money
Electronic Numerical Integrater and Computer (AEBE) .... ENIAC
Electronic Print (ADWA) .... E-print
Electronic Public Health Development Project (ADWA) ...... EPHDP
Electronic Publishing (ADWA) .... e-publishing
Electronic Publishing Clearing Services .... ePCS
Electronic Purse (ADWA) .... e-purse
Electronic Records Management .... ERM
Electronic Reservations Service Provider [Travel industry] (TRID) .... ERSP
Electronic Retailing (ADWA) .... e-tailing
Electronic Site (ADWA) .... e-site
Electronic Stamp (ADWA) .... e-stamp
Electronic Store (ADWA) .... e-store
Electronic Ticket [Travel industry] (TRID) .... E ticket
Electronic Ticket Delivery Network [Travel industry] (TRID) .... ETDN
Electronic Trader (ADWA) .... e-trader
Electronic Visualization Laboratory .... EVL
Electronic Wallet (ADWA) .... e-wallet
Electronic Welfare (CCCA) .... EW
Electronics Lock Overhead [NASA] (SPST) .... EO
Electronics Module (ADWA) .... ELM
Electrooculograph (DIPS) .... EOG
Electro-Oculography (ADWA) .... EOG
Electro-Optic Phase Modulation (CARB) .... EOPM
Electro-Sleep Therapy (DIPS) .... EST
Electrostatic Dissipative (SARE) .... ESD
Electrostimulation of the Brain (DIPS) .... ESB
Element Control Workstation [NASA] (SPST) .... ECWS
Elemental Carbon (CARB) .... EC
Elementary (NTIO) .... elem
Elementary School Principals' Association of Washington .... ESPAW
Elevated (NTIO) .... el
Elevated Railroad (ADWA) .... el
Elevation (ADWA) .... el
Elevation (ADWA) .... elev
Elevation Difference Accuracy (CARB) .... EDA
Eligible (ADWA) .... elig
Elipitically (ADWA) .... elipt
Elite Pharmaceuticals [AMEX symbol] (SG) .... ELI
Elizabethan (ADWA) .... Eliz
Eloquent, Inc. [NASDAQ symbol] (SG) .... ELOQ
eLoyalty Corp. [NASDAQ symbol] (SG) .... ELOY
Elvis Aaron Presley (ADWA) .... EAP
eMachines, Inc. [NASDAQ symbol] (SG) .... EEEE
eMagin Corp. [AMEX symbol] (SG) .... EMA
Embryo Toxic Factor (ADWA) .... ETF
Embryo Toxicity Assay (ADWA) .... ETA
Emcor Group .... EMCG
e-MedSoft.com [AMEX symbol] (SG) .... MED
eMerge Interactive 'A' [NASDAQ symbol] (SG) .... EMRG
Emergency (ADWA) .... emer
Emergency (ADWA) .... EMGY
Emergency Action Plan (SARE) .... EAP
Emergency Action Room (CCCA) .... EAR
Emergency Authorities Database [Department of Defense] (DEMM) .... EADB
Emergency Care Unit (ADWA) .... ECU
Emergency Command and Control System (DEMM) .... ECCS
Emergency Contraceptive .... EC
Emergency Coordinating Officer [Department of Emergency Management]
  (DEMM) .... ECO
Emergency Department Physician (NUJO) .... EDP
Emergency Housing Consortium .... EHC
Emergency Isolation Device (HEAS) .... EID
Emergency Management Preparedness and Assistance Trust Fund
  (DEMM) .... EMPATF
Emergency Management Training Center (DEMM) .... EMTC
Emergency Medical Response Agency (ADWA) .... EMRA
Emergency Medical Services for Children (ADWA) .... EMSC
Emergency Medicine Assembly (ADWA) .... EMA
Emergency Medicine Bulletin Board System (ADWA) .... EMBBS
Emergency News Center (DEMM) .... ENC
Emergency Operation (ADWA) .... EO
Emergency Preparedness Liaison Officer (DEMM) .... EPLO
Emergency Response Intervention Card (HEAS) .... ERIC
Emergency Response Plan (SARE) .... ERP
Emergency Satellite Communications System (DEMM) .... ESATCOM
Emergency Shutdown Device (HEAS) .... ESD
Emergency Support Function [Department of Emergency Management]
  (DEMM) .... ESF
Emergency Support Team [National Guard] (DEMM) .... EST
Emergency Travel (TRID) .... EMER
Emerging Company (ADWA) .... ec
Emerging Healthcare Organization (ADWA) .... ENO
EMI Music Publishing .... EMI
Emission Standards Division (AUEG) .... ESD
Emissions Prediction and Policy Analysis .... EPPA
Emotional/Behavioral Disorder .... EBD
Emotional Quotient (ADWA) .... EQ
Empire (ADWA) .... emp
Employers' Liability Compulsory Insurance (HEAS) .... ELCI
Employment Consultants Institute (COBU) .... ECI
Employment Department (HEAS) .... ED
Employment Department Group (HEAS) .... EDG
Employment Medical Adviser (HEAS) .... EMA

Employment Medical Division (HEAS) .... EMD
Employment Nursing Adviser (HEAS) .... ENA
Empress (ADWA) .... emp
Empty Spiracles-Related Retinal-Homeobox .... Erx
Encapsidated Adenovirus Minichromosome .... EAM
Encoder-Decoder (AEBE) .... endec
Encore (ADWA) .... ENC
Encrypting File System [Computer science] .... EFS
Encyclopedia (ADWA) .... ency
Encyclopedia (NTIO) .... encyc
End of Activity (ADWA) .... EOA
End of Irradiation (ABAC) .... EOI
End of Thread (ADWA) .... EOT
End Office Code (CGWS) .... NXX
End to End System .... EES
End User Terminal .... EUT
End-Effector Exchange System (ABAC) .... EEES
Endocardium (ADWA) .... EN
Endocrine (ADWA) .... endo
Endometriosis (ADWA) .... ENDO
Endometriosis Research Center (ADWA) .... ERC
Endorsement Request (TRID) .... ERQ
Endotrachial (ADWA) .... ET
Energizer Holdings [NYSE symbol] (SG) .... ENR
Energy Active Zones of the Ocean (CARB) .... EAZO
Energy Division (CARB) .... ED
Energy Module (SPST) .... EM
Energy per Bit to Noise (CCCA) .... EB/NO
Energy Policy Act (ADWA) .... EPAct
Energy-Balance Bowen Ratio (CARB) .... EBBR
Enforcement Liaison Certification for Transport of Explosives (HEAS) .... ELCTEX
Engine Failure At or After Take-Off [Aviation] (PIAV) .... EFATO
Engine Pressure Ratio Transmitter (HLLA) .... EPRT
Engineer (ADWA) .... e
Engineer (NTIO) .... eng
Engineer (ADWA) .... engr
Engineering (ADWA) .... engg
Engineering (NTIO) .... engin
Engineering All Risks (MARI) .... EAR
Engineering and Installation (CCCA) .... E&I
Engineering Computer-Aided Design .... ECAD
Engineering Integrity Society (COBU) .... EIS
Engineering Research Facility (ADWA) .... ERF
Engineering Scab Melter (ABAC) .... ESM
Engineering Test Satellite-VIII [Developed to study geostationary satellite bus
  technologies] .... ETS-VIII
English (ADWA) .... Eng
English as a Second Language Oral Assessment .... ESLOA
English Breakfast (TRID) .... EB
English for Academic Purposes .... EAP
Enhanced Cordless Base (CGWS) .... ECB
Enhanced Data Rate for Global Evolution .... EDGE
Enhanced Data Rates for Global Evolution .... EDGE
Enhanced Digital Access Communications System (CGWS) .... EDACS
Enhanced Expanded Memory System (ADWA) .... EEMS
Enhanced Graphics Adapter (AEBE) .... EGA
Enhanced Graphics Array (ADWA) .... EGA
Enhanced Proportional Rate Control Algorithm .... EPRCA
Enhanced Readiness Test (ABAC) .... ERT
Enhanced Recognition and Sensing Radar (ADWA) .... ERASER
Enhanced Sludge Washing (ABAC) .... ESW
Enhanced Specialized Mobile Radio (CGWS) .... ESMR
Enhanced Target Generator (CTAS) .... ETG
Enhanced Time Division Multiple Access (CGWS) .... E-TDMA
Enlisted (ADWA) .... enl
Enoch & Cie [Publisher] .... ENO
Enroute High Altitude Chart [Aviation] (PIPO) .... EHAC
Enroute Low Altitude Chart [Aviation] (PIPO) .... ELAC
Enroute Minimum Safe Altitude Warning [Aviation] (PIPO) .... E-MSAW
Enroute Mission Planning and Rehearsal System [Army] .... EMPRS
Ensign (NTIO) .... Ens
Enter Day Stop Order (ADWA) .... EDS
Enteroinvasive Escherichia Coli (ADWA) .... ETEC
Enterprise for the Environment E4E
Entity-Relationship Object-Oriented Specifications (ITCA) .... EROOS
Entomology (ADWA) .... entom
EntrePort Corp. [AMEX symbol] .... ENP
Entropy Unit (ABAC) .... eu
Environment (ADWA) .... environ
Environment Agency (HEAS) .... EA
Environment Canada .... EC
Environment of Evolutionary Adaptedness .... EAA
Environmental Auditors Registration Association (COBU) .... EARA
Environmental Change Network .... ECN
Environmental Communications Network .... ECONET
Environmental Criteria and Assessment Office (AUEG) .... ECAO
Environmental Education .... EE
Environmental Education Association of Washington .... EEAW
Environmental Hazards and Health Effects (ADWA) .... EHHE
Environmental Health Information Services (ADWA) .... EHIS
Environmental Health Review (ADWA) .... EHR
Environmental Impairment Liability Insurance (SARE) .... EIL
Environmental Law Monthly [A publication] .... Env LM
Environmental Law Reports [A publication] .... Env LR

Environmental Lead Laboratory Proficiency Analytical Testing (SARE) .... ELLPAT
Environmental Lead Proficiency Analytical Testing Program .... ELPAT
Environmental Librarian's Network (ADWA) .... ELN
Environmental Monitoring and Mitigation Plan (ABAC) .... EMMP
Environmental Monitoring Systems Laboratory [*Environmental Protection Agency*] (CARB) .... EMSL
Environmental Risk Assessment (SARE) .... ERA
Environmental Sustainability Initiative .... ESI
Environmental Systems Science Centre .... ESSC
Environmental Technology Building (ABAC) .... ETB
eOn Communications [*NASDAQ symbol*] (SG) .... EONC
Epidemiology and Medical Statistics Unit (HEAS) .... EMSU
Epidermal Nevus Syndrome .... ENS
Episcopal (NTIO) .... Episc
Episcopalian (ADWA) .... Episc
Epistle (ADWA) .... Epis
Epistle (ADWA) .... Epist
Eprise Corp. [*NASDAQ symbol*] (SG) .... EPRS
Equal Access End Office (CCCA) .... EAEO
Equal Opportunities Review [*A publication*] .... EOR
Equal Opportunities Review Discrimination Law Case Digest [*A publication*] .... EOR Dig
Equal Transit Rate (ADWA) .... ETR
Equation (ABAC) .... eq
Equations (ADWA) .... eq
Equatorial South America (CARB) .... ESA
Equilization (MLOA) .... EQL
Equipment Improvement Project .... EIP
Equipment Interface Development .... EID
Equipment Support Module (ADWA) .... ESM
Equivalence (ADWA) .... equiv
equivalent (ABAC) .... eq
Equivalent (NTIO) .... equiv
Equivalent-Damage Index (CARB) .... EDI
Erasable Optical Disk (ITCA) .... EO
Erbium (ABAC) .... Er
Erroneously (ADWA) .... erron
Error (ADWA) .... e
Error Checking and Correcting Random-Access Memory .... ECC RAM
Error Detection Unit (CCCA) .... EDU
Escape (NTIO) .... Esc
Escape Self-Contained Breathing Apparatus (SARE) .... ESCBA
Esdras (ADWA) .... Esdr
Eskimo (ADWA) .... Esk
Esophageal Ultrasonography (ADWA) .... EUS
Essential Field Artillery Task [*Army*] .... EFAT
Essential Fire Support Task [*Army*] .... EFST
Established (ADWA) .... estab
Estate (ADWA) .... est
Estimated Approach Time [*Aviation*] (PIAV) .... EAT
Estimated Maximum Loss (MARI) .... EML
Estimated Maximum Probable Loss (MARI) .... EMPL
Estimated Quantitation Limit (ABAC) .... EQL
Estimation and Assessment of Substance Exposure (HEAS) .... EASE
Estonia (NTIO) .... Est
Estonian (ADWA) .... Est
Ethernet Data Link (ADWA) .... EDL
Ethiopian (ADWA) .... Eth
Ethnic/Racial Minority Fellowship Programs (ADWA) .... EMFP
Ethnologist (ADWA) .... ethnol
Ethylene (RIMS) .... Eth
Ethylene Diamine Pyrocatechol .... EDP
Ethylene Glycol Methyl Ether (PIPO) .... EGME
Ethyleneglycotetraacetic Acid (ADWA) .... EGTA
Ethylene-Propylene Terpolymer (SARE) .... EPDM
Etruria (ADWA) .... Etr
Etymology (NTIO) .... etym
Euphemistic (ADWA) .... euphem
Euphonium .... euph
European Arctic Stratospheric Ozone Experiment (CARB) .... EASOE
European Business Aircraft Association (PIAV) .... EBAA
European Centre for Space Law (CARB) .... ECSL
European Council of General Aviation Support (PIAV) .... ECOGAS
European Currency Unit (NTIO) .... ecu
European Large Magnetic Field Facility .... ELMF
European Network for Research on Global Change (CARB) .... ENRICH
European Norms (SARE) .... EN
European Optical Society .... EOS
European Patent Organisation (HEAS) .... EPO
European Policy Committee (HEAS) .... EPC
European Question Committee (HEAS) .... EQC
European River Ocean System (CARB) .... EROS
European Social Fund (HEAS) .... ESF
European Space Research and Technology Centre (CARB) .... ESTEC
European Space Research Technology Center (CCCA) .... ESTEC
European Telephone Service (CCCA) .... ETS
Evacuation .... evac
Evaluation (ADWA) .... eval
Evaluation Module (AEBE) .... EVM
Evangelical (ADWA) .... evang
Evangelist (ADWA) .... evan
Evaporate (ADWA) .... evap
Evapotranspiration of Applied Water (ADWA) .... ETAW
Even If Used (RIMS) .... EIU

Evening (ADWA) .... ev
Evening (ADWA) .... eve
Event Free Survival [*Medicine*] .... EFS
Event Number Translator .... ENT
Evidence-Based Medicine .... EBM
Evidence-Based Practice Centers (ADWA) .... EPC
Evolutionary Algorithm (IDAI) .... EA
Evolutionary Programming (IDAI) .... EP
Evolving Systems [*NASDAQ symbol*] (SG) .... EVOL
Exahertz (ADWA) .... EHz
Examination (ADWA) .... ex
Examination (ADWA) .... exam
Examination for Professional Psychology Programs (DIPS) .... EPPP
Examining for Aphasia [*J. Eisenson*] (DIPS) .... EFA
Excellent (NTIO) .... exc
Except (ADWA) .... exc
Except as Otherwise Herein Provided (MARI) .... eohp
Excess Baggage (TRID) .... XBAG
Excess Mileage Surcharge [*Travel industry*] (TRID) .... EMS
Exchange (NTIO) .... exch
Exchange Order [*Travel industry*] (TRID) .... XO
Exchange-Traded Funds .... ETFS
Excitatory Tendency (DIPS) .... E
Exclamation (ADWA) .... exclaim
Excluding (ADWA) .... excl
Exclusive Economic Zone of Indonesia (CARB) .... ZEEI
Execution Reference Time (CCCA) .... ERT
Execution Statement (ITCA) .... EXEC
Executive (NTIO) .... ex
Executive Office of the Governor (DEMM) .... EOG
Executive Recruitment Association (COBU) .... ERA
Executive Support Branch (HEAS) .... ESB
Executive Women's Golf Association (ADWA) .... EWGA
Executor (ADWA) .... exor
Executor (ADWA) .... ext
Executrix (ADWA) .... exrx
Exelixis, Inc. [*NASDAQ symbol*] (SG) .... EXEL
Exemplary Voluntary Effort (ABAC) .... EVE
Exercise Countermeasure (SPST) .... EC
Exercise Stress Testing .... EST
Exercise-Associated Muscle Cramping .... EMAC
EXFO Electro-Optical Engineer [*NASDAQ symbol*] .... EXFO
Expanded Localizer (PIPO) .... EXLOC
Expanded Polystyrene (HEAS) .... EXP
Expatriate (ADWA) .... expat
Expected Approach Time (PIPO) .... EAT
Expected Departure Clearance Time (PIPO) .... EDCT
Expected Time of Completion (RIMS) .... ETC
Expected Time of Departure (RIMS) .... ETD
Expected Time of Sailing (RIMS) .... ETS
Expedited Response Action (ABAC) .... ERA
Expenses (NTIO) .... ex
Experience Balance [*Used in Rorschach tests*] (DIPS) .... Exp
Experienced (ADWA) .... expd
Experiment (ADWA) .... exp
Experiment (ADWA) .... expt
Experiment Center (ARMP) .... EC
Experimental (ADWA) .... exptl
Experimental Group (DIPS) .... E
Experimenter's Analysis Facility (ADWA) .... EAF
Expiration (NTIO) .... ex
Expires (NTIO) .... ex
Explicit Forward Congestion Indication [*Telecommunications*] (MLOA) .... EFCI
Explicit Forward Congestion Notification [*Telecommunications*] (MLOA) .... EFCN
Explicit Rate (MLOA) .... ER
Exploratory Research (ABAC) .... ER
Explorer Platform [*NASA*] .... EP
Explosive Cutting Tape .... ECT
Explosives Act 1875 (HEAS) EA75
Explosives Inspectorate (HEAS) .... EI
Explosives Notified Body (HEAS) .... ENB
Explosives Safety Transport Committee (HEAS) .... ESTC
Exponent (ADWA) .... exp
Export .... expt
Export Administration .... EA
Export Enforcement .... EE
Express (NTIO) .... ex
Expressing (ADWA) .... expr
Expressway (ADWA) .... expwy
Expressway (NTIO) .... expy
Extended (NTIO) .... ext
Extended Address Set (CCCA) .... EAS
Extended Global System for Mobile Communication (CGWS) .... E-GSM
Extended High Priority Command (ADWA) .... EHPC
Extended Life Tire (ADWA) .... EXLITE
Extended Precision Vector (ADWA) .... EPV
Extended Range Operations (PIAV) .... EROPS
Extended Services Communications Manager [*IBM Corp.*] .... ESCM
Extended Technology (ITCA) .... ET
Extension (TRID) .... XTN
Extension Markup Language [*Computer science*] (ITCA) .... XML
Extensity, Inc. [*NASDAQ symbol*] (SG) .... EXTN
External Blood Loss (ADWA) .... EBL
External Cavity Diode Laser (ARMP) .... ECDL
External Chemical Messenger (DIPS) .... ECM

External Configuration Model (MLOA) .... ECM
External Diploma Program .... EDP
External Ratio (ABAC) .... ER
External Training (HEAS) .... ET
External-Beam Radiation Therapy (ADWA) .... EBRT
Extinction (DIPS) .... ext
Extra (ADWA) .... E
Extra .... ex
Extra Fancy .... exfcy
Extra Jumbo .... exjbo
Extra Large .... exlge
Extra Long .... exlong
Extra Mileage Allowance [*Travel industry*] (TRID) ... EMA
Extra Player [*Baseball term*] (NDBD) .... EP
Extra Seat [*Travel industry*] (TRID) .... EXST

Extra-Contractual Obligations (MARI) .... ECO
Extraction Procedure Toxicity .... EPTox
Extraction Procedure Toxicity Test (SARE) .... EP TOX
Extraocular Motion (ADWA) .... EOM
Extraocular Motion Full (ADWA) .... EOMF
Extraocular Movements (DAVI) .... XOM
Extrapyramidal Involvement (DIPS) .... EPI
Extratemporal-Lobe-Epilepsy (DAVI) .... XTLE
Extraterrestrial Solar Spectral Irradiance (ADWA) .. ETSR
Extravehicular Life Support System (ADWA) .... ELSS
Extremity (ADWA) .... ext
Extroversion Sensing Feeling Judging (ADWA) .... ESFJ
Extroversion Sensing Feeling Perception (ADWA) .... ESFP
Extroversion Sensing Thinking Judging (ADWA) ...... ESTJ
Extroversion Sensing Thinking Perception (ADWA) ... ESTP
Ezekiel (ADWA) .... Ezk

F
By Meaning

F ratio (DIPS) .... F
Fabulous (ADWA) .... fab
Face-Centered Cubic (ABAC) .... fcc
Facilities (ADWA) .... fac
Facilities Change Notice (ABAC) .... FCN
Facility Control Office (CCCA) .... FCO
Facility Effluent Monitoring Plan (ABAC) .... FEMP.
Facility Inventory Assessment (ABAC) .... FIA
Facilities and Operations (ABAC) .... F&O
Facsimile (NTIO) .... fac
Factories Act 1961 (HEAS) FA61
Factory and Agricultural Inspectorate Division (HEAS) .... FAID
Factory Inspectorate Circular (HEAS) .... FIC
Factory Inspectorate Minute (HEAS) .... FIM
Factory Inspectorate Note (HEAS) .... FIN
Factory Inspectorate Specialist Minute (HEAS) .... FISM
Facultative/Obligatory (MARI) .... Fac/Oblig
Fahrenheit (ADWA) .... Fah
Fahrenheit (NTIO) .... Fahr
Fail (ADWA) .... F
Failure Detection Electronics (ADWA) .... FDE
Fair .... fr
Fair Market, Inc. [NASDAQ symbol] (SG) .... FAIM
Falling Down Rolling on the Floor Laughing (ADWA) .... FDROTFL
Familial Adenomatous Polyposis .... FAP
Familial Polyposis Coli Gene [Medicine] .... FAP
Familiar (NTIO) .... fam
Family Care International (ADWA) .... FCI
Family Channel (ADWA) .... FAM
Family Court Reporter [A publication] .... FCR
Family Law Quarterly [A publication] .... Fam LQ
Family Law Reports [A publication] .... FLR
Family Limited Partnership .... FLIP
Family Resources .... FAMR
Family Support Plan .... FSP
Fan Magazine (ADWA) .... fanzine
Fancy (ADWA) .... fcy
Far East (CARB) .... FEA
Far Infrared and Submillimeter Telescope .... FIRST
Faraday (ADWA) .... Far
Fargo Electronics [NASDAQ symbol] (SG) .... FRGO
Farm Service Agency .... FSA
Farm Services Agency (DEMM) .... FSA
Farthing (ADWA) .... f
Fascicle (ADWA) .... fas
Fashion Technology .... FT
Fast Atmospheric Signature Code (ARMP) .... FASCODE
Fast Auroral Snapshot Explorer .... FAST
Fast Low-Angle Shots .... FLASH
Fast Patrol Craft, Air Cushion [Navy] .... PCFA
Fast Patrol Craft, Hydrofoil [Navy] .... PCFH
Faster Than Light (NTIO) .... ftl
Fastnet Corp. [NASDAQ symbol] (SG) .... FSST
Fast-Spiking .... FS
Father (NTIO) .... Fr
Father-in-Law (ADWA) .... FIL
Fathom (ADWA) .... fath
Fathom (NTIO) .... fth
Fathoms (RIMS) .... FMS
Fatigue Decreased Proficiency [NASA] (SPST) .... FDP
Fear Survey Schedule II [Psychology] (DIPS) .... FSS II
Federal (NTIO) .... fed
Federal Advisory Committee .... FAC
Federal Agricultural Mortgage Corporation (ADWA) .... FAMC
Federal Assessment Team [Department of Emergency Management]
(DEMM) .... FasT
Federal Aviation Administration Logistics Center (ADWA) .... FAALC
Federal Bulletin Board (ADWA) .... FBB
Federal Credit Policy Working Group .... FCPWG
Federal Emergency Management Information System (ABAC) ..... FEMIS
Federal Emergency Response Team (DEMM) .... FERT
Federal Energy Technology Center .... FETC
Federal Financial Managers Council .... FFMC
Federal Geologic Mapping Project (CARB) .... FEDMAP
Federal Hazard Mitigation Officer (DEMM) .... FHMO
Federal Information Exchange, Inc. .... FEDIX

Federal Laboratory Consortium (ABAC) .... FLC
Federal National Radio System (DEMM) .... FNARS
Federal National Teletype System (DEMM) .... FNATS
Federal National Voice System (DEMM) .... FNAVS
Federal Response Plan (DEMM) .... FRP
Federal Technology Service .... FTS
Federal Technology Transfer Act (AUEG) .... FTTA
Federal Water Pollution Control Act [1972] (CARB) .... FWPCA
Federated (ADWA) .... fed
Federated Council for Internal Medicine (ADWA) .... FCIM
Federation (ADWA) .... fedn
Federation of Animal Science Societies .... FASS
Federation of Chiropractic Licensing Boards (ADWA) .... FCLB
Federation of Historical Bottle Clubs (ADWA) .... FHBC
Feed Test Algorithm (ABAC) .... FTA
Feedback Threshold (CCCA) .... FTH
Feet per Minute (PIAV) .... fpm
Feet per Second (ABAC) .... ft/s
Felicity [Television program title] .... FEL
Feline Attention Deficit Disorder .... FADD
Feline Infectious Anemia (ADWA) .... FIA
Feline Leukemia Virus (ADWA) .... FeLV
Feline Lower Urinary Tract Disorder .... FLUTD
Fellow of the American College of Medical Practice Executives
(ADWA) .... FACMPE
Fellow of the American College of Nuclear Physicians (ADWA) ..... FACNP
Fellow of the Australian Library and Information Association ..... FALIA
Female (NTIO) .... fem
Feminine (ADWA) .... f
Feminist Legal Studies [A publication] .... Fem LS
Femtosecond (ABAC) .... fs
Fenfluramine [Medicine] (DIPS) .... FEN
Fennoscandian Ice Sheet .... FIS
Fermilab Main Injector .... FMI
Ferroelectric .... FLC
Fetal Alcohol Network (ADWA) .... FAN
Fetal Heart Rhythm [Medicine] (ADWA) .... FHR
Fetal Valproate Syndrome .... FVS
Fetus at Risk [Medicine] (DIPS) .... FAR
Feudalism (ADWA) .... feud
Fiber Channel Standard [Computer science] (ITCA) ...... FCS
Fiberoptic Bronchoscope .... FOB
Fiber-Reinforced Polymer .... FRP
Fibroblast Growth Factor-2 .... FGF-2
Fibromyalgia Syndrome .... FMA
Fibromyalgia Syndrome .... FMS
Fiction (NTIO) .... fict
Fictitious (ADWA) .... fict
Fidelity (ADWA) .... fid
Fidelity Guarantee [Insurance] (MARI) .... FG
Field Action Request (CTAS) .... FAR
Field Consultant Group (HEAS) .... FCG
Field Emission Device (ADWA) .... FED
Field Evaluation (CTAS) .... FE
Field Lysimeter Testing Facility (ABAC) .... FLTF
Field Management Unit (HEAS) .... FMU
Field Operations Computer System (HEAS) .... FOCUS
Field Operations Directorate (HEAS) .... FOD
Field Portable .... FP
Field Programmable Logic Device (AEBE) .... FPLD
Field Record Form (ABAC) .... FRF
Field Scientific Support Unit (HEAS) .... FSSU
Field Sobriety Test (SARE) .... FST
Field Task Proposal (ABAC) .... FTP
Field-Emission Transistor (ABAC) .... FET
Fielding Percentage [Baseball term] (NDBD) .... FP
Field-Work Proposal (ABAC) .... FWP
Figural Bottle Opener Collectors (ADWA) .... FBOC
Figuratively (ADWA) .... fig
Figures and Captions .... FC
Film Bagged .... flmb
Film Wrapped .... flmw
Film Wrapped .... flmwrpd
Filter Bank Combiner Radiometer (CCCA) .... FBCR
Final Approach Point (PIPO) .... FAP
Final Approach Segment (PIPO) .... FAS

Final Control Point (PIPO) ... FCP
Final Payment (TRID) ... FP
Finance and General Purposes Committee (HEAS) ... F&GPC
Finance and Planning Unit (HEAS) ... FPU
Finance Efficiency and Planning Division (HEAS) ... FEPD
Finance Unit (HEAS) ... FINU
Financial Aid Form Need Analysis Report ... FAFNAR
Financial Management Accounting System (HEAS) ... FMAS
Financial Markets Development ... FMD
Financial Need Analysis Report ... FNAR
Financial Reconstruction Commission ... FRC
Financially Independent (ADWA) ... fin indep
Financially Secure (ADWA) ... fin sec
Fine Grain (ADWA) ... FG
Finger Skin Temperature (HEAS) ... FST
Finish (ADWA) ... fin
Finished Room over Garage ... FROG
Finite Element Model of Material Transport through Aquifers (CARB) ... FEMA
Finland (NTIO) ... Fin
Finnish (ADWA) ... Fin
Finnish (ADWA) ... Finn
Fire and Accident [*Insurance*] (MARI) ... F/A
Fire and Allied Perils [*Insurance*] (MARI) ... F&AP
Fire and Explosion (HEAS) ... F&Ex
Fire Break Door (MARI) ... FD
Fire, Collision, Overturning, and Derailment [*Insurance*] (MARI) ... FCOD
Fire Control (ADWA) ... FC
Fire Extinguishing Appliances (MARI) ... FEA
Fire Fighting (RIMS) ... FiFI
Fire Island Association ... FIA
Fire Island National Seashore ... FINS
Fire Pond, Inc. [*NASDAQ symbol*] (SG) ... FIRE
Fire Precautions Act 1971 (HEAS) ... FPA71
Fire Risk on Freight [*Insurance*] (MARI) ... frof
Fire Risk Only [*Insurance*] (MARI) ... FRO
Fire Safety Officer (HEAS) ... FSO
Fireplace (ADWA) ... fireplc
Firewall Forward (PIPO) ... FWF
First Access Channel (CGWS) ... FIRSTCHA
First Available (TRID) ... FRAV
First City Bank [*AMEX symbol*] (SG) ... FBX
First Paging Channel (CGWS) ... FIRSTCHP
First Paragraph ... FP
First Scan ... FS
First Stage Digital Multiplexer (CCCA) ... FSDM
First World Communic 'B' [*NASDAQ symbol*] (SG) ... FWIS
First-Class Hotel (TRID) ... FHTL
Fiscal Year to Date (ABAC) ... FYTD
Fiscal Year Work Plan (ABAC) ... FYWP
Fish Information Network (CARB) ... FIN
Fish Kill (AUEG) ... FK
Fisheries Task Force ... FTF
Fit for Duty Evaluation (DIPS) ... FFDE
Fitted with Auxiliary Engine (MARI) ... Aux
Five Year Master Objectives Program (CCCA) ... FYMOP
Five Year Program (CCCA) ... FYP
Five-Hydroxytrptamine [*Chemical name of serotonin*] (DIPS) ... 5HT
Five-Hydroxytryptophan [*Chemical precursor to serotonin*] (DIPS) ... 5HTP
Fixed Base Operation (PIPO) ... FBO
Fixed Disk (ADWA) ... FDISK
Fixed Head Star Tracker ... FHST
Fixed Head Star Trackers ... FHST
Fixed Time Division Multiple Access (CCCA) ... FTDMA
Fixed-Ratio Schedule of Reinforcement (DIPS) ... FR
Fixing Note (RIMS) ... F/N
Flag, Ownership, or Management (MARI) ... FOM
Flag Telecom Hldgs. [*NASDAQ symbol*] (SG) ... FTHL
Flame Resistant (SARE) ... FR
Flameproof (HEAS) ... FLP
Flammable Gas Tank Safety (ABAC) ... FGTS
Flammables and Gas Policy Unit (HEAS) ... FLAGU
Flat ... flt
Fleet Command Control (CCCA) ... FCC
Fleet Operational Center (CCCA) ... FOC
Fleet Operations (CCCA) ... FLTOPS
Fleet Replacement Squadron [*Military*] ... FRS
Fleet Street Reports [*A publication*] ... FSR
FleetBoston Financial ... FBF
Flexible Film Isolator (HEAS) ... FFI
Flexible Satellite Communications Systems Simulator (CCCA) ... FSCSS
Flexileave (HEAS) ... FL
Flight (TRID) ... flt
Flight Data Management Unit (HLLA) ... FDMU
Flight Increment Training Load [*NASA*] (SPST) ... FITL
Flight Interruption Manifest [*Travel industry*] (TRID) ... FIM
Flight Management Control and Display Unit (HLLA) ... FMCDU
Flight Management Guidance Envelope Computer (HLLA) ... FMGEC
Flight Operations Maintenance Management System [*NASA*] (SPST) ... FOMMS
Flight Planned Route (PIPO) ... FPR
Flight Situation Display ... FSD
Flight Visibility (PIPO) ... FV
Floating Rate Collateralized Mortgage Obligation ... FRCMO
Flood Boundary Floodway Map (ADWA) ... FBFM
Flood Insurance Study (ADWA) ... FIS
Flood Mitigation Assistance Program (DEMM) ... FMAP
Floodway Hazard Boundary Map (ADWA) ... FHBM
Floor (NTIO) ... fl
Floor Plate-Conditioned Culture Medium ... FPCM
Florida Administrative Code (DEMM) ... FAC
Florida Department of Law Enforcement (DEMM) ... FDLE
Florida Department of Transportation (DEMM) ... FLDOT
Florida Electrical Cooperative Association (DEMM) ... FECA
Florida Emergency Information Line (DEMM) ... FEIL
Florida Highway Patrol (DEMM) ... FHP
Florida Housing Finance Agency (DEMM) ... FHFA
Florida Marine Patrol (DEMM) ... FMP
Florida National Guard (DEMM) ... FLNG
Florida State Agency for Surplus Property (DEMM) ... FLSASP
Florida State Fire College (DEMM) ... FSFC
Florida-Caribbean Cruise Association (TRID) ... FCCA
Flow Controlled Virtual Circuit (MLOA) ... FCVC
Flow-Injection Analysis System (ABAC) ... FIAS
Fluency (DIPS) ... f
Flugelhorn ... flg
Fluid Applied Asphalt (ABAC) ... FAA
Fluid Dram (NTIO) ... fl dr
Fluid Ounce (NTIO) ... fl oz
Fluid System Design [*NASA*] (SPST) ... FSD
Fluidic Self-Assembly [*Allied Technology*] ... FSA
Fluids Utility Distribution System [*NASA*] (SPST) ... FUDS
Fluorescent Multilayer Disc ... FMD
Fluorescent Multilayer Disk ... FMD-ROM
Fluoresence Lifetime Imaging Microscopy ... FLIM
Fluoro-2, 4-Dinitrobenzene (ADWA) ... FDNB
Flute ... fl
Fly [*Baseball term*] (NDBD) ... F
Fly Wheels ... F/W
Fly-by-Night (HLLA) ... FBN
Flying Surgeon (NUJO) ... FS
Flying Training Organisation (PIAV) ... FTO
Flyout [*Baseball term*] (NDBD) ... F
Focal Distance (NTIO) ... f
Foldback Current Limiter (ADWA) ... FCL
Folding Articulated Square Truss (SPST) ... FAST
Folio (NTIO) ... fol
Folios (ADWA) ... ff
Food Allergy Survivors Together (ADWA) ... FAST
Food and Agriculture Forum ... FAF
Food and Environmental Protection Act (HEAS) ... FPA
Food, Drugs, and Cosmetics (NTIO) ... FD&C
Food for the Hungry (ADWA) ... FH
Food for the Hungry International (ADWA) ... FHI
Food, Nutrition, and Consumer Service ... FNCS
Food Safety Advisory Centre (HEAS) ... FSAC
Food Safety Network ... ESNet
Food Science and Human Nutrition ... FSHN
Foolscap (ADWA) ... fcap
Foolscap (ADWA) ... fcp
Foot-Candle (NTIO) ... fc
Foot-Candle (ABAC) ... ft-c
Foot-Lambert (ABAC) ... ft-L
Foot-Lambert (DIPS) ... ftl
Foot-Pound (NTIO) ... ft-lb
For a Second [*Internet dialog*] ... FAS
For Declaration Purposes Only (MARI) ... FDO
For Future Reference [*Internet dialog*] ... FFR
For Our Guidance (RIMS) ... FOG
For Sale ... FS
For Trade ... FT
For Your Guidance (RIMS) ... FYG
Forced Expectorant Volume [*Medicine*] ... FEV
Fore and Aft (ADWA) ... f and a
Forecast (PIAV) ... fcst
Forecast Generator [*Canadian natural language generation system*] (IDAI) ... FOG
Foreign (NTIO) ... for
Foreign Language and Area Studies ... FLAS
Form of Payment (TRID) ... FOP
Form Response [*Used in Rorschach test scoring*] (DIPS) ... F
Formal Dining Room (ADWA) ... FDR
Formula Air Racing Association (PIAV) ... FARA
Formula One Management ... FOM
ForSoft Ltd. ... FORS
Fortissimo (ADWA) ... ff
Fortississimo (ADWA) ... fff
Fortnightly Operational Minute (HEAS) ... FOM
Forward (NTIO) ... fwd
Forward Air Controller [*Military*] ... FAC
Forward Analog Control Channel (CGWS) ... FOCC
Forward Analog Voice Channel (CGWS) ... FVC
Forward Error Control (CCCA) ... FEC
Forward Support Company [*Military*] ... FSC
Forwarding Agents' Certificate of Receipt [*Insurance*] (MARI) ... FCR
Forwarding Agents' Certificate of Transport [*Insurance*] (MARI) ... FCT
Forward-Swept Wing ... FSW
Foster Care ... FC
Foul Fly [*Baseball term*] (NDBD) ... F
Foundation Damage (ADWA) ... FD
Foundation Fighting Blindness (ADWA) ... FFB
Foundation for Health Care Quality (ADWA) ... FHCQ

Foundation for the Accreditation of Hematopoietic Cell Therapy
(ADWA) .... FAHCT
Foundation for the Advancement of Innovative Medicine (ADWA) .... FAIM
Foundation of the American Association of Gynecologic Laparoscopists
(ADWA) .... FAAGI
Foundries Industry Advisory Committee (HEAS) .... FIAC
Four-Door Car (TRID) .... FDOR
Fourier Amplitude-Sensitivity Test (CARB) .... FAST
Fraction Actually Burned (CARB) .... FAB
Fraction Actually Degrades (CARB) .... FAD
Fraction Burned Annually (CARB) .... FB
Fraction of Agri-Residue Burned in Fields (CARB) .... FABF
Fraction of Waste Water Treated Anaerobically (CARB) .... FWWTA
Fractional Antedating Goal Response (DIPS) .... FAGR
Fractional Cloud Cover (ARMP) .... FCC
Fracture Control Plan (SPST) .... FCP
Fragmentation Order [*Army*] .... FRAGO
Frame Discard (MLOA) .... FD
France Pacific Territories National Committee for Pacific Economic
Cooperation .... FPTPEC
Franchise (MARI) .... fch
Free Aids Advice Counseling Treatment Support (ADWA) .... FAACTS
Free Alongside Steamer (MARI) .... FAS
Free Carrier (RIMS) .... FCA
Free Discharge (RIMS) .... FDIS
Free Format (CARB) .... FF
Free In and Out Stowed and Trimmed (RIMS) .... FIOST
Free in Trimmed (RIMS) .... FIT
Free of Accident Reported (MARI) .... FAR
Free of any Extra Insurance (RIMS) .... Free Ex Ins
Free of Capture, Seizure, Strikes, Riots, and Civil Commotions
[*Insurance*] (MARI) .... FCSSRCC
Free of Claims [*Insurance*] (MARI) .... FOC
Free of Damage Absolutely [*Insurance*] (MARI) .... FODabs
Free of Particular Average Absolutely (MARI) .... FPA Abs
Free of Particular Average Unless Caused By (MARI) .... FPA
Free of Reported Casualty [*Insurance*] (MARI) .... FRC
Free of Strikes, Riots, and Civil Commotion [*Insurance*] (MARI) .... FSR&CC
Free Sale (TRID) .... FS
Free Steered Vehicle (HEAS) .... FSV
Free Troposphere (CARB) .... FT
Free-Column Volume (ABAC) .... FCV
Freestanding Ambulatory (ADWA) .... FAC
Freezing Level (ARMP) .... FZL
Freezing Point (NTIO) .... fp
Freight, Demurrage, and Defence [*Insurance*] (MARI) .... FDD
Freight Demurrage Deadfreight (RIMS) .... FDD
Frequency-Shift Keying .... fsk
Frequent Traveler (TRID) .... FQTV
Fresh Water (RIMS) .... Fr wa

Fresh Water Arrival Draft (RIMS) .... FWAD
Fresh Water Damage [*Insurance*] (MARI) .... fwd
Fresh Water Departure Draft (RIMS) .... FWDD
Friction Horsepower (ADWA) .... fhp
Friday Holidays Included (RIMS) .... FHINC
Friendly Ice Cream [*AMEX symbol*] .... FRN
Friends of Mineralogy .... FM
Frit Slurry Transport (ABAC) .... FST
From (NTIO) .... fm
From the Ground Up (MARI) .... FGU
Front-End Hardward Emulator (ADWA) .... FEHEM
Frontier Science Research Conferences .... FSRC
Frontline Commun. Cv'B' Pfd. [*AMEX symbol*] (SG) .... FNT Pr
Frontline Communications [*AMEX symbol*] (SG) .... FNT
Fuel System Controller (HLLA) .... FSC
Fuel-Cell Energy .... FCL
Fuel-Cladding Chemical Interaction (ABAC) .... FCCI
Fuel-Oil Blend (ABAC) .... FOB
Full Authority Digital Electronic Control .... FADEC
Full Contract Value [*Insurance*] (MARI) .... FCV
Full Duplex .... FDX
Full Economic Cost .... FEC
Full Extraocular Movement (ADWA) .... FEOM
Full Operational Assessment (CTAS) .... FOA
Full Route Clearance [*Aviation*] (PIPO) .... FRC
Full Turbulence Simulation (CARB) .... FTS
Fully Integrated Groups (ADWA) .... FIGS
Functional Analytic Causal Model (DIPS) .... FACM
Functional Behavioral Assessment .... FBA
Functional Directory (HEAS) .... FD
Functional Group .... FG
Functional Magnetic-Resonance-Imaging (DIPS) .... fMRI
Functional Work Recording (HEAS) .... FWR
Functionally Equivalent Unit (SPST) .... FEU
Functions and Requirements (ABAC) .... F&R
Fund for African and African-American Cultural and Educational Solidarity,
Inc. .... FACES
Fund for UFO Research, Inc. .... FUFOR
Fundamental Expenditure Review (HEAS) .... FER
Fungal Mitochondrial Genome Project .... FMGP
Furlong (NTIO) .... fur
Furnished (NTIO) .... furn
Furniture Industry Research Association (HEAS) .... FIRA
Further Extended Three-Letter Acronym (ADWA) .... FETLA
Future Combat System [*Army*] .... FCS
Future Ground Combat Systems [*Army*] .... FGCS
Fuzzy Associative Memory (IDAI) .... FAM
Fuzzy Neuron Syndrome .... FNS
Fuzzy Rule Approximation (IDAI) .... FRA
Fuzzy Singleton Inference (IDAI) .... FSI

By Meaning

G
By Meaning

G & C Music Corporation .... G&C
G. Schirmer, Inc. [*Publisher*] .... GS
Gain to System Noise Temperature (CCCA) .... G/T
Galaxy Evolution Explorer .... GALEX
Galileo Extended Mission .... GEM
Gallons per Day (ABAC) .... gal/d
Gallons per Hour (PIAV) .... gph
Gallons per Minute (ABAC) .... gal/min
Gallons per Minute (ABAC) .... gpm
Gallons per Second (ABAC) .... gal/s
Gallons per Second (ABAC) .... gps
Game-Winning Run Batted In [*Baseball term*] (NDBD) ... GWRBI
Gamma-Ray Bursters .... GRB
Gamma-Weighted Two-Stream Approximation (ARMP) ..... GWTSA
Gas Accumulation Over Spreading Pools (HEAS) .... GASP
Gas Analysis System for Metabolic Analysis of Physiology [*NASA*]
  (SPST) .... GASMAP
Gas Chromatography .... GC
Gas Heater (CARB) .... GH
Gas Phase Etching .... GPE
Gas Producer .... GP
Gas Release Event (ABAC) .... GRE
Gate Acceptance Rate (CTAS) .... GAR
Gauss (ABAC) .... g
Gay, Lesbian, and Straight Education Network .... GLSEN
Gay-Related Immune Deficiency (DIPS) .... GRID
GBI Capital Management [*AMEX symbol*] (SG) .... GBC
GE Aircraft Engines .... GEAE
Gearless (RIMS) .... GLESS
Gemini (NTIO) .... GEM
Gondor (NTIO) .... gen
Gender Identity (DIPS) .... GI
Gender Role (DIPS) .... GR
General Ability (DIPS) .... G
General Admission (NTIO) .... G
General Average Deposit (MARI) .... GAD
General Average Loss (MARI) .... GAL
General Aviation Awareness Campaign (PIAV) .... GAAC
General Aviation Manufacturers Association (PIAV) ...... GAMA
General Aviation Safety Information Leaflet (PIAV) ...... GASIL
General Aviation Visual Flight Forecast (PIAV) .... GAFOR
General Circuit Interface .... GCI
General Development Procedure Order (HEAS) .... GDPO
General Education Degree (DIPS) .... GED
General Employee Radiation Training (SARE) .... GERT
General Flying Test (PIAV) .... GFT
General, Organic, and Biochemistry .... GOB
General Packet Radio Service .... GPRS
General Packet Radio System .... GPRS
General Problem Solving (IDAI) .... GPS
General Purpose Facilities (ABAC) .... GPF
General Purpose Satellite System (CCCA) .... GPSS
General Purpose Simulation Program [*Computer science*] (ITCA) ... GPSP
General Regression Neural Network (IDAI) .... GRNN
General Research Equipment (ABAC) .... GRE
General Support Services Contractor (ABAC) .... GSSC
General Telephone & Electric Company (CCCA) .... GTE
General Third Party [*Insurance*] (MARI) .... GTP
General World Radio Administrative Conference (CCCA) .... GWRAC
Generalized Additive Model (IDAI) .... GAM
Generalized Logic Diagram (IDAI) .... GLD
Generalized Trace Facility [*Computer science*] (ITCA) ..... GTF
Generally Accepted Accounting Principles .... GAAP
Generally Accepted System Security Principles [*Computer science*]
  (ITCA) .... GSSP
Generally Regarded as Safe (NTIO) .... GRAS
Generation Data Group [*Computer science*] (ITCA) .... GDG
Generic Cell Rate Algorithm (MLOA) .... GCRA
Generic Intelligence Control System (ABAC) .... GICS
Generic Phased Array Radar Simulator (CCCA) .... GPARS
Generic Spacecraft Analyst Assistant (IDAI) .... GenSAA
Genesis (NTIO) .... Gen
Genetically Engineered Machine (ABAC) .... GEM
Genetically Modified Plant (CARB) .... GMP
Genstar Therapeutics [*AMEX symbol*] (SG) .... GNT
Genuity, Inc. 'A' [*NASDAQ symbol*] .... GENU

Geodesy Satellite (CARB) .... Geosat
Geographic .... Geog
Geographical Information System (ARMP) .... GIS
Geographical Rotation (RIMS) .... GEOROT
Geographical Service Area (CGWS) .... GSA
Geography (NTIO) .... geog
Geology (NTIO) .... geol
Geometry (NTIO) .... geom
Geophysical and Environmental Fluid Dynamics .... GEFD
Geophysical Data Facility .... GDF
Geophysical Focus Area (ARMP) .... GFA
Georgian .... GN
Geospace Environment Modeling (CARB) .... GEM
Geostationary Earth Observation (CARB) .... GEO
Geostationary Imaging Fourier Transform Spectrometer [*NASA's proposed
  launch date is 2003*] .... GIFTS
Geostationary Observatory Earth Satellite (CCCA) ..... GOES
Geostationary Operational Environmental Satellite M [*NASA*] ... GOES-M
Geostationary Operational Environmental Satellite N [*NASA*] ... GOES-N
Geostationary Operational Environmental Satellite O [*NASA launch date
  proposed for April 2004*] .... GOES-O
Geostationary Orbiting Environmental Satellite .... GOES
Geostationary Satellite Precipitation Data Centre (CARB) .... GSPDC
Geosynchronous Space Based Radar (CCCA) .... GSBR
German (NTIO) .... Germ
German North Sea (RIMS) .... GNS
Gerund (NTIO) .... ger
Gesell Developmental Schedules [*Clinical method for the study of
  sensorimotor growth of preschool children*] (DIPS) ..... GSCH
Gifted with Special Needs .... GSN
Giga Media Ltd. [*NASDAQ symbol*] (SG) .... GIGM
Gill (NTIO) .... gi
Gimbaled Dish Antenna (CCCA) .... GDA
Gland Manufacturers' Technical Committee (HFAS) ...... GMTC
Glareshield Control Panel (HLLA) .... GCP
Glasgow Coma Scale [*Medicine*] .... gcs
Glaxo Wellcome .... GW
glissando (NTIO) .... gliss
Global Advisor .... GA
Global Air Traffic Management (HLLA) .... GATM
Global Broadcast Services .... GBS
Global Change Master Directory [*NASA*] .... GCMD
Global Change Research Information Office .... GCRIO
Global Climate Change Digest [*A publication*] .... GCCD
Global Earth Radiation Budget .... GERB
Global Energy and Water Experiment (ARMP) .... GEWEX
Global Environmental and Ecological Simulation of Interactive System
  (CARB) .... GENESIS
Global Environmental Research .... GER
Global Indicator (TRID) .... GI
Global Navigation Satellite Sensor Unit (HLLA) .... GNSSU
Global Navigation System (HLLA) .... GNS
Global Observation Information Network (CARB) .... GOIN
Global Ocean Flux (CARB) .... GOF
Global Ozone Monitoring Instrument (CARB) .... GOMI
Global Positioning/Inertial Reference System (HLLA) .... GPIRS
Global Positioning System Sensor Unit (HLLA) .... GPSSU
Global Seismic Network (CARB) .... GSN
Global Sources [*NASDAQ symbol*] (SG) .... GSOL
Global Surface Radiation Network (CARB) .... GSRN
Global Trigger .... GLB TRG
Glockenspiel .... glock
Glyphosate-Tolerant Soya Beans .... GTSB
Glyphosate-Tolerant Soybeans .... GTSB
Goal Orientation (DIPS) .... GO
GoAmerica, Inc. [*NASDAQ symbol*] (SG) .... GOAM
Golay Sequential Coding (CGWS) .... GSC
Golf and Travel Industry Association (TRID) .... GTIA
Good and Safe Port Both Ends (RIMS) .... GASBEND
Good Health is Good Business (HEAS) .... GHGB
Good Merchantable Brand (MARI) .... Gmb
Good Merchantable Quality (MARI) .... Gmq
Good Partial Remission [*Medicine*] .... GPR
Good Practices Standard (ABAC) .... GPS
Goods in Bad Order (MARI) .... gbo
Goods in Transit (MARI) .... GIT

Gordon Occupational Check List II [*A checklist of 240 descriptions of activities related to occupations that do not require a college degree, developed by L.V. Gordon*] (DIPS) .... GOCL-II
Gordon Research Conferences .... GRC
Government Communications Systems Department (SPST) .... GCSD
Government Information Technology Services .... GITS
Government of India (CARB) .... GOI
Government Research Establishment .... GRE
Government Research Laboratories .... GRL
Grade .... Grd
Grade of Service (CGWS) .... GoS
Gradient Angle (PIPO) .... GA
Graduate Medical Education .... QME
Graduate Research, Internship, and Fellowwhhip .... GRIF
Graduated (NTIO) .... grad
Graduated and Reciprocated Initiatives in Tension Reduction [*C. Osgood*] (DIPS) .... GRIT
Grain Inspection, Packers, and Stockyards Administration .... GIPSA
Gram Molecular Volume (ABAC) .... gmv
Grand Slam [*Baseball term*] (NDBD) .... GS
Grant Prideco [*NYSE symbol*] (SG) .... GRP
Graphics Interchange File [*Computer science*] (ITCA) .... GIF
Graphics Performance Characterization (AEBE) .... GPC
Graphics Processor Command Interface .... GPCI
Grapple Fixture (SPST) .... GF
Gravity Field and Steady State Ocean Circulation Explorer .... GOCE
Gravity Pipe [*A specialized computer*] .... GRAPE
Gravity Probe B .... GPB
Grazing Incidence Infrared (ABAC) .... GIIR
Great (NTIO) .... gr
Great Atlantic and Pacific Tea Company (NTIO) .... A&P
Great Lakes Fishery Trust .... GLFT
Greater Boston Youth Symphony Orchestras (ROAS) .... GBYSO
Greatest Commom Divisor (NTIO) .... gcd
Greatest Common Factor (NTIO) .... gcf
Greek (NTIO) .... Gr
Green Arrow .... GA
Green Bank Telescope (ROAS) .... GBT
Green Lantern .... GL
Greenhouse Effect Detection Experiment (CARB) .... GEDEX
Greenwich Standard Time (NTIO) .... GST

Grid Organizational Development (DIPS) .... grid OD
Gromerular Filtration Rate .... GFR
Gross Arrived Damaged Value (MARI) .... GADV
Gross Arrived Sound Value (MARI) .... GASV
Gross Laden Weight (HEAS) .... GLW
Gross Tonnage (RIMS) .... Brt
Gross Written Premiums [*Insurance*] (MARI) .... GWP
Ground Controlled Descent (ROAS) .... GCD
Ground Electro-Optical Deep Space Surveillance System (CCCA) .... GEODS
Ground Mobile Command Capability (CCCA) .... GMCC
Ground Operations and Logistics Integration Panel [*NASA*] (SPST) .... GOLIP
Ground Point of Interception (PIPO) .... GPI
Ground to Air (PIPO) .... G/A
Ground Window Display Utility [*NASA*] (SPST) .... GWDU
Ground-Based Software Tool (HLLA) .... GBST
Groundspeed [*Aviation*] (PIAV) .... G/S
Groundwater Surveillance (ABAC) .... GWS
Group Dispatch Number (CGWS) .... GDN
Group Inclusive Tour [*Travel industry*] (TRID) .... GIT
Group Personnel Unit (HEAS) .... GPU
Group Seat Request [*Travel industry*] (TRID) .... GPST
Group Soviet Forces Germany (CCCA) .... GSFP
GT Group Telecom 'B' [*NASDAQ symbol*] (SG) .... GTTLB
Guadelupe (NTIO) .... Guad
Guam Army National Guard .... GUARNG
Guarantee (NTIO) .... guar
Guaranteed (NTIO) .... guar
Guaranteed Group Rate [*Travel industry*] (TRID) .... GG rate
Guest Investigator .... GI
Guest Observer .... GO
Guidance Memoranda (HEAS) .... GM
Guidance Note (HEAS) .... GN
Guide Star Catalog .... GSC
Guide to Integrated Information Literacy Skills [*A publication*] .... GIILS
Guided Affected Imagery (DIPS) .... GAI
Guided Missile Patrol Combatant [*Navy*] .... PGG
Guiding Light [*Television program title*] .... GL
Gulf Stream Locale (CARB) .... GSL
Gun to Target .... GT
GunMar Music [*Publisher*] .... GM
Gunning Transceiver Logic (AEBE) .... GTL
Gynecology (NTIO) .... gyn

H
By Meaning

Hadron-Electron Ring Accelerator .... HERA
Half Demurrage Weather Timed Saved (RIMS) .... HDWTS
Half Despatch Lay Time Saved Both Ends (RIMS) .... HDLTSBENDS
Half Energy Width .... HEW
Halstead-Reitan Neuropsychological Test Battery [*Intended to measure brain functioning*] (DIPS) .... HRNTB
Hamburg Ocean Carbon Cycle .... HAMOCC
Hammond Organ .... Horg
Hanaro Telecom ADS [*NASDAQ symbol*] (SG) .... HANA
Hand Held Monitor (HEAS) .... HAM
Hand Portable Unit (CGWS) .... HPU
Handspring, Inc. [*NASDAQ symbol*] .... HAND
Harbor Patrol Boat [*Navy*] .... PSB
Hard Disk (AEBE) .... HD
Hard to Find .... HTF
Hard X-Ray Detector .... HXD
Hardware Compatibility [*Computer science*] .... HCL
Hardy-Rand-Rittler [*Test for color blindness*] (DIPS) ... HRR
Harmless Bulk Fertilizer (RIMS) .... HBF
Harmonica .... hca
Harmonised Electronic Data Set (HEAS) .... HEDSET
Harmonium .... hmn
Harp .... hp
Harrier Review Panel [*Military*] .... HaRP
Harvard Business School Association (COBU) .... HBSA
Harvard International Law Journal [*A publication*] .... HILJ
Harwell Acid Rain Model .... HARM
Hatch (RIMS) .... HA
Have Cancelled [*Travel industry*] (TRID) .... HX
Hawaii (NTIO) .... Ha
Hawaii Visitors and Convention Bureau (ROAS) .... HVCB
Hawaiian Studies .... HAWNA
Hawthorne Army Depot [*Umatilla, Oregon*] .... HWAD
Hazard Communication (SARE) .... HazCom
Hazard Evaluation Laboratory Limited [*Herts, England*] . HEL
Hazard Installation (HEAS) .... HI
Hazard Mitigation (DEMM) .... HAZMIT
Hazard Mitigation Grant Program (DEMM) .... HMGP
Hazard Mitigation Officer [*Department of Emergency Management*] (DEMM) .... HMO
Hazardous Installation Group (HEAS) .... HIG
Hazardous Installation Policy Unit (HEAS) .... HIPU
Hazardous Materials Business Plans (SARE) .... HMBP
Hazardous Materials Emergency Preparedness (DEMM) .. HMEP
Hazardous Materials Indentification Guide (SARE) .... HMIG
Hazardous Substance (SARE) .... HS
Hazardous Substances Consent (HEAS) .... HzSC
Hazardous Waste Control Law [*California*] (SARE) ...... HWCL
Hazardous Waste Information System (SARE) .... HWIS
Hazardous Waste Inspectorate (HEAS) .... HWI
Hazardous Waste Management Units (SARE) .... HWMU
Hazards (PIPO) .... H
Header Error Check (MLOA) .... HEC
Heading (PIAV) .... Hdg
Headquarters (NTIO) .... hdqrs
Head-Related Transfer Functions .... HRTF
Health and Safety Advice Centre (HEAS) .... HASAC
Health and Safety Co-Ordinating Group (HEAS) .... HASCOG
Health & Safety Officer (SARE) .... HSO
Health and Safety Policy Liaison (HEAS) .... HSPL
Health Care Coordination Initiative [*Federal Government of Canada, Veterans Affairs*] .... HCCI
Health Care Quality Improvement Program .... HCQIP
Health Circular (HEAS) .... HC
Health Education and Adult Literacy .... HEAL
Health Effects Assessment (AUEG) .... HEAS
Health Hazard Evaluation (HEAS) .... HHE
Health Information Resources Service .... HIRS
Health Insurance Portability & Accountability Act .... HIPAA
Health Notice (HEAS) .... HN
Health Physics Technician (ABAC) .... HPT
Health Policy Division (HEAS) .... HPD
Health Risk Review (HEAS) .... HRR
Health Service Support Plan [*Army*] .... HSSPLAN
Healthcare Integrated Svcs. [*AMEX symbol*] (SG) .... HII
Healthcare Open Systems and Trials .... HOST

Heat-Dissipation Unit (ABAC) .... HDU
Heating Rate (ARMP) .... HR
Heavy Fuel (RIMS) .... HVFL
Heavy Lift Capability .... HLC
Heavy Metal Scraps (RIMS) .... HMS
Heavy Rare-Earth Elements .... HREE
Heavy Tarnish .... H/Y
Heavy Weathering .... H/W
Heckelphone .... heck
Heckler & Koch .... H&K
Hectometer (ABAC) .... hm
Height (NTIO) .... hgt
Held to Maturity .... HTM
Helicopter Association International (TRID) .... HAI
Helicopter Deck (RIMS) .... HELDK
Helping Educators Link Learners Online .... HELLO
Helsinki Exchanges Group Ltd Oy .... HEX
Hepatitis B Immunoglobulin (HEAS) .... HBIG
Heptachlor (ABAC) .... HC
Heptachlor Epoxide (ABAC) .... HCE
Her Highness (NTIO) .... HH
Her Majesty (NTIO) .... HM
Her Majesty's Agricultural Inspectorate (HEAS) .... HMAI
Her Majesty's Explosives Inspectorate (HEAS) .... HMEI
Her Majesty's Industrial Pollution Inspectorate for Scotland (HEAS) .... HMIPIS
Her Majesty's Inspectorate of Mines (HEAS) .... HMIM
Her Majesty's Nuclear Installations Inspectorate (HEAS) . HMNII
Her Royal Highness (NTIO) .... HRH
Herald Tribune [*A publication*] .... HT
Hermes Robotic Arm .... HeRA
Heterocyclic Aromatic Amines .... HAA
Heterocyclicamine (ABAC) .... HCA
Hexachlorobutadiene (ABAC) .... HCB
Hexadecimal (AEBE) .... hex
Hexagon (NTIO) .... hex
Hierarchic Sequential Access Method [*Computer science*] (ITCA) .... HSM
Hierarchical Mixtures of Experts (IDAI) .... HME
Hierarchical Sequential Organization [*Computer science*] (ITCA) ..... HS
Hierarchical Storage Management [*Computer science*] .. HSM
High Availability Cluster Multi-Processing [*IBM Corp.*] . HACMP
High Density Line Conditioning Module .... HDLCM
High Density Subscriber Loop (CGWS) .... HDSL
High Energy Corona (ABAC) .... HEC
High Energy Solar Spectroscopic Imager [*NASA*] .... HESSI
High Fidelity Simulation Model (SPST) .... HFSM
High Frequency Data Link (HLLA) .... HFDL
High Intensity Approach Lighting [*Aviation*] (PIAV) ..... HIAL
High Intensity Runway Edge Lights (PIPO) .... HIRL
High Intensity Strobe Light [*Aviation*] (PIAV) .... HISL
High Latitude (ARMP) .... HL
High Level Languages Operations per Second (CCCA) ... HLOS
High Performance Computer .... HPC
High Resolution Camera .... HRC
High Resolution Dynamics Limb Sounder .... HIRDLS
High Resolution Surveillance System (CCCA) .... HRSS
High Resolution Transmission Molecular Absorption Database (CARB) .... HITRAN
High Rise .... HR
High Speed Photometer .... HSP
High Tempature Melter (ABAC) .... HTM
High Temperature Elongation .... HTE
High Vapor Pressure Metals (ABAC) .... HVPM
High-Altitude Aerial Photograph (CARB) .... HAAP
High-Altitude Lidar Sensing Station (CARB) .... HALSS
High-Density Disk [*Computer science*] (ITCA) .... HDD
High-Dose Reference Laboratory (CARB) .... HDRL
High-Efficiency Metal Fiber (ABAC) .... HEMF
Higher Education Affairs Directorate .... HEAD
Higher Education Coordinating Board .... HECB
Higher Intermediate Point (TRID) .... HIP
High-Intensity Lights (PIPO) .... HI
Highlands Restricted Area (PIAV) .... HRA
High-Level Defense Waste (ABAC) .... HLDW
High-Level Design Language (AEBE) .... HDL
High-Level Waste Solidification (ABAC) .... HLWS
Highly Flammable Liquid (HEAS) .... HFL

Highly Sensitive Person .... HSP
High-Occupancy Toll Lane .... HOT
High-Precision Liquid Chromatography (CARB) .... HPLC
High-Pressure Isolation .... HPI
High-Resolution Field-Ionization Mass Spectrometry (ABAC) .... HRFIMS
High-Resolution Limited Area Model (ARMP) .... HIRLAM
High-Resolution Microwave Sounding Unit (CARB) .... HMSU
High-Resolution Microwave Spectrometer Sounder (CARB) .... HIMSS
High-Resolution Optical Instrument (CARB) .... HROI
High-Resolution Transmission (ARMP) .... HITRAN
High-Temperature Superconducting .... HTS
Highway (NTIO) .... hwy
Highway Patrol (SARE) .... HP
Hilly Terrain (CGWS) .... HT
Hindi (NTIO) .... Hind
Hispanic Broadcasting 'A' [NYSE symbol] .... HSP
Historical (NTIO) .... hist
Historical Canadian Climate Database (CARB) .... HCCD
Historical Tank Content Estimate (ABAC) .... HTCE
Hit by Pitch [Baseball term] (NDBD) .... HBP
Hit by Pitch [Baseball term] (NDBD) .... HP
Hit Probability .... Ph
HLM Design [AMEX symbol] (SG) .... HMD
Hold [Baseball term] (NDBD) .... H
Holds List [Travel industry] (TRID) .... HL
Holistic Nurse Certified (NUJO) .... HNC
Home Area Customer Dialing (ROAS) .... HACD
Home Audio Video Interoperability .... HAVi
Home Electronic Systems (HEAS) .... HES
Home Grocer.com, Inc. [NASDAQ symbol] (SG) .... HOMG
Home Phoneline Networking Alliance .... HPNA
Home Pregnancy Test .... HPT
Home Public Lands Mobile Network (CGWS) .... HPLMN
Homestead .... HO
Homestead Air Reserve Base (DEMM) .... HARB
Honda New Model Center .... HNMC
Honduras (NTIO) .... Hon
Hong Kong Committee for Pacific Economic Cooperation .... HKCPEC
Hops per Second (CCCA) .... HPS

Horizontal Takeoff Horizontal Landing .... HTHL
Horizontal Takeoff Vertical Landing .... HTVL
Horticultural (NTIO) .... hort
Host Behavior Functional Group .... HBFG
Host Computer System (CTAS) .... HCS
Host Processor/Bus Interface Dedicated (SPST) .... HPBID
Host-on-Demand [Computer science] (ITCA) .... HOD
Hot Mix Asphaltic Concrete (ABAC) .... HMAC
Hot Section Inspection [Aviation] (PIPO) .... HSI
Hotel Electronic Distribution Network Association (TRID) ...... HEDNA
Hotel Reservations Network 'A' [NASDAQ symbol] (SG) .... ROOM
Hour (NTIO) .... h
House .... Hse
House-Tree-Person (DIPS) .... HTP
Housing Law Reports [A publication] .... HLR
Houston Automatic Spooling Program [Computer science] (ITCA) .... HASP
HPSC, Inc. [AMEX symbol] .... HDR
Human Capital Exchange .... HCE
Human Figure (DIPS) .... H
Human Health and the Environment (SARE) .... HH&E
Human Mesenchymal Stem Cells .... hMSC
Human Resources Professionals Association of Ontario [Canada] .... HRPAO
Human Resources Unit (HEAS) .... HRU
Human Rights Law Journal [A publication] .... HRLJ
Human T-Cell Leukemia Virus (NTIO) .... HTLV
Humble, Old, Unattractive, Nonverbal, and Dumb (DIPS) .... HOUND
Hurricane Andrew Recovery and Reconstruction Trust Fund (DEMM) ..... HARRTF
Hybrid .... h
Hybrid Fiber Coaxial .... HFC
Hydraulic Conductivity (ABAC) .... HC
Hydrogen Chloride (ABAC) .... HCl
Hydrological Radar Experiment .... HYREX
Hydrostatic Release Unit (TRID) .... HRU
Hyperbaric Lighting Set [NASA] (SPST) .... HLS
Hyperion Bay [Television program title] .... HB
Hypertext Transport Protocol (CARB) .... http
Hypervelocity Impact (SPST) .... HVI
Hypotenuse (NTIO) .... hyp
Hypothesis (NTIO) .... hypoth
Hypothetical Construct (DIPS) .... HC

I

By Meaning

123

Inner Detector ... ID
Inner Diameter (NTIO) ... id
Inner Magnetosphere Explorer [*NASA*] ... IMEX
Inorganic Monomeric Aluminum (CARB) ... IM-A1
Input Output Buffer Information Specification (AEBE) ... IBIS
Input/Output Configuration Program [*Computer science*] (ITCA) ... IOCP
Input Port (CCCA) ... IP
Inshell ... ins
InSilicon Corp. [*NASDAQ symbol*] (SG) ... INSN
In-Situ Propellant Production ... ISPP
Inspection Time (DIPS) ... IT
Inspiration of Astronomical Phenomena ... INSAP
Installation and Check Out (CTAS) ... I/CO
Installation Control Specification [*Computer science*] (ITCA) ... ICS
Instant (NTIO) ... inst
Instantaneous Radiative Flux (ARMP) ... IRF
Instantaneous Radiative Transfer (CARB) ... IRF
Institute Builders Risk Clause (MARI) ... IBC
Institute Cargo Clauses (MARI) ... ICC
Institute for Atmospheric Radioactivity [*Feiberg, Germany*] (CARB) ... IAR
Institute for British Business (COBU) ... IBB
Institute for Computational Earth System Science ... ICESS
Institute for Employment Studies (COBU) ... IES
Institute for Palestine Studies ... IPS
Institute for the Study of Contract with Non-Human Intelligence ... ISCNI
Institute Freight Clause (MARI) ... IFC
Institute of Biological Engineering ... IBE
Institute of Biology of the Southern Seas ... IBSS
Institute of Careers Guidance (COBU) ... ICG
Institute of Employment Studies (HEAS) ... IES
Institute of Environmental Managers (COBU) ... IEM
Institute of Group Analysis (COBU) ... IGA
Institute of Hospital Engineering (COBU) ... IHospE
Institute of Industrial Market Research (COBU) ... IIMR
Institute of Investment Managers and Research (COBU) ... IIMR
Institute of Logistics (COBU) ... ILOG
Institute of Management (COBU) ... IM
Institute of Management Development Alumni Associates (COBU) ... IMDAA
Institute of Museum and Library Services ... IMLS
Institute of Physics (COBU) ... IPhys
Institute of Population Research [*Beijing University*] ... IPR
Institute of Project Management (COBU) ... IPM
Institute of Sales and Marketing Management (COBU) ... ISMM
Institute Port Risk Clause (MARI) ... IPRC
Institute Yacht Clause (MARI) ... IYC
Institution of Diagnostic Engineers (COBU) ... IDiagE
Institution of Electrical Designers (COBU) ... IED
Institution of Gas Engineers (COBU) ... IGasE
Institution of Structural Engineers (COBU) ... IStructE
Institutional Admissions Testing Program ... IATP
Institutional Summary Data Service ... ISDA
Instructional Management Systems ... IMS
Instructional Manual ... inst
Instructor (NTIO) ... instr
Instrument Definition Document ... IDD
Instrument Detection Limit (ABAC) ... IDI
Instrument Flow Diagram (ABAC) ... IFD
Instrument Performance Model (ARMP) ... IPM
Instrument Rating [*Aviation*] (PIAV) ... IR
Instrument Remote Controller (PIPO) ... IRC
Instrument Team (ARMP) ... IT
Instrumentation and Control (ABAC) ... I&C
Insurance Corporation of British Columbia ... ICBC
Integrated Atmospheric Deposition Network ... IADN
Integrated Avionics Architecture, Requirements, and Design (SPST) ... IAARD
Integrated Avionics Computer (HLLA) ... IAC
Integrated Baseline System (ABAC) ... IBS
Integrated Call Management ... ICM
Integrated Cloud Liquid (CARB) ... ICL
Integrated Computer Environment (ABAC) ... ICE
Integrated Conservation and Development Project ... ICDP
Integrated Demonstration (AUEG) ... ID
Integrated Demonstration Coordinator (ABAC) ... IDC
Integrated Electronic Control Centre (HEAS) ... IECC
Integrated Exposure Uptake Biokinetic Model (SARE) ... IEUBK
Integrated Information Sy. [*NASDAQ symbol*] (SG) ... IISX
Integrated Liquid Water (ARMP) ... ILW
Integrated Master Measurement and Command List (SPST) ... IMMCL
Integrated Military Airlift Planning System (CCCA) ... IMAPS
Integrated Performance and Risk Management ... IPRM
Integrated Power Management ... IPM
Integrated Program (ABAC) ... IP
Integrated Program Coordinator (ABAC) ... IPC
Integrated Program Manager (ABAC) ... IPM
Integrated Program Plan (ABAC) ... IPP
Integrated Program Scheduling Standard Document (SPST) ... IPSSD
Integrated Provider Organization ... IPO
Integrated Resource Planning (ABAC) ... IRP
Integrated Service Network ... ISN
Integrated Services Digital Network-Basic Rate Interface (CGWS) ... ISDN-BRI
Integrated Services Digital Network-Primary Rate Interface (CGWS) ... ISDN-PRI
Integrated Services Digital Network-User Part (CGWS) ... ISDN-UP
Integrated Target Weather System (CTAS) ... ITWS
Integrated Terrain Unit (CARB) ... ITU
Integrated Truss Assembly [*NASA*] (SPST) ... ITA
Integrated Water Vapor (ARMP) ... IWV
Intellectual Property Quarterly [*A publication*] ... IPQ
Intelligent Computer-Aided Instruction (IDAI) ... ICAI
Intensive Care Baby Unit (ROAS) ... ICBU
Intensive Field Observation (ARMP) ... IFO
Intensive Operational Period (ARMP) ... IOP
Intent to Deny ... ITD
Intentional Walk [*Baseball term*] (NDBD) ... IW
Inter Process Communication (CTAS) ... IPC
Interaction-Process Analysis (DIPS) ... IPA
Interactive Call Distribution (ROAS) ... ICD
Interactive Collaborative Environment ... ICE
Interactive Data Language ... IDL
Interagency Alternative Dispute Resolution Working Group ... IADRWG
Interagency Education Research Initiative ... IERI
Inter-Agency Electronic Grants Committee ... IAEGC
Interaural Intensity Differences ... IID
Inter-Bank Organisation and Methods Association (COBU) ... IBOMA
Interceptor Body Armor [*Military*] ... IBA
Intercom (PIAV) ... i/c
Interdisciplinary American Studies ... IAS
Interest (NTIO) ... i
Interest Rate Risk ... IRR
Interested Party Information ... IPI
Interface (CTAS) ... I/F
Interface Design Document (CTAS) ... IDD
Interference Calibration Blank (ABAC) ... ICB
Interim Airborne Target Acquisition System (CCCA) ... IATAS
Interim Alternative Educational Setting ... IAES
Interim Full Operating Capability (CCCA) ... IFDC
Interim Local Management Interface ... ILMI
Interim Standard 41 for North American Inter-Switch Signaling (CGWS) ... IS-41
Interim Standard 54 for the First North American Dual-Mode Time Division Multiple Access Cellular System (CGWS) ... IS-54
Interim Standard 88 for the Narrowband Advanced Mobile Phone System Cellular System (CGWS) ... IS-88
Interim Standard 136 for North American Time Division Multiple Access Cellular Access (CGWS) ... IS-136
Interim STandard for Code Division Multiple Access Cellular Service (CGWS) ... IS-95
Interim Use Manual (SPST) ... IUM
Interim Voice Response System (PIPO) ... IVRS
Interior Design Engineering (SPST) ... IDE
Interlibrary Loan (AUEG) ... ILL
Intermediate Care Unit (NUJO) ... IMC
Intermediate Facility (ARMP) ... IF
Intermediate Frequency (ABAC) ... if
Intermediate Fuel Oil (RIMS) ... IFO
Intermediate Level School ... ILS
Intermediate-Size Car (TRID) ... ICAR
Intermediate-Size Station Wagon (TRID) ... IWGN
Intermountain Rural Electrical Association ... IREA
InterMune Pharmaceuticals [*NASDAQ symbol*] (SG) ... ITMN
International (TRID) ... IN
International Advisory Group ... IAG
International Airlines Travel Agency Network (TRID) ... IATAN
International Association of School Librianship ... IASL
International Association of World Tourism (TRID) ... IAWT
International Biophysical Program (CARB) ... IBP
International Bluegrass Music Museum ... IBMM
International Business Machines Personal Computer (CARB) ... IBM PC
International Centre for Alpine Environments [*Chambery, France*] (CARB) ... ICALPE
International Centre for Equatorial Atmospheric Research [*Indonesia*] (CARB) ... ICEAR
International Centre for Fundamental Physics in Moscow ... ICFPM
International Centre for Research in Agroforestry ... ICRAF
International Christian Chamber of Commerce (COBU) ... ICCC
International Code Assessment and Applications Programme (HEAS) ... ICAP
International Commission on Continental Erosion (CARB) ... ICCE
International Commission on Ground Water (CARB) ... ICGW
International Committee of the Red Cross ... ICRC
International Committee on Atmosphere-Soil-Vegetation Relations (CARB) ... ICASVR
International Communications Conference (CCCA) ... ICC
International Computer Communications Conference (CCCA) ... ICCC
International Conference on Few-Body Problems in Physics ... IUPAP
International Countermeasures Handbook (CCCA) ... ICH
International Dark-Sky Association ... IDA
International Electronic Component Qualification ... IECQ
International English Language Testing System ... IELTS
International Environmental Commitments ... IEC
International Forum of Travel and Tourism Advocates (TRID) ... IFTAA
International Gamma-Ray Astrophysics Laboratory [*Sponsored by European Space Agency*] ... INTEGRAL
International Geoscience and Remote Sensing Society (CARB) ... IGRSS
International Heliospheric Study (CARB) ... IHS
International Institute for Democracy and Electoral Assistance ... IDEA
International Institute of Information Design (CARB) ... IIID
International Law Enforcement Telecommunications Seminar ... ILETS
International Linear Collider ... ILC
International Livestock Research Institute ... ILRI
International Loss Control Institute (SARE) ... ILCI
International Marine Insurance Union (MARI) ... IMIU
International Meteor Organization ... IMO

International Mobile Telecommunications Association (CGWS) .... IMTA
International Occupational Hygiene Society (SARE) .... IOHS
International Organization of the Network Layer (ITCA) .... IONL
International Psychoanalytic Association .... IPA
International Route Charge [*Travel industry*] (TRID) .... IRC
International Society for Ecosystem Health .... ISEH
International Society for Optical Engineering .... SPIE
International Society for Technology in Education .... ISTE
International Society of Regulatory Toxicology and Pharmacology .... ISRTP
International Society of Travel and Tourism Educators (TRID) .... ISTTE
International Standard Work Code .... ISWC
International Standards Organization (CGWS) .... ISO
International Telecommunications Union-Radio Sector (CGWS) .... ITU-R
International Test Conference (AEBE) .... ITC
International Travel Agent Guild (TRID) .... ITAG
International Tropospheric Ozone Year (CARB) .... ITOY
International Union of Biochemistry and Molecular Biology (CARB) .... IUBMB
International Union of Electrical Workers .... IUE
International Union of Geodesy and Geophysics (CARB) .... IUGG
International Water Management Institute .... IWMI
Internet Access Provider .... IAP
Internet Activities Board (MLOA) .... IAB
Internet Architect Holdrs. Tr. [*AMEX symbol*] (SG) .... IAH
Internet Call Manager .... ICM
Internet Capital Group .... ICG
Internet Control Messaging Protocol (ITCA) .... ICMP
Internet Directory of Advisors and Consultants (COBU) .... IDAC
Internet Infrastruct Holdrs. Tr. [*AMEX symbol*] (SG) .... IIH
Internet Learning Agent (IDAI) .... ILA
Internet Network Information Center .... Internic
Internet Presence Provider .... IPP
Internet Rapid Application Development (ITCA) .... IRAD
Internet Security Advisors Group .... ISAG
Internetwork Address Sub-Group .... IASG
Internetwork Broadcast Sub-Group .... IBSG
Internetwork Broadcast/Unknown Functional Group .... IBUFG
Interpersonal Psychotherapy (DIPS) .... IPT

Interpolated Schedule of Reinforcement (DIPS) .... INTER
Interrogate Friend or Foe (CCCA) .... IFF
Interrogative (NTIO) .... interrog
Intersegmental General Education Transfer Curriculum .... IGETC
Intersil Holdings 'A' [*NASDAQ symbol*] (SG) .... ISIL
Inter-Symbol Interference (AEBE) .... ISI
Intervening Variable (DIPS) IV
interWAVE Communic. Intl. [*NASDAQ symbol*] (SG) .... IWAV
Inter-Working Function (MLOA) .... IWF
IntraBiotics Pharmaceuticals [*NASDAQ symbol*] (SG) .... IBPI
Intransitive (NTIO) .... intrans
Introversion I
Intrusion Countermeasures Electronics .... ICE
Inventory Update Rule (SARE) .... INUR
Investigational New Animal Drug Application .... INADA
Investor Relations Society (COBU) .... IRS
Investors in People (HEAS) .... IiP
Involuntary Nervous System (DIPS) .... INS
Iodine Absorber (ABAC) .... IA
Ionospheric Plasma and Electrodynamics Instrument (CARB) .... IPEI
Iowa Educational Media Association .... IEMA
Iowa Youth and Families Project .... IYFP
iParty Corp. [*AMEX symbol*] (SG) .... IPT
IPI, Inc. [*AMEX symbol*] (SG) .... IDH
Iris Pigmentepithelium .... IPE
Irish Law Times [*A publication*] .... ILT
Irish Reports [*A publication*] .... IR
Iron Pipe Standard (SARE) .... IPS
Irrespective of Percentage (MARI) .... iop
Island (NTIO) .... Isl
Island View [*Travel industry*] (TRID) .... ISLVW
Isotype On-Line Separator .... ISOLDE
Issues Screening Board [*NASA*] (SPST) .... ISB
Isthmus (NTIO) .... isth
Italian (NTIO) .... It
Italian Space Agency (CARB) .... ISA
Italic (NTIO) .... Ital
Italicize (NTIO) .... ital

By Meaning

J

By Meaning

J. Curwen & Sons [Publisher] .... CUR
J. Robert Oppenheimer .... JRO
Jacket .... jkt
Jamaica (NTIO) .... Jam
Jammer (CCCA) .... J
Jammer Locator Detector (CCCA) .... JLD
Jammer-to-Noise Ratio (CCCA) .... JNR
Japan (NTIO) .... Jap
Japan Air System .... JAS
Japan National Committee for Pacific Economic Cooperation .... JANCPEC
Japanese Earth Observing Satellite (CARB) .... JEOS
Japanese Earth Observing System (CARB) .... JEOS
Japanese Polar-Orbiting Platform (CARB) .... JPOP
Jitter Equivalent Target (CCCA) .... JET
Job Performance Assistance (SPST) .... JPA
John F. Kennedy International Airport (NTIO) .... JFK
John Hancock Fin'l Svcs. [NYSE symbol] (SG) .... JHF
Johnson Space Center Astronomical Society .... JSCAS
Joint Account (NTIO) .... J/A
Joint Advisory Committee Report (HEAS) .... JACR
Joint Analysis and Design (ABAC) .... JAD
Joint Bi-Level Image Experts Group .... JBIG
Joint Contingency Force Advanced Warfighting Experiment [Army] ..... JCF AWE
Joint Fire Research Organisation (HEAS) .... JFRO
Joint Hulls Committee (MARI) .... JHC
Joint Implementation Network (CARB) .... JIN
Joint Industry Board for the Electrical Contracting Industry (HEAS) .... JIB
Joint Reconnaissance Structure (CCCA) .... JRS
Joint Research Centre (HEAS) .... JRC
Joint Safety Assurance Working Group [NASA] (SPST) .... JASWG
Joint Service General Purpose Mask [Army] .... JSGPM

Joint Services Communications Element (CCCA) .... JSCE
Joint Services Test Plan (CCCA) .... JSTP
Joint Standing Committee Report (HEAS) .... JSCR
Joint Statement of Work (ABAC) .... JSOW
Joint Strategic Integrated Planning Staff (CCCA) .... JSIPS
Joint Tactical Radio System [ARMY] .... JTRS
Joint Technology Program (CCCA) .... JTP
Joint Transmission Services Information Network .... JTSIN
Joint United States Canadian Air Defense Study (CCCA) .... JUSCADS
Joint Vaccine Acquisition Program .... JVAP
Joint Variable Message Format .... JVMF
Journal (NTIO) .... jour
Journal of Artificial Intelligence [A publication] .... JAI
Journal of Banking and Finance Law and Practice [A publication] .... JBFL&P
Journal of Business Law [A publication] .... JBL
Journal of Law and Society [A publication] .... JLS
Journal of Legal History [A publication] .... JLH
Journal of the American College of Cardiology [A publication] (ROAS) .... JACC
Journal of the Association for Computing Machinery [A publication] .... JACM
Jumbo .... jbo
Jump (NTIO) .... J
Junction (NTIO) .... junc
Junction Adhesion Molecule .... JAM
Junior (NTIO) .... jun
Junior Leader Training [Boy Scouts of America] .... JLT
Junior Suite [Travel industry] (TRID) .... JRSTE
Just Kidding [Online dialog] .... JK
Just My Opinion [Online dialog] .... JMO
Just-Noticeable Difference (DIPS) .... jnd
Juvenile (NTIO) .... juv
Juvenile Delinquent (NTIO) .... JD

K

By Meaning

Kahunen-Loeve [*Mathematics*] (CCCA) .... KL
Kamioka Liquid Scintillator Anti-Neutrino Detector .... KamLAND
Kansas City Southern Industries, Inc. .... KCSI
Karaoke Jockey .... KJ
Karat (NTIO) .... kt
Karlsruhe-Rutherford Medium-Energy Neutrino Experiment .... KARMEN
Kaufman Adolescent and Adult Intelligence Test (DIPS) .... KAIT
Keep Alone if Possible [*Travel industry*] (TRID) .... KIP
Keep to Top of Mast (RIMS) .... KTM
Kentucky Commonwealth Virtual Library .... KCVL
Kentucky School Media Association .... KSMA
Kernelized Secure Operating System (CCCA) .... KSOS
Kerry Blue Terrier (ROAS) .... KBT
Key Display Call Indicator .... KDCI
Kilcalorie (NTIO) .... Kcal
Kilo High Level Language Operations per Second (CCCA) .... KHLOS
Kilo Hops per Second (CCCA) .... KHPS
Kilobar (ABAC) .... kbar
Kilocycle (AEBE) .... KC
Kiloelectron Volt (ABAC) .... KeV
Kilogram (NTIO) .... K
Kilowatt (NTIO) .... kw
Kilowatt-Hour (NTIO) .... kwhr

Kinesthetic Aftereffect (DIPS) .... KAE
King Pharmaceuticals [*NYSE symbol*] .... KG
King's Police and Fire Services Medal for Distinguished Service
   [*British*] .... KPFSM
King's Police Medal for Distinguished Service [*British*] .... KPM
King's Police Medal for Gallantry [*British*] .... KPM
Knight Bachelor [*British*] .... KB
Knight Grand Cross of the Equestrian Order of the Holy Sepulchre of
   Jerusalem .... KGCHS
Knock-for-Knock (MARI) .... KK
Knot (ABAC) .... kn
Knowledge Discovery in Databases (IDAI) .... KDD
Knowledge Discovery in Text (IDAI) .... KDT
Kodak Flashpix Image Format .... FPX
Kolmogorov-Smirnoff Tests (DIPS) .... KS
Kongcha [*Publisher*] .... KON
Koo Energy Ken .... KEK
Koopman's Theorem .... KT
Korea National Committee for Pacific Economic Cooperation .... KOPEC
Kos Pharmaceuticals .... KOSP
Krispy Kreme Doughnuts [*NASDAQ symbol*] (SG) .... KREM
Kroger Equity [*NYSE symbol*] (SG) .... KE
Krypton (ABAC) .... Kr

L
By Meaning

L90, Inc. [NASDAQ symbol] (SG)	LNTY
La Palma Observatory	LPO
Laboratory Animal Allergy (HEAS)	LAA
Laboratory Animal Resources	LAR
Laboratory Animal Sciences	LAS
Laboratory Control Sample (ABAC)	LCS
Laboratory Port [NASA] (SPST)	LP
Laboratory Studies in Atmospheric Chemistry	LSAC
Labrador (NTIO)	Lab
Lactic Dehydrogenase	LDH
Laidlaw Global [AMEX symbol]	GLL
Lake (NTIO)	Lk
Lambda Index (DIPS)	L
Land Cover (CARB)	L/C
Land Information System (CARB)	LIS
Landau-Kleffler Syndrome	LKS
Landing Platform Helicopter (CCCA)	LPH
Landing Ship Mechanized (CCCA)	LSM
Land-Ocean Interaction Study	LOIS
Language Across the Curriculum	LAC
Language Disordered	LD
Language Learning Disorder	LLD
Language MOS Evaluation Program [Army]	LMEP
Language Score (DIPS)	L
Language Textbook	lxb
Language-Acquisition Device (DIPS)	LAD
Lante Corp. [NASDAQ symbol] (SG)	LNTE
Laquer Stains	LAQ STNS
Large Array for Millimeter Astronomy	LAMA
Large Millimetre and Submillimetre Array	LMSA
Large Quantity Generator (AUEG)	LQG
Large Range (RIMS)	LR
Large Submillimeter Array	LSA
Large-Area Chemical Sensor (ABAC)	LACS
Larger	lgr
Large-Volume Sampling (CARB)	LVS
Laser Retroreflector (CARB)	LR
Laser Retroreflector Array (CARB)	LRA
Lasers and Electro-Optics Applications Program	LEAP
Lashed Secured Dunnage (RIMS)	LSD
Last Called Directory Number (ROAS)	LCDN
Last Compliance Time	LCT
Last Glacial Maximum	LGM
Last Open Water (RIMS)	LOW
Last Paging Channel (CGWS)	LASTCHP
Lastminute.com plc ADS [NASDAQ symbol] (SG)	LMIN
L.A.T. Sportswear [AMEX symbol] (SG)	FLD
Late Middle Paleolithic	LMP
Late Run	L/R
Late-Inning Pressure Situation [Baseball term] (NDBD)	LIPS
Latitude (NTIO)	lat
Launch Grapnel Hook	LGH
Lawrence Hall of Science	LHS
Lawson Gould [Publisher]	L-G
Layday Cancelling Date (RIMS)	LAYCAN
Layer	lyr
Lead in Lighting System (PIPO)	LDIN
Lead Radial (PIPO)	LR
Leading Lanthanum Zirconate Titanate	PLZT
Leaking Underground Fuel Tank (SARE)	LUFT
Leap Wireless International	LWIN
Learning Assistance Program	LAP
Learning Disabled (NTIO)	LD
Learning Resource Interchange	LRN
Learning Station.com	LSC
Learning Subspace Method (IDAI)	LSM
Learning Vector Quantization (IDAI)	LVQ
Least Absolute Deviation (IDAI)	LAD
Least Common Denominator (NTIO)	lcd
Least Common Multiple (NTIO)	lcm
Least Frequency Used Memory [Computer science] (ITCA)	LFU Memory
Least General Generalization (IDAI)	LGG
Least Median Squares (ARMP)	LMS
Least-Perceptible Difference (DIPS)	lpd
Left Field [Baseball term] (NDBD)	lf
Left On [Baseball term] (NDBD)	LO
Left Ventricular End-Diastolic Dimension [Medicine]	LVEDd
Left Ventricular Shortening Fraction [Medicine]	LVSF
Left-Handed Batter [Baseball term] (NDBD)	LHB
Legal Nurse Consultant (NUJO)	LNC
Legato (NTIO)	leg
Legends of Batman	LOB
Legitimate (NTIO)	legit
Leisure Accident Surveillance System (HEAS)	LASS
Less Commonly Taught Languages	LCTLs
Letter of Credit (NTIO)	L/C
Letter of Indemnity (RIMS)	LOI
Lettered	LTRD
Leukaemia Research Fund [British]	LRF
Level 8 Systems	LVEL
Levorotatory [Organic chemistry] (DIPS)	L
Lexicon Genetics [NASDAQ symbol] (SG)	LEXG
Liberal (NTIO)	lib
Liberation (NTIO)	lib
License Condition (HEAS)	LC
Licensed Chemical Dependency Counselor (NUJO)	LCDC
Licensed Industrial Hygienist (SARE)	LIH
Licensed Psychiatric Technician (NUJO)	LPT
Licensed Respiratory Care Practitioner (NUJO)	LRCP
Licensed Respiratory Care Technician (NUJO)	LRCT
Lidar/Radiometer (CARB)	LIRAD
Life Cycle Cost Impact Worksheet (SPST)	LCCIW
Life Cycle Cost Management (SPST)	LCCM
Life Data (DIPS)	Ldata
Life Point, Inc. [AMEX symbol] (SG)	LFP
Lift to Drag Ratio (PIPO)	L/D
Lifted Index (ARMP)	LI
Light	lgt
Light Aircraft Maintenance Schedule (PIAV)	LAMS
Light Amplification by Stimulated Emission of Radiation (HEAS)	LASER
Light Shield (SPST)	LS
Light Weathering	L/W
Light-Duty Utility Arm (ABAC)	LDUA
Lighter Than Air Airship (PIPO)	LA
Lightning Imaging Sensor (CARB)	LIS
Lightning Sensor System (HLLA)	LSS
Lights	LTS
Lightspan Partnership [NASDAQ symbol] (SG)	LSPN
Likely Preferred Options (ADAC)	LPO
Liminal Sensitivity (DIPS)	LS
Limited Edition	Limit Ed
Limulus Amebocyte Lysate [Medicine]	LAL
Lincoln Near-Earth Asteroid Research	LINEAR
Lincoln Space Experiment (CCCA)	LSE
Line Build Out [Telecommunications] (MLOA)	LBO
Line by Line (ARMP)	LBL
Line Drive [Baseball term] (NDBD)	L
Line Replaceable Item (CTAS)	LRI
Linear Magnetic Drive (CCCA)	LMD
Linguistics (NTIO)	ling
Link Access Protocol-Balanced (MLOA)	LAP-B
Link Encapsulation (MLOA)	LE
Liquefied Petroleum Gas Association (HEAS)	LPGA
Liquid (NTIO)	liq
Liquid Crystal on Silicon (AEBE)	LCOS
Liquid Rocket Booster	LRB
Liquid Waste Disposal Facility (ABAC)	LWDF
Liquid-Fed Ceramic Melter (ABAC)	LFCM
Liquid-Fed Minimelter (ABAC)	LFMM
Liquor (NTIO)	liq
List of Classified and Authorised Explosives (HEAS)	LOCAE
Literacy Volunteers of Massachusetts	LVM
Little British Car	LBC
Little Person	LP
Little Rubber Feet (MLOA)	LRF
Living Room (NTIO)	lr
Lloyd's Open Form (RIMS)	LOF
Loading Capacity (RIMS)	LC
Lobular Carcinoma in Situ	LCIS
Local (PIPO)	LCL
Local Area and Transport Area (CCCA)	LATA
Local Area Augmentation System (HLLA)	LAAS

Local Authority Circular (HEAS) .... LAC
Local Authority Unit (HEAS) .... LAU
Local Automatic Intercept System .... LAIS
Local Career Development Panels (HEAS) .... LCDP
Local Common Channel Interoffice Signaling (ROAS) .... LCCIS
Local Distribution Center (CCCA) .... LDC
Local Emergency Coordinator (SARE) .... LEC
Local Enforcement Agency (SARE) .... LEA
Local Hazard Mitigation Officer [*Department of Emergency Management*]
    (DEMM) .... LHMO
Local Interstellar Medium .... LISM
Local Liaison Committee (HEAS) LLC
Local Selling Fare [*Travel industry*] (TRID) .... LSF
Local Subscriber Switch (CCCA) .... LSS
Local Time Clock .... LTC
Localizer Type Directional Aid (PIPO) .... LDA
Location Administrative Officer (SARE) .... LAO
Location Radiation Protection Officer (SARE) .... LRPO
Locator (PIPO) .... LOC
Lockheed Electronic Systems Company (SPST) .... LESC
Logility Value Chain Solution .... LVCS
London Chamber of Commerce and Industry Examinations Board .... LCCIEB
London Financial Studies .... LFS
London Fire and Civil Defence Authority (HEAS) .... LFCDA
London Stock Exchange (SG) .... Lo
London Stock Exchange [*England*] .... LONDON SE
Long Delay-Code Excited Linear Prediction .... LD-CELP
Long Period Variable .... LPV
Long Range Guided Missile (CCCA) .... LRGM
Long Reach Manipulator (ABAC) .... LRM
Long-Bout .... LB
Longitude (NTIO) .... long
Long-Range Transboundary Air Pollution .... LRTAP
Loose .... lse
Losing Pitcher [*Baseball term*] (NDBD) L
Loss and Prevention Council (HEAS) .... LPC
Loss Damage Waiver [*Travel industry*] (TRID) .... LDW
Loss of Cell Delineation (MLOA) .... LCD
Loss of Frame (MLOA) .... LOF
Loss of Pointer .... LOP

Lost Workday Injury and Illness (SARE) .... LWDII
Lotus Translation Services for Sametime .... LTSS
Loudeye Tech [*NASDAQ symbol*] (SG) .... LOUD
Low Acid Canned Food .... LACF
Low Altitude (PIPO) L
Low Altitude Alert System [*Aviation*] (PIPO) .... LAAS
Low Drag Multi/Wire Antenna (CCCA) .... LDMWA
Low Energy Ion Ring .... LEIR
Low Level Control Module [*NASA*] (SPST) .... LLCM
Low Level Vault (ABAC) LLV
Low/Medium Frequency (PIPO) .... L/MF
Low Particle Concentration .... LPC
Low Profile Combined Distributing Frame (ROAS) .... LPCDF
Low Temperature Loop (SPST) .... LTL
Low-Energy Photon (ABAC) .... LEP
Low-Energy Photon Spectroscopy (ABAC) .... LEPS
Lower .... lwr
Lower Anchors and Tethers for Children [*Car seat safety term*] .... LATCH
Lower Heating Value (CARB) .... LHV
Lower Hold (RIMS) .... Lo Ho
Lower Large Intestine (ABAC) LLI
Lowest Current Rate (RIMS) .... LCR
Lowest Observed Effect Level (HEAS) .... LOEL
Lowest Obtainable Quantification (ABAC) .... LOQ
Lowest-Feasible Concentration (ABAC) .... LFC
Low-Level Radioactive Mixed Waste (ABAC) .... LLRMW
Low-Level Waste Treatment System (ABAC) .... LWTS
Low-Molecular-Weight Organic Acid (ABAC) .... LMWA
Low-Resolution Picture Transmission (CARB) .... LRPT
Low-Volume Sampler (CARB) .... LVS
Luminex Corp. [*NASDAQ symbol*] (SG) .... LMNX
Luminous Energy (DIPS) .... Q
Luminous Flux (DIPS) .... f
Lumpectomy [*Medicine*] Lx
Lunar Transient Phenomenon .... LTP
Lute .... lu
Luxury Car (TRID) .... LCAR
Luxury Hotel (TRID) .... LHTL
Lymphocyte Depleted [*Medicine*] .... LD
Lymphocyte Predominant [*Medicine*] .... LP

M
By Meaning

Mach (NTIO) .... M
Machine (NTIO) .... mach
Machine Bath Collection .... MBC
Machinery Breakdown (MARI) .... MBD
Magnetic Levitation (TRID) .... maglev
Magnetism and Magnetic Materials .... MMM
Magneto Photo Luminescence .... MPL
Magnetron .... mag
Magnovox Research Laboratories (CCCA) .... MRL
Mail Stop Identification Number (ABAC) .... MSIN
Mailbox (ROAS) .... MBX
Mail.com .... MAIL
Main Geophysical Observatory [*Russia*] (CARB) ...... MGO
Maine (NTIO) .... Me
Maintenance Data Acquisition Unit (HLLA) .... MDAU
Maintenance Monitor Console (CTAS) .... MMC
Maintenance Requirements Documents (CTAS) .... MRD
Maisonette .... Masnte
Major Accident Prevention Policy (HEAS) .... MAPP
Major Acquisition Review (CTAS) .... MAR
Major Area of Responsibility .... MAR
Major Damage History [*Aviation*] (PIPO) .... MDH
Major General (NTIO) .... Maj Gen
Major Hazards Assessment Unit (HEAS) .... MHAU
Major Hazards Legislation Working Party (HEAS) .... MHLW
Major League Baseball Players Alumni Association (NDBD) .... MLBPAA
Major League Baseball Properties (NDBD) .... MLBP
Major Trading Area (CGWS) .... MTA
Malaysia National Committee for Pacific Economic Cooperation .... MANCPEC
Malcolm Music [*Publisher*] .... MAL
Malicious Damage (MAHI) .... MA
Malicious Damage (MARI) .... MD
Malta Stock Exchange .... MALTA SE
Mammoth .... Mam
Man Machine (CGWS) .... MM
Man Month Equivalents (SPST) .... MME
Man Year Equivalent (SPST) .... MYE
Managed Query Environment [*Computer science*] (ITCA) ...... MQE
Management (NTIO) .... mgmt
Management and Administration Regulations (HFAS) ...... MAR
Management and Operating (AUEG) .... M&O
Management and Operations (ABAC) .... M&O
Management Arrangements Feasibility Study (HEAS) ...... MAFS
Management Engineering Plan (CCCA) .... MFP
Management Information Database (CGWS) .... MIB
Management Operations (SPST) .... MO
Management Summary Report (ABAC) .... MSR
Manager (NTIO) .... mgr
Managing Owner (RIMS) .... MO
Mandatory Investigation (HEAS) .... MI
Mandatory Reporting (HEAS) .... MR
Mandolin .... man
Maneuvering at Critically Slow Airspeed [*Aviation*] (PIPO) ...... MCA
Manic Depression .... M-D
Manitoba Health Research Council [*Canada*] .... MHRC
Manned Orbital Maneuvering Vehicle .... MOMV
Mansion .... MN
Manual Berthing Mechanism [*NASA*] (SPST) .... MBM
Manually Controlled Barrier (HEAS) .... MCB
Manufactured (NTIO) .... manuf
Manufacturers Services [*NYSE symbol*] .... MSV
Manufacturing Assessment and Planning Package (SPST) ...... MAAPP
Manufacturing Enterprise Model .... MEM
Manufacturing Support Item .... MSI
Maracas .... MRC
Margun Music [*Publisher*] .... MG
Marimba .... mba
Marine Aerosol and Gas Exchange Experiment .... MAGE
Marine and War Risks [*Insurance*] (MARI) .... M&W
Marine Aviation Campaign Plan .... MACP
Marine Aviation Logistics Support Program .... MALSP
Marine Aviation Weapons and Tactics Squadron 1 ...... MAWTS-1
Marine Corps Aviation Refresher Training .... MCAVRET
Marine Corps University .... MCU
Marine Corps Warfighting Lab .... MCWL
Marine Insurance Act (MARI) .... MIA

Marine Life Information Network for Britain & Ireland .... MarLIN
Marine Optical Buoy (ROAS) .... MOBY
Marine Protected Area .... MPA
Marine Science and Technology .... MAST
Marine Stratus (ARMP) .... MS
Marine Technology Support Unit (HEAS) .... MaTSU
MarineMax .... HZO
Marital Opportunity Ratio (DIPS) .... MOR
Maritime (NTIO) .... mar
Maritime Surveillance Capability (CCCA) .... MSC
Marker Beacon (PIPO) .... MB
Market Access and Compliance .... MAC
Market Value of Portfolio Equity .... MVPE
Marketing Education .... ME
Marketing Society (COBU) .... MS
Markov Chain Monte Carlo (IDAI) .... MCMC
Markov Decision Problem (IDAI) .... MDP
Mars Climate Orbiter [*NASA*] .... MCO
Mars Observer Camera .... MOC
Mars Observer Laser Altimeter .... MOLA
Mars Polar Lander .... MPL
Martinique (NTIO) .... Mart
Marvel Universe .... MU
Marvell Technology Group [*NASDAQ symbol*] .... MRVL
Masculine (NTIO) .... m
Masculine (NTIO) .... masc
Mass Bias Correction (ABAC) .... MBC
Mass Casualty [*Military*] .... MASCAL
Mass Migration Response (DEMM) .... MMR
Mass Spectral Detector (ABAC) .... MSD
Mass Spectroscopy .... MS
Massachusetts Adult Literacy and Technology Team ...... MALTT
Massachusetts Alliance of Adult Learners .... MAAL
Massachusetts Association of Teachers of English to Speakers of Other Languages .... MATSOL
Massachusetts Board of Library Commissioners ..... MBLC
Massachusetts Coalition for Adult Education .... MCAE
Massachusetts Corporation for Educational Telecommunications .... MCET
Massachusetts Immigrant and Refugee Advocacy Coalition .... MIRA
Massachusetts Job Council .... MJC
Master Alarm Light Panel [*NASA*] (SPST) .... MALP
Master of Industrial Safety (SARE) .... MIS
Master Sergeant (NTIO) .... M Sgt
Master's in Social Work .... MSW
Material Accounting Center (ABAC) .... MAC
Material Processing Platform (SPST) .... MPP
Materials Interaction Test (ADAC) .... MIT
Materials Management Plan (ABAC) .... MMP
Materials Research Society .... MRS
Mates' Receipt (RIMS) .... m/r
Mathematics (NTIO) .... math
Mathematics, Engineering, and Science Achievement (ABAC) ...... MESA
MatrixOne, Inc. [*NASDAQ symbol*] (SG) .... MONE
Maximum Amount Subject (MARI) .... MAS
Maximum Average Pressure .... MAP
Maximum Burst Size (MLOA) .... MBS
Maximum Doping Limit .... MDL
Maximum Elevation Figure [*Aviation*] (PIPO) .... MEF
Maximum Permissible Working Pressure (HEAS) ... MPWP
Maximum Probably Flood (ABAC) .... MPF
Maximum Street Load (CTAS) .... MSL
McCarthy Screening Test [*Intended to diagnose academic potentials and disabilities*] (DIPS) .... MST
MDZ, Inc. [*NYSE symbol*] (SG) .... MDZ
Mean (DIPS) .... m
Mean Productive Time Between Assists .... MTBAP
Mean Productive Time Between Failures .... MTBFP
Mean Sea Level (PIAV) .... msl
Mean Time Between Incident .... MTBI
Measurement and Improvement of Manufacturing Capacity .... MIMAC
Mechanics (NTIO) .... mech
Mechanism Control Unit (SPST) .... MCU
Media 100 .... MDEA
Media-Access Control (AEBE) .... MAC
Mediacom Communic. 'A' [*NASDAQ symbol*] (SG) ...... MCCC
Medial Geniculate Body (DIPS) .... MGB

Median (DIPS) ... Mdn
Median Deviation (DIPS) ... Md D
Medical (NTIO) ... med
Medical Aid (NTIO) ... Medicaid
Medical Care (NTIO) ... Medicare
Medical Communications for Combat Casualty Care [*Army*] ... MC4
Medical Equipment Set [*Army*] ... MES
Medical Removal Protection (SARE) ... MRP
Medical Research and Materiel Command [*Army*] ... MRMC
Medical Support Unit [*Department of Emergency Management*] (DEMM) ... MSU
Medicare Payment Assessment Commission ... MedPAC
Mediterranean ... ME
Mediterranean (NTIO) ... Med
Mediterranean Fruit Fly (NTIO) ... medfly
Medium Expendable Launch Vehicle (CARB) ... MELV
Medium Power Homing (PIPO) ... MH
Medium Resolution Imaging Spectrometer (CARB) ... MERS
Medium Scale Integrated Circuit ... MSI
Medium-Class Explorer ... MIDEX
Medix Resources [*AMEX symbol*] (SG) ... MXB
Meet and Assist [*Travel industry*] (TRID) ... MAAS
Meetings Industry Association (COBU) ... MIA
Mega High Level Language Operations per Second (CCCA) ... MHLOS
Mega-Gauss ... MG
Megawatt-Day (ABAC) ... MWd
Megawatt-Year (ABAC) ... MWyr
Melanocortin-4 Receptor (DIPS) ... MC4-R
Melrose Place [*Television program title*] ... MP
Melter Cell (ABAC) ... MC
Melter Feed Tank (ABAC) ... MFT
Membership (NTIO) ... mem
Memorandum of Participation (ARMP) ... MOP
Memorandum of Understanding ... MOU
Memory Control Block (ROAS) ... MCB
Memory Controller Hub ... MCH
Memory-Operating Characteristic Curve (DIPS) ... MOCC
Mental Deficiency (DIPS) ... MD
Mental Status Examination Report (DIPS) ... MSER
Merchant Broker (RIMS) ... MB
Mercury Deposition Network ... MDN
Mercury Surface, Space Environment, Geochemistry and Ranging Mission [*NASA launch date proposed for March 2004*] ... MESSENGER
Meridian (NTIO) ... mer
Mesh Sacks ... mshsks
Message Distribution Module (CCCA) ... MDM
Message Processing Display System (CCCA) ... MPDS
Message Transfer Protocol (CGWS) ... MTP
Message Type (CGWS) ... MT
Metal Active Gas (HEAS) ... MAG
Metal Ferroelectric Metal Insulator Semiconductor ... MFMIS
Metal Forming Machinery Makers' Association (HEAS) ... MFMMA
Metal-Insulator-Semiconductor Transistor (CCCA) ... MIST
Metallophone ... met
Metawave Communications [*NASDAQ symbol*] (SG) ... MTWV
Meteorological and Aeronautical Presentation System (CTAS) ... MAPS
Meteorological Research Flight ... MRF
Meteorological Research Unit ... MRU
Meteorology ... Meteor
Meter Fix (CTAS) ... MF
Meter Fix Acceptance Rate (CTAS) ... MFAR
Meter Fix Crossing Time (CTAS) ... MFT
Methamphetamine (NTIO) ... meth
Methane Recovery (CARB) ... MR
Methods for the Detection of Toxic Substances in Air (HEAS) ... MDTSA
MetLife's Intelligent Text Analyzer [*Textual analysis of life insurance applications*] (IDAI) ... MITA
Metric Deadweight Tons (RIMS) ... MDWT
Metric Ton (NTIO) ... mt
Metric Ton of Metal (ABAC) ... MTM
Metric Tonnes (RIMS) ... MTONS
Metropolitan (NTIO) ... metro
Metropolitan Area Network ... MAN
Metropolitan Association of Professional Travel Agents (TRID) ... MAPTA
Metropolitan Electrical League of New Jersey ... MELN
Metropolitan Readiness Tests-Sixth Edition [*J. R. Nurss*] (DIPS) ... MRT 6
meVC Draper Fisher Jurvest Fd. [*NYSE symbol*] ... MVC
Mexican (NTIO) ... Mex
Mexican-American (NTIO) ... Mexamerican
Mexico National Committee for Pacific Economic Cooperation ... MXCPEC
Mezzo Forte (NTIO) ... mf
Mezzo Soprano ... Mz
Michigan Association for Media in Education ... MAME
Michigan Association of Non-Public Schools ... MANS
Michigan Sportsmen Against Hunger ... MSAH
Michigan Steelhead and Salmon Fisherman's Association ... MSSFA
Michigan Youth Hunter Education Challenge ... MYHEC
Micorsoft Installer [*Computer science*] ... MSI
Micro (NTIO) ... mc
Microclimate Cooling System (HEAS) ... MCCs
Microhenry ... mH
Micrometer (ABAC) ... m
Microscopy, Microscopic Superconducting Quantum Interference Devices ... microSQUID
Microsoft Cluster Server ... MSCS
Microsoft Management Console ... MMC
Microvolt ... mV
Microwatt ... mW
Microwave Humidity Sounder (CARB) ... MHS
Microwave Radiometer (CARB) ... MWR
Microwave Remote Sensing Laboratory (CARB) ... MIRSL
Microwave Scanning Radiometer (CARB) ... MSR
Microwave Temperature Profiler (ARMP) ... MTP
Microwave Temperature Sounder (CARB) ... MTS
Microwave Unit (CARB) ... MU
Mid-Atlantic Regional Air Management Association ... MARAMA
Middle Atmosphere Nitrogen Trend Assessment ... MANTRA
Middle Compass Locator (PIPO) ... ML
Middle East (CARB) ... MDE
Middle Level Student Activities Association ... MLSAA
Middle Zone (HEAS) ... MZ
Midpoint (DIPS) ... MP
Mid-Roll Change Capability ... MRC
Midwest Agents Selling Travel (TRID) ... MAST
Midwest Area (SARE) ... MWA
Midwestern Higher Education Commission ... MHEC
Milan Stock Exchange (SG) ... ML
Mild Traumatic Brain Injury ... MTBI
Mildly Mentally Retarded ... MMR
Miles per Gallon (NTIO) ... mpg
Milestone Description Sheet (ABAC) ... MDS
Military ... mil
Military Assistance for Civil Disturbance [*Department of Defense*] (DEMM) ... MACDIS
Military Emergency Diversion Airfield (PIAV) ... MEDA
Military Middle Airspace Radar Service (PIAV) ... MMARS
Military Operations in Urban Terrain [*Army*] ... MOUT
Military Operations on Urban Terrain ... MOUT
Military Science ... MSCI
Military Terminal Control Area (PIAV) ... MTCA
Military Utility Assessment ... MUA
Military-Oriented Protective Posture ... MOPP
Millennium Eco-Communities [*Canada*] ... MEC
Miller Assessment for Preschoolers (DIPS) ... MAPS
Milliamp (AEBE) ... ma
Milligram (DIPS) ... Mg
Millihenry (AEBE) ... mh
Millilambert (DIPS) ... ml
Milliliter (AEBE) ... ml
Millimeter-Wave Imaging Radiometer (ARMP) ... MIR
Millimicron (DIPS) ... m
Million Barrels of Oil (ABAC) ... MBO
Million Instructions per Second (NTIO) ... MIPS
Million Tonne (CARB) ... MT
Million Tonnes of Carbon Equivalent (CARB) ... MTCE
Million Tonnes of Coal Replacement (CARB) ... MTCR
Millions of Instructions per Second ... mips
Millon Adolescent Clinical Inventory (DIPS) ... MACI
Millon Clinical Multiaxial Inventory-III (DIPS) ... MCMI-III
Mils per Year (ABAC) ... mpy
Mineral Ash Free (ABAC) ... MAF
Mini Points of Presence ... Mini-POPs
Miniature Warning Light (HEAS) ... MWL
Minimal Audible Field (DIPS) ... MAF
Minimal Audible Pressure (DIPS) ... MAP
Minimum Description Length Principle (IDAI) ... MDLP
Minimum Detectable Flux ... MDF
Minimum Detectable Level ... MDL
Minimum Detectable Radiance (ARMP) ... mdr
Minimum Detectable Radiance (CARB) ... MDR
Minimum Essential Back Up (CCCA) ... MEBU
Minimum Funding Requirement ... MFR
Minimum/Maximum (RIMS) ... MIN/MAX
Minimum Message Length (IDAI) ... MML
Minimum Navigation Performance Specification Airspace (PIPO) ... MNPS
Minimum Rate [*Travel industry*] (TRID) ... MINR
Minimum Sector Altitude [*Aviation*] (PIPO) ... MSA
Minimun Sector Altitude [*Aviation*] (PIAV) ... MSA
Mining Certification Service (HEAS) ... MCS
Mining Equipment Certification Service (HEAS) ... MECS
Mining Inspectorate (HEAS) ... MI
Minnesota Multiphasic Personality Inventory-2 (DIPS) ... MMPI-2
Minnesota Multiphasic Personality Inventory-Adolescent (DIPS) ... MMPI-A
Minnesota Pollution Control Agency ... MPCA
Minnesota Spatial Relations Test (DIPS) ... MSRT
Minnesota Telephone Association (CGWS) ... MNTA
Minor (NTIO) ... min
Minor Planets Electronic Circular ... MPEC
Minority On-Line Information Service ... MOLIS
Mint on Card ... MOC
Mint on Mint Card ... MOMC
Mir Sample Return Experiment [*NASA*] (SPST) ... MSRE
Misconnection [*Travel industry*] (TRID) ... MSCN
Missile Impact and Gaseous Explosions (HEAS) ... MIGE
Missing at Random (IDAI) ... MAR
Missing Completely at Random (IDAI) ... MCAR
Missing Insects Department ... MID
Missing Parts ... M/P
Missing Time Experience ... MTE
Mission Defined Unit Assemblage [*Army*] ... MDUA
Mission, Enemy, Terrain, Troops, and Time [*Military*] ... METT-T

Mission Engagement Area [*Military*] ... MEA
Mission Equipment Cargo Support Launch Site Installation [*NASA*] (SPST) ... MECSLSI
Mission Specific Data Set [*Army*] ... MSDS
Mississippi Association for Adult and Community Education ... MAACE
Missouri Association of School Librarians ... MASL
Missouri Valley Electric Association ... MVEA
Mitochrondrial [*Medicine*] ... mt
Mitochrondrial Neurogastrointestinal Encephalomyopathy ... MNGIE
Mixed ... mxd
Mixed Schedule of Reinforcement (DIPS) ... MIX
Mixed Waste Project (ABAC) ... MWP
Mixture-of-Experts (IDAI) ... ME
Mobile Access Part (CGWS) ... MAP
Mobile Allocation (CGWS) ... MA
Mobile Allocation Channel Number (CGWS) ... MACN
Mobile Allocation Index (CGWS) ... MAI
Mobile Allocation Index Offset (CGWS) ... MAIO
Mobile Assisted Hand-Over (CGWS) ... MAHO
Mobile Augmented Reality System ... MARS
Mobile Country Code (CGWS) ... MCC
Mobile Emergency Communication System (CCCA) ... MECS
Mobile Emergency Radiological Laboratory (DEMM) ... MERL
Mobile Emergency Response System (DEMM) ... MERS
Mobile Equipment (CGWS) ... ME
Mobile Network Code (CGWS) ... MNC
Mobile Network Computing Protocol (AEBE) ... MCNP
Mobile Station Class Mark (CGWS) ... MSCM
Mobile Station Integrated Service Digital Network Number (CGWS) ... MSISDN
Mobile Station Roaming Number (CGWS) ... MSRN
Mobile Subscriber Indentification Number (CGWS) ... MSIC
Mobile Telephone Exchange (CGWS) ... MTX
Mobile Telesystems OJSC ADS [*NYSE symbol*] ... MBT
Mobile Terminated Call (CGWS) ... MTC
Mobile/Transportable (CCCA) ... MT
Mobile-Originated Call (CGWS) ... MOC
Modal Identification Experiment [*NASA*] (SPST) ... MIE
Model Accreditation Plan (AUEG) ... MAP
Moderate Mental Retardation (DIPS) ... MMR
Moderate Rate [*Travel industry*] (TRID) ... MODR
Moderate Room [*Travel industry*] (TRID) ... MOD
Moderato (NTIO) ... mod
Modern Human Origins ... MHO
Modified Hazard Ranking System (ABAC) ... MHRS
Modular Automated Parking System [*Developed by Robotic Parking*] (IDAI) ... MAPS
Modular Avionics Unit (HLLA) ... MAU
Modular Power Subsystem ... MPS
Modulation Coding and Compression (CCCA) ... MCC
Modulation, Coding, Compression and Encryption (CCCA) ... MCCE
Modulation Semiconductor Structure ... MSS
Modulation Transfer Function Area (DIPS) ... MTFA
Module Vertical Access Kit [*NASA*] (SPST) ... MVAK
Molecular Emission (SARE) ... ME
Molecule (NTIO) ... mol
Momento of Intimacy, Laughter and Kinship ... MILK
Monastery (NTIO) ... mon
Mongolia (NTIO) ... Mong
Monitored Line Program (SPST) ... MLP
Monozygotic Twins (DIPS) ... MZ
Monozygotic Twins Reared or Raised Apart (DIPS) ... MZa
Monozygotic Twins Reared or Raised Together (DIPS) ... MZt
Monsignor (NTIO) ... Msgr
Mont Saint-Hilaire ... MSH
Monthly Overtime (RIMS) ... MOT
Monthly Variance Report (ABAC) ... MVR
Montreal Stock Exchange (SG) ... Mo
More Able Autistic Persons ... MAAP
More Abled Autistic Persons ... MAAP
More or Less Charterer's Option (RIMS) ... MOLCHOP
More or Less Owner's Option (RIMS) ... MOLOO
Morocco (NTIO) ... Mor
Morphology-Dependent Stimulated Raman Scattering (CARB) ... MDSRS
Most General Common Instance (IDAI) ... MGCI
Most General Unifier (IDAI) ... MGU
Mostly ... mstly
Motor Oil Volatility ... MOV
Motor Rifle (CCCA) ... MR
Motor Vehicle Body Repair (HEAS) ... MVBR
Motor Vehicle Repair (HEAS) ... MVR
Motorized Yacht (TRID) ... MY
Movement Response [*Used in Rorschach test scoring*] (DIPS) ... M
Multi-Access Cable Billing System ... MACBS
Multi-Access Reservations System [*Travel industry*] (TRID) ... MARS
Multi-Agent System (IDAI) ... MAS
Multiangle Imaging Spectroradiometer (ARMP) ... MISR
Multiangle Light Scattering ... MALS
Multicast Address Resolution Server (MLOA) ... MARS
Multicast Server (MLOA) ... MCS
Multichannel Distributed Bridge (CCCA) ... MDB
Multi-Channel Intelligent/Intercept Announcement System [*Telecommunications*] ... MCIAS
Multi-Cultural Environmental Science Education Centers (ABAC) ... MESEC
Multidimensional Database (IDAI) ... MDDB
Multidisciplinary Evaluation ... MDE
Multidrug-Resistant ... MDR
Multi-Engine Instrument (PIPO) ... MEI
Multi-Ethnic Study of Atherosclerosis ... MESA
Multifactorial (DIPS) ... MF
Multifilter Radiometer (ARMP) ... MFR
Multifilter Rotating Shadowband Radiometer (CARB) ... MFRSR
Multifrequency Imaging Microwave Radiometer (CARB) ... MIMR
Multifunctional Exercise Device (SPST) ... MFED
Multifunctional on-the-Move Secure Adaptive Integrated Communications [*Military*] ... MOSAIC
Multi-Line Call Detail (ROAS) ... MLCD
Multimedia Cable Networking Systems (AEBE) ... MCNS
Multimedia-Based Training ... MBT
Multi-Mission Spaceccraft ... MMS
Multimodal, Interactive Note Pad ... Mipad
Multimodal Therapy [*Arnold Lazarus*] (DIPS) ... MMT
Multi-Modular Fluid Filtration System ... MMFFS
Multimonitored Electroconvulsive Treatment (DIPS) ... MMECT
Multi-National Investigations Cooperative on Aerial Phenomena ... MICAP
Multinfarct Dementia (DIPS) ... MID
Multiple Antenna Profiler Radar (ARMP) ... MAPR
Multiple Assessment Programs and Services ... MAPS
Multiple Cloud Base Height (ARMP) ... MCBH
Multiple Correlation (DIPS) ... R
Multiple Hazard Analysis [*Department of Emergency Management*] (DEMM) ... MHA
Multiple Layer Perceptron (IDAI) ... MLP
Multiple Level Security (CCCA) ... MLS
Multiple Linear Regression Analysis ... REGRE
Multiple Loop Sidelobe Canceller (CCCA) ... MLSC
Multiple Mirror Observatory ... MMT
Multiple Project Assurance ... MPA
Multiple Schedule of Reinforcement (DIPS) ... MULT
Multiple Sclerosis Society of Canada ... MSSC
Multiple-Choice (DIPS) ... MC
Multiple-Code-Shift Keying (CCCA) ... MCSK
Multiple-Rate Processor (CCCA) ... MRP
Multiplexer (PIPO) ... MUX
Multi-Protocol Label Switching (MLOA) ... MPLS
Multipurpose Automatic Control Equipment (HEAS) ... MACE
Multi-Rate Digital Subscriber Line (AEBE) ... MDSL
Multi-Sensory Developmental Delays ... MSDD
Multispectral Thermal Imager ... MTI
Multi-Use Remote Manipulator Development Facility [*NASA*] (SPST) ... MRMDF
Multi-User Device (ABAC) ... MUD
Multivariate Adaptive Regression Spline (IDAI) ... MARS
Multi-Walled Carbon Nanotube ... MWNT
Munchausen Syndrome by Proxy [*Child abuse*] (DIPS) ... MSP
Municipal (NTIO) ... mun
Municiple [*Bond*] (NTIO) ... muni
Music (NTIO) ... mus
Music Copyright Reform Group ... MCRG
Music Sales Corporation [*Publisher*] ... MS
Musical Instrument Digital Interface (AEBE) ... MIDI
Mutual Aid Agreement (DEMM) ... MAA
Mutual Assured Destruction (CCCA) ... MAD
Mutual UFO Network, Inc. ... MUFON
Myopia (DIPS) ... My

N
By Meaning

Network Clock Signal (CCCA) .... NCS
Network Element (MLOA) .... NE
Network Emergency Co-Ordinator (HEAS) .... NEC
Network Equipment-Building System .... NEBS
Network Flow Diagrams (CTAS) .... NFD
Network Interface Function (SPST) .... NIF
Network Interworking Function (MLOA) .... NIWF
Network Load Balancing .... NLB
Network Management (MLOA) .... NM
Network Management Entity (MLOA) .... NME
Network Management Layer (MLOA) .... NML
Network Management Station (MLOA) .... NMS
Network Performance Analyzer [Computer science] (ITCA) ... NPA
Network Solutions .... NSI
Network Station Manager .... NSM
Network Voice Conferencing Protocol (CCCA) ...... NVCP
Network Voice Protocol (CCCA) .... NVP
Neural Crest Stem Cell .... NCSC
Neurologically Unique .... NU
Neurosurgical Critical Care Unit (NUJO) .... NCCU
Neuroticism .... N
Neutral (NTIO) .... neut
Neutral Buoyancy Laboratory [NASA] (SPST) .... NBL
Neutralized Cladding Removal Waste (ABAC) ...... NCRW
Neutralized Current Acid (ABAC) .... NCA
Neutralized Current Acid Waste (ABAC) .... NCAW
Neutrino Oscillation Magnetic Detector .... NOMAD
Neutrinos at the Main Injector [Fermilab] .... NuMI
Neutrinos at the Tevatron .... NuTeV
Neutron Porosity (CARB) .... NP
Neutron-Star/Black-Hole .... NS/BH
New Account Memorandum .... NAM
New Arrival Information [Travel industry] (TRID) ..... NAR
New Earth Observation Projects .... NEOP
New Energy and Industrial Technology Development Organization .... NEDO
New England Marine Research Laboratory (ABAC) ... NEMRL
New Focus [NASDAQ symbol] .... NUFO
New Foreign Launch (CCCA) .... NFL
New Hebrides (NTIO) .... New Hebr
New Mexico (NTIO) .... N Mex
New Substances Notification (SARE) .... NSN
New Testament (NTIO) .... New Test
New York Board of Trade .... NYBOT
New York Online Virtual Electronic Library .... NOVEL
New Zealand Committee of the Pacific Economic Cooperation
   Council .... NZPECC
New Zealand Stock Exchange .... NZSE
Newfoundland (NTIO) .... Newf
Nextel Partners 'A' [NASDAQ symbol] (SG) .... NXTP
Next-Generation Radar (ARMP) .... NEXRAD
Nhan Dan Newspaper [A publication] .... ND
Nickel (NTIO) .... N
Niger [African nation] (NTIO) .... Nig
Niku Corp. [NASDAQ symbol] (SG) .... NIKU
Nimbo Stratus (PIAV) .... NS
Nippon Telephone and Telegraph-Mobile Cellular System (CGWS) .... NIT-MCS
No Action Taken on Communication [Travel industry] (TRID) ... NAC
No Box .... NB
No Computed Data (HLLA) .... NCD
No Connection [Travel industry] (TRID) .... NOCN
No Damage History [Aviation] (PIPO) .... NDH
No Middle Initial (NTIO) .... nmi
No Rate [Travel industry] (TRID) .... NR
No Rate Specified [Travel industry] (TRID) .... NRS
No Record [Travel industry] (TRID) .... NRC
No Risk after Landing (MARI) .... NRAL
No Risk after Shipment (MARI) .... nras
No Risk to Attach till on Rail (MARI) .... NRTOR
No Risk to Attach till Waterborne (MARI) .... NRTWB
No Risk until on Board (MARI) .... nrtb
No Risk until Waterborne (MARI) .... nrtor
No Show [Travel industry] (TRID) .... NOSH
No Stock Number Assigned .... NSNA
No Traffic Rights [Travel industry] (TRID) .... NOTR
No Value Indicated [Stamp collecting] .... NVI
No Window Glazing .... NG
Noise Equivalent Target (CCCA) .... NET
Nominative (NTIO) .... nom
Non Coasting Drive .... NCD
Non Significant Result [Medicine] .... NSR
Non-Agricultural Pesticides Panel (HEAS) .... NAPP
Non-Avalanche-Related Snow-Immersion Death ... NARSID
Non-Broadcast Multiple Access .... NBMA
Non-Compulsory Reporting Point (PIPO) .... NCRP
Non-Conforming End Office (CCCA) .... NCEO
Non-Continuous Action (CCCA) .... NCA
Non-Cooperative Identification (CCCA) .... NCID
Non-Cumulative (SG) .... noncm
Nondairy Cattle (CARB) .... NDC
Non-Directional Radio Beacon (PIPO) .... NDB
Nonintegrated Two-Stage Liquid (ABAC) .... NTSL
Non-Interactive Display (CCCA) .... NID
Nonlinear Mesoscopic Elastic .... NME
Non-Linear Operator (CCCA) .... NLO
Nonlinear Principal Components Analysis (IDAI) ... NLPCA

Non-Linear Refraction .... NLR
Nonlinear Resonant Ultrasound Spectroscopy ... NRUS
Non-Linear Time Sequence (ABAC) .... NLT
Non-Maturing Balance .... NMB
Non-Negative Least Squares (ARMP) .... NNLS
Non-Negative Matrix Factorization .... NMF
Non-Participating Provider .... Non-par
Nonprofit Organization .... org
Nonrapid Eye Movement (DIPS) .... nREM
Non-Revenue Passenger [Travel industry] (TRID) ... NRP
Non-Roster Invitee [Baseball term] (NDBD) .... NRI
Non-Sea-Salt (CARB) .... nss
Non-Smoking Seat [Travel industry] (TRID) .... NSST
Non-Stockpile Chemical Material Program [Army] ... NSCMP
Nonverbal Learning Disability .... NLD
Non-Verbal Learning Disability .... NVLD
Non-Voting (SG) .... nonvtg
Nordic Gene Bank (CARB) .... NGB
Normal (NTIO) .... norm
Normalized Radial Basis Function (IDAI) .... NRBF
Normalized Relative Backscatter (ARMP) .... NRB
Norman (NTIO) .... Nor
North (NTIO) .... no
North (NTIO) .... nor
North American Air Defense Master Plan (CCCA) ... NAADMP
North American Association of Central Cancer Registries ... NAACCR
North American Cellular Network (CGWS) .... NACN
North American Datum of 1927 (CARB) .... NAD 27
North American Digital Cellular (CGWS) .... NADC
North American Numbering Council (CGWS) ...... NANC
North American Numbering Plan (CGWS) .... NANP
North American Official Airline Guide (TRID) ... NAOAG
North American Research Strategy for Tropospheric Ozone ... NARSTO
North American Veterinary Technician Association ... NAVTA
North Atlantic Area (SARE) .... NAA
North Atlantic Route Chart (PIPO) .... NARC
North Atlantic Tracks (HLLA) .... NAT
North Atlantic Traffic (PIPO) .... NAT
North Carolina Department of Agriculture (ROAS) ... NCDA
North Carolina Mobile Home Association .... NCMHA
North Dakota (NTIO) .... N Dak
North of England Children's Cancer Research Unit ... NECCR
North Plains Area (SARE) .... NPA
North Slope Borough (ARMP) .... NSB
Northern Africa (CARB) .... NAF
Northern Association of Management Consultants (COBU) ... NAMC
Northern Consultancy Association (COBU) .... NCA
Northern Ireland (NTIO) .... N Ire
Northern Rocky Mountain Wolf Recovery Plan ... NRMWRP
Northern Slope of Alaska (CARB) .... NSA
Northwest Land Information System Network (CARB) ... NWLISN
Northwest Natural Resource Technologies Consortium ... NNRTC
Norton Internet Security [Symantec Corp.] .... NIS
Norwegian Continental Shelf (RIMS) .... NCS
Norwegian Cruise Lines (TRID) .... NCL
Norwegian International Shipsregister (RIMS) .... NIS
Norwegian Maritime Directorate (RIMS) .... NMD
Norwegian Space Center (CARB) .... NSC
Not Diagnosed with Anything .... NDA
Not Entered (MARI) .... NE
Not Exceeding (MARI) .... ne
Not North Of (RIMS) .... n N
Not of Specific Origin .... NOSO
Not Otherwise Diagnosed .... NOD
Not Reconfirmed [Travel industry] (TRID) .... NRCF
Not Under Repair (MARI) .... NUR
Notice Given Arrival Date (MARI) .... NGAD
Notice of Commencement (SARE) .... NOC
Notice of Interest (DEMM) .... NOI
Notice of Proposed Rulemaking .... NPRM
Notices to Airmen (PIAV) .... Notam
Notifiable Installation (HEAS) .... NI
Notification of Accidents and Dangerous Occurrences Regulations 1980
   (HEAS) .... NADOR
Notification of Ammunition Reclassification [Military] ... NAR
Notification of Installations Handling Hazardous Substances Regulations
   1982 (HEAS) .... NIHHS
Notions, Oddities, Doodads & Delights of Yesterday ... NODDY
Notre Dame (NTIO) .... ND
Nova Scotia Library Association .... NSLA
Novello & Co. [Publisher] .... NOV
Nuclear, Biological, and Chemical Center .... NBCC
Nuclear, Biological, and Chemical Warning .... NBCWARN
Nuclear Forces Communications Satellite (CCCA) ... NFCS
Nuclear Fuel Services Corporation (ABAC) .... NFSC
Nuclear Magneton (ABAC) .... nm
Nuclear Power Plant Consultant (IDAI) .... NPPC
Nuclear Propulsion Initiative (ABAC) .... NPI
Nuclear Reactor Regulation (ABAC) .... NRR
Nuclear Science Abstracts (ABAC) .... NSA
Nuclear Services Corporation (ABAC) .... NSC
Nuclear Test Ban Treaty (CCCA) .... NTBT
Nuclear Weapon Site (CCCA) .... NWS
Nuclear Weapons Employment Acquisition Master Plan (CCCA) ... NWEAMP
Null Hypothesis Significance Testing (DIPS) ...... NHST

Number Assignment Module (CGWS) .... NAM
Number Book .... nmb
Number Factor (DIPS) .... N
Number of Additional Words Coming (CGWS) .... NAWC
Number of Pitches [*Baseball term*] (NDBD) .... NP

Numerical Ability (DIPS) .... N
Numerical Technologies [*NASDAQ symbol*] (SG) .... NMTC
Numerical Weather Prediction Model (CARB) .... NWPM
Nurse Education Act .... NEA
Nurse Prescriber (NUJO) .... NP

By Meaning

Oakland Athletics [*Baseball team*] (NTIO) .... As
Objective Grating Electronics (SPST) .... OGE
Object-Oriented Database Management System .... ODBMS
Obligatory .... OB
Obscene (NTIO) .... obs
Observation and Fields of Fire, Cover, and Concealment, Obstacles and Movement, Key Terrain, and Avenues of Approach [*Military*] .... OCOKA
Observation, Orientation, Decision, Action .... OODA
Obstetrical Gynecological Nurse Practitioner (NUJO) .... OGNP
Obstruction [*Baseball term*] (NDBD) .... obs
Obstruction (PIAV) .... obst
Obstruction Clearance Limit [*Aviation*] (PIPO) .... OCL
Occasional .... occ
Occasionally (NTIO) .... occas
Occidental (NTIO) .... occ
Occupation Level Crossing (HEAS) .... OLC
Occupational and Environmental Safety Management .... OESM
Occupational Health Maintenance Program (SARE) .... OHMP
Occupational Violent Crime (HFAS) .... OVC
Occurrence Report (ABAC) .... OR
Ocean Circulation and Climate Advanced Modelling .... OCCAM
Ocean Margin Exchanges (CARB) .... OMEX
Ocean View (TRID) .... OCNVW
Oceaneering Technology Integration (ABAC) .... OTECH
Oceanfront (TRID) .... OCNFT
Oceania (CARB) .... OCN
Ocular Motor Apraxia .... OMA
Office of Academic Affairs .... OAA
Office of American Indian Trust .... OAIT
Office of Antiboycott Compliance .... OAC
Office of Business Liaison .... OBL
Office of Communications, Education, and Public Affairs (AUEG) .... OCEPA
Office of Environmental Restoration (AUEG) .... OER
Office of Planning and Environment (ABAC) .... OPE
Office of Planning and Integration (ABAC) .... OPI
Office of Public Health and Science .... OPHS
Office of Risk Assessment and Cost-Benefit Analysis .... ORACBA
Office of Rural Health Policy .... ORHP
Office of Safety Assessment (ABAC) .... OSA
Office of Small Business Programs .... OSBP
Office of Strategic Industries & Economic Security .... SIES
Office of Superintendent of Public Instruction .... OSPI
Office of Technical Financial Assistance (ABAC) .... OTFA
Office of Technology Integration (ABAC) .... OTI
Office of Transportation Technologies .... OTT
Officer (NTIO) .... off
Official Establishment Inventory .... OEI
Official Hotel Guide (TRID) .... OHG
Official Journal (HEAS) .... OJ
Official Recreation Guide (TRID) .... ORG
Official Scorer [*Baseball term*] (NDBD) .... OS
Official Tour Directory (TRID) .... OTD
Offshore Minerals Management Program .... OMM
Ohio Gun Collectors Association .... OGCA
Oil Recovery (RIMS) .... OILREC
Oklahoma Telecommunications Interlibrary System (AUEG) .... OTIS
On Request (PIAV) .... o/r
On-Base Average [*Baseball term*] (NDBD) .... OBA
Onboard Data Interfaces and Network [*NASA*] (SPST) .... ODIN
Onboard Short Term Plan [*NASA*] (SPST) .... OSTP
Oncology Certified Nurse (NUJO) .... OCN
Oncology Nursing Foundation .... ONF
ONI Systems [*NASDAQ symbol*] .... ONIS
Online Computer Library Center .... OCLC
Online Information Exchange [*Association of American Publishers*] .... ONIX
Online Service Provider .... OSP
Ontario Federation of Agriculture [*Canada*] .... OFA
Ontario Ministry of Agriculture and Food [*Canada*] .... OMAF
Ontario Ministry of Agriculture, Food and Rural Affairs .... OMAFRA
Ontario Ministry of Environment and Energy [*Canada*] .... OMEE
Ontario Ministry of Natural Resources [*Canada*] .... OMNR
Ontario Soil and Crop Association [*Canada*] .... OSCIA
Ontology Markup Language (IDAI) .... OML
Onvia.com, Inc. [*NASDAQ symbol*] (SG) .... ONVI
Onwards (RIMS) .... ONW
Open .... opn

Open Access .... OA
Open Access Same-Time Information System .... OASIS
Open Crossing (HEAS) .... OC
Open Frame Motor .... OFM
Open Heart Intensive Care Unit (NUJO) .... OHICU
Open Shelter Deck (RIMS) .... OSD
Open Technology Support Unit (HEAS) .... OTSU
Open Window .... opnwndo
Operating Code [*Computer science*] (ITCA) .... Opcode
Operating Environment (CTAS) .... OE
Operating System/Virtual Storage 1 [*Computer science*] (ITCA) OS/VS1
Operating System/Virtual Storage 2 [*Computer science*] (ITCA) OS/VS2
Operation (NTIO) .... op
Operation Minute (HEAS) .... OM
Operational Circular (HEAS) .... OC
Operational Data Store [*Computer science*] (ITCA) .... ODS
Operational Exposure Guide .... OEG
Operational License Stage (CARB) .... OLS
Operational Line Scanner (CARB) .... OLS
Operational Requirements Analysis (SPST) .... ORA
Operational Safety Analysis Report (ABAC) .... OSAR
Operational Strategy Unit (HEAS) .... OSU
Operational Tempo [*Military*] .... OPTEMPO
Operations and Robotics (SPST) .... O&R
Operations and Service (CCCA) .... O&S
Operations Branch (HEAS) .... OB
Operations Management Consultant [*Department of Emergency Management*] (DEMM) .... OMC
Operations Management Forum (HEAS) .... OMF
Operator Console Monitor .... OCM
Operator's License Number (SARE) .... OLN
Opposing Force .... OpFor
Optical (NTIO) .... opt
Optical Character Reader Equipment (CCCA) .... OCRE
Optical Detection (ABAC) .... OD
Optical Gravitational Lensing Experiment .... OGLE
Optical Inter-Orbit Communications Engineering Test Satellite [*Sponsored by European Space Agency and Japan Space Agency*] .... OICETS
Optical Networks, Inc. .... ONI
Optical Sensor (CARB) .... OPS
Optimal Waste Loading (ABAC) .... OWL
Option Adjusted Spread .... OAS
Optizon Liquid Phase Sintering Experiment [*NASA*] (SPST) .... OLIPSE
Opus 360 Corp. [*NASDAQ symbol*] (SG) .... OPUS
Or Best Offer (NTIO) .... obo
OraPharma, Inc. [*NASDAQ symbol*] (SG) .... OPHM
Orchestra .... Orch
Order of Burma .... OB
Order-Disorder Transition .... ODT
Ordinal (NTIO) .... ord
Ordinary .... ord
Ordinary Radial Basis Function (IDAI) .... ORBF
Oregon (NTIO) .... Or
Oregon Administrative Rules (SARE) .... OAR
Organic (NTIO) .... org
Organic Electroluminescent (AEBE) .... OEL
Organic, Inc. [*NASDAQ symbol*] (SG) .... OGNC
Organic Variable (DIPS) .... OV
Organic Wash Waste (ABAC) .... OWW
Organismic Variable (DIPS) .... OV
Organization for the Promotion and Advancement of Small Telephone Companies (CGWS) .... OPASTCO
Organized Baseball (NDBD) .... OB
Organometallic .... OM
Original Estimated Time of Arrival (CTAS) .... OETA
Original Response (DIPS) .... O
Originally (NTIO) .... orig
Ornithology (NTIO) .... ornith
Orofacial Dyskinesia (DIPS) .... OFD
Orthogonal Transform Coding (CCCA) .... OTC
Orthopaedic Nurse Certified (NUJO) .... ONC
Orthopedic (NTIO) .... orth
OSCA, Inc. [*NASDAQ symbol*] .... OSCA
OTG Software [*NASDAQ symbol*] (SG) .... OTGS
Other Federal Agencies (ABAC) .... OFA
Other Government Departments (HEAS) .... OGD

Other Person (TRID) .... OP
Other Project Costs (ABAC) .... OPC
Other Service Information (TRID) .... OSI
Other Times (PIPO) .... O/T
Other Times (PIAV) .... o/t
Other-Total Ratio [*B. Mullen*] (DIPS) .... OTR
Out of City Indicator .... OCI
Out of Service (PIPO) .... OTS
Outback Steakhouse [*NYSE symbol*] .... OSI
Outer Detector .... OD
Outer Diameter (NTIO) .... od
Outer Fix (CTAS) .... OFX
Outer Membrane Phospholipase A .... OMPLA
Outer Segment .... OS
Outer Zone (HEAS) .... OZ
Outfielder [*Baseball term*] (NDBD) .... OF
Outgoing Calls Barred (CGWS) .... OCB
Output (PIPO) .... O/P

Output and Performance Analysis (HEAS) .... OPA
Output and Performance Measures (HEAS) .... OPM
Output Port (CCCA) .... OP
Outside Sales (TRID) .... OS
Outside Sales Support Network (TRID) .... OSSN
Over Aged (RIMS) .... OA
Overall Survival [*Medicine*] .... OS
Overload Class (CGWS) .... OLC
Ovulation .... O
Ovulation Prediction Kit .... OPK
Owner Requirements Table (HLLA) .... ORT
Owners (RIMS) .... OW
Owner's Option (RIMS) .... OO
Oxford Air Training School [*British*] (PIAV) .... OATS
Oxford and Cambridge Universities (NTIO) ..... Oxbridge
Oxford Committee for Famine Relief (NTIO) ...... Oxfam
Oxford GlycoSciences .... OGS
Oxygen Depletion Sensor .... ODS
Ozone Monitor Comparison System (CARB) .... OMCS

P

By Meaning

Pacific (NTIO) .... Pacif
Pacific Airmotive Corporation .... PAC
Pacific Car and Foundry .... PCF
Pacific Daylight Time (AEBE) .... PDT
Pacific Digital Cellular (CGWS) .... PDC
Pacific Economic Outlook .... PEO
Pacific Food Outlook .... PFO
Pacific Island Nations .... PIN
Pacific Project Phoenix P3
Pacific Stock Exchange (SG) .... P
Pacific Telecom, Incorporated .... PTI
Pacific Trade and Development Conference .... PAFTAD
Package Processing Point .... PPP
Packaged Ice [AMEX symbol] .... ICY
Packaging and Industrial Polymers [E.T. DuPont] .... PIP
Packaging and Transport of Radioactive Materials (HEAS) .... PATRAM
Packaging Corp. America [NYSE symbol] (SG) .... PKG
Packaging, Handling, Storage, and Transportability ...... PHS&T
Packaging, Storage, and Containerization Center .... PSCC
Packard BioScience [NASDAQ symbol] (SG) .... PBSC
Packed .... pack
Packed .... pkd
Packed Binary Coded Decimal (ROAS) .... PBCD
Packet (NTIO) .... pkt
Packet Data Unit (MLOA) .... PDU
Packet Send Sequence Number .... PS
Pad .... PD
Paediatric Oncology Nurses Forum [British] .... PONF
Paging and Access Grant Channel (CGWS) .... PAGCH
Paging Channel (CGWS) .... PCH
Paint Template .... PNT
Pakistan Air Force .... PAF
Palestine (NTIO) .... Pal
Pall Aircraft Porous Media .... PAPM
Palladium .... PD
Palletized Loading System .... PLS
Palm, Inc. [NASDAQ symbol] (SG) .... PALM
Pan American Standards Committee .... PASC
Panel and Shelf .... P&S
Panel Study of Income Dynamics .... PSID
Panic Disorder (DIPS) .... PD
Paninternational .... PNI
Panorama .... pan
Panzer Abwewp Hubschrauber [Attack Helicopter] .... PAHZ
Paradoxical Intention [V. E. Frankl] (DIPS) .... PI
Paraglider Research Vehicle .... PARREV
Parallax Second (NTIO) .... pc
Parallel Distributed Processing (DIPS) .... PDP
Parallel to Series Converter .... PSC
Parallel Virtual Machine Daemon (CTAS) .... PVMD
Parametric Data Base .... PDB
Paranitrophenal .... PNP
Parapet Foxhole .... PARFOX
Parents and Friends of Lesbians and Gays [An association] ... PARENTS FLAG
Parimeter Array Radar .... PAR
Paris Stock Exchange (SG) .... Pa
Parish Nurse (NUJO) .... PN
Parking Orbit Inspection [NASA] .... POI
Parliament (NTIO) .... parl
Parsons Brinckerhoff-Tudor-Bechtel .... PBTB
Part Number .... P/N
Part Number Configuration Summary .... PCS
Partial Mission Capability [Time] .... PMC
Partial Mission Capable-Supply .... PMCS
Partial Neutralization Feed (ABAC) .... PNF
Partial Packet Discard (MLOA) .... PPD
Partial Pressure Carbon Dioxide PPCO2
Partial Refund Message [Travel industry] (TRID) .... PRM
Partial Reinforcement (DIPS) .... PR
Partial Reinforcement Effect (DIPS) .... PRE
Partial Reward (DIPS) .... PR
Partial-Zero-Emission-Vehicle .... PZEV
Participate in the Lives of America's Youth .... PLAY
Participle (NTIO) .... p
Participle (NTIO) .... part
Particle Beam .... PB

Particle Image Velocimeter (ABAC) .... PIV
Particle Modulator Radiometer (CARB) .... PEM
Particles and Waves (SPST) .... P&W
Particulate Inorganic Carbon (CARB) .... PIC
Partner Relationship Management .... PRM
Partnership in Global Learning .... PGL
Part-of-Speech (IDAI) .... POS
Parts List .... P/L
Parts Management System .... PAMS
Parts Order Form .... POF
Parts per Trillion by Volume (CARB) .... pptv
Parts Selection List (SPST) .... PSL
Party of Five [Television program title] Po5
Pascal [Unit of measure] .... PA
Pass Separately .... PASEP
Passe Partout International .... PPI
Passenger (TRID) .... psgr
Passenger Name Record [Travel industry] (TRID) .... PNR
Passenger Network Services Corporation (TRID) .... PNSC
Passenger Now Recorded [Travel industry] (TRID) .... PNR
Passenger Profile Record [Travel industry] (TRID) .... PPR
Passenger Service Agent [Travel industry] (TRID) .... PSA
Passenger Service Representative [Travel industry] (TRID) ... PSR
Passenger Will Contact [Travel industry] (TRID) .... PWCT
Passengers .... PAX
Passengers (PIAV) .... pax
Passive (NTIO) .... pass
Passive Aircraft Surveillance System .... PASS
Passive Angle Attack .... PAT
Passive Coherent Locating System (CCCA) .... PCLS
Passive Correlation Track-On-Jam [Department of Defense] ..... PCTOJ
Passive Geodetic Satellite .... PAGEOS
Pasture Systems and Watershed Management Research Lab ..... PSWMRL
Patellofemoral Knee Brace [Medicine] .... PFB
Patented (NTIO) .... patd
Patersons [Publisher] .... PAT
Path Overhead Indicator (MLOA) .... POI
Path Terminating Equipment .... PTE
Pathfinder Instruments for Cloud and Aerosol Spacebourne Observations-Climatologie Etneduedes des Nuages et des Aerosols [NASA's proposed launch date is March 2003] .... PICASSO-CENA
Pathology Expert Interpretative Reporting System (IDAI) ... PEIRS
Patient Environment Program [Medicine] .... PEP
Patient Protective Wrap .... PPW
Patient Service Records System .... PSRS
Patriot Information Control Center .... PATRIOT ICC
Patrol Combatant Missile Hydrofoil [Navy] .... PHM
Patrol Escort [Navy] .... PG
Patrol Hydrofoil Missileship [Navy] .... PHM
Patrol Ship [Navy] .... PGF
Patrol Vessel Gunboat [Navy] .... PG
Patter Recognition Technique .... PRT
Pauling and Harrischfeger .... PH
Pay and Allowances .... PA
Pay-As-You-Go .... PAYGO
Payload .... P/L
Payload and Servicing Accommodations [NASA] (SPST) ... P&SA
Payload Data Services System (SPST) .... PDSS
Payload Diameter .... PD
Payload Mission Integration Contract [NASA] .... PMIC
Payload Type Identifier .... PTI
Payment Transaction Application Layer [Computer science] (ITCA) ... PTAL
Payroll Personnel System .... PPS II
PC Holdings ADS [NYSE symbol] (SG) .... PC
P-Channel Metal-Oxide Semiconductor .... P-MOS
PeaCe Pill [Slang for Phencyclidine] (DIPS) .... PCP
Peaceful Nuclear Explosive .... PNE
Peacetime Airborne Reconnaissance Program .... PARPRO
Peacetime Force Material Request .... PTFMR
Peacetime Utilization Program .... PUP
Peak (NTIO) .... Pk
Peak Cell Rate (MLOA) .... PCR
Peak Horizontal Acceleration .... PHA
Peak Horizontal Velocity .... PHV
Peak Operating Valve .... POV
Peak-to-Peak [Value] .... P-P

Peak-to-Peak (AEBE) ... p-p
Pediatric Advanced Life Support (NUJO) ... PALS
Pediatric Oncology Group ... POG
Peer Review Panel (ABAC) ... PRP
Peer Review Systems, Inc. ... PRS
Pendulous Integrating Gyroscope ... PIG
Pendulous Integrating Gyroscope Accelerometers ... PIGA
Penetration Aids ... PENAIDS
Penetration of the Gray Electronics Market ... PENGEM
Peninsula (NTIO) ... pen
Penthouse (TRID) ... PTHSE
People's Republic of China Satellite ... PRCS
Per Day Pro-Rata (RIMS) ... PDPR
Per Geard Hatch (RIMS) ... PGH
Per Hatch per Day (RIMS) ... PHPD
Per Person, Double Occupancy [*Travel industry*] (TRID) ... PPDO
Per Weather Working Day (RIMS) ... PWWD
Per Workable Hatch (RIMS) ... PWH
Perceived Noise Decibels ... PNDB
Percent (NTIO) ... pct
Percentile (DIPS) ... P
Percutaneous Transmyocardial Revascularization [*Medicine*] ... PTMR
Perfectly Matched Layer (ARMP) ... PML
Perfluorooctane Sulfonate ... PFOS
Performance Analysis Report ... PAR
Performance and Demonstration ... P&D
Performance Assessment Matrix (SARE) ... PAM
Performance Assessment Scientific Support (ABAC) ... PASS
Performance Evaluation (ABAC) ... PE
Performance Management Operations Manager ... PMOM
Performance Management System (HLLA) ... PMS
Performance Measurement ... PM
Performance Monitoring Function ... PMF
Performance Monitoring Program (CCCA) ... PMP
Performance Operating Characteristic (DIPS) ... POC
Performance Partnership Agreement (SARE) ... PPA
Performance Review Institutes ... PRI
Performance Summary Sheet ... PSS
Peribacteriod Membrane (CARB) ... PBM
Peril Insured Against (MARI) ... PIA
Periodic Armaments Planning System ... PAPS
Periodic Evaluation Record (DIPS) ... PER
Periodic Leg Movements in Sleep (DIPS) ... PLMS
Periodic Maintenance Information Cards ... PMIC
Periodic Personnel Reports ... PPREP
Periodical ... per
Peripheral Adapter Module Replacement Item (CTAS) ... PAMRI
Peripheral Blood Stem Cell Transplant [*Medicine*] ... PBSCT
Peripheral Connection Interface ... PCI
Peripheral Control Unit Diagnostic [*Program*] ... PCUD
Peripheral Target Position (ABAC) ... PTP
Peri-Urethral Diathermy [*Medicine*] ... PUD
Permanent (NTIO) ... perm
Permanent Normal Trade Relations ... PNTR
Permanent Steering Group ... PSG
Permanent Virtual Channel ... PVC
Permeability Invariable ... PERMINVAR
Permit to Work (HEAS) ... PTW
Perpendicular to Orbital Plane ... POP
Perpendicular-to-Orbit Plan ... POP
Pershing II ... PH
Person with Cystic Fibrosis ... PWCF
Personal Access Communications System (CGWS) ... PACS
Personal Accident Coverage [*Travel industry*] (TRID) ... PAC
Personal Air Communications Technology (CGWS) ... PACT
Personal Analog Computer ... PAC
Personal Answer Line ... PAL
Personal Breathing Zone (HEAS) ... PBZ
Personal Computer (AUEG) ... PC
Personal Computer Aircraft Training Device ... PCATD
Personal Computer Manufacturer Interface Adaptor ... PCMIA
Personal Damage Waiver (TRID) ... PDW
Personal Disposition [*G. W. Allport*] (DIPS) ... PD
Personal Financial Planner ... PEP
Personal Injury Protection (TRID) ... PIP
Personal Messaging Unit (CGWS) ... PMU
Personal Property Inventory Report ... PPIR
Personal Smoke Device ... PSD
Personnel Administrative Center ... PAC
Personnel Advice Notes (HEAS) ... PAN
Personnel and Pay Services Division ... PPSD
Personnel Command [*Army*] ... PERSCOM
Personnel Deployment and Distribution Management System ... PERDDIMS
Personnel Information Retrieval System ... PIRS
Personnel Performance and Training Program ... PPTP
Personnel Planning Integration Report ... PPIR
Personnel Services Delivery Unit (HEAS) ... PSDU
Personnel Support Agency ... PSA
Personnel Surety and Security Program ... PSSP
Personnel Training ... PT
Personnel, Training and Force Development ... PTFD
Personnel Work Plan (HEAS) ... PWP
Perspective Digital Map Generator ... PDMG
Peruvian National Committee for Pacific Economic Cooperation ... PERUPEC
Peso (NTIO) ... p
Pesticide Exposure Group of Sufferers (HEAS) ... PEGS
Pesticides Incidents Appraisal Panel (HEAS) ... PIAP
Pesticides Registration Section (HEAS) ... PRS
Pet in Cabin [*Travel industry*] (TRID) ... PETC
Peter Group Leader ... PGL
Pets.com, Inc. [*NASDAQ symbol*] (SG) ... IPET
Pharmacy Benefits Manager ... PBM
Pharmacy Corporation of America ... PCA
Phase Alternating Line [*Telecommunications*] (MLOA) ... PAL
Phase Alternation Line Delay ... PALD
Phase Change Dual Compact Disk Drive [*Computer science*] (ITCA) ... PD-CD Drive
Phase Coherent Sinusoidal Frequency Shift Keying (CCCA) ... PCSFSK
Phase Tracking Loop ... PTL
Phased Array Radar for Overland Surveillance ... PHAROS
Phased Program Planning ... PPP
Phencyclidine (NTIO) ... PCP
Philadelphia Electric Company ... PECo
Philadelphia Stock Exchange (SG) ... Ph
Philemon [*Biblical*] ... PHM
Philippians [*Biblical*] ... PHIL
Philippine Pacific Economic Cooperation Committee ... PPECC
Philippine Stock Exchange ... PSE
Philosphy (NTIO) ... phil
Phonetic (NTIO) ... phon
Phonetic Letter Spell Out (CCCA) ... PLSO
Photochemical Assessment Monitoring Stations ... PAMS
Photoconductive ... PC
Photoelectron ... pe
Photographic ... PHOTO
Photographic Area and Location System ... PALS
Photographic Intelligence ... PHOINT
Photographic Interpretation ... PI
Photographic Interpretation Report ... PIR
Photographic Master ... PM
Photographic Peak Analysis ... PPA
Photographic Processing and Interpretation Facility ... PPIF
Photographic Radar Intelligence ... PRI
Photographics Laboratory Usage Reporting ... PLUR
Photography (NTIO) ... photog
Photolimited Yield ... PLY
Photomagnet Electric ... PME
Photosynthetically Available Radiation (CARB) ... PAR
Phrase (NTIO) ... phr
Phrase Book ... phr
Physical (NTIO) ... phys
Physical Damage Division ... PDD
Physical Education for Progress [*Act*] ... PEP
Physical Layer Convergence Protocol (MLOA) ... PLCP
Physical Medium (MLOA) ... PM
Physical Operators Foreign Area Data System ... PFADS
Physical Research Laboratory (CARB) ... PRL
Physical Security Equipment Action Group ... PSEAG
Physical Teardown Evaluation ... PTD/E
Physical Teardown/Maintenance Evaluation ... PTME
Physically Handicapped Children's Program ... PHCP
Physician Data Services ... PDS
Pico ... P
Picofarad ... PF
Picosecond ... PS
Picosecond Transient Grating Spectroscopy ... PTGS
Picowatts ... PW
Picture Element (AEBE) ... pixel
Picture Element [*Computer science*] (ITCA) ... Pixel
Picture Exchange Communication System ... PECS
Picture-in-Picture ... PIP
Pilot Landing Air Television ... PLAT
Pilot Landing Assistance Television ... PLAT
Pilot Pulse ... PP
Pilot Pulse Missile ... PPM
Pilot Scale Ceramic Melter (ABAC) ... PSCM
Pilot Scale High Temperature Melter (ABAC) ... PSHTM
Pilot Weather Report (PIPO) ... PIREP
Pilotless Aircraft ... PA
Pilotless Drone Missile [*Department of Defense*] ... PQM
Pioneer [*A publication*] ... PIO
Pioneer Aerodynamic Systems ... PAS
Pioneer-Central Division [*Bendix*] ... PCD
Pioneers Across America for Alzheimer's Research [*An association*] ... PAAAR
Pioneers Across America for Alzheimer's Research [*An association*] ... PAAR
Pipe Flexibility [*Stress Analysis Program*] ... PIPEFLEX
Pipeline Inspection Notification System (PIAV) ... PINS
Pipelines Inspectorate (HEAS) ... PIPI
Piping and Pipe Band Society of Ontario [*Canada*] ... PPBSO
Piping Program ... PIPEMAID
Pirmasens Communications and Electronics Maintenance Center ... PCMC
Pitch and Yaw ... P&Y
Pitch Control ... P/C
Pitch Dynamic Pressure ... Q-alpha
Pitch Radio Adjustment Device ... PRAD
Pitch Radio Controller ... PRC
Pitcher (NTIO) ... P
Pittsburgh Paint and Glass [*Company*] ... PPG
Place of Receipt (MARI) ... POR
Placement Research Service ... PRS

By Meaning

Plain	PN
Plan for Congressional and Public Affairs	PCPA
Plan Objectives Memorandum (CCCA)	POM
Plan of Work (HEAS)	PoW
Plane Parallel Approximation (AHMP)	PPA
Planned Maintenance Subsystem	PMS
Planned Product Improvement	P2I
Planned Speed Indicator	PSI
Planner Epitaxiel Passivated	PEP
Planning and Analysis (ABAC)	P&A
Planning and Tracking Group	PTG
Planning Authority (HEAS)	PA
Planning, Programming, and Budgeting Structure	PPBS
Planning Tracking Working Group	PTWG
Planning Unit (HEAS)	PU
Plant Simulation Code (ABAC)	PSC
Plant Specific Emission Limit (SARE)	PSEL
Plasma Arc Centrifugal Treatment	PACT
Plasma Display System	PDS
Plasma Electron Profiles, Symmetric	PEPS
Plasma Energy Recycle and Conversion	PERC
Plasma-Desorption Mass Spectrometry (ABAC)	PDMS
Plastic Chip Carrier (AEBE)	PCC
Plate Appearance [Baseball term] (NDBD)	PA
Plateau (NTIO)	Plat
Platform Equipment Deck	PED
Platform for Privacy Preferences	P3P
Platinum	PT
Platoon Package Program	PPP
Player Relations Committee [Baseball] (NDBD)	PRC
PlayStation 2 [Video game console]	PS2
Please Be Brief [Internet dialog]	PBB
Plotter	PLOT
Plural (NTIO)	plur
Plutonium	PU
Pneudraulic	PNEUD
Pneumatic Tube	P-Tube
Pneumatically Installed Stabilized Earth	PISE
Pockel's Readout Optical Memory	PROM
Pocket Monsters [Nintendo Co., Ltd.]	Pokeman
Pocket Radio Network (CCCA)	PRNET
Poetry in the Branches [Program]	PITB
Pogo Suppression System [NASA]	POGO
Point (NTIO)	Pt
Point of Turnaround [Travel industry] (TRID)	POT
Point-Hour Ratio (DIPS)	PHR
Point-to-Point Protocol over Ethernet	PPPoE
Poise [Unit of measure]	P
Poison Inhalation Hazard (SARE)	PIH
Poland Efficient Lighting Project	PELP
Polar Air-Snow Experiment (CARB)	PASE
Polar Atmospheric and Snow Chemistry (CARB)	PASC
Polar Atmospheric Chemistry (CARB)	PAC
Polar Satellite Data Processing Centre (CARB)	PSDPC
Polar Scientific Research Institute for Marine Fisheries and Oceanography [Russian]	PINRU
Polar to Analog	PA
Polaris Industrial Team [Navy]	PIT
Police Service Pistol	PSP
Policy Unit Support Unit (HEAS)	PUSU
Polite (NTIO)	pol
Political Science	POLSC
Politician (NTIO)	pol
Politico-Military Administrative Affairs [Committee]	PMAA
Pollution Prevention	P2
Pollution Standards Index (SARE)	PSI
Polonium	Po
Polyactide [Chemistry term]	PLA
Polycylic Aromatic Hydrocarbons	PAC
Polycystic Ovarian Syndrome	PCOS
Polycystic Ovaries	PCO
Polygon	PY
Polygram [Publisher]	POL
Polymer Education	POLYED
Polynuclear Aromatic Hydrocarbon (ABAC)	PNA
Polynuclear Aromatic Hydrocarbons (SARE)	PAH
Polysomnography (DIPS)	PSG
Pontine Geniculate Occipital (DIPS)	PGO
Pool View (TRID)	PLVW
Poor Box	PB
Poor Decals	PD
Poor Foam	PF
Port Charles [Television program title]	PC
Port Financial [NASDAQ symbol] (SG)	PORT
Port Protection Device [Computer science] (ITCA)	PPD
Port Risks (MARI)	PR
Port Taxes (TRID)	PT
Port Thermal Radiator (SPST)	PTR
Portable Breathalyzer Test (SARE)	PBT
Portable Computer and Communications Association (CGWS)	PCCA
Portable Field Trainer/Evaluator	PFTE
Portable Fire Extinguisher (SPST)	PFE
Portable Work Station (SPST)	PWS
Porte-Avion Nucleaire	PAN
Port-Wine Stain	PW

Position Accuracy	PA
Position Homing Indicator	PHI
Position Location Reporting System Terminal	PT
Position of Intended Movement	PIM
Position Sensor	P SNSR
Positioning Azimuth Determining System	PADS
Positioning/Navigation	POS/NAV
Positive Control Launch (CCCA)	PCL
Positive Control Turnaround Point (CCCA)	PCTAP
Positive Emitter-Coupled Logic (AEBE)	PECL
Positive Indentification and Direction Finding Equipment	PI/DE
Positive Negative	PN
Positive Negative, Positive Negative Transistor Magnetic Logic	PTML
Possible Duplicate Message (TRID)	PDM
Possible Maximum Loss (MARI)	PML
Possible Nuclear Underground Test Site	PNUTS
Post Award Contract [Department of Defense]	PA
Post Deployment Software Support	PDSS
Post Deployment Software Support Center	PDSSC
Post Flight Checklist	PFC
Post Landing	P/L
Post Manufacture Checkout	PMC
Post Meridian	PM
Post Mobilization Deployment List [Department of Defense]	PMDL
Post Office Protocol Mail	POPMail
Postage and Handling (NTIO)	p&h
Postage Validation Imprinter	PVI
Postal, Telephone, and Telegraph	PTT
Post-Employment Services Demonstration	PESD
Posterior Oblique Ligaments [Medicine]	POL
Post-Operational Analysis and Exercise Review [Program]	PACER
Postoperative Expert Medical System (IDAI)	POEMS
Potential (DIPS)	E
Potentiometer Synchronometer	PS
Potentiometric Stripping Analysis (ABAC)	PSA
Potomac General Research Group	PGRG
Potomac Research, Incorporated	PRI
Pounds per Square Inch per Second	PSIS
Power and Servo Assembly	PSA
Power as an Integral Variable	PAIV
Power Control Register	PCR
Power Conversion	PC
Power Convulsion Unit	PCU
Power Distribution and Control	PD&C
Power Factor Correction	PFC
Power Generation Section	PGS
Power Generators, Incorporated	PGI
Power Input Filter Assembly	PIFA
Power Jets, Limited	PJL
Power Management and Distribution Palmdale [California]	PMD
Power Reactant Supply and Distribution	PRSD
Power Reactant System	PRS
Power Sources Center of Excellence	PSCOE
Power Station Two	PS2
Power Supply/Fuel Cell	PS/FC
Power System Computation Conference	PSCC
Power-On Reset (AEBE)	POR
Practical Intelligence (DIPS)	p
Practice Training Index	PTI
Praseodymium	PR
Pratt and Whitney	PW
Preburner	P/B
Precategorical Acoustic Storage (DIPS)	PAS
Precipitable Water (CARB)	PW
Precipitation (CARB)	PRC
Precipitation Static	P-STATIC
Precise Software Solutions [NASDAQ symbol]	PRSE
Precision Acquisition of Vehicle Entry and Phased Array Warning System	PAVE-PAWS
Precision Acquisition System	PAS
Precision Asrania Range Target Acquisition and Control	PARTAS
Precision Drop Glider	PDG
Precision Infrared Radiometer (ARMP)	PIR
Precision Locator Strike System Intelligence Augmentation System	PIAS
Precision Machinery Commercialization	PMC
Precision Measurement Equipment	PME
Precision of Process (DIPS)	h
Precision Products, Incorporated	PPI
Precision Radar Approach (PIPO)	PRA
Pre-Columbian Art Research Institute	PARI
Precombat Checks and Inspections [Army]	PCI
Predicate (NTIO)	pred
Predictive Model Markup Language (IDAI)	PMML
Preference (SG)	Pref
Preference (NTIO)	pref
Preferential Arrival Route [Aviation] (PIPO)	PARL
Preferred (SG)	Pfd
Preferred Arrival Route (CTAS)	PAR
Preferred Equity Redemption Cumulative Stock	PERCS
Preferred Machine Assist [Computer science] (ITCA)	PMA
Preferred Noise Criterion [L. L. Beranek] (DIPS)	PNC
Preferred Provider Network	PPN
Pre-Flight	P/F
Preflight	PR
Preflight Acceptance Checkout Equipment-Launch Vehicle [NASA]	PACE-LV

Preflight Test Bus ... PETB
Pre-Invitation Notice ... PIN
Prelaunch Certification Test ... PLCT
Preliminary Acceptance Tests ... PAT
Preliminary Award Letter System ... PALS
Preliminary Damage Assessment [*Department of Emergency Management*] (DEMM) ... PDA
Preliminary Design Review ... PDR
Preliminary Endangerment Assessment (SARE) ... PEA
Preliminary Flight Rated Test ... PFRT
Preliminary Maintenance Inspection [*Department of Defense*] ... PMI
Preliminary Marksmanship Instruction [*Army*] ... PMI
Preliminary Program Management Plan ... PPMP
Preliminary Qualification Analysis ... PQA
Preliminary Qualitative and Quantitative Personnel Requirements Information ... PQQPRI
Preliminary Site Assessment (SARE) ... PSA
Preliminary System Package Program ... PSPP
Premarksmanship Instruction [*Army*] ... PMI
Premate Verification System Test [*NASA*] ... PVST
Premium Income (MARI) ... PI
Premodulation ... PRE-MOD
Pre-Operational ... PRE-OP
Prepaid Ticket Advice [*Travel industry*] (TRID) ... PTA
Preparatory (NTIO) ... prep
Preparticipation Physical Examination ... PPE
Preprimer ... pprm
Pre-Processeur de Signal [*Computer*] [*French*] ... PPS
Presbyterian (NTIO) ... Presb
Presence Sensing Device Initiation (SARE) ... PSDI
Present (NTIO) ... pres
Present Position Indicator ... PPI
Present Weather Sensor (ARMP) ... PWS
Present Working Estimate (ABAC) ... PWE
Preservation and Packaging Committee ... PPC
Preservation and Packing ... P&P
President of Board for Inspection and Survey ... PREINSURV
Presidential Communications Support Office (CCCA) ... PCSO
Presidential Reorganizational Project ... PRP
President's Advisor for Science ... PAC
President's Committee of Advisors on Science and Technology ... PCAST
President's Private Sector Survey ... PPSS
Pressure (HLLA) ... Ps
Pressure Ageing Vessel (ABAC) ... PAV
Pressure Modulator Infrared Radiometer (CARB) ... PMIR
Pressure Reduction Valve ... PRV
Pressure Regulation ... PR
Pressure Regulation Valve ... PRV
Pressure Relief Valve ... PRV
Pressure-Modulator Cell (CARB) ... PMC
Pre-Stock Point ... PSP
Prevent Significant Deterioration ... PSD
Preventive Maintenance and Self-Help [*Program*] ... PM/SH
Preventive Maintenance Instruction [*Department of Defense*] ... PMI
Preventive Maintenance Periodic [*Inspection*] ... PMP
Preventive Maintenance Services ... PMS
Preventive Medicine Measures ... pmm
Previous (NTIO) ... prev
Previous Owner ... PO
Priced Exhibit Processing System ... PEPS
Priceline.com ... PCLN
Prices Square Parts List-Pre-Operational ... PSPL Pre-Op
Price-to-Earnings ... P/E
Primary (NTIO) ... prim
Primary Adhesively Bonded Structure Techniques ... PABST
Primary Aromatic Amine (ABAC) ... PAA
Primary Dispersal Base (CCCA) ... PDB
Primary Domain Controller [*Computer science*] ... PDC
Primary Inventory Cutoff Data [*Supply*] ... PICD
Primary Level Field Activities ... PLFA
Primary Memory (DIPS) ... PM
Primary Power Unit ... PPU
Primary Reasoning (DIPS) ... R
Prime ... P
Prime Input Development ... PID
Prime Mission Equipment ... PME
Prime Power Group ... PPG
Prime Response [*NASDAQ symbol*] (SG) ... PRME
Prime Systems Contractor ... PSC
Primer ... prm
Principal and Interest (NTIO) ... p & i
Principal Reducing Credit ... PRC
Principal Reducing Option ... PRO
Print Punch ... P/P
Printed Control Board ... PCB
Printing Industry Advisory Committee (HEAS) ... PIAC
Prior (SG) ... Pr
Priorities Analysis Group ... PAG
Priority Academic Student Skills ... PASS
Priority Control (MLOA) ... PC
Priority High Interest Tactical Air Acoustic Forecast Prediction ... PHITAP
Priority Planning Grid (ABAC) ... PPG
Priority Problem Areas ... PAA
Priority Timing Module ... PTM
Prise Ombilicale Derniers Instants ... PDI
Prisoner of War/Missing Personnel ... POW/MP
Prisoners and Community Working Together [*Institute*] ... PACT
Private Automatic Branch Exchange [*Computer science*] (ITCA) ... PBAX
Private Branch Exchange ... PBX
Private First Class [*Military*] (NTIO) ... Pfc
Private Line Network (CCCA) ... PLN
Private Mobile Radio (CGWS) ... PMR
Private Mobile Radio Service (CGWS) ... PMRS
Prize Energy [*AMEX symbol*] (SG) ... PRZ
Probabilistic Context Free Grammar (IDAI) ... PCFG
Probabilistic Neural Network (IDAI) ... PNN
Probabilities Expert Systems Knowledge and Inference (IDAI) ... PESKI
Probability (DIPS) ... p
Probability Discrete Automation ... PDA
Probability of a Single Failure Causing Other Failures within a Three-Pack [*Department of Defense*] ... PM
Probability of Bit Error (CCCA) ... PBE
Probability of Character Error (CCCA) ... PCE
Probability of Correct Message Receipt (CCCA) ... PCMR
Probability of Detection [*Department of Defense*] ... PD
Probability of Error (CCCA) ... PE
Probability of False Alarm [*Department of Defense*] ... PFA
Probability of Incurring Estimated Cost ... PIE COST
Probability of Leakage through Overlay ... PLO
Probability of Leakage through Underlay ... PLU
Probability of Missed Message (CCCA) ... PMM
Probability of No Penetration [*NASA*] (SPST) ... PNP
Probability of Single Shot Engagement Kill [*Military*] ... PSSEK
Probability of Wrong Message (CCCA) ... PWM
Probability Percentage (PIAV) ... PROB
Probable Error (DIPS) ... pe
Probably Approximately Correct (IDAI) ... PAC
Probex Corp. [*AMEX symbol*] (SG) ... PRB
Problem Analysis ... PA
Problem Identification Form (ARMP) ... PIF
Problem Oriented Medical Guidance System ... PROMIS
Problem Report Squawk Sheet ... PRSS
Problem Review Board (ARMP) ... PRB
Problem Space ... PS
Problem Trouble Report (CTAS) ... PTR
Procedure Change Unit ... PCU
Procedure Description Language ... PDL
Proceedings of the American Mathematical Society [*A publication*] ... PAMS
Proceedings of the National Electronics Conference [*A publication*] ... PNEC
Proceedings of the National Symposia [*A publication*] ... PDIS
Process Assembly Languages ... PAL
Process Asset Library ... PAL
Process Control Laboratory (ABAC) ... PCL
Process Design Analysis [*Program*] ... PDA
Process Facility Modification (ABAC) ... PFM
Process Status Word ... PSW
Processeur Militaire Francais [*French*] ... PMF
Process-Induced Defect ... PID
Processing and Display System (CCCA) ... PDS
Processing Index Terms ... PIT
Processor Control Panel ... PCP
Processor Input/Output ... PI/O
Processor Tape Reader ... PTR
Procurement Coordination Committee ... PCC
Procurement Technical Assistance ... PTA
Procurement, Value, Economy, Reliability ... PROVER
Procuring Contracting Officer/Administrative Contracting Officer ... PCO/ACO
Prodedure Change List ... PCL
Producers Alliance for Cinema & Television ... PACT
Producibility Engineering Plan [*Air Force*] ... PEP
Product Assurance Data System (SPST) ... PADS
Product Assurance Discrepancy Report ... PADR
Product Assurance Test and Evaluation ... PAT&E
Product Configuration Item ... PCI
Product Consistency Test (ABAC) ... PCT
Product Definition Data Requirements (SPST) ... PDDR
Product Improved ... PI
Product Improvement Verification Test ... PIVT
Product Reliability Improvement Program ... PRIP
Product Removal (ABAC) ... PR
Product Requirements Plan ... PRP
Product Verification Test-Government ... PVT-G
Production Acceptance Test and Evaluation ... PAT&E
Production Acceptance Test and Evaluation ... PATE
Production and Deployment ... P&D
Production and Research Property [*Department of Defense*] ... P&RP
Production, Configuration, Integration ... PCI
Production Control Centers ... PCC
Production Development Change Notice ... PDCN
Production Environmental Testing ... PET
Production Program, Douglas ... PPD
Production Prototype Test ... PPT
Production Qualification Testing ... PQT
Production Reliability Verification Test ... PRVT
Production Validation Testing ... PVT
Productional Operational Capability ... POC
Profan Test Assessment [*NASA*] ... PTA
Profession Military Education [*Department of Defense*] ... PME
Professional (NTIO) ... prof
Professional Advisory Committee (DIPS) ... PAC

Professional and Career Education for Early Childhood	PACE
Professional Data Service, Incorporated	PDSI
Professional Development of Officers Study	PDOS
Professional Development Scheme (HEAS)	PDS
Professional Rights and Responsibilities	PRR
Professional Scholarly Publishing	PSP
Professional Staffs Branch (HEAS)	PSB
Professional Women's Rodeo Association	PWRA
Professor	P
Program Activity Transmission	PAT
Program Advisory Group	PAG
Program Analysis Report	PAR
Program Announcement	PA
Program Budget Guidance	PGB
Program Control Output	PCO
Program Controlled Input	PCI
Program Coordinator	PC
Program Counter Register	PCR
Program Counterpart Office	PCO
Program Design Document (CTAS)	PDD
Program Evaluation and Review Techniques Costs	PERT COST
Program Extension Key [Computer science] (ITCA)	PA KEY
Program for Understanding Neurological Diseases	PFUND
Program Function Key [Computer science] (ITCA)	PF KEY
Program Function Keyboard	PFK
Program Interrupter	PI
Program Load Unit	PLU
Program Maintenance Office	PMO
Program Management Assistance Group	PG
Program Management Documents	PMD
Program Management Instruction [Department of Defense]	PMI
Program Management Organization (HLLA)	PMO
Program Management Review	PMR
Program Manager's Office	PMO
Program Manager's Recommended Program	PMRP
Program Master Plan [Department of Defense]	PMP
Program Performed	PP
Program Peripheral Subsystems (CCCA)	PPS
Program Planning and Control (SPST)	PP&C
Program Quality Acceptance (SPST)	PQA
Program Resources Catalog	PRC
Program Review Change Board	PRCB
Program Support Center	PSC
Program Technical Report (CTAS)	PTR
Program Test Director (CCCA)	PTD
Programmable Display Pushbuttons	PDP
Programmable Link Adapter	PLA
Programmable Machine Interface	PMI
Programmable Universal Machine for Assembly [Robot]	PUMA
Programme for the Inspection of Steel Components (HEAS)	PISC
Programmed Automatic Communications Equipment Requirements	PACER
Programmed Information Center	PIC
Programmed Logic for Automatic Teaching Operation	PLUTO
Programmed Requirement	PR
Programming Language for Interactive Teaching	PLANIT
Programming Requirements Process Specifications	PRPS
Programming Support Environment	PSE
Programming Support Library	PSL
Programs Advancing Citizenship Education [Institute]	PACE
Progression Free Survival [Medicine]	PFS
Progressive Airframe Rework	PAR
Project Data Coordinator	PDC
Project de Norme	PN
Project Development (ABAC)	PD
Project Director	PD
Project Execution Guidelines (ABAC)	PEG
Project for Interface Compatibility	PIC
Project Identification Code	PID
Project in Trouble (CCCA)	PIT
Project Lead Time	PLT
Project Management (ABAC)	pm
Project Management Control System	PMCS
Project Management Plan (ABAC)	PMP
Project Management Review	PMR
Project Management System Assessment	PMSA
Project Manager, Advanced Attack Helicopter	PMAAH
Project Manager, Advanced Scout Helicopter	PMASH
Project Manager, Air	PMA
Project Manager, Aircraft Survivability Equipment	PMASE
Project Manager Allocation Chart	PMAC
Project Manager Control Board	PMCB
Project Manager for Nuclear [Munitions]	PMNUC
Project Manager, Navigation and Control	PMNAVCON
Project Manager, Remotely Piloted Vehicles [Department of Defense]	PMRPV
Project Manager System	PMS
Project Manager, Training Devices	PM TRADE
Project Manager, Utility Tactical Transport Aircraft System	PMUTTAS
Project Manager's Office	PMO
Project Master Schedule	PMS
Project of Ocean Rafts System for Hydrogen Economy	PORSHE
Project Office Business Operations	POBO
Project Order Action Required	POAR
Project Planning Document (ABAC)	PPD
Project Quality Engineer	PQE
Project Specification Group Engineer	PSGE
Prolactin (DIPS)	PrL
Promethium	PM
Promissory Note (NTIO)	p/n
Promotion Dossier (HEAS)	PD
Promotion Research Committee	PRC
Pronoun (NTIO)	pron
Propagation Delay (MLOA)	PD
Propellant Injection Pressure	PT
Propellant Seal	PS
Propellants and Explosives	PE
Propeller Technical Committee	PTC
Proper (NTIO)	prop
Property Clearance Assessment (SARE)	PCA
Property Disposal Agency	PDA
Property Disposal Organization	PDO
Property Disposal Request (ABAC)	PDR
Property Management System (TRID)	PMS
Property Type	PT
Prophyria Catanba Tarda [Medicine]	PCT
Proportional, Integral, and Differential Gain (SPST)	PIDG
Proportional Integral Derivation	PID
Proportional Integration Derivation	PID
Proportional Navigation Guidance	PNG
Proportional Representation Society	PRS
Proposal Evaluation Program	PEP
Proprietary (NTIO)	pty
Propulsion and Terrain Vehicle Engineering [NASA]	PTVE
Propulsion Module Attach Assembly [NASA] (SPST)	PMAA
Propulsion Module Attach Structure [NASA] (SPST)	PMAS
Propulsion Research Corporation	PRC
Prosecuting Attorney (NTIO)	pros atty
Prostate Cancer Prevention Trial [Medicine]	PCPT
Prostate, Lung, Colorectal, and Ovarian [Cancers]	PLCO
Prostate-Specific Membrane Antigen [Medicine]	PSMA
Prosthetic Intradithelial Neodlasia [Medicine]	PIN
Protactinium	PA
Protect as Restricted Data	PARD
Protect Our Mountain Environment [Colorado]	POME
Protected Reservation [Travel industry] (TRID)	PROT
Protected Tube-Launched Optically Tracked Wire-Guided Anti-Tank Missile Vehicle	PVT
Protection	Protect
Protection Action Recommendation [Department of Emergency Management] (DEMM)	PAR
Protection Security Service	PSS
Protective Structure	PS
Protein Disulphide Isomerase	PDI
Protocol Analysis System (ABAC)	PAS
Protocol Capability Indicator (CGWS)	PCI
Prototype Adaptation Toolkit (CTAS)	PAT
Prototype Program Office	PPO
Prototype Qualification Test	PQT
Proverb	PR
Province (NTIO)	prov
Provincial Standard Time (TRID)	PST
Provisioned Item Orders	PIO
Provisioning	PROV
Provisioning Technical Data	PTD
Proximity Warning Instrument	PWI
Prudential plc ADS [NYSE symbol]	PUK
Psalms	PS
Pseudo Aircraft Simulation (CTAS)	PAS
Pseudoachondroplastic Spondyloepiphysial Dysplasia (DIPS)	PAD
Pseudo-Noise, Pseudo-Random Binary String/Stream (CGWS)	PN-PRBS
Pseudo-Sense Switch	PSS
PSi Technologies Hldg. ADS [NASDAQ symbol] (SG)	PSIT
Psychiatric Nurse Practitioner (NUJO)	PNP
Psychoanalysis (DIPS)	Psa
Psychokinesis (DIPS)	Pk
Psychological Stress Evaluation	PSE
Psychology (NTIO)	psych
Psychopathy Checklist-Revised [R. Hare] (DIPS)	PCL-R
Psychopharmacology Demonstration Project [Department of Defense] (DIPS)	PDP
Public Affairs Detachment	PAD
Public Affairs Specialist	PAS
Public and Commercial Services Union (HEAS)	PCS
Public Assistance Officer (DEMM)	PAO
Public Charter (TRID)	PC
Public Disclosure Commission	PDC
Public Health Officer Inspector (HEAS)	PHO
Public Information Zone (HEAS)	PIZ
Public Involvement (ABAC)	PI
Public Key Infrastructure	PKI
Public Land Mobile Network (CGWS)	PLMN
Public Safety Building (SARE)	PSB
Public Use Micro Sample	PUMS
Public-Area Branch Exchange (AEBE)	PABX
Publication Applicability List [Navy]	PAL
Publication Illustration Request	PIR
Publications Reliability Inspection Sheet	PRIS
Publications Ships Assistance Team [Navy]	PUBSAT
Public-Sector Net Borrowing	PSNB
Publishing Information Bulletin	PIB
Pull-Up, Push-Out	PUPO

Pulse Code Modulation [*Microwave System*]	PCM
Pulse Code Modulation Microwave [*System*]	PCM
Pulse Compression System	PCS
Pulse Height Analyzed	PHA
Pulse Interference Elimination	PIE
Pulse Ratio Modulator	PRM
Pulse Repetition Time	PRT
Pulse Width	pw
Pulsed Integrating Pendulum	PIP
Pulsed Intense Plasma for Experimental Research	PIPER
Pulse-Duration Modulation-Frequency Modulation	PDMFM
Pulsepower Systems Incorporated	PSI
Pumps (RIMS)	PU
Punched Card Request	PCR
Pupil Personnel Services	PPS
Purchase Change Order Request	PCOR
Purchase Enquiry (RIMS)	P/E
Purchase Memorandum	PM
Purchase Part Tab Card	PPTC
Purchase Parts Data Sheet	PPDS
Purchase Parts Material Request	PPMR
Purchase Requisition	PR
Purchased Part	PP
Purdue Aeronautics Corporation	PRD
Pure Resources [*NYSE symbol*]	PRS
Push Button	P/B
Pyramid	pyr
Pyramid Cartons	pyrcrts
Pyrotechnic Optical Plume Simulation	POPS
Pyrotechnic Substitute Monitor	PSM

Q

By Meaning

QS Communications ADS [*NASDAQ symbol*] (SG) .... QSCG
Quad (TRID) .... qd
Quad with Bath (TRID) .... QADB
Quad with Shower (TRID) .... QADS
Quad without Bath or Shower (TRID) .... QADN
Quadrature .... Q
Quadrature Overlapped Raised Cosine (CCCA) .... QORC
Quadrature Phase Subcarrier .... QCW
Quadruple Neuromuscular Facilitation (DIPS) .... QNF
Quadrupole-Ioffe-Configuration .... QUIC
Qualification Test .... QUAL TEST
Qualification Testing .... QT
Qualitative Research Requirement .... QRR
Quality and Reliability .... QR
Quality and Reliability Assurance Laboratory of the Marshall Space Flight
  Center [*NASA*] .... QUAL
Quality Assurance .... Q/A
Quality Assurance and Revalidation .... QA&R
Quality Assurance Committee (HEAS) .... QAC
Quality Assurance Management Plan (ABAC) .... QAMP
Quality Assurance Specialist, Ammunition Specialist .... QASAS
Quality Check .... QC
Quality Control Program Plan (CTAS) .... QCPP
Quality Development Requirements Information .... QDRI
Quality Improvement Team (ABAC) .... QIT
Quality Measurement Experiment (ARMP) .... QME
Quality Readiness Review .... QRR
Quantitation Limit (ABAC) .... QL
Quantitative Electroencephalograph (DIPS) .... qEEG
Quantitative Electrophysiological Battery (DIPS) .... QEB
Quantitative Risk Assessment (SARE) .... QRA
Quantitative Test (DIPS) .... Q
Quantity Distance-Interline Distance .... QD-IL

Quantized Gate Video .... QGIV
Quantum Effect Devices [*NASDAQ symbol*] (SG) .... QEDI
Quantum Electronics [*A publication*] .... QE
Quantum Electronics and Applications Society .... QECA
Quantum Electronics and Laser Science Conference .... QELS
Quarries National Interest Group (HEAS) .... QNIG
Quarter (NTIO) .... quar
Quarterly Cost and Operational Effectiveness Analysis Forecast .... QCF
Quarterly Return Group (HEAS) .... QRG
Quarterly Review .... QR
Quarters After Contract Award .... QACA
Quartzsite Integrated Acoustic Engine Test .... QIAET
Quasi-Alloy of Zirconium .... QAZ
Quasi-Triennial Oscillation (CARB) .... QTO
Queen Anne Villa .... QV
Queen's Police Medal for Distinguished Service [*British*] ...... QPM
Queue Difference (CCCA) .... QD
Quick Action Engineering Order .... QAEO
Quick Erection Dome .... QED
Quick Flashing (PIPO) .... QK
Quick Look .... Q/L
Quick Look Data Assessment System .... QUIDAS
Quick Perusal .... QP
Quick Position Oriented Event .... QPOE
Quick Reaction Project .... QRP
Quick Return on Investment Program .... QRIP
Quick Total Ozone Manning Spectrometer [*NASA*] .... QuikTOMS
Quiet Reliable Generators .... QRG
Quin with Bath (TRID) .... QINB
Quin with Shower (TRID) .... QINS
Quin without Bath or Shower (TRID) .... QINN
Quinoline (CARB) .... QN
Qwest Communications Intl. [*NYSE symbol*] (SG) .... Q

149

R
By Meaning

Race Relations and Equal Opportunity .... RR&EO
Radar Action Message Processor .... RAMP
Radar Altimeter .... R/A
Radar Altitude Warning System [*Air Force*] .... RAWS
Radar Analysis of Noise and Clutter .... RANC
Radar Attenuation, Noise and Clutter (CCCA) .... RANC
Radar Bomb Evaluation [*Air Force*] .... RHBVAL
Radar Computer .... RC
Radar Data Converter .... RDC
Radar Data Processor .... RDP
Radar Diagnostic Control System .... RDCS
Radar Diagnostic Operational Processor .... RDOP
Radar Echo Simulation Subsystem .... RESS
Radar Group .... RG
Radar Homing Guidance Intercept .... RHOGI
Radar Improvement Proposal .... RIP
Radar Interface and Scheduling Control (CCCA) .... RISC
Radar Maintenance Control .... RMC
Radar Netting System .... RNS
Radar Planning Device .... RPD
Radar Shelter .... RS
Radar Transmitter Group .... RTG
Radar Warning System .... RWRS
Radar Wind Profiler (ARMP) .... RWP
Radial Keratotomy .... R/K
Radial Structure Plot (ABAC) .... RSP
Radiated Intelligence .... RINT
Radiation Area Monitor (ABAC) .... RAM
Radiation Exposure Status .... RES
Radiation Generating Device (ABAC) .... RGD
Radiation Protection Adviser (HEAS) .... RPA
Radiation Protection Officer .... RPLL
Radiation Protection Technician (ABAC) .... RPT
Radiation Therapy (DAVI) .... XRT
Radio Altitude (HLLA) .... RA
Radio Amplification by Simulated Emission of Radiation System .... RASERS
Radio Atmospheric Study Centre (CARB) .... RASC
Radio Beacon (PIPO) .... RBN
Radio Code Test Speed on Response .... RCTSR
Radio Communications Coordinator (CCCA) .... RCC
Radio Deployment Option [*Department of Defense*] .... RDO
Radio Direction Indicator (HLLA) .... RDI
Radio Electronic [*Combat*] .... REL
Radio Frequency Channel (CGWS) .... RFC
Radio Frequency Intelligence .... RFI
Radio Frequency Surveillance (CCCA) .... RFS
Radio Management Unit (PIAV) .... RMU
Radio Port (CGWS) .... RP
Radio Port Control Unit (CGWS) .... RPCU
Radio Resource (CGWS) .... RR
Radio Signaling Link (CGWS) .... RSL
Radio Telephone .... R/T
Radioactive Containment Exclusion Clause [*Insurance*] (MARI) ...... RACE
Radioactive Liquid Fed Ceramic Melter (ABAC) .... RLFCM
Radioactive Mixed Waste (ABAC) .... RMW
Radioactive Waste Collection Tank (ABAC) .... RWCT
Radioisotopic Thermoelectric Generator .... RTG
Radiological Control (ABAC) .... RadCon
Radiological Officer [*Department of Emergency Management*] (DEMM) ...... RO
Radioplane [*Company*] .... RP
Radius of Safety .... Rs
Radius Vector Axis .... R-BAR
Radon .... RN
Radon Contractor Proficiency (AUEG) .... RCP
RADVision, Ltd. [*NASDAQ symbol*] (SG) .... RVSN
Rainfall Anomaly Index (CARB) .... RAI
Rambus Direct RAM .... RDRAM
Ranch .... RA
Random Access Burst (CGWS) .... RAB
Random Access Channel (CGWS) .... RACH
Random Access Indestructive Advanced Memory .... RANDAM
Random Acts of Kindness .... RAoK
Random Area Navigation (PIPO) .... RNAV
Random Early Discard (MLOA) .... RED
Random Path Infrared .... REPAIR
Random Walk .... RWALK

Randomized Clinical Trial (DIPS) .... rCT
Range and Evaluation Guidance for Approach and Landing .... REGAL
Range Antiarmor Antipersonnel Weapon System .... RAAWS
Range Data Measurement System .... RDMS
Range Destruction Officer .... RDO
Range Instrumentation Division .... RID
Range Location Clutter .... RLCL
Range Location in Correlator .... RLC
Range Location Skin .... RLS
Range Measurement System .... RMS
Range Minimum Commanded .... RMINC
Range Minimum Control .... RMC
Range Operator .... RO
Range Rate to Target .... R DOT
Range Safety .... R/S
Range-Gated Pulse Doppler .... RGPD
Rank Correlation (DIPS) .... P
Ransom and Kidnap [*Insurance*] (MARI) .... R&K
Rapid Model Development Environment .... RMDE
Rapid Radiative Transfer Model (ARMP) .... RRTM
Rapid Reaction Deployable Command Control Communications
   (CCCA) .... RRDCCC
Rapid Sequential Visual Presentation (DIPS) .... RSVP
Rate Range Indicator .... RRI
Rate Sensitive Assets/Rate Sensitive Liabilities .... RSA/RSL
Rational Emotive Behavior Therapy [*A. Ellis*] (DIPS) .... REBT
Rational Emotive Therapy [*A. Ellis*] (DIPS) .... RET
Raw Material Support Group .... RMSG
Rawlings Official [*Baseball term*] (NDBD) .... RO
Reacquisition .... REACQ
Reaction Motors, Incorporated .... RMI
Reactional Biography [*A. Anastasi*] (DIPS) .... RB
Reactive Attachment Disorder .... RAD
Reader .... rdr
Readiness Capability .... REDCAP
Reading Quotient (DIPS) .... Rdq
Readout and Relay .... R/R
Real Time .... R/T
Real Time Computation Center [*NASA*] .... RTCC
Realistic Air Defense Evaluation System .... RADES
Receipt, Storage, and Issue .... RS&I
Receive Counter .... R Counter
Receive Only (PIPO) .... R
Receive Only (PIPO) .... R/O
Received Signal Strength Indicator (CGWS) .... RSSI
Receiver (PIAV) .... Rx
Receiver/Exciter .... R/E
Receiver Timing Counter .... RTC
Receiver/Transmitter (PIPO) .... RT
Receive-to-Transmit .... R/T
Receiving Inspection .... R/I
Receiving Quality Assurance Card .... RQAC
Receptive Service Operator (TRID) .... RSO
Recharge .... RK
Reciprocal Electrical Council, Inc. .... RECI
Recognition by Components [*I. Biederman*] (DIPS) .... RBC
Reconfirmed (TRID) .... RR
Reconnaissance Attack Squadron [*Air Force*] .... RVDP
Reconnaissance Attack Squadron [*Navy*] .... RVHA
Reconnaissance Patrol Combatant [*Navy*] .... PGR
Reconnaissance/Surveillance .... R/S
Reconnaissance, Surveillance, and Target Acquisition [*Military*] ...... RSTA
Reconstitutable and Enduring Command Control Communicatons
   (CCCA) .... RECCC
Record Association System .... RAS
Record Descriptive Word [*Computer science*] (ITCA) .... RDW
Record Locator (TRID) .... RLOC
Recorder Cycle .... RC
Records Turnover Package (ABAC) .... RTP
Recover, Reconstitute, Reload & Restrike [*Military*] (CCCA) R4
Recovery Support Plan .... RSP
Recreation (NTIO) .... rec
Recreational Vehicle .... R/V
Red Integrated Strategic Operations Plan .... RISOP
Red Poppy [*Publisher*] .... RP
Redeemable (SG) .... Red

Redeployment of Forces to Germany	REFORGER
Rediated Emission	RE
Rediff.com India ADS [*NASDAQ symbol*]	REDF
Redstone Shielding Information Center [*NASA*]	RSIC
Reduce Number in Party [*Travel industry*] (TRID)	RNP
Reduced Vertical Separation Minimums (PIPO)	RVSM
Redundant Array of Inexpensive Disks [*Computer science*] (ITCA)	Raid
Redwood Employees Protection Program	REPP
Reengineering Task Force	PTF
Refer (NTIO)	ref
Reference Assembly Sequence (SPST)	RAS
Reference My Letter (TRID)	REML
Reference My Telegram (TRID)	REMT
Reference Our Cable (RIMS)	ROC
Reference Our Telex (RIMS)	ROTLX
Reference Quality Level	RQL
Reference Your Cable (RIMS)	RYC
Reference Your Letter (TRID)	REYL
Reference Your Telegram (TRID)	RYT
Reference Your Telex (RIMS)	RYTLX
Reflectance Ratio Cloud Test (CARB)	RRCT
Reflector in Space (CARB)	RIS
Refractive Backscattering	RBS
Refresher Fleet Training [*Navy*]	REFTRA
Refugee Liaison Office	RLO
Regent (NTIO)	reg
Regent Communications [*NASDAQ symbol*] (SG)	RGCI
Regional Air Quality Coordinating Committee	RAQCC
Regional Cerebral Blood Flow (DIPS)	RCBF
Regional Commerce Growth Association	RCGA
Regional Food and Drug Director	RFDD
Regional Investment Bankers Association	RIBA
Regional Science Research Institute	RSRI
Register Memory Address	RMAD
Register.com, Inc. [*NASDAQ symbol*] (SG)	RCOM
Registered Environmental Health Specialist (SARE)	REHS
Registered Geologist (SARE)	RG
Registered Industrial Hygienist (SARE)	RIH
Registered Kinesiotherapist (NUJO)	RKT
Registered Nurse First Assistant (NUJO)	RNFA
Registered Nurse Recruiter (NUJO)	RNR
Registered Occupational Hygiene Technologist (SARE)	ROHT
Registered Occupational Hygienist (SARE)	ROH
Registered Professional Industrial Hygienist (SARE)	RPIH
Registered Psychiatric Nurse (NUJO)	RPN
Registered Pulmonary Function Technician (NUJO)	RPFT
Registered Radiation Protection Technologist (SARE)	RRPT
Registor Logic	RL
Reglements sur l'Assurance de la Quality [*Quality Assurance Regulation*] [*French*]	RAQ
Regular Pulse Excitation (CGWS)	RPE
Regulation	R
Rehabilitation Through Photography	RTP
Reinitialization	REINT
Reinitialization Time	RIT
Reix Limen [*Absolute Threshold*] [*German*] (DIPS)	RL
Rejection and Disposition Request	RDR
Related Deviation Standard (ABAC)	RDS
Relational Online Analytic Processing (IDAI)	ROLAP
Relative Bearing Indicator [*Aviation*] (PIAV)	RBI
Relative Partial Sum of Squares (CARB)	RPSS
Relative Percent Accuracy (ABAC)	RPA
Relative Percent Difference (ABAC)	RPD
Relay Assembly Group [*Air Force*]	RAG
Relay Mirror Experimental Satellite (CARB)	RMES
Release (TRID)	RLSE
Release for Handling by Your Agency (TRID)	RHYA
Releasing (TRID)	RLNG
Reliability and Maintainability	RM
Reliability and Maintainability Prediction and Notification Tool (SPST)	RAMPAT
Reliable Broadcast Toolkit (ROAS)	RBT
Reliable Service Area (CGWS)	RSA
Religion (NTIO)	rel
Remain over Night (PIAV)	RON
Remarks (TRID)	RMKS
Remote Access Terminal [*NASA*]	RAT
Remote Amplifier and Adaptation Box	RAAB
Remote Antenna Driver (CGWS)	RAD
Remote Antenna Signal Processor (CGWS)	RASP
Remote Area Conflict Information Center	RACK
Remote Bar Code System	RBCS
Remote Carrier Module	RCM
Remote Clinical Communications System	RCCS
Remote Cloud Sensing (ARMP)	RCS
Remote Communications Center	RCC
Remote Data Protocol [*Computer science*]	RDP
Remote Defect Indicator (MLOA)	RDI
Remote Desktop Protocol	RDP
Remote Ecological Monitoring of the Seafloor	REMOTS
Remote Ground Station (CCCA)	RGS
Remote Line Concentrating Module	RLCM
Remote Minefield Identification and Display System	REMIDS
Remote Monitoring [*Computer science*] (ITCA)	Rmon
Remote Monitoring Subsystem (CTAS)	RMS

Remote Operator Vehicle [*Nautical*]	ROV
Remote Sensing (CARB)	RS
Remote Sensor	REMS
Remote Station Automation [*System*] [*Air Force*]	RSA
Remote Station Communications Equipment Interface	RSCEI
Remote Storage Management [*Computer science*]	RSM
Remote Subscriber Switch (CCCA)	RSS
Remote Unit Power	RMU PWR
Remotely Piloted Aircraft (CARB)	RPA
Rendered	R
Rendezvous and Recovery	RAR
Rendoring Safe Procedures	RSP
Rentech, Inc. [*AMEX symbol*] (SG)	RTK
Repair Part	RP
Repeat Previous Transaction (TRID)	RPT
Replacement New Box	RNB
Replacement New Foam	RNF
Replacement Production Reactor (ABAC)	RPR
Reply by Letter	REPLTR
Reply to Duplicate Booking Enquiry [*Travel industry*] (TRID)	RDB
Report Crossing [*Aviation*] (PIPO)	RX
Report of Shipment	REPSHIP
Report on the In-Process Review	RIPR
Reportable Item Code	RIC
Reporting District (SARE)	RD
Reporting Party (SARE)	RP
Reports Control System	RCS
Reproductive Endocrinologist	RE
Republic (NTIO)	rep
Republic Aircraft Corporation	RAC
Republic of South Africa (CARB)	RSA
Republic of The Gambia (NTIO)	Gam
Republican Leadership Council	RLC
Repurchase Transactions	REPOS
Request for Check	RFC
Request for Engineering Instructions	REI
Request for Plan	RFP
Request for Proposal (TRID)	RFP
Request for Reply (TRID)	RQR
Request for Support	RS
Request is Desired (TRID)	RQID
Request Seat [*Travel industry*] (TRID)	RQST
Requested That	RETAT
Required Collaborative Research Experience (CARB)	RCRE
Requirement (NTIO)	req
Requirement Appraisal Work Group	RAWG
Requirements	REQMTS
Requirements and Product Design [*Phase*]	RPD
Requirements Assessment Group	RAG
Requirements for Total Mobilization	RETMOD
Requirements Inventory Sheet	RIS
Requisition and Invoice/Shipping Document	RI/SD
Research and Development Advisory Council	RDAC
Research and Development Center	RDC
Research and Development Planning Summary [*Methodology*]	R&DPS
Research Assistant	RA
Research Council	RC
Research, Development, and Acquisition Specialties Committee	RDASC
Research Development Associates (CCCA)	RDA
Research, Development, Test, and Evaluation Obligation Phase Plan [*Department of Defense*]	RDOPP
Research Fellow	RF
Research Institute for Mathematical Sciences [*Japan*]	RIMS
Research Planning Section (HEAS)	RPS
Research Scale Meter (ABAC)	RSM
Research Strategy Unit (HEAS)	RSU
Research Student	RS
Research Volume (ABAC)	RV
Research Volume Cost (ABAC)	RVC
Reservation (NTIO)	RES
Reservation (NTIO)	res
Reservations Sales Agent (TRID)	RSA
Reserve Component Advisory Group	RCAG
Reserve Component Allocation System	RCAS
Reserve Component Civilian Acquired Skills Program	RCCASP
Reserved Seat [*Travel industry*] (TRID)	RS
Reservoir Level Sensor	RLE
Resident Integrated Logistics Support Team	RILST
Residual Excited Linear Predictive (CGWS)	RELP
Resistance	R
Resolution Trust Company (NTIO)	RTC
Resolver-to-Digital (AEBE)	R-D
Resource	Resour
Resource Allocation Notice (SPST)	RAN
Resource Center Information System (AUEG)	RCIS
Resource Management System	RMS
Resource Recovery Act	RRA
Respective Rights and Interests (MARI)	RR&I
Respiration Rate	RR
Respiratory Protective Equipment (HEAS)	RPE
Respiratory Technician (NUJO)	RT
Response Amplitude (DIPS)	A
Response Analysis Processor	RAP
Response Operating Characteristic (DIPS)	ROC
Response Shock (DIPS)	RS

Response Surface Matrix .... RSM
Responsible Young Drivers [*An association*] .... RYD
Restructured Armored Division .... RAD
Reticular Formation (DIPS) .... rf
Retinol .... Rol
Retired Activities Offices [*Navy*] .... RAO
Retired International Business Machine Program .... RIP
Retiree Activity Days .... RAD
Retirees to Eliminate Source Income State Tax .... RESIST
Retractable Gear [*Aviation*] (PIPO) .... RG
Retrieval of Calling Line Directory Number .... RCLDN
Retrofit Change Action Request .... RCAR
Retrofit Change Drawings .... RCDS
Retrofit Modification Kit .... RMK
Return Transportation .... RETRANS
Return Verandah Villa .... RV
Reunion Industries [*AMEX symbol*] (SG) .... RUN
Re-Usable Benchmarking Environment (AEBE) .... RUBEN
Revenue Accounting Office .... RAO
Reverse Analog Control Channel (CGWS) .... RACC
Reverse Analog Voice Channel (CGWS) .... RVC
Reverse Command Channel (ROAS) .... RCC
Reverse Digital Traffic Channel (CGWS) .... RDTC
Reverse Traffic Channel Digital (CGWS) .... RTC
Review Advisory Group .... RAG
Review and Analysis .... RA
Review and Planning Conference .... RAPC
Review Board for Release of Materiel for Issue .... RBRMI
Review of Regulation (HEAS) .... RoR
Revised (NTIO) .... rev
Revised Beta Examination, Second Edition [*C. E. Kellogg, N. W. Morton*] (DIPS) .... BetaII
Rewind (NTIO) .... rew
Reynolds Army Community Hospital [*Fort Sill*] .... RACH
Rhetoric (NTIO) .... rhet
Rhode Island Educational Media Association .... RIEMA
Rhode Island Lines .... RIL
Riddles .... rid
Ridiculously High Frequency (HLLA) .... RHF
Right Angle Program .... RAP
Right Field (NTIO) .... rf
Right Fielder [*Baseball term*] (NDBD) .... rf
Right Half Plane (CCCA) .... RHP
Right Turn .... RT
Right-Handed Batter [*Baseball term*] (NDBD) .... RHB
Right-Handed Pitcher [*Baseball term*] (NDBD) .... RHP
Rigid Disk Drive System .... RDDS
Rijn-Schelde-Verolme .... RSV
Riot and Civil Commotion [*Insurance*] (MARI) .... r&cc
Ripple Down Rules (IDAI) .... RDR
Risk Assessment Liaison Group (HEAS) .... RALG
Risk Assessment Tool (HEAS) .... RISKAT
Risk Management (ABAC) .... RM
Risk Management Agency .... RMA
Risk Mitigation Experiment [*NASA*] (SPST) .... RME
Risk Reduction Factor (ABAC) .... RRF
River (NTIO) .... Riv
River Mile (CARB) .... RM
River Monitor [*Navy*] .... RM
Riverbed Acoustical Laboratory .... RAL
Riverdeep Group ADS [*NASDAQ symbol*] (SG) .... RVDP
Rivermead Behavioral Memory Test [*B. Wilson*] (DIPS) .... RBMT

Riverside Telescope Makers Conference [*California*] .... RTMC
Road March [*Marine Corps*] .... RM
Roadside .... RS
Roadstead Patrol Boat [*Navy*] .... RPB
Robotic Optical Transient Search Equipment .... ROTSE
Robotic Optical Transient Search Experiment I .... ROTSE-I
Robotics Test-Bed [*Program*] .... RTB
Rochester Applied Science Association .... RASA
Rochester Theory Center .... RTC
Rock Mechanics and Explosives Research Center .... RMERC
Rocket Troops and Artillery .... RTA
Rockwell Hardness Number (ABAC) .... RHN
Rockwell Ship Systems, Australia .... RSSA
Rocky Flats Publication [*Rockwell International*] .... RFP
Rodent Impact Program [*Detroit, MI*] .... RIP
Roger Received and Understood .... RGR
Rogers Corp. [*NYSE symbol*] (SG) .... ROG
Role Construct Repertory Test [*G. A. Kelly*] (DIPS) .... REP Test
Roll Rate .... P
Romanian Society for Mathematical and Physical Sciences [*Romania*] .... RSMPS
Rome Stock Exchange (SG) .... Ro
Root Mean Squared (SARE) .... RMS
Rosman [*North Carolina*] .... ROS
Rotary Joints Motor Controller [*NASA*] (SPST) .... RJMC
Rotatable Wing Assembly .... RWA
Rotating Beacon (PIPO) .... RB
Rotating-Combustion Engine .... RCENGINE
Rotational Aftereffect (DIPS) .... RAE
Rough Set Data Analysis (IDAI) .... RSDA
Route Server Functional Group .... RSFG
Routing Logic Radio Interface Unit .... RLRIU
Row Cottage .... RC
Royal Armoured Corps Centre [*British*] .... RACC
Royal Australian Air Force .... RAN
Royal Australian Navy Experimental Laboratory .... RANEL
Royal Institute of Technology [*Sweden*] .... RIT
Royal Naval and Royal Marine Forces Reserve Decoration [*British*] .... RD
Royal Netherlands Meteorological Institute (CARB) .... RNMI
Royal Society Study Group (HEAS) .... RSSG
Rubber Industry Advisory Committee (HEAS) .... RUBIAC
Runaway Centerline Lights [*Aviation*] (PIPO) CL
Runway .... R/W
Runway (PIAV) .... rwy
Runway Acceptance Rate (CTAS) .... RAR
Runway Edge Lights (PIPO) .... RL
Runway Point of Interception (PIPO) .... RPI
Rural .... RA
Rural Area (CGWS) .... RA
Rural Cellular Association (CGWS) .... RCA
Rural Economic and Community Development .... RECD
Rural Electric Cooperative .... REC
Rural Housing Service .... RHS
Rural Information Center Health Service .... RICHS
Rural Utilities Service .... RUS
Russian (NTIO) .... Rus
Russian Military News Agency .... AVN
Russian National Committee for Pacific Economic Cooperation .... RNCPEC
Rust Federal Services Northwest (ABAC) .... RFSNW
Rust Federal Services of Hanford, Inc. (ABAC) .... RFSH
Rust, Oxidation, Discoloration [*Insurance*] (MARI) .... ROD
Ruth .... RU
Ruthenium .... RU
Rydberg [*Unit of measure*] .... RY

S
By Meaning

S1 Corp.	SONE
Saab Variable Compression	SVC
Saba Software [*NASDAQ symbol*] (SG)	SABA
Sabbath (NTIO)	Sab
Sacrifice [*Baseball term*] (NDBD)	sac
Saddle Bronc Riding [*Rodeo term*]	SB
Sadomasochism (DIPS)	SM
Sadomasochistic (DIPS)	SM
Safe, Arm, Fuze, and Fire	SAFE
Safe, Arming, and Fuzing	SAF
Safe Medical Devices Act [*Food and Drug Administration*]	SMDA
Safe Operating Practice	SOP
Safe Ports (RIMS)	SP
Safe Use Determination (SARE)	SUD
Safeguard	SAF
Safeguard Logistics Command	SAFLOG
Safeguard Project Officer	SAFPO
Safety and Arming	S&A
Safety and Enforcement Statistics (HEAS)	SES
Safety and Loss Prevention (HEAS)	S and LP
Safety Appliance Illustration (HEAS)	SAI
Safety Approval Form (SARE)	SAF
Safety Arming Device	SAD
Safety Coordinator	SC
Safety Environment Institute (HEAS)	SEI
Safety Evaluation Document (ABAC)	SED
Safety Information Bulletin (HEAS)	SIB
Saigon Time Weekly [*A publication*]	STW
Saigon Times Daily [*A publication*]	STD
St. Petersburg (RIMS)	SPB
Salt Water Arrival Draft (RIMS)	SWAD
Salt Water Departure Draft (RIMS)	SWDD
Same Clock Timing (MLOA)	SCT
Samoa Observatory (CARB)	SMO
Sample Analysis Form (ABAC)	SAF
Sample Exchange Evaluation (ABAC)	SEE
Sample Job (ABAC)	SJ
Sample Management Office (AUEG)	SMO
Sample Stabilizer (ABAC)	SS
San Antonio Air Logistic Center [*Air Force*]	SAALC
San Francisco Art Institute	SFAI
Santa Barbara Community College [*California*] (ROAS)	SBCC
Satellite, Air, Surface, Subsurface Tactical Information Exchange Subsystem	SASSTIXS
Satellite and Missile Observation System	SAMOS
Satellite Communications (PIAV)	satcoms
Satellite Data Relay	SADR
Satellite Landing System (HLLA)	SLS
Satellite Operation Command and Control (CARB)	SOCC
Satellite Ranging Facility	SRF
Satellite Signal Receiver (CCCA)	SSR
Satellite Ticket Printer Network (TRID)	STPN
Saturday (NTIO)	Sa
Saturdays, Sundays, Holidays Excepted (RIMS)	SATSHEX
Saturdays, Sundays, Holidays Excepted (RIMS)	SSHEX
Saturdays, Sundays, Holidays Included (RIMS)	SATSHINC
Saturdays, Sundays, Holidays Included (RIMS)	SSHINC
Saturn/Apollo [*NASA*]	S/A
Saudi Arabian Land Forces	SALF
Saudia Air Force Material Study	SAMS
Savvis Communications [*NASDAQ symbol*] (SG)	SVVS
Sawlog Harvest (CARB)	SAW
Saxon (NTIO)	Sax
S-Band Linear Collider	SBLC
Scanning Hall Probe Microscope	SHPM
Scanning Spectral Polarimeter (CARB)	SSP
Scanning Tunneling Microscopy	STM
SCG Holdings [*NASDAQ symbol*] (SG)	ONNN
Schedule/Actual	S/A
Schedule Change (TRID)	SC
Schedule Exchange Data Message (TRID)	SEDM
Schedule Optimization Study (ABAC)	SOS
Scheduled Time of Arrival (CTAS)	STA
Scheduled Time of Departure (CTAS)	STD
Scheduling and Review Procedures	SARP
School Ability Tests (DIPS)	SAT
School Achievement Test (DIPS)	SAT
School Bus (ROAS)	SBUS
School District	SD
School of Aviation Medicine [*Air Force*]	SAM
School of Environment Studies	SES
School-to-Career	STC
School-to-Work	STW
Science Applications International	SAI
Science Baseline Document	SBD
Science Budget	SB
Science Committee	SC
Science Fiction (NTIO)	sci-fi
Science, Mathematics, Engineering, and Technology	SME&T
Science Payload	S/P
Science Teacher and Research Scientist [*Fellowships*]	STaRS
Science Teams in Rural Environments for Aquatic Management Studies	STREAMS
Science Technology & Engineering Preview Summer [*1997*]	STEPS
Science, Technology, and Research Students [*Program*]	STARS
Science Textbook	sctx
Science to Achieve Results	STAR
Scientific and Technical Communications Committee	SATCOM
Scientific and Technical Information	S&TI
Scientific Committee for Veterinary Measures Relating to Public Health	SCVPH
Scorpio (NTIO)	SCO
Scottish and Newcastle Lymphoma Group	SNLG
Scottish Natural Heritage	SNH
Scottish UFO Research	SRUFO
Scout Executive [*Boy Scouts of America*]	SE
Scoutmaster [*Boy Scouts of America*]	SM
Scratching, Denting, Marring, Chipping [*Insurance*] (MARI)	SDMC
Screen-Based Telephone (ROAS)	SBT
Scribner Encyclopedia of American Lives [*A publication*]	SEAL
Scripps Institution of Oceanography [*University of California at San Diego*]	SCRIPPS
Sea Based [*Navy*]	SB
Sea Based Anti-Ballistic Missile Intercept System [*Navy*]	SABMIS
Sea Food Meal (TRID)	SFML
Sea Level (PIAV)	sl
Sea Surface Height (CARB)	SSHT
Sea View (TRID)	SVW
Sea Water Damage [*Insurance*] (MARI)	SWD
Sealed Double-Ring Infiltrometer (ABAC)	SDRI
Sealed Storage Cask (ABAC)	SSC
Search and Rescue Coordination [*FAA*]	SARCC
Search and Rescue Homing	SARAH
Search and Reserve (CCCA)	SAR
Search Look Strategy (CCCA)	SLS
Search of Associative Memory [*R. M. Shiffrin*] (DIPS)	SAM
Seasonal Year (CARB)	SY
Second in Command [*Aviation*] (PIPO)	SIC
Second Level Domain	SLD
Second Stage Digital Multiplexer (CCCA)	SSDM
Second-Class Hotel (TRID)	SHTL
Secret	S
Secret Identity Key (CGWS)	Ki
Secretary (NTIO)	sec'y
Secretary of the Air Force for Research and Development	SAF/RD
Secure Digital	SD
Secure Digital Modem (CCCA)	SDM
Secure Electronic Mail	S/MIME
Secure Voice Element (CCCA)	SVE
Security Affairs Support Association	SASA
Security Certification Working Group (CCCA)	SCWG
See You Later (ADWA)	CYL
Seed End	SE
Seeker Antenna	SA
Segment (SPST)	s
Segment (TRID)	SGMT
Segment Status Message (TRID)	SSM
Seiler Algorithmic Oriented Language Digitally	SADSAC
Selected Acquisition Review	SAR
Selected Ion Monitoring (ABAC)	sim
Selected Nuclear Option (CCCA)	SNO
Selectica, Inc. [*NASDAQ symbol*] (SG)	SLTC

Selection Index [*H. J. Eysenck*] (DIPS) ... D
Selective Call Forwarding ... SCF
Selective Class of Call Screening (CGWS) ... SCCS
Selective Equipment Removal System (ABAC) ... SERS
Selective Estrogen Receptor Modulator [*Medicine*] ... SERMS
Selective Ion Electrode (ABAC) ... SIE
Selective Message Routing (CCCA) ... SMR
Self Discharger (RIMS) ... SELFDISCH
Self-Amortizing Project ... SAP
Self-Assessment (DIPS) ... SA
Self-Containing ... SC
Self-Help Group (DIPS) ... SHG
Self-Instructional Training (DIPS) ... SET
Self-Perceived Communication Competence ... SPCC
Self-Statement Training (DIPS) ... SST
Semantic Pragmatic Disorder ... SPD
SEMCO Energy [*NYSE symbol*] (SG) ... SEN
Semiactive Homing ... SAH
Semi-Active Laser Guided Projectiles ... SAL GP
Semiautomated Command-to-Line-of-Sight ... SACLOS
Semi-Automated Range, Azimuth, and Height ... SARAH
Semi-Automatic Ground Environment (CCCA) ... SAGE
Semi-Automatic Switch Center (CCCA) ... SASC
Semiconductor Generic Manufacturing Requirements Specification ... SGMRS
Seminary (NTIO) ... sem
Semiquantitative (ABAC) ... SQA
Semitic (NTIO) ... Sem
Senate (NTIO) ... sen
Senior District Executive [*Boy Scouts of America*] ... SDE
Senior Executive Vice President ... SEVP
Senior Information Resource Management Officer (AUEG) ... SIRMO
Senior Inspector (HEAS) ... SI
Senior Lecturer ... SL
Senior Management Review (HEAS) ... SMR
Senior Patrol Leader [*Boy Scouts of America*] ... SPL
Senior Professional Baseball Association (NDBD) ... SPBA
Senior Research Fellow ... SRF
Sensation Level of Sound (DIPS) ... SL
Sensation Unit (DIPS) ... SU
Sense and Destroy Armor Missile ... SADARM
Sensors for the Water Industry Group ... SWIG
Sensory Integration Dysfunction ... SID
Sensory Integrative Dysfunction ... SID
Sensory-Information Store (DIPS) ... SIS
September (NTIO) ... Sep
Sequenced Flashing Lights (PIPO) ... SFL
Sequenom, Inc. [*NASDAQ symbol*] (SG) ... SQNM
Serial Number (PIPO) ... S/N
Serious Adverse Event [*Medicine*] ... SAE
Serotonin Reuptake Inhibitor [*Medicine*] (DIPS) ... SRI
Server-Gated Cryptography [*Computer science*] ... SGC
Serves (TRID) ... SRVS
Service Acquisiton Review Council ... SARC
Service Assessment Pool (ABAC) ... SAP
Service Coordinator ... SC
Service Data Link [*Computer science*] (ITCA) ... SDL
Service de la Surveillance Industrielle de'Armement [*France*] ... SAIR
Service Information (TRID) ... SI
Service Level Agreement (HEAS) ... SLA
Service Specific Connection Oriented Protocol ... SSCOP
Service Specific Convergence Sublayer ... SSCS
Service Specific Coordination Function ... SSCF
Service Switching Point (CGWS) ... SSP
Serviceability Level Indication Processing [*Computer science*] (ITCA) ... SLIP
Set-Top Box (AEBE) ... STB
Severe Expressive Language Delay ... SELD
Severe Weather Avoidance Procedures (CTAS) ... SWAP
Severely Emotionally Disturbed ... SED
Severely Errored Cell Block ... SECB
Severely Errored Seconds (MLOA) ... SES
Sexual-Orientation Disturbance (DIPS) ... SOD
Sexual-Response Cycle (DIPS) ... SRC
Sforzando (NTIO) ... sf
Shack ... SH
Shaken Infant Syndrome ... SIS
Shallow-Water Equations (CARB) ... SWE
Shareable Courseware Object Reference Model [*Computer science*] ... SCORM
Shares (SG) ... shs
Shawnee Press [*Publisher*] ... SHA
Sheet Metal and Plastics ... SMP
Ship Alteration Inventory List [*Navy*] ... SAIL
Ship Repairer's Liability [*Insurance*] (MARI) ... SRL
Shipalt [*Navy*] ... S/A
Shipboard Armament Inventory List [*Navy*] ... SAIL
Shipping and Handling (NTIO) ... s&h
Ships Anti-Missile Systems Operability Test ... SAMSOT
Ship-to-Objective Maneuver ... STOM
Short Airfield Tactical ... SATRAK
Short Approach Light System Sequenced Flashing Lights (PIPO) ... SALSF
Short Contact Time (ABAC) ... SCT
Short Life Memorandum (HEAS) ... SLM
Short Message Service Call Broadcast (CGWS) ... SMSCB
Short Supply ... SS
Short-Bout ... SB
Short-Rotation Intensive Culture (CARB) ... SRIC
Shortwave Radiation (ARMP) ... SWR
Shortwave Spectroradiometer (ARMP) ... SWS
Shutout [*Baseball term*] (NDBD) ... ShO
Shuttle Mission Training Facility [*NASA*] (SPST) ... SMTF
Siegfried and Roy Masters of the Impossible ... SARMOTI
Sigma Theta Tan International ... STTI
Signal and Telecommunications (HEAS) ... S&T
Signal Band Energy in the Main Lobe ... SBML
Signal Band Indication ... SBI
Signal Passed at Danger (HEAS) ... SPAD
Signal to Jam (CCCA) ... S/J
Signal to Noise Ratio (DIPS) ... s/n
Signaling Controller (CGWS) ... SC
Signaling Point (CGWS) ... SP
Signaling System Number (CGWS) ... SSN
Signaling Tone (CGWS) ... ST
Signalling Channel Link Protocol ... SCLP
Signing and Releasing Bill of Lading (RIMS) ... S/R B/L
Silencer of Death Domains ... SODD
Silicon Labs [*NASDAQ symbol*] (SG) ... SLAB
Siliconware Precision ADS [*NASDAQ symbol*] ... SPILA
Silt Density Index ... SDI
Silverline Technologies 'A' [*NYSE symbol*] ... SLT
Simple Programmable Logic Device (AEBE) ... SPLD
Simplified Omnidirectional Approach Light System (PIPO) ... SODALS
Simplified Short Approach Light System with Sequenced Flashing Lights (PIPO) ... SSALF
Simplified Tax and Wage Reporting System ... STAWRS
Simulated Air-to-Air Combat ... SAAC
Simulated Analog Computer ... SADSAC
Simulated High-Level Waste Slurry (ABAC) ... SHLWS
Simulated Waste Access to Ground Water (AUEG) ... SWAG
Simulation Test and Exercise (CCCA) ... STEX
Simultaneous (PIPO) ... S
Simultaneous Auroral Multi-Balloons Observations (CARB) ... SAMBO
Since Chrome Major Overhaul [*Aviation*] (PIPO) ... SCMOH
Since Factory Remanufacture [*Aviation*] (PIPO) ... SFRM
Since Hot Section (PIPO) ... SHS
Since Overhaul [*Aviation*] (PIPO) ... SOH
Since Prop Overhaul [*Aviation*] (PIPO) ... SPOH
Since Top Overhaul [*Aviation*] (PIPO) ... STOH
Sine (NTIO) ... sin
Singapore Aircraft Industries ... SAI
Singapore National Committee for Pacific Economic Cooperation ... SINCPEC
Single (TRID) ... sgl
Single Acquisition Unit ... SAU
Single Address Assembly Machine Language ... SAAL
Single Attachment Concentrator [*Computer science*] (ITCA) ... SAC
Single Channel Objective Terminal (CCCA) ... SCOT
Single Channel Transponder Injection System (CCCA) ... SCTIS
Single Deck (RIMS) ... SID
Single Event Effect (SPST) ... SEE
Single Fronted ... SF
Single Gauss Point (CARB) ... SGP
Single Photon Emission Computerised Tomography ... SPECT
Single Room with Bath (TRID) ... SGLB
Single Room with Shower (TRID) ... SGLS
Single Room without Bath (TRID) ... SGLN
Single-Channel Distribution Bridge (CCCA) ... SDB
Single-Major-Locus Model (DIPS) ... SML
Single-Stage-to-Orbit ... SASSTO
Singular (NTIO) ... s
Sister (NTIO) ... Sr
Site Acceptance Test (CTAS) ... SAT
Site Activation ... S/A
Site Activation Requirements Documents ... SARD
Site Characterization Plan (ABAC) ... SCP
Site Characterization Report (ABAC) ... SCR
Site Management System (ABAC) ... SMS
Site Operations Log (ARMP) ... SOL
Site Platform Processing Facility (SPST) ... SPPF
Site Program Manager (ARMP) ... SPM
Situation Awareness Beacon with Reply ... SABER
Situation Comedy (NTIO) ... sitcom
Sixteen Personality Factor Questionnaire [*R. B. Cattell*] (DIPS) ... 16PF
Size-Resolving (CARB) ... SR
Skillcentre (HEAS) ... SC
Slavic (NTIO) ... Slav
Slight Tarnish ... SLT
Slop Tanks (RIMS) ... SLPTA
Slovak Air Force ... SAF
Small Acoustic Device Simulating an Aircraft Carrier [*Navy*] ... SADSAC
Small Agency Council ... SAC
Small Airfield Tactical ... SATRAK
Small and Medium Enterprise ... SME
Small Business Set Aside ... SBSA
Small Computer Standard Interface ... SCSI
Small Mission for Advanced Research in Technology [*Sponsored by European Space Agency*] ... SMART-1
Small Outline Diode ... SOD
Small Outline Package ... SOP
Small Scale High Temperature Melter (ABAC) ... SSHTM
Small Scale Melter (ABAC) ... SSM
Small System Executive/Virtual Storage Extended [*Computer science*] (ITCA) ... SSCS/VSE

Smallest Space Analysis (DIPS) ... SSA
Smith-Magenis Syndrome ... SMS
Smoke/Aerosol Working Group ... SAWG
Smoking Seat (TRID) ... SMST
Smooth-Pursuit Eye Movements (DIPS) ... SPEM
Snow-Covered Area (CARB) ... SCA
Social (NTIO) ... soc
Social Accountability International ... SAI
Social Age (DIPS) ... SA
Social Science ... SSCI
Social Services ... SOSER
Social Studies ... sst
Social-Skills Training (DIPS) ... SST
Societe Anonyme Telecommunication [*French*] ... SAT
Society for Accelerator and Velocity Apparatus ... SAVA
Society for the Preservation and Encouragement of Barber Shop Quartet Singing in America ... SPEBSQUA
Society for the Social Sciences ... SASS
Society of Authors ... SoA
Society of Nuclear Medicine Education and Research Foundation ... SNMER
Society of Pension Consultants (COBU) ... SPC
Society of Professional Engineering Employees in Aerospace ... SPEEA
Society of Rheology ... SoR
Socioeconomic Data and Applications Center ... SEDAC
Software & Information Industry Association ... SIIA
Software Architecture Review (SPST) ... SAR
Software Configuration Control System (ROAS) ... SCCS
Software Development (CTAS) ... SD
Software Development Integration Laboratory (SPST) ... SDIL
Software Integration and Test (SPST) ... SI&T
Software Maintenance Engineer ... SME
Software Management and Assurance Program (SPST) ... SMAP
Software Review (CTAS) ... SR
Software Specification Document ... SSD
Software Technologies [*NASDAQ symbol*] (SG) ... STCS
Software Verification Facility (SPST) ... SVF
Sol-Air Tres Courte Portee [*Very Short Range Ground to Air*] ... SATCAP
Solar Influence (CARB) ... SI
Solar Neutrino Problem ... SNP
Solar Radiance Transmittance Interferometer (ARMP) ... SORTI
Solaris Network Cache and Accelerator ... SNCA
Sold Inside, Ticketed Inside [*Travel industry*] (TRID) ... SITI
Sold Inside, Ticketed Outside [*Travel industry*] (TRID) ... SITO
Sold Outside, Ticketed Inside [*Travel industry*] (TRID) ... SOTI
Sold Outside, Ticketed Outside [*Travel industry*] (TRID) ... SOTO
Solenoid Driver Output (SPST) ... SDO
Solicitation ... SOL
Solicitor's Office (HEAS) ... SO
Solid State Uninterruptible Power Source (CCCA) ... SSUPS
Solid Waste Act (SARE) ... SWA
Solid Waste Information and Tracking System (ABAC) ... SWITS
Solid Waste Information System (SARE) ... SWIS
Solid Waste Technology Support (ABAC) ... SWTS
Solidified High-Level Waste (ABAC) ... SHLW
Solidified Intermediate-Level Waste (ABAC) ... SILW
Soliloquy (NTIO) ... sol
Soluble Unreactive Phosphorus (CARB) ... SUP
Solvent Alternatives Guide ... SAGE
Solvent Extract Conductivity ... SEC
Somalia (NTIO) ... Som
Song Book ... son
Sonicport.com, Inc. [*AMEX symbol*] (SG) ... SPO
Sony/Philips Digital Interface ... S/PDIF
Sophomore (NTIO) ... soph
Sound Installed ... SND
Sound User Interface ... SUI
Sound Wave File ... WAV
Source and Application of Funds Report ... SAFR
Source Reduction Review Project ... SRRP
Source Routing Bridging [*Telecommunications*] (MLOA) ... SRB
South African National Committee for Oceanographic Research ... SANCOR
South Florida Water Management District ... SFWMD
South Western Bell Telephone (ROAS) ... SWBT
Southdown ... SDW
South-East Consortium for International Development [*Washington, D.C.*] ... SECID
Southeastern Association of Regulatory Utility Commissioners ... SARUC
Southern (NTIO) ... so
Southern California Seismograph Network ... SCSN
Southern Oscillation Index (CARB) ... SOI
Southern Weed Science Society ... SWSS
Southwest Oncology Group ... SWOG
Southwest Townships [*South Africa*] (NTIO) ... Soweto
Southwest Washington Educational Development Consortium ... SWEDC
Southwestern Bell Mobile Service ... SBMS
Soviet (NTIO) ... Sov
Soviet Battlefield Development Plans ... SBDP
Soviet Light Machine Gun ... PK
Soviet Mobile Rocket Technical Base ... PRTB
Space Astrophysics Group ... SAG
Space Based Surveillance System (CCCA) ... SBSS
Space Interferometry Mission [*NASA*] ... SIM
Space Network (CARB) ... SN
Space Requested (TRID) ... SQ
Space Station Control Center [*NASA*] (SPST) ... SSCC
Space Station Element [*NASA*] (SPST) ... SSE
Space Station Furnace Facility [*NASA*] (SPST) ... SSFF
Space Station Pricing Model [*NASA*] (SPST) ... SSPM
Space Station Proximity Operations Trainer [*NASA*] (SPST) ... SPOT
Space Station Quality [*NASA*] (SPST) ... SSQ
Space Station Research Facility Assessment Review [*NASA*] (SPST) ... SSRFAR
Space Station Utilization Advisory Subcommittee [*NASA*] (SPST) ... SSUAS
Space Support Equipment [*NASA*] (SPST) ... SSE
Space Surveillance Center (CCCA) ... SSC
Space-Based Infrared [*Missile system*] ... SBIR
Space-Based System Simulation ... SBSIM
Spacecraft Adapter [*NASA*] ... S/A
Spacecraft Array for Michelson Spatial Interferometer ... SAMSI
Spacial Division Multiple Access (CGWS) ... SDMA
Spanish ... SP
Spanish (NTIO) ... Span
Spares Acquisition Improvement Program ... SAIP
Spares Acquisition Integrated with End Item Production ... SAIP
Spatial Relations (DIPS) ... S
Speaking Across-the-Curriculum ... SAC
Special (NTIO) ... spec
Special Access Program Oversight Committee ... SAPOC
Special Ammunition Storage Point ... SASP
Special Assignment Airlift Mission [*Air Force*] ... SAAM
Special Astronautical Requirement ... SAR
Special Case Waste (ABAC) ... SCW
Special Edition ... Spec Ed
Special Exemption Order (HEAS) ... SEO
Special Factor (DIPS) ... s
Special Mode Group (CGWS) ... SMG
Special Needs Gifted ... SNG
Special Sensor Microwave (CARB) ... SSM
Special Service Requirement (TRID) ... SSR
Special Topic ... ST
Special Weapons Attack Team (NTIO) ... SWAT
Special Work Permit (ABAC) ... SWP
Specialized Common Carrier Service (ROAS) ... SCCS
Speciated Non-Methane Organic Compound ... SNMOC
Specific Application Software Elements (SPST) ... SASE
Specific Factor (DIPS) ... s
Specific Fuel Consumption [*Aviation*] (PIAV) ... sfc
Specific Growth Rate (CARB) ... SGR
Spectronic Automatic Fire Extinguishing ... SAFE
Spectrum Analyzer ... SA
Speech and Language Impaired ... SLI
Speech Impairment ... SI
Speech Interface Assessment Method (DIPS) ... SIAM
Speech Therapy ... ST
Speech Tolerance Level (DIPS) ... TL
Spherical Equivalent Diameter (ABAC) ... SED
Spherical Harmonic Spatial Grid (CARB) ... SHSG
Spigadoro, Inc. [*AMEX symbol*] (SG) ... SRO
Sponsoring Agency ... SA
Sporting Arms and Ammunition Manufacturers Institute ... SAAMI
Spot Profile Analysis Low Energy Electron Diffraction ... SPA-LEED
Spray Advisor Genetic Algorithm ... SAGA
Springfield Arsenal ... SA
Square Feet (NTIO) ... sf
Stability and Support Operation [*Army*] ... SASO
Staff Side (HEAS) ... SS
Staff Welfare Officer (HEAS) ... SWO
Stage Unique Requirements Report (SPST) ... SURR
Stainless Steel (ABAC) ... SS
Standalone Dedicated Control Channel (CGWS) ... SDCCH
Standard Army Intermediate Level Supply ... SAILS
Standard Army Missile ... SAM
Standard Avionics Integrated Fusing ... SAIF
Standard Color Display (ROAS) ... SCD
Standard Cubic Feet per Minute (ABAC) ... scfm
Standard Dutch Hull Form (MARI) ... SDHF
Standard Quick Release Universal Interface Device (SPST) ... SQUID
Standard Solar Model ... SSM
Standard Stimulus (DIPS) ... S
Standardization and Interoperability ... S&I
Standardized Monitoring Framework (AUEG) ... SMF
Standardized Unexpected Earnings ... SUE
Standards of Learning ... SOL
Standby ... S/B
Standby Attitude Indicator ... SAI
Standing Advisory Committee on Pilot Licensing (PIAV) ... SACP
Stanford Positron Electron Accelerating Ring ... SPEAR
Stanford Telecommunications, Inc. (CCCA) ... STI
Stanford-Binet Intelligence Scale (DIPS) ... SB
Stanford-Binet IV [*Test*] (DIPS) ... SB IV
Star Media Network ... STRM
Star Trek ... ST
Star Wars ... SW
Start of Message (CCCA) ... SOM
Starting Pitcher [*Baseball term*] (NDBD) ... SP
State and Local Relations (AUEG) ... SLR
State Children's Health Insurance Program ... S-CHIP
State Nurses Association ... SNA
State Veterinary Service ... SVS
Statement of Charges ... SC
Statement of Facts (RIMS) ... SOF

Station Class Mark (CGWS) .... SCM
Station Crew Procedures Management Plan [*NASA*] (SPST) .... SCPMP
Stationary Source Enforcement (SARE) .... SSE
Statistics (NTIO) .... stats
Statutory Instrument (HEAS) .... SI
Statutory Regulation Order (HEAS) .... SRO
Steer Roping [*Rodeo term*] .... SR
Steer Wrestling [*Rodeo term*] .... SW
Sterile Alpha Motif .... SAM
Sterilization Advance Development Laboratory .... SADL
Sternberg Triarchic Abilities Test (DIPS) .... STAT
Stick and Click (MLOA) .... SC
Stick and Turn (MLOA) .... ST
Stilwell Financial [*NYSE symbol*] .... SV
Stimulus (DIPS) .... S
Stimulus as Coded (DIPS) .... SAC
Stimulus Sampling Theory (DIPS) .... SST
Stimulus-Organism-Response (DIPS) .... SOR
Stock Control Number Approval Form [*Department of Defense*] .... SAF
Stone Undifferentiated .... S
Stop Pirating Internationally Now [*An association*] .... SPIN
Stopover (TRID) .... STVR
Storage Networks, Inc. [*NASDAQ symbol*] .... STOR
Storm Water Pollution Prevention Plan SWP3
Stormwater Monitoring Program (SARE) .... SWMP
Strait (NTIO) .... Str
Stranded, Stunk, or Burnt [*Insurance*] (MARI) .... SS or B
Strategic Air Command Automated Command and Control System [*Air Force*] .... SACCS
Strategic Air Command Digital Network [*Air Force*] .... SACDIN
Strategic Air Command Teletypewriter Network [*Air Force*] .... SACTTYNET
Strategic Air Relocatable Processing Facility .... SARPF
Strategic and Theater Command and Control Systems (CCCA) .... STCCS
Strategic Communications System (CCCA) .... SCS
Strategic Configured Load [*Military*] .... SCL
Strategic Connectivity (CCCA) .... SC
Strategic Connectivity Communications (CCCA) .... SCC
Strategic Defensive Architecture (CCCA) .... SDA
Strategic Project Planning and Assessment (SPST) .... SPP&A
Strategic Rail Authority [*London, England*] .... SRA
Strategic Targeting Activities Reporting System (AUEG) .... STARS
Stratos Lightwave [*NASDAQ symbol*] .... STLW
Stratospheric Limb Infrared Emission Spectrometer (CARB) .... SLIES
Stratospheric Wind Infrared Limb Sounder (CARB) .... SWIRLS
Straw:Grain .... S:G
Stream Class (CTAS) .... SC
Streaming SIMD Extension .... SSE
Stress Analysis of Axisymmetric Solids Version II .... SAAS II
Stress-Innoculation Training (DIPS) .... SIT
Strictly Private (ABAC) .... SP
Strike Out (NTIO) .... so
Strike Warnings [*Military*] .... STRIKWARN
Strikeout, Called [*Baseball term*] (NDBD) .... KC
Strikeout, Swinging [*Baseball term*] (NDBD) .... KS
Strikes, Riots, and Civil Commotions [*Insurance*] (MARI) .... SR&CC
Strikes, Riots, Civil Commotions, and Malicious Damage [*Insurance*] (MARI) .... SR&CC&MD
Stripped Mortgage-Backed Security .... SMBS
Strong Interest Inventory (DIPS) .... SII
Strong-Campbell Interest Inventory Form of the Strong Vocational Interest Blank (DIPS) .... SVIB-SCII
Strontium Recovery (ABAC) .... SrR
Struck Submerged Object [*Insurance*] (MARI) .... SSO
Structural Analysis Program Version 4 .... SAP IV
Structural Analysis Program Version 4 .... SAPVERSION 4
Structured Analysis Design Technique .... SADT
Structured Written Interview Technique (DIPS) .... SWIT
Structures and Materials .... S&M
Stub-Series Terminated Logic (AEBE) .... SSTL
Student (NTIO) .... stud
Student/Community Enrichment Activity Program .... SCEAP
Student Development .... SD
Student Learning Improvement Grant .... SLIG
Student Performance Level .... SPL
Students' Evaluation of Teaching (DIPS) .... SET
Studio (TRID) .... STO
Sub-Arctic Summer (ARMP) .... SAS
Sub-Arctic Winter (ARMP) .... SAW
Subassembly .... S/A
Subcarrier Adapter (AEBE) .... SCA
Subcommunity .... SC
Subcontractor Management Analysis and Integration Team (SPST) .... SMAIT
Subject File (HEAS) .... SF
Subject to Acceptance (MARI) .... S/A
Subject to Approval (MARI) .... s/a
Subject to Approval No Risk (MARI) .... sanr
Subject to Enough Merchandise (RIMS) .... STEM
Subjective Units of Distress (DIPS) .... SUD
Subjunctive (NTIO) .... subj
Submarine (NTIO) .... sub
Submarine Launched Ballistic Missile .... SLBM
Submerged Bed Scrubber (ABAC) .... SBS
Subscriber Identity Module (CGWS) .... SIM
Subscriber Identity Module Expert Group (CGWS) .... SIMEG
Subscriber Line Control Circuit (AEBE) .... SLCC

Substitute Senate Bill .... SSB
Subsurface Barrier (ABAC) .... SSB
Suburb (NTIO) .... sub
Subversion and Espionage Directed Against the Army .... SAEDA
Sudan (NTIO) .... Sud
Suffix (NTIO) .... suff
Sulfur Polymer Cement (ABAC) .... SPC
Sulfuric Acid-Ozone Mixture .... SOM
Sulphur Nitrogen Aerosol Regional Experiment .... SNARE
Summary Basis of Approval .... SBA
Sun Microsystems Computer Corporation (ROAS) .... SMCC
Sunday (NTIO) .... Su
Sunday Communic. ADS [*NASDAQ symbol*] (SG) .... SDAY
Sunset Beach [*Television program title*] .... SUN
Super Kamiokande .... SK
Super Stream Class (CTAS) .... SSC
Super Ultra-Low Emission Vehicle .... SULEV
Superficial Feet (RIMS) .... SF
Superfund Chemical Analysis Data System (AUEG) .... SCADS
Superintendent (NTIO) .... super
Superintending Specialist Inspector (HEAS) .... SSI
Superior Canal Dehiscence Syndrome [*Medicine*] .... SCDS
Superior Labral Anterior and Posterior [*Medicine*] .... SLAP
Superior Room (TRID) .... SUP
Superlative (NTIO) .... sup
Superman, the Animated Series .... STAS
Supersonic Airborne Infrared Measurement Safety .... SAIMS
Supervising Authority .... SA
Supervisory Audio Tone (CGWS) .... SAT
Supplemental Assembly (SPST) .... SA
Supplementary Information (TRID) .... supl info
Supplementary Medical Insurance .... SMI
Supplementary Service (CGWS) .... SS
Supplies and Accounts .... SA
Supply and Transportation .... S&T
Supply of Machinery Safety Regulations (HEAS) .... SMR
Support Availability Multi-System Operational Model .... SAMSON
Support Concept .... SC
Support Equipment Data Base (SPST) .... SEDB
Suppress Enemy Air Defense [*Army*] .... SEAD
Suppressed-Conductivity Ion Chromatography (ABAC) .... SCIC
Surface Air .... SA
Surface Burst Electromagnetic Pulse .... SBEMP
Surface Environmental Surveillance (ABAC) .... SES
Surface Photoconductivity .... SPC
Surface Storage Facility (ABAC) .... SURF
Surface to Air Missile-Development .... SAM-D
Surface Towed Array Sensor System (CCCA) .... SURTASS
Surface Water (AUEG) .... SW
Surface-to-Air .... S/A
Surface-to-Air Antimissile .... SAAM
Surgical and Cardiovascular Intensive Care Unit (NUJO) .... SCVICU
Surplus (NTIO) .... sur
Surveillance and Warning (CCCA) .... SW
Survey of Management Practices [*C. L. Wilson*] (DIPS) .... SMP
Survivability and Vulnerability Improvement .... SAVIM
Survivable and Endurable (CCCA) .... S/E
Surviving Missile Surveillance Study (CCCA) .... SMSS
Survivor Administration Assistance Service .... SAAS
Sustainable Cell Rate (MLOA) .... SCR
Sustainable Development of Small Island Developing States (CARB) .... SIDS
Swaziland (NTIO) .... Swaz
Swedish Board for Technical Accreditation (CARB) .... SWEDAC
Swedish Official Measure (RIMS) .... SOM
Swiss Exchange .... SWX
Switch Fabric (MLOA) .... SF
Switchboard, Inc. [*NASDAQ symbol*] (SG) .... SWBD
Switches and Crossings (HEAS) .... S&C
Switching System [*Telecommunications*] (MLOA) .... SS
Symbolic Language for Automated Verification and Execution [*Computer science*] (ITCA) .... SLAVE
Symphony .... Sym
Synchronize .... sync
Synchronous .... SYNC
Synchronous Data Hierarchy (AEBE) .... SDH
Synchronous Data-Link Control .... SDSI
Synchronous Digital Transmission Network (CCCA) .... SDTN
Synchronous Residual Time Stamp .... SRTS
Synchro-to-Digital (AEBE) .... S-D
Synonym (NTIO) .... syn
Synoptic Optical Long-Term Investigations of the Sun .... SOLIS
Synthetic Operative Radar .... SAR
System Acquisition .... SAC
System Actuation Monitoring .... SAM
System Advisory Group (CCCA) .... SAG
System Analysis .... SA
System Analysis Organization .... SAO
System Approach to Training .... SAT
System Architectural and Trade Study .... SATS
System Associates, Incorporated .... SAI
System Authentication Facility [*Computer science*] (ITCA) .... SAF
System Control and Data Acquisition .... SCADA
System Control Block (ROAS) .... SCB
System Control Facility .... SCF
System Design Team (CTAS) .... SDT

System Engineer (CTAS)	SE
System Extension Release 1 [*Computer science*] (ITCA)	SE1
System Extension Release 2 [*Computer science*] (ITCA)	SE2
System Functional Requirements Description (CCCA)	SFRD
System Identification (CGWS)	SID
System Integration Design Specification (CCCA)	SIDS
System Level Specification (CTAS)	SLS
System Maintenance Console (CTAS)	SMC
System Maintenance Monitoring Console (CTAS)	SMMC
System Manager Console (CTAS)	SMC
System Manager's Console Graphical User Interface (CTAS)	SMC-GUI
System of Automatic Processing and Indexing Reports	SAPIR
System of Automation of Material Plans for Army Material	SAMPAM
System Planning and Engineering Working Group (CCCA)	SPEWG
System Preparation	SysPrep
System Preparation Tool	SysPrep
System Programmable Gate Array	SPGA
System Response (CGWS)	SRES
System Support Element (CCCA)	SSE
System Time Generator (CCCA)	STG
Systematic Desensitization (DIPS)	SD
Systematic Rational Restructuring (DIPS)	SRR
Systemic Accident Cause Analysis (HEAS)	SACA
System-Programmable Gate Array (AEBE)	SPA
Systems Analysis Recording (CTAS)	SAR
Systems Approach to Managing Bureau of Ships Acquisition [*Navy*]	SAMBA
Systems Development Team (CTAS)	SDT
Systems Engineering and Integration (CTAS)	SEI
Systems Integration and Avionics (SPST)	SI&A
Systems Management Functional Area [*Computer science*] (ITCA)	SMFA
Systems Planning Corp. (CCCA)	SPC
Systems Product [*Computer science*] (ITCA)	SP

By Meaning

T

By Meaning

Tablespoon (NTIO)	tbsp
Taco Bell	TB
Tactical Air Control Post (CCCA)	TACP
Tactical Airspace Integration System [Army]	TAIS
Tactical Force Command Center (CCCA)	TFCC
Tactical Intelligence Photo Interpretation (CCCA)	TIPI
Tactical Nuclear Force Security & Survivability (CCCA)	TNFSS
Tactical Unmanned Aerial Vehicle [Military]	TUAV
Tagged Cell Rate (MLOA)	TCR
Take-Off (PIPO)	T/O
Take-Off Configuration (PIPO)	TOC
Takeoff Minimum [Aviation] (PIPO)	T
Taking Inward Pilot (RIMS)	TIP
Taking Outward Pilot (RIMS)	TOP
Tale-Brown Obsessive-Compulsive Scale (DAVI)	TBOCS
Tandem Auto-Transplants [Medicine] (DAVI)	TAT
Tandem Schedule of Reinforcement (DIPS)	TAND
Tangential Radiation Therapy (DAVI)	TRT
Tangential Sensitivity Signal (CCCA)	TSS
Tank Advisory Panel (ABAC)	TAP
Tank Waste Characterization Plan	TWCP
Tank Waste Remediation System	TWRS
Tank-Automotive and Armaments Command [Army]	TACOM
Tanks (RIMS)	TA
Tanox, Inc. [NASDAQ symbol] (SG)	TNOX
Tapered Steroid Dosing Package [Medicine] (DAVI)	TSDP
Tar Creosote (HFAS)	TC
Target Dry Weight (DAVI)	TDW
Target Plasma Concentration [Medicine] (DAVI)	TPC
Targeted Nutritional Intervention	TNI
Tarsal Tunnel Decompression [Medicine] (DAVI)	TTD
Taskforce on Amphibian Declines and Deformities	TADD
Task-Oriented Dialogue Understanding System (DIPS)	TDUS
T-Complex Responder [Medicine]	TCR
Teaching Research Fellow	TRF
Team Conference (DAVI)	TC
Team Roping [Rodeo term]	TR
Technical Analysis/Cost Estimate (CCCA)	TA/CE
Technical Assistance Contractor (CTAS)	TAC
Technical Data and Documentation (SPST)	TD&D
Technical Integration Forum	TIF
Technical Performance Specification (CCCA)	TPS
Technical Safety Requirement (SARE)	TSR
Technical Staffs Branch (HEAS)	TSB
Technical Steering Panel	TSP
Technical Support Management Assistance (CCCA)	TSMA
Technical Task Plan	TTP
Technical Task Plans (AUEG)	TTP
Technology Development (AUEG)	TD
Technology Flavors and Fragrances [AMEX symbol] (SG)	TFF
Technology Literacy Challenge Fund	TLCF
Technology Unit (HEAS)	TU
Telaxix Communications [NASDAQ symbol] (SG)	TLXS
Tele 1 Europe ADS [NASDAQ symbol] (SG)	TEUR
Telecommunication Alarm-Sequence Analyzer (IDAI)	TASA
Telecommunications	Telecomm
Telecommunications and Information Industry Forum	TIIF
Telephone Exchange (PIPO)	TELEX
Telephone Managers Association (COBU)	TMA
Telerobotic Electrical Power Subsystem [NASA] (SPST)	TEPS
Teletype Adaptor Module (CCCA)	TAM
Telocity, Inc. [NASDAQ symbol] (SG)	TLCT
Telomerase (DAVI)	TS
Temazepam [Medicine] (DAVI)	TMZ
Temozolomide [Medicine] (DAVI)	TZ
Temperate East Asia (CARB)	TEA
Temperate South America (CARB)	TSA
Temperature and Pulse (DAVI)	T&P
Temperature by Mouth (DAVI)	TM
Temperature Profiling (ARMP)	TP
Templeton [Publisher]	TPL
Tempo Music [Publisher]	TPO
Temporary Denial Order	TDO
Temporary Mobile Service Identity (CGWS)	TMSI
Temporary Portacaval Anastomosis [Medicine] (DAVI)	TPA
Temporary Protection Order (SARE)	TPO

Temporary Visit (DAVI)	TV
Temporomandibular Dysfunction [Medicine] (DAVI)	TMD
Temporoparietal (DAVI)	TP
Tenderness, Asymmetry, Restricted Motion, and Tissue Texture Changes [Medicine] (DAVI)	TART
Tennessee Wildlife Resources Agency (CARB)	TWRA
Tension (DAVI)	TEN
Tension and Nervousness (DAVI)	T&N
Terabits per Second	Tbps
Terlipressin [Medicine] (DAVI)	TER
Term Birth Appropriate for Gestational Age (DAVI)	TBAGA
Term Birth, Living Female (DAVI)	TBLF
Term Birth, Living Male (DAVI)	TBLM
Term Newborn (DAVI)	TNB
Terminal Access Control System (CCCA)	TACS
Terminal Area Forecast (PIAV)	TAF
Terminal Cancer (DAVI)	TC
Terminal Control Area (PIAV)	TCA
Terminal End Point Indentifier [Computer science] (ITCA)	TEI
Terminal Equipment Identifier (CGWS)	TEI
Terminal Extension (DAVI)	TE
Terminal Handling Charge (MARI)	THC
Terminal Handling Cost (RIMS)	THC
Terminal Instrument Approach Procedures (PIPO)	TERPS
Terminal Knee Extension (DAVI)	TKE
Terrace House	TC
Terrain Awareness and Warning System	TAWS
Terrain Awareness System	TAWS
Terrestrial Ecosystems (CARB)	TECO
Test and Electrical Characterization	TEC
Test Dose (DAVI)	TD
Test of Early Reading Comprehension (DAVI)	TERC
Test of Variable Attention	TOVA
Test Status Review (CTAS)	TSR
Test Tape (DAVI)	TT
Testicular Cancer (DAVI)	TC
Testing Memorandum (HEAS)	TM
Testosterone to Epitestosterone Ratio (DAVI)	T/E
Tetanus-Diphtheria Toxoid [Medicine] (DAVI)	Td
Tethered Cord Syndrome	TCS
TeV-Energy Superconducting Linear Accelerator	TESLA
Texas Library Association	TLA
Text File Extension	txt
Text Retrieval Data System (AUEG)	TRDS
Textured Particle System	TPS
Thailand National Committee for Pacific Economic Cooperation	TNCPEC
Thallim Threadmill (DAVI)	TTDM
Thallium-Graded Exercise Test (DAVI)	TGXT
Thames Water (HEAS)	TW
Theater Army Command Multichannel System (CCCA)	TACMS
Theater War Architecture (CCCA)	TWA
Thematic Organization Point (DIPS)	TOP
Theophylline Serum Concentration (DAVI)	TSC
Theorem Proving System (IDAI)	TPS
Theoretical Arrival Time (MLOA)	TAT
Theoretical Orthogonal Function (CARB)	TOF
Theory of Distributed Associative Memory [B. B. Murdock] (DIPS)	TODAM
Theory of Mind	TOM
Therapeutic Activities Aide (DAVI)	TAA
Therapeutic Community (DIPS)	TC
Therapeutic Massage Therapist (NUJO)	MST
Therapeutic Outcomes Monitoring (DAVI)	TOM
Therapeutic Pass (DAVI)	TP
Therapeutic Recreation (DAVI)	TR
Therapeutic Recreation Specialist (DAVI)	TRS
Theraputty (DAVI)	T putty
Therapy-Related Acute Myelogenous Leukemia [Medicine] (DAVI)	TAML
There is No Evidence of Malignancy (DAVI)	TINEM
Thermal Electric Holding Facility [NASA] (SPST)	TEHOF
Thermal Expansion Difference (ABAC)	TED
Thermal Model Generator (SPST)	TMG
Thermal Radiation Analyzer System (SPST)	TRASYS
Therma-Wave, Inc. [NASDAQ symbol] (SG)	TWAV
Thermolysin-Like Metalloendopeptidase [Medicine] (DAVI)	TME
Thermo-Nuclear War (CCCA)	TNW

Thermosphere Ionosphere-Mesosphere-Electrodynamics General Circulation Model .... TIME-GCM
Thermosphere-Ionosphere-Mesosphere Energetics and Dynamics .... TIMED
Thesaurus of Graphics Materials .... TGM
Thick Ascending Limb of Henle's Loop [*Medicine*] (DAVI) .... TAHL
Thin Quad Flat-Pack (AEBE) .... TQFP
Thioguanine and Cytarabine [*Medicine*] (DAVI) .... TC
Thioguanine and Cytarabine [*Medicine*] (DAVI) .... TCA
Thiotepa (DAVI) .... TSPA
Thiotepa, Bleomycin, and Vinblastine [*Medicine*] (DAVI) .... TBV
Third Generation 3G
Thompson Ramo Wooldridge, Inc. (CCCA) .... TRW
Thompson Thematic Apperception Test [*C. E. Thompson*] (DIPS) .... TTAT
Thoracic Circumference (DAVI) .... TC
Thoracic Electrical Bioimpedance .... TEB
Thoracic Lumbar Sacral Orthosis [*Medicine*] (DAVI) .... TLSO
Thoracolumbosacral Spinal Orthosis [*Medicine*] (DAVI) .... TLSSO
Thornton Leadership Council .... TLC
Thought Process (DAVI) .... TP
Threat-Image Projection .... TIP
Three-Dimensional Nephanalysis (ARMP) 3DNEPH
Threshold Limit Value (CARB) .... TLV
Throughfall (CARB) .... TF
Throughout Hospitalization (DAVI) .... TOH
Thrust Reverser [*Aviation*] (PIPO) .... T/R
Thruster (RIMS) .... THR
Thyroglossal Duct [*Medicine*] (DAVI) .... TGD
Thyrotopin-Binding Inhibitory Immunoglobulins [*Medicine*] (DAVI) .... TTII
Tiagabine (DAVI) .... TGB
Tiazofurin (DAVI) .... TCAR
Ticarcillin-Clavulanate [*Medicine*] (DAVI) .... TC/CL
Tick-Borne Encephalitis Virus (DAVI) .... TBEV
Ticket Designator (TRID) .... TD
Ticket Exchange Notice [*Travel industry*] (TRID) .... TEN
Ticket Number [*Travel industry*] (TRID) .... TKNO
Ticket Order Exception [*Travel industry*] (TRID) .... TOE
Ticket Time Limit [*Travel industry*] (TRID) .... TKTL
Ticketed Point Mileage [*Travel industry*] (TRID) .... TPM
Tiger Cub [*Boy Scouts of America*] .... TC
Time Charter Party (RIMS) .... TCP
Time Charter Trip (RIMS) .... TCT
Time Code Bits per Sample (CCCA) .... TB/S
Time Distribution Record (ABAC) .... TDR
Time Division Duplex (CGWS) .... TDD
Time Generation Unit (SPST) .... TGU
Time Hopped (CCCA) .... TH
Time Hopped Narrow Beam (CCCA) .... THNB
Time of Non-Redundant Sample (CCCA) .... TNRS
Time to Repetition and Time to Echo in Spin (DAVI) .... TR/TE
Time to Treatment Failure (DAVI) .... TTF
Time to Waypoint (HLLA) .... TTW
Time Weighted Average Gap .... TWAG
Time-Averaged Urea Concentration [*Medicine*] (DAVI) .... TAUC
Timelife Graphical User Interface (CTAS) .... TGUI
Time-Limited Psychotherapy (DIPS) .... TLP
Time-Resolved Ion Correlation .... TRIC
Tincture (DAVI) .... tinct
Tirapazamine (DAVI) .... TPZ
Titan Systems Corp. (CCCA) .... TSI
To Be Documented (CTAS) .... TBD
To Be Named (RIMS) .... TBN
To Be Named (RIMS) .... TOBENA
To Be Renamed (RIMS) .... TBR
To-Be-Remembered (DIPS) .... TBR
Tobramycin and Ticarcillin [*Medicine*] (DAVI) .... T&T
Tocodynamometer (DAVI) .... TOCO
Todd's Paralysis (DAVI) .... TP
Toe Touch as Tolerated (DAVI) .... TTAT
Tolerance Level (DIPS) .... TL
Tolonium Chloride (DAVI) .... TC
Toluene .... Tol
Tongue Jaw Neck (DAVI) .... TJN
Tonic Labyrinthine Reflex [*Medicine*] (DAVI) .... TLR
Tonometry Applanation [*Medicine*] (DAVI) .... Ta
Tonometry by Applanation [*Medicine*] (DAVI) .... TAP
Tonsillectomy (DAVI) .... TLT
Tool Interface Plate .... TIP
Tool Kit (CTAS) .... Tk
Toronto Stock Exchange (SG) .... To
Toronto Virtual Enterprise [*Project*] (IDAI) .... TOVE
Total (TRID) .... TOTL
Total Air Temperature (HLLA) .... TAT
Total Aircraft Information System (HLLA) .... TAIS
Total Airport Management System (HLLA) .... TAMS
Total Anorectal Reconstruction [*Medicine*] (DAVI) .... TAR
Total Average [*Baseball term*] (NDBD) .... TA
Total Bilirubin (DAVI) .... Tbili
Total Bilirubin [*Medicine*] (DAVI) .... TOT BILI
Total Colon Examination (DAVI) .... TCE
Total Daily Dose [*Medicine*] (DAVI) .... TDD
Total Direct Cost .... TDC
Total Direct Diffuse Radiometer (CARB) .... TDDR
Total Energy Expended [*Medicine*] (DAVI) .... TEE
Total Episode of Illness (DAVI) .... TEI
Total Extraperitoneal [*Medicine*] (DAVI) .... TEP

Total Glottic Transverse Laryngectomy [*Medicine*] (DAVI) .... TGTL
Total Intravenous Anethesia [*Medicine*] (DAVI) .... TIVA
Total Ion Electropherogram .... TIE
Total Ionizing Dose (CCCA) .... TID
Total Joint Arthroplasty [*Medicine*] (DAVI) .... TJA
Total Knee Prosthesis (DAVI) .... TKP
Total Knee Replacement Left (DAVI) .... TKRL
Total Knee Replacement Right (DAVI) .... TKRR
Total Linux Coverage .... TLC
Total Loss of Vessel Only [*Insurance*] (MARI) .... TLVO
Total Non-Methane Organic Compound .... TNMOC
Total Organic Gas .... TOG
Total Organic Nitrogen (CARB) .... TON
Total Path Length (CTAS) .... TPL
Total Placental Estrogens [*Medicine*] (DAVI) .... TPE
Total Productive Manufacturing .... TPM
Total Program Cost Analysis Tool (SPST) .... TOPCAT
Total Range of Motion (DAVI) .... TROM
Total Serum Bilirubin [*Medicine*] (DAVI) .... TSB
Total Serum Solids (DAVI) .... TSS
Total Time Aircraft and Engine (PIPO) .... TTAE
Total Time Since New [*Aviation*] (PIPO) .... TTSN
Total Tumor Mass (DAVI) .... TTM
Total Ultrafiltration [*Medicine*] (DAVI) .... TUF
Total Urinary Nitrogen [*Medicine*] (DAVI) .... TUN
Total User Cell Difference (MLOA) .... TUCD
Total-Body Magnesium (DAVI) .... TBMg
Total-Body Phosphorus (DAVI) .... TBP
Total-Body Protein (DAVI) .... TBP
Total-Dietary Fiber (DAVI) .... TDF
Totally Dissolved Solid (SARE) .... TDS
Total-Retinal Detachment (DAVI) .... TRD
Touch and Stay (MARI) .... t&s
Touchdown Zone [*Aviation*] (PIPO) .... TDZ
Touchdown Zone and Centerline Lighting [*Aviation*] (PIPO) .... TDZ/CL
Touchdown Zone Lighting [*Aviation*] (PIPO) .... TDZL
Touch-Verbal (DAVI) .... T/V
Tour Operator Program (TRID) .... TOP
Tour Order [*Travel industry*] (TRID) .... TO
Tourist Hotel (TRID) .... THTL
Toward Other Planetary Systems Science Working Group .... TOPSSWG
Townhouse .... TwnHse
Toxaphene .... TOX
Toxic (HEAS) .... T
Toxic Interstitial Pneumonitis [*Medicine*] (DAVI) .... TIP
Toxic Pits Cleanup Act (SARE) .... TPCA
Toxicokinetics (DAVI) .... TK
Toxicology Network (AUEG) .... TOXNET
Toxicology Review Panel .... TRP
Tracheal Collar [*Medicine*] (DAVI) .... TC
Tracheobronchomalacia [*Medicine*] (DAVI) .... TBM
Tracheostomy Mask [*Medicine*] (DAVI) .... T/MA
Tracheotomy Bar (DAVI) .... T-bar
Tracheotomy Set (DAVI) .... T set
Track and Hold (AEBE) .... T/H
Track Safety Working Group (HEAS) .... TSWG
Tracking and Data Acquisition (SPST) .... T&DA
Tracking Data Relay Satellite System .... TDRSS
Trade Policy Forum .... TPF
Trade Union Side (HEAS) .... TUS
Trademark .... tm
Trader.com NV 'A' [*NASDAQ symbol*] (SG) .... TRDR
Trade-Related Aspects of Intellectual Property .... TRIPS
Trade-Related Intellectual Property Rights .... TRIPS
Traditional Neighborhood Development .... TND
TRADOC System Manager-Soldier .... TSM-Soldier
Traffic and Associated Channel (CGWS) .... TACH
Traffic Channel/Full Rate Speech (CGWS) .... TCH/FS
Traffic Channel/Half Rate Speech (CGWS) .... TCH/HS
Traffic Collision Alerting Device .... TCAD
Traffic Management Coordinator (CTAS) .... TMC
Traffic Management Coordinator-Graphical User Interface (CTAS) .... TMC-GUI
Traffic Management Station (CTAS) .... TMS
Traffic Management Systems Interface (CTAS) .... TMI
Traffic Shaping [*Telecommunications*] (MLOA) .... TS
Trailing Umbilical System (SPST) .... TUS
Trainable Mental Defective (DIPS) .... TMD
Trained Participating Father (DAVI) .... TPF
Training and Development (TRID) .... T&D
Training Information and Communication Enhancement .... TICE
Training Liaison Inspector (HEAS) .... TLI
Training Manager (HEAS) .... TM
Training Needs Statement [*Military*] .... TNS
Training Officer (DEMM) .... TO
Trajectory Synthesis (CTAS) .... TS
Tramcinolone and Nystatin [*Medicine*] (DAVI) .... TNT
Trans Canada Trail .... TCT
Transanal Endoscopic Microsurgery (DAVI) .... TEM
Transbronchoscopic Balloon Tipped [*Medicine*] (DAVI) .... TBT
Transcatheter Oily Chemoembolization [*Medicine*] (DAVI) .... TOCE
Transcerebellar Diameter (DAVI) .... TCD
Transcontinental Control Area (PIPO) .... TCTA
Transcortical Motor Aphasia (DIPS) .... TMA
Transcortical Sensory Aphasia (DIPS) .... TSA
Transcranial Doppler (DAVI) .... TCD

Transcription [*Medicine*] (DAVI) .... Tx
Transcystic Duct [*Medicine*] (DAVI) .... TCD
Transesophageal Atrial Paced [*Medicine*] (DAVI) .... TAP
Transesophageal Echocardiography [*Medicine*] (DAVI) .... TE
Trans-European Express (TRID) .... TEE
Transfer Module Controller .... TMC
Transform and Lighting .... T&L
Transfusion-Associated Graft-Versus-Host Disease (DAVI) .... TA-GVHD
Transient Episodes of Myocardial Ischemia [*Medicine*] (DAVI) ...... TEMI
Transient Evoked Otoacoustic Emission [*Medicine*] (DAVI) ...... TEOAE
Transient Infrared Emission Spectroscopy .... TIRS
Transient Neonatal Diabetes Mellitus [*Medicine*] (DAVI) .... TNDM
Transient Neurologic Symptoms (DAVI) .... TNS
Transient Radicular Irritation [*Medicine*] (DAVI) .... TRI
Transient Respiratory Distress of the Newborn (DAVI) ...... TRDN
Transistor Electrical Characterization and Analysis Program ...... TECAP
Transition Level (PIPO) .... TLV
Transition Line Model .... TLM
Transition Primer .... trprm
Transitional Automated Ticket [*Travel industry*] (TRID) ...... TAT
Transitional Care Unit (DAVI) .... TCU
Transitional Stored Ticket [*Travel industry*] (TRID) .... TST
Transjugular Intrahepatic Portosystemic Shunt [*Medicine*] (DAVI) ...... TIPSS
Transmissible Spongiform Encephalopathy .... TSE
Transmission (PIAV) .... xmsn
Transmission Convergence [*Telecommunications*] (MLOA) .... TC
Transmission Electron Microscopy .... TEM
Transmitted Electron .... TE
Transmitted Electron Detection .... TED
Transmitter (PIAV) .... Tx
Transnasal Endoscopic Ethmoidectomy [*Medicine*] (DAVI) ...... TEE
Trans-Neptunian Object .... TNO
Trans-Neptunian Objects .... TNO
Transplant-Related Coronary-Artery Disease (DAVI) ...... TCAD
Transponder (HLLA) .... XPDR
Transponder (PIAV) .... xpdr
Transportable Air Lift Control Element (CCCA) .... TALCE
Transportation Adjudication Panel .... TAP
Transportation Administrative Service Center .... TASC
Transportation and Handling (SPST) .... T&H
Transportation Coordinators'-Automated Information Movements System II
     [*Army*] .... TC-AIMS II
Transrectal Electroejaculation [*Medicine*] (DAVI) .... TE
Transrectal Needle Biopsy Prostate (DAVI) .... TRNBP
Transrectal Ultrasonography of the Prostate [*Medicine*] (DAVI) ...... TRUSP
Transrectal Ultrasound [*Medicine*] (DAVI) .... TU
Transthoracic Echocardiography [*Medicine*] (DAVI) ...... TTE
Transtracheal Catheter (DAVI) .... TTC
Transtracheal Jet Ventilation [*Medicine*] (DAVI) .... TTJV
Transureteroureterostomy [*Medicine*] (DAVI) .... TUU
Transurethral Extraction [*Medicine*] .... TUE
Transurethral Incision of Bladder Neck [*Medicine*] (DAVI) ...... TUIBN
Transurethral Microwave Thermotherapy [*Medicine*] (DAVI) ...... TUMT
Transurethral Needle Ablation [*Medicine*] (DAVI) .... TUNA
Transurethral Needle Biopsy of Prostate [*Medicine*] (DAVI) ...... TNBP
Transurethral Prostatic Resection [*Medicine*] (DAVI) .... TUPR
Transurethral Resection of Vesical Neck [*Medicine*] (DAVI) ...... TURVN
Transurethral Thermo-Ablation Therapy [*Medicine*] (DAVI) T3
Transurethral Valve [*Medicine*] (DAVI) .... TUV
Transurethral Vaporization of the Prostate [*Medicine*] (DAVI) ...... TUVP
Transverse Cardiac Diameter [*Medicine*] (DAVI) .... TCD
Transverse Electric (CCCA) .... T&E
Transverse Relaxation-Optimized Spectroscopy .... TROSY
Trap, Neuter, and Return .... TNR
Trauma Center (DAVI) .... TC
Trauma Related Injury Severity Score (DAVI) .... TRISS
Trauma Skull (DAVI) .... T Skull
Travel Agency Commission (TRID) .... TAC

Travel Agent (TRID) .... TA
Travel Agent Automated Deduction (TRID) .... TAAD
Travel Agents of Suffolk County [*New York*] (TRID) ...... TASC
Travel Industry Association (TRID) .... TIA
Travel Industry Association of Georgia (TRID) .... TIAG
Travel Intermediary Designator Service (TRID) .... TIDS
Travel Service Intermediary (TRID) .... TSI
Traversing and Elevating .... T&E
Treated Effluent Disposal Facility .... TEDF
Treating Physician (DAVI) .... TP
Treatment .... trmt
Treatment Authorization Number (DAVI) .... TAN
Treatment Improvement Protocol (DIPS) .... TIP
Treatment Investigational New Drug (DAVI) .... TIND
Treatment Related Mortality (DAVI) .... TRM
Trend Virus Control System .... TVCS
Trendelenburg (DAVI) .... T-berg
Trendelenburg (DAVI) .... TRND
Trendwest Resorts [*NASDAQ symbol*] (SG) .... TWRI
Trial of Void (DAVI) .... TOV
Triamcinolone (DAVI) .... TMCN
Trieger Dot Test (DAVI) .... TDT
Trifluorotoluene .... TFT
Triglycerides (DAVI) .... TRIG
Triple (TRID) .... tpl
Triple with Bath (TRID) .... TRPB
Triple with Shower (TRID) .... TRPS
Triple without Bath (TRID) .... TRPN
Trofosfamide (DAVI) .... TROFO
Troglitazone [*Medicine*] (DAVI) .... TGZ
Tropical Easterly Jet (ARMP) .... TEJ
Tropical Ocean-Atmosphere (CARB) .... TOA
Tropical Phagedenic Ulcer [*Medicine*] (DAVI) .... TPU
Tropical Western Pacific Ocean (CARB) .... TWPO
Tropospheric Emission Spectrometer (ARMP) .... TES
Tropospheric Ozone Research (CARB) .... TOR
True Knot in Cord [*Medicine*] (DAVI) .... TKIC
True Track (PIAV) .... TT
True Vocal Fold (DAVI) .... TVF
Trunk Key Generator (CCCA) .... TKG
Tumor Chemosensitivity Assay [*Medicine*] (DAVI) .... TCA
Tumor Lysis Syndrome [*Medicine*] (DAVI) .... TLS
Tumor-Inducing Hypercalcemia (DAVI) .... TIH
Tunable Diode Laser Spectroscopy (CARB) .... TDLS
Tunneling Electron Microscopy .... TEM
Tupperware .... TUP
Turbine Vessel (TRID) .... TV
Turbo Direct Injection .... TDI
Turn and Slip Indicator [*Aviation*] (PIPO) .... T&S
Turn Coordinator (PIPO) .... TC
Turning Against Self (DAVI) .... TAS
Turnstone Systems [*NASDAQ symbol*] (SG) .... TSTN
Tutor I
Twin Room with Bath (TRID) .... TWNB
Twin Room with Shower (TRID) .... TWNS
Twin Room without Bath (TRID) .... TWNN
Twisting and Bending (MARI) .... TB
Two Wide-Angle Imaging Neutral-Atom Spectrometers [*NASA*] ...... TWINS
Two-Dimensional Cloud (ARMP) 2DC
Two-Door Car (TRID) .... TDOR
Two-Phase Integrated Thermal System (SPST) .... TPITS
Two-Way Data Link (HLLA) .... TWDL
Two-Way Interface (CTAS) .... TWI
Type and Crossmatch [*Medicine*] (DAVI) .... T&C
Type and Crossmatch (DAVI) .... T&M
Type and Hold (DAVI) .... T&H
Typical Absence Seizures [*Medicine*] (DAVI) .... TAS
Typing Manager (HEAS) .... TM
Tyrosine Kinase Activity (DAVI) .... TKA

UbiQui Tel, Inc. [*NASDAQ symbol*]	UPCS
Ubrandit.com [*AMEX symbol*] (SG)	UBI
UFO Information Retrieval Center	UFOIRC
UFO Newsclipping Service	UFONS
UFO Research Australia	UFORA
UFO Research Institute of Canada	UFORIC
Ufology Research of Manitoba [*Canada*]	UFOROM
Ulster Defence Regiment Medal	UD
Ultra High Frequency (HLLA)	UHF
Ultra Violet/Visible	UV/vis
Ultrafiltration Volume (DAVI)	UFV
Ultra-High-Throughout Screening	UHTS
Ultra-Low Penetration Air (SARE)	ULPA
Ultraluminous Far Infrared Galaxies	ULIRG
Ultra-Rapid Opiate Detoxification [*Medicine*] (DAVI)	UROD
Ultrasonic	U/S
Ultrasonic Mist (DAVI)	USM
Ultrasound-Guided Compression Repair (DAVI)	UGCR
Ultrasound-Guided Vascular Access (DAVI)	UGVA
Ultraviolet Lithography	UVL
Ultraviolet Spectral Radiometer (ARMP)	UVSR
Ultraviolet Type A (CARB)	uv-A
Ultraviolet Type B (CARB)	uv-B
Ultraviolet-Visible [*Spectroscopy*] (CARB)	uv-vis
Umbilical Cord Blood [*Medicine*] (DAVI)	UCB
Umbilical Cord Prolapse [*Medicine*] (DAVI)	UCP
Umbilical Hernia (DAVI)	UH
Unable to Determine (DAVI)	UTD
Unable to Locate (DAVI)	UTL
Unable to Obtain (DAVI)	UTO
Unable to Reach (TRID)	UTR
Unassisted Diastolic Pressure (DAVI)	UDP
Unassisted Putout [*Baseball term*] (NDBD)	U
Unassisted Systolic Pressure [*Medicine*] (DAVI)	USP
Unattended Power Source (CCCA)	UPS
Unattended Ticket Delivery Network (TRID)	UTDN
Unconditioned Response (DIPS)	UnCR
Unconditioned Stimulus (DAVI)	UDS
Unconscious (DAVI)	UC
Unconscious (DIPS)	UCs
Uncontainerable Goods (MARI)	UNICON
Uncontrolled Hemorrhagic Shock [*Medicine*] (DAVI)	UCHS
Unconventional Stellar Aspect	USA
Uncrossed (DAVI)	UNC
Undelivered (DAVI)	UNDEL
Under Elbow (DAVI)	UE
Under One Roof (MARI)	UOR
Under Repair (MARI)	U/R
Underground Storage Tank (SARE)	UGST
Undersea Surveillance System (CCCA)	USS
Underwater Sound Laboratory	USL
Underwater Test Facility (SPST)	UWTF
Underwater Unidentified Objects	UUO
Underwriter (MARI)	U/W
Undetermined Origin (DAVI)	UO
Undifferentiated Embryonal Sarcoma [*Medicine*] (DAVI)	UES
Undifferentiated Respiratory Disease (DAVI)	URD
Unemployment Insurance Benefits (DAVI)	UIB
Unfavorable History (DAVI)	UH
Unfractionated Heparin [*Medicine*] (DAVI)	UFH
Unicom (PIPO)	U
Unidentified Atmospheric Phenomenon	UAP
Unified Medical Language System (IDAI)	UMLS
Unified Modeling Language [*Computer science*] (ITCA)	UML
Uniform Computer Information Transactions Act	UCITA
Uniform Fire Code (SARE)	UFC
Uniform Manifest (SARE)	UM
Uniform Resource Indicator	URI
Unilateral Posterior Lumbar Interbody Fusion [*Medicine*] (DAVI)	UPLIF
Union of Concerned Scientists	UCS
Unipolar (DAVI)	UP
Unique Physician Identification Number (DAVI)	UPIN
Unit Telescope 1	UT1
United Aerial Phenomenon Agency	UAPA
United Baseball League (NDBD)	UBL
United Food & Commercial Workers	UFCW
United Global Com	UGC
United Kingdom Hazard Information System (HEAS)	UKHIS
United Nations Command Security Battalion-Joint Security Area	UNCSB-JSA
United Nations Commission on International Trade Law (MARI)	UNCITRL
United Nations Economic Committee (CARB)	UNEC
United Nations Global Change Research Program (CARB)	UNGCRP
United Nations Office for Project Services	UNOPS
United Nations Political Affairs (CARB)	UNP
United Nations Sanctions	UNS
United Nations Technical Assistance Board (CARB)	UNTAB
United Pan-Europe Communications	UPC
United Pan-European Communications [*Amsterdam*]	UPC
United Services for Handicapped (DAVI)	USH
United States Air Tour Association	USATA
United States Food and Drug Administration (SARE)	USFDA
United States Global Change Research Program Office (CARB)	USGCRPO
United States League [*Baseball*] (NDBD)	USL
United States National Committee for Pacific Economic Cooperation	USNCPEC
United States National Map Accuracy Standard (CARB)	USNMAS
United States/North Atlantic Treaty Organization	US/NATO
U.S. On-Orbit Segment (SPST)	USOS
U.S. Plastic Lumber [*NASDAQ symbol*] (SG)	USPL
United States Possessions Possessions Society [*Founded in 1978*]	USPPS
U.S. Science Operations Center (SPST)	USOC
United States Service Office of Investigation	USCSOI
United States Society of Ecological Economics	USSEE
United States Travel Agent Registry (TRID)	USTAR
United States Unilateral Control (CCCA)	USUC
United Telecommunications Council (CGWS)	UTC
United Wireless Communications Consortium (CGWS)	UWCC
Universal Blood Donor (DAVI)	UBD
Universal Communications (PIPO)	UNICOM
Universal Communications Language	UCL
Universal Credit Card Charge Form (TRID)	UCCCF
Universal Grammar (DIPS)	UG
Universal Joint [*Medicine*] (DAVI)	UJ
Universal Personal Telecommunications (CGWS)	UPT
Universal Synchronous Receive/Transmit (CCCA)	USYNR/T
Universal Time Coordinates (ARMP)	UTC
Universal Travel Voucher (TRID)	UTV
Universities and Colleges Employers Association	UCEA
University Fellow	UF
University Lecturer	UL
University of Cambridge Local Examinations Syndicate	UCLES
University of Houston-Clear Lake [*Texas*]	UHCL
University of Montana	UM
University of Oregon	UO
University of Phoenix Online	UOPX
Univl Access [*NASDAQ symbol*] (SG)	UAXS
Unknown Primary Carcinoma (DAVI)	UPC
Unless Sooner Commenced (RIMS)	USC
Unless Used (RIMS)	UU
Unless Used in Which Case Time Actually Used to Count (RIMS)	UUIWCTAUTC
Unlettered	UNLTRD
Unlicensed Assistive Personnel	UAP
Unmanned Aerospace Vehicle (CARB)	UAV
Unmanned Automated Vehicle	UAV
Unpainted	U/P
Unpressurized Berthing Mast [*NASA*] (SPST)	UBM
Unrelated (DAVI)	url
Unrelated Cord Blood Transplant [*Medicine*] (DAVI)	UCBT
Unreviewed Safety Question	USQ
Unreviewed Safety Question Determination	USQD
Unserviceable (PIPO)	U/S
Unserviceable [*Aviation*] (PIAV)	u/s
Until Gone (DAVI)	UG
Unusual Facial Features (DAVI)	UFF
Upon Arrival Patient Found (DAVI)	UAPF
Upper Aerodigestive Tract [*Medicine*] (DAVI)	UADT
Upper Air Observation (CARB)	UAOB
Upper Airway Sleep Apnea (DAVI)	UASA
Upper and Lower (DAVI)	U/L
Upper Arm (DAVI)	U ARM
Upper Exposure Limit (HEAS)	UEL

Upper Extremity Somatosensory Evoked Potential (DAVI) .... UESEP
Upper Flight Information Region (PIPO) .... UIR
Upper Gastrointestinal Tract (DAVI) .... UGIT
Upper Gastrointestinal with Small Bowel Follow Through (DAVI) .... UGI
Upper Heyford Mandatory Radio Area [*British*] (PIAV) .... UHMRA
Upper Left Sternal Border (DAVI) .... ULSB
Upper Lid (DAVI) .... UL
Upper Lid, Left Eye (DAVI) .... ULLE
Upper Lid, Right Eye (DAVI) .... ULRE
Upper Normal Levels [*Medicine*] (DAVI) .... UNL
Upper Range Limit (CARB) .... URL
Upper Thames River Conservation Authority [*Canada*] .... UTRCA
Upper Troposphere-Lower Stratosphere .... UTLS
Uproar, Inc. [*NASDAQ symbol*] (SG) .... UPRO
Uptake (DAVI) .... UPT
Upwelling Solar Radiation (ARMP) .... USR
Uracil and Tegafur [*Medicine*] (DAVI) .... UFT
Urban Air Toxics Monitoring Program .... UATMP
Urban/Industrial (CCCA) .... U/I
Urban Regeneration of the Environment .... URGENT
Urban Search and Rescue [*Department of Emergency Management*]
   (DEMM) .... USAR
Urban Wastewater Directive .... UWWD
Urea Breath Test (DAVI) .... UBT
Urea Cycle Enzymopathy [*Medicine*] (DAVI) .... UCE
Urgent Center Weather Advisory (PIPO) .... UCWA
Uric Acid (DAVI) .... UR AC
Uric Acid (DAVI) .... URIC A
Urinalysis and Microscopy (DAVI) .... UA&M
Urinary Glucose (DAVI) .... UG

Urinary Gonadotropin Peptide (DAVI) .... UGP
Urinary Osmolality [*Medicine*] (DAVI) .... Uosm
Urinary Output (DAVI) .... UOP
Urinary Retention (DAVI) .... UR
Urinary-Tract Malformation [*Medicine*] (DAVI) .... UTM
Urine, Glucose, and Ketones (DAVI) .... UGK
Urine Immunoelectrophoresis [*Medicine*] (DAVI) .... UIEP
Urobilinogen (DAVI) .... UROB
Urogenital Atrophy [*Medicine*] (DAVI) .... UGA
Urokinase Intracoronary [*Medicine*] (DAVI) .... UKIC
Urologist (DAVI) .... UROL
Use Classes Order (HEAS) .... UCO
Use of Work Equipment Directive (HEAS) .... UWED
Useful Field of View (DAVI) .... UPOV
User Channel (CGWS) .... UCH
User Code Document (ROAS) .... UCD
User Display Segment (CCCA) .... UDS
User Interface Environment (SPST) .... UIE
User Performance Requirements (CGWS) .... UPR
User Preferred Routing (CTAS) .... UPR
User Terminal Element (CCCA) .... UTE
User Worked Crossing (HEAS) .... UWC
Users' Tree of Knowledge [*Computer science*] .... uTOK
User-to-Network Interface (MLOA) .... UNI
Usual Body Weight (DAVI) .... UBW
Usual State of Good Health (DAVI) .... USOGH
Usual State of Health (DAVI) .... USOH
Uterine Papillary Serous Carcinoma [*Medicine*] (DAVI) .... UPSC
Utilization and Operations (SPST) .... U&O
UTStarcom, Inc. [*NASDAQ symbol*] (SG) .... UTSI

V
By Meaning

Vacant Land VL
Vaccine Research Center [*National Institutes of Health*] .... VRC
Vaccines for Children (DAVI) .... VFC
Vacuum Bottom .... VB
Vacuum Extraction Delivery [*Medicine*] (DAVI) .... VED
Vacuum Extractor (DAVI) .... VAC EXT
Vagotomy and Antrectomy [*Medicine*] (DAVI) .... V&A
Vagotomy and Gastroenterotomy [*Medicine*] (DAVI) .... V&G
Validation Therapy (DAVI) .... VT
Value Added Procedure (ARMP) .... VAP
ValueClick, Inc. [*NASDAQ symbol*] (SG) .... VCLK
Values Lifestyle Groups (DIPS) .... VALS
Vancomycin-Peak [*Medicine*] (DAVI) .... VANCO/P
Vancomycin-Trough [*Medicine*] (DAVI) .... VANCO/T
Vancouver Stock Exchange (SG) Vc
Vanilla Milkshake (DAVI) .... VMS
Vapor Sampling System .... VSS
Vaporization Laser Ablation of the Prostate [*Medicine*] (DAVI) .... VLAP
Variable Hydrologic Source Area (CARB) .... VHSA
Variable Life-Adjusted Display (DAVI) .... VLAD
Variable Stimulus (DIPS) V
Variance (DIPS) V
Variance of Resident Time (DAVI) .... VRT
Variance Ratio (DIPS) .... F
Variant Creutzfeldt-Jakob Disease [*Medicine*] .... vCJD
Variation (PIAV) .... var
Variation Coefficient (DIPS) V
Varicella Vaccine (DAVI) .... VAR
Varus Derotational Osteotomy [*Medicine*] (DAVI) .... VDO
Vascular Access Flush Device [*Medicine*] (DAVI) .... VAFD
Vascular Dementia [*Medicine*] (DAVI) .... VaD
Vascular Dementia (DIPS) .... VAD
Vascular Endothelial Growth Factor-2 .... VEGF-2
Vascular Occlusive Episode [*Medicine*] (DAVI) .... VOE
Vascularized Patellar Tendon [*Medicine*] (DAVI) .... VPT
Vasoconstrictor Assay [*Medicine*] (DAVI) .... VCA
Vasodepressor Syncope [*Medicine*] (DAVI) .... VDS
Vastus Lateralis Release [*Medicine*] (DAVI) .... VLR
Vecuronium [*Medicine*] (DAVI) .... VEC
Vegetable Protein Diet Plus Fiber (DAVI) .... VPDF
Vegetation Canopy Lidar Mission [*NASA*] VCL
Vehicle Analysis and Integration Team [*NASA*] (SPST) .... VAIT
Vehicle in Question .... VIQ
Vehicle Sampling System .... VSS
Vein Graft Myringoplasty [*Medicine*] (DAVI) .... VGM
Vein of Galen Aneurysmal Dilatation [*Medicine*] (DAVI) .... VGAD
Vein of Galen Aneurysmal Malformation [*Medicine*] (DAVI) ..... VGAM
Velo-Cardio-Facial-Syndrome .... VCFS
Velocity Common Carotid Artery [*Medicine*] (DAVI) .... VCCA
Velocity Internal Carotid Artery [*Medicine*] (DAVI) .... VICA
Velopharyngeal Incompetence [*Medicine*] (DAVI) .... VPI
Venereal Disease [*Medicine*] (DIPS) .... VD
Venous Access Port [*Medicine*] (DAVI) .... VAP
Venous Blood Gas (DAVI) .... VBG
Venous Filling Time (DAVI) .... VFT
Venous Pressure Module [*Medicine*] (DAVI) .... VPM
Venous Resistance (DAVI) .... VR
Venous Thromboembolic Disease [*Medicine*] (DAVI) .... VTED
Venovenous Bypass [*Medicine*] (DAVI) .... VVB
Ventilated Mask [*Medicine*] (DAVI) .... VM
Ventilation-Perfusion Lung Scan [*Medicine*] (DAVI) .... VPLS
Ventilator Dependent Respiratory Failure [*Medicine*] (DAVI) ...... VDRF
Ventilator Rehabilitation Unit (DAVI) .... VRU
Ventricular (DAVI) V
Ventricular Atrial Distal Coronary Sinus [*Medicine*] (DAVI) ...... VADCS
Ventricular Atrial Height Right Atrium [*Medicine*] (DAVI) ...... VAHRA
Ventricular Atrial His Bundle Electrocardiogram [*Medicine*] (DAVI) ...... VAHBE
Ventricular Atrial Proximal Coronary Sinus [*Medicine*] (DAVI) ...... VAPCS
Ventricular Extrasystoles (DAVI) .... VES
Ventricular Premature Activation (DAVI) .... VPA
Ventricular Premature Depolarization [*Medicine*] (DAVI) .... VPD
Ventricular Premature Depolarization Contraction [*Medicine*] (DAVI) ...... VPDC
Ventricular Tachycardia/Fibrillation [*Medicine*] (DAVI) .... VT/VF
Ventricular Tachycardia Non-Sustained [*Medicine*] (DAVI) ...... VT-NS
Ventricular Tachycardia Sustained [*Medicine*] (DAVI) .... VT-S
Ventriculoatrial Shunt [*Medicine*] (DIPS) .... VA

Ventromedial Nucleus of the Hypothalamus [*Medicine*] (DIPS) ...... VMH
Verbal Ability (DIPS) V
Verbalize Understanding (DAVI) .... V/U
Verification Loads Analysis (SPST) .... VLA
Verification Logic Network (SPST) .... VLN
Verification Requirements Traceability Matrix (CTAS) .... VRTM
Versa Module Europe .... VME
Versata, Inc. [*NASDAQ symbol*] (SG) .... VATA
Versatile Integrated Avionics (HLLA) .... VIA
Vertebral (DAVI) V
Vertel .... VRTL
Vertex (DAVI) .... VE
Vertical and Centric (DAVI) .... V&C
Vertical Assault Element [*Military*] .... VAE
Vertical Banded Gastroplasty [*Medicine*] (DAVI) .... VBGP
Vertical Navigation (PIPO) .... VNAV
Vertical Navigation (PIAV) .... Vnav
Vertical Short Takeoff and Landing (PIPO) .... VSTL
Vertical Speed Indicator/Traffic, Resolution Advisory [*Honeywell*]
   (HLLA) .... VSI/TRA
Vertical Subcondylar Oblique [*Medicine*] (DAVI) .... VSO
Very Far Radiation (CARB) .... vfr
Very High Frequency (CARB) .... vhf
Very High Performance Backbone Network System .... vBNS
Very Large Hadron Collider .... VLHC
Very Large Scale Integration (CCCA) .... VLSI
Very Large Submillimeter Array .... VLSA
Very Low Birth Weight Preterm Neonate (DAVI) .... VLBWPN
Very Short Below Elbow (DAVI) .... VSBE
Very-Late Antigen (DAVI) .... VLA
Vesicle Neck Contracture (DAVI) .... VNC
Vesico Ureteral Junction [*Medicine*] (DAVI) .... VUJ
Vesicoureteral [*Medicine*] (DAVI) .... VU
Vessel Pay Dues (RIMS) .... VPD
Veterans Health Administration .... VHA
Veterinary Manual .... vman
Viasystems Group [*NYSE symbol*] (SG) .... VG
Vibration (DAVI) .... vib
Vibration (PIPO) .... VIB
Vicinity Corp. [*NASDAQ symbol*] (SG) .... VCNT
Victim's Information Bureau Service (DAVI) .... VIBS
Victorian UFO Research Society [*Australia*] .... VUFORS
Video Conferencing (MLOA) VIC
Video Distribution System (CCCA) .... VDS
Video Lead Locator VLL
Video on Demand (MLOA) .... VoD
Video Teleconferencing System (SPST) .... VITS
Video, Voice, Image, and Data .... VIVID
Video-Assist Thoracoscopy [*Medicine*] (DAVI) .... VAT
Vienna Expert System for Parental Nutrition of Neonates [*Design of
   nutritional feeding regimens for newborn infants*] (IDAI) ...... VIF-PNN
Vietnam Economic News [*A publication*] .... VEN
Vietnam Investment Review [*A publication*] .... VIR
Vietnam National Committee for Pacific Economic Cooperation ...... VNCPEC
Vietnam News [*A publication*] .... VN
Villa VI
Vinblastine, Bleomycin, and Cisplatin [*Medicine*] (DAVI) ...... VBP
Vincristine, Doxorubicin, and Cyclophosphamide [*Medicine*] (DAVI) ...... VADRIAC
Vincristine, Doxorubicin, and Cyclophosphamide [*Medicine*] (DAVI) ...... VDC
Vincristine, Etoposide, Prednisone, and Doxorubicin [*Medicine*] ...... OEPA
Vinflunine (DAVI) .... VFL
Vinorelbine (DAVI) .... VNB
Violence and Eloper (DAVI) .... V/E
Viragen, Inc. [*AMEX symbol*] (SG) .... VRA
Viral (DAVI) V
Viral Haemorrhagic Fever [*Medicine*] (HEAS) .... VHF
Viral Rhinosinusitis [*Medicine*] (DAVI) .... VRS
Virginia Educational Media Association .... VEMA
Virtual Channel VC
Virtual Channel Flow Control (MLOA) .... VCFC
Virtual Collaborative Environment .... VCE
Virtual Communications Driver (ROAS) .... VCD
Virtual Machine Entry [*Computer science*] (ITCA) .... VM/E
Virtual Machine/Extended Architecture [*Computer science*] (ITCA) ...... VM/XA
Virtual Manufacturing Enterprise .... VME
Virtual Path Connection Identifier .... VPCI

Virtual Rain Gauge (DEMM)	VRG
Virtual Subnet (MLOA)	VS
Virus Control System	VCS
Visible Emissions Observation (SARE)	VEO
Visible Infrared Scanner (CARB)	VIRS
Visible Infrared Scanning Radiometer (CARB)	VIRSR
Vision Left Eye (DAVI)	VLE
Visited Location Register (CGWS)	VLR
Vista Response (DIPS)	V
Visteon Corp. [*NYSE symbol*]	VC
Visual Acuity, Left Eye (DAVI)	VAOS
Visual Acuity, Right Eye (DAVI)	VAOD
Visual Analogue Self Assessment Scales for Pain Intensity (DAVI)	VASPI
Visual Audio Tool (MLOA)	VAT
Visual Basic Syntax	VBScript
Visual C Environment [*Computer science*] (ITCA)	VICE
Visual Descent Point (PIPO)	V
Visual Exempted (PIPO)	VE
Visual Fields Full to Confrontation (DAVI)	VFFC
Visual Fields Intact (DAVI)	VFI
Visual Impairment Service (DAVI)	VIS
Visual Internal Urethrotomy [*Medicine*] (DAVI)	VIU
Visual Motor Integration (DAVI)	VSI
Visual Perception (DAVI)	VP
Visual Reinforcement Audiometry (DAVI)	VRA
Visual Search Task (DAVI)	VST
Visual Signs Quality of Life (DAVI)	VSQOL
Visually Impaired	VI
Visually Induced Motion Sickness	VIMS
Vital Capacity (DAVI)	VIT CAP
Vital Signs Normal (DAVI)	VSN
Vital Signs Stable, Afebrile [*Medicine*] (DAVI)	VSSAF
Vitamin D Dependency Rickets Type I (DAVI)	VDDR I
Vitamin D Dependency Tickets Type II (DAVI)	VDDR II
Vitamin K Deficiency Bleeding (DAVI)	VKDB
Vitran Corp. [*AMEX symbol*] (SG)	VVN
Vitreal Corneal Touch Syndrome (DAVI)	VCTS
Vitreous Infusion Suction Cutter (DAVI)	VISC
Vocabulary	voc
Vocal Cord Dysfunction (DAVI)	VCD
Vocational English as a Second Language	VESL
Vocational Rahabilitation Program (DAVI)	VRP
Vocational Rehabilitation Counselor (DAVI)	VRC
Vocational Rehabilitation Therapy Assistant (DAVI)	VRTA
Vocational Skills Assessment and Development Program (DAVI)	VSADP
Vocational Skills Center	VSC
Voice Activity Detection (CGWS)	VAD
Voice Application Language [*Computer science*]	VAL
Voice Control (CGWS)	VOX
Voice Controlled Switch (CGWS)	VCS
Voice Mobile Attenuation Code (CGWS)	VMAC
Voice Operated (PIPO)	VOX
Voice-Coil Motor (AEBE)	VCM
Voice-In/Voice-Out	VIVO
Void On-Call to Operating Room (DAVI)	VOCOR
Volar Intercalated Segmental Instability (DAVI)	VISI
Volatile Organic Analyzer (SPST)	VOA
Volt	v
Volt Ohm Milliameter	VOM
Voltage Common-Collector (AEBE)	VCC
Voltage Dependent Anion Channel	VDAC
Volume Parts per Million	vppm
Volume Picture Element (AEBE)	voxel
Volume Pressure Response (DAVI)	VPR
Volume to be Infused (DAVI)	VTBI
Volume-Guaranteed Pressure Option [*Medicine*] (DAVI)	VGPO
Voluntary Safety Cases (HEAS)	VSC
Voluntary Termination of Pregnancy (DAVI)	VTOP
Volunteer Transport Service (DAVI)	VTS
Vomiting and Diarrhea (DAVI)	V&D
Voting Trust Certificates (SG)	vtc
Votorantim CeluLose ADS [*NYSE symbol*] (SG)	VCP
Vulva and Vagina [*Medicine*] (DAVI)	V-V
Vulvovaginal Candidiasis [*Medicine*] (DAVI)	VVC
Vyyo, Inc. [*NASDAQ symbol*] (SG)	VYYO

W
By Meaning

Wait for Overhead Message (CGWS)	WFOM
Wakefield Inventory (DAVI)	WKI
Walk-In Emergency Department (DAVI)	WIED
Walking Heel (DAVI)	WH
Walking Speed (DAVI)	WS
Walking Tank (DAVI)	WT
Walk-Through Performance Testing (DIPS)	WTPT
Wall Chart	wch
Wall Motion Index (DAVI)	WMI
Walter Reed Biosystematics Unit (ROAS)	WRBU
Ward Confinement (DAVI)	WC
Warehouse Management System	WMS
Warm and Dry (DAVI)	W/D
Warm Compresses and Lid Scrubs (DAVI)	WC/LC
Warm, Moist (DAVI)	WM
Warm Moist Dressings (DAVI)	WMD
Warm Moist Packs (DAVI)	WMP
Wash (DAVI)	W
Washington Area Wideband System (CCCA)	WAWS
Washington Association of Marketing Educators	WAME
Washington Association of School Administrators	WASA
Washington Association of Secondary School Principals	WASSP
Washington Association of Vocational Administrators	WAVA
Washington Association of Vocational Education Special Needs Personnel	WAVESNP
Washington Education Association	WEA
Washington Library Media Association	WLMA
Washington School Counselor Association	WSCA
Washington State Business Education Association	WSBEA
Washington State Federation of Teachers	WSFT
Washington State Labor Council	WSLC
Washington State Parent/Educator Partnership Project	WSPEP
Washington State School Directors' Association	WSSDA
Washington Vocational Agriculture Teachers Association	WVATA
Washington Vocational Association	WVA
Waste Compliance Plan	WCP
Waste Discharge Requirements (SARE)	WDR
Waste Gas Assembly (SPST)	WGA
Waste Ice Release and Removal System (SPST)	WIRRS
Waste Water Outflow (CARB)	WWO
Wastewater Treatment (AUEG)	WWT
Water Quality Analysis System (AUEG)	WQAS
Water Quality Parameters (AUEG)	WQP
Water Recovery Management (SPST)	WRM
Water User Fee	WUF
Water Vapor (ARMP)	WV
Water Vapor Profiling (ARMP)	WVP
Water Vapor Radiometer (CARB)	WVR
Water View (TRID)	WTRVW
Watershed Initiative Network	WIN
Watershed Model (AUEG)	WSM
Watson-Barker Listening Test	WBLT
Wave Length Shifter	WLS
Weakness and Fatigue (DAVI)	W/F
Weakness, Atrophy, and Fasciculation [Medicine] (DAVI)	WAF
Weapons and Tactics Instructor [Military]	WTI
Wearable Speech Processor (DAVI)	WSP
Weather Observing Station (PIPO)	WOS
Web Methods, Inc. [NASDAQ symbol] (SG)	WEBM
Web-Based Electronic Design (AEBE)	WELD
Web-Based Management	WBM
Web-Based Training	WBT
Webelos Assistant [Boy Scouts of America]	WA
Webelos Den Leader [Boy Scouts of America]	WDL
Webelos Leader Outdoor Training [Boy Scouts of America]	WLOT
Websense, Inc. [NASDAQ symbol] (SG)	WBSN
Wechsler Adult Intelligence Scale-Third Edition [Test] (DIPS)	WAISIII
Wechsler Intelligence Scale for Children-Third Edition [Test] (DIPS)	WISCIII
Wechsler Preschool and Primary Scale of Intelligence-Revised [Test] (DIPS)	WPSSIR
Weekly Radiation Therapy (DAVI)	WRT
Weeks by Ultrasound (DAVI)	WBUS
Weight Activated Locking Knee (DAVI)	WALK
Weight and Temperature (PIAV)	WAT
Weight Loss (DAVI)	WL
Weighted Fair Queuing (MLOA)	WFQ
Weighted Nonlinear Least Squares (DAVI)	WNLS
Weighted Usable Area (CARB)	WUA
Weighted-Average Life	WAL
Weintraub Music [Publisher]	EWM
Welcome Back [Internet dialog]	WB
Well Child Care (DAVI)	WCC
Wellhead Protection (AUEG)	WHP
West Coast Environmental Law Association	WCELA
West Coast Environmental Law Research Foundation	WCELRF
West Nile Fever (DAVI)	WNF
Westergren Erythrocyte Sedimentation Rate (DAVI)	WESR
Western Antarctic Peninsula	WAP
Western Governors' Association (AUEG)	WGA
Western Pacific	WestPac
Western Society of Weed Science	WSWS
Western Sydney Amateur Astronomical Group	WSAAG
Wet to Dry (DAVI)	W-T-D
What You See is What You Get (ITCA)	WSIWYG
Wheelchair (TRID)	WCHR
Wheelchair Passenger Cannot Negotiate Stairs (TRID)	WCHS
Wheelchair Passenger Immobile (TRID)	WCHC
Wheeled Walker (DAVI)	WW
Wheezes (DAVI)	WHZ
When, Where Ready (RIMS)	WWR
Whether in Berth or Not (RIMS)	WIBON
Whether in Port or Not (RIMS)	WIPON
Whirlpool Bath (DAVI)	WHPB
White Coat Effect (DAVI)	WCE
White Coat Hypertension (DAVI)	WCH
White Divorced Female (DAVI)	WDF
White Divorced Male (DAVI)	WDM
White Female Living Child (DAVI)	WFLC
White House Emergency Plan (CCCA)	WHEP
White Male Living Child (DAVI)	WMLC
White Matter Lesions (DAVI)	WML
White Paper Account (HEAS)	WPA
White Separated Female (DAVI)	WSepF
White Separated Male (DAVI)	WSepM
White Single Female (DAVI)	WSF
White-Faced Hornet (DAVI)	WFH
Whitehall Jewellers [NYSE symbol] (SG)	JWL
Whole Blood Volume (DAVI)	WBV
Whole Body Vibration (HEAS)	WBV
Whole Tomography Slice (DAVI)	WTS
Whole Wheat Bread (DAVI)	WWBrd
Whole-Body Count	WBC
Whole-Tree Harvest (CARB)	WTH
Wide Area Calling Plan (CGWS)	WACP
Wide Local Excision [Medicine] (DAVI)	WLE
Wide Open (DAVI)	WO
Wide Range Destillate (RIMS)	WRD
Wideband Code Division Multiple Access (CGWS)	WB-CDMA
Wideband Code Division Multiple Access	WCDMA
Willingness to Communicate	WTC
Winchester Center-Fire	WCF
Window Glazing	GLZ
Window, Icon, Menu, Pointer	WIMP
Window Manager (SPST)	WM
Windows File Protection [Computer science]	WFP
Windows Management Instrumentation	WMI
Windows Media Audio	WMA
Windows Media Player	WMP
Windows Script Host [Computer science]	WSH
Winland Electronics [AMEX symbol] (SG)	WEX
Winning Pitcher [Baseball term] (NDBD)	W
Wire Rods in Coils (RIMS)	WRIC
Wireless Access Communications System (CGWS)	WACS
Wireless Application Protocol	WAP
Wireless Carrier (CGWS)	WC
Wireless Data Forum (CGWS)	WDF
Wireless Dealers Association (CGWS)	WDA
Wireless Ethernet Compatibility Alliance	WECA
Wireless Industry Association (CGWS)	WIA
Wireless LAN Alliance (CGWS)	WLA
Wireless Local Loop (CGWS)	WLL
Wireless Office Telephone System (CGWS)	WOTS

Wireless Service Provider (CGWS) .... WSP
Wireless Switching Center (CGWS) .... WSC
Wisconsin Educational Media Association .... WEMA
Wisconsin Public Service .... WPS
Without Guarantee (RIMS) .... WOG
Witness Systems [*NASDAQ symbol*] (SG) .... WITS
Women's Cancer Information Project (ADWA) .... CanCom
Women's Health Care Nurse Practitioner (NUJO) .... WHCNP
Women's Health Nurse Practitioner (NUJO) .... WHNP
Women's Network for Entrepreneurial Training .... WNET
Wood Badge [*Boy Scouts of America*] .... WB
Word Error Rate (IDAI) .... WER
Word of Day (CCCA) .... WOD
Word Superiority Effect [*J. M. Cattell*] (DIPS) .... WSE
Word-Tag Model (IDAI) .... WTM
Work at Home Mom .... WAHM
Work Capacity Assessment (DAVI) .... WCA
Work Capacity Specialist (DAVI) .... WCS
Work of Engineering Construction (HEAS) .... WEC
Work Related Upper Limb Disorders [*Medicine*] (HEAS) .... WRULD
Work Simplification (DAVI) .... WS
Work Status (DAVI) .... WS
Work Stimulation (DAVI) .... WS
Workbook .... wkb

Working Group on Ionising Radiations (HEAS) .... WGIR
Working Integrated Product Team .... WIPT
Workplace Contact Officer (HEAS) .... WCO
Work-Related Upper-Extremity Disorder (DAVI) .... WRUED
World Anti-Doping Agency .... WADA
World Equity Benchmarks .... WEBS
World Precision Instruments .... WPI
World Quest Networks [*NASDAQ symbol*] (SG) .... WQNI
World Radiation Center (CARB) .... WRC
World Series [*Baseball term*] (NDBD) .... WS
World Travel and Tourism Council (TRID) .... WITC
World Wide Christian Literature .... WWCL
Worldwide Official Airline Guide (TRID) .... WOAG
Worthington Indus. [*NYSE symbol*] (SG) .... WOR
.... W&S
Wound & Skin (DAVI)
Wright's Anaesthesia and Critical Care Resources on the Internet
(ADWA) .... ACCRI
Write to Operator/Write to Operator with Reply [*Computer science*]
(ITCA) .... WTO/WTOR
Writing Across the Curriculum .... WAC
Writing Book .... wrtg
Wrong Box .... WB
Wyeth-Ayerst Laboratories (DAVI) .... W-A
Wyoming Cloud Radar (ARMP) .... WCR

X-Y-Z
By Meaning